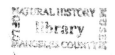

Smithsonian at the Poles

Contributions to
International Polar Year Science

Igor Krupnik, Michael A. Lang,
and Scott E. Miller
Editors

A Smithsonian Contribution to Knowledge

Smithsonian Institution
Scholarly Press
WASHINGTON, D.C.
2009

This proceedings volume of the Smithsonian at the Poles symposium, sponsored by and convened at the Smithsonian Institution on 3–4 May 2007, is published as part of the International Polar Year 2007–2008, which is sponsored by the International Council for Science (ICSU) and the World Meteorological Organization (WMO).

Published by Smithsonian Institution Scholarly Press

P.O. Box 37012
MRC 957
Washington, D.C. 20013-7012
www.scholarlypress.si.edu

Cover design: Piper F. Wallis

Cover images: (top left) Wave-sculpted iceberg in Svalbard, Norway (Photo by Laurie M. Penland); (top right) Smithsonian Scientific Diving Officer Michael A. Lang prepares to exit from ice dive (Photo by Adam G. Marsh); (main) Kongsfjorden, Svalbard, Norway (Photo by Laurie M. Penland).

Library of Congress Cataloging-in-Publication Data

Smithsonian at the poles : contributions to International Polar Year science / Igor Krupnik,
  Michael A. Lang, and Scott E. Miller, editors.
    p. cm.
  ISBN 978-0-9788460-1-5 (pbk. : alk. paper)
   1. International Polar Year, 2007–2008.   2. Polar regions—Research—Congresses.
3. Research—Polar regions—Congresses.   4. Arctic regions—Research—Congresses.
5. Antarctica—Research—Congresses.   6. Polar regions—Environmental
conditions—Congresses.   7. Climatic changes—Detection—Polar regions—Congresses.
I. Krupnik, Igor.   II. Lang, Michael A.   III. Miller, Scott E.

G587.S65 2009
559.8—dc22   2008042055

ISBN-13: 978-0-9788460-1-5
ISBN-10: 0-9788460-1-X

∞ The paper used in this publication meets the minimum requirements of the American National Standard for Permanence of Paper for Printed Library Materials Z39.48–1992.

Contents

Foreword

On behalf of Smithsonian colleagues and as a tropical biologist, I extend a warm welcome to this International Polar Year 2007–2008 science symposium. The commonality between poles and tropics is their shared image of "remoteness" that keeps them removed from the thoughts of society that sponsors our research. In fact, we believe that the poles and tropics are now "canaries in the coalmine," because they are at the forefront of global change.

We face a desperate task of educating society that our global problems are not restricted to the densely populated areas of the United States, Europe, and Asia. We must increase our understanding of how polar regions affect the habitability of our planet through long-term monitoring and observations of short-term cyclical changes, geosphere/atmosphere interactions, and interconnectivity of physical, biological, and social systems.

Coming to Washington in 2007 to adopt a broader set of science responsibilities than I previously had at the Smithsonian Tropical Research Institute, I have found a multitude of polar interests throughout the Smithsonian. I highlight the following Smithsonian programs, which you will learn more about during this Smithsonian symposium.

The U.S. Antarctic Meteorite Program is headed by Tim McCoy, Department of Mineral Sciences, National Museum of Natural History. Since 1976, Smithsonian, NSF and NASA have supported the accession of over 12,000 meteorite specimens from the Antarctic ice sheets in an attempt to better understand the history of our solar system.

The U.S. Antarctic Program Invertebrate Collections are deposited in the National Museum of Natural History and currently number over 900,000 specimens. Archival samples from the Palmer Long-Term Ecological Research site are now also included. Rafael Lemaitre, Chairman of the Invertebrate Zoology Department, reports that this program (co-sponsored by SI and NSF) has loaned over 170,000 specimens in 138 separate lots to researchers in 22 countries since 1995.

Antarctic photobiology has been co-sponsored by NSF and the Smithsonian Environmental Research Center since 1990. Patrick Neale, Principal Investigator, investigates the colonial alga (*Phaeocystis antarctica*) that dominates spring blooms in a polynya well within the ozone hole, exposing plankton to elevated UV-B. The continuous daylight characteristic of this time of year has implications for the regulation of DNA repair, most of which normally occurs at night.

The Northern Latitudes Invasions Biology Program, directed by Gregory Ruiz of the Smithsonian Environmental Research Center has documented the northward spread into six Alaskan regions of several nonnative species. Emerging data suggest that polar systems are certainly vulnerable to invasions. Experimental analyses and modeling of the environmental tolerance of known nonnative species and their capacity to colonize polar systems are underway.

The National Zoological Park's Olav Oftedal is studying Weddell Seal energetics in Antarctica. This study of seal capital expenditure (reliance on stored reserves), lactation energetics and the importance of food intake relies on a novel multimarker approach. The relative importance of these expenditures and energy transfer to pups, in the evolution of a mixed capital and income breeding strategy, is being evaluated.

The NSF's U.S. Antarctic Diving Program has been managed since 2001 by Michael Lang in the Smithsonian's Office of the Under Secretary for Science through an Interagency Agreement. During this period the program reports an average of 35 scientific divers per year logging a total of over 4,800 under-ice dives while enjoying a remarkable safety record and scientific productivity. Smithsonian ice diving courses are taught regularly at the Svalbard Arctic Marine Laboratory.

Astrophysical results include first light achieved with the NSF 10-m South Pole Telescope, 16 February 2007, obtaining maps of Jupiter at wavelengths at 2 mm and 3 mm. The Antarctic Submillimeter Telescope and Remote Observatory was operated by Antony Stark of the Smithsonian Astrophysical Observatory since 1995 as part of the Center for Astrophysical Research in Antarctica, under NSF agreement.

The Arctic Studies Center of the National Museum of Natural History was established by the Department of Anthropology's William Fitzhugh in 1988, with a second office operating since 1995 in Anchorage. Its focus is on cultural heritage studies and indigenous knowledge of sea ice, marine mammals and Arctic climate change. The recent exhibit "Arctic: A Friend Acting Strangely" premiered in 2006 at the Natural History Museum.

The United States marked the start of International Polar Year (IPY) 2007–2008 with an opening event hosted by the National Academies and the National Science Foundation on 26 February 2007. IPY is a global research effort to better understand the polar regions and their climatic effect on Earth. The research completed during IPY 2007–2008 will provide a baseline for understanding future environmental change. *Smithsonian at the Poles: Contributions to International Polar Year Science* is one of the major inaugural science symposia of this IPY. It is also one of the first efforts in disseminating scientific knowledge and research inspired by IPY to be undertaken and published during this IPY period.

Another Smithsonian-initiated conference, *Making Science Global: Reconsidering the Social and Intellectual Implications of the International Polar and Geophysical Years*, will convene in November 2007. *Making Science Global*, an NSF-supported conference, explores the impetus for (and the impact upon) science, society, and culture of the IPYs of 1882–1883 and 1932–1933, and the International Geophysical Year of 1957–1958. It is devoted to sharing historical perspectives that might be useful to those involved in the current IPY. Sessions will explore the origins of these campaigns, their political dimensions, and their consequences. Specific themes include the place of the poles in human imagination, the role of polar exploration in discipline formation, cultural nationalism, politics, and transnationality. Additionally, there are sessions planned on the emergence of the modern geosciences, the uses of new technologies to explore the poles, changing assessments of the nature of human cultures in high latitudes, and polar contributions to environmental awareness. The final session of the conference, *Polar History: Perspectives on Globalization in the Geosciences*, is a plenary session at the annual meeting of the History of Science Society.

The Antarctic Treaty Summit: Science-Policy Interactions in International Governance will be co-sponsored by the Smithsonian Institution and will be convened at the National Museum of Natural History from 30 November through 3 December 2009. This summit celebrates the fiftieth anniversary of the signature-day for the Antarctic Treaty in the city where it was adopted *"in the interest of all mankind."*

I would like to thank the NSF Office of Polar Programs for its support of this symposium and the Symposium Committee Michael Lang, Scott Miller, Igor Krupnik, Bill Fitzhugh, Rafael Lemaitre, Pat Neale, and Tony Stark and the symposium speakers for their efforts.

Ira Rubinoff
Smithsonian Institution
Acting Under Secretary for Science
3 May 2007

Executive Summary

Smithsonian at the Poles: Contributions to International Polar Year Science presents the proceedings of an interdisciplinary symposium dedicated to the opening of International Polar Year (IPY) 2007–2008 and hosted by the Smithsonian Institution on 3–4 May 2007. The volume reflects partnerships across various Smithsonian research units engaged in polar research as well as collaboration with U.S. government agencies with active IPY 2007–2008 programs, including the National Science Foundation (NSF), the National Aeronautics and Space Administration (NASA), the National Oceanic and Atmospheric Administration (NOAA), and the Department of the Interior (DOI). *Smithsonian at the Poles* is the first of many publications by Smithsonian scientists and curators and their collaborators envisioned in association with U.S. scholarly and public programs for IPY.[1]

The *Smithsonian at the Poles* symposium was convened by the Smithsonian Institution's Office of the Under Secretary for Science (OUSS) with major support from NSF. The three symposium co-Chairs—Igor Krupnik, Department of Anthropology, National Museum of Natural History (NMNH), and Michael Lang and Scott Miller, both of OUSS—relied on support from many scientists and curators active in polar research in both the Arctic and Antarctic regions. The Symposium Committee included the three co-Chairs as well as Antony Stark (Smithsonian Astrophysical Observatory), William Fitzhugh (Department of Anthropology, NMNH), Rafael Lemaitre (Department of Invertebrate Zoology, NMNH), and Patrick Neale (Smithsonian Environmental Research Center). The committee members were designated Chairs of the individual symposium sessions and coordinators of the corresponding sections in this volume.

On May 3, 2007, Paul Risser, then Acting Director of NMNH, opened the *Smithsonian at the Poles* symposium. The first plenary session was concluded with an address by Ira Rubinoff, then Acting Under Secretary for Science. The agenda included plenary session presentations by Robert W. Corell (Heinz Center), Robert W. Wilson (SAO), Donal T. Manahan (University of Southern California) and William W. Fitzhugh (NMNH); six concurrent thematic sessions (IPY Histories and Legacies, People and Cultures, Systematics and Biology of Polar Organisms, Methods and Techniques of Under-Ice Research, Environmental

Change and Polar Marine Ecosystems, and Polar Astronomy: Observational Cosmology) and panel discussions; an evening public cinematic event presented by Adam Ravetch and Norbert Wu; and a keynote presentation by James W. C. White (University of Colorado, Boulder). The first ever Smithsonian polar science assembly that covered both the Arctic and Antarctica, *Smithsonian at the Poles* featured more than 200 scholars, members of the public, agency representatives from the Smithsonian, NSF, NOAA, numerous U.S. universities, Australia, and Germany.

The symposium was originally pledged in 2005 by the Office of the Under Secretary for Science in addition to an educational exhibit on Arctic climate change, *Arctic: A Friend Acting Strangely* (2006), access to the Smithsonian polar collections, and the use of the Smithsonian facilities for IPY-related public activities (Anonymous, 2005; Krupnik, 2006). The Smithsonian Institution is pleased to contribute this summary of the Institution's research around the Poles.[2]

ACKNOWLEDGMENTS

The National Science Foundation contributed funding in support of this polar science symposium under Grant No. 0731478 to Michael A. Lang, Principal Investigator, Smithsonian Office of the Under Secretary for Science.

NOTES

1. The *Smithsonian at the Poles* symposium was part of the IPY 2007–2008, a joint initiative of the International Council for Sciences (ICSU) and the World Meteorological Organization (WMO). Scholars from more than 60 nations participated in some 250 projects under the IPY 2007–2008 science program.

2. More details related to the symposium program are available on the symposium website at www.si.edu/ipy, the official U.S. site www.ipy.gov, in Smithsonian Institution press releases, and in the news media.

LITERATURE CITED

Anonymous. 2005. U.S. Arctic Research Plan. Biennial Revision: 2006–2010. *Arctic Research of the United States*, 19 (Fall–Winter):20–21.

Krupnik, I. 2006. Smithsonian Institution. *Arctic Research of the United States*, 20:142–146.

"Smithsonian at the Poles": A 150-Year Venture

The Smithsonian Institution has a strong legacy of International Polar Year (IPY) activities dating to the first IPY in 1882–1883. The first two Smithsonian Secretaries, Joseph Henry (1846–1878) and Spencer F. Baird (1878–1887), were strong proponents of the advancement of science in the polar regions and of the disciplines that eventually formed the core of the program for that first IPY: meteorology, astronomy, geology, and natural history, as well as studies of the polar residents and their cultures.

By the first IPY, the Smithsonian had forged partnerships with federal agencies, private organizations, and individual explorers active in polar regions (Baird, 1885a; 1885b). For instance, the Signal Office of the then U.S. War Department was in charge of preparations for U.S. IPY missions to Barrow (1881–1883) and Lady Franklin Bay (1881–1884), supported by expedition scientists whom the Smithsonian helped to select and train. The Institution also offered its facilities and libraries, and the expertise of its curators to the returning IPY parties and was granted most of the American IPY-1 natural science and ethnological collections, expedition photographs, and personal memorabilia returning from the North. As a result, the Smithsonian's early natural history collections from Barrow, Alaska, are among the most comprehensive in the world, as are those from Labrador, accessioned in 1884. The Smithsonian published two monographs as contributions to its *Annual Reports of the Bureau of Ethnology* series and many shorter papers that described the collections accessioned from the IPY missions to Alaska and Canada (Murdoch, 1892; Turner, 1894; Fitzhugh, 1988; Loring, 2001). These Smithsonian holdings are now a source of knowledge to scientists and cultural information to indigenous communities, who view the early IPY collections as their prime heritage resource.

The Smithsonian's involvement in the second International Polar Year 1932–1933 and in the International Geophysical Year (IGY) 1957–1958 (originally planned as the "third IPY") was modest, although the National Air and Space

Museum (NASM) houses a substantial collection related to the space explorations from the IGY era.

Since the 1970s, the Smithsonian has been actively engaged in Antarctic research, initially through hosting (since 1976) the U.S. Antarctic Meteorite Program, a cooperative effort with NASA and NSF aimed at collection, curation, and long-term storage of meteorites recovered from the Antarctic ice sheets by U.S. scientists. Today, curators of the NMNH Department of Mineral Sciences classify each of the meteorites accessioned and publish the results in the *Antarctic Meteorite Newsletter*, issued biannually by NASA's Johnson Space Center.

For decades, the Smithsonian has focused sociocultural and heritage studies on the indigenous people of the Arctic, supported by its long-established tradition of cultural research in the North and its northern ethnographic collections from Alaska, Canada, Greenland, and Siberia. Since 1988, these efforts have been spearheaded through the creation of the Smithsonian's polar cultural studies unit, the Arctic Studies Center (ASC) at NMNH's Department of Anthropology. Under a cooperative agreement with the Anchorage Museum of History and Art, the ASC operates its Alaskan regional office in Anchorage.

In the 1990s, NMNH agreed to host the national Antarctic invertebrate collection for the NSF United States Antarctic Program (USAP), which now also incorporates the Palmer Long-Term Ecological research (LTER) voucher specimens. Now totaling over 900,000 specimens, 170,000 specimens have been loaned in 138 separate lots to polar researchers in 22 countries. The precursor of this collection was the Smithsonian Oceanographic Sorting Center, which processed over 38 million polar specimens and distributed them to the scientific community between 1965 and 1992 (Moser and Nicol, 1997).

One of the Smithsonian's long-term polar ventures is its astrophysical projects at the South Pole station in Antarctica. The Smithsonian Astrophysical Observatory's (SAO) Antarctic projects have included the Antarctic Submillimeter Telescope and Remote Observatory (AST/RO) operated by SAO 1995–2007 as part of the Center for Astrophysical Research in Antarctica, under NSF agreement. Now SAO collaborates on several projects using the newly built South Pole Telescope (SPT), a 10-m diameter telescope for millimeter and submillimeter observations. The SPT holds the promise of making a significant breakthrough in our understanding of the universe and of physics in general by surveying the entire southern sky, one-third of the celestial sphere, and potentially discovering 30,000 new clusters of galaxies during the next two to three years. This data will provide substantially improved

measures of "dark energy," the newly discovered force that is driving the acceleration of the universe.

Since 2001, the Smithsonian Scientific Diving Program (SDP), established by the Office of the Under Secretary for Science in 1990, has managed the NSF Office of Polar Programs—sponsored scientific diving activities at the U.S. Antarctic McMurdo and Palmer Stations and from the research vessels *L.M. Gould* and *N.B. Palmer*. On average, 35 scientists have dived under ice each year through USAP dive program. More than 4,800 scientific ice dives were logged during 2000–2005. Formal ice diving training is provided by the SDP through biannual ice diving courses in Ny-Ålesund, Svalbard. The USAP scientific diving exposures enjoy a remarkable safety record and proven scientific productivity as an underwater research tool. Polar diving history spans only 60 years, since the United States' first major post-war Antarctic venture and the invention of the scuba regulator, and was thus not represented well until this fourth IPY.

Smithsonian scientists are actively engaged in IPY 2007–2008 projects from astrophysical observations at the South Pole to the use of Smithsonian collections in educational and knowledge preservation programs in indigenous communities across the Arctic. Ongoing projects include: the Photobiology and Solar Radiation Antarctic Research Program, supported by the Smithsonian Environmental Research Center (SERC) and NSF; Northern Latitudes Invasions Biology (NLIB) by SERC's Invasions Biology Program; NMNH's professional collections management services provided for the NSF USAP and the international scientific community through the "USNM Polar Invertebrate Online Databases"; investigations of Weddell seal energetics, supported by NSF and conducted by the Smithsonian's National Zoological Park; and bipolar international polar diving safety research in Svalbard and McMurdo Station (Lang and Sayer, 2007).

For the fourth IPY in 2007–2008, there was Smithsonian representation in all interagency planning meetings. Igor Krupnik served on the first U.S. National IPY Committee in 2003–2005 (NAS, 2004) and since 2004 on the Joint Committee for IPY 2007–2008, the international steering body that supervises planning and implementation, to represent social and human studies.

By its very nature, each International Polar Year is an invitation to the history of science, polar research, and the legacy of polar exploration. Launched approximately every 50 years (or after 25 years in the case of International Geophysical Year 1957–1958), these international ventures create incentives for scientists to test earlier records and to revisit the studies of their predecessors. Each new initiative offers an unparalleled vantage point into the advancement of science, scholarly planning, and collaboration since the previous IPY. The "Smithsonian at the Poles" symposium of 2007 and this resulting volume are the most recent Smithsonian contributions to the ever-growing influence and inspiration of the International Polar Year.

LITERATURE CITED

Baird, S. F. 1885a. Report of Professor Baird, Secretary of the Smithsonian Institution, for 1883. *Annual Report of the Board of Regents of the Smithsonian Institution, Showing the Operations, Expenditures, and Condition of the Institution for the Year 1883.* Washington, D.C.: Government Printing Office.

———. 1885b. Report of Professor Baird, Secretary of the Smithsonian Institution, for 1884. *Annual Report of the Board of Regents of the Smithsonian Institution, Showing the Operations, Expenditures, and Condition of the Institution for the Year 1884.* Washington, D.C.: Government Printing Office.

Fitzhugh, W. W. 1988. "Introduction to the 1988 Edition." In *Ethnological Results of the Point Barrow Expedition*, ed. John Murdoch, pp. xiii–xlix. Washington, D.C.: Smithsonian Institution Press.

Lang, M. A., and M. D. J. Sayer, eds. 2007. *Proceedings of the International Polar Diving Workshop.* Svalbard, 15–21 March 2007. Washington, D.C.: Smithsonian Institution.

Loring, S. 2001. Introduction to Lucien M. Turner and the Beginnings of Smithsonian Anthropology in the North. In *Ethnology of the Ungava District, Hudson Bay Territory*, L. M. Turner, pp. vii–xxxii. Washington, D.C.: Smithsonian Institution Press.

Moser, W. E., and J. Nicol. 1997. The National Museum of Natural History. *Antarctic Journal of the United States*, 23:11–16.

Murdoch, J. 1892. "Ethnological Results of the Point Barrow Expedition." In *Ninth Annual Report of the Bureau of Ethnology 1887–88*, pp. 1–441. Washington, D.C.: Government Printing Office (2nd ed., 1988, Smithsonian Institution Press).

National Academy of Sciences Polar Research Board. 2004. *A Vision for the International Polar Year 2007–2008.* Washington, D.C.: National Academies Press.

Turner, L. 1894. "Ethnology of the Ungava District, Hudson Bay Territory." In *Eleventh Annual Report of the Bureau of Ethnology, 1889–1890*, ed. J. W. Powell, pp.159–350. Washington, D.C.: Government Printing Office.

Advancing Polar Research and Communicating Its Wonders: Quests, Questions, and Capabilities of Weather and Climate Studies in International Polar Years

James R. Fleming and Cara Seitchek

ABSTRACT. Since its inception, the Smithsonian Institution has been a leader in advancing science and communicating its wonders. It functioned as a "national center for atmospheric research" in the nineteenth century and served as a model for the founding of the U.S. Weather Bureau. Its archives and collections document Smithsonian support and involvement over the years in many of the early weather and climate science initiatives: in both the first and second International Polar Years; in the founding of the Arctic Institute of North America and the National Academy of Sciences Conference on the Antarctic; and in the International Geophysical Year in 1957–1958. This presentation examines science, technology, and public opinion surrounding weather and climate research at both poles, from the middle of the nineteenth century through the first and second International Polar Years and the International Geophysical Year, up to the current International Polar Year 2007–2008.

INTRODUCTION

During the past two centuries, the scientific study of weather and climate has changed repeatedly and dramatically. In different eras, telegraphy, radio, rocketry, electronic computing, and satellite meteorology have provided new capabilities for measuring, monitoring, modeling, and theorizing about the atmosphere. While the scale and sophistication has changed, what has not changed is the need for cooperative efforts spanning the largest areas possible—including the poles. Over the years, polar science has served as a very positive example of international peaceful cooperation. The first International Polar Year (IPY-1) of 1882–1883 involved 11 nations in a coordinated effort to study atmospheric changes and "electrical weather" as shown by magnetic disturbances and the polar lights. These efforts were confined to surface observations (Heathcote and Armitage, 1959). In IPY-2 of 1932–1933, 40 nations were involved in a global program to study meteorology, magnetism, and radio science as related to the ionosphere, using instrumented balloons to reach altitudes as high as 10 kilometers (Laursen, 1959). The International Geophysical Year (IGY) of 1957–1958 involved 67 nations in what the British astronomer and geophysicist Sydney Chapman (1888–1970) called, "the common study of our planet by all nations for the benefit of all." Using rockets, new earth-orbiting satellites, and a variety of other techniques, scientists studied

James R. Fleming, Science, Technology, and Society Program, Colby College, 5881 Mayflower Hill, Waterville, ME 04901, USA. Cara Seitchek, Woodrow Wilson International Center for Scholars, 1300 Pennsylvania Avenue, NW, Washington, DC 20004-3027, USA. Corresponding author: J. R. Fleming (jfleming@colby.edu). Accepted 29 May 2008.

the interaction of the sun and the earth, with a special focus on Antarctica (Chapman, 1959a:102). These international cooperative efforts serve as benchmarks for meteorological efforts in high latitudes and help reveal larger issues concerning the continuity and interconnectedness of the science and technology of weather and climate research. Indeed, each successive IPY was based upon the technological innovations of its era and was informed by cutting-edge scientific theories and hypotheses. The launch of the current IPY of 2007–2008, involving more than 60 nations, provides an occasion to look back and to look beyond for larger messages about weather and climate research, the interrelationships created by international science, and the connection between science, technology, and popular culture.

HISTORICAL PRECEDENTS

Cooperative scientific observations date to the early seventeenth century. In the closing decades of the eighteenth century in Europe, and slightly later in Russia and the United States, serious attempts were made to broaden the geographic coverage of weather observations, standardize their collection, and publish the results. Individual observers in particular locales dutifully tended to their journals, and networks of cooperative observers gradually extended the meteorological frontiers. A century before

IPY-1, the Societas Meteorologica Palatina (1781–1795), an international organization whose members represented the chief European scientific institutions, collected observations from a network of 57 stations extending from Siberia to North America and southward to the Mediterranean. The observers, who received instruments, forms, and instructions free of charge, sent their results to Mannheim, Germany, where they were published *in extenso* (Cassidy, 1985:8–25; Societas Meteorologica Palatina, 1783–1795). Many subsequent projects emulated their example.

In the 1830s Sir John Herschel (1791–1872), then in Cape Town, South Africa, initiated the practice of collecting extensive hourly geophysical measurements on "term days"—36-hour periods surrounding the dates of the equinoxes and solstices. The measurements, according to a common plan, were taken simultaneously from widely dispersed stations in order to obtain knowledge of the "correspondence of [the] movements and affections [of the atmosphere] over great regions of the earth's surface, or even over the whole globe" (Herschel, 1836). These efforts were patterned after the Göttingen Magnetic Union, which also used term days and instituted a vast network of magnetic observers operating on a common plan. As with the IPYs, which cited these precedents in instituting its own term days, simultaneous observations were meant to foster both scientific understanding and peaceful international cooperation.

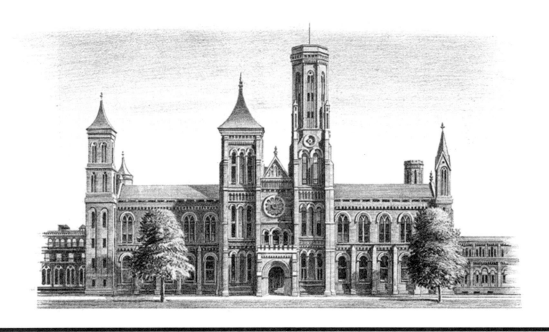

FIGURE 1. Smithsonian Institution ca. 1860, home of the Meteorological Project. Source: Smithsonian Institution.

James P. Espy (1785–1860), the first meteorologist employed by the U.S. government, captured the basic difference between the lone astronomer and the needs of the gregarious meteorologist:

The astronomer is, in some measure, independent of his fellow astronomer; he can wait in his observatory till the star he wishes to observe comes to his meridian; but the meteorologist has his observations bounded by a very limited horizon, and can do little without the aid of numerous observers furnishing him contemporaneous observations over a wide-extended area. (Espy, 1857:40)

Espy worked closely with Joseph Henry (1797–1878), the first secretary of the Smithsonian Institution, to create a meteorological network of up to 600 volunteer observers, reporting monthly, that spanned the entire United States and extended internationally. Some telegraph stations also cooperated, transmitting daily weather reports to Washington, D.C., where the information was posted on large maps in the Smithsonian Castle (Figure 1) and at the U.S. Capitol. The Smithsonian meteorological project provided standardized instruments, uniform procedures, free publications, and a sense of scientific unity; it formed a "seedbed" for the continued growth of theories rooted in data. To increase knowledge of the atmosphere, it sponsored original research on storms and climate change; to diffuse knowledge, it published and

distributed free reports, instructions, and translations. It soon became the U.S. "national center" for atmospheric research in the mid-nineteenth century, as well as a clearinghouse for the international exchange of data (Fleming, 1990:75–94).

Nineteenth-century meteorology benefited from many of the leading technologies and theories available at the time, which, in turn, fueled public expectations about weather prediction. Telegraphy provided instantaneous transmission of information, at least between stations on the grid, and connected scientists and the public in a vast network of information sharing.

Nineteenth-century meteorology, climatology, and other areas of geophysics were undoubtedly stimulated by telegraphic communications that enabled simultaneous observations, data sharing, and timing of phenomena such as auroras, occultations, and eclipses. The vast amounts of gathered data also encouraged scientists to experiment with new ways of portraying the weather and other phenomena on charts and maps (Anderson, 2006). In an effort to enhance both the understanding and prediction of weather phenomena, Yale professor Elias Loomis (1811–1889) searched for "the law of storms" governing storm formation and motion (Figure 2) (Fleming, 1990:77–78, 159). He also mapped the occurrence, intensity, and frequency of auroras from global records, providing a preview of what might be accomplished by observing at high latitudes (Figure 2) (Shea and Smart, 2006).

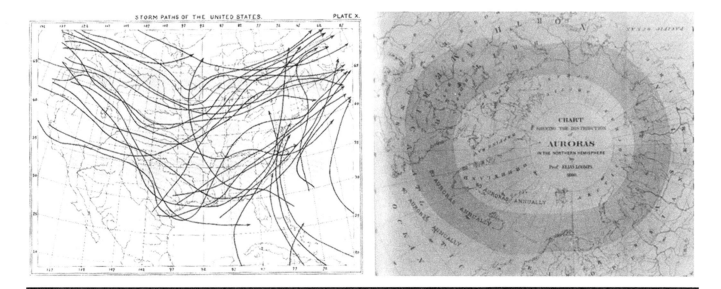

FIGURE 2. Charts by Elias Loomis, ca. 1860. (left) Trajectories of storms entering northeastern USA. Source (Fleming 1990, 159); (right) Frequency of aurora borealis sightings; darker band shows at least 80 auroras annually (http://www.phy6.org/Education/wloomis.html).

Public demand for weather-related information worldwide led to the establishment of many national services by the 1870s. In the United States, the Army Signal Office was assigned this task and soon took the lead in international cooperation. In 1873, the U.S. proposed that all nations prepare an international series of simultaneous observations to aid the study of world climatology and weather patterns. This suggestion led to the *Bulletin of International Simultaneous Observations*, which contained worldwide synoptic charts and summaries of observations recorded at numerous locations around the world (Figure 3) (Myer, 1874:505). Beginning in 1871, the U.S. National Weather Service issued daily forecasts, heightening public expectations that weather could be known—and in some cases, prepared for—in advance. The increasing density and geographic extent of information becoming available in meteo-

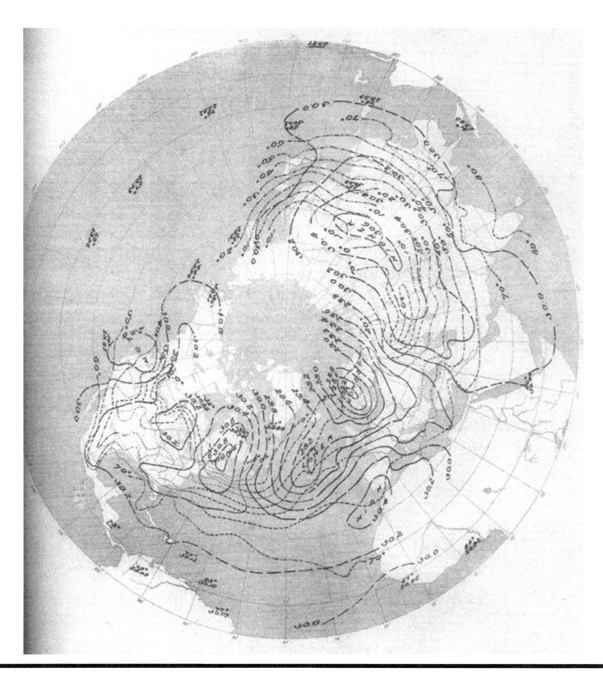

FIGURE 3. International Synoptic Chart: Observations cover the Northern Hemisphere, except for the oceans and polar regions. Dashed lines indicate projected or interpolated data. Source: U.S. Army Signal Office, *Bulletin of International Meteorology*, 28 January 1884.

rology fueled hopes that the scientific enterprise would soon encompass the entire globe, including the polar regions.

THE FIRST INTERNATIONAL POLAR YEAR

The IPY-1 resulted from the ideas of the Austrian naval officer and polar explorer Karl Weyprecht (1838–1881) and the organizational skills of Georg von Neumayer (1826–1909), director of the German Hydrographical Office, along with Heinrich Wild (1833–1902), director of the Central Physical Observatory in St. Petersburg. Weyprecht, who co-directed the unsuccessful 1872 Austro-Hungarian North Pole Expedition, argued that decisive scientific results could only be obtained by research stations distributed over the Arctic regions and charged with the task of obtaining one year's series of reliable meteorological and geophysical observations made with the same methods (Barr, 1983:463–483). Weyprecht wrote in 1875:

The key to many secrets of Nature . . . is certainly to be sought for near the Poles. But as long as Polar Expeditions are looked upon as merely a sort of international steeple-chase, which is primarily to confer honour upon this flag or the other, and their main objective is to exceed by a few miles the latitude reached by a predecessor, these mysteries will remain unsolved. (Weyprecht, 1875:33)

Weyprecht formulated six principles of Arctic research: (1) Arctic exploration is of greatest importance for a knowledge of the laws of nature; (2) geographical discovery is of serious value only when linked to scientific exploration; (3) detailed Arctic topography is of secondary importance; (4) the geographic pole is of no greater importance for science than other high-latitude locations; (5) favorable locations for stations are near high-intensity phenomena; and (6) isolated series of observations are of limited value (Baker, 1982).

Weyprecht's ideas were institutionalized in 1879 with the establishment of the International Polar Commission at the German Hydrographical Office, chaired by von Neumayer. The IPY-1, launched just one year after Weyprecht's death, brought together a cast of hundreds, eventually resulting in 11 nations placing 12 stations around the North Pole and two near the South Pole (Figure 4) (Anonymous, 1884).

The scientists in IPY-1 practiced a form of coordinated Humboldtean science; that is, they emulated the exhaustive methods of the famed German scientific traveler Alexander von Humboldt (1769–1859), who took precision measurements of natural phenomena. The expeditions set out with an ambitious agenda and tracked data for fields as diverse as meteorology, magnetism, glaciology, oceanography, sea ice studies, geomorphology, phytogeography, exploration, mapping, ethnography, and human geography. They made observations in conditions of hardship, hunger, extreme cold, severe gales, blinding drifting snow, and continuous darkness, with frozen instruments often coated with ice.

Each station established its own identity while retaining its position in the greater network. The station at Point Barrow (Figure 5), established by the U.S. Army Signal Service, also served as a crucial part of the Smithsonian Institution's natural history and ethnographic studies (Burch, this volume; Crowell, this volume; Krupnik, this volume). The Kara Sea observations were conducted on sea ice when the Norwegian steamer *Varna* became beset. The *Varna* and a Danish relief vessel *Dijmphna* gathered data for the entire IPY. The *Varna* eventually sank after being crushed by the moving ice. The signal service station at Fort Conger, Lady Franklin Bay (Figure 5), originally conceived as a base from which a U.S. expedition might reach the North Pole, met with tragedy. The expedition lost 19 of 25 men when resupply efforts failed in 1883–1884. Yet its leader, Lt. Adolphus Greely (1844–1935),

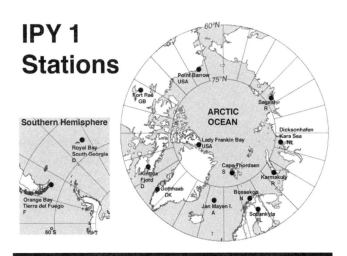

FIGURE 4. The IPY-1 Stations (and their sponsoring countries) during 1881–1884. Arctic (clockwise): Sagastyr (Russia, R), Kara Sea near Dicksonhafen (Netherlands, NL), Karmakuly (Russia), Sodankyla (Finland, FL), Bossekop (Norway, N), Cape Thordsen (Sweden, S), Jan Mayen Island (Austria, A), Godthaab (Denmark, DK), Lady Franklin Bay/Fort Conger (USA), Kingua Fjord (Germany, D), Fort Rae (Great Britain, GB), Point Barrow (USA); Southern Hemisphere: Orange Bay, Tierra del Fuego (France, F) and Royal Bay, South Georgia Island (Germany). Source: original graphic, after Barr, 1985.

FIGURE 5. U.S. IPY-1 stations at (left) Point Barrow, Alaska, and (right) Fort Conger, Lady Franklin Bay, Canada. Source: Wood and Overland 2007.

who nearly starved to death himself, took steps to protect the instruments and data.

Despite hardships and limitations, each expedition published a final report accompanied by numerous scientific articles and popular accounts. The IPY-1 data were intended to enable the creation of new synoptic charts that could connect polar weather conditions to those in lower latitudes. Yet ultimately, the network of only 12 stations scattered north of 60 degrees latitude was spread too thin (cf. Wood and Overland, 2006). Alfred J. Henry (1858–1931), chief of the meteorological records division of the U.S. Weather Bureau, observed that the "gap between the polar stations and those of the middle latitudes [was] entirely too wide to span by any sort of interpolation and thus the relationship of polar weather to the weather of mid-latitudes failed of discovery." Noted geographer Isaiah Bowman (1878–1950) commented in 1930, "The first polar explorers could go only so far as the state of technology and theory permitted" (Bowman, 1930: 442).

Still there were modest accomplishments, for example, in expanded knowledge of the weather in the Davis Strait between Canada and Greenland and the influence of the Gulf Stream in northern latitudes. IPY-1 data were also used in 1924 to construct circumpolar charts for planning "Aeroarctic," the international airship expedition to the Russian Arctic, conducted in 1931 (Luedecke, 2004). In 2006, a systematic reanalysis and reevaluation of IPY-1 data provided insights on climate processes and points of comparison with subsequent Arctic climate patterns. While the stations showed that sea-level pressures and

surface air temperatures were indeed influenced by large-scale hemispheric circulation patterns, in the end, the data lacked sufficient density and the time period was too short to allow for any fundamental discoveries in meteorology or earth magnetism (Wood and Overland, 2006).

TOWARD THE SECOND INTERNATIONAL POLAR YEAR

As the fiftieth anniversary of the IPY approached, the leading edge of 1930s technology, particularly aviation and radio, provided scientists with new capabilities for collecting data and collaborating with colleagues on projects of global scale. New theories and new organizations supported the geosciences, while public expectations for weather and climate services continued to rise. The "disciplinary" period in meteorology began in the second decade of the twentieth century, rather late compared to parallel developments in other sciences, but just in time to inform planning for IPY-2. Meteorologists in World War I were trained to analyze and issue battlefield weather maps; to take hourly measurements conducive to launching and defending against poison gas attacks; and to collect data on upper-air conditions, especially winds, to help calculate the trajectories of long-range artillery shells (Bates and Fuller, 1986:15–19; Fuller, 1990:9–15). By using pilot balloons with theodolite trackers and electrical timers, observers could track the winds and atmospheric conditions aloft.

Meteorologists also provided critical support for aviation and benefited, especially after the war, by data collection from instrumented aircraft, using wing-mounted aerometeorographs that continuously recorded atmospheric data. By 1920, the Bergen school of meteorology in Norway had firmly established the principles of air-mass analysis. Of greatest relevance to polar meteorology are the massive domes of clear cold air called *continental arctic air masses* that sweep across Canada and Siberia, dramatically influencing the weather in lower latitudes. The so-called polar air masses—both continental and maritime—are also significant weather-makers, although they originate below the Arctic Circle. Also, using newly available information on the vertical structure of the atmosphere, Bergen meteorologists identified inclined surfaces of discontinuity separating two distinct air masses, most notably the polar front that spawns many severe winter storms (Figure 6). These conceptual models, combined with objective techniques of weather map analysis and the hope of someday solving the complex equations of atmospheric motion governing storm dynamics, breathed new theoretical life into what had been a largely empirical and applied science (Friedman, 1982).

Radio technology also provided new scientific capabilities. Since magnetic disturbances and auroral displays interfered with radio transmission and telephone wires, radio equipment could be used to detect these phenomena and measure their strength. Radio also provided precise time signals to coordinate simultaneous measurements and communication links that allowed the polar stations to stay in touch with each other and with supporters in lower latitudes (Figure 7, left). Balloon-borne radiosondes

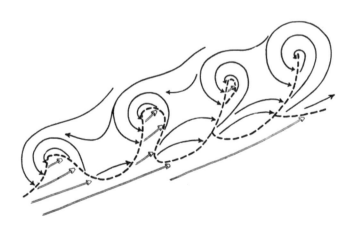

FIGURE 6. Norwegian model of the polar front through a series of cyclones (Bjerknes and Solberg, 1922).

used miniature transmitters to send pressure, temperature, and humidity to earth from altitudes as high as 10 kilometers. (Figure 7, right). Special sondes were outfitted to take measurements of cosmic rays, ultraviolet light, ozone, and other data previously gathered with self-registering balloonsondes; this provided a significant advantage since it was almost impossible to recover meteorographs launched in remote polar areas (DuBois et al., 2002).

Public expectations about climate and weather broadened as radio broadcasts of weather conditions became commonplace. As weather broadcasts increased, so did the number of people employed in weather reporting. Radio in the mid-1920s created the "weather personality," which became an established role at many stations. One of the first weather personalities was E. B. Rideout at station WEEI that started broadcasting from Boston in 1924 (Leep, 1996).

Early commercial airlines also benefited from the improved weather data. An airways weather service provided valuable information to pilots and dispatchers in support of commercial aviation, which navigated by landmarks and instrument readings.

In 1927, based on significant technological advances, new theories of dynamic meteorology, and rising public expectations, the German meteorologist Johannes Georgi (1888–1972) raised the issue of a possible second International Polar Year. Two years later, the International Conference of Directors of Meteorological Services at Copenhagen approved the following resolution:

Magnetic, auroral and meteorological observations at a network of stations in the Arctic and Antarctic would materially advance present knowledge and understanding [of these phenomena] not only within polar regions but in general ... this increased knowledge will be of practical application to problems connected with terrestrial magnetism, marine and aerial navigation, wireless telegraphy and weather forecasting. (C. Luedecke, 2006, cited with author's permission)

IPY-2 was held in 1932–1933, the fiftieth anniversary of IPY-1. Although a worldwide economic depression limited participation, some 40 nations sent scientific teams to reoccupy the original stations and open new ones. Research programs were conducted in meteorology, terrestrial magnetism, atmospheric electricity, auroral physics, and aerology using the newest technologies of radio communication. As in previous field programs, certain periods, now called "international days," were designated for intensive, around-the-clock observations. Even in that era, scientists detected signs of Arctic warming.

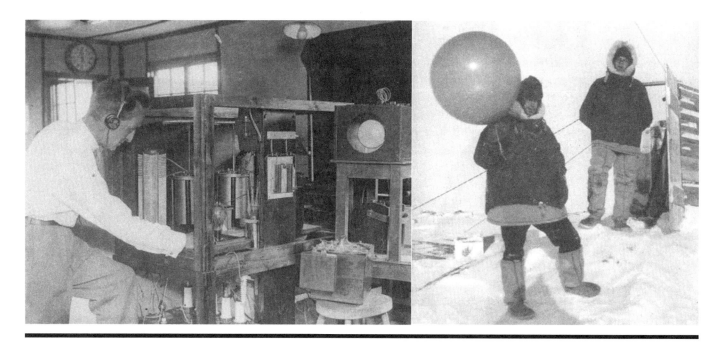

FIGURE 7. (left) W. C. Brown operating radio equipment at Simavik, Norway, during IPY-2 (http://www.wdc.rl.ac.uk/ionosondes/history/IPY. html); (right) John Rea, left, and Stuart McVeigh launching a radiosonde at Chesterfield Inlet, Hudson Bay, Canada, in winter. Source: University of Saskatchewan Archives.

Also, the Second Byrd Antarctic Expedition of 1933–1935—that coincided with, and expanded beyond, IPY-2—brought new focus to Antarctica. It established a year-round meteorological station on the Ross Ice Shelf and captured public attention through live weekly radio broadcasts. Several additional IPY-2 stations in low latitudes added to the worldwide nature of the effort.

The IPY-2 benefited from a sense of interconnectedness stimulated by the International Union of Geodesy and Geophysics (IUGG), a nongovernmental, scientific organization founded in 1919 to promote both disciplinary advances and the ultimate unity of the planetary sciences. The polar front theory also provided focus. As Isaiah Bowman remarked, IPY-2 meteorologists, especially those trained in Norwegian methods, were "inspired by a profound curiosity as to the suspected influence of weather conditions in high latitudes upon (or interaction with) those of the temperate regions as well as the tropics" (Bowman, 1930:442). The IPY-2 accomplishments included simultaneous measurements at multiple stations; higher temporal and spatial resolution, including the vertical; and new instrumentation such as radiosondes, ionosondes, rapid-run magnetometers; and accurate timing of global current patterns for magnetic storms. Reporting included the launch of the *Polar Record* in 1931, an international journal on

polar research published in Cambridge, UK, numerous scientific papers, articles, personal accounts, data archives, and a comprehensive IPY-2 bibliography published in 1951, just in time for planning the IGY (Laursen, 1951). However, an expected summary publication for IPY-2 was not produced until 1959 (Laursen, 1959), and a part of the IPY-2 instrumental data was lost at its major international depository in Copenhagen, presumably during World War II.

THE DAWN OF THE INTERNATIONAL GEOPHYSICAL YEAR

World War II swelled the ranks of practicing meteorologists and introduced new technologies originally developed for the military. Rockets provided a new means for accessing upper levels of the atmosphere, broadening the scope of data collection. Not only could instruments be sent high into and even beyond the atmosphere to take measurements, but also cameras could travel to new heights to send back images of the earth. Electronic computers, designed to crack codes, calculate shell trajectories, and estimate bomb yields, were applied to problems of geophysical modeling, while radar enabled scientists to visualize weather patterns remotely. An important aspect of this new technological age was atmospheric nuclear testing, which injected radionuclide "tracers" into the environment. Meteorology, climatology, and aeronomy—"the atmospheric sciences"—benefited intellectually from an influx of new talent from fields such as mathematics, physics, chemistry, and engineering.

The same technology that provided remote-imaging capabilities for scientists was also used in broadcasting to reach the general public. While long-range weather forecasts and even weather control were distinct possibilities, the public was growing apprehensive about the meteorological effects of atmospheric nuclear testing and increasingly visible levels of smoke and smog. Scientists were increasingly interested in the interconnected workings of the global environment, while military planners sought new geophysical capabilities (Fleming, 2000).

American physicist Lloyd Berkner (1905–1967) suggested that IPY-3 take place 25 years after IPY-2. His colleague, Sidney Chapman, who suggested that the event be called the International Geophysical Year, served as president of Comité Spécial de l'Année Géophysique Internationale (CSAGI), which coordinated the effort internationally. In his presidential remarks, Chapman (1959b) emphasized the earth's fluid envelope and the continuing need for widespread simultaneous observations:

The main aim [of the IGY] is to learn more about the fluid envelope of our planet—the atmosphere and oceans—over all the earth and at all heights and depths. The atmosphere, especially at its upper levels, is much affected by disturbances on the sun; hence this also will be observed more closely and continuously than hitherto. Weather, the ionosphere, the earth's magnetism, the polar lights, cosmic rays, glaciers all over the world, the size and form of the earth, natural and man-made radioactivity in the air and the seas, [and] earthquake waves in remote places will be among the subjects studied. These researches demand widespread simultaneous observation.

The IGY logo emphasized the influence of the sun on the earth, scientific focus on Antarctica, and the hope that geophysical satellites would soon be placed in orbit (Figure 8). The breadth of the program was certainly made possible by new technological developments in transportation, communication, and remote sensing. Teams of observers equipped with the latest scientific instruments were deployed around the globe—some to the ends of the earth in polar regions, on high mountaintops, and at sea—to study earth processes. The effort in Antarctica alone involved hundreds of people in logistically complex

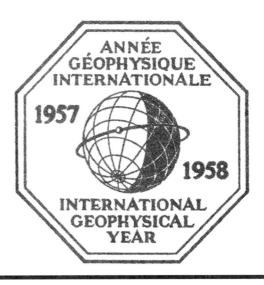

FIGURE 8. The IGY logo adopted in 1955 and used on IGY instruments and publications. Source: U.S. National Academy of Sciences.

and expensive expeditions. While Earth-orbiting satellites were in their infancy, *Explorer 1* and *Explorer 3* brought immediate geophysical results that fundamentally altered our understanding of the planet—the discovery of the Van Allen radiation belts (National Research Council, 2007). The IGY's 18 months of comprehensive global research resulted in other accomplishments as well, including the charting of ocean depths and currents, an in-depth study of Antarctic ice sheets, and, notably, the beginnings of global CO_2 monitoring efforts. The IGY captured scientific center stage at the time and generated many technical and popular publications. Its organizers, recognizing that the international interchange of geophysical data was "the immediate and specific end of its vast scientific program," also made careful provisions for its preservation in the World Data Centers (Odishaw, 1962).

The IGY was actually the twenty-fifth anniversary of IPY-2. Had there been a full fiftieth anniversary, it would have occurred in 1982–1983, well into the era of Earth satellite observations that by then were providing complete coverage of many global atmospheric processes. In the late 1970s, the Global Atmospheric Research Program (GARP) was gearing up for the Global Weather Experiment (GWE)—at the time the largest fully international scientific experiment ever undertaken—linking in situ and satellite data to computer modeling in an attempt to improve operational forecasting, determine the ultimate range of numerical weather prediction, and develop a scientific basis for climate modeling and prediction. In this experiment,

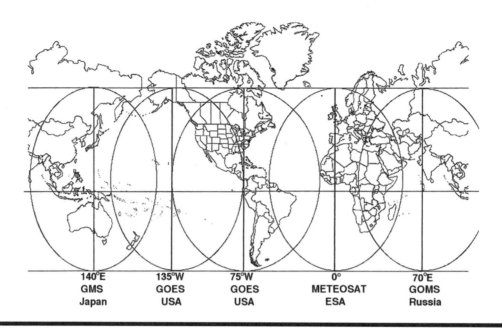

FIGURE 9. During the Global Weather Experiment of 1979, five international geostationary satellites supported global mid-latitude observations of cloud-tracked winds. (GMS = Geostationary Meteorological Satellite; GOES = Goestationary Operational Environmental Satellites; METEOSAT, ESA = a meteorological satellite (European Space Agency); GOMS = Geostationary Operational Meteorological Satellite)

worldwide surface and upper-air observations from satellites, ships, land stations, aircraft, and balloons were combined with global coverage provided by five geostationary satellites operated by the United States, Russia, Japan, and the European Space Agency (ESA) (Figure 9). Polar orbiting satellites covered the rest of the globe. This experiment was followed by the World Climate Research Programme (WCRP), which began in 1980. Today, it can be said that the global observing system provides the equivalent of a GWE of data every day (National Research Council, 2007). The challenge today lies in analyzing, assimilating, and archiving the massive flows of data.

CONCLUSIONS—TOWARD IPY 2007–2008

As we enter the International Polar Year of 2007–2008, today's scientists are heirs to a grand research tradition. With more than 60 nations participating, the current IPY has a broad interdisciplinary focus on environmental change. Six scientific themes provide a framework for IPY 2007–2008 (Allison et al., 2007:13):

1. Status: to determine the present environmental status of the polar regions;

2. Change: to quantify and understand past and present natural environmental and social change in the polar regions and to improve projections of future change;
3. Global linkages: to advance understanding on all scales of the links and interactions between polar regions and the rest of the globe, and of the processes controlling these;
4. New frontiers: to investigate the frontiers of science in the polar regions;
5. Vantage point: to use the unique vantage point of the polar regions to develop and enhance observatories from the interior of the earth to the sun and the cosmos beyond; and
6. The human dimension: to investigate the cultural, historical, and social processes that shape the sustainability of circumpolar human societies and to identify their unique contributions to global cultural diversity and citizenship.

The current IPY is supported by the latest technologies including computer models of ice sheet dynamics, ice cores reaching all the way to bedrock, and advanced surface, airborne, and satellite sensors that measure ice thickness, surface elevation, mass balance, and subsurface conditions. Recently, scientists have discovered rapid changes in ice sheets. The latest collapse of the Larsen B ice shelf in Antarctica in 2002, captured only because of frequent coverage by satellite imagery, illustrated this dynamic on astonishingly short time scales. These new "bits" of knowledge carry weighty implications: The rapid transfer of ice from the continental ice sheets to the sea could result in a significant rise of sea level. Because of the global implications of the changes at the poles for ecosystems and human communities everywhere, IPY 2007–2008 science aims to reach a wide audience, train a new generation of polar researchers, and galvanize public opinion through the associated education, outreach, and communication efforts.

The 125-year history of polar scientific quests, like the much longer history of cooperative observations, involves scientific research questions, technological (including logistic) capabilities, and public perceptions. Since 1882–1883, all IPY ventures have been about science done in extreme conditions, fruitful international cooperation, arctic air masses and polar fronts, melting ice caps, and rising sea levels. That is, the IPY studies are essentially "about us." Each successive IPY has been based upon the technological innovations of its era and the leading scientific theories and hypotheses developed by its time.

In 1881 at the start of IPY-1, the Russian meteorologist Heinrich Wild observed that "the good and favorable idea of Weyprecht . . . has survived the calamities of war, the discords of nations, the obstacles of jealous people, and the death of the author" (Baker, 1982:284). Today, in spite of intervening world wars and numerous discords and obstacles, this statement still rings true. The International Polar Year 2007–2008 is solidly grounded in scientific cooperative efforts for the increase and diffusion of knowledge. Its goal, like those of its predecessors, is to advance research and communicate its wonders. It also aims to preserve the habitability of the planet. Joseph Henry would be pleased.

LITERATURE CITED

Allison, I., M. Béland, K. Alverson, R. Bell, D. Carlson, K. Dannel, C. Ellis-Evans, E. Fahrbach, E. Fanta, Y. Fujii, G. Glasser, L. Goldfarb, G. Hovelsrud, J. Huber, V. Kotlyakov, I. Krupnik, J. Lopez-Martinez, T. Mohr, D. Qin, V. Rachold, C. Rapley, O. Rogne, E. Sarukhanian, C. Summerhayes, and C. Xiao. 2007. The Scope of Science for the International Polar Year 2007–2008. *World Meteorological Organization, Technical Document* 1364. Geneva: World Meteorological Organization.

Anderson, K. 2006. "Mapping Meteorology." In *Intimate Universality: Local and Global Themes in the History of Weather and Climate*, ed. J. R. Fleming, V. Jankovic, and D. R. Coen, pp. 69–92. Sagamore Beach, Mass.: Science History Publications.

Anonymous. 1884. The International Polar Stations. *Science*, 4:370–372.

Baker, F. W. G. 1982. The First International Polar Year, 1882–1882. *Polar Record*, 21:275–285.

Barr, W. 1983. Geographical Aspects of the First International Polar Year, 1882–1883. *Annals of the Association of American Geographers*, 73:463–483.

———. 1985. The Expeditions of the First International Polar year, 1882–1883. *The Arctic Institute of North America, Technical Paper* 29. Calgary, Alberta, Canada: University of Calgary.

Bates, C. C., and J. F. Fuller. 1996. *America's Weather Warriors, 1814–1985.* College Station: Texas A&M University Press.

Bjerknes, J., and H. Solberg. 1922. Life Cycle of Cyclones and the Polar Front Theory of Atmospheric Circulation, *Geofysiske Publikationer* 3(1):3–18.

Bowman, I. 1930. Polar Exploration. *Science*, n.s., 72:439–449.

Burch, Ernest S., Jr. 2009. "Smithsonian Contributions to Alaskan Ethnography: The IPY Expedition to Barrow, 1881–1883." In *Smithsonian at the Poles: Contributions to International Polar Year Science*, ed. I. Krupnik, M. A. Lang, and S. E. Miller, pp. 89–98. Washington, D.C.: Smithsonian Institution Scholarly Press.

Cassidy, D. C. 1985. Meteorology in Mannheim: The Palatine Meteorological Society, 1780–1795. *Sudhoffs Archiv: Zeitschrift für Wissenschaftsgeschichte*, 69:8–25.

Chapman, S. 1959a. *IGY: Year of Discovery.* Ann Arbor: University of Michigan Press.

———. 1959b. Presidential Address, 28 January 1957. *Annals of the International Geophysical Year*, 1:3–5.

Crowell, Aron L. 2009. "The Art of Iñupiaq Whaling: Elders' Interpretations of International Polar Year Ethnological Collections." In *Smithsonian at the Poles: Contributions to International Polar Year Science*, ed. I. Krupnik, M. A. Lang, and S. E. Miller, pp. 99–114. Washington, D.C.: Smithsonian Institution Scholarly Press.

DuBois, J. L., R. P. Multhauf, and C. A. Ziegler. 2002. *The Invention and Development of the Radiosonde with a Catalog of Upper-Atmospheric Telemetering Probes in the National Museum of American History.* Smithsonian Studies in History and Technology, No. 53. Washington, D.C.: Smithsonian Institution Press.

Espy, J. P. 1857. *Fourth Meteorological Report.* U.S. Senate, Ex. Doc. 65, 34th Cong., 3rd sess. Washington, D.C.

Fleming, J. R. 1990. *Meteorology in America, 1800–1870.* Baltimore: Johns Hopkins University Press.

———, ed. 2000. Geophysics and the Military. *Historical Studies in the Physical and Biological Sciences* 30(2). [Special issue]

Friedman, R. M. 1982. Constituting the Polar Front, 1919–1920. *Isis*, 74:343–362.

Fuller, J. F. 1990. *Thor's Legions.* Boston: American Meteorological Society.

Heathcote, N., and A. Armitage. 1959. The First International Polar Year (1882–1883). *Annals of the International Geophysical Year*, 1:6–100.

Herschel, J. 1836. Report of the Meteorological Committee of the South African Literary and Scientific Institution. *Edinburgh New Philosophical Journal*, 21:239–246.

Krupnik, Igor. 2009. "'The Way We See It Coming': Building the Legacy of Indigenous Observations in IPY 2007–2008." In *Smithsonian at the Poles: Contributions to International Polar Year Science*, ed. I. Krupnik, M. A. Lang, and S. E. Miller, pp. 129–142. Washington, D.C.: Smithsonian Institution Scholarly Press.

Laursen, V. 1951. *Bibliography for the Second International Polar Year 1932–3.* Copenhagen, Denmark: Horsholm Bogtrykkeri.

———. 1959. The Second International Polar Year. *Annals of the International Geophysical Year*, 1:211–234.

Leep, R. 1996. "The American Meteorological Society and the Development of Broadcast Meteorology." In *Historical Essays on Meteorology, 1919–1995*, ed. J. R. Fleming, pp. 481–507. Boston: American Meteorological Society.

Luedecke, C. 2004. The First International Polar Year (1882–83): A Big Science Experiment with Small Science Equipment. *History of Meteorology,* 1:55–64.

———. 2006. Changing Trends in Polar Research as Reflected in the History of the International Polar Years. Unpublished manuscript. Institute for History of Science and Technology, University of Hamburg, Germany.

Myer, A. J. 1874. *Annual Report of the U.S. Army Signal Office, 1874.* Washington, D.C.

National Research Council. 2007. *Earth Observations from Space: The First 50 Years of Scientific Achievements.* Washington, D.C.: National Academies Press.

Odishaw, H. 1962. What Shall We Save in the Geophysical Sciences? *Isis,* 53:80–86.

Shea, M. A., and D. F. Smart. 2006. Compendium of the eight articles on the "Carrington Event" attributed to or written by Elias Loomis in the *American Journal of Science,* 1859–1861. *Advances in Space Research,* 38(2):313–385.

Societas Meteorologica Palatina. 1783–1795. *Ephemerides,* 12 vols.

Weyprecht, K. 1875. Scientific Work on the Second Austro-Hungarian Polar Expedition, 1872–4. *Royal Geographical Society Journal,* 45:19–33.

Wood, K. R., and J. E. Overland. 2006. Climate Lessons from the First International Polar Year. *Bulletin of the American Meteorological Society,* 87:1685–1697.

———. 2007. Documentary Image Collection from the First International Polar Year, 1881–1884. http://www.arctic.noaa.gov/aro/ipy-1/Frontpage.htm (accessed 2 November 2007).

Cooperation at the Poles? Placing the First International Polar Year in the Context of Nineteenth-Century Scientific Exploration and Collaboration

Marc Rothenberg

ABSTRACT. The first International Polar Year (IPY) of 1882–1883 came at the end of a half-century of efforts at collaborative and/or cooperative research among the scientific communities of Europe and the United States. These efforts included the Magnetic Crusade, a cooperative endeavor to solve fundamental questions in terrestrial magnetism; a variety of plans for international cooperation in the gathering of meteorological data; the observations of the transits of Venus; and the establishment of the Smithsonian's international network to alert astronomers of new phenomena. It was also a half century when scientific exploration of the polar regions was still problematic in terms of the safety and survival of the investigator. This paper will look at scientific cooperation and earlier Polar research as the background for the first IPY, with special emphasis on the leadership role taken by the Smithsonian Institution.

INTRODUCTION

The first International Polar Year (IPY), which included 14 expeditions sponsored by 11 countries (12 expeditions to the North Polar Region, 2 to the South Polar Region), was a landmark event in the history of polar science. During the half-century leading up to the coordinated research efforts of 1882–1883, scientific research in the Polar Regions had been very problematic. Survival, let alone the successful completion of observations, was uncertain. The use of trained specialists was a rarity. Instead, research was usually conducted as a sideline to the primary objectives or mission of the expedition, which were geographical discovery, by a scientifically inclined explorer, military officer, or physician who made observations or collected specimens on a limited basis. Attempting to reach higher latitudes was an end in itself, a form of international competition, independent of any scientific return (Barr, 1983:464).

The catalyst for the transformation from competition and exploration to cooperation and scientific research was Karl Weyprecht, the Austrian explorer who first suggested the IPY. It was Weyprecht's "drive, ambition, and connections" which were essential in bring the idea of an international, cooperative attack on the problems of polar science to fruition, although he died in 1881, before the IPY was officially launched (Barr, 1983:464).

Marc Rothenberg, Historian, National Science Foundation, 4201 Wilson Boulevard, Arlington, VA 22230, USA (mrothenb@nsf.gov). Accepted 29 May 2008.

It is important, however, not to claim too much for the first IPY. It did not launch science on an entirely new path of international cooperation. That was already a well-trod path by the last quarter of the nineteenth-century, and many of the programs of the Smithsonian Institution, for example, incorporated some aspect of international cooperation. If it proved "that international scientific ventures were possible on a large scale," as C. J. Taylor (1981:376) contended, it was just one of many proofs. If it demonstrated that scientists could cooperate in spite of national differences at a time that when international relations were fraught with danger (Budd, 2001:50–51), so too did scientists in a variety of other disciplines cooperate during this era in order to further research on a number of different scientific questions.

The IPY was organized at the end of a half century marked by efforts at collaborative research or other forms of cooperation in the physical sciences among and between the scientific communities of Europe and the United States. These efforts included the Magnetic Crusade, a collaborative endeavor to solve fundamental questions in terrestrial magnetism; a variety of plans for international cooperation in the gathering of meteorological data; the establishment of the Smithsonian's international network to alert astronomers of new phenomena; and the many expeditions sent out throughout the world to observe the transits of Venus. The level of cooperation ranged from simply improving communication among scientists to establishing common standards for recording observations.

This urge to cooperate across national boundaries in the nineteenth century was not limited to the world of science. It was an integral part of the Victorian-era Euro-American society. Perhaps this urge was most clearly expressed through the organization of international congresses. For example, no less than 32 international congresses met in conjunction with the 1878 Exposition at Paris. The various agendas included cooperation, coordination, standardization, exchange of information, best methods for the gathering of statistics, and efforts at common solutions for common problems. The congresses ranged in subject area from legal issues, such as international copyright, patent rights, and legal medicine to social issues, such as prevention of cruelty to animals, the treatment of alcoholism, guidelines for military ambulance service, and aid to the blind and deaf. Science was not left out. Among the scientific fields to hold congresses in Paris that year were geometry, anthropology, ethnography, botany, geology, and meteorology. Included on the agendas of the scientific congresses were such issues as simultaneity of observations and uniform nomenclatures. There was also

a congress to discuss the possibility of the adoption of a uniform system of weight, measures, and coinage (United States, 1880:1:455–464).

In this paper, I will briefly summarize the various nineteenth-century efforts at international collaboration and cooperation in science, with particular attention to the role played by the Smithsonian Institution and its leader, Joseph Henry. From this discussion, it should be evident that a proposal for international cooperation to solve a scientific question, such as the proposal for the first IPY, would not appear to be a startling new idea to European or American physical and earth scientists in the 1870s or 1880s. In fact, just the opposite was true; by the last quarter of the nineteenth century, efforts at cooperation were the norm, not the exception. The story is not one of inevitable success. Sometimes the efforts at cooperation failed. The general movement of the international physical science community, however, was toward better communication and coordination. Rather than look at the IPY as a new beginning, it is more accurate, I believe, to look at it as a culmination. What occurred with the first IPY was not a revolution in international science, but the transformation of polar science; it began to more closely resemble the norm in international science.

MAGNETIC CRUSADE

The first great international effort at coordinating physical science research in the nineteenth century was the Magnetic Crusade, which focused on the international gathering of terrestrial magnetic observations (Cawood, 1977; 1979). The roots of the Magnetic Crusade lay in the appreciation by early nineteenth-century scientists that the variations of the earth's magnetic field were extremely complex. Driven by both the desire to understand geomagnetic activity and the hope of creating a practical system of navigation through geomagnetic observations, observers created an informal system of contacts "to provide a degree of order in the sometimes spasmodic and rather uncoordinated work—and of course, to exchange information" (Cawood, 1979:496).

Although Alexander von Humboldt put together a loose association of magnetic observatories linked through Paris, which had been the center of terrestrial magnetic observations early in the century, a more important, and more formal, system was organized in the German-speaking world. Carl Friedrich Gauss and Wilhelm Weber founded a system in 1834 under the name of the Göttingen Magnetische Verein. Inspired by the work on the Continent, the

COOPERATION AT THE POLES? • 15

British Association for the Advancement of Science agreed, in 1838, to establish its own system. Led by Samuel Hunt Christie, John Herschel, Humphrey Lloyd, and Edward Sabine, the British Association system consisted of 10 observatories, with coverage expanded to include the British colonies and India (with the cooperation of the East India Company). The British system coordinated with 23 other observatories scattered in the Russian Empire, Asia, North America, North Africa, and Europe, all of whom were funded by their respective governments, except for those in the United States funded by academic institutions (Girard College and Harvard University). Also part of this effort was a British naval expedition to make observations in Antarctica, led by James Clark Ross (1839–1843).

There were some limitations to the international cooperation. Although the British system synchronized observations using Göttingen Mean Time, as suggested by the Göttingen Magnetische Verein, so that data could be compared, there was no formal collaboration. The Paris Observatory acted independently of its other European counterparts. Nonetheless, by the time the Crusade formally ended in 1848, there was a firmly established network of magnetic observatories in Europe, throughout the British Empire, and in the United States that continued to make observations and exchange data. Other observatories later joined in the cooperative venture, including that of the Smithsonian Institution (Rhees, 1859:27–29). Most importantly, as Cawood argued, the Magnetic Crusade demonstrated "that large-scale operations could be organized and carried through" (1979:516). Even Taylor, who argued for the significance of the IPY in the demonstration of the possibilities of large-scale international cooperation, admitted that the Magnetic Crusade "provided many precedents for subsequent global scientific endeavours" (1981:370).

METEOROLOGICAL COOPERATION

Weather does not respect political boundaries, and many meteorologists realized the need for cooperation. German meteorologists took the lead, with such organizations as the Süddeutsche Meteorologische Verein (1841), the Könglich Preussische Meteorologische Institut (1847), and the Norddeutsche Seewarte (1872). These organizations had relatively limited geographical coverage, however, and were international only because of the political fragmentation of the German scientific community (Fleming, 1990:165–166).

A more significant international approach to meteorological observations took place in the United States. Per-

haps not coincidently, it was first directed by a physicist who was an active geomagnetic observer, who had cooperated with the Magnetic Crusade, and was aware of the rewards and challenges of international cooperation. Not only had Joseph Henry received practical advice on observing from Edward Sabine while in England in 1837 (Reingold et al., 1979:312–313), but he also "had conversation with Mr[.] Christie on the subject of establishing magnetic observator[i]es to cooperate with those established by Humboldt" (Reingold et al., 1979:303). Joseph Henry became the first secretary of the Smithsonian Institution in 1846 and established a program that placed an emphasis on the coordination of large-scale research projects, arguing that there were no other institutions in the United States equipped to do so. The first such project Henry embraced was the development what Elias Loomis, one of Henry's consultants in meteorology, characterized as "a grand meteorological crusade" for collecting meteorological observations (Smithsonian Institution, 1848:207).

The system devised by Henry had two distinct but interrelated components, both requiring cooperation. The first was a system of observers who—using standard apparatus, techniques, and forms to the greatest extent possible—maintained monthly logs of weather conditions that were sent to the Smithsonian for reduction. These logs were used to understand climate and weather tendencies over the long term. From the onset, it was recognized that "to give this system its greatest efficiency, the co-operation of the British government and of the Hudson's Bay Company [in Canada] is absolutely indispensable" (Smithsonian, 1848:207). Both the British government and the private Hudson's Bay Company quickly agreed to cooperate (Fleming, 1990:123). The program soon expanded throughout North and Central America. Observers were recruited in Bermuda, Mexico, all the Central American countries, and throughout the West Indies, frequently drawing, in the latter two regions, upon Americans residing overseas (Smithsonian Institution, 1872:68–69). The second component was the use of the telegraph to forward data on weather in real time to the Smithsonian, allowing, in the late 1850s, for the publication of the first scientifically based weather forecasts in newspapers and the first publicly posted weather maps. These forecasts were based on the conclusions drawn from the monthly data logs. Unlike the data gathering, the forecasting only lasted a few years and ended before the dream of making it international was accomplished. Among the obstacles it ran into was the realization by the commercial telegraph companies that weather data was a valuable commercial commodity; the companies wanted to charge for the use of the lines (Fleming, 1990: 145; Rothenberg et al., 2007:102).

Henry's international system worked in part because there were no government meteorologists involved who felt the need to protect their own national systems. Instead, Henry was relying on an international network of independent observers. Two efforts bracketing Henry's establishment of the Smithsonian network demonstrated that meteorology was not yet ready for extended international cooperation.

In 1845, an international meeting of scientists interested in terrestrial magnetism and meteorology was held in conjunction with the meeting of the British Association for the Advancement of Science. Efforts to establish some sort of coordination of meteorological observations, akin to the Magnetic Crusade, ran into a very serious obstacle. The government meteorologists of the various European nations had too much invested in their own systems to lay them aside for some common system. As Edward Sabine remembered two decades later (1866:30), the government meteorologists "manifested so marked a disposition . . . to adhere to their respective arrangements in regard to instruments, times of observation, and modes of publication," as to make it clear the time for a uniform system "had not then arrived."

Another effort came a few years later. Matthew Fontaine Maury, a naval officer, oceanographer, and director of the Naval Observatory (Williams, 1963) was a keen student of meteorology. For example, he had independently recognized the possibilities presented for weather forecasting by the telegraph almost as early as Henry had (Fleming, 1990: 109). In 1851, a request from the British government to the United States government on behalf of the Royal Engineers, who were conducting meteorological observations throughout the empire, ended up being forwarded to Maury for a response. The Royal Engineers had suggested the need to establish a uniform system of recording meteorological data. Maury attempted to expand this request into a broad international cooperative venture covering both nautical and terrestrial meteorology. What this venture demonstrated was that the European meteorological community was still not yet ready for such a bold stroke. Although Maury did manage to organize an 1853 meeting in Brussels to which 10 nations sent representatives, the roadblocks to international exchange of information, let alone real cooperation, were still huge. The sole major accomplishment of the meeting was the agreement that nations that did not use centigrade as the standard scale for temperature would add that scale to the standard thermometer (Fleming, 1990: 107–109; Anderson, 2005:245).

After 1870, a new player in American and international meteorology appeared. Albert J. Myer, the commander of the United States Army Signal Corps, seized on the transmission of storm information as a worthy responsibility for a military organization facing budget cuts. Eventually the Smithsonian transferred its system to the Signal Corps (Hawes, 1966).

Myer's organization came to the forefront of American meteorology just when the international community was becoming more open to the possibilities of broad cooperation. At the 1872 meeting of the Gesellschaft deutscher Naturforscher und Ärzte in Leipzig, meteorologists called for an international gathering to further standardization and cooperation for terrestrial observations. The result was the 1873 congress in Vienna, which ultimately attracted representatives from 20 nations. At the Vienna Congress, Myer's proposal for international simultaneous observations was agreed to, leading to the *Bulletin of International Simultaneous Observations*, first published by the Signal Office in 1875 (Hawes, 1966). There were, however, still obstacles to be overcome, such as the continuing conflict between the metric and English systems of measurement (Anderson, 2005:246). Even so, the discussions had begun (Luedecke, 2004) and, with the second international meteorological congress of 1879, held in Rome, "a pattern of voluntary cooperation between meteorologists on international problems" had been established which bypassed the national meteorological organizations (Weiss, 1975:809).

COOPERATION IN ASTRONOMY

Henry and the Smithsonian were involved in other international cooperative efforts, for example in astronomical communication. As the quantity and quality of telescopes increased in the nineteenth century, so did the number of comets and asteroids discovered. C. H. F. Peters, professor of astronomy at Hamilton College in upstate New York, a prolific discoverer of asteroids, was aware of the importance of the dissemination of observations to other astronomers to aid in the calculation of orbits (or even the relocation of the object). Because he was also German-born and educated, he was in closer touch with his colleagues on the European continent than most of his colleagues in American observatories (Rothenberg, 1999) He wrote to Henry in January 1872, suggesting a system of communicating discoveries among the world's astronomers using the Atlantic cable and the land telegraph systems of the U.S. and Europe. Peters's system would be modeled after the Smithsonian international exchange system for publications, in which the Smithsonian served as the intermediary between American scientists and scientific institutions seeking to distribute their publications throughout the world, and their foreign counterparts seeking to distribute publications in the United States. In the case of astronomy, the Smithsonian would serve as the American node, receiving announcements of discoveries and distributing them to two proposed European nodes—the observatories at Leipzig and Vienna—and vice versa. Given Henry's well-known inclination to support international cooperation, Peters expressed his optimism that the Smithsonian would be willing to pick up the cost of trans-Atlantic telegraph transmission (Rothenberg et al., 2007:447)

Henry, responding as Peters had anticipated, immediately began seeking support for Peters's plan. It took eighteen months for Peters's proposal to be fully implemented, in part because Henry wanted to avoid having science pay for the use of the telegraph. Within a year, Henry had secured the support of Cyrus Field, the father of the Atlantic cable, and William Orton, president of Western Union, for free employment of the Atlantic Cable and the telegraph system in the United States for the transmission of astronomical data. By February 1873 the Smithsonian had begun transmitting information to the Royal Greenwich Observatory for further dissemination to Europe, and through the Associated Press, to astronomers throughout the United States. On the other side of the Atlantic, the European state telegraph companies eventually also agreed to carry the data free of charge. By May 1873 that Henry was able to announce the launching of the system, with European nodes at the major national observatories: Greenwich, Paris, Berlin, Vienna, and, a little later, Pulkova. Working out some of the confusion over which of the observatories had what reporting responsibilities took some time to work out, as did developing a standard lexicon, but by 1883, when Spencer Baird, Henry's successor at the Smithsonian, turned the responsibility for the U.S. node over to Harvard College Observatory, the information exchange was world-wide. Approximately fifty European observatories were linked to Harvard's counterpart in Europe, the observatory at Kiel, and connections had also been made with observatories in South America, Australia, and South Africa (Rothenberg et al., 2007, 448; Jones and Boyd, 1971:197).

TRANSITS OF VENUS

Transits of Venus, the observation from Earth of the passage of that planet across the face of the sun, are rare astronomical events. Two occur eight years apart, with a gap of over a century between pairs. Because of their application in establishing the astronomical unit, the distance between the earth and the sun, which is the essential yardstick for solar system astronomy, the astronomical community was very eager to take advantage of the opportunities provided by the transits of 1874 and 1882. Ultimately, 13 nations sent out observing expeditions to observe one or both transits. A number of nations established government commissions to oversee the efforts, including the United States. Astronomers exchanged copies of their observing protocols and coordinated with each other in selecting observing sites (Dick, 2004; Duerbeck, 2004; Dick, 2003:243, 265).

Planning had begun as early as 1857, with the publication of Astronomer Royal George B. Airy's suggestions of possible observing sites (Airy, 1857). Among the desirable locations, from an astronomical perspective, was Antarctica. For the first time, there was serious discussion of establishing a scientific observing site in Antarctica.

But the transits occurred in December. Were astronomical observations in Antarctica that time of year practical? Scientists were divided. Airy, using information provided him from Edward Sabine, concluded that "December is rather early in the season for a visit to this land, but probably not too early, as especially firm ice will be quite as good for these observations as dry land" (1857:216). He called for a reconnaissance ahead of time to test whether it was practical to establish an observing station in the Polar Regions. J. E. Davis, a British naval officer and Arctic explorer, was even more optimistic, although very realistic as to the difficulties. He developed a plan in 1869 for observations of the 1882 transit from Antarctica, but noted in his presentation to the Royal Geographical Society (1869), that such observations would have required the observing parties to winter over. There was insufficient time to find a safe harbor and establish the observing station prior to the transit. In the case of the 1882 observers, Davis argued that they should be landed in late 1881 with sufficient supplies to last two years, even though the plan was to have them picked up in about a year. It was necessary to leave a margin of error. He did warn of the problematic weather conditions, describing the weather as "either very bad or very delightful" (1869:93). To Davis, it was a gamble worth taking, but it seemed less attractive to astronomers who were going to be making once in a lifetime observations. In contrast to Davis and Airy, Simon Newcomb, the leading American astronomer and a member of the American Transit of Venus Commission, was much more pessimistic. He rejected the idea of astronomical observations from "the Antarctica continent and the neighboring islands . . . because a party can neither be landed nor subsisted there; and if they could, the weather would probably prevent any observations from being taken" (1874:30).

Although observations were not made from the continent of Antarctica, the 1874 transit was observed by parties from Britain, Germany, France, and the United States from stations on islands within the Antarctic Convergence, including Kerguelen (Newcomb apparently thought Kerguelen sufficiently north not to be considered "a neighboring island") and Saint-Paul. The 1874 observations were only moderately successful because of weather problems (Bertrand, 1971:258; Duerbeck, 2004;). But the seeds were planted for a more extensive investigation of the Antarctic. Davis had argued from the beginning that the Antarctic stations should also "obtain a series of observations in meteorology and other branches" (1869: 93), while the American expedition conducted biological and geological collecting which "resulted in a significant contribution to the scientific knowledge of the Antarctic" (Bertrand, 1971:255). Although the combination of the uncertainty of the weather and the difficulties, dangers, and expense of sending parties to Antarctica seemed to have discouraged most further efforts in that direction for the 1882 transit, Germany sent an expedition to South Georgia for the dual purpose of conducting transit of Venus observations and other observations as part of the IPY (Duerbeck, 2004:14).

Later observers have recognized the significance of the transit of Venus expeditions in establishing a precedent for later cooperative research in Antarctica. Julian Dowdeswell of the Scott Polar Research Institute has called these observations of 9 December 1872, "the earliest example of international coordination in polar science and a clear precursor to the first IPY" (Dowdeswell, 2007). The geographer Kenneth Bertrand also argues that the transit observations belong to the history of Antarctic research, although he skips over the IPY, because it was primarily an Arctic venture, and contends that the international program for observing the transit was a "predecessor of the International Geophysical Year" (1971:255).

POLAR STUDIES: SURVIVING THE ELEMENTS AND MORE

So if the first IPY was not a path breaking forerunner of later international cooperative research programs, what was its significance? It was 'Polar.' That may seem obvious, but at the time when it was organized, uncertainty hung over Polar research, at least in the United States. The question might be asked: would any effort to gather data in the Polar Regions be a waste of human and scientific resources?

The United States, and especially the Smithsonian, had supported scientific research in the Arctic during the three decades prior to the IPY (Lindsay, 1993; Sherwood, 1965; Fitzhugh, this volume). Some of this could be solidly placed under the heading of international cooperation, though not at the level exemplified by the first IPY. For example, the Smithsonian had developed strong ties with the British Hudson's Bay Company, and in a spirit of international cooperation, company employees had collected natural history specimens and made meteorological observations. In addition, Francis L. McClintock, a British Polar explorer, had turned his Arctic meteorological observations over to the Smithsonian for reduction (Rothenberg et al., 2004:142, 143).

The Smithsonian had also arranged for the reduction and publication of the geophysical observations made by two U.S. polar endeavors, the second Elisha Kent Kane expedition (1853–1855) and the I. I. Hayes expedition (1860–1861). The apparatus used in the latter expedition were on loan from the Smithsonian (Rothenberg et al., 2004:142–144). In addition, the Smithsonian encouraged natural history research at relatively lower latitudes in Alaska as part of its broader program of supporting the scientific exploration of the American West (Fitzhugh, this volume; Goetzmann, 1966). Among the collectors were Robert Kennicott, working in conjunction with the Western Union Telegraph Company's survey of a telegraph route across Alaska, and W. H. Dall, who was Kennicott's successor and then served with the U.S. Coast Survey (Rothenberg et al., 2007:128, 397). Both were very closely associated with the Smithsonian and its northern research and collecting program (Fitzhugh, this volume).

Polar research was dangerous, as Henry admitted in 1860, requiring "much personal inconvenience and perhaps risk of life" (Rothenberg et al., 2004:141). That opinion was no doubt further reinforced by the death of Kennicott in 1866 and the disaster of the U.S. Polaris Expedition, led by Charles Francis Hall, in 1871. This latter expedition has been renown in the history of exploration because of the debate over whether the expedition's scientist/physician murdered the commander (Loomis, 1991). But beyond the human cost, the expedition's failure temporarily dashed the hopes of the American scientific community for governmental support for intensive research in the Polar region.

Although it has been claimed that Hall, an experienced Arctic explorer, was "lacking credibility as a man of science" (Robinson, 2006:76), he had received the endorsement of Joseph Henry during the debate over who would lead the expedition (Rothenberg et al., 2007:288). There was no question that science was to be a part of the expedition. The legislation which established the expedition, and provided an appropriation of $50,000 for it, ordered that "the scientific operations of the expedition be prescribed in accordance with the advice of the National Academy of Sciences" (United States, 1871:251). That advice, including the selection of the scientist, Dr. Emil Bessels, a zoologist, came primarily from Henry, as president of the National Academy of Sciences, and his Assistant Secretary at the Smithsonian, Spencer F. Baird, who chaired the Academy committee for the expedition. In his report on the preparation for the scientific aspect of the expedition, Henry acknowledged that Hall's primary mission was "not of a scientific character" and that to have attached "a full corps of scientific observers" to it would have been inappropriate (Rothenberg et al., 2007:352). Officially, he recognized the reality of the politics of exploration and was willing to settle for having Bessels and a few junior observers on the expedition, armed with instructions from some of the leading scientists in the United States on collecting data and specimens in astronomy, geophysics, meteorology, natural history, and geology. Unofficially, Henry had the expectation that if the Polaris Expedition was successful, Congress could be persuaded to follow up the triumph with an appropriation "for another expedition of which the observation and investigation of physical phenomena would be the primary object" (Rothenberg et al., 2007:355). But with the failure of the Polaris Expedition in 1871, the hope of additional Congressional funding was dashed. It would be another decade before another U.S. government-sponsored expedition would be sent to the polar region, and it would occur under the auspices of the first IPY in 1881.

Participation by the United States in the first IPY in 1881–1884 was coordinated by U.S. Army Signal Corps, which was experienced in conducting meteorological observations. However, the Smithsonian was in charge of many aspects of the U.S. IPY scholarly program and laid claim to all its resulting 'natural history' collections (Krupnik, this volume). The eastern U.S. mission, on Ellesmere Island, under the command of Lt. Adolphus Greely, was a reasonable success from the perspective of its scientific observations and data returned. But the expedition was plagued by mutiny, bad luck, and poor judgment, and more than two-thirds of the participants perished. In contrast, the Alaskan (Point Barrow) mission, commanded by Lt. P. Henry Ray, had an uneventful time, returning valuable scientific data and abundant natural history and

ethnology collections with little fuss (Burch, this volume; Crowell, this volume; Krupnik, this volume). Furthermore, the little fuss that accompanied Ray's expedition may be the most important aspect of it and the reason why it was a turning point in the history of American scientific ventures in the polar regions. For the first time, an expedition "made survival in the Arctic wastes at 70° below zero look routine to Americans" (Goetzmann, 1986:428). That survival was at least a reasonable expectation was a necessary premise to further scientific exploration of the polar regions.

CONCLUSION

There is an important caveat to this apparent success story of increasing science cooperation. An agreement for international cooperation was not always followed by implementation. As one representative to the unsuccessful 1853 Brussels conference noted, when the delegates returned home, "every one followed his own plan and did what he pleased" (Fleming, 1990:109). Even after the founding of the International Meteorological Organization in 1879, conflict was avoided by the issuing of "resolutions and recommendations that national weather services could, and often did, ignore" (Edwards, 2004:827).

In addition, William Budd (2001) was correct in identifying the same half century between roughly 1835 and 1885, which I argue was marked by increased efforts at scientific cooperation, as also a half century of intense international rivalry. And that rivalry is the flip side of the history of scientific cooperation. Prestige and glory were strong motivations for participating in collaborative ventures. National scientific communities could, and frequently did, point to the activities of international rivals to encourage their governments to provide financial support for research. Participation in certain international endeavors, such as the Magnetic Crusade or the transit of Venus observations, the argument went, was absolutely necessary if a nation was to maintain status within the international community. Scientists would use the activities of other governments to shame their own to action. As Cawood noted, the willingness of the Norwegian Parliament to fund a geomagnetic expedition in 1828, while at the same time denying the funds for the erection of a royal residence, "became an almost obligatory precedent to be quoted in all British pleas for the government backing of terrestrial magnetism" (1979:506). Cawood warned, moreover, that there was "a very narrow dividing line between international cooperation and international rivalry"

(1979:518). When international relations soured, or nationalistic emotions increased, the presence of government funding and the recognition of the domestic political value of scientific success could possibly result in national factors overwhelming the cooperative, international aspects of research. International cooperation in meteorology suffered from the unwillingness of government-funded scientists to turn their backs on the immense investment they had made in their own systems and accept a foreign system. It remains to see, when historians look back, whether rivalry or cooperation will be the dominant theme for the latest International Polar Year in 2007–2009.

LITERATURE CITED

Airy, George B. 1857. On the Means which Will Be Available for Correcting the Measure of the Sun's Distance, in the Next Twenty-Five Years. *Monthly Notices of the Royal Astronomical Society*, 17:208–221

Anderson, Katharine. 2005. *Predicting the Weather: Victorians and the Science of Meteorology*. Chicago: Chicago University Press.

Barr, William. 1983. Geographical Aspects of the First International Polar Year, 1882–1883. *Annals of the Association of American Geographers*, 73:463–484.

Bertrand, Kenneth J. 1971. *Americans in Antarctica, 1775–1948*. New York: American Geographical Society.

Budd, W. F. 2001. "The Scientific Imperative for Antarctic Research." In *The Antarctic: Past, Present and Future,* ed. J. Jabour-Green and M. Haward, pp. 41–59. Antarctic CRC Research Report 28.

Burch, Ernest S., Jr. 2009. "Smithsonian Contributions to Alaskan Ethnography: The IPY Expedition to Barrow, 1881–1883." In *Smithsonian at the Poles: Contributions to International Polar Year Science*, ed. I. Krupnik, M. A. Lang, and S. E. Miller, pp. 89–98. Washington, D.C.: Smithsonian Institution Scholarly Press.

Cawood, John. 1977. Terrestrial Magnetism and the Development of International Collaboration in the Early Nineteenth Century. *Annals of Science*, 34:551–587.

———. 1979. The Magnetic Crusade: Science and Politics in Early Victorian Britain. *Isis*, 70:493–518.

Crowell, Aron L. 2009. "The Art of Iñupiaq Whaling: Elders' Interpretations of International Polar Year Ethnological Collections." In *Smithsonian at the Poles: Contributions to International Polar Year Science*, ed. I. Krupnik, M. A. Lang, and S. E. Miller, pp. 99–114. Washington, D.C.: Smithsonian Institution Scholarly Press.

Davis, J. E. 1869. On Antarctic Discovery and Its Connection with the Transit of Venus. *Journal of the Royal Geographical Society*, 39:91–95.

Dick, Steven J. 2003. *Sky and Ocean Joined: The U.S. Naval Observatory, 1830–2000*. Cambridge, U.K.: Cambridge University Press.

———. 2004. The American Transit of Venus Expeditions of 1874 and 1882. In *Proceedings of IAU Colloquium No. 196*, pp. 100–110. Cambridge, U.K.: Cambridge University Press.

Dowdeswell, Julian. U.K.—Scott Polar Research Institute, International Polar Year Outreach Project. http://www.spkp.se/ipy/ipyou03.htm (accessed 7 September 2007).

Duerbeck, Hilmar W. 2004. The German Transit of Venus Expeditions of 1874 and 1882: Organizations, Methods, Stations, Results. *Journal of Astronomical History and Heritage*, 7:8–17.

Edwards, Paul N. 2004. "A Vast Machine": Standards as Social Technology. *Science*, 304:827.

Fitzhugh, William W. 2009. "'Of No Ordinary Importance': Reversing Polarities in Smithsonian Arctic Studies." In *Smithsonian at the Poles: Contributions to International Polar Year Science*, ed. I. Krupnik, M. A. Lang, and S. E. Miller, pp. 61–78. Washington, D.C.: Smithsonian Institution Scholarly Press.

Fleming, James Rodger. 1990. *Meteorology in America, 1800–1870*. Baltimore: Johns Hopkins University Press.

Goetzmann, William H. 1966. *Exploration and Empire: The Explorer and the Scientist in the Winning of the American West*. New York: Alfred A. Knopf.

———. 1986. *New Lands, New Men: America and the Second Great Age of Discovery*. New York: Viking.

Hawes, Joseph M. 1966. The Signal Corps and Its Weather Service, 1870–1890. *Military Affairs*, 30:68–76.

Jones, Bessie Zaban, and Lyle Gifford Boyd. 1971. *The Harvard College Observatory: The First Four Directorships*. Cambridge, Mass.: Harvard University Press.

Krupnik, Igor. 2009. "'The Way We See It Coming': Building the Legacy of Indigenous Observations in IPY 2007–2008." In *Smithsonian at the Poles: Contributions to International Polar Year Science*, ed. I. Krupnik, M. A. Lang, and S. E. Miller, pp. 129–142. Washington, D.C.: Smithsonian Institution Scholarly Press.

Lindsay, Debra J. 1993. *Science in the Subarctic: Trappers, Traders, and the Smithsonian Institution*. Washington, D.C.: Smithsonian Institution Press.

Loomis, Chauncy C. 1991. *Weird and Tragic Shores: The Story of Charles Francis Hall, Explorer*. Lincoln: University of Nebraska Press.

Luedecke, Cornelia. 2004. The First International Polar Year (1882–83): A Big Science Experiment with Small Science Equipment. *History of Meteorology*, 1:55–64.

[Newcomb, Simon]. 1874. The Coming Transit of Venus. *Harper's New Monthly Magazine*, 50:25–35.

Reingold, Nathan, Arthur P. Molella, Marc Rothenberg, Kathleen Waldenfels, and Joel N. Bodansky, eds. 1979. *The Papers of Joseph Henry*. Volume 3. Washington, D.C.: Smithsonian Institution Press.

Rhees, William J. 1859. *An Account of the Smithsonian Institution, Its Founder, Building, Operations, Etc., Prepared from the Reports of Prof. Henry to the Regents, and Other Authentic Sources*. Washington, D.C.: Thomas McGill.

Robinson, Michael F. 2006. *The Coldest Crucible: Arctic Exploration and American Culture*. Chicago: University of Chicago Press.

Rothenberg, Marc. 1999. Peters, Christian Henry. *American National Biography,* 17:391–392.

Rothenberg, Marc, Kathleen W. Dorman, Frank R. Millikan, Deborah Y. Jeffries, and Sarah Shoenfeld, eds. 2004. *The Papers of Joseph Henry*. Volume 10. Sagamore Beach, Mass.: Science History Publications.

———, eds. 2007. *The Papers of Joseph Henry*. Volume 11. Sagamore Beach, Mass.: Science History Publications.

Sabine, Edward. 1866. Note on a Correspondence between Her Majesty's Government and the President and Council of the Royal Society Regarding Meteorological Observations to Be Made by Land and Sea. *Proceedings of the Royal Society of London*, 15:29–38.

Sherwood, Morgan. 1965. *Exploration of Alaska, 1865–1900*. New Haven, Conn.: Yale University Press.

Smithsonian Institution. 1848. *Annual Report of the Board of Regents of the Smithsonian Institution for 1847*. Washington, D.C.: Tippen and Steeper.

———. 1872. *Annual Report of the Board of Regents of the Smithsonian Institution for 1868*. Washington, D.C.: Government Printing Office.

Taylor, C. J. 1981. First International Polar Year, 1982–83. *Arctic,* 34: 370–376.

United States. 1871. *The Statutes at Large and Proclamations of the United States of America, from December 1869 to March 1871.* Boston: Little, Brown, and Company.

United States, Commission to the Paris Universal Exposition. 1880. *Reports of the United States Commissioners to the Paris Universal Exposition, 1878.* Volume 1. Washington, D.C.: Government Printing Office.

Weiss, Edith Brown. 1975. International Responses to Weather Modification. *International Organization,* 29:805–826.

Williams, Francis L. 1963. *Matthew Fontaine Maury, Scientist of the Sea.* New Brunswick, N.J.: Rutgers University Press.

The Policy Process and the International Geophysical Year, 1957–1958

Fae L. Korsmo

ABSTRACT. By the post–World War II era, the U.S. federal government's role in science had expanded considerably. New institutions, such as the Office of Naval Research and the National Science Foundation, were established to fund basic science. Technological breakthroughs that had provided the instruments of war were recognized as having important economic, civilian applications. Understanding the earth's environment, including the extreme polar regions, the upper atmosphere, and the ocean depths, was recognized as key to enhancing a nation's communications, transportation, and commerce. The IGY developed in part from such national interests, but became a huge international undertaking. The process of international negotiations leading up to and during the IGY set a precedent for organizing cooperative scientific undertakings and enshrined norms and practices for sharing data and resources. Further, the IGY demonstrated the importance of communicating results across political, disciplinary, and societal boundaries. Fifty years later, the organizers of the International Polar Year embraced these values.

INTRODUCTION

Legacies of the Third International Polar Year, more commonly known as the International Geophysical Year (IGY) of 1957–1958, include the launch of the first artificial Earth-orbiting satellites, the negotiation of the Antarctic Treaty, the establishment of the World Data Center system, the discovery of the Van Allen belts, and the long-term measurements of atmospheric carbon dioxide and glacial dynamics (Sullivan 1961; Korsmo 2007b). While the outcomes of the IGY are well known, the social and political processes that led to the IGY are less studied. One of the best sources from a policy perspective is a small pamphlet produced by the Congressional Research Service (Bullis 1973). Another source is the U.S. National Academy of Sciences voluminous IGY Archive in Washington, D.C., in addition to other archives containing the papers of IGY scientists and government sponsors. Some IGY participants have contributed their recollections in oral histories (e.g., Van Allen, 1998; see Acknowledgements), an excellent source of information on what it was like to be a researcher or an administrator before, during, and after the IGY.

This chapter draws on archival collections, biographies, oral histories, and secondary sources to ask the question, What lessons can IGY teach us about

Fae L. Korsmo, National Science Foundation, Office of the Director, Arlington, VA 22230, USA (fkorsmo@nsf.gov). Accepted 29 May 2008.

organizing and carrying out a large-scale, international, and multidisciplinary science program? The IGY helped to establish a precedent for the post–World War II conduct of international science, particularly as organized campaigns of international years or decades. In addition, the U.S. organizers of the IGY within the National Academy of Sciences left a well-organized archive of documentation, including a set of full transcripts from executive committee meetings. It is as if they wanted to be studied, since they purposely recorded their daily conversations, arguments, and decisions. As a political scientist, I find this record irresistible. When it comes to setting science agendas, building coalitions to advocate for programs, and making sure that commitments for funding and other support are made and kept, it is seldom one has access to so complete a record of events. Even as we find ourselves in the midst of the [Fourth] International Polar Year 2007–2008, it is not too late to learn from the IGY.

Policy can be thought of as a set of processes, including the setting of the agenda (the list of problems or subjects to which the decision-makers are paying serious attention at any given time); the specification of alternatives from which a choice is to be made; an authoritative choice among the alternatives, and the decision itself (Kingdon, 1995). In the process of setting the agenda or advocating for alternatives, those motivated by the outcomes form coalitions and engage in coordinated behavior based on common beliefs or motivations (Sabatier and Jenkins-Smith, 1999). Policy entrepreneurs—advocates willing to invest their resources to promote an alternative in return for anticipated future gain—look for opportunities to link solutions to problems, using what they know about the relevant coalitions and decision-makers. They are the classic integrators, creating connections among people, problems, alternatives, and decisions. Once a decision is made, then the question becomes, Who will implement the decision? There must be a credible commitment among institutions (and by "institutions," I mean the rules and norms that groups of people live by, which may or may not be embodied in organizations) to match subsequent actions with authoritative choices (North and Weingast, 1989). In the follow-through, the rules of the game and lines of accountability become crucial.

The IGY, on the one hand a daring and audacious plan to make the entire earth—surface, oceans, and atmosphere—the topic of concerted studies, and on the other hand a series of small, incremental decisions taken independently by numerous small groups, can be understood as a set of policy processes. A retrospective analysis of what worked enabled us to compare these IGY lessons with the science planning we are doing now. Was the IGY simply a product of its time or are there enduring legacies in terms of how we construct and conduct coordinated research programs? In terms of process, this chapter provides some of the highlights. First, however, it is helpful to examine the political context of the IGY in comparison to the other Polar Years.

THE POLITICAL CONTEXT

All of the Polar Years occurred in periods of relative peace and political stability, when international organizations had emerged in a new or reconstituted fashion (e.g., from periods of inactivity during wartime or economic depression) and when powerful nations were not distracted by the drain of soldiers and armaments. The idea for a First Polar Year or coordinated polar studies, for example, emerged within the Austro-Hungarian Empire in the early 1870s but only gained traction with other major powers after the 1878 Congress of Berlin had settled the Balkan War (Baker, 1982). The idea for a Second Polar Year was raised in 1927 and the studies took place in 1932–1933, fifty years after the First Polar Year (Baker, 1982; Nicolet, 1984). The Great Depression, followed by the outbreak of World War II and the untimely death of the International Polar Year Commission's President D. LaCour in 1942 resulted in a lengthy delay in publishing the results from the Second Polar Year. By the end of World War II, science and technology, as well as politics, had changed. The main factor that separates the IGY from the first two Polar Years was the existence of nuclear weapons and the beginnings of the Cold War between East and West. Understanding, detection, and development of nuclear weapons became a driving force for investment in the physical sciences following World War II. The Arctic, as geographer Paul Siple pointed out in 1948, afforded a straight line of attack to the Soviet Union (Siple, 1948). The United States began to conduct top-secret overflight missions to determine whether the Soviet forces were staging long-range bombers in the frozen north (Hall, 1997). The artificial Earth-orbiting satellites that emerged from the IGY were useful in studying the upper atmosphere but also provided a means of checking on enemy activities (Day, 2000). Basic science and military objectives both were motivations. The debate among historians has centered on how inextricably linked the motivations were for participating scientists and institutions. As in the first two Polar Years, international scientific organizations, such as the International Meteorological Congress in the 1870s and the International Council of Scientific Unions in the 1930s, played a key role in providing stable, reliable fora in which to build coalitions and collaborations. However, individuals—our policy entrepreneurs—also were required to initiate and carry out ambitious programs.

AGENDA SETTING: FIRST, SET A DATE

It sounds easy to set a date but even this requires some thought. How many declared international years of *this* and decades of *that* pass unnoticed? There has to be a reason for the date, preferably a reason tied to the proposed activity, an agenda that establishes the urgency of action within a specific time frame. What is the scientific justification for an "international year"? Unless the urgency appeals to a community of scientists beyond the initially small group of advocates, it will be difficult to affix a convincing time period for intense activity.

Setting a date, then, requires the ability to persuade others and build coalitions of advocates and future performers—those who will carry out the activity. Building the coalitions requires access to other potential supporters who can help to make the case. Access comes through networks of contacts, including committees, boards, and other fora.

It helps to start with venues that allow for the exchange of ideas. Most sources place the beginning of the IGY at the home of Dr. James Van Allen, in Silver Spring, Maryland in the spring of 1950 (Sullivan, 1961; Van Allen, 1997 and 1998). Trained as a nuclear physicist, Van Allen (1914–2006) was well known for the development of the proximity fuze during World War II. He became involved in the use of rockets to study the upper atmosphere immediately following the war, instrumenting captured and refurbished German V-2 rockets to study cosmic radiation, the ionosphere, and geomagnetism. At the time of Chapman's visit, Van Allen headed up a high-altitude research group at Johns Hopkins University, Applied Physics Lab. Shortly thereafter, Van Allen would go to the University of Iowa, where he would spend most of his professional career as a professor of physics (American Institute of Physics, 2000). While in Maryland, he and his wife Abigail hosted a dinner on 5 April 1950 for British geophysicist Sydney Chapman (1888–1970). Chapman, a theoretical physicist interested in the earth's magnetic phenomena, had participated in the Second Polar Year of 1932–1933. He was well known for his work on magnetic storms, and would come to spend a great deal of time in the United States, at the University of Alaska Fairbanks, the High Altitude Observatory in Boulder, Colorado, and

University of Michigan (Good, 2000). He was to start his lengthy U.S. sojourn at Caltech. In April 1950, Chapman was in the United States on his way to join a Caltech study on the upper atmosphere. Van Allen described the gathering as "one of the most felicitous and inspiring" that he had ever experienced. Also present at the dinner was Lloyd Berkner, a former radio engineer who had been on Admiral Byrd's 1928–1930 Antarctic expedition. Berkner had both science and policy in his background. According to Van Allen,

> The dinner conversation ranged widely over geophysics and especially geomagnetism and ionospheric physics. Following dinner, as we were all sipping brandy in the living room, Berkner turned to Chapman and said, "Sydney, don't you think that it is about time for another international polar year?" Chapman immediately embraced the suggestion, remarking that he had been thinking along the same lines himself. (Van Allen, 1998:5)

Chapman also observed that the years 1957–1958 would be a time of maximum solar activity, so the time frame for the Third Polar Year was settled. The properties of the upper atmosphere, including the relationships among magnetic storms, cosmic rays, and solar activity intrigued scientists. The military, in particular, was interested in very-high-frequency scatter technology for reliable low-capacity communication that could avoid the disruptions caused by solar emissions, magnetic storms, and auroras. The perturbations emanated from high latitudes. Choosing a year of maximum solar activity for a new international polar venture made scientific sense for atmospheric physicists interested in understanding more about these high-latitude phenomena. Furthermore, as Chapman explained later (1960, 313) and may well have noted at the Van Allen residence, technological improvements in instrumentation and rocketry had now enabled scientists to probe much deeper into the atmosphere. The time was ripe. Was the Berkner-Chapman exchange rehearsed? Perhaps. But the main point is that there were many opportunities for leading scientists to get together and persuade one another of the need for an intense research campaign (Kevles, 1990). One of the main venues in the United States after World War II was the Joint Research and Development Board, renamed the U.S. Research and Development Board in 1947. Led by Vannevar Bush, the Research and Development Board combined civilian researchers and military personnel in determining and coordinating research priorities for the Department of Defense. Bush was President of the Carnegie Institution of Washington and had led the Joint Committee on New Weapons and Equipment during the war. Widely respected today as the author of *Science—The Endless Frontier* (Bush, 1945), a book that stressed the importance of basic research in the United States, Bush represented the transition from wartime science—applications focused on immediate problems of winning the war—to peacetime science—research into fundamental questions for the sake of discovery.

The Research and Development Board's committees and their subcommittees and panels took up scientific problems that the military identified—or civilian scientists identified for them. They covered the physical, medical, biological, and geophysical sciences (U.S. National Archives and Records Administration, n.d.). Vannevar Bush tapped Lloyd Berkner (1905–1967) to run the Research and Development Board as its executive secretary. Berkner, profiled in Allan Needell's excellent biography (2000), had a rich experience in ionospheric research, government consulting, and national security. He had been to Antarctica in 1928–1930. He was not afraid to speak out publicly on science policy. He was perfect example of a policy entrepreneur: breaking down boundaries between government agencies and between government and other sectors of society, exploiting every opportunity for bringing solutions—in this case technological breakthroughs and scientific programs—to problems. In the world of agenda setting, solutions, carried in the pockets of entrepreneurs, go searching for problems. While we are left with the impression that Berkner first introduced the idea of a Third International Polar Year at the Van Allen home in April 1950, undoubtedly he had broached the topic before, perhaps on the Research and Development Board, using his previous Antarctic experience and his knowledge of postwar developments in international science policy.

Berkner was not the only science entrepreneur in the postwar science world. One can also think of Swedish meteorologist Carl Gustav Rossby (1898–1957), who called the attention of the U.S. military to the climate warming occurring in the 1920s through the 1940s (e.g. Rossby 1947). His fellow Swede, glaciologist Hans W. Ahlmann (1889–1974), studied the properties of glaciers as indicators of climate variation. Rossby urged the U.S. military to take advantage of Ahlmann's knowledge as the military searched for expertise on high-latitude operations. Because the Arctic represented the shortest distance between the United States and Soviet territory, Rossby and Ahlmann knew they had the attention of the U.S. military planners. Using solid ice for planes and other military transport was fine as long as the ice was not melting; a warming trend would require a change in strategy. In a way, it was Ahlmann who helped

to set the science agenda for the IGY's approach to glaciology. Using mountain glaciers, Ahlmann measured accumulation, ablation, and regime (the grand total of a glacier's entire accumulation and net ablation) and recommended simultaneous measurements in different climates (Kirwan et al., 1949). In 1946, he called for exact measurements to be made on the ice sheets: temperatures at different depths, seismic methods to compute thickness, and detailed observations of stratification of annual layers. The only way to do this systematic comparison in different parts of the world was through international cooperation (Ahlmann, 1946). Ahlmann's frequent calls for this style of comparative work eventually led to the Norwegian-British-Swedish Antarctic Expedition of 1949–1952, the first scientific traverse in the Antarctic interior. This traverse served as a model for the IGY expeditions to Antarctica (Bentley, 1964). Of course, the U.S. had political reasons for a scientific presence in Antarctica; the existence of competing territorial claims and concerns about possible Soviet claims ensured the Antarctic would have a place on the IGY agenda (U.S. National Security Council, 1957).

How did the Third Polar Year, originally envisioned as a high-latitude, upper-atmosphere research campaign, become the International Geophysical Year? In the process of enlisting support among the international scientific societies, Chapman and Berkner found a strong preference for a global program encompassing additional geographical regions and physical science disciplines. To attain widespread support, Chapman and Berkner skillfully embraced a much broader geophysical agenda.

The international science scene after World War II included a reconstituted International Council of Scientific Unions (ICSU), a body where membership was both by nation-state and by international scientific union, e.g., the International Union of Geodesy and Geophysics (IUGG). The national member might be a national academy or a government agency with research responsibilities. Berkner and Chapman first presented the idea for the Third International Polar Year to the constituent scientific unions that made up a "Mixed Commission on the Ionosphere" under ICSU (Beynon, 1975:53). These unions included the IUGG, International Astronomy Union (IAU), International Union of Pure and Applied Physics (IUPAP), and International Union of Radio Science (URSI) (Beynon, 1975:53). The unions, in turn, presented the proposal to the ICSU General Assembly, and ICSU, in turn, invited the World Meteorological Organization (WMO) to participate as well as the national organizations adhering to ICSU. (Note that this pattern of approaching international scientific organizations first ICSU, then the WMO, was also used to prepare for the International Polar Year 2007–2008). By 1953, there were 26 countries signed up to participate in what came to be known as the International Geophysical Year 1957–1958. The disciplines included practically all the earth, atmosphere, and oceanic sciences, covering many parts of the globe beyond the polar regions (Nicolet, 1984). The price of coalition building beyond the minimum one needs to win an objective is that the agenda—the set of interesting science questions and topics—becomes expansive and unwieldy.

Political scientists have theorized that a minimum winning coalition—the number of political parties, representatives, or individuals needed to win a particular competition such as an election—will prevail in democratic politics given a zero-sum situation of clear winners and losers (Riker, 1962). Surplus coalition members may bring instability and demands that cannot be met. While coalition theory has been a lively topic of debate and study in the political science literature (e.g., Cusack et al., 2007), I believe it is a useful concept outside the realm of electoral politics to analyze the building of science coalitions, which are not necessarily zero-sum endeavors.

Did Berkner, Chapman, and their allies know that they needed to build a large umbrella? Their intentions are not explicit, but they may have felt that they needed as much support as possible from the international scientific organizations in order to press their case at home for an IGY. To prevent the science agenda from becoming too diffuse, barriers to entry have to be established. By 1954, the international IGY organizing committee (set up by ICSU in 1952 and known as CSAGI after its French name, Comité Spécial de l'Année Géophysique Internationale) established criteria for IGY proposals. Priority would be given to projects with at least one of the following characteristics:

1. Problems requiring concurrent synoptic observations at many points involving cooperative observations by many nations.
2. Problems in geophysical sciences whose solutions would be aided by the availability of synoptic or other concentrated work during the IGY.
3. Observations of all major geophysical phenomena in relatively inaccessible regions of the Earth that can be occupied during the IGY because of the extraordinary effort during that interval (the Arctic and Antarctic).
4. Epochal observations of slowly varying terrestrial phenomena (International Council of Scientific Unions, 1959).[1]

These were not arbitrary or unreasonable criteria, since they still permitted a variety of disciplines and conformed in the main with the justification for a coordinated program confined to an 18-month time period, from July 1957 until December1958. Each discipline fitting the criteria had a reporter, whose responsibilities included working with the appropriate scientific union to organize the program for that discipline. The program for each discipline was first outlined by an IGY Committee created by the appropriate scientific union or by some other ICSU body. Detailed coordination of the program, such as the issuance of instruction manuals for the taking of measurements, was the responsibility of the reporter. The overall direction was the responsibility of the CSAGI Bureau (Bullis, 1973; Nicolet, 1984; see Appendix 1).

The CSAGI Bureau members, reporters, and members of the CSAGI General Assembly all served based on their scientific field and their professional standing in the ICSU unions rather than based on nationality. Representation on the basis of science rather than nationality enabled CSAGI and the committees to focus on the nature of the work to be done. This model set a precedent in subsequent ICSU and joint ICSU/WMO scientific campaigns, most recently in IPY 2007–2008. A separate Advisory Council, composed of one delegate from each national IGY committee, assisted with practical arrangements such as finances, regional meetings, access to foreign territory and facilities, bilateral exchanges, and the collection and storage of data. The national committees, through the Advisory Council, were responsible for implementation (Bullis, 1973).

The use of national committees for the IGY ensured that government agencies—both as sources of funding and as authorities—would be involved in science planning from the beginning. Decisions about what was to be funded were made at the national level, so that the IGY amounted to a loosely coordinated set of parallel (or simultaneously run) national programs. The structure of parallel science committees and the advisory council at the international level enabled realistic commitments to be made on the spot.

The U.S. National Academy of Sciences assembled the IGY national committee of 19 members (see Appendix 2; Atwood 1952) in early 1953 and it included government scientists, operational agencies such as the National Weather Bureau, funding agencies, and the military agencies that would provide personnel and logistics. The U.S. national committee formed special technical panels to plan the science and evaluate proposals sent to the National Science Foundation. Including the operational agencies ensured that whatever academic scientists had in mind could be compared to what was possible on the ground.

The National Science Foundation (NSF), established with a very small budget in 1950, was charged to be the official IGY funding agency in the United States, the one that would carry forward and coordinate the IGY budget for the U.S. government. The director of the NSF, Alan Waterman, enthusiastically supported and lobbied for the IGY, no doubt seeing an opportunity for the small agency to gain visibility and resources (Korsmo and Sfraga, 2003). Internationally, UNESCO helped out financially (Bullis, 1973). As an independent, nonmilitary agency, the NSF offered a credible funding source both here in the United States and internationally, in an era where military funding—accompanied by classification and secrecy—was the prime source of most geophysical research. The IGY was to be civilian in character, with the scientific results shared in the open literature. Nevertheless, the logistics for fieldwork and of course the satellite program would be shouldered by the military agencies.

What about political and monetary support for the IGY? Where was the money coming from? That is where solutions go searching for problems. In order to persuade nonspecialists to fund the large-scale nonmilitary science program, the U.S. National Committee for the IGY had to move beyond agenda-setting and coalition building with scientists and executive branch agencies to approach the U.S. Congress and respond to congressional concerns about the public value of science.

LINK SOLUTIONS TO PROBLEMS: THE STATE OF SCIENCE EDUCATION IN THE UNITED STATES

The National Academy of Sciences' IGY Archive provides evidence that the U.S. National Committee for the IGY reached out to many audiences and answered the hundreds of inquiries received from teachers, students, media, and members of the public. The archive contains, for example, a copy of a letter to an elementary school student who had written of his ambition to become a "space man." Hugh Odishaw (1916–1984), another entrepreneurial character and, as the Executive Director to the U.S. National Committee, the architect of the Committee's information strategy, replied with a two-page letter:

I was happy to receive your well-written letter, and to learn of your interest in becoming a "Space Man." While you are in elementary school, you won't have to choose your own subjects

of course. Later on, when you to go high school and college, you will want to take as many Mathematics and Science courses as possible, together with courses in English, History, and other subjects which will help to make you a well-rounded person, as well as a possible "Space Man."

The letter goes on to recommend reading all the materials assigned by the student's teacher in addition to other books such as Ronald Fraser's *Once Round the Sun* (H. Odishaw, letter to J. Bunch, 15 April 1958, in Chron. file, IGY Office of Information, National Academy of Sciences IGY Collection, Washington, D.C.).

Odishaw's response to the young student is typical of the care with which the U.S. National Committee's Office of Information answered the mail. During the IGY, about a dozen people worked in this Office, maintaining close contact with media, schools, government agencies, Congress, private industry, and professional societies.

Well before the IGY began in 1957, the U.S. National Committee for the IGY thought about providing education materials and general information about the exciting "experiments in concert" that were about to begin. Broadly accessible information about the IGY was necessary background for the National Science Foundation's IGY budget request, but also there was a sense of urgency regarding the state of science education in the country. In its 30 November 1956 issue, the magazine *U.S. News and World Report* focused on education and science, noting the disparity between the Soviet Union and the United States in the size of the workforce engaged in technical and engineering jobs. One of the articles in this issue, by chemist and businessman Arnold Beckman (who developed the first commercially successful pH meter), leveled the all-too-familiar complaints about the American school system: it has failed to anticipate and prepare for the increasing need for more scientists and engineers; its science teachers are not competent to teach science; and its teacher certification requirements pay more attention to how to teach rather than mastery of the subject matter (Beckman, 1956).

Beckman was not the only one calling for improvements in science and mathematics education across the United States. The U.S. Congress raised the same concerns to the National Science Foundation and the IGY Committee. As recounted to Hugh Odishaw by S. Paul Kramer, a consultant to Odishaw who attended the congressional hearings, Senator Everett Dirksen (R–Illinois) urged the IGY scientists to involve the high schools and colleges in real time: "I would not like to see available information embalmed until the year and a half is over," said Dirksen. "I would like to see it move out where it will do good." Senator Warren Magnuson (D–Washington) reminded the National Science Foundation that education and public outreach were well within the scope of the Foundation's mandate: "I know from having authored the bill. The real reason for approving it was this sort of thing" (S. P. Kramer, correspondence to H. Odishaw, 6 March 1957, in Chron. file, IGY Office of Information, National Academy of Sciences IGY Collection, Washington, D.C.). In response, the IGY organizers worked with publishers, universities specializing in teacher training, and organizations such as the Science Service to develop educational pamphlets, teacher guides, posters, and classroom activities. An example of one of IGY posters on the Oceans that also appeared in a pamphlet is reproduced in Figure 1. The IGY organizers also produced a film series, *Planet Earth*, released in 1960, for use in schools and for educational television (U.S. National Committee for the IGY, 1960; Korsmo, 2004).

There was little if any dissent on the need for an education and information campaign; the organizers believed it was the right thing to do. The arguments that emerged from the archival records were about the best ways of doing it (Korsmo, 2004).

FULFILLING THE COMMITMENTS: DATA, PUBLICATION, AND RESULTS

The justification for having a Third International Polar Year, which became the International Geophysical Year, only twenty-five years after the Second Polar Year of 1932–1933 rested in part on the many advances made in techniques of geophysical observation, including radio communications and aviation (Chapman, 1960). If new techniques of analysis, including advances in instrumentation and processing, seem adequate to push for large-scale data collection, then how does one go about it on a worldwide scale? Who takes responsibility to collect, process, and share the data in useable formats?

This was the question faced by the designers of the International Geophysical Year. The U.S. National Committee for the IGY met for the first time on 27 March 1953 in Washington, D.C. In Berkner's absence on the first day, the participants expressed their doubts. There were at least two problems: first, the question of whether the Soviet Union would participate at all, and second, the problem of secrecy and classification of geophysical data that existed in the United States (Gerson, 1953; Needell, 2000).

How could you have a worldwide program when the Soviet Union and its allies were not involved? With Stalin's death earlier that month, on 6 March 1953, the question hung in the air: Would the Soviet Union open up? At the time, the Soviet Union belonged to the World Meteorological Organization and the International Astronomical Union, but not to ICSU or other ICSU member unions. There was hardly any data exchange between the United States and its allies and the Soviet Union except for routine weather observations. On the other hand, the United States also classified much of its data; the entire polar program funded by the military, for example, How could the United States expect the Soviet Union to supply data when we withheld ours? All high-latitude ionospheric data—the original focus of the Third Polar Year as proposed by Berkner and Chapman back in 1950—were considered classified in the United States.

The U.S. National Committee for the IGY was not the only committee to raise the problem of classification and secrecy. In May 1953, the U.S. Research and Development Board's Geophysics Committee also raised the issue to the army, navy, and air force (U.S. Research and Development Board, 1953). The Geophysics Committee made a distinction between basic data—"the elementary building blocks of scientific progress in the earth sciences"—and the end products, such as reports that might be used for military or national security purposes. Free access to the data, insisted the Committee, was necessary for scientific progress.

The designers of the IGY deliberately decided in favor of a science program with free and open data exchange. Indeed, they saw IGY as a means to loosen up the secrecy classifications in their own country in addition to encouraging better data flow from other nations.

By the fall of 1954, it became clear that the Soviet Union would indeed participate in the IGY, so Berkner instructed the U.S. National Committee to prepare a description of all the data that the United States was prepared to gather and exchange. The idea was to get standardized instruments to record multiple observations taken at frequent intervals in many parts of the world. These observations would be recorded, analyzed, synthesized, and preserved in usable formats for further study. As Berkner told the U.S. National Committee in 1953, "Let our measurements be designed so that repeats during the 4th [Geophysical Year] will be valuable" (Gerson, 1953).

The idea of the world data centers also came up early in the IGY planning process (Chapman, 1955). The United States volunteered to host one, which became a distributed system involving several universities and research institutions all over the country, and then the Soviet Union followed suit. A third world data center was established for Europe and Japan. Multiple data sets in different parts of

FIGURE 1. The Oceans, IGY Poster. National Academy of Sciences, 1958.

the world were encouraged to ensure against catastrophic destruction of a single center and to make the data accessible to researchers in different parts of the world.

While the national IGY committees were responsible for delivering timely and quality data, the world data centers were responsible for the safekeeping, reproduction, cataloging, and accessibility of the data. Anyone engaged in research was to be given access. If you could get yourself into the host country and up to the door of the data center, you could not be turned away (P. Hart, personal communication). We know there were gaps, and the limits of East–West cooperation became immediately apparent in the satellite program. However, the rules of the game were in place, establishing norms of behavior that lasted well beyond the IGY.

Finally, the IGY publications included but went much further than peer reviewed scientific journals. The *Annals of the IGY*, 48 volumes published by Pergamon Press between 1959 and 1970 (International Council of Scientific Unions, 1959; Fleagle, 1994:170), record not only the results of the research, but also the process of developing the IGY—the international meetings, the world data center guidelines, and the resolutions. This was a self-conscious documentation effort, and we are still benefiting from that today. We have journalists' accounts such as Walter Sullivan's *Assault on the Unknown* (1961). Upon completion of the IGY research, Sullivan was given virtually unfettered access to the IGY field projects and documentation.

The establishment of the world data centers and the constant encouragement by the U.S. National Committee for researchers to publish and share their results in many forms demonstrated to many audiences the ability of science organizations to live up to their commitments. The world data centers, which continue to function today, were instrumental in continuing the legacy of the IGY: coordinated, international science to understand the interactions of atmospheric, oceanic, and terrestrial processes. While entrepreneurs initiated schemes and linked solutions to problems, the thousands of people who carried out the work and contributed results gave credibility to the geophysical sciences, both in the United States and in other countries. Sufficient trust had been established to begin the demilitarization of geophysics.

CONCLUSION

The IGY can teach us something about both process and results. The ways in which Berkner, Chapman, Odishaw, and many others pursued the activities of agenda-setting, linking solutions to problems, and establishing a pattern of credible commitments, turned a casual conversation among a few experts into a whirlwind series of international expeditions and experiments. There are many other ways of looking at the IGY. Elsewhere, I have compared my approach to the story of the blind men and the elephant. After they felt different parts of the animal, they each proclaimed the elephant looked like a tree trunk, a snake, and a fan (Korsmo, 2007a). The policy sciences are useful in deciding what rules of decision-making and allocation of resources work the best for different types of projects in different contexts. The context I chose here was primarily based in the United States, but it would be quite valuable to compare both current and historical science policy evolution in other countries during the time of the IGY.

This symposium is an important step in the documentation of our present efforts in the International Polar Year 2007–2008. Due to the precedents set by the IGY and its successors, such as the International Years of the Quiet Sun (1964–1965) and the Upper Mantle Project (1962–1970), we have international frameworks for scientific cooperation as well as a history of data sharing and long-term environmental observations.

While the IGY did not include social sciences, it supported a surprising amount of geography and natural history associated with the study of ice sheets and mountain glaciers. The umbrella was large enough to include these projects and contribute to our knowledge of alpine and Arctic ecosystems. The glaciology program of the IGY was a bridge between the physical and biological sciences, paving the way for programs such as UNESCO's International Hydrological Decade, 1965–1974 (Kasser 1967; Muller 1970). In a similar fashion, the social and human studies included in the present International Polar Year 2007–2008 are a bridge between science and policy. Their inclusion (e.g., Krupnik et al., 2005) provides even more opportunity for self-reflection and evaluation of what lessons and legacies we will leave for the future.

ACKNOWLEDGMENTS

I am grateful to several IGY 1957–1958 participants, including Pembroke Hart and Phillip Mange, for their insights and recollections. I also wish to thank the archivists and staff of the following institutions for their assistance in locating and accessing the archival and oral history collections used in this research: Sydney Chapman Papers, University of Alaska Fairbanks, Elmer E. Rasmuson Library, Alaska and Polar Regions Collections; Nathaniel C. Gerson Papers and Alan T. Waterman

Papers, U.S. Library of Congress, Manuscripts Division; IGY Collection at the U.S. National Academy of Sciences Archives; Oral History Collection, Niels Bohr Library and Archives, Center for History of Physics, American Institute of Physics; Polar Archival Program, Ohio State University Libraries; and U.S. Research and Development Board Collection, Record Group 330, Entry 341, U.S. National Archives and Records Administration. This material is based on work supported by the National Science Foundation (NSF) while I was working at the foundation. Any opinions, findings, and conclusions expressed in this article are those of the author and do not necessarily reflect the views of NSF.

APPENDIX 1

THE CSAGI BUREAU MEMBERS AND REPORTERS, IPY 1957–1958

The following list demonstrates the breadth of disciplines and expertise represented among the international IGY leadership (Nicolet, 1984:314).

CSAGI Bureau

S. Chapman, President (UK)
L. Berkner, Vice President (USA)
M. Nicolet, Secretary General (Belgium)
J. Coulomb, Member (France)
V. Beloussov, Member (USSR)

CSAGI Discipline Reporters

World Days (when intensive measurements would be taken)—A. H. Shapley (USA)
Meteorology—J. Van Mieghem (Belgium)
Geomagnetism—V. Laursen (Denmark)
Aurora and Airglow—S. Chapman (UK), with F. Roach and C. Elvey (USA)
Ionosphere—W. J. G. Beynon (UK)
Solar Activity—Y. Ohman (Sweden)
Cosmic Rays—J. A. Simpson (USA)
Longitudes and Latitudes—J. Danjon (France)
Glaciology—J. M. Wordie (UK)
Oceanography—G. Laclavére (France)
Rockets and Satellites—L. V. Berkner (USA)
Seismology—V. V. Beloussov (USSR)
Gravimetry—P. Lejay (France)
Nuclear Radiation—M. Nicolet (Belgium)

APPENDIX 2

MEMBERS OF THE FIRST U.S. NATIONAL COMMITTEE FOR IPY 1957–1958

The following list of U.S. IGY leadership shows a mixture of disciplinary and professional society representation and the direct involvement of U.S. government agencies (Atwood, 1952).

Chair

J. Kaplan, representing the U.S. National Committee of the International Union of Geodesy and Geophysics

Members

L. H. Adams, Geophysical Laboratory, Carnegie Institution of Washington
Henry Booker, International Scientific Radio Union (URSI)
Lyman W. Briggs, National Geographic Society
G. M. Clemence, U.S. Naval Observatory
C. T. Elvey, Geophysical Institute, University of Alaska
John A. Fleming, American Geophysical Union
Nathaniel C. Gerson, Cambridge Research Directorate, U.S. Air Force
Paul Klopsteg, National Science Foundation
F. W. Reichelderfer, U.S. Weather Bureau and World Meteorological Organization
Elliot B. Roberts, U.S. Coast and Geodetic Survey
Alan H. Shapley, U.S. Bureau of Standards
Paul A. Siple, representing U.S. National Committee of the International Geography Union, Association of American Geographers, and General Staff, U.S. Army
Otto Struve, representing U.S. National Committee of the International Astronomy Union
Merle Tuve, Department of Terrestrial Magnetism, Carnegie Institution of Washington
Lincoln Washburn, Snow, Ice, and Permafrost Research Establishment, U.S. Corps of Engineers, and the Arctic Institute of North America

Ex-officio Members

Wallace W. Atwood Jr., Director, Office of International Relations, National Academy of Sciences-National Research Council
Lloyd V. Berkner, Member, Special Committee for the International Geophysical Year
J. Wallace Joyce, Deputy Science Advisor, U.S. Department of State

NOTE

1. In a similar fashion, the planners of the 2007–2008 International Polar Year came up with a framework that established criteria for participation. This not only provided guidance for researchers who were considering whether to write proposals, but also the existence of criteria conveyed to a broader audience, including policy-makers at the national level, the seriousness and purposefulness of the upcoming science campaign (Rapley et al., 2004).

LITERATURE CITED

Ahlmann, H. W. 1946. Glaciological Methods. *Polar Record*, 4(31): 315–319.

American Institute of Physics. 2000. Finding Aid to the James A. Van Allen Papers, 1938–1990. University of Iowa, Iowa City. http://www.aip.org/history/ead/19990077.html (accessed 18 September 2007).

Atwood, W. W., Jr. 1952. Letter to Chairmen of U.S. National Committees of International Scientific Unions, 9 December 1952. In Folder "Organization USNC 1952." National Academy of Sciences, IGY Archive, Washington, D.C.

Baker, F. W. G. 1982. A Century of International Interdisciplinary Cooperation. *Interdisciplinary Science Reviews*, 7(4):270–282.

Beckman, A. O. 1956. "A Businessman's View on the 'Failure' of Education." *U.S. News and World Report*, 30 November 1956, 83–89.

Bentley, C. R. 1964. "The Structure of Antarctica and Its Ice Cover." In *Research in Geophysics*, ed. H. Odishaw, vol. 2, pp. 335–389. Cambridge, Mass.: MIT Press.

Beynon, W. J. G. 1975. U.R.S.I. and the Early History of the Ionosphere. *Philosophical Transactions of the Royal Society of London. Series A, Mathematical and Physical Sciences*, 280:47–55.

Bullis, H. 1973. *The Political Legacy of the International Geophysical Year*. Washington, D.C.: U.S. Government Printing Office.

Bush, V. 1945. *Science—The Endless Frontier*. Washington, D.C.: National Science Foundation. [Reprinted in 1990]

Chapman, S. 1955. Letter to Merle Tuve, 8 January. Box 53, Folder 103, "Data Processing" in "Sydney Chapman Papers." Alaska and Polar Regions Collections, Elmer E. Rasmuson Library, University of Alaska, Fairbanks.

Chapman, S. 1960. From Polar Years to Geophysical Year. *Studia geophysica et geodaetica*, 4:313–324.

Cusack, T. R., T. Iversen, and D. Soskice. 2007. Economic Interests and the Origins of Electoral Systems. *American Political Science Review*, 101(3):373–391.

Day, D. A. 2000. "Cover Stories and Hidden Agendas: Early American Space and National Security Policy." In *Reconsidering Sputnik: Forty Years Since the Soviet Satellite*, ed. R. D. Launius, J. M. Logsdon, and R. W. Smith, pp. 161–195. Amsterdam: Harwood Academic Publishers.

Fleagle, R. G. 1994. *Global Environmental Change: Interactions of Science, Policy, and Politics in the United States*. Westport, Conn.: Praeger.

Gerson, N. C. 1953. "1st USNC Meeting, 27 March 1953." Box 8, Folder 1, "N. C. Gerson Papers." Manuscripts Division, Library of Congress, Washington, D.C.

Good, G. A. 2000. "Biographical Note." In *Guide to the Sydney Chapman Papers*. Alaska and Polar Regions Collections, Elmer E. Rasmuson Library, University of Alaska Fairbanks. http://nwda-db.wsulibs.wsu.edu/findaid/ark:/80444/xv48580#bioghistID (accessed 18 September 2007).

Hall, R. C. 1997. The Truth about Overflights. *Quarterly Journal of Military History*, 9(3):24–39.

International Council of Scientific Unions. 1959. *Annals of the International Geophysical Year*, Vol. 1. New York: Pergamon Press.

Kasser, P. 1967. Fluctuations of Glaciers, 1959–1965. *Technical Papers in Hydrology*, 1. Paris: UNESCO (ICSI).

Kevles, D. J. 1990. Cold War and Hot Physics: Science, Security, and the American State, 1945–56. *Historical Studies of the Physical Sciences*, 20(2):238–264.

Kingdon, J. W. 1995. *Agendas, Alternatives, and Public Policies*. 2nd ed. New York: Addison-Wesley Educational Publishers.

Kirwan, L. P., C. M. Mannerfelt, C. G. Rossby, and V. Schytt. 1949. Glaciers and Climatology: Hans W:son Ahlmann's Contribution. *Geografiska Annaler*, 31:11–20.

Korsmo, F. L. 2004. Shaping Up Planet Earth: The International Geophysical Year (1957–1958) and Communicating Science through Print and Film Media. *Science Communication*, 26(2):162–187.

———. 2007a. The International Geophysical Year of 1957 to 1958. *Science, People and Politics* 2 (January 2007). http://www.gavaghan-communications.com/korsmoigy.html (accessed 14 September 2007).

———. 2007b. The Genesis of the International Geophysical Year. *Physics Today*, 60(7):38–43.

Korsmo, F. L., and Sfraga, M. P. 2003. From Interwar to Cold War: Selling Field Science in the United States, 1920s–1950s. *Earth Sciences History*, 22(1):55–78.

Krupnik, I., M. Bravo, Y. Csonka, G. Hovelsrud-Broda, L. Müller-Wille, B. Poppel, P. Schweitzer, and S. Sörlin. 2005. Social Sciences and Humanities in the International Polar Year 2007–2008: An Integrating Mission. *Arctic*, 58(1):91–97.

Müller, F., ed. 1970. Perennial Ice and Snow Masses: A Guide for Compilation and Assemblage of Data for a World Inventory; Variations of Existing Glaciers: A Guide to International Practices for Their Measurement. *Technical Papers in Hydrology*, 5. Paris: UNESCO (ICSI).

National Academy of Sciences. 1958. *Planet Earth: The Mystery with 100,000 Clues*. Washington, D.C.: National Academy of Sciences.

Nicolet, M. 1984. The International Geophysical Year (1957–1958): Great Achievements and Minor Obstacles. *GeoJournal*, 8(4):303–320.

Needell, A. 2000. *Science, Cold War, and the American State: Lloyd V. Berkner and the Balance of Professional Ideals*. Washington, D.C.: Smithsonian Institution and Harwood Academic.

North, D. C., and B. R. Weingast. 1989. Constitutions and Commitment: The Evolution of Institutions Governing Public Choice in Seventeenth-Century England. *The Journal of Economic History*, 49(4):803–832.

Rapley, C., R. Bell, I. Allison, R. Bindschadler, G. Casassa, S. Chown, G. Duhaime, V. Kotlyakov, M. Kuhn, O. Orheim, P. C. Pandey, H. K. Petersen, H. Schalke, W. Janoschek, E. Sarukhanian, Z. Zhang. 2004. A Framework for the International Polar Year. ICSU IPY 2007–2008 Planning Group. http://216.70.123.96/images/uploads/framework.pdf (accessed 19 September 2007).

Riker, W. 1962. *The Theory of Political Coalitions*. New Haven, Conn.: Yale University Press.

Rossby, C. G. 1947. Letter to Executive Secretary, Joint Research and Development Board, 21 April 1947. Research and Development Board, Record Group 330, Entry 341, Box 452, Folder 2. National Archives and Record Administration, College Park, Md.

Sabatier, P. A., and H. C. Jenkins-Smith. 1999. "The Advocacy Coalition Framework: An Assessment." In *Theories of the Policy Process*, ed. P. A. Sabatier, pp. 117–166. Boulder, Colo.: Westview Press.

Siple, P. 1948. "Memorandum to Robert B. Simpson, 14 April 1948," p. 4. Record Group 330, Entry 341, Box 452, Folder 1. U.S. National Archives and Records Administration, College Park, Md.

Sullivan, W. 1961. *Assault on the Unknown: The International Geophysical Year*. New York: McGraw-Hill.

U.S. National Archives and Records Administration, n.d. "Finding Aid" to Record Group 330, Entry 341, "Office of the Secretary of Defense, Research and Development Board." U.S. National Archives and Records Administration, College Park, Md.

U.S. Research and Development Board. 1953. Memorandum from the Board, 23 May, in General Correspondence, Box 33. "Alan T. Waterman Collection." Library of Congress, Washington, D.C.

U.S. National Committee for the IGY. 1960. Press release, 17 November 1960. National Academy of Sciences IGY Archive, Office of Information, Series 12, Planet Earth Films Chron. File. National Academy of Sciences, Washington, D.C.

U.S. National Security Council. 1957. Statement of Policy by the National Security Council on Antarctica. NSC 5715/1. 29 June. Contained in NSC Series, Policy Papers Subseries, Eisenhower Library. Abilene, Kans.

Van Allen, J. A. 1997. Interview with B. Shoemaker, November 18, 1997. Transcript. Oral History Collection, Ohio State University, Columbus.

———. 1998. Genesis of the International Geophysical Year. *The Polar Times*, 2(11):5.

Preserving the Origins of the Space Age: The Material Legacy of the International Geophysical Year (1957–1958) at the National Air and Space Museum

David H. DeVorkin

David DeVorkin, National Air and Space Museum, Smithsonian Institution, P.O. Box 37012, MRC 311, Washington, DC 20013-7012, USA (devorkind@si.edu). Accepted 29 May 2008.

ABSTRACT. In July 1966, the 89th Congress (H.R. 6125) laid out the charge defining the new Smithsonian National Air and Space Museum: to " memorialize the national development of aviation and space flight; collect, preserve, and display aeronautical and space flight equipment of historical interest and significance; serve as a repository for scientific equipment and data pertaining to the development of aviation and space flight; and provide educational material for the historical study of aviation and space flight." Under this umbrella statement, the Museum has been actively collecting artifacts and documentary evidence in the area of the earth and space sciences, as well as in astronomy, that helps to preserve the social, cultural, intellectual, and material legacy of the enterprise. The paper examines the holdings pertaining to the IGY era (1957–1960) presently in the NASM collection. It discusses how some of these items were identified, selected, and collected, as a means of offering a preliminary appraisal of the historical value of the collection. It highlights a suite of objects built by James Van Allen's Iowa group and discusses their historical significance.

THE IGY

The International Geophysical Year (IGY) of 1957–1958 was conceptualized at a small dinner party in April 1950, held at the home of James A. Van Allen in Silver Spring, Maryland. As Walter Sullivan recorded at the time, and as Fae Korsmo and many others have reminded us more recently (Sullivan, 1961; Korsmo, 2007; this volume), out of this meeting grew a plan to coordinate observations relevant to the geosciences over all parts of the globe, and, for the first time, conduct significant soundings of the upper reaches of the earth's atmosphere and ionosphere. Considering that three members of the party, notably Van Allen, Lloyd Berkner, and Sydney Chapman, later to become key players in IGY, were primarily concerned with studying the ionosphere, it is not surprising that they organized the means to pursue its global characteristics using all available technologies (Needell, 2000). Their plan was aided and abetted by Cold War priorities for developing the capabilities of space flight to aid global reconnaissance, and in fact became driven by those priorities, modified in complex ways by the foreign policy and national security strategies of the major participating nations (McDougall, 1985; Bulkeley, 1991).

Out of this complex mixture of scientific and national security priorities, both the Soviet Union and the United States announced plans to orbit artificial satellites during the IGY, and both made good on their promise, though in a manner, and especially an order, that surprised and deeply disturbed a large portion of world's media and propelled a space race between the two superpowers that fuelled the first decade of what has been called the Space Age.

A substantial historical literature exists recounting the IGY and the origins of the space age (Pisano and Lewis, 1988; Marson and Terner, 1963; McDougall, 1985) Our purpose here is not to recount this history nor to delineate the Smithsonian Institution's participation in space research, but rather to describe holdings at the National Air and Space Museum (NASM) pertaining to space flight activities during the International Geophysical Year (1957–1958). This paper discusses specifically how the Smithsonian National Air and Space Museum (NASM) has participated in preserving the material heritage of this legacy—a legacy that might be seen someday as a major factor leading to the existence of the Museum itself. We begin by situating the act of cultural preservation within the mission of the Smithsonian, and then conclude with an assessment of efforts to preserve the material legacy of the IGY.

ON MUSEUM PRESERVATION

Institutions like the NASM collect for a variety of purposes, both immediate and long term. One can only speculate about why, precisely, a material legacy will be important for our descendents, say 400 years from now; whether they are specialists in science and its history, or whether they are educated and inquisitive nonspecialists. Will they think well of us for making the effort to preserve a material legacy, one that can be "read" without the intervention of media-specific technologies? Or will they possess technologies undreamt of today for seeking out the answers to historical questions that transcend the material legacy, and regard our efforts as ultimately futile?

The mission, defined by legislation that brought the NASM into existence, claims that the Institution has a responsibility to "memorialize the national development of aviation and space flight" (U.S. House of Representatives, 1946). That is what we indeed do, and as I have argued elsewhere, the survival of a physical artifact will, in and of itself, help to stimulate questions about our times someday, and may even, conceivably, help to answer questions about our lives and times (DeVorkin, 2006a; 2006b). As more than one observer has noted recently, commenting

about the significance of objects displayed in museums and the motives for the curators to put them on display; "Their presence there is the message. . . . It is still all about visibility." (Kennicott, 2007:C1)

From the beginning, NASM's charge has been to "serve as the repository for, preserve, and display aeronautical and space flight equipment and data of historical interest and significance to the progress of aviation and space flight, and provide educational material for the historical study of aviation and space flight and their technologies" (U.S. House of Representatives, 1946) Since this is a formal process with oversight, NASM curators periodically create and review collections plans that rationalize the effort. But curators are also keenly aware of the fact that they are, in some way, making choices and hence are filtering history. After all, taking the existentialist's point of view, as Oxford's Jim Bennett and others have observed from time to time "museum collections . . . show you not what there was but what was collected." (Bennett, 2004),

This statement is a simple fact of life, of means, motives, and of circumstance. Unlike the natural history disciplines, whose collections stand at the very core of their research interests, and in fact define them, forming the data banks from which they ask questions and draw conclusions, collections of space history reflect something rather different. They reflect cultural and institutional needs to preserve the material heritage of ourselves, a very recent past still very much alive in its human participants and in its institutions, and of which we are part, our contemporary national heritage. Deciding what to collect and preserve, then, involves as much issues of a symbolic nature, the need to memorialize, as it does intellectual issues relating to any disciplinary goals, past, present, or future, and so the questions historians ask about culture transcend the specimens they preserve. Collections are not comprehensive of their culture and are the result of choices, personal preferences, biases, and both political and financial limitations.

So what is it that institutions like museums do when they collect and preserve? The economic anthropologist tells us that the act of collection by institutions is a formal method of removing objects from the commodity sphere—the sphere of use, speculation, and trade—and placing them into a singularized and sacralized sphere (Kopytoff, 1986). This is definitely what we try to do at the Smithsonian and it is reflected in our Collections Rationales, our arguments over what to collect. Indeed, over the past years, some curators have repeatedly worried that if we do not maintain control of objects deemed to be of historical value coming out of the Nation's space program, relics bought and paid for by taxpayers, they will be sold as excess property and become commodities for speculation by collectors and agents. In more recent times, as our ability to collect has met serious financial, personnel, and storage limitations, this concern has diminished somewhat and there is now healthy consideration of establishing a means to distribute the responsibility of preservation. This includes establishing a "national strategy" of sharing the responsibility for preserving the heritage among many institutions. But ultimately, we generally accept the view that what it is we are doing by collecting is making this material heritage accessible to future generations in a manner that will stimulate interest and remembrance of an historical era or event.

A clear symptom of this rationale for sacralization and protection from the commodity sphere comes from a unique agreement the Smithsonian Institution maintains with NASA, the "NASA/NASM Transfer Agreement" (Agreement, 1967). This document asserts that any object on NASA's inventories that is deemed by a select committee of NASA program managers and specialists to be historic and excess to present agency needs must be offered first to the National Air and Space Museum for its collection. The NASM will then deliberate and decide upon collection. If it agrees, the object is transferred to the Smithsonian inventory. If not, it goes on the normal "excess property" listings and can be transferred to other agencies, or sold to the public. It is the existence of this agreement that gives the Space History collection at NASM its special responsibility. Even though the IGY-era collections predate the agreement, many came to the Museum as a result of its existence, well after the close of the era.

There is yet another aspect of collecting in Space History that warrants attention here that adds to its unique character and will help us evaluate our IGY-era collections. Many of the most important objects, those responsible for the actual science performed, are not available for collection and never will be. They were launched, and were either consumed through use or by re-entry, or are now in orbits that make them inaccessible. What we can collect, therefore, are surrogates for the "real thing." They may be very close in form and function, like flight backups, but they are not the actual objects that made the historic observations or performed the historic feats, such as the first soft landing on the moon, Mars, Titan, or an asteroid. There are exceptions, of course, such as the panoramic camera from *Surveyor* III that was returned to Earth by *Apollo* 12 astronauts (NASM Catalogue number I19900169001; hereafter, just the alphanumerical code will be used: "I" for incoming loan, "A" for accession). There are objects returned from Shuttle missions, as well as objects that returned to earth by design, like the particle collectors aboard *Stardust*, and interplanetary probes that were launched and might someday be captured and returned, like the third *International Sun-Earth Explorer* (ISEE-3).

In addition to its special relationship with NASA, and its unique responsibilities, NASM must still justify what it collects both internally and externally. Individuals rarely rationalize why they collect what they collect but institutions, especially public ones, must provide clear and cogent rationalizations in order to gain the support to identify, collect, and preserve. One need only consider the large costs involved in collection and preservation, and the long-term commitment an institution or a culture is willing to make in supporting such efforts. Thus, given this mandate, and limitations, how representative is "what was collected" to "what there was"?

THE TIME BOUNDARIES OF THE IGY LEGACY

The legacy of the International Geophysical Year (IGY) of 1957–1958 predates NASA, of course, though many of the objects that one can describe as belonging to the IGY era came from NASA, which inherited the legacy upon its formation in August 1958 and retained much of it for years at its visitor centers and in storage. We can roughly limit the IGY-era legacy in space by establishing its beginning as the material legacy growing out of planning for the IGY since the early 1950s (see Korsmo, this volume), to the launch of *Explorer VII* in October 1959, *Vanguard III* in September 1959, and two *Discoverer* launches (VII and VIII) through 20 November 1959 (Green and Lomask, 1970). *Explorer VII* was the last Army Ballistic Missile Agency (ABMA) satellite and was transferred to NASA. It represents the end of the legacy started by *Sputnik* 1 and *Explorer* 1 and the IGY context, even though transfer of all programs to NASA took place with NASA's creation in the fall of 1958 via the National Aeronautics and Space Act. The major American programs linked to the IGY era include *Vanguard* (I–III), *Explorer* (I–VII), *Pioneer* (I–IV), and the military programs known as Project *SCORE* and *Discoverer* (I–VIII). Russian programs included *Sputnik* (I–III) and *Luna* (I–III).

THE NASM COLLECTION

More than 200 objects in the national collection can be associated with IGY-era space-related activities. These reside in several NASM sub-collections, including rocketry and propulsion, the space sciences, memorabilia, international, and social and cultural collections. There are partial-scale and full-scale models, replicas, engineering models, components, medals, badges, and ephemera (collectibles). In this review, we consider only the artifact collections, not flat materials in our library and archives, including monographs, serials, technical publications, print and film resources, as well as extensive manuscript collections or oral histories (see http://www.siris.si.edu/ and http://www.nasm.si.edu/research/arch/collections.cfm).

IGY-RELATED COLLECTIONS: PREPARING FOR THE IGY

In addition to numerous examples of early sounding rocket payloads for both atmospheric and space research—such as ultraviolet spectrographs, X-ray detectors, magnetometers, varieties of halogen quenched particle flux counters, mass spectrometers, temperature and pressure sensors, and cameras built for V-2, Viking, Aerobee and ARCAS flights from the late 1940s through the 1950s—the NASM collection preserves objects intended specifically for use during the IGY, such as a visual Project Moonwatch telescope (A19860036000) (Figure 1) and the first Baker-Nunn satellite tracking camera (A19840406000) mounted in Arizona. The most curious object, symbolic of the aspirations of S. Fred Singer, one of the original members of the group that conceived the IGY, is MOUSE (Minimal Orbital Unmanned Satellite, Earth), a full-scale design concept model for an artificial satellite (A19731670000). It carries two Geiger counters for cosmic-ray studies, photocells, telemetry electronics, and a rudimentary magnetic data storage element (Figure 2). The rocketry collection has examples of small sounding rockets derived from barrage ordnance technology, such as the Loki-Dart (A19750183000; 0184000), and various combinations that were used in the 1950s for atmospheric measurements and as payloads under Skyhook balloons for extreme high-altitude soundings by the University of Iowa and by the Navy.

IGY-RELATED COLLECTIONS: *SPUTNIK*

In addition to one of the first full-scale models of *Sputnik* 1 on loan to the Smithsonian from the Soviet Union/Russia (I19900388002), as well as the original electrical arming pin removed from the flight unit just before launch (I19971143001), the Museum holds six objects relating to the flight, all in the collectible category and ranging from a cigarette lighter and commemorative pin to medals and a music box. There are no holdings relating to, or informing, the technical characteristics of any of the early

FIGURE 1. Project Moonwatch telescope (A19860036000), preserved and on display at the NASM's Hazy Center. Amateurs and commercial organizations alike built thousands of instruments of this type; they exist in many forms. The Smithsonian Astrophysical Observatory created and coordinated the Moonwatch program to produce preliminary orbital elements of the first satellites. (NASM photograph)

FIGURE 2. S. Fred Singer's full-scale concept model for an artificial satellite (A19731670000). (Eric Long photograph, NASM)

Sputniks. There is nothing in the collection pertaining to Project *Luna.*

IGY-Related Collections: Project Vanguard

The NASM collection has seven objects identified as Vanguard 1 backup models, test models, replicas, and display models (A19580115000 through A19830244000). Among these is the original test vehicle TV-3 (Figure 3), which was recovered after the launch vehicle crashed onto the launchpad on 6 December 1957 (A19761857000). The object was acquired from John P. Hagen (1908–1990), the former Project Vanguard manager, in the spring of 1971

and placed on exhibit in the Smithsonian's Arts & Industries Building. After NASM opened in July 1976, visitors encountered it in the outstretched hand of an unhappy and concerned 12-foot tall "Uncle Sam." It now resides in a case near the Museum's Vanguard rocket, a TV-2BU (Figure 4, center) that had been prepared for launch by the Martin Company on 3 September 1957 but was delayed and then cancelled. Vanguard 1 was launched on a near duplicate rocket; the markings on the NASM version were changed to be identical to those of the flight vehicle by the Naval Research Laboratory, which then donated the rocket to the Smithsonian Institution in 1958 (A19580114000). There are also three elements of various stages of the

FIGURE 3. Examination of the original TV-3 satellite in March 2008, by members of the Naval Research Lab team who designed and built it, on the eve of the fiftieth anniversary of the first successful Vanguard flight. The object was opened to allow inspection for identification of components, search for undocumented experiments, and to assess its state of preservation. Martin Votaw, left, Roger Easton, right. (Photograph courtesy Judith Pargamin)

FIGURE 4. Vanguard launch vehicle TV-2BU on display at NASM in the "Missile Pit." (NASM photograph by Eric Long)

Vanguard propulsion system in the collection, as well as a set of 18 electrical and electronic radio instruments used in a Vanguard Minitrack station (A19761036000). There is one instrumented replica of the Vanguard Lyman Alpha satellite, also called SLV-1, that failed to orbit in May 1958, and two versions of Vanguard III, including Vanguard 3, also called Magne-Ray Satellite, and finally the Vanguard Magnetometer satellite that did fly, designated SLV-5 or Vanguard 3a (A19751413000; 1407000; 1412000). It was placed in orbit in December 1959 and was equipped with two X-ray detectors and micrometeoroid detectors.

The instrumented Vanguards do preserve many of the technical parameters of the early flight objects. They were built generally by the same people, using the same jigs and materials, which produced the flight objects at the Naval Research Laboratory. Some of the craft have Lyman alpha and X-ray detectors identical to, or very similar to those used by NRL scientists in sounding rocket flights throughout the 1950s (DeVorkin, 1996).

IGY-Related Collections: Explorer

There are more than two dozen objects in the collection relating to some form of Explorer satellite between Explorers I through VII, and dozens more UV and X-Ray detectors identical to those flown by groups at NRL, Iowa and elsewhere. This collection contains objects with a high degree of historical accuracy and significance, and preserves some of the most detailed technical characteristics of the first flight objects. Of great historical significance is a suite of objects recently acquired from George H. Ludwig, one of James Van Allen's graduate students at the time the Iowa group became engaged in preparing for the first Explorers. The primary object Dr. Ludwig donated was built as an engineering model for the payload for the first fully instrumented Vanguard flight (Figure 5), and then became the template for the redesign effort at the Jet Propulsion Laboratory after Army Ordnance was given the green light to proceed with a launch after the failure of the Vanguard TV-3 launch (A20060086000). As both Van Allen and Ludwig have noted in various recollections (Van Allen, 1983:55–57), the package was designed for a 20-inch Vanguard sphere but was within parameters easily adaptable to a 6-inch diameter cylindrical chamber compatible with the dimensions of the scaled-down Sergeant solid rocket of the sort that ABMA had been placing on Jupiter test flights. So when a flight on a Jupiter-C became possible in the wake of the Vanguard failure, and after Von Braun promised Eisenhower that the Army could orbit something useful within 90 days, Ludwig packed his bags and his family and brought their Vanguard payload to JPL for modification into what would be called at first "Deal 1." The object in the collection includes electronic and mechanical elements of the initial "Deal" payloads designed and built by the University of Iowa. In addition, Ludwig donated versions of the separate electronic components before they would have been "potted" or electronically sealed for flight. All of these components had been in Ludwig's possession since they were built in the late 1950s, with the exception of short intervals when the components were at JPL under his care. Their provenance, in other words, is unquestioned, and he has provided extensive documentation attesting to their historical role in the early Explorer series.

Possibly the most significant corrective to our documentation of IGY-era artifacts in the NASM collection

came as a result of Ludwig's assistance. In 1961, the Jet Propulsion Laboratory transferred what it claimed was a fully instrumented flight spare of Explorer 1 to the Smithsonian Institution (A19620034000). Attached to an empty fourth-stage Sergeant rocket, it was initially displayed in the Smithsonian's Arts & Industries building to symbolize the United States' first successful artificial satellite. It became a centerpiece of the NASM Milestones gallery upon opening in 1976, having toured briefly just before the opening (Figure 6). In 2005, acting upon an inquiry from Ludwig (2005a), who was then searching out all surviving cosmic-ray Geiger counter detectors inventoried in Van Allen's Iowa laboratory that supplied the first Explorers, the Collections Management staff of NASM, led by Karl Heinzel, removed the object from display for dismantling (Figure 7), conservation evaluation, and inspection. It was empty (Figure 8).

Naturally, we reported this fact back to Ludwig, after taking detailed photographs of the interior instrument frame, wiring and markings. The micrometeoroid detector was in place, wrapped around the external shell, but not any of the associated electronics. Nothing from the cosmic ray package survived. But there were clear markings that at one time, the instrument frame had held "Payload II" as those words appeared in red (Figure 8). Ludwig's highly detailed documentary record showed, immediately, that this was indeed the flight backup for "Deal 1" that was sent back to Van Allen's Iowa laboratory for inspection and testing, and then was returned to JPL later in 1958. The

FIGURE 5. George Ludwig examining his engineering model for the payload for the first fully instrumented Vanguard flight and became the template for the Explorer 1 payload. (NASM photograph by Dave DeVorkin)

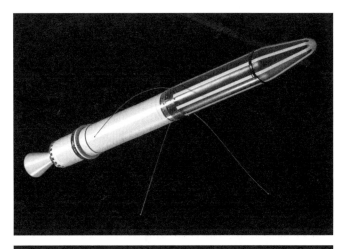

FIGURE 6. Explorer 1 (A19620034000), initially displayed in the Smithsonian's Arts & Industries building, became a centerpiece in NASM's Milestones gallery upon opening in 1976. Opening it for inspection revealed it was a true backup but was devoid of instrumentation. (NASM photograph)

FIGURE 7. Inspection and conservation evaluation of Explorer 1 (A19620034000) by Matthew Nazarro, specialist at the NASM's Paul E. Garber Restoration Facility. (NASM photograph)

cosmic-ray package donated by Ludwig in 2006 was indeed the Vanguard payload that served as template for the flight version of Deal 1. Ludwig is not absolutely positive that his donated package was originally inside the spacecraft we display today in Milestones, but it is identical in nature (Ludwig, 1959, 1960, 2005).

IGY-RELATED COLLECTIONS: PIONEER

Van Allen's group was also engaged to instrument a series of Pioneer flights under Air Force auspices that were aimed at the moon. Although not successful in this goal, three of them managed to detect the complete inner and outer structures of the Earth's radiation belts, as well as confirm the profound influence that solar activity has on the Earth's radiation environment. The first Pioneer reached 70,000 miles altitude, less than a third the distance to the Moon, but failed to achieve either orbital or escape velocity and so re-entered the earth's atmosphere and was destroyed. The Pioneer 1 replica in the collection was reconstructed out of original parts that failed to meet flight specifications (A19640665000). Two examples of the smaller Pioneer IV are also in the collection. One is a cutaway model showing the instrumentation and housekeeping elements, and the other is a fully instrumented flight spare (A19751426000; A19620018000).

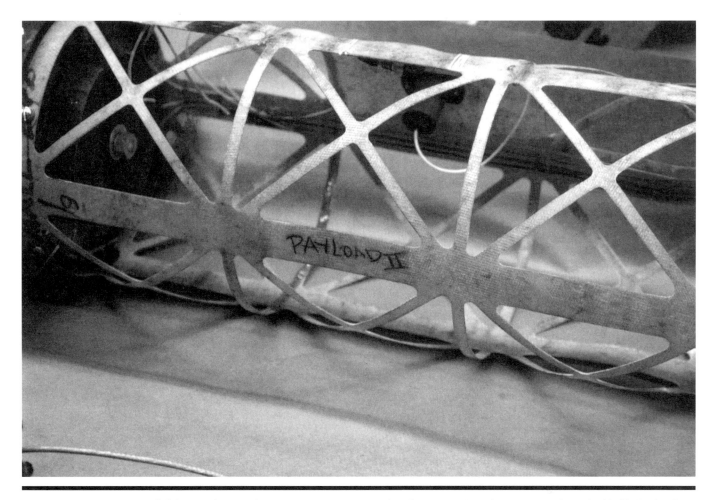

FIGURE 8. Inspection revealed that Explorer 1 (A19620034000) was empty but that at one time, the instrument frame had held "Payload II." (NASM photograph.)

IGY-RELATED COLLECTIONS: LAUNCH VEHICLES AND SUPPORT EQUIPMENT

The NASM Collection boasts probably the strongest collection of IGY-era launch vehicles in the world. As noted above, a full and virtually complete multi-stage Vanguard TV-2BU is preserved, as well as examples of turbo-pumps and engines. In addition, the precursors to its various stages are in the collection, including a full-scale Viking rocket that was prepared for display in the early 1950s using real components from the Glenn L. Martin Company and Reaction Motors inventories. A Jupiter-C missile, donated by the Army in 1959, dominates NASM's "Missile Pit" (Figure 4, left) and is capped by a complete array of scaled-down Sergeant rockets in a configuration identical to that used for the launch of Explorer 1 (A19590068000).

Numerous Aerobee and Aerobee-Hi components, along with a complete unit, document the most prolific sounding rocket in history. The collection also contains many smaller solid rockets, most with tactical air-to-ground and ground-to-air origins, and even one example of the multistage *Farside,* a gigantic balloon-launched rocket system created for the Air Force Office of Scientific Research for extreme high-altitude non-orbital flights in the fall of 1957 (A19680013000).

Although there are several Loki-based multistage systems in the collection, we lack a fully articulated "Rockoon" system consisting of a Skyhook-balloon, connecting hardware, radio telemetry control, and a small solid-fuelled rocket, such as a Loki or Loki-Dart. These systems, in the hands of James Van Allen's Iowa team, as well as various NRL groups, carried cosmic-ray detector payloads to high altitudes at a wide range of geographic latitudes during the IGY.

IGY-Related Collections: Individuals

There is little question today that the one name that will survive from the IGY in historical accounts written in future centuries will be James Van Allen. From a cursory analysis of newspaper coverage of the IGY era based upon a Proquest survey conducted by Sam Zeitlin, 2007 NASM Summer intern, Van Allen's name stands out above all others as most frequently cited or referred to. A significant region of space surrounding the earth has been named for him, the "Van Allen belts," a term which at this writing garners more than 78,000 "hits" in a simple Google search. So it is reasonable to ask: What have we done to preserve the material legacy of James Van Allen at NASM?

Van Allen was a Regents' Fellow at the Smithsonian in 1981, spending much of the academic year preparing a personal scientific memoir and submitting himself to some 18+ hours of oral history interviews by NASM curators and historians (SAOHP, NASM Archives). He also participated in several symposia and seminars (Hanle and Von del Chamberlain, 1981; Mack and DeVorkin, 1982; Van Allen, 1983). He was then planning for the organization of his papers at Iowa, where they would be housed, and engaged NASM staff in an advisory capacity to appraise the collection. Out of this intimate contact, Van Allen eventually donated a small selection of objects that both informs and symbolizes his career. In the early 1990s, he donated a casing from a World War II–era Mark 58 radio proximity fuze for antiaircraft artillery fire control (Figure 9). The fuze had been partly cut open to display the microelectronic components (A19940233000). He was part of the wartime effort to design, test, and build these fuzes,

FIGURE 9. World War II–era Mark 58 radio proximity fuze for anti-aircraft artillery fire control designed by the Applied Physics Laboratory group that included Van Allen. (NASM photograph)

and Van Allen played a significant role in bringing them into operation through tours with the fleet in the Pacific. The experience and expertise he gained managing his portion of this program served him well after the war when he devoted much of his energies to building delicate and complex arrays of Geiger counters for rocket flights aboard captured German V-2 missiles, then Aerobees, and especially the innovative balloon-launched Loki-Dart systems (Figure 10) he developed at Iowa that subjected payloads to huge accelerations and confined quarters reminiscent of the fuze-equipped 5-inch shells (Figure 9). He also donated a complete flight backup payload for Explorer IV; the first payload designed with knowledge of the existence of the trapped radiation field, and thereby employed new Anton detectors that had smaller cross sections, as well as two small scintillation detectors. Van Allen also asked

FIGURE 10. James Van Allen holding a balloon-launched Loki-Dart payload developed at Iowa. (James A. Van Allen Papers, The University of Iowa Libraries, Iowa City, Iowa; c. 1950s)

his Iowa staff to refurbish a plaque bearing a gold-plated flight-spare tape recorder that commemorated the flight of Explorer III, the first to be able to record and ultimately transmit a continuous record of the radiation fields it was encountering, and the first to show unambiguously the presence of the inner regions of trapped radiation.

Some 17 objects in the collection preserve the character of the Explorer 1–4 series and Van Allen's contribution. Among them is a flight spare radio transmitter for Explorer 1, donated by Henry L. Richter, former head of the JPL group that built these units. Richter found that JPL had discarded this unit some years later, and saved it from oblivion. But the surviving mercury-cell batteries in the unit had seriously corroded the overall structure, so Richter removed the corrosive elements, fully documented the process he took to neutralize and restore the structure, and donated the object to the museum in 1997 (A19980115000).

Van Allen is not the only pioneer space scientist to be represented in the collection. Objects relating to the efforts of two groups at the Naval Research Laboratory headed by Richard Tousey and Herbert Friedman, over the period starting with V-2 flights and lasting through the 1960s and 1970s, have also been preserved and are on display (DeVorkin, 1992; 1996).

GENERAL OBSERVATIONS

It should be evident from this brief reconnaissance of IGY-era objects in the NASM collection that, even though our holdings may be impressive, they are not the result of a single rational process or any consistent, premeditated program to preserve IGY history. Some of the objects exist because they were part of the developmental process leading to the flight instrument. Others are replicas or facsimiles created to symbolize the historic event (Figure 11). Most were collected with little or no apparent priority given to engineering, scientific or symbolic value, though they had to possess at least one of those qualities. Some objects came to us serendipitously, some due to our intrinsic visibility and centrality to national preservation. Some were collected as the result of judicious inquiry, but not to the extent of specifically collecting the IGY era.

There were, however, some consistently applied schemes. For instance, we planned out a collection documenting 30 years of electronic ultraviolet and X-ray detector development by Herbert Friedman's group at the Naval Research Laboratory (1949–1980s); there was a similar program tracing the evolution of ultraviolet detectors for solar research

FIGURE 11. Inspection of a replica of Vanguard 1 that had been modified to hold a solar powered audio system for demonstrating the "beeping." (NASM photograph)

with rockets over the same period by members of Richard Tousey's NRL group, and the efforts of similar teams were devoted to aeronomy and ionospheric physics in the 1950s at NRL, the Applied Physics Laboratory, at the University of Colorado, at the Air Force Cambridge Research laboratory, and elsewhere (DeVorkin, 1992; 1996; Hirsh, 1983; Schorzman, 1993). Collections arising from these efforts produced a large set of oral and video-histories, as well as a considerable cache of non-record archival material, all a result of our search for representative artifacts documenting the origins of the space sciences in the United States. Many of them bordered on IGY interests and activities, but did not center on them.

Even so, our collection does reflect the enormous excitement and public impact of the first years of the Space Age. We do meet the goal of memorialization, for instance, because at any one time our collections of multiple examples of Explorer 1 and Vanguard 1 spacecraft replicas are on loan to museums across the United States, in Europe, Asia, and Australia. More than a dozen examples of IGY-era artifacts are presently on display at NASM, as well as the new NASM facility at Dulles, the Udvar Hazy Center.

So as we ask questions about the IGY during this season of commemoration, at the beginning of the new International Polar Year 2007–2008, I hope we will continue to ask how well our collections inform the historical actors, events, episodes and eras that made up the IGY. Where did the expertise come from that allowed our nation to respond to *Sputnik* and that framed the character of that response? What sorts of technologies were bought to bear? And what was the nature of the infrastructure created to facilitate space-borne research? If our present commemoration efforts do not adequately answer these sorts of questions, hopefully future historians will succeed in the effort, asking questions stimulated in part by our material legacy.

LITERATURE CITED

U.S. House of Representatives. 1946. 70th Congress, 2nd Session, 12 August, Chapter 955, Public Law 79–722. *Department of Space History Collections Rationale, 2005.* [The word *space* was added in the 1960s and serves as basis for the Museum's Mission Statement, 29 July 1996.]

Agreement. 1967. "Agreement Between the National Aeronautics and Space Administration and the Smithsonian Institution Concerning the Custody and Management of NASA Historical Artifacts," signed 10 March 1967. In the introduction to *Space History Division Collections Rationale, 2005.*

Bennett, J., 2004. "Scientific Instruments." In *Research Methods Guide,* Department of History and Philosophy of Science, 12 March. Cambridge, U.K. Cambridge University.

Bulkeley, R. P., 1991. *The Sputniks Crisis and Early United States Space Policy.* Bloomington: Indiana University Press.

DeVorkin, D. H. 1992. *Science with a Vengeance: How the Military Created the U.S. Space Sciences after World War II.* New York: Springer-Verlag. (Reprinted 1993, paperback study edition.)

———. 1996. "Where Did X-Ray Astronomy Come From?" *Rittenhouse,* 10:33–42.

———. 2006a. "The Art of Curation: Collection, Exhibition, and Scholarship." In *Showcasing Space,* ed. M. Collins and D. Millard, pp. 159–168. East Lansing: Michigan State University Press.

———. 2006b. "Space Artifacts: Are They Historical Evidence?" In *Critical Issues in the History of Spaceflight,* ed. S. J. Dick and R. D. Launius, NASA SP-2006–4702, pp. 573–600. Washington, D.C.: National Aeronautics and Space Administration (NASA).

Green, C. M., and M. Lomask, 1970. *Vanguard: A History.* NASA SP-4202, Appendix 3, pp. 290–293. Washington, D.C.: NASA.

Hanle, Paul, and Von del Chamberlain, eds., 1981. *Space Science Comes of Age.* Washington, D.C.: Smithsonian Institution.

Hirsh, R. 1983. *Glimpsing an Invisible Universe: The Emergence of X-ray Astronomy.* Cambridge, U.K.: Cambridge University Press.

Kennicott, Philip. 2007. "At Smithsonian, Gay Rights Is Out of the Closet, into the Attic." *Washington Post* (8 September 2007), C1; C8.

Kopytoff, Igor, 1986. "The Cultural Biography of Things: Commoditization as Process." In *The Social Life of Things: Commodities in Cultural Perspective,* ed. Arjun Appadurai, pp. 64–91. Cambridge, U.K.: Cambridge University Press.

Korsmo, Fae L. 2007. "The Genesis of the International Geophysical Year," *Physics Today,* 70 (2007), 38–44.

———. "The Policy Process and the International Geophysical Year, 1957–1958." In *Smithsonian at the Poles: Contributions to International Polar Year Science,* ed. I. Krupnik, M. A. Lang, and S. E. Miller, pp. 23–34. Washington, D.C.: Smithsonian Institution Scholarly Press.

Ludwig, George H. 1959. "The Instrumentation in Earth Satellite 1958 Gamma." MSc diss., February, SUI-59-3, State University of Iowa, Iowa City.

———. 1960. "The Development of a Corpuscular Radiation Experiment for an Earth Satellite." Ph.D. diss., August, SUI-60-12, State University of Iowa, Iowa City.

———. 2005. Letter to D. H. DeVorkin, 26 September. Curatorial Artifact Files A20060086000. Deed of Gift 1476 (26 January 2006). Smithsonian Institution, Washington D.C.

Mack, Pamela E., and D. H. DeVorkin. 1982. Conference Report on Pro-Seminar in Space History. *Technology and Culture,* 23, No. 2(April):202–206.

Marson, Frank M., and Janet R. Terner. 1963. *United States IGY Bibliography, 1953–1960; an Annotated Bibliography of United States Contributions to the IGY and IGC (1957–1959).* Washington, D.C.: National Academy of Sciences-National Research Council.

McDougall, Walter A. 1985. *The Heavens and the Earth: A Political History of the Space Age.* New York: Basic Books.

Needell, Allan A. 2000. *Science, Cold War and the American State: Lloyd V. Berkner and the Balance of Professional Ideals.* Amsterdam: Harwood Academic in association with the National Air and Space Museum, Smithsonian Institution.

Pisano, Dominick A., and Cathleen S. Lewis, eds. 1988. *Air and Space History: An Annotated Bibliography.* New York: Garland.

Space Astronomy Oral History Project (SAOHP). 1981–1986. Smithsonian Institution, National Air and Space Museum, Archives Division, MRC 322, Washington, D.C.

Schorzman, T. A., ed. 1993. *A Practical Introduction to Videohistory.* Malabar, Fla.: Krieger.

Sullivan, Walter A. 1961. *Assault on the Unknown; the International Geophysical Year.* New York: McGraw-Hill.

Van Allen, J. A. 1983. *Origins of Magnetospheric Physics.* Washington, D.C.: Smithsonian Institution Press.

Wilson, J. Tuzo, 1961. "Foreword by Lloyd V. Berkner." In *I.G.Y., the Year of the New Moons.* New York: Knopf.

From Ballooning in the Arctic to 10,000-Foot Runways in Antarctica: Lessons from Historic Archaeology

Noel D. Broadbent

ABSTRACT. The author discusses three archaeological investigations of historic sites in the polar regions. The first site is that of the Solomon A. Andrée expedition camp on White Island, Svalbard. This fateful ballooning expedition to the North Pole in 1897 was the first experiment in polar aeronautics. Andrée and his colleagues gave their lives but opened the door to polar flight, the backbone of polar logistics today. The other site, East Base, on Stonington Island off the Antarctic Peninsula, served the 1939–1941 U.S. Antarctic Service Expedition, under Admiral Richard Byrd, the first U.S. government–sponsored scientific and aerial mapping effort in Antarctica. In 1992, a team of archaeologists documented and secured the site that had been recently recognized as an historic monument by the Antarctic treaty nations. The third site is Marble Point on Victoria Land across from Ross Island and McMurdo Station. In conjunction with the IGY 1957–1958, a massive effort was put into laying out a 10,000-foot year-round runway and creating a fresh water reservoir and other base facilities. It was one of the premier locations for strategic aviation in Antarctica. The site was archaeologically surveyed and original engineering documentation from 1956–1957 offers superb baselines for studying permafrost, erosion, and human disturbances in the Antarctic environment. These types of sites are in situ monuments to human courage, ingenuity, and perseverance on a par with NASA's exploration of space. They require careful management and protection following the same principles as historic sites within the United States and in other nations.

INTRODUCTION

There is a seemingly limitless public interest in polar exploration. This fascination is one of the greatest resources we have for support of polar science: Public enthusiasm for polar history and exploration should be actively acknowledged in projects of these kinds. With volunteer help led by professional archaeologists on regular tour ships, site documentation and cleanup efforts could be carried out on a scale that would otherwise be impossible to achieve.

This paper is about international polar history and heritage along with science and technology in context. We are now embarked on the Fourth International Polar Year. In addition to projects in the natural and physical sciences, focusing especially on issues of global change, there are a number of themes in anthropology and archaeology, and new historic archaeology projects are being initiated at both poles.

Noel D. Broadbent, Arctic Studies Center, Department of Anthropology, National Museum of Natural History, Smithsonian Institution, P.O. Box 37012, MRC 112, Washington, DC 20013-7012, USA (broadbentn@si.edu). Accepted 29 May 2008.

The three archaeological studies presented here span 60 years of aviation history from before the period of fixed-wing aircraft to the International Geophysical Year in 1957–1958. They also relate to competing national interests in the polar regions including Nordic rivalries, U.S. and German conflicts over Antarctic territories during World War II, and Cold War strategic thought in the southern hemisphere.

Historic archaeology is based on the theories and methods of traditional archaeology but applies these to historic periods (South, 1977; Orser, 2004; Hall and Silliman, 2006). One great advantage of historic archaeology over prehistoric archaeology is that it can be matched with written sources that may reveal, among other things, the motives behind various endeavors and the details of planning and consequent successes and failures. However, written history tends also to focus on the larger picture of given events and can be biased by political, social, or other concerns of the times. Physical evidence and archaeological analysis can be used not only to test hypotheses about historical events but also, of equal importance, to provide information about the daily lives of individuals that rarely make it into historical accounts.

Global warming, one of the great scientific concerns of today regarding polar ecosystems, is having profound impacts on archaeological sites. These sites are subject to increasingly severe weathering and erosion damage. Warmer conditions have also made them more accessible to tourism, as well as to looting. Documentation of these sites is urgently needed. This is exemplified by the Andrée site in Svalbard, Norway. While such efforts have intrinsic value in and of themselves, the importance of these investigations extends beyond that, inasmuch as the sites themselves can provide baselines for measuring the effects of climate change over time. This is the case of the two Antarctic sites, East Base and Marble Point.

THREE CASE STUDIES

The first study was an investigation of the S. A. Andrée ballooning expedition to the North Pole in 1897 (Andrée, Strindberg, and Fraenkel, 1930). This study was undertaken in 1997–2000 as a purely scientific investigation into the causes of death of these Swedish polar explorers and to document their campsite (Broadbent, 1998; 2000a; 2000b). The centennial of this expedition was 1997, and the project was supported by the Royal Swedish Academy of Science and the Nordic Research Council for the Humanities within the framework of a larger history of science program (Wråkberg, 1999).

The second study was undertaken in 1992 as an Antarctic environmental cleanup and cultural heritage management project. The United States Congress allocated environmental funds in 1991 to facilitate the cleanup of old American bases in Antarctica. One of these bases, East Base on the Antarctic Peninsula dating to 1940, is the oldest remaining American research station in Antarctica. The archaeological project was conducted through the auspices of the Division of Polar Programs at the National Science Foundation in collaboration with the National Park Service (Broadbent, 1992; Broadbent and Rose, 2002; Spude and Spude, 1993).

The third study, Marble Point, was directly related to the International Geophysical Year of 1957–1958. Marble Point is situated across the Antarctic continent from East Base and near the large American research station at McMurdo Sound. An enormous engineering effort had been put into building a 10,000-foot runway at Marble Point. This base was, nevertheless, abandoned when the U.S. Navy found its sea approach extremely difficult for supply ships. With the aid of volunteers from McMurdo in 1994, it was possible to map the remains of the SeaBee (Navy Construction Battalion Unit or CBU) base camp at Marble Point (Broadbent, 1994). It was in this context that the science that had gone into the prospecting of the airfield became apparent, as well as the impacts that construction had left on the landscape.

The combination of history, archaeology, and natural science is an exceptionally productive approach to understanding the past and applying this knowledge to modern research questions.

THE ANDRÉE NORTH POLE EXPEDITION IN 1897

The Andrée expedition is one of the most intriguing in polar history. Solomon August Andrée (1856–1897) worked at the Swedish patent office. He had become fascinated by ballooning after visiting the U.S. centennial celebration in Philadelphia in 1876. On returning to Sweden, he devoted himself to designing hydrogen balloons that could be used for exploration and aerial mapping. His greatest effort was put into the design of the *Eagle*, which was intended to take him and two colleagues to the North Pole using southerly winds. A balloon building and hydrogen generating facility were built on Dane Island in northwestern Svalbard in 1896 (Capelotti, 1999). The first attempt on the North Pole was aborted because of poor winds and gas leakage. A new team consisting of Andrée, Nils Strindberg, and Knut Fraenkel (replacing Nils Ekholm) launched in the *Eagle* on 11 July 1897. They were never seen alive again. Interestingly enough, Nils Ekholm, who quit the project which he felt was too risky, was seen by many as a coward and his decision is still being debated in Sweden. He went on to become one of Sweden's most prominent meteorologists.

In 1930, the bodies of Andrée, Strindberg, and Fraenkel were found at their campsite on White Island in eastern Svalbard (Lithberg, 1930). The bodies were returned to Sweden, cremated, and buried in Stockholm following an almost royal funeral and national day of mourning (Lundström, 1997). An exhibit of their equipment was shown at Liljevalch's Art Hall in Stockholm in 1931 (*Fynden på Vitön*, 1931). Remarkably, their diaries and notes, as well as undeveloped roles of Kodak film, had survived. A number of negatives could be developed and these images provide a haunting picture of their ordeal.

The balloon had gone down on the sea ice on 14 July 1897. Because of icing the balloon could simply not stay aloft and after 33 hours of misery the decision was made to land. They had reached 82° 56′ north latitude (Figure 1). They were well equipped with sleds and a boat and from 14 July until 5 October they trekked on the sea ice, first east-

FIGURE 1. The *Eagle* shortly after landing on the sea ice at 82° 56′ N on 14 July 1897. Andrée and Fraenkel are looking at the balloon. The image was developed from a roll of Kodak film recovered from White Island in 1930. (Photo by Nils Strindberg, courtesy of Andrée Museum. Gränna)

wards, making little real distance because of the ice drift, then southwards. They were planning on wintering in a comfortable snow house near White Island and celebrated the king's birthday on September 18 with a meal of seal meat, liver, kidneys, brains, and port wine. They were in fine spirits. Then disaster struck when the ice fractured under their snow house. Luckily the weather was good. They systematically gathered their equipment and supplies and were forced to go ashore on White Island where they set up a new camp. The last note in their diaries has a date of 17 October. There is little in the diaries about being in a critical situation. There were no last words or explanations, letters to their loved ones or to their sponsors. It seems that they had no inkling that they were in danger of dying. By comparison, Robert Falcon Scott and his companions took the time to leave a number of letters when they understood their situation. They knew at some future date their camp and bodies would be found. As Andrée and his companions were now on dry land one would assume that, if they had known that all was lost, they would have done the same. They were well aware that the world had been watching them and considerable national prestige was at stake, particularly since the Swedish king, Oskar II, and Alfred Nobel were official sponsors.

Strindberg's body was found in 1930, half buried in a rock crevice near the campsite, indicating that he had been the first to die. Fraenkel lay dead in the tent and Andrée lay on the rock shelf above the tent.

There have been many theories but no conclusive evidence for how or why they had died. The campsite that had been mapped during the recovery in 1930 had been largely buried in snow and ice (Lithberg, 1930). Warming trends in the Arctic made it likely that the site would be better exposed today. A new investigation in connection with the centennial of the expedition was organized and subsequently funded.

FIELDWORK IN 1998

The first project expedition to Svalbard was undertaken in 1998 on the Norwegian research vessel *Lance* through the auspices of the Swedish Polar Research Secretariat and the Royal Academy of Sciences. The participants included science historian Sverker Sörlin, the director of the Andrée Museum, Sven Lundström, Nordic Museum ethnographer and polar historian, Rolf Kjellström, archaeology student Berit Andersson, and the author. The team visited White Island for one day and mapped the immediate camp area using standard mapping techniques and photography.

The site, as hoped, was found to be totally free of ice and snow cover and even the margins of the tent were still discernable in the sandy soil. Embedded in the tent depression were frozen remnants of clothing. Driftwood, bamboo, silk shreds, metal fragments, and other small debris were scattered on the soft sand. Even fragments of bone, certainly polar bear and seal bone, but possibly even human, were found (Figure 2). The area surrounding the site also produced artifacts, including opened food tins from the expedition.

With this archaeological potential, a follow-up project was proposed in order to map the site using digital technology and to conduct a soil chemistry analysis in order to map the non-visible areas of the camp and evidence of camp use. It was reasoned that low levels of phosphates, by-products of defecation, urination, and animal carcasses, could also reflect length of site use. Magnetic susceptibility would tell us about burning on the site. A pile of driftwood still lies near the tent site and had been collected by the Andrée team as construction material as well as for fuel.

From the initial inspection it was possible to verify the archaeological potential of the site and its surroundings. Although most objects had been collected in the 1930s, the ground was still littered with small debris including silk and bamboo from the balloon and boat, tin openers and various metal fragments. This micro-deposition reflected the extent of the former campsite. The tent and its half frozen floor deposits presented an excellent opportunity for study.

Among the most interesting conclusions of the survey was that this campsite had been well chosen. It was on well-drained sandy soil and protected by a rocky outcrop. There was a small stream nearby. In addition, the camp was situated well back from the shore and away from areas where polar bears would prowl. Considerable effort had clearly been put into choosing this spot and substantial piles of logs had also been assembled for dwelling construction and/or fuel. We know from a note in Andrée's journal that the camp had been named "Camp Minna" after his mother.

FIELDWORK IN 2000

Having received permission by the Norwegian authorities to conduct the study, we returned on the Swedish chartered ship *Origo* to White Island on 19 August 2000 (Broadbent and Olofsson, 2001).

The goal of the investigation of the Andrée site was to archaeologically document the camp and its surround-ings and to assess the potential causes of their deaths. The men did not appear to be either ill-equipped or desperate on going ashore on 5 October 1897. They had established a good campsite on dry ground. They had fuel for their stoves, ammunition, food, and medicines.

With this goal in mind, a new potential for analysis at the site emerged in 2000. Mark Personne, MD, of the Stockholm Poison Center, had just published an article in the *Swedish Journal of Medicine* in which he assessed the symptoms of the three men that could be gleaned from their diaries (Personne, 2000). Suicide, murder, depression, trichinosis, hypothermia, carbon monoxide poisoning, alcohol/fuel poisoning, and so on had been proposed in the past, but Personne deduced that the most probable cause of death for all three men was botulism poisoning.

Botulism Type E is common in the Arctic and is found on the skin of marine mammals that pick it up from bottom sediments and in the near-shore environment. It is tasteless and odorless and among the most deadly poisons in nature. Once ingested, death occurs within 24–36 hours (Personne, 2000, plus references). As a neurotoxin, it affects the central nervous system. For our purposes, although the bacteria would be long gone, it was technically possible to identify the botulism toxins in the soils of the camp, namely in the area of the tent floor. Testing this theory thus became a new target of the investigation.

The first setback was to discover that the campsite was now buried under as much as 30 centimeters of ice. Snows from the previous two winters had melted into a hard mass which could only be hacked out with difficulty. That evening a heavy snow storm with gale-force winds hit the island and the team was unable to go ashore for two days. Some 20–30 inches of snow now covered the island and the initial survey plans, which had already rendered several interesting finds, including one of the three sled yokes from the expedition, were not possible. The planned excavation of the tent floor to test Personne's theory was also no longer possible. The focus returned to the topographic mapping of the site and sampling for phosphates and magnetic susceptibility. Ground level could still be determined with our measuring rod and soil samples could still be collected.

WHAT THE SOILS REVEALED

The Andrée camp on White Island is situated at 80° 05′ N and 31° 26′ E. The camp was about 175m from the shore in sandy terrain and adjacent to a 3m high stone outcrop. The site area covers about 250 square meters. From

FIGURE 2. The Andrée campsite in 1998 was completely exposed. Fragments of the balloon, clothing, and other items were visible. (Photo by Noel Broadbent)

the perspective of soil chemistry, the site is analogous to the environment of Late Post Glacial hunters living near the ice margins of Scandinavia 9,000 years ago. In an environment like this, almost all organic and phosphate-containing materials were brought to the site by man or beast. Indications of burning were certainly an indication of human presence. Small groups of hunters slaughtering and subsisting on animals left relatively high phosphate deposits in the same types of soils. These inorganic phosphates bind with the soil and remain for thousands of years. Citric acids releases the phosphate and this can be measured using colorimetric (phosphorous-molybdate)–based methods. Johan Olofsson provided the expertise for soil sampling and analysis (Broadbent and Olofsson, 2001).

The human body processes 1–2 g of phosphorus per day (Devlin, 1986). In addition to the deposition of food residues, especially bones, urination and defecation contribute to the buildup of phosphate in the soil. The longer a site is occupied, the greater will be the phosphate enrichment. This buildup is expected to be greatest in the site center or adjacent to the center. Since this is a relative measure, differences of 5 percent or more are considered significant as related to offsite normal background sample values. The team collected 240 soil samples in the camp area.

Phosphate is measured in phosphate degrees, mg P_2O_5 per 100 g dry soil. The mean phosphate enrichment in the site center was 17 ± 9 P° with a range of 38–2 P°. The highest values were actually to the north of the camp

margin and associated with water pooling that was a natural process. The average off site values were 11 ± 11 P° with a range of 38–1 P°.

Although the site areas averaged slightly higher than the control samples, this was due to natural drainage on the site rather than human activity. In fact, the map of phosphate values shows that the immediate tent area no enrichment whatsoever. This is strong evidence that they had not been active on the site for very long before death overcame them.

Magnetic susceptibility (MS) on the campsite averaged 5 ± 4 SI which is comparable to the off site control measurement of 4 ± 2 SI. One sample on the site measured 40 SI because of a rusty flake in the soil sample and this raised the average campsite value. MS is measured in SI units per 10 g of soil using a Bartington MS2B measure cell (Thomson and Oldfield, 1986).

Magnetic susceptibility rendered no evidence of fires and the low phosphate values suggest that the site had hardly been used.

The three men had arrived on the island on 5 October 1897 in relatively good shape, searched out an excellent campsite, collected heavy driftwood logs for construction of a hut, and then died within hours of each other. They managed a simple burial of the youngest member of the expedition, Nils Strindberg, and then barely made it back to the tent where they collapsed. Andrée was found with a Primus Stove, which was easily re-lit after 33 years in the snow. Fraenkel was lying on or beside, not in, his sleeping bag.

The Personne hypothesis on botulism poisoning could not be tested but remains the most probable cause of the sudden death of all three men. The lack of final words and letters in the otherwise preserved papers supports the idea as well. With exposure to a neurotoxin, the men would have been quickly immobilized and were apparently unable to write. Oddly enough, Fraenkel was found still wearing his dark glasses in spite of the low light in early October. Light sensitivity is another symptom of botulism (Personne, 2000). A follow-up sampling of the site might one day help prove this theory.

Andrée and his companions still capture the imagination of the public, especially in Sweden. The fact remains that Andrée was the first pioneer of polar flight and aerial photography in the polar regions. While in some quarters he is viewed as a "balloonatic" who knew this was going to end in disaster, to others he is revered as a genius of balloon design. In 2000, the same year of the investigation of his campsite on White Island, an English adventurer, David Hempelman Adams, launched his hot air balloon, the *Britannic Challenger*, from Longearbyn in Svalbard. He reached the North Pole and most of the way back in 133 hours, thus proving that Andrée's plan had been feasible all along.

Every year the Andrée campsite is visited by numerous tour groups. We noted during our first visit in 1998 that the soft soils of the site were badly disturbed and the area between the site and the shore was dimpled with thousands of deep footprints.

EAST BASE AND THE UNITED STATES ANTARCTIC SERVICE EXPEDITION (1939–1941)

In 1939, President Franklin Roosevelt appointed Rear Admiral Richard E. Byrd to command the U.S. Antarctic Service Expedition. Roosevelt was well aware of German territorial interests in Antarctica; that same year the German Antarctic Expedition on the seaplane tender *Swabenland* claimed 200,000 square miles of territory, including Crown Princess Maerta Land, which had been a Norwegian claim. Most important coastal points were marked with swastikas and flags dropped from aircraft. Germany invaded Norway in 1940 (Broadbent and Rose, 2002).

Two American bases were quickly established in Antarctica in 1940: West Base under the command of Paul Siple, and East Base under the command of Richard Black (Black, 1946a, 1946b). West Base was built on the Bay of Whales and has been lost in the sea, but East Base, built on Stonington Island off the Antarctic Peninsula (68° 28' S, 67° 17' W), still stands.

East Base was hastily abandoned on 22 March 1941 under the looming threat of war. The 26 men, with a smuggled puppy and a pet bird—Giant Petrel, later donated the

FIGURE 3. The abandoned East Base on Stonington Island, Antarctica. The Science Building with its weather tower and the Bunkhouse building were intact. The crate containing a spare engine for the Curtis Wright Condor biplane can be seen in front of the Science Building. (Photo by Noel Broadbent, 1992)

National Zoo in Washington, D.C.—abandoned the base and flew out to the ice edge in their Curtis Wright Condor biplane, which also had to be abandoned. The *USS Bear* then took them back to the United States, and some nine months later the United States was at war with Japan and Germany.

Stonington Island was reoccupied by the Falklands Islands Dependencies in 1946 and subsequently used by the British Antarctic Service until 1970 (Walton, 1955). East Base itself, although badly vandalized by ship crews from Chile and Argentina, was reoccupied by the Ronne Antarctic Research Expedition (RARE) in 1947–1948 (Ronne 1949; 1979). The RARE expedition was a private venture under the leadership of Finn Ronne who had been second in command at East Base in 1940. The RARE expedition was unique because this was the first time women (Jackie Ronne and the chief pilot's wife, Jennie Darlington) were to winter over in Antarctica (Ronne, 1950; Darlington and McIlvaine, 1956).

All three expeditions conducted important research and determined that this part of the continent was indeed a peninsula and not an island (Ronne, 1949: English, 1941; Wade, 1945). Interest in the historic value of the site was noted by Lipps in the late 1970s (Lipps, 1976, 1978). East Base was recognized as an historic site (#55) by the Antarctic Treaty Nations in 1989.

In 1991, U.S. National Park Service archaeologist, Catherine Blee (later Spude), and NPS historian, Robert Spude, were taken to the island by NSF to conduct a survey and develop a management plan for the site. In 1993, the author led a team, including archaeologist and hazardous waste expert, Robert Weaver, and staff from the U.S. Antarctic Research Program Base at Palmer Station and British Antarctic Survey personnel from Rothera Station. We were there to follow through on the NPS recommendations. These included cleanup and documentation of debris, removal of hazardous materials, repairs of doors, windows, and roofs and the storage of artifacts. In addition, warning and information signs were made for the site and its buildings and an interpretive panel with a description of the station and historic photographs was put on display in the Science Building (Figure 3).

The team worked on the site from 20 February until 3 March 1992. The grounds were cleaned and capped with fresh beach stones, the buildings repaired as far as possible and one building became an artifact storage facility. A collection of some 50 artifacts, including old maps, tools, mittens, films, bottles, bunk plates and dog tags with names, scientific specimens, medical supplies and other items were brought back and are now kept at

FIGURE 4. Noel Broadbent recording a cold-weather mask at East Base in 1992. In the foreground are old weather maps found at the site. (Photo by Michael Parfit)

the Naval Historical Center, U.S. Naval Yard, in Washington D.C. (Figure 4).

A small museum, one of the most remote museums in the world (Iijima, 1994), was set up in the Science Building with and a brass plaque with the names of the 1940–1941 and 1947–1948 expedition members that had been donated by the National Geographic Society. A guest book was left in the museum together with an American flag.

A spare engine for the Curtis Wright Condor biplane still rests in its original crate in front of the museum. There is even a World War I vintage light tank with an air-cooled aircraft engine, a failed experiment in winter traction (Figure 5). The first tourists arrived in 29 December 1993 onboard the *Kapitan Khlebnikov*. In 1994, Jackie Ronne, widow of Finn Ronne, and their daughter, Karen Tupek, visited the site and left more photos and texts for the museum and the bunkhouse.

The East Base project was conducted as a cleanup and historical archaeological project. It was the first U.S. effort in historic archaeology in Antarctica that set a precedent for how sites of these types can be managed (Parfit, 1993). Sites in the East Base area were made environmentally safe and worthy of tourism and are lasting memorials to polar science. More than 100 cruise ships now visit Antarctica every year and there is still an urgent need to document and manage many historic sites around the continent. Preservation conditions have left items in pristine condition and the continent is littered with aircraft, vehicles, and buildings. This is one of the greatest challenges of cultural resource management and ideally should be conducted as collaborative international efforts.

FIGURE 5. The gap between Stonington Island and the Northeast glacier, 1992. As late as in the 1970s, an ice bridge connected the island to the Antarctic Peninsula; it had been the major reason for choosing the island as a base in 1940. The changes reflect rapid warming in the region. (Photo by Noel Broadbent)

MARBLE POINT, ANTARCTICA

The final project to be discussed is a small archaeological endeavor but one encompassing a huge site, that of a 10,000-foot-long airfield and base at Marble Point in Victoria Land, across from Ross Island and the large American base at McMurdo Sound.

While making site visits to researchers supported by the social sciences program as NSF, the author had the opportunity to carry out a survey of Marble Point on 22 January 1994. With the help of volunteers from McMurdo, we mapped the site of the Navy Seabee (CBRU) camp established in 1957. There were numerous foundations of "Jamesway" huts, trash dumps, oil spills, roads, and other features. Large vehicles, graders, and rollers had also been left behind. A reservoir dam been built at the foot of the glacier (Figures 6 and 7a–e). The U.S. Navy (Operation Deep Freeze I) supported American scientists in Antarctica during the 1957–1958 International Geophysical Year and this base was part of the effort. More than 40 nations participated in the IGY and the Antarctic was studied by teams from the United States, Great Britain, France, Norway, Chile, Argentina, Japan, and the USSR. Marble Point was both a research site and an ideal place for an airfield. It was also a jumping-off point for researchers working in the Dry Valleys.

Rear Admiral George J. Dufek championed the airfield construction. In an Airfield Feasibility Study film (CNO-5–1958), he pointed out the strategic significance such an airfield for the southern hemisphere. Aircraft could

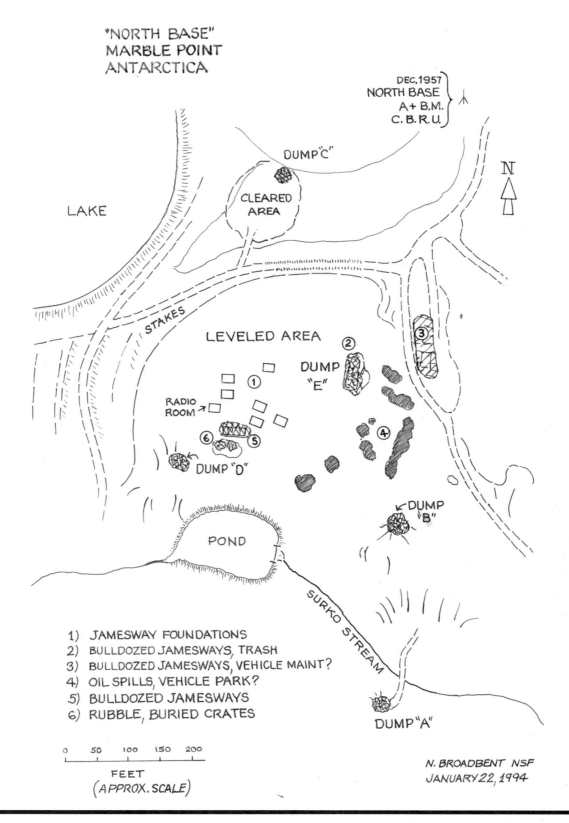

FIGURE 6. Archaeological map of the Navy SeaBee camp "North Base" from 1957 at Marble Point, Victoria Land, Antarctica. Map shows locations of "Jamesway" huts, trash dumps, roadways, and oil-spill areas where vehicles had been parked. (Produced by Noel Broadbent, January 22, 1994)

(a)

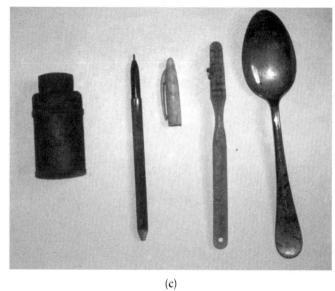

(c)

(b)

(d)

(e)

FIGURES 7a–e. Selection of items found at Marble Point and the remarkable preservation of paper and fabrics. (a) The newspaper cartoons from 1960 still have bright colors. These simple things, large and small, tell us about daily life and work at the base. (Photo by Noel Broadbent).

be rapidly deployed to South America, Africa, and other points north. The sea ice runways used at McMurdo were limited to only part of the year and had to be rebuilt each season. Further, while clearly advantageous for aviation, the icy coast of Victoria Land proved difficult for ships to use and the shores were shallow. The 10,000-foot runway was never finished. Notably, however, the first "wheels on dirt" landing of an aircraft in Antarctica took place here when a Navy VXE-6 squadron *Otter* landed with Sir Edmund Hillary onboard. He had just reached the South Pole in an overland tractor convoy.

Marble Point is a weather station and helicopter refueling station today. In the 1980s, when the Chinese program was considering the site as a potential research station, the VXE-6 commander, Captain Brian Shumaker, had new stakes placed along the runway to assert continuing American presence there. It remains an American site today, and is, without question, the best place for a year-round airfield on the continent. It is a rocky promontory located 50 miles from McMurdo Station, and an adjacent land strip serves as a helicopter refueling station in support of U.S. Antarctic program research.

Our survey of the Marble Point area revealed that an enormous engineering study had been conducted there in 1956–1957 by the U.S. Navy. There were test trenches in the permafrost, test pads established with the sensors still in place, and detailed reports by engineers and scientists. In all, the studies encompassed geology, pedology, permafrost studies, seismic studies, hydrology, glaciology, sea ice and sea bed studies, and polar engineering. This material provides an unparalleled 50-year baseline for studying changes in the Antarctic environment and the effects of human impacts over time.

SUMMARY AND CONCLUSIONS

Archaeology offers unique opportunities for research on polar history. In addition to adding new substance to material culture remains and a greater focus on individuals, the documentation of in situ features is a necessary prerequisite for historic site preservation. The loss of sites in the Arctic due to climate change is an enormous problem and increased erosion along Arctic beaches and rivers is destroying thousands of years of Arctic prehistory and history. These regions have been little documented as compared with the lower latitudes. New highly perishable artifacts and human remains are melting out of glaciers around the world.

The Andrée expedition study was conducted as a research project on the causes of the deaths of these explorers. As an immensely popular figure in Nordic history, hundreds of visitors visit the campsite every year, made even more accessible by global warming. Management of sites like this will require greater protection, but at the same time we must help facilitate visitors' needs through marked pathways, signs, and better information.

The second project, at East Base, was a cleanup and management effort that also served to document and protect the site. This kind of project should continue to be international in scope. In 1992, John Splettstoesser published an article in *Nature* regarding the melting of the Northeast glacier at East Base as evidence of rapid global warming (Splettstoesser, 1992). One of the principal reasons Stonington Island has been chosen as a base in 1940 was that the glacier connected the island to the peninsula. Today the glacial bridge has vanished and the island is separated by a wide gap of open water. The bridge had been there as late as the 1970s. Human presence at places like Stonington Island has, in other words, inadvertently given us baseline observations for documenting rapid climate change effects.

Finally, Marble Point, even as a small mapping effort, further reveals the indirect scientific value of former bases. This site is literally a climate-change data goldmine. The engineering baseline data from sites like this, collected for entirely unrelated reasons, are of great value for understanding human impacts in polar environments.

Polar flight plays a major part in these three investigations. Andrée was the first pioneer of polar flight. Byrd was at the forefront of polar aviation and in 1946–1947, after World War II was also instrumental in Operation Highjump. Ronne mapped 450,000 square miles of Antarctica in 1947–1948. Marble Point was the site of the first dirt runway landing and still remains the largest land airfield ever conceived of in Antarctica. Aviation was at the core of mid-twentieth-century exploration and the transition from dog sleds to aircraft has left an amazing legacy of technology at both poles.

The "old politics" of polar research, and the technological efforts put into them, are closely akin to those of international climate change research of today. The International Geophysical Year in 1957–1958 was, after all, conducted during the heat of Cold War.

The Arctic Ocean has, once again, drawn the close attention of the eight polar nations—the United States, Canada, Russia, Sweden, Norway, Finland, Iceland, Denmark/Greenland—as well as all other nations highly dependent on gas and oil. The Antarctic, as international territory, is still a place where national presence is deemed critical. It would not be an exaggeration to state that the past is truly prelude to the most significant issues of the modern era. To ignore this history is to fail to recognize why the polar regions have long played such an important part in the economic and political history of the western world.

EPILOGUE

Since the logistical costs of archaeological projects in the polar regions are so great, they are rarely possible to carry out. A potential model for achieving a more comprehensive approach to documentation and cleanup could be to use volunteers under expert supervision on regularly scheduled tourist vessels. This would provide meaningful experiences for the public, facilitate polar heritage management, and offer unique opportunities for the tourist industry. This idea is currently being discussed by a consortium of polar historians and archaeologists. The Smithsonian has several sites of interest that would be ideal places to begin. One is the old town of Barrow, site of U.S. efforts in the original IPY in 1881–1883, and a second site is Fort Conger on Ellesmere Island, used in 1881 by the Greely Expedition

LITERATURE CITED

Andrée, S. A., Nils Strindberg, and Knut Fraenkel. 1930. Med Örnen mot polen. Sällskapet för antropologi och geografi. Stockholm: Albert Bonniers Förlag.

Black, Richard B. 1946a. Narrative of East Base, U.S. Antarctic Expedition, 1939–1941, 27 Dec. 1960, Accession III-NNG-57, R 126, National Archives-CP. Washington, D.C.

———. 1946b. "Geographical Operations from East Base, United States Antarctic Service Expedition 1939–1941," *Proceedings of the American Philosophical Society*, 89:4–12.

Broadbent, Noel D. 1992. Project East Base: Preserving Research History in Antarctica. *NSF Directions*, 5:1–2.

———. 1994. An Archaeological Survey of Marble Point, Antarctica. *Antarctic Journal of the United States*, 29:3–6.

———. 1998. *Report on a preliminary archaeological investigation of the Andrée expedition camp on White Island, Spitsbergen, 1998.* "Lance" Expedition of the Swedish Program for Social Science Research in the Polar Regions, 16–24 August 1998. Manuscript, Department of Archaeology, University of Umeå, Sweden.

———. 2000a. Archaeological Fieldwork at Andréenäset, Vitön, Spitsbergen—A Preliminary Report. *Swedartic 2000*, pp. 62–64. Stockholm: Swedish Polar Research Secretariat.

———. 2000b. Expedition Vitön i Andrées spår. *Populär arkeologi* nr. 4, 2000:19–22.

Broadbent, Noel D., and Johan Olofsson. 2001. *Archaeological Investigations of the S. A. Andrée Site, White Island, Svalbard 1998 and 2000.* UMARK 23. Arkeologisk rapport. Institutionen för arkeologi och samiska studier. Umeå universitet, Sweden.

Broadbent, Noel D., and Lisle, Rose. 2002. Historical Archaeology and the Byrd Legacy. The United States Antarctic Service Expedition, 1939–31. *The Virginia Magazine of History and Biography 2002*, 110(2):237–258.

Capelotti, P. J. 1999. Virgohamna and the Archaeology of Failure. *The Centennial of S. A. Andrée's North Pole Expedition*, ed. U. Wråkberg, pp. 30–43. Stockholm: Kungl. Vetenskapsakademien.

Darlington, Jennie, and J. McIlvaine. 1956. *My Antarctic Honeymoon: A Year at the Bottom of the World*. New York: Doubleday and Company.

Devlin, T. M. ed. 1986. *Textbook of Biochemistry with Chemical Correlations*. Second edition. New York: Wiley.

English, R. A. J. 1941. Preliminary Account of the United States Antarctic Expedition, 1939–1941. *Geographical Review*, 31:466–478.

Fynden på Vitön. Minnesutställning över S. A. Andrée, Nils Strindberg och Knut Fraenkel anordnad i Liljevalchs konsthall. 1931. Liljevalchs konsthall, katalog nr. 90. Stockholm.

Hall, M., and S. Silliman, eds. 2006. *Historical Archaeology*. Oxford, U.K.: Blackwell.

Iijima, G. C. 1994. Our Most Remote Museum. *Odyssey*, 3:41–42.

Lipps, J. H. 1976. The United States, "East Base," Antarctic Peninsula. *Antarctic Journal of the United States*, 11:215.

———. 1978. East Base, Stonington Island, Antarctic Peninsula. *Antarctic Journal of the United States*, 1978:231–232.

Lithberg, Nils. 1930. "The Campsite on White Island and Its Equipment." In *Med Örnan mot polen*, ed. S. A. Andrée, Nils Strindberg, and Knut Fraenkel, pp. 189–227. Stockholm: Sällskapet för antropologi och geografi.

Lundström, Nils. 1997. *"Var position är ej synnerligen god . . . Andrée expeditionen i svart och vitt."* Stockholm: Carlssons Bokförlag.

Orser, Charles E. 2004. *Historical Archaeology*. Upper Saddle River, N.J.: Pearson Education.

Parfit, Michael, and Robb Kendrick. 1993. Reclaiming a Lost Antarctic Base. *National Geographic Magazine*, 183:110–26.

Personne, Mark. 2000. Andrée-expeditionens män dog troligen av botulism. *Läkartidningen 97*, 12:1427–1431.

Ronne, Finn. 1949. *Antarctic Conquest: The Story of the Ronne Expedition 1946–1948*. New York: G. P. Putnam's Sons.

———. 1950. Women in the Antarctic, or the Human Side of Scientific Expedition. *Appalachia*, 28:1–15.

———. 1979. *Antarctica, My Destiny: A Personal History by the Last of the Great Polar Explorers*. New York: Hastings House.

South, Stanley. 1977. *Method and Theory in Historical Archaeology*. New York: Academic Press.

Splettstoesser, John. 1992. Antarctic Global Warming? Nature, 355:503.

Spude, Catherine Holder, and Robert L. Spude. 1993. *East Base Historic Monument, Stonington Island/Antarctic Peninsula: Part I: A Guide for Management; Part II: Description of the Cultural Resources and Recommendation*, NPS D-187, National Park Service. Denver: United States Department of the Interior.

Thomson, R., and F. Oldfield. 1986. *Environmental Magnetism*. London: Allen and Unwin.

Wade, F. A. 1945. An Introduction to the Symposium on Scientific Results of the United States Antarctic Service Expedition, 1939–1941. *Proceedings of the American Philosophical Society*, 89:1–3.

Walton, E. W. K. 1955. *Two Years in the Antarctic*. London: Lutterworth Publishers.

Wråkberg, Urban, ed. 1999. *The Centennial of S. A. Andrée's North Pole Expedition*. Stockholm: Royal Swedish Academy of Sciences.

"Of No Ordinary Importance": Reversing Polarities in Smithsonian Arctic Studies

William W. Fitzhugh

ABSTRACT. The founding of the Smithsonian in 1846 offered the promise of scientific discovery and popular education to a young country with a rapidly expanding western horizon. With its natural history and native cultures virtually unknown, Smithsonian Regents chartered a plan to investigate the most exciting questions posed by an unexplored continent at the dawn of the Darwinian era. Prominent issues included the origins and history of its aboriginal peoples, and this thirst for knowledge that led the young institution into America's subarctic and Arctic regions. The Yukon, Northwest Territories, and Alaska were among the first targets of Smithsonian cultural studies, and northern regions have continued to occupy a central place in the Institution's work for more than 150 years. Beginning with Robert Kennicott's explorations in 1858, Smithsonian scientists played a major role in advancing knowledge of North American Arctic and Subarctic peoples and interpreting their cultures. Several of these early enterprises, like the explorations, collecting, and research of Edward Nelson, Lucien Turner, John Murdoch, and Patrick Ray in Alaska and Lucien Turner in Ungava, either led to or were part of the first International Polar Year of 1882–1883. Early Smithsonian expeditions established a pattern of collaborative work with native communities that became a hallmark of the institution's northern programs. This paper presents highlights of 150 years of Smithsonian work on northern peoples with special attention to themes that contributed to Smithsonian Arctic studies during International Polar/Geophysical Year events, especially 1882–1883 and 2007–2008.

HISTORICAL CONTRIBUTIONS

The International Polar Year (IPY) 2007–2008 provides an opportunity to explore how the Smithsonian has served for the past 150 years as a repository of Arctic knowledge and a center for northern research and education. When Robert Kennicott arrived in the Mackenzie District in 1859 to make natural history and ethnology collections for the Smithsonian, science in the North American Arctic was in its infancy. By the time the first IPY began in 1882, the Smithsonian had investigated parts of the Canadian Arctic and Subarctic and the Mackenzie District. Further, it had sent naturalists to the Northwest Coast, the Aleutians, western Alaska, and nearby Chukotka in Siberia and was on its way toward developing the largest well-documented Arctic anthropological and natural history collection in the world. By its close in 1883–1884 major

William W. Fitzhugh, Arctic Studies Center, Department of Anthropology, National Museum of Natural History, Smithsonian Institution, P.O. Box 37012, MRC 112, Washington, DC 20013-7012, USA (Fitzhugh@si.edu). Accepted 9 May 2008.

IPY-related field programs in Barrow, Ellesmere Island, and Ungava had been or were nearly completed and collecting projects in Kodiak and Bristol Bay were underway. The cumulative results established the Smithsonian as the pre-eminent scholarly institution of its day in the fields of northern natural and anthropological science.

In the 125 years since IPY-1, northern collecting, research, publication, and education programs have given the Smithsonian an Arctic heritage of immense value to scholars, Natives and northern residents, and interested public around the world. It is a world, moreover, in which Arctic issues have steadily moved from the exoticized periphery of global attention to a well-publicized central focus, as a result of changes in geopolitics, climate, and governance. We are hearing about the north now more than ever before, and this trend is accelerating as global warming strikes deeper into polar regions, transforming oceans, lands, and lives.

Elsewhere I explored how nineteenth-century Smithsonian Arctic scientists laid the foundation for the field of museum anthropology (Fitzhugh, 1988a; 2002a) and public presentation and exhibition of Arctic cultures at the Institution during the past 125 years (Fitzhugh, 1997). Here I review some of the themes that contributed to Smithsonian Arctic studies during International Polar/Geophysical Year events, especially 1882–1983 and 2007–2008. My purpose is not only to illustrate how long-term Smithsonian research, collecting, and exhibition has contributed to Arctic social and natural science, but also to explore how these historical assets contribute to understanding a region undergoing rapid, dynamic social and environmental change.

FOUNDATIONS OF ARCTIC SCIENCE

Heather Ewing's recent book, *The Lost World of James Smithson* (Ewing, 2007), reveals the Smithsonian's reclusive founder as more intellectual and politically active than previously thought but provides few clues as to what his bequest mandate intended. Accordingly, setting the course for the young Smithsonian fell to its first Secretary, Joseph Henry (1797–1878), and his scientific assistant, Spencer Baird (1823–1887), who followed Henry as Secretary and presided during the years of IPY-1. Both Henry and Baird shared in establishing natural science and cultural studies at the Smithsonian and gave early priority to northern studies, which Henry judged "of no ordinary importance" (Smithsonian Institution Annual Report [SIAR], 1860:66). In fact, during the Smithsonian's earli-

est years, it is surprising how much energy went into research and publication on Arctic subjects, including Elisha Kent Kane's meteorological, tidal, and magnetic studies; McClintock's and Kane's searches for Franklin; and solar observations and natural history collecting in Labrador and Hudson Bay during the 1850s.

Drawing on his previous experience as a regent of the New York University and his association with ethnologists Henry Schoolcraft and Lewis Henry Morgan, Henry was instrumental in laying groundwork for what was to become the field of museum anthropology at the Smithsonian (Fitzhugh, 2002a). In fact, Henry believed that cultural studies would eventually develop into a discipline as rigorous as the natural sciences, and for this reason instructed Baird to include ethnology among the tasks of naturalists he hired as field observers and collectors. Baird believed taxonomic and distributional studies of animals and plants in northwestern North America would reveal relationships with Asia and lead to understanding their origins and development, and he came to believe that "ethnological" collections could also reveal deep history.

In 1859, a gifted young protégée of Baird's named Robert Kennicott (1835–1866) became the first of "Baird's missionaries" (Rivinus and Youssef, 1992:83; Fitzhugh, 2002a) sent north to begin this grand task (Lindsay, 1993). Kennicott spent 1859 to 1862 in the Hudson Bay Territory and Mackenzie District making the first carefully documented natural history collections from any North American Arctic region. Assisted by Natives and Hudson Bay Company agents, he also collected more than 500 ethnological specimens from Inuvialuit (Mackenzie Eskimo) and Dene Indians, as swell as linguistic data, myths and oral history, and ethnological observations. In his report to the Regents on 1861, Henry noted the collections being submitted by the factors of the Hudson's Bay Company, "taken into connexion with what Mr. Kennicott is doing, bid fair to make the Arctic natural history and physical geography of America as well known as that of the United States" (SIAR, 1862:60). A year later Henry reported (SIAR, 1863:39), "This enterprise has terminated very favorably, the explorer having returned richly laden with specimens, after making a series of observations on the physical geography, ethnology, and the habits of animals of the regions visited, which cannot fail to furnish materials of much interest to science."

In 1860, when Kennicott first began to explore west from the Mackenzie into Russian America territory, only southern and western Alaska had been previously explored ethnologically by Russians, and northern and eastern Alaska was nearly unknown (Sherwood, 1965; James,

1942). Ethnological collecting had been conducted sporadically in coastal and southwest Alaska since ca. 1800 by Russia and its agents [e.g., Lavrentii Zagoskin (1842–1844)]. In 1839–1849, purposive but not scientifically directed ethnological museum collecting was carried out by Ilya G. Voznesenskii for the Russian Academy of Sciences (Black, 1988; Fitzhugh, 1988a; Kuzmina, 1994; Fitzhugh and Chaussonnet, 1994).

In 1865, the Western Union Telegraph Company was pushing an overland telegraph line to Europe via the Yukon River, Bering Strait, and Siberia. That year Baird asked Kennicott to direct the scientific activity of the survey with assistance from William Healy Dall, Henry W. Elliott, and several other naturalists (Figure 1; Collins, 1946; Fitzhugh and Selig, 1981). While making the first scientifically documented American collections from interior and coastal Alaska north of the Aleutians, the project collapsed after Kennicott's death on the Yukon River in May 1866, and the subsequent completion of a transatlantic cable by a rival company the following July. Nevertheless, the Western Union survey produced the first scientifically documented American collections from Alaska, trained the first American scholars of Alaska, and led to the first English-language books on "the great land" written by Henry W. Elliott (1886), Frederick Whymper (1869), and William Healy Dall (1870).

In the early 1870s, Baird and Dall began to implement a more ambitious Alaskan collecting venture. Realizing the Smithsonian could not finance a sustained endeavor by itself, Baird recruited government agencies like the U.S. Army Signal Service, Hydrographic Office, and War Department to employ Smithsonian naturalists as weather and tidal observers at government stations throughout the newly purchased territory. Their activities produced a vast collection of meteorological, geographical, natural historical, and anthropological data that, supplemented by photography after 1880 (Fitzhugh, 1998c), laid the scientific bedrock for later studies in Alaska and northern Quebec.

FIGURE 1. Frederick Whymper's illustration of the Western Union Telegraph Survey team battling ice on the Yukon River below Nulato in 1866 in Eskimo *umiaks* in spring 1866. (From Whymper, 1869)

While Baird's collecting and publication programs were an unqualified success, only part of Baird's and Henry's original plan was ever realized. Documentation of endangered cultures and languages fulfilled their science plan and provided materials for further study, following Henry's expectation that new methods and techniques would lead to creating a "hard" science of anthropology. This prospective view from the mid-nineteenth century is still our optimistic view at the turn of the twenty-first century but it probably will never be realized. Progress in anthropological science has come in different directions: Ethnology and cultural anthropology have not merged with the natural or hard sciences as Baird and Henry predicted. Rather, Smithsonian anthropology proceeded to develop in other directions: the study of human remains and forensics; archaeology (long one of Henry's interests but one that was impossible to conduct with the method and theory available in the late nineteenth century); and another set of anthropological fields not imagined by them at all—heritage, ethnicity, and cultural identity.

SMITHSONIAN ACTIVITIES IN IPY-1 (1881–1884)

As the first IPY approached, the Smithsonian had conducted work throughout most regions of Alaska south of the Bering Strait: James G. Swan had collected on the Northwest Coast in the 1850–1880s; Robert Kennicott in British America in 1859–1862 and in interior Alaska, 1865–1866; William Healy Dall in western Alaska and the Aleutians, 1865–1885; Lucien Turner in St. Michael, 1871–1877, and the Aleutians, 1877–1878; and Edward W. Nelson had just completed studies in the Yukon, Kuskokwim, and Bering Strait in 1877–1881 (Figure 2). Several other collecting projects were proceeding in southern Alaska, but none had been carried out north of Bering Strait.

The 1881 voyage of the Revenue Cutter *Corwin* briefly visited the coast between the Bering Strait and Barrow with a scientific team including Edward W. Nelson, John Muir, and Irving Rosse, reaching as far east as the Inuit settlement of Ooglamie at today's Barrow, and as far west as Herald and Wrangel Islands in the Chukchi Sea and Wankarem on the Arctic coast of Siberia. The visit to Barrow was only two days, and Nelson's diary notes that he had difficulty making collections and gathering information. Barrow people had been dealing with European whalers for almost three decades and knew how to drive hard bargains.

FIGURE 2. Ceremonial mask representing Tunghak, Spirit of the Game, collected by Edward W. Nelson from the Lower Yukon River, undergoing conservation in 2003. (NMNH 33118)

As documented in accompanying papers in this volume, the Smithsonian's major collection focus in IPY-1 were Barrow and Ungava Bay. Given the Institution's interest in Alaska, Barrow became the primary target of a major effort directed by Lt. Patrick Henry Ray with the assistance of John Murdoch, a Smithsonian employee who carried out ethnological studies (Ray, 1885; Murdoch, 1892; Burch, 2009, this volume; Crowell, 2009, this volume). The Barrow project filled the last major gap in the Smithsonian's survey coverage of Alaska and, second only to Nelson's work, made the most important contribution to science. Living for two full years in a weather station near the native village, Murdoch concentrated his efforts on ethnological collecting and reporting. Like Nelson, he collected vocabularies and linguistic data, but he did not venture out on long trips with Native guides or show much interest in oral history and mythology (Burch, 2009, this volume; A. Crowell, Arctic Studies Center, personal communication, 2007). Murdoch's more remote approach led him to be duped by Natives who sold him artifacts they constructed hastily for sale or had composited from unmatched materials, inserting stone scrapers in ivory handles that had no blades or embellishing ancient ivory objects with new designs.

Nevertheless, while Murdoch was not as perceptive a cultural observer, his work received great notice in the developing profession of anthropology. Boas' *The Central Eskimo* (1888a), also published by the Smithsonian, made Murdoch's *Ethnological Results of the Point Barrow Expedition* (1892) the first study of a Western Arctic Eskimo group. More importantly, Murdoch's monograph directly addressed the scholarly debates about Eskimo origins and migrations and utilized a scientific method, making specific comparisons of Alaskan Eskimo customs and material objects with those known from the Canadian Arctic and Greenland. When Nelson's (1899) monograph, *The Eskimos About Bering Strait*, appeared several years later, it was not fully appreciated by anthropologists because Nelson was a biologist and his highly descriptive study did not address the Eskimo origin controversy (Fitzhugh, 1988b). As a result, until the 1980s most scholars did not comprehend the importance of differences between Yup'ik and Iñupiat material culture, art, and language that these monographs clearly illustrated. Even Boas, who made much of cultural continuities in Raven mythology, art, and folklore between Northwest Coast and Northeast Asia (Boas, 1903, 1905, 1933; Bogoras, 1902), failed to recognize that these features were also present in the geographically intermediate Yup'ik Bering Sea and Iñupiat Eskimo area; he continued throughout his life to promote the idea that Eskimos were recent arrivals to the Bering Strait from Canada (Boas, 1888b, 1905; see below). It was not until much later that Yup'ik Eskimo culture began to be understood as a distinct Eskimo tradition with stronger ties to the south than to Iñupiat and other Arctic coast Eskimo cultures, and with a legacy from ancient Eskimo cultures of the Bering Sea (Fitzhugh, 1988c; Dumond, 2003).

Other projects also made important contributions to the Smithsonian's IPY-1 program even though they were not part of the official IPY agenda. Charles MacKay's collections from the Signal Service Station at Nushugak in Bristol Bay (1881–1883) contained fascinating materials from the border between Yup'ik, Aleut, and Alutiiq cultures, complementing S. Applegate's materials from Unalaska and nearby regions (1881–1885). However, none of these collections was ever published or exhibited, and the early ethnography of this boundary region is still poorly known today. More prominent is the work of William J. Fisher who contributed materials from southern Alaska and Kodiak Island throughout the 1880s (Crowell, 1992). Like Applegate and MacKay, Fisher did not prepare reports; however, his collection became the subject of intensive recent study and exhibition (Crowell et al., 2001). Two other projects also were "official" Smithsonian IPY ventures (Krupnik, 2009, this volume). Adolphus Greely's ill-fated scientific explorations at Fort Conger, Lady Franklin Bay, Ellesmere Island in High Arctic Canada, were a massive undertaking organized by the U.S. Signal Service in 1882–1883 (Barr, 1985), for which Spencer Baird served as scientific advisor. Although the expedition ended in disaster, it obtained important scientific observations. Many of the weather, aurora, and meteorological observations were archived at the Smithsonian, which also received a few natural history and ethnological specimens, along with the team's scientific instruments. Today the Barrow and Fort Conger weather records serve as important benchmarks for long-term study of climate change (Wood and Overland, 2006). The third official Smithsonian IPY-1 field study, Lucien Turner's ethnological work among the Innu and Inuit of Ungava Bay in northern Quebec during 1882–1884, produced a trove of important ethnological materials from both Innu (Naskapi) and Inuit (Eastern Eskimo) groups, as well as natural history and photographic records (Turner 1894; Loring, 2001a, 2009, this volume).

BUILDING ON IPY-1: MUSEUM EXHIBITION, RESEARCH, AND ANTHROPOLOGICAL THEORY

By 1890, the great era of synoptic Smithsonian natural history-based collecting had passed and attention began to be devoted to publishing, collection work, building a specialized scientific staff, and presenting American cultures to the world. Following the 1893 Chicago Columbian Exposition, a series of world's fairs exhibited living Eskimos and other northern peoples together with displays of museum collections to wide audiences in Chicago, New Orleans, St. Louis, Buffalo, and other locations. The Smithsonian's Arctic ethnography collections were featured in many of these exhibitions, and some of the displays were later installed in the Smithsonian's permanent galleries. This was the era of the dramatic life-group diorama reconstructions pioneered by the Smithsonian's famous artist-geologist William Henry Holmes. His Polar Eskimo group for the Buffalo fair in 1901 became one of the most popular exhibits after the National Museum of Natural History opened in 1910 and remained on view for nearly 100 years (Figure 3; Ewers, 1959:513–525; Fitzhugh, 1997).

Concurrent with growth of exhibitions and new architecture on the Washington Mall, the Smithsonian began to build its curatorial staff and hire its first professionally trained anthropologists. The Bureau of American Ethnology founded by John Wesley Powell in 1879 as a center for anthropological field surveys, research, and publication (Hinsley, 1981) was the first Smithsonian entity staffed by anthropologists. In 1891, Powell's linguistic surveys and subsequent synthesis produced the first linguistic map of North America, a tour de force of early museum research that seemed to establish language as the guiding structure

FIGURE 3. The Polar Eskimo of Smith Sound, Greenland, display—created by William Henry Holmes for the Buffalo Exposition in 1901 and on exhibit since then at the National Museum of Natural History—was dismantled in October 2004. Robert Peary Jr. of Qaanak (at right), the Inuit grandson of the American explorer who collected some of the materials for this exhibit, was present for the event. (Courtesy Department of Anthropology, Smithsonian Institution)

for cultural diversity. However, by 1893, Otis Mason's study of material culture collections across North America showed both congruence and discontinuity across linguistic boundaries (Figure 4). Eskimo collections figured prominently in his work, demonstrating gradual stylistic changes in dress, implements, kayaks, and other equipment (Mason, 1891, 1896, 1902; Ewers, 1959:513–525)—except in Greenland, where 200 years of exposure to European culture had produced a radical departure from traditional Central and Western Eskimo clothing and design. Mason concluded that tribal material culture and language groups were not always synchronous, as Powell had supposed, but more closely followed C. Hart Merriam's biogeographic life zones. But even here discontinuities resulted from external influence, migration, language capture and loss, and other cultural and historical factors. Mason's "culture area" con-

cept was a direct outgrowth of museum-based research on the Smithsonian's Arctic IPY-1 collections and remains one of the underpinnings of anthropological theory today. As analysis of the Smithsonian's pan-North American Arctic collections progressed, it seemed that anthropology was drifting further from the pure science Henry predicted it would become.

NEW SCIENCE ARRIVES: PHYSICAL ANTHROPOLOGY AND ARCHAEOLOGY

These gropings toward the development of anthropological science did not become fully professionalized until Aleš Hrdlička (1869–1943), the father of American physical anthropology, joined the Smithsonian in 1903 and be-

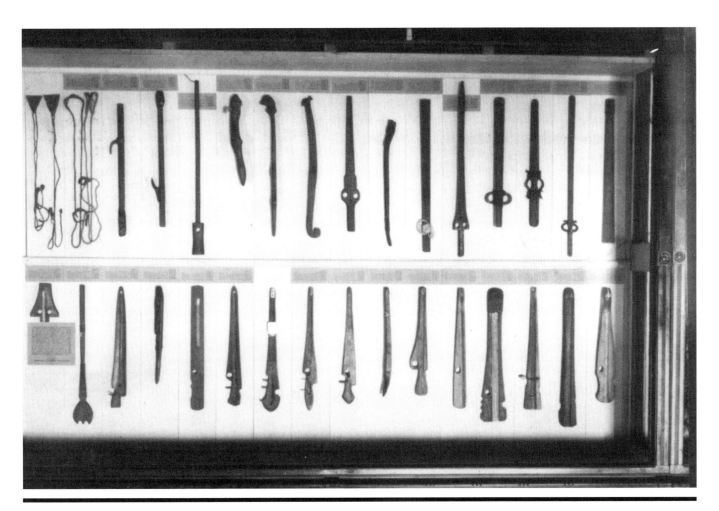

FIGURE 4. This spear thrower display was assembled by Otis Mason to demonstrate spatial changes in artifact types across culture and space, analogous to biological species distribution. North American Eskimo throwers (bottom row) are arranged from Alaska (left) to Greenland and Labrador (right). These and many other Eskimo artifacts demonstrate systematic style change from west to east. (Courtesy Department of Anthropology, Smithsonian Institution)

gan to study the question of Indian and Eskimo origins with new methods and discipline applied to human skeletal remains. Hrdlička's Alaskan work utilized methods of field collecting offended native people, and are seen today as outrageously insensitive, and his scientific results, while interesting in their day, have been largely superseded (Scott, 1994). Perhaps his most lasting contribution was recruitment of T. Dale Stewart and Henry B. Collins to the Smithsonian staff in the mid 1920s. Stewart refined Hrdlička's osteological methods and inherited Hrdlička's mantle while Collins took a different path, bringing archaeology into the forefront of studies of Eskimo origins through his pioneering stratigraphic excavations on St. Lawrence Island in the 1930s (Collins, 1937, 1951). Here an unbroken sequence of changing artifact forms, art styles, house types, and economies demonstrated a

long history of local development interrupted periodically by Asian influences over the past 2,000 years. Hrdlička's, Stewart's, and Collins' early work in Alaska was conducted largely without reference to the Smithsonian's early IPY collections and research products and without reference to IPY-2 and IGY 1957–1958 program efforts, with which Smithsonian scientists had little involvement (Krupnik, 2009, this volume).

PUBLIC "DISCOVERY" OF ESKIMO ART

In 1973, the Institution's IPY-1 ethnological collections from Barrow and Collin's prehistoric archaeological materials from Bering Strait resurfaced suddenly and dramatically with the refined cachet of "Eskimo art" when the National Gallery of Art opened its groundbreaking exhibition *The Far North: 2000 Years of American Indian and Eskimo Art* (Collins, 1973). C. D. Lewis, curator of sculpture at the Gallery, was assigned to curate the exhibition, and I assisted his search for northern art among the Smithsonian's Arctic collections. The experience was life-changing. Acquaintance with the collections, coupled with the phenomenal success of the exhibit, convinced me that the Smithsonian "attic" housed treasures of interest not only to anthropologists and Native constituencies but also to a far broader audience. To paraphrase former Smithsonian Secretary S. Dillon Ripley's reference to the Institution's musical instrument collections, we needed to take the Arctic treasures out of their storage cabinets and make them "sing."

In the late 1970s, I began to do that, and with William C. Sturtevant started meeting with anthropologists from the Soviet Academy of Science's Institute of Ethnography to plan an exhibit on the cultures of Siberia and Alaska. Political difficulties caused periodic delays, and it did not open until 1988, in the early phase of the Gorbachev revolution known as *perestroika* (Fitzhugh, 2003). During the years while *Crossroads* was gestating, Susan Kaplan and I created an exhibit based on the ethnological collections made by Edward W. Nelson in 1877–1881 from western Alaska and Bering Strait. *Inua: Spirit World of the Bering Sea Eskimo* (Fitzhugh and Kaplan, 1983) explored the art, culture, and history of the Yup'ik peoples of southwest Alaska. The exhibit (Figure 5) and catalog illustrated the extraordinary beauty and workmanship of Yup'ik and Bering Strait Iñupiat culture. After opening at the Smithsonian in 1982, *Inua* toured to Anchorage, Fairbanks, Juneau, and other cities in North America. Later, Kaplan and I created a mini-*Inua* version that toured to

FIGURE 5. E. W. Nelson collections from 1877–1881 in a hunting ritual display in *Inua: Spirit World of the Bering Sea Eskimo*. (1983 photograph; courtesy Arctic Studies Center, Smithsonian Institution)

small museums and culture centers in Alaska, Canada, and Greenland (Fitzhugh and Kaplan, 1983). Eventually a third version, "Euro-*Inua*" (Figure 6), was developed by Susan Rowley for a tour across eastern and northern Europe and Iceland (Rowley, 1988).

After the long hiatus following Collins' work in the 1930s, these 1980s exhibits and publications brought Smithsonian Alaska collections to a wide audience in North America and to the rest of the world, especially to Alaska residents and native villages. They also brought us to the attention of Ted Stevens, U.S. Senator from Alaska. Early in 1980 while I was preparing *Inua*, I had occasion to give his wife, Ann Stevens, a tour of the Smithsonian's Alaskan collections in what was then a very dusty Natural History Museum attic. A few days later, the Senator called for his own tour, during which he remarked, "Bill, we have to find a way to get these collections back to Alaska." The IPY-1 and other early Alaskan collections indeed had a captivating power, and it was growing year by year. That tour and the senator's remark gave me my marching orders for the next twenty-five years and in time led to a dedicated Smithsonian program reconnecting its historic collections with Alaska and its Native peoples.

As I explored the Smithsonian attic, I was amazed to discover how little the collections were known. In those days the Smithsonian's attic was a virtual King Tut's tomb before excavation—quiet, dusty, and full of splendid things! The Smithsonian had never hired an Arctic ethnol-ogist, and Hrdlička, Collins, and Stewart had not strayed far from their osteological and archaeological disciplines. The few scholars aware of the collections knew them only from small black and white illustrations in Nelson's and Murdoch's monographs. Ronald Senungetuk, an artist on the staff of the University of Alaska in Fairbanks who came to Washington in 1981 to consult on the *Inua* exhibit, may have been the first Alaska Native to inspect them firsthand.

During the late 1980s, we completed arrangements to launch *Crossroads of Continents: Cultures of Siberia and Alaska* (Fitzhugh and Crowell, 1988). The exhibit (Figure 7) was based on a reciprocal exchange that paralleled the history of the collections: The earliest objects from Alaska had been gathered during the Russian–America era and had been stored at the Museum of Anthropology and Ethnography in Leningrad since the 1840s, whereas the earliest Siberian materials had been gathered by Franz Boas' Jesup North Pacific Expedition and were held by the American Museum of Natural History in New York.

FIGURE 6. Catalogs issued for the mini-*Inua* exhibitions that toured small museums in Alaska in 1983–1984 (Fitzhugh and Kaplan, 1983) and in Europe 1988–1989 (Rowley, 1988). (2008 photograph; courtesy Arctic Studies Center, Smithsonian Institution)

FIGURE 7. *Crossroads of Continents* combined Russian collections from Alaska with American collections from Siberia in an integrated exhibition featuring the history, culture, and art of the peoples of the North Pacific rim. (1988 photograph; courtesy Arctic Studies Center, Smithsonian Institution)

Logistics, geography, political barriers, and lack of publication and scholarly exchange, to say nothing of native awareness, had made it impossible to synthesize a larger view of the traditional cultures of the North Pacific 'crossroads' region. Every one of the 650 specimens was jointly selected and researched by teams from both sides during yearly visits financed by the International Research and Exchanges Board (IREX). Co-curated with Aron Crowell and assisted by Valérie Chaussonnet, Sergei Arutiunov, Sergei Serov, Bill Holm, James VanStone, and many others, including Igor Krupnik, this exhibit put us in direct contact with Soviet scholars and laid the groundwork for future research, publication, conferences, and exhibit ventures. The show toured in Alaska and the lower 48 and was the first joint U.S.–Soviet exhibition in which American and Soviet/Russian materials were published in a single catalog and comingled in a single display (Fitzhugh, 2003).

In the early 1990s, following precedent established by the mini-*Inua* exhibits, Valérie Chaussonnet organized a small version of *Crossroads* called *Crossroads Alaska* that toured towns across Alaska (Chaussonnet, 1995; Carlo et al., 1995). Unfortunately, when it came time to transfer the large *Crossroads* exhibit to Russia, economic and security conditions had deteriorated so much that the tour was cancelled. Nevertheless, as a substitute, in 1996 we arranged for a smaller exhibit *Crossroads Siberia* (Krupnik, 1996) to tour cities in the Russian Far East, curated by Igor Krupnik, who had come to work at the Arctic Studies Center in 1991. This was probably the first anthropology exhibit to travel in Siberia, as well as the first Alaska Native artifacts to be seen in the Russian Far East.

A WIDENING FOCUS: ARCTIC STUDIES CENTER AND CIRCUMPOLAR ANTHROPOLOGY

In 1988, the Smithsonian received congressional support for creating a special unit called the Arctic Studies Center (ASC) in the National Museum of Natural History, enabling a series of new research, education, and publication ventures that have been described in annual ASC newsletters and on the website (www.mnh.si.edu/arctic). Building anew on the IPY-1 legacy and new *Crossroads* partnerships, in 1992 a 10-year archival research and publication project titled "Jesup II" was initiated with United States, Russian, Japanese, and Canadian partners (Krupnik and Fitzhugh, 2001; Kendall and Krupnik, 2003). To fulfill Boas' original vision of the scope of the Jesup expedition (Boas, 1903)—a vision thwarted by bureaucracy and logistics during the expedition and by Soviet fiat excluding the Ainu from the *Crossroads* exhibition—with Japanese and Ainu scholars, we produced a comprehensive Ainu exhibition and catalog drawing on collections and archives in museums in North America and Japan (Fitzhugh and Dubreuil, 1999).

Concurrent with the opening of field opportunities in Russia after 1990, the ASC began a re-study of culture themes that motivated circumpolar theories of Arctic peoples in the early twentieth century (Gjessing, 1944; Bogoras, 1902, 1929; Fitzhugh, 1975; Dumond, 2003) with new fieldwork in the lower Ob River and Yamal Peninsula. Supported by a grant from Amoco Eurasia Corporation, we conducted archaeological surveys and ethno-archaeology of Nenets reindeer-herders in Western Siberia (Fedorova et al., 1998; Fitzhugh, 1998a; 1998b; Fitzhugh and Golovnev, 1998; Haakanson, 2000; Fedorova, 2005) combined with several museum-focused heritage projects, exhibits, and catalogs (Krupnik and Narinskaya, 1998; Krupnik, 1998; Pika, 1998). Subsequently, with Andrei Golovnev and Vladimir Pitul'ko, we searched for pre-Eskimo sites eastward from Yamal along the Arctic coast to Bering Strait, inspired by Leonid Khlobystin's pioneering work (Khlobystin, 2005) and assisted excavations at an 8,000-year-old Mesolithic site on Zhokhov Island (Pitul'ko, 2001). Although the results did not reveal evidence of proto-Eskimo culture, they helped explain why earlier researchers believed Eskimo adaptations and art had originated in these regions (Larsen and Rainey, 1948; Fitzhugh, 1998a) and helped fill a large gap in circumpolar archaeology (Fitzhugh, 2002b). Later our research and public programs gap in the North Atlantic was filled by production of a major exhibition titled *Vikings: the North Atlantic Saga*, which opened in 2000 and toured to various locations in North America (Fitzhugh and Ward, 2000).

REVITALIZING THE SMITHSONIAN–ALASKA CONNECTION

Beginning in the early 1990s, the reprinting of Nelson's and Murdoch's monographs and new interest created by the Alaska tours of *Inua* and *Crossroads* and their mini-exhibit versions resulted in a major revitalization of the Smithsonian–Alaska connection. Unlike the earlier focus on collecting and research, these efforts were based on collection interpretation, education, and public access. Whereas earlier work involved primarily a one-way transfer of Alaskan objects and information to Smithsonian coffers for use in research, publication, and exhibitions, the emerging emphasis used the Smithsonian treasures to engage Native groups and individuals in two-way collaborative studies and publication, along with joint curation of exhibitions, museum training, and re-documentation of the Smithsonian's early object and archival collections (Fienup-Riordan, 1996, 2007; Loring, 1996).

The overwhelming interest exhibited by Alaskans to early Smithsonian collections helped spark a revival of interest in traditional native culture, and in the early 1990s we began to explore the idea of opening a regional office to formalize a new permanent Smithsonian–Alaska connection. In April 1994, we opened an office at the Anchorage Museum of History and Art and shortly after, Aron Crowell joined the ASC as local director and launched archaeological research, museum training, exhibition, and teaching projects.

As the Alaska office took shape, back in Washington the ASC staff collaborated on collection projects with the National Museum of Natural History (NMNH) Repatriation Office, which was working with Alaska Native groups on the return of human remains collected by Hrdlička, Stewart, Collins, and others in the early 1920–1930s. More than 3,500 skeletal remains were transferred back to Native groups between 1990–2007, together with associated grave goods and religious objects (Bray and Killion, 1994; http://anthropology.si.edu/repatriation). ASC staff began to work with Native groups to document old archival and ethnographic collections from Alaska, and by 2001 these "knowledge repatriation" projects (Crowell et al., 2001; Loring, 2001b, 2008; Krupnik, 2004, 2005) blossomed into the Alaska Collection Project, bringing Alaska Natives into contact with Smithsonian collections for intensive study and re-documentation, with the ultimate aim of loaning them back to Alaska for study and exhibition.

In 1994 Crowell began an exhibition project with the William J. Fisher Alutiiq ethnographic collection from the Kodiak Island area gathered in 1880–1885 during the first IPY era, but never previously published or exhibited. The resulting exhibit—*Looking Both Ways: Heritage and Identity of the Alutiiq People*—and its catalog and website, co–curated by Crowell with Alutiiq leaders and organized with the Alutiiq Museum (Crowell et al., 2001; Pullar, 2001), helped catalyze the movement by Alutiiq peoples to rejuvenate Kodiak cultural traditions in art, oral history, language, and material culture (Crowell, 2004; Clifford, 2004).

The collections and observations garnered as well as the re-publication (with new data) of the Nelson, Murdoch, and Turner monographs, and presentation of exhibitions and new illustrated catalogs have proven important both for science and historical legacies. For instance, without historical baseline information from archaeological sites, it is impossible to determine the significance of climate shifts or assess the effects of long-term cultural and environmental change. Further, preservation of traditional artifacts, customs, and oral histories and presentation of these materials through exhibitions and other venues have given Alaska Natives a window into a past that had been largely forgotten or was considered irrelevant to the modern day (Kaplan and Barsness, 1986; Fitzhugh, 1988c; Chaussonnet, 1995).

Now nearing its fifteenth year, the Smithsonian relationship with the Anchorage Museum is poised to take another giant step forward. With funding from the Rasmuson Foundation and others, the Anchorage Museum has constructed a new wing to house an expanded ASC office and research suite. A major part of this wing will be a Smithsonian exhibition hall displaying nearly 650 anthropological objects loaned from the Smithsonian's National Museum of Natural History and the National Museum of the American Indian (Figure 8). The collections have

FIGURE 8. Unangan consultants (from left) Daria Dirks, Marie Turnpaugh, Vlaas Shabolin, and Mary Bourdukofsky study a painted wooden shield from Kagamil in the Aleutian Islands, Alaska (ASCN11:3). Native experts—young and old—have helped to redocument the objects with new information, stories, songs, and native language, and the process has helped to find new routes to the past. (2003 photograph; courtesy Arctic Studies Center, Smithsonian Institution)

FIGURE 9. The Ralph Applebaum Associates rendition of the Native Cultures exhibition to open in 2010 in the Smithsonian Gallery of the expanded Anchorage Museum.

been selected by teams of exhibit designers, conservators, and Alaska Native experts under the curatorial direction of Aron Crowell and will open in 2010 (Figure 9). A pilot exhibit titled *Sharing Knowledge* and a website of the same name have been created (Figure 10; http://alaska. si.edu) and expanded educational programs are planned as part of a new phase of the Smithsonian's commitment to Alaska and its cultures and peoples.

INTO THIN AIR: ARCTIC STUDIES AND IPY 2007–2008

The convergence of the Smithsonian's effort to forge a new relationship with Native and other constituencies in Alaska and across the circumpolar north featured in many current International Polar Year projects is hardly a coincidence. Just as the Smithsonian's work with northern peoples has evolved over the past fifteen years, so too have biologists, oceanographers, and other natural scientists begun to recognize the need for active involvement of northern residents in the enterprise of polar science. For the first time since IPY-1, the 2007–2008 IPY includes social science as a major research focus as well as—for the

FIGURE 10. The Arctic Studies Center's Alaska office prepared *Sharing Knowledge: the Smithsonian Alaska Collections* (http:// alaska.si.edu) in collaboration with Native elders and Second Story Interactive Studio provides interactive assess to historic collections enriched by new Native documentation and oral history.

FIGURE 11. View of National Museum of Natural History exhibition *Arctic: A Friend Acting Strangely,* documenting the impacts of climate change on Arctic animals, landscapes, peoples, and cultures in ancient and modern times. (Photo by Chip Clark, NMNH)

first time in polar research—direct participation by northern peoples (Krupnik et al., 2004; Krupnik and Hovelsrud, 2006; Allison et al., 2007; NOAA, 2008; www.ipy.org).

Back in Washington, as preparations for the 2007–2008 IPY began to take shape amid the growing realization that climate warming was altering the Arctic world in ways that had never been imagined, the ASC curated an exhibit exploring the forces at work in this regional expression of global change (Figure 11). *Arctic: A Friend Acting Strangely* (2006), produced by the ASC with assistance from NOAA, NSF, NASA climate scholars as a major component of the U.S. Interagency Arctic Research Policy Committee's SEARCH (Study of Arctic Environmental Change) Program, presented the science of Arctic warming and its effects on marine and terrestrial systems, animals, and people. Special attention was given to human observations of changes in the Arctic, such as rising temperatures, reductions in permafrost and sea ice, increases

in coastal erosion, shorter winters and longer summers, shifts in animal distributions, and the possible local extirpation of some species important for human subsistence (NOAA, 2008; http://forces.si.edu/arctic; www.arctic.noaa .gov). The exhibit helped focus the national climate debate from exclusive attention to geophysical drivers of global warming to its human and social "face" by illustrating the massive changes underway in the Arctic, long before such effects are expected to become pronounced at lower latitudes. Many of these issues are subjects of ongoing IPY science initiatives. The ASC activities most closely associated with these efforts are found in Aron Crowell's research into culture and climate history in the Gulf of Alaska region (Crowell and Mann, 1998; Crowell, 2000; Crowell et al., 2003), William Fitzhugh's (1998a, 2002b; Fitzhugh and Lamb, 1984) work on long-term culture and environmental change and human-environmental interactions in the circumpolar region, and Igor Krupnik's (Krupnik and

Jolly, 2002; Huntington et al., 2004; Krupnik et al., 2004; Krupnik, 2006) collaborative projects on indigenous observations of sea ice, animal, and climate change in the Bering Sea, and Stephen Loring's (1996, 1998; 2001a; 2001b; 2008; Loring and Rosenmeier, 2005) work with indigenous community science and education.

It is clear that global warming, as dramatically demonstrated during the 2007 summer melt season, is going to be the most serious environmental issue facing the world in the coming century. Building upon the Smithsonian's long history of anthropological and archaeological collecting and research, the ASC has the capability for deep-time and broad panoramic studies of culture and environmental change. The Institution's ethnographic collections and archival records provide information on how northern peoples in many regions of the north have adapted to regional variation and changing conditions. Its archaeological collections, particularly from Alaska—as well as its recent long-term studies in the Eastern Arctic and Subarctic, the Russian North, Scandinavia, and most recently in Mongolia—provide cultural and environmental information on past changes of climate, environment, and culture that form the basis for studies and educational programs informing current conditions and trends. Movements of prehistoric and historic Indian and Eskimo cultures in Labrador, responses of past and present sea mammal hunters on St. Lawrence Island to changing sea ice and animal distributions, and cultural changes seen in Russia and Scandinavia have been taking place for thousands of years. One of the challenges of IPY 2007–2008 is to apply knowledge of these and similar records to the conditions we are facing today, and to assist local government and people living in these regions in making sensible choices for the future.

The Smithsonian's long history of northern studies from Kennicott's first steps in the Mackenzie District in 1858 to the modern day; its collections, research, and public programs; and its contemporary collaboration with northern communities and peoples give it unique capacity for contributions in this IPY and in this time of rapid social and environmental change. After 150 years of drawing upon the north as a source of collections and scholarly research exemplified in the Institution's first IPY efforts, Smithsonian science and education have shifted the polarity of its collecting, science, and educational activities back into the north so that its resources can contribute to meeting the challenges that lie ahead through the direct involvement of Alaskan and other Arctic people. Smithsonian scholars still research and publish at the forefront of their fields, curate collections, and work with the public in many capacities; but sharing the Smithsonian's historic collections and archives and opening its facilities as venues for education and expanded awareness have become the guiding star for this new phase in our history. Nothing could be more important or more worthy of the course established by our founders in the earliest days of the Institution, for whom Arctic research is, as Henry deemed, "of no ordinary importance."

ACKNOWLEDGMENTS

This paper owes much to the long-term support and intellectual stimulation provided by the Smithsonian's dedicated staff, particularly of the Department of Anthropology and its Collections Program staff, who have managed and maintained the Arctic collections and supported the many exhibitions and outreach programs conducted by the ASC since the early 1980s. Susan Kaplan (Bowdoin College), Valérie Chaussonnet, Aron Crowell (ASC), Natalia Fedorova (Museum-Exhibit Center, Salekhard, Russia), Andrei Golovnev (Institute of History and Archaeology, Ekaterinburg, Russia), Susan Kaplan (Bowdoin College), Igor Krupnik (ASC), Stephen Loring (ASC), Noel Broadbent (ASC), Vladimir Pitul'ko (Institute of the History of Material Culture, St. Petersburg, Russia), Susan Rowley (University of British Columbia), Ruth Selig (NMNH), Elisabeth Ward (University of California, Berkeley; formerly with ASC), and Patricia Wolf (Anchorage Museum of History and Art) have been of great assistance and inspiration as friends and colleagues and contributed to programs and ideas expressed above. Of course, nothing would have been possible without the tradition of scholarship and service maintained by the Smithsonian since its founding. I also thank my ASC colleagues Igor Krupnik, Aron Crowell, Stephen Loring, and anonymous reviewers for helpful comments on earlier drafts.

LITERATURE CITED

Allison, I., M. Béland, K. Alverson, R. Bell, D. Carlson, K. Darnell, C. Ellis-Evans, E. Fahrbach, E. Fanta, Y. Fujii, G. Glasser, L. Goldfarb, G. Hovelsrud, J. Huber, V. Kotlyakov, I. Krupnik, J. Lopez-Martinez, T. Mohr, D. Qin, V. Rachold, C. Rapley, O. Rogne, E. Sarukhanian, C. Summerhayes, and C. Xiao. 2007. The Scope of Science for the International Polar Year 2007–2008. *World Meteorological Organization, Technical Documents* 1364. Geneva.

Barr, William. 1985. The Expeditions of the First International Polar Year, 1882–1883. *The Arctic Institute of North America, Technical Paper* 29. Calgary, Alberta, Canada: University of Calgary.

Black, Lydia. 1988. "The Story of Russian America." In *Crossroads of Continents: Cultures of Siberia and Alaska*, ed. William W. Fitzhugh and Aron Crowell, pp. 70–82. Washington, D.C.: Smithsonian Institution Press.

Boas, Franz. 1888a. "The Central Eskimo." In *Sixth Annual Report of the Bureau of American Ethnology for the Years 1884–1885*, pp. 399–669. Washington, D.C.: Government Printing Office.

———. 1888b. The Eskimo. *Proceedings and Transactions of the Royal Society of Canada for the Year 1887*, 5(2):35–39.

———. 1903. The Jesup North Pacific Expedition. *American Museum Journal*, 3(5):72–119.

———. 1905. "The Jesup North Pacific Expedition." In *Proceedings of the International Congress of Americanists, 13th Session*, pp. 91–100. Easton, Pa.: Eschenbach .

———. 1933. "Relations between North-West America and North-East Asia." In *The American Aborigines: Their Origins and Antiquity*, ed. Diamond Jennes, pp. 355–370. Toronto: University of Toronto Press.

Bogoras, Waldemar. 1902. The Folklore of Northeastern Asia as Compared with That of Northwestern North America. *American Anthropologist*, 4(4):577–683.

———. 1929. Elements of the Culture of the Circumpolar Zone. *American Anthropologist*, 31(4):579–601.

Burch, Ernest S., Jr. 2009. "Smithsonian Contributions to Alaskan Ethnography: The IPY Expedition to Barrow, 1881–1883." In *Smithsonian at the Poles: Contributions to International Polar Year Science*, ed. I. Krupnik, M. A. Lang, and S. E. Miller, pp. 89–98. Washington, D.C.: Smithsonian Institution Scholarly Press.

Bray, Tamara L., and Thomas W. Killion, eds. 1994. *Reckoning with the Dead: The Larsen Bay Repatriation and the Smithsonian Institution*. Washington, D.C.: Smithsonian Institution Press.

Carlo, Jean, Valérie Flannagan, and Stephen Loring. 1995. Crossroads Alaska. *Arctic Studies Center Newsletter*, 4:1–2.

Chaussonnet, Valerie, ed. 1995. *Crossroads Alaska: Native Cultures of Alaska and Siberia*. Washington, D.C.: Arctic Studies Center, Smithsonian Institution.

Clifford, James. 2004. Looking Several Ways: Anthropology and Native Heritage in Alaska. *Current Anthropology*, 45(1):1–43.

Collins, Henry B. 1937. *Archaeology of St. Lawrence Island, Alaska*. Smithsonian Miscellaneous Collections, 96(1). Washington, D.C.: Smithsonian Institution.

———. 1946. Wilderness Exploration and Alaska's Purchase. *The Living Wilderness*, 11(19):17–18.

———. 1951. The Origin and Antiquity of the Eskimo. *Annual Report of the Smithsonian Institution, 1950*, pp. 423–467. Washington D.C.: Smithsonian Institution.

———. 1973. "Eskimo Art." In *The Far North: 2000 Years of American Indian and Eskimo Art*, ed. Henry B. Collins, Frederica De Laguna, Edmund Carpenter, and Peter Stone. Washington, D.C.: National Gallery of Art.

Collins, Henry B., Frederica De Laguna, Edmund Carpenter, and Peter Stone. 1973. *The Far North: 2000 Years of American Indian and Eskimo Art*. Washington, D.C.: National Gallery of Art.

Crowell, Aron L. 1992. Post-Contact Koniag Ceremonialism on Kodiak Island and the Alaska Peninsula: Evidence from the Fisher Collection. *Arctic Anthropology*, 29(1):18–37.

———. 2000. Maritime Cultures of the Gulf of Alaska. *Journal of American Archeology*, 17/18/19:177–216.

———. 2004. Terms of Engagement: The Collaborative Representation of Alutiiq Identity. *Etudes/Inuit/Studies*, 28(1):9–35.

———. 2009. "The Art of Iñupiaq Whaling: Elders' Interpretations of International Polar Year Ethnological Collections." In *Smithsonian at the Poles: Contributions to International Polar Year Science*, ed. I. Krupnik, M. Lang, and S. Miller, pp. XX–XX. Washington, D.C.: Smithsonian Institution Scholarly Press.

Crowell, Aron L., and D. H. Mann. 1998. *Archaeology and Coastal Dynamics of Kenai Fjords National Park, Alaska*. Anchorage: Department of the Interior, National Park Service.

Crowell, Aron L., D. H. Mann, and M. Matson. 2003. Implications of "Punctuated Productivity" for Coastal Settlement Patterns: A GIS Study of the Katmai Coast, Gulf of Alaska. *Alaska Journal of Anthropology*, 2(1):62–96.

Crowell, Aron L., Amy F. Steffian, and Gordon L. Pullar, eds. 2001. *Looking Both Ways: Heritage and Identity of the Alutiiq People*. Fairbanks: University of Alaska Press.

Dall, William Healy. 1870. *Alaska and Its Resources*. Boston: Little and Shepard.

Dumond, Don. 2003. "The So-Called 'Eskimo Wedge': A Century after Jesup." In *Constructing Cultures Then and Now: Celebrating Franz Boas and the Jesup North Pacific Expedition*, ed. Laurel Kendell and Igor Krupnik, pp. 33–48. Washington, D.C.: Arctic Studies Center, Smithsonian Institution.

Elliott, Henry W. 1886. *Our Arctic Province: Alaska and the Seal Islands*. New York: Charles Scribner's Sons.

Ewers, John C. 1959. A Century of American Indian Exhibits at the Smithsonian Institution. *Annual Report of the Smithsonian Institution, 1958*. Washington, D.C.: Smithsonian Institution.

Ewing, Heather. 2007. *The Lost World of James Smithson: Science, Revolution, and the Birth of the Smithsonian*. New York: Bloomsbury.

Fedorova, Natalia. 2005. *Zelinii Yar: Arkeologicheskii Komplekc Epoxi Crednevekob'ia v Severnom Priob'e / Kollektiiv Avtorov*. 368c. Ekaterinburg and Salekhard: Russian Academy of Sciences.

Fedorova, Natalia, Pavel A. Kosintsev, and William W. Fitzhugh. 1998. *"Gone into the Hills": Culture of the Northwestern Yamal Coast Population in the Iron Age*. Russian Academy of Sciences, Ural Division, Institute of History and Archaeology; Institute of Plant an Animal Ecology. Washington, D.C.: Arctic Studies Center, Smithsonian Institution.

Fienup-Riordan, Ann. 1996. *Agayuliyararput: Kegginaqut, Kangiit-Ilu—Our Way of Making Prayer: Yup'ik Masks and the Stories They Tell*. Seattle: University of Washington Press.

———. 2007. *Yuungnaqpiallerput: The Way We Genuinely Live*. Seattle: University of Washington Press.

Fitzhugh, William W. 1988a. "Baird's Naturalists: Smithsonian Collectors in Alaska." In *Crossroads of Continents: Cultures of Siberia and Alaska*, ed. William W. Fitzhugh and Aron Crowell, pp. 89–96. Washington, D.C.: Smithsonian Institution Press.

———. 1988b. Introduction and Appendices. In *Ethnological Results of the Point Barrow Expedition*, by John Murdoch. Classics in Smithsonian Anthropology. Washington, D.C.: Smithsonian Institution Press.

———. 1988c. "Persistence and Change in Art and Ideology in Western Alaskan Cultures." In *The Late Prehistoric Development of Alaska's Native Peoples*. Alaska Anthropological Association Monograph 4, pp. 81–105. Santa Fe, N.Mex.: Aurora Press.

———. 1997. "Ambassadors in Sealskins: Exhibiting Eskimos at the Smithsonian." In *Exhibiting Dilemmas: Issues of Representation at the Smithsonian*, ed. Amy Henderson and Adrienne Kaeppler, pp. 206–245. Washington, D.C.: Smithsonian Institution Press.

———. 1998a. Searching for the Grail: Virtual Archeology in Yamal and Circumpolar Theory. *Publications of the National Museum, Ethnographic Series*, 18:99–118. Copenhagen: Danish National Museum.

———. 1998b. "Ancient Times: Yamal among Circumpolar Cultures." In *Living Yamal: Cultural Legacy of Yamal at the Arctic-Antarctic Exhibit in Bonn (1997–1998) Catalog*, ed. Igor Krupnik and Natalya Narinskaya. Washington, D.C.: Arctic Studies Center, Smithsonian Institution and I. S. Shemanovsky Regional Museum of the Yamal-Nenets Area.

———. 1998c. "The Alaska Photographs of Edward W. Nelson, 1877–1881." In *Imaging the Arctic*, ed. J. C. H. King and Henrietta Lidchi, pp. 125–142. London: British Museum Press.

———. 2002a. "Origins of Museum Anthropology at the Smithsonian Institution and Beyond." In *Anthropology, History, and American Indians: Essays in Honor of William Curtis Sturtevant*, ed. William L. Merrill and Ives Goddard, pp. 179–200. Smithsonian Contributions to Anthropology, No. 44. Washington, D.C.: Government Printing Office.

———. 2002b. "Yamal to Greenland: Global Connections in Circumpolar Archaeology." In *Archaeology: the Widening Debate*, ed. Barry Cunliffe, Wendy Davies, and Colin Renfrew, pp. 91–144. Oxford: Oxford University Press.

———. 2003. "Heritage Anthropology in the 'Jesup-2' Era: Exploring North Pacific Cultures through Cooperative Research." In *Constructing Cultures Then and Now: Celebrating Franz Boas and the Jesup North Pacific Expedition*, ed. Laurel Kendall and Igor Krupnik, pp. 287–306. Contributions to Circumpolar Anthropology, 4. Washington, D.C.: Arctic Studies Center, Smithsonian Institution.

Fitzhugh, William W., ed. 1975. *Prehistoric Maritime Adaptations of the Circumpolar Zone*. International Congress of Anthropological and Ethnological Sciences. The Hague: Mouton.

Fitzhugh, William W., and Valérie Chaussonnet, eds. 1994. *Anthropology of the North Pacific Rim*. Washington, D.C.: Smithsonian Institution Press.

Fitzhugh, William W., and Aron Crowell, eds. 1988. *Crossroads of Continents: Cultures of Siberia and Alaska*. Washington, D.C.: Smithsonian Institution Press.

Fitzhugh, William W., and Chisato Dubreuil, eds. 1999. *Ainu: Spirit of a Northern People*. Washington D.C.: Arctic Studies Center, Smithsonian Institution and University of Washington Press.

Fitzhugh, William W., and Andrei Golvonev. 1998. The Drovyanoy 3 Shaman's Cache: Archaeology, Ethnography, and "Living Yamal." *Arctic Anthropology*, 35(2):177–198.

Fitzhugh, William W., and Susan A. Kaplan. 1983. *Inua: Spirit World of the Bering Sea Eskimo*. Smithsonian Traveling Exhibition Service. Washington, D.C.: Smithsonian Institution Press.

Fitzhugh, William W., and Henry Lamb. 1984. Vegetation History and Culture Change in Labrador Prehistory. *Journal of Arctic and Alpine Research*, 17(4):357–370.

Fitzhugh, William W., and Ruth O. Selig. 1981. "The Smithsonian's Alaska Connection: 19th-Century Explorers and Anthropologists." In *The Alaska Journal: A 1981 Collection*, pp. 193–208. Anchorage: Alaska Northwest Publishing Co.

Fitzhugh, William W., and Elisabeth Ward. 2000. *Vikings: The North Atlantic Saga*. Washington, D.C.: Smithsonian Institution Press.

Gjessing, Gutorm. 1944. The Circumpolar Stone Age. *Acta Arctica* 2.

Haakanson, Sven D., Jr. 2000. Ethnoarchaeology of the Yamal Nenets, Utilizing Emic and Etic Evidence in the Interpretation of Archaeological Residues. Ph.D. thesis, Department of Anthropology, Harvard University, Cambridge, Massachusetts.

Hinsley, Curtis. 1981. *Savages and Scientists: The Smithsonian Institution and the Development of American Anthropology 1846–1910*. Washington, D.C.: Smithsonian Institution Press.

Huntington, Henry, Terry Callaghan, Shari Fox, and Igor Krupnik. 2004. Matching Traditional and Scientific Observations to Detect Environmental Change: A Discussion on Arctic Terrestrial Ecosystems. *AMBIO, Journal of the Human Environment, Special Report*, 13: 18–23.

James, James Alton. 1942. The First Scientific Exploration of Russian America and the Purchase of Alaska. *Northwestern University Studies in the Social Sciences* 4. Evanston, Ill.: Northwestern University Press.

Kaplan, Susan A., and Kristin J. Barsness. 1986. *Raven's Journey: The World of Alaska's Native People*. Philadelphia: University of Pennsylvania, University Museum.

Kendall, Laurel, and Igor Krupnik, eds. 2003. *Constructing Cultures Then and Now: Celebrating Franz Boas and the Jesup North Pacific Expedition*. Contributions to Circumpolar Anthropology, 1. Washington, D.C.: Arctic Studies Center, Smithsonian Institution.

Khlobystin, Leonid P. 2005. *Taymyr: The Archaeology of Northernmost Eurasia*. Trans. Leonid Vishniatski and Brois Grudinko, ed. William W. Fitzhugh and Valdimir Pitul'ko. Contributions to Circumpolar Anthropology, 5. Washington, D.C.: National Museum of Natural History, Smithsonian Institution.

Krupnik, Igor. 1996. *Perekrestkii Kontinentov: Kul'turii Korenniikh Narodov Dal'nezo Vostoka I Alaskii*. Trans. from the English by N. A. Aleiinukova, ed. Igor Krupnik. Washington, D.C.: Arctic Studies Center, Smithsonian Institution.

———. 1998. "Foreword." In *The Land of Yamal. Photographs of the Yamal Expeditions of Vladimir Evladov, 1926–1936*, comp. T. I. Pika. Bilingual Russian–English Catalog. Moscow: Sovetskii Sport.

———. 2004. Knowledge Repatriation: Anthropologists Share Cultural Resources with Beringia Native Communities. In *Beringia: Northern Expanses/Severnya Prostory*, 1–2:66–68.

———. 2005. "When Our Words Are Put to Paper": Heritage Documentation and Reversing Knowledge Shift in the Bering Strait Region. *Etudes/Inuit/Studies*, 29(1):67–90.

———. 2006. "We Have Seen These Warm Weathers Before: Indigenous Observations, Archaeology, and the Modeling of Arctic Climate Change." In *Dynamics of Northern Societies*. Proceedings of the SILA/NABO Conference on Arctic and North Atlantic Archaeology. *National Museum of Denmark Publications in Archaeology and History*, 10:11–21.

———. 2009. "'The Way We See It Coming': Building the Legacy of Indigenous Observations in IPY 2007–2008." In *Smithsonian at the Poles: Contributions to International Polar Year Science*, ed. I. Krupnik, M. A. Lang, and S. E. Miller, pp. 129–142. Washington, D.C.: Smithsonian Institution Scholarly Press.

Krupnik, Igor, and William W. Fitzhugh, eds. 2001. *Gateways: Exploring the Legacy of the Jesup North Pacific Expedition, 1897–1902*. Contributions to Circumpolar Anthropology, 1. Washington, D.C.: Arctic Studies Center, Smithsonian Institution.

Krupnik, Igor, and Grete K. Hovelsrud. 2006. IPY 2007–08 and Social/Human Sciences: An Update. *Arctic*, 59(3):341–348.

Krupnik, Igor, Henry Huntington, Christopher Koonooka, and George Noongwook, eds. 2004. *Watching Ice and Weather Our Way*. Washington, D.C.: Arctic Studies Center, Smithsonian Institution, Savoonga Whaling Captains Association, and Marine Mammal Commission.

Krupnik, Igor, and Dyanna Jolly, eds. 2002. *The Earth Is Faster Now: Indigenous Observations of Arctic Environmental Change*. Fairbanks, Alaska: Arctic Research Consortium of the United States and Arctic Studies Center, Smithsonian Institution.

Krupnik, Igor, and Natalia Narinskaya, eds. 1998. *Living Yamal/Zhivoy Yamal*. Bilingual exhibit catalog from *Arktis und Antarktis* Exhibit (1997–1998) in Bonn, Kunst- und Augsstellungs Halle, pp. 96–99. Washington, D.C.: Arctic Studies Center, Smithsonian Institution and I. S. Shemanovsky Regional Museum of the Yamal-Nenets Area.

Kuzmina, Liudmila P. 1994. "The Jesup North Pacific Expedition: A History of Russian–American Cooperation." In *Anthropology of the North Pacific Rim*, ed. Valerie Chaussonnet and William Fitzhugh, pp. 63–78. Washington, D.C.: Smithsonian Institution Press.

Larsen, Helge, and Frohlich Rainey. 1948. Ipiutak and the Arctic Whaling Hunting Culture. *Anthropological Papers of the American Museum of Natural History*, 42. New York: American Museum of Natural History.

Lindsay, Debra. 1993. *Science in the Subarctic: Trappers, Traders, and the Smithsonian Institution.* Washington, D.C.: Smithsonian Institution Press.

Loring, Stephen. 1996. Community Anthropology at the Smithsonian. American Anthropological Association. *Anthropology Newsletter,* October: 23–24.

———. 1998. "Stubborn Independence: An Essay on the Innu and Archaeology." In *Bringing Back the Past, Historical Perspectives on Canadian Archaeology,* ed. Pamela Jane Smith and Donald Mitchell, pp. 259–276. Mercury Series Archaeological Survey of Canada Paper 158. Hull, Quebec: Canadian Museum of Civilization.

———. 2001a. "Introduction to Lucien M. Turner and the Beginnings of Smithsonian Anthropology in the North." In *Ethnology of the Ungava District, Hudson Bay Territory* by Lucien Turner, pp. vii–xxxii. Washington, D.C.: Smithsonian Institution Press.

———. 2001b. "Repatriation and Community Anthropology: The Smithsonian Institution's Arctic Studies Center." In *The Future of the Past: Archaeologists, Native Americans, and Repatriation,* ed. Tamara Bray, pp. 185–200. New York: Garland.

———. 2008. "The Wind Blows Everything Off the Ground: New Provisions and New Directions in Archaeological Research in the North." In *Opening Archaeology: the Impact of Repatriation on the Discipline,* ed. Thomas Killion, pp. 181–194. Santa Fe, N.Mex.: School of American Research.

———. 2009. "From Tent to Trading Post and Back Again: Smithsonian Anthropology in Nunavut, Nunavik, Nitassinan, and Nunatsiavut—The Changing IPY Agenda, 1882–2007." In *Smithsonian at the Poles: Contributions to International Polar Year Science,* ed. I. Krupnik, M. A. Lang, and S. E. Miller, pp. 115–128. Washington, D.C.: Smithsonian Institution Scholarly Press.

Loring, Stephen, and Leah Rosenmeier, eds. 2005. *Angutiup ânguanga/Anguti's Amulet.* Truro, Nova Scotia: Eastern Woodland Publishing, Milbrook First Nation.

Mason, Otis P. 1891. The Ulu, or Woman's Knife, of the Eskimo. *Annual Report of the United States National Museum for 1890,* pp. 411–416. Washington, D.C.: Government Printing Office.

———.1896. Influence of Environment upon Human Industries or Arts. *Annual Report of the United States National Museum for 1890.* Part I, pp. 639–665. Washington, D.C.: Government Printing Office.

———. 1902. Aboriginal American Harpoons: A Study in Ethnic Distribution and Invention. *Annual Report of the United States National Museum for 1900,* pp. 189–304. Washington, D.C.: Government Printing Office.

Murdoch, John. 1892. Ethnological Results of the Point Barrow Expedition. *Ninth Annual Report of the Bureau of American Ethnology 1887–88.* Washington, D.C.: Government Printing Office.

National Oceanic and Atmospheric Administration (NOAA). 2008. *NOAA at the Poles: International Polar Year 2007–2008. Exploring and Understanding a Changing Planet During the 4th International Polar Year 2007–2008.* CD and website presentation.

Nelson, Edward W. 1899. The Eskimos about Bering Strait. *Eighteenth Annual Report of the Bureau of American Ethnology, 1896–1897.* Washington, D.C.: Government Printing Office. (Reprinted 1983, Smithsonian Institution Press.)

Pika, T. I. 1998. *The Land of Yamal: Photographs of the Yamal Expeditions of Vladimir Evladov, 1926–1936.* Bilingual Russian-English Catalog. Moscow: Sovetskii Sport.

Pitul'ko, Vladimir V. 2001. Terminal Pleistocene–Early Holocene Occupation in Northeast Asia and the Zhokhov Assemblage. *Quaternary Science Review,* 20:267–275.

Pullar, Gordon. 2001. "Contemporary Alutiiq Identity." In *Looking Both Ways: Heritage and Identity of the Alutiiq People,* ed. Aron Crowell, Amy Steffian, and Gordon Pullar, pp. 73–98. Fairbanks: University of Alaska Press.

Ray, Patrick Henry. 1885. "Ethnological Sketch of the Natives of Point Barrow." In *Report of the International Polar Expedition to Point Barrow, Alaska, in Response to the Resolution of the House of Representatives of December 11, 1884,* Part III, pp. 35–60. Washington, D.C.: Government Printing Office.

Rivinus, E. F., and E. M. Youssef. 1992. *Spencer Baird of the Smithsonian Institution.* Washington, D.C.: Smithsonian Institution Press.

Rowley, Susan. 1988. *Inua: Spirit World of the Bering Sea Eskimo.* Catalog for an exhibition presented by the United States of America. Washington, D.C.: Smithsonian Institution and United States Information Agency.

Scott, G. Richard. 1994. "Teeth and Prehistory on Kodiak Island." In *Reckoning with the Dead: The Larsen Bay Repatriation and the Smithsonian Institution,* ed. Tamara L. Bray and Thomas W. Killion, pp. 67–75. Washington, D.C.: Smithsonian Institution Press.

Sherwood, Morgan. 1965. *Exploration of Alaska 1865–1900.* New Haven, Conn.: Yale University Press.

Smithsonian Institution Annual Report (SIAR). 1860. Smithsonian Institution Annual Reports and United States National Museum Annual Reports, 1866–1996. Smithsonian Institution Archives, Washington, D.C. SIA Acc. 98-159.

Smithsonian Institution Annual Report (SIAR). 1862. Smithsonian Institution Annual Reports and United States National Museum Annual Reports, 1866–1996. Smithsonian Institution Archives, Washington, D.C. SIA Acc. 98-159.

Smithsonian Institution Annual Report (SIAR). 1863. Smithsonian Institution Annual Reports and United States National Museum Annual Reports, 1866–1996. Smithsonian Institution Archives, Washington, D.C. SIA Acc. 98-159.

Turner, Lucien. 1894. Ethnology of the Ungava District, Hudson Bay Territory. *Eleventh Annual Report of the Bureau of American Ethnology for the Years 1889–1890,* ed. John Murdoch, pp. 159–350. Washington, D.C.: Government Printing Office.

Whymper, Frederick. 1869. *Travel and Adventure in the Territory of Alaska.* New York: Harper and Bros.

Wood, Kevin R., and James E. Overland. 2006. Climate Lessons from the First International Polar Year. *Bulletin of the American Meteorological Society,* 87:1685–1697.

WEBSITE RESOURCES

Smithsonian Institution
   http://anthropology.si.edu
   http://anthropology.si.edu/repatriation
   www.mnh.si.edu/arctic
International Polar Year
   www.ipy.org
Arctic: A Friend Acting Strangely
   http://forces.si.edu/arctic
National Oceanographic and Atmospheric Administration
   www.arctic.noaa.gov
Sharing Knowledge, ASC Alaska Collection Project
   http://alaska.si.edu

Yup'ik Eskimo Contributions to Arctic Research at the Smithsonian

Ann Fienup-Riordan

ABSTRACT. The following pages review four research trips to Smithsonian collections made by Yup'ik community members between 1997 and 2003. In each case, Yup'ik elders had the opportunity to examine ethnographic material gathered from southwest Alaska in the late-nineteenth and early-twentieth centuries. Most had seen similar objects in use locally when they were young and provided rich commentary not only on the significance of particular tools and pieces of clothing, but on the traditional way of life and worldview that flourished in southwest Alaska in the 1920s and 1930s. Although much has changed since these elders came of age—the introduction of organized religion, formal education, and a wage economy—a rich and vibrant oral tradition remains. Through sharing knowledge in collections as well as working with museum professionals to bring objects home to Alaska for exhibition, elders seek not only to remind their younger generations of their rich heritage, but to declare the ingenuity and compassion of their ancestors to all the world.

INTRODUCTION

Yup'ik Eskimo men and women first gained awareness of Smithsonian collections in 1982, with the opening of Bill Fitzhugh and Susan Kaplan's groundbreaking exhibition, *Inua: Spirit World of the Bering Sea Eskimo* (Fitzhugh and Kaplan, 1982) in Anchorage. Prior to the opening of the Yup'ik mask exhibit, *Agayuliyararput/Our Way of Making Prayer* in 1996, elders worked with photographs of objects, but few entered museums to see the real thing. Since then, Yup'ik elders have had unprecedented opportunities to visit and view Smithsonian collections, including one- and two-week research trips to the National Museum of the American Indian in 1997 and 2002, and the National Museum of Natural History in 2002 and 2003.

Inua and *Agayuliyararput* opened doors, and those who entered found an unimagined array of artifacts, which most had viewed only briefly when they

Ann Fienup-Riordan, Arctic Studies Center, 9951 Prospect Drive, Anchorage, AK 99516, USA (riordan@alaska.net). Accepted 9 May 2008.

were young. All were deeply moved by what they saw. Elders also recognized the potential power of museum collections to communicate renewed pride and self-respect to a generation of young people woefully ignorant of the skills their ancestors used to survive.

Finally, in 2003 the Calista Elders Council began to actively search for ways to bring museum objects home. Repatriation was not the issue, as ownership of objects was not the goal. Rather the Council sought "visual repatriation"—the opportunity to show and explain traditional technology to contemporary young people. The results of their work in Smithsonian collections has not only enriched our understanding of nineteenth-century Yup'ik technology in unprecedented ways but also laid the foundation for the exhibition *Yuungnaqpiallerput (The Way We Genuinely Live): Masterworks of Yup'ik Science and Survival,* bringing Yup'ik materials home to Alaska in this Fourth International Polar Year.

SOUTHWEST ALASKA

The Yukon-Kuskokwim region, a lowland delta the size of Kansas, is the traditional homeland of the Yupiit, or Yup'ik Eskimos. The region's current population of more than 23,000 (the largest native population in Alaska) lives scattered in 56 villages, ranging between 200 and 1,000 persons each, and the regional center of Bethel with a population of nearly 7,000 (Figure 1). Today this huge region is crosscut by historical and administrative boundaries, including two dialect groups, three major Christian denominations, five school districts, two census areas, and three Alaska Native Claims Settlement Act (ANCSA) regional corporations. Villages each have an elementary and a secondary school, city government or traditional council, health clinic, church or churches, airstrip, electricity, and, in some cases, running water. With 14,000 speakers of the Central Yup'ik language, the Yupiit remain among the most traditional Native Americans.

The subarctic tundra environment of the Bering Sea coast supports rich flora and fauna. An impressive variety of plants and animals appears and disappears as part of an annual cycle of availability on which Yup'ik people focus both thought and deed. Millions of birds nest and breed in the region's ample wetlands, including geese, ducks, and swans. Annual migrations of salmon and herring are major resources for both riverine and coastal hunters. Halibut, flounder, tomcod, whitefish, capelin, pike, needlefish, smelt, and blackfish seasonally appear in coastal waters and tundra lakes and sloughs, and seals, walrus, and beluga whales return each spring. Land animals abound, including moose, caribou, bear, fox, otter, Arctic hare, muskrat, and beaver, and edible greens and berries are plentiful during summer months. Prehistorically this abundance supported the development and spread of Inuit culture, and some scholars have called the coast the "cradle of Eskimo civilization."

The abundance of plants and animals in southwest Alaska allowed for a more settled life than in other parts of the Arctic. Hundreds of seasonal camps and dozens of winter settlements lined riverine highways that link communities to this day. Like the northern Inuit, the coastal Yupiit were nomadic, yet their rich environment allowed them to remain within a relatively fixed range. Each of at least a dozen regional groups demarcated a largely self-sufficient area, within which people moved freely throughout the year in their quest for food. Far from seeing their environment as the insentient provider of resources available for the taking, many Yupiit continue to view it as responsive to their own careful action and attention.

ELDERS IN MUSEUMS: FIELDWORK TURNED ON ITS HEAD

This year, 2007, marks the beginning of the Fourth International Polar Year. September 2007 also saw the opening of the exhibition, *Yuungnaqpiallerput/The Way We Genuinely Live: Masterworks of Yup'ik Science and Survival,* in Bethel, Alaska. *Yuungnaqpiallerput* was developed by the Calista Elders Council in collaboration with the Anchorage Museum with funding from the National Science Foundation. It is based on over a decade of work in museums by Yup'ik men and women, including four seminal research trips to Smithsonian collections. The following pages share highlights of how and why elders came to the Smithsonian, what they learned, and what they hope to do with this knowledge.

Yuungnaqpiallerput (Fienup-Riordan, 2007) stands squarely on the shoulders of the successful partnership that gave rise to the Yup'ik mask exhibit *Agayuliyararput/Our Way of Making Prayer* in 1996 (Fienup-Riordan, 1996). That exhibit was the culmination of efforts to understand the meaning and power of nineteenth-century masks, including masks collected by Edward Nelson and Lucien Turner, from the Yup'ik point of view. The cornerstone of that exhibition, as with *Yuungnaqpiallerput,* was information eloquently shared by Yup'ik elders during both private and public conversations, remembering the masked dances they had seen when they were young. Some had seen photographs of masks, but few had entered muse-

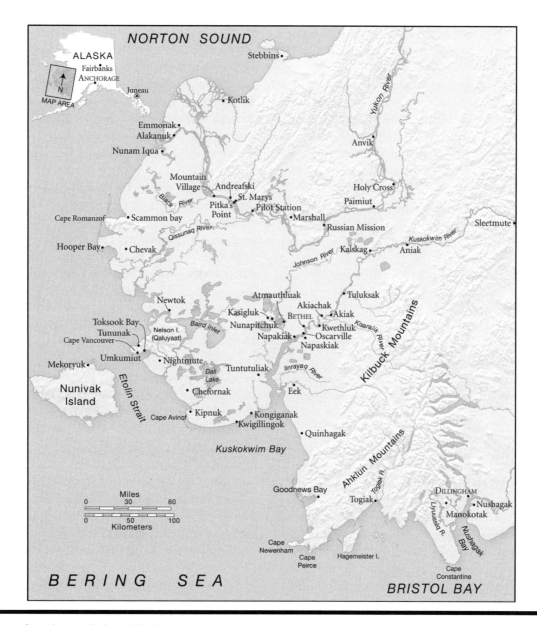

FIGURE 1. Map of Southwest Alaska, 2008. (Patrick Jankanish and Matt O'Leary)

ums to see the real thing until after the exhibit opened in Toksook Bay in January 1996.

Following *Agayuliyararput*, Yup'ik men and women have had unprecedented opportunities to visit museums and view collections. The first "Yup'ik delegation" to do serious work with Smithsonian collections was a group of six elders who, along with myself and Marie Meade, traveled to the Bronx storage facility of the National Museum of the American Indian (NMAI) for two weeks in April 1997. NMAI had invited the elders to New York as thanks for what they had shared during the Yup'ik mask exhibit, which was then on display in New York. Our visit

marked the first time Smithsonian staff extended such an invitation to Alaska Native elders. Organized in large part by Mary Jane Lenz, NMAI housed us, fed us, and shared with elders as many objects as they could during the time we had together.

Agayuliyararput opened museum doors, and those who entered found an unimagined array of artifacts, including hunting equipment, clothing, and the tools of daily life. Ironically, the objects elders found least interesting were the masks, which most had viewed only briefly when they were young. Grass socks, stone tools, and fish-skin clothing, however, excited enormous interest. All were deeply moved by what they saw and spoke repeatedly about the skill required to make and use each item. Viewing collections for the first time, the late Willie Kamkoff (April 1997) of Kotlik remarked: "Seeing these things after we arrived, our ancestors were so ingenious in making hunting tools. They didn't have iron tools, only *ciimat* [rocks]. Their tools weren't sharp, but they were amazing."

Elders also recognized the potential power of museum collections to communicate renewed pride and self-respect to a generation of younger Yup'ik men and women woefully ignorant of the skills their ancestors used to survive. Reflecting on his visit to NMAI, Paul John (September 1998) of Toksook Bay said:

We saw many objects when we visited the museum in New York, but I couldn't leave the adze and an ax for a long time. I kept going back to look at them in awe, realizing that they had been used by someone long before metal and nails were introduced. The ax had an ivory blade with a wooden handle shiny from constant sweat and oil from the hands that held it. . . .

The objects in museums are not insignificant. If we live using them as our strength, we will get closer to our ancestors' ways. And when we are gone, our grandchildren will continue to live according to the knowledge they have gained.

Elders were deeply engaged by the full range of Yup'ik technology. This point was brought home during the second major Yup'ik foray into Smithsonian collections, a visit to NMAI's Cultural Resources Center in August 2000. Three elders had been invited to choose objects for inclusion in the new museum's planned exhibit, *Our Universes*. During the first four days of their visit, they sat in a conference room and carefully described their way of life to curator Emil Her Many Horses and staff. On the last day they were invited into storage areas where all 1,000 Yup'ik objects in the museum's collections were spread before them. The elders were asked to walk through the room and choose the things that they felt best reflected the traditional Yup'ik view of the world. The Yup'ik group was the last of eight groups to make such selections. Some, like the Pueblo, had chosen 40 pieces, including many sacred ones. Others made smaller selections. The Yup'ik group circled the room, pointed enthusiastically at everything recognizably Yup'ik, and chose more than 300 objects. Masks were of interest, but the technology that had allowed their ancestors to survive was of primary importance.

This trip, planned with the help of the Calista Elders Council (CEC) and fully funded by NMAI, was preceded by a two-day gathering in Bethel, where five elders answered questions and discussed their view of the world with Emil Her Many Horses and Mary Jane Lenz. This meeting was foundational, not only for NMAI staff but for CEC, the region's primary heritage organization representing the 1,300 Yup'ik elders sixty-five and older. CEC had just begun actively documenting traditional knowledge in 1999, both during their annual Elder and Youth Conventions and interviews with individual elder experts. The format NMAI chose—a small group of elders focusing discussion on a specific topic—was an inspiration. Supported by NSF, the CEC has since held more than two dozen two- and three-day gatherings on topics chosen by CEC's board of elders, including ones on relational terms, discipline techniques, migratory waterfowl, and fall survival skills. In my 30 years work in the region, the last five years have been both the most satisfying and the most productive, seeking to answer questions Yup'ik people themselves are posing.

Aron Crowell, Director of the Arctic Studies Center's Anchorage office, organized the third Yup'ik visit to Smithsonian collections in 2002. There, three elders spent one week examining and commenting on a rich range of objects Aron selected for inclusion in the Arctic Studies Center's Anchorage exhibition, scheduled to open in 2010. Photographs and elders' observations from this important trip are available on the Arctic Studies Center's website, *Sharing Knowledge*. Again, it was deeply moving to see how much exploring collections meant to individual elders. Eighty-year-old John Phillip Sr. from Kongiganak wanted to come so badly that when stormy coastal weather closed in, he drove his snow machine more than 100 miles to Bethel to make his flight.

February 2003 was the last Yup'ik trip to work in the Smithsonian Institution's Museum Support Center (MSC). Frank Andrew, the single most knowledgeable elder I have every known, had been unable to come to Washington, D.C., in 2002 due to his wife's death. Members of the CEC staff had worked with Frank at museums in Bethel and Anchorage, but he wanted to see objects specifically from the Canineq (lower coastal) area of the Bering Sea. So, we organized this one-week trip just for him. Frank was accompanied by his son, Noah, as well as two knowledgeable elders he felt comfortable with. The Smithsonian Community Scholars program funded our travel, with additional support from the Calista Elders Council.

Prior to our week at MSC, I searched records and preselected close to 300 objects from Canineq (Nelson, 1899). The MSC staff was generous in supplying records and print outs to make this long-distance selection possible. During our stay, we recorded close to 30 hours of discussion, all in Yup'ik, producing more than 1,000 pages of transcripts. We had an additional adventure when the blizzard of

2002 hit D.C. the night before we were to fly home. Frank had noted that the Yup'ik name for the small snowflakes he saw falling was *taqailnguut*, ones that don't stop—and they didn't. Washington shut down and planes didn't fly for another three days. The elders were unconcerned, as waiting out storms was a routine part of life. Food was a potential problem, but Noah and I went "hunting" every afternoon for whatever Pennsylvania Avenue could provide—tins of smoked oysters, roast chickens, canned soup. During the days, we gathered in our largest room and told stories. I kept the recorder running, producing what Marie affectionately referred to as the Blizzard Tapes.

Not only have elders traveled to Smithsonian collections but Smithsonian collections have come home also. During our last trip to MSC, NMAI photo archivist Donna Rose gave us a fat binder of copies of the wonderful photographs made by Dr. Leuman M. Waugh, recently saved from oblivion by Igor Krupnik and Stephen Loring, among others (Krupnik and Loring, 2002; Fienup-Riordan, 2005). An especially moving account was recorded while looking at Waugh's photo of men hunting in kayaks near Frank Andrew's hometown (Figure 2). I naively asked Frank if he felt pride the first time he used a kayak. Here is what he said.

There were two men [Qilkilek and Puyulkuk] who picked on me. One was my grandfather, and the other was my cross-cousin. Getting a kayak didn't make me feel important. One of them picked on me very hard. He said that I would only eat catches that I got from other people and not my own and that I would only wear clothing that was handed down. The other one asked me why I got a kayak, one that would rot before the blood of my catch soaked it. These things that I heard were not things that make you feel good.

That was how I felt when I got a kayak, and I stopped sleeping. I didn't want to be [the way they said I would be]. I learned everything about paddling before I got a kayak by using one that wasn't mine, and I was taught how to hunt as well. I was filled with eagerness and the will to succeed.

I got a kayak during summer. They put it up on stilts. I would even go and check on it at night when it was windy, being afraid it might blow away because that old man bothered me so much. . . .

Then during [the following] spring they began to go down to the ocean. I stopped sleeping, wondering when he would let me go. They eventually began to catch sea mammals. After that, my late older sister told me that they were going to take me. I was so ecstatic because I loved to be by the ocean when I went to fetch their catches. And we would be reluctant to go back up to land sometimes. It was always calm.

FIGURE 2. An uncatalogued hand-tinted lantern slide: "Men hunting in kayaks, probably near Kwigillingok," in 1935/1936, Alaska, by Leuman M. Waugh, DDS, based on comments from Frank Andrew, 2002. Photo L02230 courtesy of National Museum of the American Indian, Smithsonian Institution.

We were getting ready to go down. . . . We walked, pulling our kayak sleds at night, and we got to the ocean just at daybreak. I saw the person who ridiculed me. His name was Qilkilek, and he was in a kayak. I never forgot what he said to me. When he saw me he said, "What are you here for? Go back up and be a urine-bucket dumper. You won't catch anything." I didn't answer.

Frank then left to hunt with his two cousins. Soon he spotted a bearded seal pup sleeping on floating ice and signaled to his cousin, who killed it. Frank then saw its mother swimming nearby. His cousin told him not to hunt it but Frank didn't want to give up. When the animal surfaced directly in front of him, Frank took aim and fired.

I shot it immediately and hit it. I quickly harpooned it. It was very large. My poor heart was going tung-tung, and I could hear my heartbeat with my ears. I was afraid I would capsize, but I really wanted to catch it. After checking the ice, I got off on a thick spot, holding [the seal] with the harpoon. It was floating because it was very fat. I told my cousin Mancuaq to come, and he helped me.

Qallaq didn't make a sound again. We pulled it on top of the ice together and butchered it. Because it was so large, I told him to put it inside his kayak. I carried only the meat. When we got back, they came right over. Qilkilek didn't say anything. . . . They butchered it, cutting it in strips, and distributed them. That's what they do with first catches.

He asked me what I came for and told me to go back up and be the dumper of their urine buckets. They said they do that to those who they were encouraging because they want their minds to be stronger, those who they goaded toward success.

Frank's narrative is an unprecedented account, not only of what took place, but of the mixture of excitement, humility, and determination he felt when ridiculed by men whose intent was not to shame him but to encourage him and prevent him from feeling overly proud and self-confident. Personal accounts are hard to elicit in gatherings and interviews. Objects and photographs have opened doors that all of my questions never could.

VISUAL REPATRIATION: "EVERYTHING THAT IS MADE CAUSES US TO REMEMBER"

To the extent that elders were personally moved by what they saw in collections, they regretted that young people in Alaska could not share their experience. Elders agreed that people cannot understand what they do not see. Frank Andrew (August 2003) spoke from personal experience: "Among the things I saw in the museum, I didn't know about things that I had not used. That's how our young people are. They don't know what they haven't seen." Neva Rivers (March 2004) of Hooper Bay agreed:

Even though they hear about them with their ears, they cannot replicate these things if they don't see them. But if our young people see what they did long ago, they will understand. They cannot come [to museums] because they are too far away, but if they bring things to Alaska, they can replicate some that they want to continue to be seen.

Again and again elders said how valuable it would be for young people to see what they were seeing. During our 2003 trip to MSC, Frank Andrew (February 2003) remarked:

Only education can keep things alive, only if a person who listens closely hears the information. These handmade items were constantly constructed when I was young by those who knew how to make them and who had the knowledge.

Men taught young men how to catch animals. These [traditional ways] were visible and did not change. Today [these ways] are no longer displayed, because we are not teaching what we were taught, even though we have the knowledge. It will not live on if it is like that.

Paul John (January 2004) agreed, "We are losing our way of life, and we need to help young people and others to better understand what they've lost. If the things that our ancestors used are shown, they will think, 'So this is what our ancestors did, and I can do what my ancestors did, too.'"

Statistics bear out elders' view that contemporary young people lack knowledge of and appreciation for the values and technical skills that made life both possible and meaningful on the Bering Sea coast in the not-so-distant past. Southwest Alaska has one of the highest suicide rates in the nation, primarily young men and women in their twenties. Rates of poverty, alcohol abuse, and domestic violence are also disproportionately high. The rapid changes before and after Alaska statehood in 1959 shook the moral foundation of Yup'ik community life to its core. These problems run deep, and knowledge and pride in their past is one among many elements needed for a solution. Joan Hamilton (November 2003) of Bethel said simply, "Many people here are displaced by alcohol, but if we learn about ourselves from our elders, our minds will improve."

The truth of Frank Andrew's and Paul John's words was brought home to me personally in April 2003 when I listened to Jeffery Curtis, a Toksook Bay high-school student, speak publicly about his recent visit to Anchorage. He said how glad he was to have the opportunity to visit the University of Alaska that he hoped someday to attend. He said that he planned to study science because his ancestors had no science, and he wanted to learn what white people could teach. Jeff comes from a proud and talented family, and his grandfather, Phillip Moses, is a master kayak builder with expert knowledge on many aspects of Yup'ik technology. Jeff knows this, but nowhere has he learned to respect his grandfather's knowledge as "science."

Phillip Moses had likewise given me food for thought six months before, during work in collections at the Anchorage Museum. I had undergone retinal surgery two weeks earlier and could still only half-see out of one eye. As we worked together, my partner Alice Rearden handed Phillip a pair of wooden snow goggles, painted black on the inside with long, thin slits to let in the light. Phillip smiled, passed them to me to examine, and then launched into an enthusiastic explanation of how these goggles were the original "Yup'ik prescription sunglasses." Half-listening, I held the goggles to my eyes, and for the first time since surgery, I could see! As I digested the sophisticated design—thin slits that focused the light like a pinhole camera, enhancing the user's vision—I could hear Phillip relating in Yup'ik how the goggles worked both to reduce glare and to help a hunter see far. Phillip, like many elders, was well aware of the goggles' properties, yet I know of no reference in the literature on southwest Alaska regarding the capacity of snow goggles to improve distance vision. Like Phillip, many living elders can articulate the fundamentals of Yup'ik technology. How powerful it would be to bring their clear descriptions home to a younger generation, both Native and non-Native.

Finally, in 2003, the Calista Elders Council began to search for ways to respond to the desire of their board of elders to bring museum objects home. Repatriation was not the issue, as ownership of objects was not the goal. Rather, "visual repatriation" was what they sought—the opportunity to show and explain traditional technology to contemporary young people.

Just as the Yup'ik community had looked to the Anchorage Museum in 1993 when beginning work on the Yup'ik mask exhibit, it again turned to the museum, which energetically embraced their project. Planning meetings formally began in August 2003 with a combination of National Science Foundation and Anchorage Museum Association support. The first meeting took place in Bethel in August 2003. There, a team of twelve Yup'ik elders and educators—including Frank Andrew and Paul John— gathered to plan a comprehensive exhibit of nineteenth-century Yup'ik technology.

First, we discussed what kinds of objects the Yup'ik community would want to see. The answer was "everything." This was no surprise, given the elders' all-inclusive choices three years before at NMAI. What followed did surprise me, although in retrospect it should not have. I spoke briefly about the mask exhibit that many of us had worked on together ten years earlier, saying that since that exhibit had focused on Yup'ik spirituality, we could take this opportunity to focus on Yup'ik science. I said that this exhibit could be what *Agayuliyararput/Our Way of Making Prayer* was not. I was reminded politely but firmly that Yup'ik tools and technology were also "our way of making prayer." Yup'ik team members did not view their traditional technology and spirituality as separable, and a valuable contribution of our exhibit would be to show how their ancestors lived properly, without this separation. Elsie Mather explained, "Long ago our beliefs and our way of life weren't seen as separate. But nowadays, they look at those two as separate. In this exhibit, we should remember that and try to help people understand. If our exhibit becomes a reality, it will be taught that their ways of life and their beliefs were one."

Our second task was to name the exhibit. This was done with serious deliberation. After several suggestions, Frank Andrew spoke: "The way of our ancestors is called *yuungnaqsaraq* ['to endeavor to live']. When using all the tools together, only a person who is trying to survive will use them to live. That's the name, and our ancestors used it all the time, *ciuliamta yuungnaquciat* [our ancestors' way of life]." Paul John agreed: "Back when Yup'ik people were really surviving on their own, they took care of themselves, trying to follow their traditions."

Mark John then added a crucial observation, restating the Yup'ik phrase in the present tense:

We could make it more personal rather than distant. It could be *yuungnaqpiallerput* [the way we genuinely live], which includes us, too. We are part of all that is being displayed. In the villages, people still utilize those ways, even though they may be using different materials. We're not distancing ourselves from our ancestors.

Paul John concluded: "That *yuungnaqpiallerput* is perfect as a title. We really did try to live and survive the real way."

Discussion continued on which objects people thought most important to include. Paul John again mentioned the adze and the ax, as well as the fire-making tools he had admired in New York. Frank Andrew spoke of the kayak and of that most essential tool, the *negcik* (gaff), which he referred to as "life hook." Andy Paukan remembered the powerful sinew-backed bow, and Marie Meade recalled the finely sewn clothing and ceremonial regalia she had seen in collections. Paul John emphasized the importance of including the drum as a metaphor for the continued vitality of the Yup'ik way of life. Frank Andrew concluded: "The reverberation of the drum kept everyone together."

Elders also enthusiastically supported the inclusion of newly made examples of traditional technology, including a kayak, fish trap, seal-gut parka, and bearskin boat. Living elders had the skills to make these tools, and, once again, many people thought that elders mentoring young people in these techniques had the potential not only to transfer specific skills but also to shape lives.

Another issue was how to organize the objects. A recurrent theme was the continued importance of the seasonal cycle of activities, both in the past and today. They suggested that this cycle be used as the foundation for the exhibit. This simple but elegant mandate is what we have followed. Our story begins with preparation in the village and moves through spring, summer, fall, and early-winter harvesting activities. We then return to the winter village, where activities today, as in the past, focus on sharing the harvest and on renewal for the coming year.

To tell this story, our exhibit includes examples of the most important features of nineteenth- and early-twentieth-century Yup'ik technology. It draws from a number of major collections of Yup'ik material culture in the United States and Europe, as well as from many less known but equally important collections. Some of our best pieces, however, come from the Smithsonian, including pieces collected by Edward Nelson, William Healey Dall, and A. H. Twitchell. Without Smithsonian collections, we could not tell our story.

"WE HAVE NO WORD FOR *SCIENCE*"

In choosing a "science" focus for their exhibition, Yup'ik community members continue to advocate for respect for their knowledge systems. The perceived gap between Yup'ik indigenous knowledge and western science is enormous. Clearly, there are differences; but understanding the links can deepen our appreciation of both Yup'ik and western thought (Kawagley, 1995).

When describing Yup'ik masks and ceremonies, elders made it clear that in the past they had no separate category for "religion." Everyday acts were equally "our way of making prayer." Similarly, discussions of hunting and harvesting activities make no separation between a person's technical and moral education. Frank Andrew (February 2003) remarked that "Everything has a rule, no matter what it is. Because admonitions are a part of these snow goggles, we are talking about it through these." Elsie Mather (November 2003) observed, "Our language had no word for science, yet our tools were so well designed that they allowed us to live in a land no one else would inhabit."

Yup'ik ontology promoted constant watchfulness and attention to the signs the natural world provided. A child's first task each morning was to exit the house and observe the weather. When traveling, each person depended for survival on observational skills honed from an early age.

Knowledge in the past was situated, based on observation and experience. Frank Andrew (June 2003) stated, "I only speak intelligently about things that I know here in our village. I don't know things in other villages that I didn't see, and I cannot explain them very well." What Frank does know, however, would impress any professional biologist or natural scientist. Frank and his contemporaries are gifted naturalists, engaged in classification of all aspects of the world around them, often by appearance, usefulness,

and behavior. Frank (June 2003) provided one excellent example. Previously he had talked at length about the different species of sea mammals, all of which have a one-to-one correspondence with western species classifications, including *makliit* (bearded seals), *nayit* (hair seals), *issurit* (spotted seals), *qasrulget* (ribbon seals), *asveret* (walrus), *cetuat* (beluga whales), *arveret* (bowhead whales), *arrluut* (killer whales), and *arrnat* (sea otters). He also distinguished between different age groups within individual species. For example, the general category of bearded seal (*Erignathus barbatus*) includes *maklak* or *tungunquq* (adult bearded seal), *maklassuk* (subadult bearded seal), *maklacuk* (adult bearded seal with a small body but the flippers and intestines of an adult), *qalriq* (bearded seal in rut), *amirkaq* (young bearded seal), *maklassugaq* (two-year-old bearded seal), and *maklaaq* (bearded seal pup).

Speaking to Alice Rearden and his son, Noah, both of whom he assumed understood the names for seal species and age groups, Frank added another level of detail, naming eight distinct varieties of bearded seals based on appearance and behavior, three of which I quote below:

There are many bearded seals, and they all have different names. Some are rare, like those that have long beards that curl up when released. When they come out of the water close by, it seems as though they are biting on something large with their beards curled, looking like balls. They call those bearded seals *ungagciaret* [from *ungak*, "whisker"]. . . .

Then there are bearded seals that swim on their backs. When they get to the ice, they climb up face down, gallop across, go into the water, and then reappear on their backs. They say the ones that get sleepy do that. They said that if we saw one of those we should follow it carefully. They said that it would climb on top of the ice after awhile and stop and sleep. They say to hunt it when it does that. They called those *papangluat*.

Then they say that some bearded seals would sleep and wake. When they look at their surroundings, they would curl up sitting on their stomachs with their head and hind flippers touching, turning all the way around, looking behind them, searching their surroundings. After they look all around, they finally lie down and sleep. They call those *ipuuyulit* [from *ipug-*, "to move with one's front high in the air"].

They suddenly awake and search their surroundings. They are more afraid of the area behind them. That's why they say not to approach them from behind, only by looking straight at them. We would approach them with them watching us.

Close observation and classification of the natural world are not the only things Yup'ik experts have in common with their western counterparts. At the same time elders reported important instructions that guided life, they tested rules as a means of judging their veracity. Rather than showing blind obedience to a timeless canon, Yup'ik men and women frequently describe their questioning of the principles on which they based their actions and understandings. Nick Andrew (March 2004) of Marshall described testing the admonishment that broad whitefish would become scarce if those caught in lakes were fed to dogs:

I went with my male cousin when he was a boy to check our net with dogs. We got to the net and pulled it, and there were so many broad whitefish, and we set the net again. When we finished, I told him, "Don't tell on me, cousin." I took them and gave one to each of the dogs. When they were done eating, we returned home. I told him, "I wonder how our net will do tomorrow. Come with me again." Then the next day, we checked our net. We pulled it, and it was heavy. We saw that we caught more than before. [Whitefish] don't become scarce in lakes since they stay and don't have anywhere to go. But they warned us not to throw them around or discard them carelessly.

Yup'ik experimentation extended to technology. Men and women learned to construct and work with tools through constant trial and error. Kwigillingok elder Peter John (February 2003) noted:

We tried to learn to make things. We took them by ourselves and examined them. We Yupiit are like that. We listen to and watch those who are working.

Sometimes when we try to work, we don't do a good job and stop working on it. When we try the next time, it looks better. Then we repeatedly make other ones. We just don't do it once. That is the way to learn.

Working in museum collections, one cannot fail to be impressed by the varied tool types and clothing patterns Yup'ik men and women created. There was a tool for every purpose. When Western technology was introduced, Yup'ik craftsmen embraced many labor-saving devices. If a new tool broke, time-tested materials were often used to fix it, as when a commercially made boat propeller was replaced by one fashioned from bone. The late Jim VanStone went so far as to dub Inuit peoples "gadget ridden." They knew their materials well and displayed impressive inventiveness in using them to advantage. Trial and error played a central role in Yup'ik learning and discovery.

The perspectives shared by elders show important differences from and similarities with western science. Yup'ik knowledge was and is geared primarily to functions and outcomes. It is critical to know how to achieve some

specific end so that resources necessary for survival and well-being may be acquired effectively. Western science is primarily aimed at developing and testing hypotheses to understand what is happening within and between variables. However, the two are complementary in that Yup'ik science is the result of significant trial and error that has produced acceptable outcomes, while western science can explain how these outcomes were achieved.

Yup'ik technology can demonstrate scientific principles in new and exciting ways by matching such practical outcomes to the phenomena they were designed to address. Moreover, the fact that Yup'ik science produced such outcomes prior to their conceptual bases is critical in understanding how "science" as a process must be carefully evaluated both on hypothesis testing and on manifested outcomes. Such a collaboration is especially important for science education in Alaska, where it can make the subject more relevant and effective.

At our last exhibit-planning meeting, steering committee members articulated the purpose of the exhibit in their own words. Elsie Mather stated, "It will show the proven ways of tools and processes Yup'ik people used to survive and let people see the common ways we share the knowledge of our environment." Joan Hamilton said, "It will help people understand science and how it is part of everyday life, and it will communicate how much knowledge of the world Yup'ik people needed to survive." There is a great deal of misunderstanding regarding how science works as a process unto itself. The value of considering western scientific approaches side by side with those of Yup'ik traditional knowledge to close the gap between academic venues and the general public cannot be overstated. Yup'ik grade-school principal Agatha John (March 2004) of Toksook Bay articulated the dilemma of her generation: "When I was in school I hated science. I couldn't understand it. Not only was it in another language [English], but all the examples were foreign. If we begin to speak of 'Yup'ik science,' we will give our children something they can understand."

In closing, I would like to return to Yup'ik motivations for traveling to the Smithsonian, sharing information, and seeking to borrow objects to display in Alaska and beyond during this Fourth International Polar Year. They hope to create an exhibition that will teach about the Yup'ik way of life—the animals and plants they rely on, the tools they used to survive, and the values that animate their lives. Perhaps more important, their work at the Smithsonian teaches us about the generosity and compassion of men and women who shared their knowledge, not only to inform us but to enrich all our lives and allow us to live genuinely.

ACKNOWLEDGMENTS

I am indebted first and foremost to the Yup'ik men and women who generously shared their knowledge, and to Calista Elders Council (CEC) language expert Alice Rearden for carefully and eloquently transcribing and translating what they said. Our work together in Alaska has been supported by the CEC with funding from the National Science Foundation. We are grateful to the many Smithsonian staff members, both at the National Museum of Natural History and at the National Museum of the American Indian, who made it possible for Yup'ik elders to work in their collections. Special thanks to Bill Fitzhugh, Smithsonian Institution, for first bringing me into the Smithsonian in the 1980s, and to both Igor Krupnik, Smithsonian Institution, and Bill Fitzhugh for the invitation to share what I learned.

NOTE ABOUT INTERVIEW DATES

Dates following Elders' names refer to the month and year discussions with them took place. Tapes are archived with the Calista Elders Council, Bethel, Alaska.

LITERATURE CITED

Fienup-Riordan, Ann. 1996. *The Living Tradition of Yup'ik Masks: Agayuliyararput/Our Way of Making Prayer.* Seattle: University of Washington Press.

———. 2005. *Yupiit Qanruyutait/Yup'ik Words of Wisdom.* Lincoln: University of Nebraska Press.

———. 2007. *Yuungnaqpiallerput/The Way We Genuinely Live: Masterworks of Yup'ik Science and Survival.* Seattle: University of Washington Press.

Fitzhugh, William W., and Susan A. Kaplan. 1982. *Inua: Spirit World of the Bering Sea Eskimo.* Washington, D.C.: Smithsonian Institution Press.

Kawagley, Oscar. 1995. *A Yupiaq Worldview: A Pathway to Ecology and Spirit.* Prospect Heights, Ill.: Waveland Press.

Krupnik, Igor, and Stephen Loring. 2002. The Waugh Collection Project: ASC Joins Efforts with the National Museum of the American Indian. *ASC Newsletter*, 10:24–25.

Nelson, Edward William. 1899. The Eskimo about Bering Strait. *Bureau of American Ethnology Annual Report for the Years 1896–1897,* Volume 18, Part 1. Washington, D.C.: Smithsonian Institution Press.

Smithsonian Contributions to Alaskan Ethnography: The First IPY Expedition to Barrow, 1881–1883

Ernest S. Burch Jr.

ABSTRACT. From 1881 to 1883, as part of the First International Polar Year, an expedition sponsored by the U.S. Signal Corps and the Smithsonian Institution operated a research station a short distance north of where the modern city of Barrow now stands. The 10 members of the expedition had the primary task of making an unbroken series of weather and magnetic observations over the two-year period, and the secondary task of studying the natural history of the Barrow area. "Natural history" included descriptions of native life and collections of material culture, in addition to studies of the fauna and flora. In this paper, I summarize the substantial contributions to our knowledge of North Alaskan Eskimo life made by members of the expedition, and evaluate them in the light of work that has been done since.

INTRODUCTION

From 1881 to 1883, as part of the first International Polar Year, an expedition sponsored jointly by the U. S. Signal Corps and the Smithsonian Institution operated a research station near Point Barrow, Alaska.[1] The members of the expedition had the primary task of making an unbroken series of weather and magnetic observations over the two-year period, and the secondary task of studying the natural history of the Barrow area. "Natural history" was understood to include descriptions of the local people and collections of their material culture, in addition to observations of the fauna and flora. In this paper, I summarize and contextualize the contributions they made to our knowledge of North Alaskan Iñupiaq Eskimo life.

Point Barrow is the northernmost point of Alaska and of the United States as a whole. It is approximately 550 kilometers north of the Arctic Circle, and 400 kilometers north of the latitudinal tree line (Figure 1). It is located in the Beaufort coastal plain ecoregion, a treeless area of very low relief having a considerable amount of surface water (Nowacki et al., 2002). Summers are short and cool, and the winters are long and cold. The climate was significantly colder in the nineteenth century than it is now. During the winter, the nearby ocean was completely frozen over; for much of the summer, it was covered with unconsolidated floating ice.

Ernest S. Burch Jr., 3601 Gettysburg Road, Camp Hill, PA 17011-6816, USA (esburchjr@aol.com). Accepted 9 May 2008.

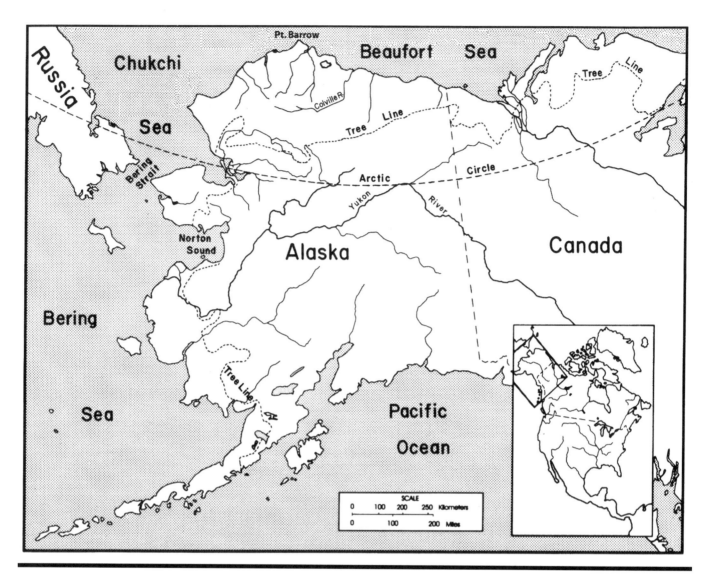

FIGURE 1. Map of Alaska.

EARLY EXPEDITIONS

The first westerners to visit the Point Barrow district were the members of a detachment from the Frederick W. Beechey expedition led by Thomas Elson, which arrived from the southwest in September 1826 (Beechey, 1831:414–442). The explorers were met with a friendly greeting from the Natives, but that was quickly followed by considerable hostility. Not only for that reason, but also because the season was dangerously far advanced, the men turned around and headed back south almost immediately.

The second western expedition to make contact with the Native people of Point Barrow was a detachment from a Hudson's Bay Company expedition sent to explore the western Arctic coast of North America. The group was led by Thomas Simpson, and it arrived at the point from the east on August 4, 1837 (Barr, 2002:70–112; Simpson, 1839; 1843). Simpson's small party was fortunate to get there when it did, because the settlement was largely unoccupied at the time. The few residents who were there were frightened and hid from the explorers. However, they were soon persuaded to come out and show themselves. Everyone got along pretty well for the few hours that the explorers were there.

The next year, on July 23, 1838, a Russian expedition led by Aleksandr Kashevarov reached Point Barrow in a fleet of small boats, arriving from the southwest (VanStone, 1977:31–45). A fair number of people, with considerable hostility, met Kashevarov's party. The Russians were forced to flee in fear of their lives after just three days. Despite the brevity of his stay, Kashevarov acquired some very useful information on native life in the Barrow district. This was due to the fact that his party included an interpreter. Kashevarov is the *only* person, Native or otherwise, who has ever reported the name of the nation (Burch, 2005:11–33) whose members inhabited the Barrow district. According to what he was told, they called themselves, and were known by others, as "Kakligmiut" (VanStone, 1977:33).

Franklin Search Expeditions

The fourth western expedition to visit Point Barrow consisted of several of the ships involved in the search for the lost British explorer Sir John Franklin (Bockstoce, 1985). One of them, the depot ship H. M. S. *Plover*, under the command of Rochefort Maguire, spent the winters of 1852–1853 and 1853–1854 frozen in the ice a short distance southeast of Nuvuk, the Iñupiaq settlement on the

point (Figure 2). The British were greeted with considerable hostility. However, through wise diplomacy by the leaders on both sides, peaceful relations were established, and were maintained for the rest of the time the British were there. The information on native life acquired by the members of this expedition exceeded that of its three predecessors by several orders of magnitude.

The surgeon on the *Plover*, John Simpson, already had acquired some proficiency in the Iñupiaq language when the ship spent successive winters on Kotzebue Sound (1849–1850) and in Grantley Harbor (1850–1851), on the western end of the Seward Peninsula. He was assigned the task of learning about native life in the Barrow district, in addition to his duties as surgeon. He performed his research through almost daily contact with Nuvuk's inhabitants; this was mostly when they visited the ship, but also through his periodic visits to the village.

Simpson (1855; 1875) wrote an outstanding report on what he learned about native life. It was one of the best ethnographic accounts of any indigenous North American people to appear in the nineteenth century. Much more

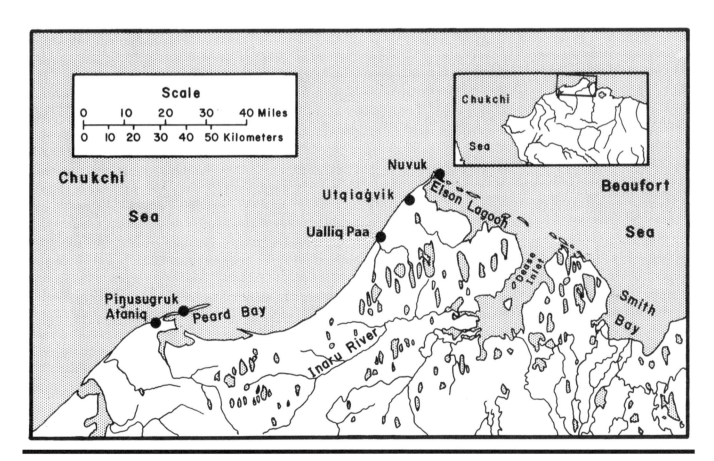

FIGURE 2. Former Iñupiaq settlements in the Barrow district, Alaska.

recently, John Bockstoce (1988) published an edited and annotated version of Captain Maguire's diary of the years spent near Point Barrow. He included in the volume a reprint of Simpson's 1855/1875 report and several other useful documents. More recently still, Simpson's (1852–1854) diary, as well as several other manuscripts written by him, became accessible in the Duke University Archives. These documents, plus others produced by people involved in the Franklin search (e.g., Collinson, 1889, Hooper, 1853, Maguire, 1857, Pim, 1853, Pullen, 1979, Seemann, 1853), contain a remarkable amount of information on native life in the Barrow district in the mid-nineteenth century. We know not only what the members of the expedition found out, but also, through the diaries, how and from whom many of them acquired their information.

THE IPY EXPEDITION[2]

The IPY expedition to Barrow arrived 27 years after the Plover left. The members of this expedition established a base on shore about 15 kilometers southwest of the point. It was near Utqiaġvik, the other main settlement of the "Kakligmiut." Its leader, Patrick Henry Ray, did not want to establish a base at Nuvuk because the only dry ground there was already taken by the native village. He also did not want to locate the base right in Utqiaġvik because he was afraid of being pestered by the Natives. So, it was set up a little more than 1 kilometer to the northeast, at the place known more recently as Browerville.

Some tension between the Natives and the researchers arose due to the fact that the commander tried to put a stop to the trade in whiskey and firearms that was being conducted with American whalers during the period when the expedition was based there (Ray, 1882b, 1882c). However, in general, the two groups got along pretty well. The commander, Patrick Henry Ray (1882a), wrote that "these people in their appearance, general intelligence and industry are superior to any native I have seen on the continent. . . ." His colleague, John Murdoch (1890a:223), said that the Eskimos were "altogether pleasant people to see and to associate with." Another colleague, Middleton Smith (1902:118), characterized them as "a good people." One does not expect to read such positive sentiments expressed by late-nineteenth century-American white men about indigenous North Americans. They help account for the expedition members' willingness to loan tools and sometimes weapons to their Iñupiaq neighbors, at least during the second year of their stay. (I have seen no evidence on what the residents of Utqiaġvik thought of the IPY people.)

The expedition members consisted of 10 men of whom five are of special importance to this paper. In what follows I summarize the individual contributions made by these five, plus one other person, and then discuss the expedition's collective results.

PATRICK HENRY RAY

Patrick Henry Ray was a first lieutenant in the 8th infantry. It is not quite clear to me just how he spent his time in Utqiaġvik. He was apparently not involved in the boring, time-consuming work of recording meteorological and magnetic observations. Instead, he managed to get out and about a fair amount of the time, both in the native village and beyond. For example, in late March and early April of both 1882 and 1883, he traveled south to the Meade River with Native companions during caribou hunting season (Ray, 1988a:lii; 1988b:lxxvii). He also visited the settlement on numerous occasions. There he was able to observe ceremonies and rituals, as well as people simply going about their daily lives (Murdoch, 1988:80, 432; Ray, 1988c:xciii).

Ray wrote informative summaries of the expedition and of his own travels inland (Ray, 1988a, 1988b), as well as a comprehensive sketch of native life (Ray, 1988c). The latter is a generally accurate document, but it is diminished by the fact that its author paraphrased and even plagiarized the work of John Simpson from 30 years earlier. There is evidence (e.g., in Murdoch, 1988:433) that Ray kept a notebook, but if he did, it has been lost.

E. P. HERENDEEN

The second person worthy of mention is Captain Edward Perry Herendeen, a whaler and trader with considerable experience in northern Alaska (J. Bockstoce, pers. comm.). Herendeen was brought along as interpreter and storekeeper. Just how effectively he acted as an interpreter is questionable. Other members of the expedition complained about being unable to communicate effectively with the Natives during the first year of their stay (e.g., Murdoch, 1988:45), and Ray (1988c:lxxxvii) stated flatly that the party had no interpreter. By the second year, each man could do fairly well on his own (Ray, 1988a:li).

Herendeen seems to have gotten out and about even more than Ray did. He attended a number of ceremonies in the village, hunted inland with Natives in both fall and winter, and visited the whaling camps on the sea ice in spring. Others (e.g., Murdoch, 1988:39, 272, 276, 364,

372, 374, 423) cite Herendeen as having provided them with information about a variety of subjects that he had to have obtained in the village or out in the country. If he kept a journal, it has been lost, and the only publication he produced that I am aware of was a piece on caribou hunting (Herendeen, 1892).[3]

GEORGE SCOTT OLDMIXON

George Scott Oldmixon was the surgeon on the expedition. In addition to treating the health problems of expedition members, he also treated many sick Natives, and he made many visits to the village for that purpose. In the process, he learned something about native health problems and their means of dealing with them. Unfortunately, he, too, is not known to have kept a journal. However, he reported some of what he learned to others, who wrote down some of what he told them. Oldmixon's one substantive contribution to the expedition's published reports was a set of height and weight measurements made of a number of Iñupiaq men and women from the two Barrow villages (Murdoch, 1988:cvii).

MIDDLETON SMITH

Middleton Smith was one of the assistants who checked the instruments and kept the records of the magnetic and meteorological observations. As far as I am aware, the only thing he wrote about the expedition was a popularized piece titled "Superstitions of the Eskimo" (Smith, 1902). Unfortunately, the article contains some erroneous information, such as the population figures on pp. 113–114. It also paints an idyllic picture of Iñupiaq life (e.g., on pp. 118–119), contributing to the stereotype of Eskimos as being happy, hard-working, fun-loving, peaceful people. In fact, like most people everywhere, they were considerably more complicated than that.

Smith also presents interesting bits of information not included in the reports of his colleagues. For example, on page 120 he reports:

When a death occurs in the village the women are not allowed, from sunset to sunrise, either to make or repair garments or to do sewing [of] any kind, except in the most urgent cases, when the work must be done while sitting within circles inscribed by the point of a knife upon the floor of the iglu.

This is the only source I am aware of that reports on a way of circumventing a taboo. It would be fascinating to know if there were others. Also of interest are Smith's accounts (pp. 127–128) of how the Natives cheated during some of their trading sessions.

JOSEPH S. POWELL

Joseph S. Powell was not a member of the IPY expedition, but he commanded the ship sent to re-supply it for the second winter. Powell's (1988) report summarizes his visit, and also contains quite a bit of interesting information about native life in Utqiaġvik. Very little of this information could have been obtained first-hand, however. Powell was at Utqiaġvik for only a week, and at least some of the time was prevented from going ashore due to bad weather. Presumably, he also spent some of his time in supervisory activities onboard the ship.

Rather than basing his account on personal observation and experience, Powell relied on information conveyed to him by others, primarily Lieutenant Ray and Sergeant James Cassidy (Powell, 1988:lx). This had to have been presented to him in summary form rather than in detail, and, as a result, his report contains some useful generalizations. For example: "There are leading men whose influence depends on their wealth and the number of their relatives and friends, but no chiefs, hereditary or otherwise..." (Powell, 1988:lxi). I have never seen the subject of Iñupiaq leadership characterized more accurately or succinctly than that.

JOHN E. MURDOCH

This brings us to John E. Murdoch. A Harvard-trained naturalist, Murdoch was one of the men involved in the tedious recording of magnetic and meteorological data. Accordingly, he was not inclined to go out as much as some of his colleagues. However, it is clear from comments scattered about in his various writings that he was interested in and generally aware of what was going on in Utqiaġvik and the area around it. He became proficient enough in the Iñupiaq language for people living on Norton Sound in western Alaska, to identify him later, on the basis of his speech, as someone coming from Point Barrow (Murdoch, 1988:46). Unlike John Simpson in the 1850s, Murdoch never reached a level of linguistic proficiency at which he could discuss abstract philosophical matters, but he understood enough to know that the Eskimos had a raunchy sense of humor (Murdoch, 1988:419), and he could converse with them about a variety of day-to-day matters (e.g., Murdoch, 1988:58, 79, 384, 412, 424, 432).

In addition to his other duties, Murdoch was put in charge of cataloguing the numerous artifacts that were obtained from the Natives through barter. He wrote the catalogue of ethnological specimens and the natural history sections of the expedition's final report (1885a, 1885b), and he authored a major monograph (1988) and more than a dozen articles. The latter concerned such varied subjects as fish and fishing (1884), seal hunting (1885d), sinew-backed bows (1885e), legends (1886), native clothing and physique (1890a), counting and measuring (1890b), Iñupiaq knowledge of heavenly bodies (1890c), whale hunting (1891), and Iñupiaq knowledge of local wildlife (1898).

DISCUSSION

The primary objectives of IPY-1 were in the fields of physics and meteorology. Thus, as noted by Igor Krupnik (2009, this volume),[4] it is a curious fact that the most enduring products of the expedition to northern Alaska were its ethnographic collections and reports. Just why the members of this expedition engaged in studies of human affairs at all is not immediately clear. Of the main contributors in this area, Patrick Henry Ray, was a military man and John Murdoch was a naturalist, although both seem to have been intelligent and intellectually curious individuals. The answer to this question must lie in the considerable involvement of Spencer F. Baird, head of the Smithsonian Institution, in the expedition's planning and staffing. Baird was a biologist with wide-ranging interests, he was an avid collector personally, and, at the time, he was engaged in an ambitious program to build up the museum's collections (Henson, nd). In 1879 he oversaw the integration of the Bureau of American Ethnology with the Smithsonian, and, "with strong support from Congress, [he] encouraged the ethnologists to also collect artifacts and pursue archaeological investigations" (Henson, nd). Thus, it seems reasonable to conclude that Baird strongly encouraged/required the members of the expedition, particularly Murdoch, to conduct ethnological/ethnographic research and to bring what they acquired back to the museum. If the expedition was sent out with a set of specific ethnographic research objectives, however, no record of what it was has been discovered. We are thus forced to surmise that the various sections of Murdoch's (1988) monograph reflect a set of more or less ad hoc conceptual categories that enabled him to organize into a coherent account his own experiences and observations, as well as those reported to him by his colleagues.

Nearly all pieces of the artifact collection were obtained through barter, with "the natives bringing their weapons, clothing and other objects to the station for sale" (Murdoch, 1988:19). Since Murdoch was the person charged with recording these items, this gave him "especially favorable opportunities for becoming acquainted with the ethnography of the region" (Murdoch, 1988:19), even though he was not able to leave the station nearly as often as some of his colleagues.

Murdoch apparently hoped to do more than just collect artifacts. The following passage expresses his frustration:

It was exceedingly difficult to get any idea of the religious belief of the people, partly from our inability to make ourselves understood in regard to abstract ideas and partly from ignorance on our part of the proper method of conducting such inquiries. For instance, in trying to get at their ideas of a future life, we could only ask "where does a man go when he dies?" to which we, of course, received the obvious answer, "to the cemetery!" (Murdoch, 1988:430)

Another passage elaborates:

Occupied as our party was with the manifold routine scientific work of the station, it was exceedingly difficult to get hold of any of the traditions of the Natives, though they showed no unwillingness, from superstitious or other reasons, to talk freely about them. In the first place there were so many (to the Eskimos) more interesting things to talk about with us that it was difficult to bring the conversation round to the subject in question. Then our lack of familiarity with the language was a great hindrance to obtaining a connected and accurate version of any story. The jargon, or kind of *lingua franca*, made up of Eskimo roots and "pigeon English" grammar, which served well enough for every-day intercourse with the Natives, enabled us, with the help of expressive gestures, to get the general sense of the story, but rendered it impossible to write down an Eskimo text of the tale which could afterwards be translated. Moreover, the confusion and difficulty was still further increased by the fact that two or three people generally undertook to tell the story at once. (Murdoch, 1886:594)

The above factors resulted in the fact that the main ethnographic contribution of the IPY expedition lay in its collection of material objects, not in accounts of Native social organization, history, philosophy, or worldview. In the latter areas, John Simpson's (1855; 1875) report remains the best single source, although there are many bits and pieces of new and updated, information in the IPY documents. However, the IPY collection of artifacts was significant, the largest ever acquired in Arctic Alaska. Murdoch's massive volume, first published in 1892, is a superb adjunct to the collection itself because it provides excellent illustrations and descriptions of the objects and tells how many of them were made. It also compares items in the Barrow collection with similar artifacts acquired in other parts of the north by other expeditions.

One important contribution the IPY reports in general made was to provide evidence of changes that had occurred in the Barrow people's way of life during the 30 years since the Franklin Search Expedition. Perhaps the most striking difference was demographic. In 1853, the combined population of Nuvuk and Utqiaġvik had been about 540; 30 years later, it was less than 300 (Ray, 1988c:xcix).

The intervening years had seen the arrival of American whaling ships and trading vessels in Arctic Alaskan waters. Many of these ships stopped briefly at one or both of the Barrow villages almost every year after the Franklin Search Expedition left. The Americans brought firearms, ammunition, whisky, and epidemic diseases to the Natives. They also killed a substantial number of the bowhead whales, on which the coastal native economy was based.

Other changes resulted from the use of firearms in hunting. Previously, seal hunters had first attached themselves to a seal with a harpoon and a line, and only then killed the animal. With firearms, they killed the seal at a distance, then tried to attach a line to it for retrieval (Murdoch, 1885c). Whereas before they rarely lost a seal that had been struck, they now lost a significant number, particularly in spring.

Caribou hunting was also transformed. In the 1850s, Barrow hunters killed caribou in winter by digging pitfalls in the snow and killing the animals that fell into them. Since the snow was not deep enough in the fall to permit this, they did not hunt caribou at that time of year. By the 1880s, they could kill caribou at a distance with firearms, so they could hunt them in both fall and winter. This nearly doubled the hunting pressure on this particular resource.

POST-IPY RESEARCH

The IPY expedition took place at a time when native life in the Barrow district was beginning to come into increasing contact with members of the U. S. Revenue Marine and with an assortment of adventurers, explorers, and traders. Some of the individuals involved wrote informative descriptions of native life in the region. However, none of them conducted systematic research and none of them made any effort to relate their observations to those of the earlier IPY or Franklin Search reports (of which they probably were unaware.) This situation did not change until the 1950s, when some more serious investigations were undertaken. The major people involved in this subsequent work were Robert F. Spencer, Joseph Sonnenfeld, and Barbara Bodenhorn.

ROBERT F. SPENCER

The first researcher to build on the work of the nineteenth-century investigators was Robert F. Spencer.[5] Spencer did his research in Barrow in the early 1950s, publishing his findings in the late 1950s, and for many years afterwards (e.g., 1959, 1967–1968, 1968, 1972, 1984). Despite the late date of his field studies, the emphasis in his writing was on the "traditional" way of life, with the timeframe being left unspecified. Careful examination of both his publications and his field notes indicates that the situation he wrote about was what his informants experienced as children, in the late 1880s and 1890s (Bodenhorn, 1989:24 n. 19). It certainly was not what J. Simpson and Maguire described for the early 1850s. Thus, even though Spencer did his research some seven decades after the IPY expedition left the field, it is almost as though he did it just a few years later.

Spencer filled in two major gaps left by his predecessors. First, he paid almost as much attention to Iñupiat living inland as he did to those living along the coast (1959:3–4, 132–139). It seems hard to believe in retrospect, but until Spencer's book appeared, most anthropologists believed that Eskimos were primarily or even exclusively a coastal people. In fact, as Spencer (1959:21) pointed out, in the nineteenth century, inlanders outnumbered coast dwellers in Arctic Alaska by a ratio of about three to one. He then went on to describe (1959:62–97) in some detail the nature of the relations between the residents of the two ecological zones, showing how they were linked into a larger regional system.

Spencer's second main contribution was to give the Iñupiaq family system the attention it deserves (1959:62–96; 1967–68; 1968). Again, it seems hard to believe in retrospect, given the importance of families in Iñupiaq societies, but systematic studies of Eskimo family life were all but nonexistent at the time Spencer did his research. Spencer changed all that, and the decades following publication of his major monograph witnessed an outpouring of kinship studies in Eskimo settlements all across the North American Arctic (Burch, 1979:72).

JOSEPH SONNENFELD

Joseph Sonnenfeld is a geographer who did research in Barrow for four months in 1954, the year after Spencer left. He apparently did not know of Spencer's work at that time, and when he completed his Ph.D. thesis in 1957, he was acquainted only with Spencer's report to the granting agency. As a result, he recapitulated some of Spencer's reconstructive work. However, he was oriented much more to contemporary events than Spencer was. Thus, without really being aware of the fact, he brought the documentation of Barrow Iñupiaq life forward from the end of the nineteenth century to the middle of the twentieth.

Being a geographer, Sonnenfeld was interested primarily in ecological and economic matters. With reference to those subject areas, his Ph.D. thesis (1957) was wide ranging and informative. Unfortunately, it was never published. As far as I am aware, Sonnenfeld published only two articles on his work in Barrow, one (1959) on the history of domesticated reindeer herds in the Barrow district, the other (1960) on changes in Eskimo hunting technology.

BARBARA BODENHORN

Barbara Bodenhorn is a social anthropologist who began her research in Barrow in 1980 and who continued it for many years subsequently. More than any of her predecessors, Bodenhorn tried to learn how the community worked as a social system, and she spent enough time in it to find out. Her work focused on families, the interrelations between and among families, and the role of families in the overall economy. She has written extensively on these and related subjects (e.g., 1989, 1990, 1993, 1997, 2000, 2001).

Bodenhorn's work is only the most recent effort in more than a century and a half of ethnographic research in Barrow. No other Arctic community has been so thoroughly studied over so long a time. Viewed from this broad perspective, although their artifact collection remains unequaled, the ethnographic work of John Murdoch, Patrick Henry Ray, and the other IPY expedition members constitutes just one link in a long chain of empirical investigations. The "chain" as a whole should now become the center of someone's attention: Where else in the Arctic can one find so much good information on social change in one community over so long a time?

CONCLUSION

In conclusion, I wish to address briefly the issue of what scientific value there might be in gaining knowledge of nineteenth-century native life in Barrow. The answer lies in the value of natural experiments.

Social scientists can experiment with small numbers of people in highly restricted settings, but there is no way that we can experiment with entire societies, certainly not on any kind of ethical basis. The only way we can develop a broad understanding of how human social systems operate is by observing people going about their lives in their own ways without any interference from a researcher. This is what is "natural" about the method. The greater the diversity of the social systems that can be studied in this way, the more "experimental" the approach becomes, and the more powerful any resulting theories about the structure of human social systems are likely to be.

Arctic peoples in general, and Eskimos in particular, are important in this regard because they lived in such extreme environments. In the nineteenth century, the way of life of the Eskimos in the Barrow district stood in marked contrast to the previously recorded ways Eskimos lived in the eastern North American Arctic. This information expands our knowledge of the range of variation of Arctic social systems and, by extension, of human social systems in general. In order to be scientifically significant, though, the research on the societies in a sample of societies must be conducted in terms of a common conceptual and theoretical framework so that a systematic comparative analysis can be subsequently carried out. The Franklin Search and IPY-1 reports are fairly close to meeting that requirement, but they are only a first step. Fortunately, the information they contain is good enough and complete enough for future researchers to adapt for that purpose.[6]

NOTES

1. I thank John Bockstoce and Igor Krupnik for information and/or advice given during the preparation of this article.

2. Most of the expedition's reports, originally published in the nineteenth century, were reprinted in 1988 by the Smithsonian Institution Press. While both the earlier and later versions are listed here in the References, only the 1988 versions are cited in the text.

3. I have not seen this article myself, but I thought its existence should be recorded here.

4. Krupnik, this volume.

5. My knowledge of Spencer's work was enhanced under a grant from the National Science Foundation, Office of Polar Programs (OPP-90817922). I am grateful to that organization for its support, and to Marietta Spencer for giving me her late husband's Barrow field notes.

6. A comparative analysis of the meteorological data acquired in IPY-1 was not carried out until recently (Wood and Overland, 2006). Thus, one of the primary objectives of the first IPY was not achieved until nearly a century and a quarter after the raw data were collected.

LITERATURE CITED

Barr, William, ed. 2002. *From Barrow to Boothia. The Arctic Journal of Chief Factor Peter Warren Dease, 1836–1839.* Montreal: McGill-Queen's University Press.

Beechey, Frederick W. 1831. *Narrative of a Voyage to the Pacific and Bering's Strait to Cooperate with the Polar Expeditions Performed in His Majesty's Ship Blossom . . . in the Years 1825, 26, 27, 28.* London: Colburn and Bentley.

Bockstoce, John R. 1985. "The Search for Sir John Franklin in Alaska." In *The Franklin Era in Canadian Arctic History, 1845–1859,* ed. Patricia D. Sutherland, pp. 93–113. Mercury Series, Archaeological Survey of Canada Paper No. 131. Ottawa: National Museum of Man.

———, ed. 1988. *The Journal of Rochfort Maguire, 1852–1854: Two Years at Point Barrow, Alaska, aboard HMS* Plover *in the Search for Sir John Franklin.* 2 vols. (2nd series, nos. 169 and 170). London: Hakluyt Society.

Bodenhorn, Barbara A. 1989. "The Animals Come to Me, They Know I Share": Iñupiaq Kinship, Changing Economic Relations and Enduring World Views on Alaska's North Slope. Ph.D. diss., Department of Social Anthropology, University of Cambridge, U.K.

———. 1990. "I'm Not the Great Hunter, My Wife Is." Iñupiaq and Anthropological Models of Gender. *Études/Inuit/Studies,* 14(1–2): 55–74.

———. 1993. "Gendered Spaces, Public Places: Public and Private Revisited on the North Slope of Alaska." In *Landscape, Politics, and Perspectives,* ed. Barbara Bender, pp. 169–203. Oxford, U.K.: Berg Publishers.

———. 1997. "Person, Place and Parentage: Ecology, Identity, and Social Relations on the North Slope of Alaska." In *Arctic Ecology and Identity,* ed. S. A. Mousalimas, pp. 103–132. Los Angeles: International Society for Trans-Oceanic Research.

———. 2000. "It's Good to Know Who Your Relatives Are, but We Were Taught to Share with Everybody: Shares and Sharing among Iñupiaq Households." In *The Social Economy of Sharing: Resource Allocation and Modern Hunter-Gatherers,* ed. George W. Wenzel, Grete Hovelsrud-Broda, and Nobuhiro Kishigami, pp. 27–60. Senri Ethnological Studies No. 53. Osaka, Japan: National Museum of Ethnology

———. 2001. "'He Used to Be My Relative': Exploring the Bases of Relatedness among Iñupiaq of Northern Alaska." In *Cultures of Relatedness: New Approaches to the Study of Kinship,* ed. Janet Carstens, pp. 128–148. Cambridge, U.K.: Cambridge University Press.

Burch, Ernest S., Jr. 1979. The Ethnography of Northern North America. A Guide to Recent Research. *Arctic Anthropology,* 16(1):62–146.

———. 2005. *Alliance and Conflict: The World System of the Iñupiaq Eskimos.* Lincoln: University of Nebraska Press.

Collinson, Richard. 1889. *Journal of HMS* Enterprise *on the expedition in Search of Sir John Franklin's Ships by Behring Strait, 1850–1855.* London: Sampson, Low, Marston, Searle and Rivington.

Henson, Pamela M. n.d. Spencer F. Baird's Vision for a National Museum. http://www.siarchives.si.edu/history/exhibits/baird/bairdhm.htm (accessed 18 August 2008).

Herendeen, E. P. 1892. An Esquimaux Caribou Hunt. *Forest and Stream,* 38(Mar. 17):249.

Hooper, William H. 1853. *Ten Months among the Tents of the Tuski.* London: John Murray.

Krupnik, Igor. 2009. "'The Way We See It Coming': Building the Legacy of Indigenous Observations in IPY 2007–2008." In *Smithsonian at the Poles: Contributions to International Polar Year Science,* ed. I.

Krupnik, M. A. Lang, and S. E. Miller, pp. 129–142. Washington, D.C.: Smithsonian Institution Scholarly Press.

Maguire, Rochefort. 1857. "Narrative of Commander Maguire, Wintering at Point Barrow." In *The Discovery of the North-West Passage. . .,* 2nd edition, ed. Sherard Osborn, pp. 409–463. London: Longman, Brown, Green, Longmans & Roberts.

Murdoch, John. 1884. "Fish and Fishing at Point Barrow, Arctic Alaska." In *Transactions of the American Fish Cultural Association, Thirteenth Annual Meeting,* pp. 111–115.

———. 1885a. "Catalogue of Ethnological Specimens Collected by the Point Barrow Expedition." In *Report of the International Polar Expedition to Point Barrow, Alaska,* ed. P. H. Ray, pp. 61–87. Washington, D.C.: Government Printing Office.

———. 1885b. "Natural History." In *Report of the International Polar Expedition to Point Barrow, Alaska,* ed. P. H. Ray, pp. 89–200. Washington, D.C.: Government Printing Office.

———. 1885c. The Retrieving Harpoon: An Undescribed Type of Eskimo Weapon. *American Naturalist,* 19:423–425.

———. 1885d. Seal-Catching at Point Barrow. *Transactions of the Anthropological Society of Washington,* 3:102–108.

———. 1885e. The Sinew Backed Bow of the Eskimo. *Transactions of the Anthropological Society of Washington,* 3:168–180.

———. 1886. A Few Legendary Fragments from the Point Barrow Eskimos. *American Naturalist,* 20:593–599.

———. 1890a. Dress and Physique of the Point Barrow Eskimo. *Popular Science Monthly,* 38:222–229.

———. 1890b. Notes on Counting and Measuring among the Eskimo of Point Barrow, Alaska. *American Anthropologist,* 3:37–43.

———. 1890c. Notes on Names of the Heavenly Bodies and the Points of the Compass among the Point Barrow Eskimo. *American Anthropologist,* 3:136.

———. 1891. Whale-Catching at Point Barrow. *Popular Science Monthly,* 38:830–836.

———. 1892. Ethnological Results of the Point Barrow Expedition. *Ninth Annual Report of the Bureau of Ethnology for the Years 1887–1888.* Washington, D.C.: Government Printing Office. (Reprinted 1988, Smithsonian Institution Press.)

———. 1898. The Animals Known to the Eskimos of Northwestern Alaska. *American Naturalist,* 32 (382):720–734.

———. 1988. *Ethnological Results of the Point Barrow Expedition.* Smithsonian Classics of Anthropology Series reprint, No. 6. Washington, D.C: Smithsonian Institution Press.

Nowacki, Gregory, Page Spencer, Michael Fleming, Terry Brock, and Torre Jorgenson. 2002. *Unified Ecoregions of Alaska: 2001.* U.S. Geological Survey Open-File Report 02–297.

Pim, Bedford. 1853. "Journal." In *Narrative of the Voyage of H.M.S.* Herald *during the Years 1845–51 in Search of Sir John Franklin,* vol. II, by Berthold Carl Seemann, pp. 130–148. London: Reeve and Company.

Powell, Joseph S. 1988. "Report of the Relief Expedition of 1882." In *Ethnological Results of the Point Barrow Expedition,* pp. lv–lxiii. Smithsonian Classics of Anthropology Series reprint, No. 6. Washington, D.C.: Smithsonian Institution Press.

Pullen, H. F., ed. 1979. *The Pullen Expedition in Search of Sir John Franklin: The Original Diaries, Log, and Letters of Commander W. J. S. Pullen.* Toronto: Arctic History Press.

Ray, Patrick Henry. 1882a. Letter, Ray to the Secretary, Office of the Interior, from Barrow, May 18, 1882. Records of the International Polar Expedition to Point Barrow, Alaska. RG 27.4.6, box 5: copies of letters sent, pp. 5–6. U.S. National Archives II, College Park, Maryland.

———. 1882b. Letter, Ray to the Chief Signal Office, from Barrow, July 23, 1882. Records of the International Polar Expedition to Point

Barrow, Alaska. RG 27.4.6, box 5: copies of letters sent, pp. 11–12. U.S. National Archives II, College Park, Maryland.

———. 1882c. Letter, Ray to the Chief Signal Office, from Barrow, August 13, 1882. Records of the International Polar Expedition to Point Barrow, Alaska. RG 27.4.6, box 5: copies of letters sent. U.S. National Archives II, College Park, Maryland.

———. 1988a. "Work at Point Barrow, Alaska, from September 16, 1881, to August 25, 1882." In *Ethnological Results of the Point Barrow Expedition*, pp. l–liv. Smithsonian Classics of Anthropology Series reprint, No. 6. Washington, D.C.: Smithsonian Institution Press.

———. 1988b. "Narrative." In *Ethnological results of the Point Barrow expedition*, pp. lxix–lxxxvi. Smithsonian Classics of Anthropology Series reprint, No. 6. Washington, D.C.: Smithsonian Institution Press.

———. 1988c. "Ethnographic Sketch of the Natives of Point Barrow." In *Ethnological results of the Point Barrow expedition*, pp. lxxxvii–cv. Smithsonian Classics of Anthropology Series reprint, No. 6. Washington, D.C.: Smithsonian Institution Press.

Seemann, Berthold Carl. 1853. *Narrative of the Voyage of H.M.S. Herald during the Years 1845–51 in Search of Sir John Franklin.* 2 vols. London: Reeve and Company.

Simpson, John. 1852–1854. Point Barrow Journal, 1852–1854. John Simpson Papers, Rare Book, Manuscript, and Special Collections Library, Box 5: Accounts of voyages. Oversized. Duke University, Durham, North Carolina.

———. 1855. Observations on the Western Esquimaux and the Country They Inhabit; From Notes Taken During Two Years at Point Barrow, by Mr. John Simpson, Surgeon, R.N, Her Majesty's Discovery Ship "Plover." Great Britain. Parliament. House of Commons. *Sessional Papers, Accounts and Papers 1854–55* 35, no. 1898:917–942.

———. 1875. Observations on the Western Eskimo and the Country They Inhabit. In *A Selection of Papers on Arctic Geography and Ethnology, Reprinted and Presented to the Arctic Expedition of 1875*, pp. 233–275. (Reprint of 1855 report.) London: Royal Geographical Society.

Simpson, Thomas. 1839. Arctic Discovery. *Nautical Magazine*, 8:564–565.

———. 1843. *Narrative of the Discoveries on the North Coast of America: Effected by the Officers of the Hudson's Bay Company during the Years 1836–39.* London: R. Bentley.

Smith, Middleton. 1902. "Superstitions of the Eskimo." In *The White World*, ed. Rudolph Kersting, pp. 113–130. New York: Lewis, Scribner, and Co.

Sonnenfeld, Joseph. 1957. Changes in Subsistence among the Barrow Eskimo. Ph.D. diss., Johns Hopkins University, Baltimore, Maryland.

———. 1959. An Arctic Reindeer Industry: Growth and Decline. *The Geographical Review*, 59(1):76–94.

———. 1960. Changes in an Eskimo Hunting Technology: An Introduction to Implement Geography. *Annals of the Association of American Geographers*, 50(2):172–186.

Spencer, R. F. 1959. The North Alaskan Eskimo: A Study in Ecology and Society. *Bureau of American Ethnology Bulletin 171*. Washington, D.C.: Smithsonian Institution Press.

———. 1967–1968. Die organization der Ehe under den Eskimos Nordalaskas. *Wiener Vǫlkerkundliche Mitteilungen*, ns 9/10:13–31.

———. 1968. "Spouse Exchange among the North Alaskan Eskimo." In *Marriage, Family, and Residence*, ed. Paul Bohannan and J. Middleton, pp. 131–146. New York: Natural History Press.

———. 1972. "The Social Composition of the North Alaskan Whaling Crew." In *Alliance in Eskimo Society: Proceedings of the American Ethnological Society, 1971, Supplement*, ed. Lee Guemple, pp. 110–131. Seattle: University of Washington Press.

———. 1984. "North Alaskan Coast Eskimo." In *Handbook of North American Indians*, ed. William C. Sturtevant. Volume 5: *Arctic*, ed. David Damas, pp. 320–327. Washington, D.C.: Smithsonian Institution Press.

VanStone, James W., ed. 1977. A. F. Kashevarov's Coastal Explorations in Northwest Alaska, 1838. Trans. David H. Kraus. *Fieldiana: Anthropology*, 69.

Wood, Kevin R., and James E. Overland. 2006. Climate Lessons from the First International Polar Year. *Bulletin of the American Meteorological Society*, 87(12):1685–1697.

The Art of Iñupiaq Whaling: Elders' Interpretations of International Polar Year Ethnological Collections

Aron L. Crowell

ABSTRACT. In the northern Bering Sea and Arctic Ocean, a 2,000-year tradition of Alaska Native bowhead whaling continues to the present day as a focus of both subsistence and cultural identity. In cooperation with the Smithsonian Institution, Iñupiaq Eskimo elders are interpreting the cultural and spiritual dimensions of whaling artifacts collected during the late nineteenth century, including material gathered by the International Polar Expedition to Point Barrow, Alaska (1881–1883). These artistic objects— hunting and boat equipment, regalia for whaling ceremonies, and charms owned by whale boat captains (*umialgich*)—were acquired during decades of rapid cultural change brought about by interaction with New England whalers, traders, and Presbyterian missionaries. Nonetheless, the social values and spiritual concepts that they express have survived and are carried forward in contemporary whaling. Current research and exhibitions benefit from both Iñupiaq expertise and a rich ethnohistorical literature from Barrow and other northern communities.

INTRODUCTION

In the northern Bering Sea and Arctic Ocean, a 2,000-year tradition of Alaska Native whaling continues to the present day (Brewster, 2004; Freeman et al., 1998; McCartney, 1995, 2003). The spring bowhead hunt in particular—and the preparations and celebrations that surround it—are a focus of cultural identity and survival (Worl, 1980). There are eight contemporary Iñupiaq whaling villages: Nuiqsut, Barrow, Wainwright, Point Hope, Kivalina, Kaktovik, Wales, and Little Diomede. Two Yupik whaling communities, Gambell and Savoonga, are located on St. Lawrence Island.

In cooperation with the Arctic Studies Center (Department of Anthropology, National Museum of Natural History, Smithsonian Institution), Iñupiaq Eskimo community members are reexamining this ancient hunting heritage through the study of traditional whaling equipment in the collections of the Smithsonian Institution. This project is in part a legacy of the first International Polar Year. During the U.S. government–sponsored International Polar Expedition to Point Barrow, Alaska (1881–1883), commander Lt. Patrick Henry Ray and naturalist John Murdoch purchased more than 1,100 items from local Iñupiaq residents including a wide variety of clothing, tools, and hunting

Aron L. Crowell, Alaska Director, Arctic Studies Center, National Museum of Natural History, Smithsonian Institution, 121 W. 7th Avenue, Anchorage, AK 99501, USA (crowella@si.edu). Accepted 9 May 2008.

weapons (cf. Burch, 2009, this volume; Fitzhugh, 1988; cf. Krupnik, 2009, this volume; Murdoch, 1892; Ray, 1885). Of special significance for the present discussion is a group of about 40 objects related to bowhead whaling and whaling ceremonies. In 2002, a group of cultural advisors from Barrow—Ronald Brower Sr., Jane Brower, Kenneth Toovak, and Doreen Simmonds—visited Washington, D.C., to examine some of the Murdoch–Ray materials, as well as other collections at the National Museum of Natural History (NMNH) and National Museum of the American Indian (NMAI) (Figure 1). The latter include objects from Barrow, Point Hope, Little Diomede, and Wales that were acquired in the late nineteenth century by Edward W. Nelson, Miner Bruce, George T. Emmons, J. Henry Turner, H. Richmond Marsh, and others. Additional contributions to the indigenous documentation of these collections were made by Barrow elder and translator Martha Aiken, as well as Norton Sound region advisors Jacob Ahwinona (White Mountain) and Marie Saclamana (King Island/Nome).

This project is one focus of the Arctic Studies Center's Sharing Knowledge program, which seeks to document indigenous oral histories and contemporary knowledge about objects in the Smithsonian's Alaskan collections (Crowell and Oozevaseuk, 2006). Outcomes include the *Sharing Knowledge* website (http://alaska.si.edu) and a large collaborative exhibition on Alaska Native cultures that will open at the Anchorage Museum in 2010. In cooperation with the University of Alaska, Fairbanks, the Iñupiat Heritage Center in Barrow produced its own community-based exhibition in 2005, *The People of Whaling* (http://www.uaf .edu/museum/exhibit/galleries/whaling/index.html). Its title places whaling at the core of cultural identity, underlined by the exhibition's theme statement, which reads, "Whaling is central to our lives. We continue to teach our youth to show respect for the whale and to share the harvest with the whole community."

CONTACT AND CHANGE IN IÑUPIAQ WHALING

The Smithsonian collections were acquired during decades of rapid cultural change. The American commercial whaling fleet came to the Bering Sea in 1848 and the Barrow area in 1854 (Bockstoce, 1986). During the 1880s,

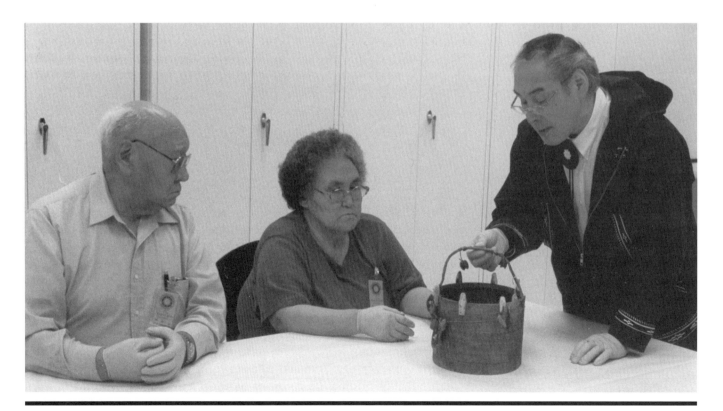

FIGURE 1. Left to right: Kenneth Toovak, Jane Brower, and Ron Brower Sr. at the National Museum of the American Indian, 2002. (Photo by Aron Crowell)

the whaling industry shifted its focus to shore-based operations that employed many Iñupiaq residents and greatly increased the direct influences of nonnative culture and economy (Cassel, 2003). Although the first shore station at Barrow was established in 1884, the year after the Point Barrow expedition ended, Murdoch noted that Native whalers had already acquired breech-loading guns for hunting caribou and "plenty of the most improved modern whaling gear" through their contacts with the commercial fleet (1892:53). The new weapons were bomb-loaded harpoons (called "darting guns") and shoulder guns that rapidly replaced traditional stone-tipped harpoons and lances. Local residents were also "now rich in iron, civilized tools, canvas, and wreck wood, and in this respect their condition is improved" (Murdoch, 1892:53). In other

ways, Murdoch observed, the community was in decline through the "unmitigated evil" of the alcohol trade, social disruption caused by the American sailors, and the effects of introduced diseases. Indigenous population losses from influenza and other epidemics were severe, and food shortages came about as caribou dwindled and whaling companies depleted whale and walrus herds. Iñupiaq willingness to sell or barter traditional items of material culture to collectors may have been related to these transformations in culture and living conditions (Fitzhugh, 1988).

Beginning in 1890, Presbyterian missionaries actively sought to suppress shamanism, whaling rituals, and hunting ceremonies, along with the spiritual concepts that underlay these practices (Figure 2). Iñupiaq *qargit*, or ceremonial houses, closed down under missionary pressure,

FIGURE 2. Men dancing in a *qargi* (ceremonial house) at Wales before the whale hunt, 1901. (Photograph by Suzanne R. Bernardi, Anchorage Museum archives B96.9.06)

ending the ceremonies that had taken place inside (Larson, 1995). The last Iñupiaq *qargi* at Point Hope became inactive in 1910, although social distinctions based on family membership in the former ceremonial houses continued to be important (Larson, 2003; VanStone, 1962; Burch, 1981). Iñupiaq whaling captains, or *umialgich*, retained their pivotal social and economic roles, as did their wives (Bodenhorn, 1990), but the once-extensive spiritual duties of these positions declined.

Despite the effects of Western contact, substantial continuities are evident between arctic whaling communities of the past and present (Anungazuk, 2003; Braund and Moorehead, 1995). The bowhead harvest is substantial, with a current allotment from the International Whaling Commission (IWC) of 56 landed whales per year, to be divided among the 10 Alaskan villages. The IWC quota is based on historic per capita averages of the subsistence harvest between 1910 and 1969 (Braund and Associates, 2007). Whaling captains and their kin-based crews and wives work throughout the year to prepare for whaling, carry out the hunt, process the catch, and distribute the meat and blubber. Whaling boats with hand-built wooden frames and skin covers are still employed in some of the villages, including Barrow. The Whale Festival or *Nalukataq* has survived and the Messenger Feast has been revived in modern form. Spiritual conceptions of whaling also persist. Ronald Brower Sr. said,

> Whalers respect their prey very highly . . . Whaling is a *very* important part of our life. In many ways, it's part of our sacred beliefs. Everything that we're doing in a year is dealing with whaling—some form of preparation, celebration, rites and rituals of whaling.[1]

Elders' commentaries in Washington provide insight into connections between modern and traditional whaling, including the deep-seated cultural view that whales are sentient beings that respond to human ritual and respect by giving themselves to feed the community.

THE ANNUAL CYCLE OF IÑUPIAQ WHALING: PAST AND PRESENT

Sources on late-nineteenth and early-twentieth-century Iñupiaq whaling include primary observations (Murdoch, 1892; Nelson, 1899; Ostermann and Holtved, 1952; Ray, 1885; Simpson, 1875; Stefánson 1919; Thornton, 1931), later anthropological and ethnohistorical reconstructions (Curtis, 1930; Rainey, 1947; Spencer, 1959; VanStone,

1962), and retrospective oral history and life stories (Brewster, 2004; Pulu et al., 1980). Most available information pertains to Barrow, Point Hope, and Wales. A brief synopsis of this diverse material, with comparisons to contemporary practices, is offered here as a foundation for the Smithsonian discussions with elders.

PREPARATIONS FOR WHALING

In the traditional whaling pattern, Iñupiaq crewmen worked through the winter and early spring in the *qargit* (ceremonial houses) owned by their captains, preparing gear for the coming hunt. Everything—harpoons, lances, floats, whaleboat (*umiaq*) frames—had to be newly made or scraped clean in the belief that no whale would approach a crew with old or dirty gear (Curtis, 1930:138; Rainey, 1947:257–258; Spencer, 1959:332–336). The captain's wife supervised the sewing of a new bearded seal or walrus hide cover for the *umiaq*; the women assigned to this task worked in an ice-block house adjacent to the *qargi*. Women made new parkas and boots for the hunters. Ritual equipment was prepared for the whaling captain's wife, including a wooden bucket with ivory ornaments and chains (Figure 3). The *umialik* (whaling captain) consulted with shamans and advisors, seeking ritual advice and portents of the season. He cleared out his ice cellar, distributing any meat from the previous year, to make way for the "parkas" or flesh of new whales, which the whale spirits shed for human use (Rainey, 1947:259; Spencer, 1959:335–336).

White beluga whales are often the first to be seen in the open water leads of early spring; at Wales, these were considered to be the bowheads' scouts, sent ahead to see if the village was clean and ready (Curtis, 1930:152). The bowheads would soon follow, and it was time to clear a path for the boats across the sea ice to the water's edge. Boat captains retrieved whaling charms that they had hidden in secret caches and caves (Spencer, 1959:338–340). When charms were placed in the *umiaq*, it became a living being. At Wales, it was said that on the night before the hunt, the boats walked out to sea using the posts of their racks as legs (Curtis, 1930:152). Before the *umiaq* was launched, the captain's wife gave it a drink of water from her bucket (Rainey, 1947:257). She herself was identified with the whale, and at Point Hope the harpooner pretended to spear her before the crew set out (Rainey, 1947:259).

Women still sew new *umiaq* covers each season in the Iñupiaq whaling communities, although the activity has moved to alternative locations; at Barrow, it takes place

FIGURE 3. *Umialik* sitting beneath whaling charms, including women's pails with ivory chains, Wales, 1901. (Photograph by Suzanne R. Bernardi, Anchorage Museum archives B96.9.05)

inside the Iñupiat Heritage Center. Clean, new gear and clothing are considered to be just as essential now as they were in the past, to show respect for the whales (Brewster, 2004; Bodenhorn, 1990). Ivory whale charms are carried onboard some *umiat*; in others, the traditional image of a bowhead is carved on the underside of the boat steerer's seat (see discussions below). Ice cellars are cleaned each spring, to make a welcoming home for the whales' bodies.

THE HUNT

Traditionally, women could not sew during the hunt because the act of stitching or cutting might entangle or break the harpoon line. A whaling captain's wife sat quietly in her house to mimic a docile whale that would be easier to catch. She would not stoop or go into an underground meat cellar, acts that could influence a wounded bowhead to go under the ice where it would be lost (Rainey, 1947: 259; Spencer, 1959:337–338).

As hunters approached a whale, the harpooner raised his weapon from an oarlock-shaped rest in the bow, thrusting it at close quarters into the animal's back. The whale dove with the harpoon head inside its body, dragging the attached line and sealskin floats. The harpooner refitted his weapon with a new head, prepared to strike again when the whale resurfaced. Other boats joined in the hunt. The whale eventually lay exhausted on the surface where it was killed with stone-tipped lances (Murdoch, 1892:275–276; Rainey, 1947:257–259)

The captain's wife greeted the whale at the edge of the ice. Singing and speaking a welcome, she poured fresh water on its snout from her ceremonial bucket (Curtis, 1930: 141; Osterman and Holtved, 1952:26; Spencer, 1969: 345; Stefánsson, 1919:389). Yupik and Siberian whaling cultures shared this practice of quenching a whale's assumed thirst for fresh water. Iñupiat traditionally gave all sea mammals they killed a drink of fresh water, and all land animals a taste of seal or whale blubber (which was rubbed on their noses), in the belief that the creatures of land and sea craved these substances that were not available to them in life (Brower, 1943:16; Rainey, 1947:267; Spencer, 1969:272; Stefánsson, 1919:389; Van Valin, 1941:199).

The contemporary spring whale hunt follows much the same course as in times past, with hunting crews camped at the ice edge by the beginning of May (Brewster, 2004: 131–163). Most crews use skin-covered *umiat* (propelled by paddles rather than motors during the hunt itself) to approach whales because the traditional hulls are much quieter in the water than wood or metal skiffs. The harpooner with his darting gun and gunner with his shoulder gun ride in the bow, ready to strike with the aim of an immediate kill. Technological innovations go beyond the adoption of these now antique weapons. Whalers use snow machines and sleds to pull their boats and gear to camp, as well as modern communications equipment to enhance the logistics and safety of the hunt. They are aided by VHF radios, walkie-talkies, GPS units, satellite phones, and Internet forecasts of ice and weather conditions. At Barrow in 1997, when shorefast ice broke away and set 142 whalers adrift in heavy snow and fog, helicopters were guided to the rescue using GPS coordinates transmitted by radio from the men on the ice (George et al., 2004).

Some of the older hunting prescriptions and prohibitions are retained, while others have faded. Today, as in the past, quiet is maintained in the whale camps because of the animals' sensitive hearing. On the other hand, cooking food on the ice is common practice now but banned under traditional norms (Rainey, 1947:259; Spencer, 1959:337).

Captains' wives try to remain peaceful and quiet to influence the whale's decision to give itself (Bodenhorn, 1990). Although she may no longer provide the customary drink of water to the whale, the captain's wife and her husband act as "good hosts" to the animal by sharing its meat with others during the *Nalukataq* celebration and at Christmas and Thanksgiving.

CEREMONIES AND CELEBRATIONS

The principal Iñupiaq whaling ceremony, *Nalukataq*, represents an unbroken tradition that extends from pre-contact times to the present (Brower, 1943:61–63; Curtis, 1930:135–160; Larson, 2003; Murdoch, 1892:272–275; Spencer, 1969:332–353; Rainey, 1947:262). *Nalukataq* follows the whaling season and is celebrated outdoors, so it was minimally affected by the decline of the ceremonial houses. Each successful *umialik* provides a feast of whale meat and *maktak* (skin and blubber) to the entire village, an act that brings great prestige. Whaleboats tipped on their sides, with the flags of each crew flying, surround the outdoor space. Feasting is followed by dancing, singing, and competitive games, including the "blanket toss" that gives the festival its name. During *Nalukataq* everyone receives new boots and parka covers.

The *Apugauti* feast marks the last time a successful whaling captain brings his boat back to shore at the end of the whaling season. It is a celebration of the boat's return. The captain raises his flag and everyone is invited to eat *mikigaq* (fermented whale meat), whale tongue, and *maktak*. Wild goose soup is also served.

Kivgiq, the Messenger Feast, is a winter dance and gift-giving festival that was once widespread across northwest Alaska and in the Yup'ik regions of Norton Sound, the Yukon–Kuskokwim Delta, and Nunivak Island (Bodfish, 1991:23–24; Burch, 2005:172–180; Curtis, 1930:146–147, 168–177, 213–214; Kingston, 1999; Lantis, 1947: 67–73; Nelson, 1899:361–363; Oquilluk, 1973:149–150; Ostermann and Holtved, 1952:103–112; Spencer, 1957: 210–228). Iñupiaq Messenger Feasts ended in the early years of the twentieth century, but North Slope Borough Mayor George Ahmaogak Sr. helped to revive the event at Barrow in 1988. Barrow's biennial celebration in February now brings visitors and dance groups from across Alaska, Russia, Canada, and Greenland.

Before a traditional Messenger Feast, leading men of a village (usually the whaling captains) sent messengers to the leaders of another community to invite them and their relatives to five days of ceremonies. At Utqiaġvik (Barrow), guests came to the *qargi* to view the great pile of gifts that they would receive, including sealskins filled with oil, weapons, sleds, and kayaks. While not specifically a whaling ceremony, *Kivgiq* was an expression of the whaling-based coastal economy and of the social dominance of the *umialgich*.

Before the disappearance of the ceremonial houses, fall and winter were a time for other whaling and hunting ceremonies. At Barrow the whaling season was followed by a feast and dance in the *qargi*, when men wore several types of masks. Few details were recorded or remembered about these dances, at least at Barrow. Murdoch purchased a dozen masks that were used in the *qargi* ceremonies, but had no opportunity to learn about their use. At Point Hope, hunting ceremonies were held each winter in the ceremonial houses until 1910 and elders' descriptions of these ceremonies were recorded by Froelich Rainey in 1940 (Rainey, 1947). Figures of whales, seals, polar bears, caribou, walrus, and birds were carved, hung in the *qargi*, and fed as part of the ritual. A mask with inset ivory eyes was hung above the oil lamp and the whaling captains vied with each other to steal it unobserved. It would be hidden in the victor's cache and used in the spring as a whaling charm.

SELECTED OBJECT DISCUSSIONS

HARPOON REST (NAULIGAQAĠVIK)

Harpoon rests were fastened inside the bows of whaling boats, as a place for the harpooner to support his weapon (Murdoch, 1892:341–343; Nelson, 1899:226; Spencer, 1959:342–343). These implements are often decorated with whale imagery and were probably regarded as hunting charms. At Wales in 1927, a wooden harpoon rest was found in one *umialik*'s old cache of whaling talismans (Curtis, 1930:138).

A walrus ivory harpoon rest from the Murdoch–Ray collection (Figure 4) is etched with images of bowhead flukes and each prong depicts a whale's head and fore body (Murdoch, 1892: fig. 348). Ronald Brower Sr. noted that on each prong the whale's back is inset with a blue bead at the center of an inscribed "X." This, he explained, is the location of the whale's life force, and the place where the harpooner aimed. Brower added that when blue is present on a hunting implement it is "part of the weapon" and not just added for beauty.[2] Blue, he said,

gives us the relationship to our spiritual beliefs, to the power of *sixa*—meaning "sky"—who controls life. *Sixa* is something bears—are carved on each side. Stories about giant eagles (or "thunderbirds") that preyed on whales, caribou, and people are found in the oral traditions of Iñupiaq, Yup'ik, Chukchi, Koryak, St. Lawrence Island Yupik, Unangan, and other North Pacific peoples (e.g. Bogoras, 1904–1909:328; Curtis, 1930:168–177; Ivanov, 1930:501–502; Jochelson, 1908:661; Nelson, 1899:445–446, 486–487). Despite their fearsome reputation, it was one of these birds, called the Eagle Mother, who is said to have taught Iñupiaq people the dances and songs of the Messenger Feast (Kingston, 1999).

Examining this harpoon rest, Jacob Ahwinona of White Mountain said,

> According to my grandpa, these birds, they're up in the big mountains back there, way up high. When they go from there, they go out to the sea and pick those whales up, just like these eagles in the rivers pick salmon up [with their talons]. That's right here, see? That bird is picking up that whale there, and then they bring them back to those high mountains. That's where they nest. And when they bring those back, those bugs that grow there eat some of the leftovers from the bird's nest. Those bugs that crawl there, my grandma said they're as big as young seals.[4]

Ahwinona reported that only a few years ago, when he was squirrel hunting at Penny River near Nome, a large shadow passed over the ground on a cloudless day, perhaps cast by one of the giant birds on its way out to the Bering Sea.

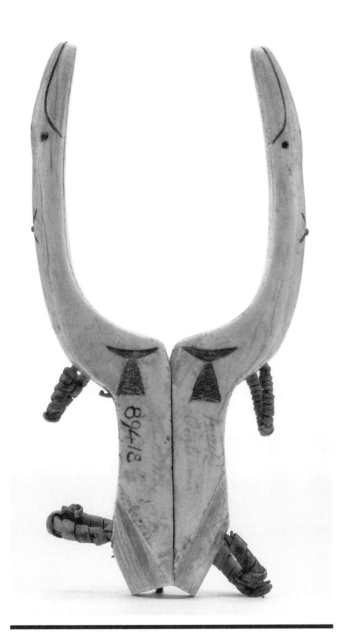

FIGURE 4. Harpoon rest, Barrow, 1881–1883, Murdoch–Ray collection. NMNH E089418. 30 cm tall.

that's both finite and infinite; you breathe it. When you look in the heavens you see blue. So blue became an important color that helped to bring a whale home.[3]

Another harpoon rest from the village of Wales (Figure 5), acquired by E. W. Nelson in 1881 (Nelson, 1899: Pl. LXXVIII–37), is made from two pieces of walrus ivory that are pinned together with ivory pegs. *Tiŋmiaqpat* ('giant eagles') in the act of catching whales are etched on the front and back, and animals with lifted paws—possibly polar

FIGURE 5. Harpoon rest, Wales, 1881, E. W. Nelson collection. NMNH E048169. 15 cm tall.

BOX FOR HARPOON BLADES
(*IKOIĠVIK*, *"STORAGE BOX"*)

A wooden container to hold and protect spare blades for the whaling harpoon was carried in the *umiaq* during hunting. Whaling captains cached the box after the whaling season, along with other hunting charms, amulets, and ritual objects (Bockstoce, 1977:102; Curtis, 1930:138–139; Kaplan et al., 1984; Kaplan and Barsness, 1986:138; Murdoch, 1892:247–250; Nelson, 1899:163, 439). Blade storage boxes were believed by Iñupiaq whalers to influence hunting success (Nelson, 1899:439) although exact conceptions about them were not historically recorded. The boxes are usually shaped like whales, but some represent other animals such as polar bears and birds.

Elders examined this whale-shaped box, collected by G. T. Emmons in about 1900 (Figure 6), as well as similar examples in the Murdoch–Ray collection (Murdoch, 1892:246–248). Its belly holds four triangular slate blades, secured beneath a wooden lid. The animal's tail is shown with cut-off tips, an apparent reference to the traditional practice of cutting off the ends of the flukes or flippers and sending them to the captain's wife to announce a successful hunt (Curtis, 1930:140–141; Rainey, 1947:260; Spencer, 1959:344). Today, as elders commented, the tips of a whale's tail are still removed but for practical reasons, to reduce drag when towing the animal at sea.

Brower likened the box to the ammunition cases that captains now carry in their boats to hold whale bombs, saying,

From a spiritual sense, my observation is that many of our whalers still retain some of the old beliefs. But instead of a box like this, we now have a whale gun box, where we have our ammunition. This would be like an ammunition box in the old days. Now we have what we call the bomb box today, where we keep all of these same types of implements, used for the purpose of killing the whale.[5]

Referring to the blade box, Kenneth Toovak said, "They're so powerful, some of these charms."[6] He remarked that they were probably owned by shamans and that Point Hope men possessed a powerful system of whaling "medicine" in which boxes like these were employed. Brower concluded,

This one is a box for the whales. The traditional beliefs deal with the spirit of the whale, and the spirit of the whale and the spirit of man are both intertwined. It is expected that whales gave themselves to the whalers. They not only are giving themselves to the whalers, but to the captain's wife, who has a ritual. Because that person maintained a clean household. Because the spirit of the whale is believed to be that of a girl.[7]

FIGURE 6. Whale-shaped box for holding harpoon blades, location unknown, 1900, G. T. Emmons collection. NMNH E204778. 45 cm long.

Brower refers here to the identification of the captain's wife with the female spirit of the whale, both evoked by the artistic imagery of the blade box. Moreover, the whale gives its life not to the whaler but to his wife, in recognition of her skills, generosity, and observance of ritual (Bodenhorn, 1990).

BOAT SEAT (*Aqutim Iksivautaŋa,* *"BOAT STEERER'S SEAT"*)

At Point Hope, wooden plaques carved with whale images were wedged inside the bow of the *umiaq*, making a small deck just in front of the harpooner. The whale figure was on the bottom side, facing downward and thus invisible. Froelich Rainey reported in 1940 that the harpooner tapped the top of the platform while he sang a song that summoned hidden whales to the surface (Lowenstein, 1993:150).

Talking about this example from the village of Wales (Figure 7), Barrow elders stated that it could be placed either in the bow of the boat (as at Point Hope) or in the stern as a seat for the boat steerer. In both places, the whale image would be on the bottom side. When used as a bow platform, Toovak said, the plaque would hold the coiled *akłunaaq* (bearded sealskin line) that attaches to the whale harpoon.

FIGURE 7. Whale plaque/seat for *umiaq*, Wales, purchased 1958. NMAI 226908.000. 42.5 cm wide.

A carved whale seat/platform belongs to the *umialik*. Toovak said, "*Uvvakii aġviqsiuqtinmakua umiaġiratiŋ piqpagipiaġataġuugait qutchiksuaġisuugait. Tavra tainna umialguruam marra suġauttaŋi.* " ("And so it is whalers really do have respect for their boats and have high regard. These are a boat captain's items.") Brower said that the im-

age of the whale is present in the boat as part of the ritual of whaling, and that its use is part of Iñupiaq sacred beliefs.[8] The practice continues, as he noted in an earlier discussion. "Some whale boats still have an ivory effigy of the whale, tied on to the boat. Or they have an effigy of the whale under the seat of the steersman in the rear of the boat."[9]

IVORY WHALING CHARMS (QAAGLIÑIQ, "CHARM," OR AANĠUAQ, "AMULET")

Murdoch collected 21 whale figures made of walrus ivory, wood, and soapstone that he identified as possible whaling charms, to be carried on the *umiaq* (Murdoch, 1892:402–405). Among these are three small carvings (3–4" long) made of darkly stained walrus ivory (Figure 8). The two smaller whales are a matched male–female pair (the far left and far right figures, respectively) and the larger figure in the center is another female, as identified by depictions of the external sex organs. Brower called this type of figure a *qaagliñiq*,[10] meaning a "charm" that could attract animals but not compel them; it has the "power of bringing." This he contrasted with more potent figures called *tuunġaq* (shaman's helping spirit), which were employed by shamans to control the animal's spirit and which have "the power of killing."[11] He and other elders used the term *aanġuaq* (amulet) more ambiguously, as a synonym for both of the above.

FIGURE 8. Ivory whaling charms, Barrow, 1881–1883, Murdoch–Ray collection. Left to right: NMNH E089324, E089325, E089323. Largest 15 cm long.

SOAPSTONE FIGURE OF WHALE (AANĠUAQ, "AMULET," OR TUUNĠAQ, "SHAMAN'S HELPING SPIRIT")

Another whale image, about 5" long, collected by Murdoch (Figure 9) appears to have been carved from the bottom of an old soapstone pot (Murdoch, 1892:404). In the discussion among elders, this figure was called both *aanġuaq* (amulet) and *tuunġaq* (shaman's helping spirit). Observing what appeared to be blood that had been rubbed on the image, Brower suggested that, "Something like this could probably be carried by the shaman, and he would add blood from the whale. And so he carries with him the life force of the whale." Comparing this object with the ivory whaling charms (above), he said, "One has more of a life force than the other. One has more strength, depending on the strength of the shaman. This one—it was used as an amulet and ensured that the whale would be caught."[12]

Returning later to the topic of shamanism, Brower said,

Kenneth [Toovak] and I were talking earlier. When I was describing those things that were used by shamans, we are reminded by our elders that that kind of life has passed. It is over. And it's something that we did not inherit, because the life has changed. The traditional lifestyle—before Christianity set in—is gone. And

FIGURE 9. Stone whaling amulet, Barrow, 1881–1883, Murdoch–Ray collection. NMNH E089557. 15 cm long.

so are the powers associated with that. Because today our people have accepted a new faith and live a different lifestyle, which does not require the old way of life in order to be successful.[13]

HEADBAND (NIAQUĠUN)

A headband acquired at Barrow by H. Richmond Marsh in 1901 is made of bleached skin, animal teeth (caribou or Dall sheep incisors), red beads, and sinew thread (Figure 10). Murdoch reported that headbands made of Dall (mountain) sheepskin with dangling stone figures of whales were "the badge of a whaleman," worn by the *umialik* and harpooner for spring preparatory rites and during the hunt itself (Murdoch, 1892:142). Some of these headbands were also decorated with mountain sheep teeth. Also at Barrow, John Simpson observed that headbands made of caribou skin and hung with caribou teeth were worn "only when engaged in whaling" (Simpson, 1875:243).

Murdoch was not able to acquire an example during the Point Barrow expedition because these articles were highly prized and rarely offered for sale. Barrow elders were not familiar with this type of headband, which is no longer worn. They suggested that it might be a woman's ornament worn during a traditional ceremony to mark the autumn equinox "when two stars appear" (*aagruuk*)—also referred to as the Iñupiaq New Year—or else during the Messenger Feast.[14]

BUCKET FOR GIVING DRINK TO WHALE (IMIQAĠVIK) AND BUCKET HANDLE (IPU)

Elders identified a wooden bucket from Wales (Figure 11) in the NMAI collection as one that may have been used by a whaling captain's wife to provide fresh water to a newly caught whale. Pails for this purpose were also made of baleen. Toovak and Brower identified the bucket's various attachments. The ivory carvings on the rim (each is a *qiñiyunaqsaun*, "ornament") represent polar bear heads and a whale. Several "hunter's items" hang on a leather cord: a polar bear tooth, a walrus tooth, part of a harpoon head, ivory weights for a bolas to hunt birds, and an ivory plug for a sealskin float. Two more float plugs (*puvuixutaŋit*) are tied to the handle. Brower suggested that all of these ornaments are symbols of success in both hunting and political leadership. "Communities respect the headman. That is indicated by making him gifts of this nature (indicates bucket), especially if he's a very successful hunter."[15]

FIGURE 10. Headband with mountain sheep or caribou teeth, Barrow, 1901, H. Richmond Marsh. NMNH E209841. 25 cm across.

FIGURE 11. Woman's ceremonial bucket, Wales, purchased 1952. NMAI 218952.000. 23 cm tall.

FIGURE 12. Handle for ceremonial bucket, Sledge Island, 1881, E. W. Nelson collection. NMNH E044690. 30 cm long.

An ivory handle with whale figures from Sledge Island (Figure 12) is from the same type of bucket. The water giving ceremony, Brower said, was to help the whale "move from the ocean to the land."[16]

Historically, these buckets served in other rituals. An *umialik*'s wife gave a drink to the whaleboat when it was launched, because the sealskin-covered *umiaq* was itself viewed as a kind of living sea mammal (Brower, 1943: 48; Rainey, 1947:257; Spencer, 1959:334; Thornton, 1931:166–167). At Point Hope, women raised their buckets to Alignuk, the Moon Man who controlled game. People said that if the water in the woman's pot was clear and clean, Alignuk would drop a whale into it, meaning that her husband would be successful in the spring hunt (Pulu

et al., 1980:15–16; Rainey, 1947:270–271; Osterman and Holtved, 1952:228). At Point Hope and Barrow, skilled craftsmen made new buckets each year for the whaling captains and their wives. These were bigger each time to show the *umialik*'s growing experience. Buckets were initiated with songs and ceremonies in the *qargi* (Rainey, 1947:245; Spencer, 1959:334).

MAN'S DANCE GLOVES (ARGAAK, "PAIR OF GLOVES")

A pair of Point Hope dance gloves collected in 1881 by E. W. Nelson (Figure 13) is made of tanned caribou skin and decorated with strings of red, white, and blue beads and with alder-dyed fringes at the wrists (Nelson,

FIGURE 13. Man's dance gloves, Point Hope, 1881, E. W. Nelson collection. NMNH E064271. 30 cm long.

FIGURE 14. Child's short summer boots for *Nalakutaq*, location unknown, 1931, donated by Victor J. Evans. NMNH E359020. 16 cm tall.

1899:38, Pl. XX–1). A keeper string to go around the neck is ornamented with copper cylinders and blue beads. According to Kenneth Toovak,

> "Sometimes a man had a special Eskimo dance song, an original song . . . *Atuutiqaġuurut taipkuagguuq atuġuuramiŋnik* ("they have short songs that they sang") . . . And he had prepared gloves for the special song that he made.

He added that these dance songs were performed at the summer whaling festival (*Nalukataq*) and winter hunting ceremonies, usually by whalers; at Point Hope songs would strictly be the property of different clans. Gloves were worn only during the dance, and then removed, a custom that continues to be observed in modern performances.[17]

CHILD'S SUMMER BOOTS (PIÑIĠAK, "PAIR OF BOOTS")

Toovak recognized a pair of short summer boots (Figure 14) as the type made for children to wear during *Nalukataq*. The thin soles are made from young bearded sealskin that has been chewed to soften and crimp the toes, sides, and heels. Jane Brower identified the uppers as bleached sealskin dyed with alder bark, while the upper trim and straps are of plain bleached skin. Ronald Brower said,

> In the old days, all the men, women, and children dressed in their finest clothes after the feast, when they were beginning to do the celebrations and dances. Everybody, after they had eaten, put on their finest clothes, including little children.[18]

DISCUSSION

Ethnological recording and collecting was assigned a lower priority than other scientific work by the leadership of the Point Barrow Expedition of 1881–1883, and it was only possible to carry it out during brief periods when ongoing magnetic and meteorological observations could be set aside. Murdoch's *Ethnological Results of the Point Barrow Expedition* (1892), for all of its gaps and flaws (especially with regard to social and ceremonial life), reflects an extraordinary effort to overcome the limitations of time and opportunity in the field (cf. Burch, 2009, this volume).

It is probably safe to say that the ultimate value of this effort was not anticipated at the time. Perhaps more evident to members of the expedition was that the Point Barrow Iñupiat were at a cultural turning point, buffeted by the growing social and economic impacts of commercial whaling. Although Murdoch felt that they were "essentially a conservative people" who remained independent and were not yet overwhelmed by change, he cataloged the new pressures on their society. In the decades after the expedition, these pressures increased with the advent of shore-based whaling stations, Presbyterian missions, food shortages, and epidemics.

What was certainly not foreseeable in 1883 was that more than a century later the northernmost Alaskan villages would still be whaling and that the practice would remain a vital center point of the culture and way of life. Due to this surprising stability, whaling objects from the late nineteenth century remain as culturally legible signposts within a continuing tradition. Some nineteenth-century types are still in current use, such as carved ivory hunting charms. Others are interpretable within a persistent conceptual frame—the reciprocal relationship between whales and people, with its obligations of ritual and respect.

Also impossible to imagine in 1883 would have been the new uses of museum collections, especially the current strong emphasis on making them accessible for Alaska Native interpretation, cultural education, and community-based exhibitions (Crowell, 2004; Clifford, 2004; Fienup-Riordan, 1996, 2005). The collaborative work presented here is only preliminary. Limited by time and resources, only a few Iñupiaq elders have so far been able to view the Smithsonian materials and only a small part of the total Murdoch–Ray collection has been surveyed. Iñupiaq consultants pointed out the necessity of involving elders from all of the whaling communities, so that each could comment on material from his or her village in greater depth. The opportunity for this will come as the objects discussed in this paper and more than 600 others from all of Alaska's indigenous cultural regions are brought to Anchorage for exhibition in 2010. The Arctic Studies Center gallery in Anchorage will be designed not only for display but also as a research center where community members can remove every object from its case for study and discussion. The Smithsonian collections, including the large number gathered as part of the first International Polar Year, represent a scientific, cultural, and historical legacy that will continue to yield new meanings.

ACKNOWLEDGMENTS

My sincerest appreciation to the following individuals who shared their expert knowledge about whaling, Iñupiaq culture, and the Smithsonian collections: Jacob Ahwinona (Kawerak Elders' Advisory Committee), Martha Aiken (North Slope Borough School District), Ronald Brower Sr (University of Alaska, Fairbanks)., Jane Brower (Iñupiat Heritage Center), Kenneth Toovak (Barrow Arctic Science Consortium), Marie Saclamana (Nome Public Schools), and Doreen Simmonds (Iñupiat History, Language, and Culture Commission). Deborah Hull-Walski (National Museum of Natural History) and Patricia Nietfeld (National Museum of the American Indian) and their staffs assisted with the collections consultations in Washington; coordinating at the Alaska end were Terry Dickey, Wanda Chin, and Karen Brewster of the University of Alaska Museum. Dawn Biddison (Arctic Studies Center, National Museum of Natural History) provided supporting research and edited the transcripts and translations of the Washington consultations. Project funding and support from the Rasmuson Foundation, National Park Service Shared Beringian Heritage Program, University of Alaska Museum, and Smithsonian Institution is gratefully acknowledged. Thanks to Igor Krupnik (Arctic Studies Center, National Museum of Natural History) and Karen Brewster (University of Alaska, Fairbanks) for reviews that helped to improve this paper.

NOTES

1. Alaska Collections/Sharing Knowledge Project, Tape 34A:096–112.
2. Alaska Collections/Sharing Knowledge Project, Tape 30A: 413–430.
3. Alaska Collections/Sharing Knowledge Project, Tape 29A: 158–172.
4. Alaska Collections/Sharing Knowledge Project, Tape 20B: 412–434.
5. Alaska Collections/Sharing Knowledge Project, Tape 29A: 052–059.
6. Alaska Collections/Sharing Knowledge Project, Tape 29A:135.
7. Alaska Collections/Sharing Knowledge Project, Tape 29A: 152–170.
8. Alaska Collections/Sharing Knowledge Project, Tape 34A: 031–116.
9. Alaska Collections/Sharing Knowledge Project, Tape 29A:063.
10. Alaska Collections/Sharing Knowledge Project, Tape 29A:378.
11. Alaska Collections/Sharing Knowledge Project, Tape 31A:166.
12. Alaska Collections/Sharing Knowledge Project, Tape 31A: 166–220.
13. Alaska Collections/Sharing Knowledge Project, Tape 32A: 148–159.
14. Alaska Collections/Sharing Knowledge Project, Tape 28A: 221–311.
15. Alaska Collections/Sharing Knowledge Project, Tape 34A: 241–334.
16. Alaska Collections/Sharing Knowledge Project, Tape 29A: 217–259.
17. Alaska Collections/Sharing Knowledge Project, Tape 28A: 003–037.
18. Alaska Collections/Sharing Knowledge Project, Tape 27A: 398–436.

LITERATURE CITED

Anungazuk, H. O. 2003. "Whaling: Indigenous Ways to the Present." In *Indigenous Ways to the Present: Native Whaling in the Western Arctic*, ed. A. P. McCartney, pp. 427–432. Salt Lake City: University of Utah Press.

Bockstoce, J. R. 1977. *Eskimos of Northwest Alaska in the Early Nineteenth Century: Based on the Beechey and Belcher Collections and*

Records Compiled during the Voyage of H.M.S. Blossom *to Northwest Alaska in 1826 and 1827*, ed. T. K. Penniman. University of Oxford, Pitt Rivers Museum Monograph Series No. 1. Oxford, U.K.: Oxprint Limited.

———. 1986. *Whales, Ice, and Men: The History of Whaling in the Western Arctic*. Seattle: University of Washington Press.

Bodenhorn, Barbara. 1990. "I'm Not the Great Hunter, My Wife Is." Iñupiat and Anthropological Models of Gender. *Études/Inuit/Studies*, 14(1–2):55–74.

Bodfish, W., Sr. 1991. *Kusiq: An Eskimo Life History from the Arctic Coast of Alaska*, ed. W. Schneider, L. K. Okakok, and J. M. Nageak. Fairbanks: University of Alaska Press.

Bogoras, W. 1904–1909. "The Chukchee." In *The Jesup North Pacific Expedition*, vol. 7, ed. F. Boas. New York: A. Stechert.

Braund, S. R., and Associates. 2007. *Quantification of Subsistence and Cultural Need for Bowhead Whales by Alaska Eskimos*. Prepared for the Alaska Eskimo Whaling Commission, Barrow. http://www.iwcoffice.org/_documents/commission/IWC59docs/59–ASW6.pdf (accessed 5 August 2007).

Braund, S. R., and E. L. Moorehead. 1995. "Contemporary Alaska Eskimo Bowhead Whaling Villages." In *Hunting the Largest Animals: Native Whaling in the Western Arctic and Subarctic*, ed. A. P. McCartney, pp. 253–280. Edmonton: Canadian Circumpolar Institute, University of Alberta.

Brewster, K., ed. 2004. *The Whales, They Give Themselves: Conversations with Harry Brower, Sr.* Fairbanks: University of Alaska Press.

Brower, C. 1943. *Fifty Years Below Zero: A Lifetime of Adventure in the Far North*, 4th ed. New York: Dodd, Mead, and Company.

Burch, Ernest S., Jr. 1981. *The Traditional Eskimo Hunters of Point Hope, Alaska: 1800–1875*. Barrow, Alaska: North Slope Borough.

———. 2005. *Alliance and Conflict: The World System of the Iñupiaq Eskimos*. Lincoln: University of Nebraska Press.

———. 2009. "Smithsonian Contributions to Alaskan Ethnography: The IPY Expedition to Barrow, 1881–1883." In *Smithsonian at the Poles: Contributions to International Polar Year Science*, ed. I. Krupnik, M. A. Lang, and S. E. Miller, pp. 89–98. Washington, D.C.: Smithsonian Institution Scholarly Press.

Cassell, M. S. 2003. "Eskimo Laborers: John Kelly's Commercial Shore Whaling Station, Point Belcher, Alaska, 1891–1892." In *Indigenous Ways to the Present: Native Whaling in the Western Arctic*, ed. A. P. McCartney, pp. 387–426. Salt Lake City: University of Utah Press.

Clifford, J. 2004. Looking Several Ways: Anthropology and Native Heritage in Alaska. *Current Anthropology*, 45(1):5–30.

Crowell, A. L. 2004. Terms of Engagement: The Collaborative Representation of Alutiiq Identity. *Études/Inuit/Studies*, 28(1):9–35.

Crowell, A. L., and E. Oozevaseuk, 2006. The St. Lawrence Island Famine and Epidemic, 1878–1880: A Yupik Narrative in Cultural and Historical Context. *Arctic Anthropology*, 43(1):1–19.

Curtis, E. S. 1930. *The North American Indian*, vol. 20, ed. F. W. Hodge. New York: Johnson Reprint Company. [Reprinted, 1970.]

Fienup-Riordan, A. 1996. *The Living Tradition of Yup'ik Masks: Agayuliyararput, Our Way of Making Prayer*. Seattle: University of Washington Press.

———. 2005. *Yup'ik Elders at the Ethnologisches Museum Berlin: Fieldwork Turned on Its Head*. Trans. M. Meade, S. Lührmann, A. Karlson, and A. Pauls. Seattle: University of Washington Press and Calista Elders Council.

Fitzhugh, W. W., ed. 1988. "Introduction." In *Ethnological Results of the Point Barrow Expedition*, by John Murdoch, pp. xiii–xlix [orig. published 1892]. Washington, D.C.: Smithsonian Institution Press.

Freeman, M. M. R., L. Bogoslovskaya, R. A. Caulfield, I. Egede, I. I. Krupnik, and M. G. Stevenson. 1998. *Inuit, Whaling, and Sustainability*. Walnut Creek, Calif.: AltaMira Press.

George, J. C., H. P. Huntington, K. Brewster, H. Eicken, D. W. Norton, and R. Glenn. 2004. Observations on Shorefast Ice Dynamics in Arctic Alaska and the Responses of the Iñupiat Hunting Community. *ARCTIC*, 7(4):363–374.

Ivanov, S. V. 1930. "Aleut Hunting Headgear and Its Ornamentation." In *Proceedings of the Twenty-third International Congress of Americanists*, New York, 1928, pp. 477–504.

Jochelson, W. 1908. "The Koryak." In *The Jesup North Pacific Expedition*, vol. 6, ed. F. Boas. New York: A. Stechert.

Kaplan, S. A., and K. J. Barsness. 1986. *Raven's Journey: The World of Alaska's Native People*. Philadelphia: University Museum, University of Pennsylvania.

Kaplan, S. A., R. H. Jordan, and G. W. Sheehan. 1984. An Eskimo Whaling Outfit from Sledge Island, Alaska. *Expedition*, 26(2):16–23.

Kingston, D. M. 1999. Returning: Twentieth-Century Performances of the King Island Wolf Dance. Ph.D. diss., University of Alaska, Fairbanks.

Krupnik, Igor. 2009. "'The Way We See It Coming': Building the Legacy of Indigenous Observations in IPY 2007–2008." In *Smithsonian at the Poles: Contributions to International Polar Year Science*, ed. I. Krupnik, M. A. Lang, and S. E. Miller, pp. 129–142. Washington, D.C.: Smithsonian Institution Scholarly Press.

Lantis, M. 1947. *Alaskan Eskimo Ceremonialism*. American Ethnological Society, Monograph 11. New York: J. J. Augustin.

Larson, M. A. 1995. "And Then There Were None: The 'Disappearance' of the *Qargi* in Northern Alaska." In *Hunting the Largest Animals: Native Whaling in the Western Arctic and Subarctic*, ed. A. P. McCartney, pp. 207–220. Edmonton: Canadian Circumpolar Institute, University of Alberta.

———. 2003. "Festival and Tradition: The Whaling Festival at Point Hope." In *Indigenous Ways to the Present: Native Whaling in the Western Arctic*, ed. A. P. McCartney, pp. 341–356. Salt Lake City: University of Utah Press.

Lowenstein, T. 1993. *Ancient Land: Sacred Whale. The Inuit Hunt and Its Rituals*. New York: Farrar, Straus and Giroux.

McCartney, A. P., ed. 1995. *Hunting the Largest Animals: Native Whaling in the Western Arctic and Subarctic*. Edmonton: Canadian Circumpolar Institute, University of Alberta.

———, ed. 2003. *Indigenous Ways to the Present: Native Whaling in the Western Arctic*. Salt Lake City: University of Utah Press.

Murdoch, J. 1892. Ethnological Results of the Point Barrow Expedition. *Ninth Annual Report of the Bureau of American Ethnology 1887–88*, pp. 3–441.Washington, D.C.: Government Printing Office.

Nelson, E. W. 1899. The Eskimo about Bering Strait. *Eighteenth Annual Report of the Bureau of American Ethnology, 1896–97*, pp. 3–518. Washington, D.C.: Government Printing Office.

Oquilluk, W. A. 1973. *People of Kauwerak: Legends of the Northern Eskimo*. Anchorage: Alaska Methodist University.

Ostermann, H., and E. Holtved, eds. 1952. *The Alaskan Eskimos as Described in the Posthumous Notes of Dr. Knud Rasmussen*. Trans. W. E. Calvert. Report of the Fifth Thule Expedition, 1921–1924, Volume 10(3). Copenhagen: Nordisk.

Pulu, T. I. (Qipuk), R. Ramoth-Sampson (Tatqavin), and A. Newlin (Ipiilik). 1980. *Whaling: A Way of Life* (Agvigich Iglaunnat Niginmun). Anchorage: National Bilingual Materials Development Center, Rural Education, University of Alaska.

Rainey, F. G. 1947. The Whale Hunters of Tigara. *Anthropological Papers of the American Museum of Natural History*, 41(2): 231–283.

Ray, P. H. 1885. "Ethnographic Sketch of the Natives of Point Barrow." In *Report of the International Polar Expedition to Point Barrow, Alaska, in Response to the Resolution of the House of Representatives of December 11, 1884*, Part III, pp. 37–60. Washington, D.C.: Government Printing Office.

Simpson, J. 1875. "Observations on the Western Eskimo and the Country They Inhabit, from Notes Taken During Two Years at Point Barrow." In *Arctic Geography and Ethnology*, pp. 233–275. London: Royal Geographic Society.

Spencer, R. F. 1959. The North Alaskan Eskimo: A Study in Ecology and Society. *Bureau of American Ethnology Bulletin 171*. Washington, D.C.: Smithsonian Institution Press.

Stefánson, V. 1919. The Stefánson–Anderson Arctic Expedition of the American Museum: Preliminary Ethnological Report. *Anthropological Papers of the American Museum of Natural History*, 14(1).

Thornton, H. R. 1931. *Among the Eskimos of Wales, Alaska, 1890–93*, ed. N. S. Thornton and W. M. Thornton, Jr. Baltimore: Johns Hopkins Press.

Van Valin, W. B. 1941. *Eskimoland Speaks*. Caldwell, Idaho: Caxton Printers.

VanStone, J. 1962. *Point Hope: An Eskimo Village in Transition*. Seattle: University of Washington Press.

Worl, R. 1980. "The North Slope Iñupiat Whaling Complex." In *Alaska Native Culture and History*, ed. Y. Kotani and W. B. Workman, pp. 305–321. Senri Ethnological Studies No. 4. Osaka, Japan: National Museum of Ethnology.

From Tent to Trading Post and Back Again: Smithsonian Anthropology in Nunavut, Nunavik, Nitassinan, and Nunatsiavut—The Changing IPY Agenda, 1882–2007

Stephen Loring

ABSTRACT. As part of the First International Polar Year, the Smithsonian Institution established a meteorological and astronomical observatory at Ft. Chimo (Kuujjuaq) in Ungava Bay in 1881–1883. Sent to man the post was the Smithsonian's most prominent northern naturalist, Lucien Turner. Turner developed a close rapport with Inuit and Innu families from whom he acquired an extraordinary array of scientific specimens and ethnological materials. While intrepid and inspired, the work of the Smithsonian's pioneering Arctic scientists reflects the biases of western scientific tradition. Northern Native peoples were viewed as part of the arctic ecosystem to be observed, cataloged, and described. For the most part, the intellectual landscape of Innu and Inuit groups was overlooked and ignored. The Smithsonian collections are a powerful talisman for evoking knowledge, appreciation, and pride in Innu and Inuit heritage and serve as one point of departure for research during the Fourth IPY in 2007–2008. Recognition that northern Natives have a mandate to participate in and inform northern research is an important change in the production of northern scientific research.

INTRODUCTION

This essay considers the changes in the practices of museum anthropology and archaeology at the Smithsonian Institution between the First IPY in 1882–1883 and the current IPY of 2007–2008. To know a place is to name it. The place we call the *Arctic* means different things to different people. A cultural construct defined by different eyes and different ways of knowing, it is both real and intangible. Archaeologist Robert McGhee (2007) calls it "the last imaginary place." It is only in the twentieth century that the technologies and the insatiable appetites of the developed world have been able to overcome environmental and logistical constraints to establish a permanent presence throughout the north. There are libraries and research institutes devoted to the complexity and variety of human experiences at high latitudes. For visitors, the Arctic is as much a cultural construct as it is a physical one, with perceptions repeatedly shaped and reshaped by time and circumstance.

One has only to consider the transformation of Arctic landscapes from the fantastic fairy-tale visions—gothic cathedrals of ice—of the early-nineteenth-century explorers, subsequently morphed by suffering and danger into the grim

Stephen Loring, Arctic Studies Center, Department of Anthropology, National Museum of Natural History, Smithsonian Institution, P.O. Box 37012, MRC 112, Washington, DC 20013-7012, USA (lorings@si.edu). Accepted 9 May 2008.

and foreboding visions of the ubiquitous and relentless ice of the post-Franklin era (Figure 1), to the modern era with its coffee-table books of stunning photography of polar bears and vast unpopulated expanses (Loomis, 1977; 1986; Grant, 1998). But the Arctic is also a homeland, and has been for thousands of years. Arctic inhabitants have evolved a remarkable and practical adaptation to the climatic and ecological extremes of the northern polar world. Indigenous knowledge—based on observation and inference and passed from generation to generation—forms an astute and perhaps surprisingly complex interpretation of

FIGURE 1. The terrible tragedy surrounding the loss of life during the U.S. North Polar Expedition (1879–1881) following on the debacle of the British Northwest Passage Expedition under Sir John Franklin (1845–1848) had soured public opinion in the United States on the benefits of polar exploration and transformed perceptions of the Arctic as a deadly and foreboding landscape. Editorial cartoon, *Frank Leslie's Illustrated Newspaper*, 20 May 1882, William Dall papers, RU7073, SI Archives. (S. Loring photograph.)

the world inhabited by indigenous northern peoples. Yet with few exceptions (e.g., Rasmussen, 1929; Rink, 1875), visiting researchers and scientists have not learned the language of their hosts and thus have been denied much of the complexity of northern perceptions that has developed over generations by indigenous peoples.

Historically, science in the north began as a handmaiden of colonial enterprise. Having developed the technology to transport them into (if not always out of) the polar regions, nineteenth-century explorers, with their passion for expanding scientific and geographic knowledge, began to collect information about the places they found themselves in. As was typical on many early and mid nineteenth-century Arctic voyages, with their winter quarters established, observatories were placed on the ice and rounds of tidal measurements, weather, and geophysical observations began. Expedition accounts are filled with observations on the phenomenology of ice and cold, as navy explorers and scientists confronted the mysteries of Arctic life and returned with their collections of natural history specimens. Also in these accounts, are anecdotal and ethnohistorical passages that provide some of the first descriptions of Native residents of the Arctic. In comparison to more complex societies elsewhere, northern band-level societies, with their more modest material remains (the very antithesis of Euro-American values of dominance, competition and wealth) were perceived as being backward and marginal, literally frozen in time. Lacking a critical self-awareness the eyes of the European explorers had yet to take the true measure of the Natives of the eastern arctic who were frequently portrayed as quaint and childlike, devoid of the quarrelsome and bellicose attitudes of some of their western and southern counterparts (Figure 2).

Gradually the accumulation of geographical knowledge, dearly bought, began to make sense of the physical mysteries of the arctic. Still little in the way of serious attention to native cultures was afforded prior to the travels of Charles Francis Hall beginning in 1860 (Hall, 1864; Loomis, 1972). More visionary than scientist, Hall had been drawn to the arctic by the continuing fascination with the fate of the lost Sir John Franklin Expedition (1845) and the possibility that survivors might yet be living amongst the Inuit. Severely curtailed by financial constraints Hall broke from the prevailing tradition of using expedition ships frozen in the ice as base stations from which to launch sledge and small-boat voyages in favor of adopting Inuit modes of travel. Hall moved in with his Nunavut hosts, learned their language, and experienced their culture as an active participant. He was fortunate

FIGURE 2. Illustrations accompanying William Edward Parry's popular accounts of his search for the Northwest Passage (1819–1834) depict the central Canadian Arctic Inuit as whimsical and childlike catered to a European perception of the polar region as a fantastic otherworldly place (Parry 1821, 1824). Detail from a Staffordshire ceramic plate, "Arctic Scenery" ca. 1835. (Photograph by S. Loring of plate in author's collection.)

in befriending an extraordinary Inuit couple, Ebierbing ("Joe") and Tookoolito ("Hannah") who provided Hall with an entrée into Inuit society and served as his guides and guardians on all of Hall's three arctic expeditions (Loomis, 1997). Hall's receptivity to Inuit testimony and acceptance of the validity of Inuit knowledge about their history and their homeland both assured his own survival and the success of his expeditions and presaged (by more than half a century) the recognition of the validity and acuity of Inuit oral knowledge by subsequent Arctic scientists and travelers (Woodman, 1991) (Figure 3).

In the eastern Arctic, it is not until nearly 20 years after Hall that the fledgling discipline of Arctic anthropology emerged as a direct consequence of the first International Polar Year with the arrival of Lucien Turner in Ungava in 1882–1884 and Franz Boas in Baffin Island in 1883–1884 (Loring, 2001a; Cole and Muller-Wille, 1984). Neither Boas nor Turner was formally trained in anthropology. Turner's first interest and abiding passion was ornithology while Boas came to the eastern arctic as a geographer. Boas' trip to Baffin Island was planned and partially sponsored by the German Polar Commission, which was then processing the data gathered from the German IPY station in Cumberland Sound (Barr, 1985). The resulting ethnographic monographs of both Boas (1885) and Turner (1894) were subsequently published by the Smithsonian Institution. These monographs have proved to be the emerging discipline of anthropology's intellectual bedrock for research pertaining to the indigenous peoples of Baffin Island and northern Quebec-Labrador, and these

FIGURE 3. Thule ground-slate whaling harpoon endblade found by Charles Francis Hall's Inuit companion Ebierbing, also known as "Esquimaux Joe." Historically, the role of Inuit guides and companions in the production of Arctic science was rarely acknowledged.SI-10153, Charles Francis Hall collection, NMNH. (S. Loring photograph)

works remain as some of the lasting triumphs of the first IPY accomplishments.

The scientific agendas of the International Polar Years, in 1882–1883, 1932–1933, and 1957–1958 have all been concerned with addressing problems of meteorology, atmospheric science, and high-latitude geophysics. Yet, ironically, arguably the most lasting accomplishments of the American contribution to the First IPY—from the Point Barrow and Ungava stations—were the collections of natural history specimens (e.g., Dunbar, 1983) and ethnographic materials that Smithsonian naturalists acquired around the fringes of their official duties as weather observers for the U.S. Army Signal Service (Murdoch, 1892; Turner, 1894; Nelson, 1899). Surprisingly, the volumes of atmospheric, oceanic, magnetic, and solar observations

gathered at the dozen IPY 1882–1883 stations did not yield the anticipated insights into global climatic and geophysical regimes (Wood and Overland, 2006). Perhaps more significant than the research results in the physical sciences was the establishment of a model for international scientific practice based on coordination and cooperation, and the recognition that the study of high latitudes (at both poles), as with the high seas, was an arena of international consequence and significance.

In company with the earth sciences and natural history, anthropology and archaeology were part of the expanding western economic, social, and intellectual hegemony of the nineteenth century. The construction of scientific knowledge about the world has, for the most part, proceeded following well-defined western notions of logic and scientific explanation as the principle explanatory process for understanding the natural world and the place of human beings therein. Now, in the twenty-first century, with much of the world's cultural and biological diversity documented in at least a preliminary fashion, anthropology faces the challenge of recognizing, articulating, interpreting, and preserving as broad a spectrum of humanity's shared cultural diversity as possible.

At the time of the first IPY, many of the indigenous peoples of North America had been swept from their traditional homelands. Secure in their northern redoubts of ice and stone, the Natives of the eastern Arctic had been spared much of the continental dislocation and genocide waged against indigenous communities in warmer climes. The inroads of European explorers, and later missionaries, whalers, and traders, had not significantly impeded traditional Inuit subsistence practices nor had they intruded far into their spiritual matters and beliefs. Under the leadership of Spencer Baird, the first curator of the U.S. National Museum and the Institution's second secretary (1878–1887), and later, John Wesley Powell (Director of the B.A.E. 1879–1902), Smithsonian anthropology—in the guise of the Bureau of American Ethnology—operated under a paradigm of salvage anthropology in the belief that Native American peoples were fated to gradually decline and disappear. Situated in the National Museum of Natural History (NMNH), Smithsonian anthropology had a decidedly materialist, collections-based orientation that was strongly influenced by biological sciences and Darwin's evolutionary doctrines. Northern native cultures were seen as being somewhat uniquely divorced from history due to their remote geography, and many theorists of the day considered them to be a cultural relic of Ice Age Paleolithic peoples, at the extremity of the scale in terms of human cultural variation.

The Smithsonian Institution's previous interests in the eastern arctic—beginning with biological studies in Hudson's Bay in the early 1860s, and support for the U.S. Eclipse Expedition to northern Labrador in 1860, as well as its close relationship with the Hudson's Bay Company (Lindsay 1993)—provided a basis for a concerted study in the Ungava region. As part of the First International Polar Year 1882–1883, the Smithsonian Institution partnered with the U.S. Signal Corps to establish meteorological and astronomical observatories at Point Barrow, Alaska, at Ft. Conger on Ellesmere Island, and at the Hudson's Bay Company Post at Fort Chimo (Kuujjuaq) in Ungava Bay (Barr, 1985). Sent to man the post at Kuujjuaq was one of the Smithsonian's most experienced northern naturalists, Lucien Turner, who had previously conducted important studies for the Smithsonian in the Aleutian Islands and Western Alaska (Turner, n.d.; 1886; Loring, 2001a).

Lucien Turner (1848–1909) was at the center of a small and talented band of young naturalists that were recruited by the Smithsonian's second secretary, Spencer Baird. An accomplished ornithologist, linguist, and taxidermist Turner reveled in the opportunities for research and collecting in the North American arctic. Baird arranged for Turner to be posted at the Hudson's Bay Company post at the mouth of the Koksoak River in Ungava Bay as a member of an IPY-sponsored meteorological observatory for the U.S. Signal Corps.

Turner's arrival at Fort Chimo in 1882 was something of a surprise for the chief factor there, as news from the outside world only arrived once a year with the annual supply ship. Not easily rebuffed, Turner quickly established his observatory and took up the responsibilities of his post (Figure 4), both those pertaining to his IPY agenda and those dictated by his Smithsonian mandate. Although constrained by the demanding regime of his observation and recording obligations, Turner was able to develop a close rapport with Inuit and Innu families visiting the post, from whom he acquired an extraordinary array of scientific

FIGURE 4. Lucien Turner at his observatory at the Hudson's Bay Company Post at Fort Chimo (near present day Kuujjuak), 1881. (SI-6968)

specimens and ethnological materials (Turner, 1888, 1894; Loring 2001a) (see Figure 5).

Unfortunately, no traces of a personal diary or letters survive from Turner's time at Fort Chimo. Diligent archival research, at the Smithsonian and Hudson's Bay Company archives, provide a few tantalizing clues to his rapport with the northern Natives he came into contact with (Loring, 2001a). However, for the most part these contacts are only dimly referred to as the source for knowledge about the local environment, animals (including mammals, birds, fish, and invertebrates), social relations, and mythology. The contemporary "intellectual landscape" of Innu and Inuit groups—the complex web of oral histories and observational knowledge pertaining to animals, weather, and the land—was largely overlooked and ignored by the IPY-era anthropologists, as their focus, stemming from the natural history approach of their missions, was to categorize and describe the material culture of the people they encountered. Despite being confined by the intellectual framework of the day, Turner's Ungava collections (as well as the collections made by Murdoch and Ray at Point Barrow in 1881–1883) have become a powerful instrument for evoking knowledge, appreciation, and pride in Innu and Inuit heritage. They serve as a point

FIGURE 5. Innu women and children visiting Lucien Turner at Fort Chimo, 1881. Photography was deemed an essential component of the work of the Smithsonian naturalists. As some of the earliest extent photographic images of northern Natives, they remain a prominent legacy of the first IPY. (SI-6977)

of departure for research during this IPY in 2007–2008, as explained below. Within the confines of their training and natural history proclivities, the Smithsonian's Arctic naturalists had a demonstrated sensitivity to some aspects of native knowledge pertaining to the cultural and biological collections they acquired, though for the most part these are brief and anecdotal notations. Today, these notes, but more significantly the objects themselves, are being reexamined and reinterpreted by descendants from the communities from which the objects had come more than a century before.

THE SHIFT IN INTELLECTUAL PARADIGM

The recognition that arctic people have an intellectual, moral, and sociopolitical mandate to participate in and inform northern research marked a fundamental and dramatic shift in the practice of scientific research in the north. It did not arrive until the 1970s and more firmly, until the 1990s (Berger, 1977; Berkes, 1999; Nadasdy, 1999; Stevenson, 1996; Nicholas and Andrews, 1997) (see Figure 6).

With the passage of the Native American Graves Protection and Repatriation Act in 1990 (NAGPRA) and the National Museum of the American Indian Act (in 1996), the intellectual landscape as it pertains to the use and study of the Native American collections has been transformed into a museum anthropology that is more inclusive, more diverse, and contingent on Native participation and expertise (Crowell et al., 2001; Fienup-Riordan, 1996, 2005a, 2005b, 2007; Loring 1996, 2001b; Swidler et al., 1997; Thomas, 2000; Watkins, 2003; 2005; Zimmerman et al., 2003). It is in this context of cooperation and respect that the agendas of Smithsonian anthropology and IPY converge as specific information about objects in the museum collection are not only interpreted by knowledgeable elders and descendant community representatives but also serve as a touchstone or gateway to discussions about traditional ecological and environmental knowledge. It thus seems appropriate, given the degree that human agency is implicated in climatic change, that anthropology for the first time has been formally recognized as a goal of IPY polar science, under its new mandate:

to investigate the cultural, historical, and social processes that shape the resilience and sustainability of circumpolar human societies, and to identify their unique contributions to global cultural diversity and citizenship. (ICSU/WHO 2007:13)

FIGURE 6. "We were *real* red-men in those days!" says Uneam Katshinak, a much revered Innu hunter, as he reminisces about being covered in blood while spearing caribou from a canoe as a boy. The continuity of traditional subsistence practices has anchored northern Native perceptions of their identity and their homeland belying the "vanishing Indian" paradigm of nineteenth-century anthropology. (S. Loring photograph at the Tshikapisk-sponsored rendezvous at Kamestastin, Nitassinan, September 2000)

SEEING AND BELIEVING: CHANGING PERSPECTIVES IN MUSEUM ANTHROPOLOGY

At the Smithsonian Institution, the climate and philosophy of *repatriation* (Loring, 2001b; 2008), coupled with the moral and inspirational presence of the new National Museum of the American Indian (NMAI), has encouraged the emergence of new practices and scholarship.

The new paradigm is evidenced by the significant numbers and variety of northern Native American and Inuit scholars, academics, artisans, and visitors who come to acknowledge, study, and appreciate the collections that were derived from their ancestors a century or more ago (Figure 7). The Smithsonian's anthropology collections acquired during the First International Polar Year in Alaska and Nunavik had languished for almost a century, awaiting an appreciation of their significance—first as objects of art with *The Far North* exhibition at the National Gallery of Art (Collins et al., 1973) and then as symbols of cultural glory and scholarly wonder in a pair of precedent-setting exhibitions, *Inua: Spirit World of the Bering Sea Eskimo* in 1982 and *Crossroads of Continents* in 1988 (Fitzhugh and Kaplan, 1982; Fitzhugh and Crowell, 1988). In opening the Smithsonian's "attic" and in returning to northern Natives an awareness of their material culture patrimony, the role of the museum has been radically transformed. Today, the Smithsonian collections at the NMNH and the NMAI form the largest holding of material culture pertaining to the heritage and history of North America's indigenous peoples. With the passage of time and the miracle of conservation, these objects have undergone an extraordinary transformation from natural history specimens and anthropological curiosities to become the foundation stones for contemporary community identity and heritage (Figure 8). The challenge of the next century is to accommodate this transformation and incorporate new perspectives and knowledge.

The future of anthropology in the museum will encourage—and necessitate—new ways of thinking about the past that would require museum anthropologists and archaeologists surrender—or negotiate—their prerogative to interpret the past. Even more important, it is incumbent upon museum professionals to learn new ways of listening, new ways of recognizing the legitimacy of other voices, and other ways of knowing and accepting oral tradition as a valid interpretive tool (Tonkin, 1992). This sea change in museum anthropology and archaeology is inherent in the programs and initiatives that Smithsonian anthropology is conducting during the time of IPY 2007–2008. A joint NMNH–NMAI exhibition project is bringing more than 500 Native Alaskan artifacts collected around the time of the First IPY to Anchorage, Alaska. The exhibit relies heavily on curatorial input from teams of Native Alaskan consultants affirming the legitimacy of their perspective, knowledge, and link to their legacy and heritage.

AN ENDANGERED PERSPECTIVE ON THE PAST

With the passing of the *Inumariit*, the knowledgeable Inuit who lived in the country in the manner of their ancestors, and the *Tsheniu Mantushiu Kantuat*, the old Innu hunters with special powers, so passes one of the last vestiges of the link to the intellectual landscape of hunting-foraging peoples. To anthropologists and even many indig-

FIGURE 7. Community-orientated collection consultation and outreach has been a core concept of the Smithsonian's Arctic Studies Center since its inception in 1991. Here George Williams, from the village of Mekoryuk on Nunivak Island, Alaska, points out construction details of a model kayak that had been collected by Henry B. Collins in 1927. Williams was part of a delegation of Nunivak elders and educators who visited the Smithsonian in March 1996. (S. Loring photograph)

FIGURE 8. A drawing of the so-called magic doll collected by Lucien Turner in 1881 from Labrador Inuit visiting the Hudson's Bay Company Post at Ft. Chimo (Kuujjuak) in Nunavik. Such unique specimens eloquently attest to the continuity of shamanistic practices in country-settings beyond the purview of missionaries and traders. Transformed into museum specimens such objects still retain a tremendous potency to inspire and inform descendant community members of the people from whom they had been acquired. (Fig. 22 in Turner 1894, Smithsonian catalog number ET982, NMNH)

enous people themselves, it becomes increasingly difficult to grasp the richness and complexity of the hunters' worlds as discerned through artifacts and museum exhibits. The insights and wisdom derived from centuries of intimate knowledge and experience on the land now exists as a much impoverished and fragmentary corpus. In Labrador, the 1918 influenza pandemic devastated Inuit communities and savaged Innu camps, killing off a generation of story-

tellers and tribal elders and often leaving camps where only children and dogs survived. Soon, much of what remains of this specialized knowledge will only reside in libraries, museum collections, and in the clues that archaeologists might deduce. However, there is yet a great potential for the practice of archaeology in the north to be informed by the knowledge and perceptions of elders, the last people to be born in snow houses and tents and to have spent much of their lives as subsistence hunters and seamstresses. The sense of urgency is palpable, as the stock of elders' knowledge and perceptions is not renewable and will not be with us much longer. Subsistence strategies are being replaced by the market economy; communal social relations predicated on reciprocity and kinship are subordinated by government mandates and initiatives. The problem can be framed in a global perspective of diminishing ecological, biological, and cultural diversity. All of which begs the question: How important are "old ways" and "traditional subsistence practices" in the modern world?

In Labrador, as elsewhere in the north, today's Innu and Inuit youth are village-dwellers. Born in hospitals and brought up in isolated rural towns, northern young people have few opportunities to acquire country experiences and knowledge. There is a huge discrepancy between the past as experienced by their grandparents and the present. However well-meaning Canadian government policies may have been in advancing schooling, health care, and old-age pensions, the results have often been disastrous (Samson, 2003; Shkilnyk, 1985). Suicide rates in Labrador Innu communities are the highest recorded in the world and substance abuse is rampant (Samson et al., 1999). Fueled by chronic unemployment and inappropriate educational development, the impoverishment of village life—devoid of country values and skills with its concomitant package of social, health and economic woes—is striking in comparison to ethnohistorical accounts which invariably describe the Innu as arrogant, self-sufficient, "tiresomely" independent, and proud (Cabot, 1920; Cooke, 1979).

KNOWLEDGE REPATRIATION AND ARCHAEOLOGY

In this situation, Smithsonian cultural research in the north becomes a component in the communities' response to the current heritage crisis and social dissolution. For the past decade, in close collaboration with Native elected officials, community leaders, and teachers, the Arctic Studies Center has pioneered community archaeology programs in Labrador with Inuit and Innu communities

(Loring, 1998; Loring and Rosenmeier, 2005). These programs have sought to develop archaeological field-schools that would provide Native youth with opportunities to experience life in the country, acquire new job skills, and foster self-esteem and pride in oneself and one's heritage. This type of enterprise, generally called "community archaeology," especially as it is practiced in the north, is rooted in applied socially conscious advocacy anthropology. In addition to addressing the special scholarly questions that archaeologists commonly pose, community archaeology seeks additional goals that strive to empower and engage communities in the recognition and construction of their own heritage. In the north in general, and in Labrador specifically, community archaeology initiatives celebrate

traditional values and share a research focus and practice that is responsible for creating and returning knowledge to communities (Lyons, 2007; Nicholas, 2006; Nicholas and Andrews, 1997), in a sense coming full circle since the years of the first IPY.

Perhaps the most important facet of community archaeology as practiced in Labrador is that it is situated outside the settlements, in the country where the knowledge, wisdom, and experience of elders is relevant and apparent (Figures 9 and 10). Fieldwork based on mutual respect and sharing among families, generations, and visiting researchers honors and encourages indigenous knowledge and different ways of knowing. The practice of community archaeology with the Innu in Nitassinan is culturally

FIGURE 9. No longer the exclusive domain of professional researchers, archaeology in the north has become a cooperative initiative between local community interests and visiting researchers. Here, community activist and former Innu Nation president Daniel Ashini, left, accompanied by Dominique Pokue, survey the ruined shorelines of former Lake Michikamats during an Innu Nation–sponsored archaeological survey of the region in 1995. (S. Loring photograph)

situated experiential education and has an important subsistence component. An awareness of animals—especially caribou—trumps the mechanics of fieldwork: Survey is as much scouting for game as it is searching for the sites where ancestors lived and hunted. The acquisition of game is an integral part of the fieldwork as young people prepare their own trap lines, catch fish, and learn from elders how to prepare food and pay proper respect to animals (Loring, 2001b; 2008). And in contrast to the practice of archaeology in the strictly scientific paradigm, the lessons of community archaeology—sharing resources and interpretations and communal decision making—could be neatly summed as "don't be bossy, don't be greedy." Beyond expanding an awareness and appreciation of indigenous knowledge and values, Smithsonian archaeology today is about being socially responsible, recognizing that the present is connected to the past, and celebrating indigenous heritage and land tenure.

CONCLUSIONS

Around the campfire or next to the tent stove, the conversation about archaeology with Native participants is tumbled together with thoughts of the weather, caribou, and seals; of the places where one went hunting, berry picking, or fishing; and of the old places where ancestors and supernatural creatures once lived. New directions

FIGURE 10. Coming full-circle in the production of knowledge about northern people and their history community archaeology returns knowledge to a local setting. Working with local youth, and informed by knowledgeable elders, such initiatives serve to celebrate and respect the continuity and experiences of Native northern hosts. Here, visiting elders from Makkovik interpret architectural features at the mid-eighteenth-century Labrador Inuit village site at Adlavik (GgBq-1) in 2002. With them is Lena Onalik (right) from Makkovik, the first professional Inuk archaeologist from Nunatsiavut. (Central Coast of Labrador Archaeological Project photo)

in the practice of archaeology in the north recognize the legitimacy of life "in the country." Because of different ways of thinking about the past, explaining the past is a basic operating assumption predicated on respect of the cultures and traditions of the people on who live (or used to live) on the land (Lorde, 1981). This collaborative approach of northern anthropological research, predicated on repatriation, recognition, and respect, suggests that the future of the past is likely to re-imagine the cultural and physical landscape of the Arctic in wholly new ways. With the passing of the last vestiges of humanity's hunting heritage, future generations will need to derive new sources for inspiration. Northern Native involvement with Arctic science might be thought to have begun with the collaboration and insights provided to early explorers and collectors, including those affiliated with the First IPY in 1882–1883. The increased awareness of the value and acuity of native knowledge and perception has radically transformed the social construction of northern science as the interests and concerns of researchers and indigenous residents alike come to share an interest in the ecological and behavioral consequences of life at high latitudes and a concern for understanding both the past and the future.

ACKNOWLEDGMENTS

William Fitzhugh (Smithsonian Institution), Igor Krupnik (Smithsonian Institution), and James Fleming (Colby College) provided helpful comments on an earlier draft.

LITERATURE CITED

Barr, William. 1985. The Expeditions of the First International Polar Year, 1882–1883. *The Arctic Institute of North America, Technical Paper* 29. Calgary, Alberta, Canada: University of Calgary.

Berger, Thomas R. 1977. *Northern Frontier, Northern Homeland: The Report of the Mackenzie Valley Pipeline Inquiry*, 2 vols. Toronto: James Lorimer in Association with Publishing Centre, Supply and Services, Canada.

Berkes, F., 1999. *Sacred Ecology: Traditional Ecological Knowledge and Resource Management*. Philadelphia: Taylor and Francis.

Boas, Franz. 1885. The Eskimo of Baffin Land. *Transactions of the Anthropological Society of Washington* 3:95–102.

Cabot, William Brooks. 1920. *Labrador*. Boston: Small, Maynard & Co.

Cole, Douglas, and Ludger Muller-Wille. 1984. Franz Boas' Expedition to Baffin Island. *Études Inuit Studies*, 8:37–63.

Collins, Henry B., Frederica de Laguna, Edmund Carpenter, and Peter Stone. 1973. *The Far North: 2000 Years of American Eskimo and Indian Art*. Washington, D.C.: National Gallery of Art.

Cooke, Alan. 1979. L'Independence des Naskapis et le caribou. In *Dossier Caribou, Ecologie et Exploitation de Caribou au Québec-*

Labrador, ed. Francois Trudel and Jean Hunt, pp. 99–104. *Recherches Amérindiennes au Québec 9*.

Crowell, Aron, Amy Steffian, and Gordon Pullar, eds. 2001. *Looking Both Ways: Heritage and Identity of the Alutiiq People*. Fairbanks: University of Alaska Press.

Dunbar, M. J. 1983. A Unique International Polar Year Contribution: Lucien Turner, Capelin, and Climatic Change. *Arctic*, 36(2):204–205.

Fienup-Riordan, Ann. 1996. *Agayuliyararput: Kegginaqut, Kangiit-Ilu "Our Way of Making Prayer": Yup'ik Masks and the Stories They Tell*. Seattle: University of Washington Press.

———. 2005a. *Yup'ik Elders at the Ethnologisches Museum Berlin: Fieldwork Turned on Its Head*. Seattle: University of Washington Press.

———. 2005b *Ciuliamta Akluit—Things of Our Ancestors*. Seattle: University of Washington Press.

———. 2007 *Yuungnaqpiallerput: The Way We Genuinely Live*. Seattle: University of Washington Press.

Fitzhugh, William, and Aron Crowell, eds. 1988. *Crossroads of Continents: Cultures of Siberia and Alaska*. Washington, D.C.: Smithsonian Institution Press.

Fitzhugh, William, and Susan Kaplan, eds. 1982. *Inua: Spirit World of the Bering Sea Eskimo*. Washington, D.C.: Smithsonian Institution Press.

Grant, Shelia. 1998. Arctic Wilderness—and Other Mythologies. *Journal of Canadian Studies* 33(2):27–42.

Hall, Charles Francis, 1864. *Life with the Esquimaux*, 2 vols. London: Sampson, Low, Son, and Marston.

ICSU (International Council for Science)/WHO Joint Committee for IPY 2007–2008. 2007. *The Scope of Science for the International Polar Year, 2007–2008*. Geneva: World Meteorological Association. http://216.70.123.96/images/uploads/lr*polarbrochurescientific_in.pdf (accessed 13 August 2007).

Lindsay, Debra. 1993. *Science in the Subarctic: Trappers, Traders and the Smithsonian Institution*. Washington, D.C.: Smithsonian Institution Press.

Loomis, Chauncey. 1972. *Weird and Tragic Shores: The Story of Charles Francis Hall, Explorer*. London: Macmillan.

———. 1977. "The Arctic Sublime." In *Nature and the Victorian Imagination*, ed. U. C. Knoepflmacher and G. B. Tennyson, pp. 95–112. Berkeley: University of California Press.

———. 1986. Arctic and Orphic. *London Review of Books*, 8(1):12–13.

———. 1997. "Ebierbing." In *Lobsticks and Stone Cairns: Human Landmarks in the Arctic*, ed. Richard C. Davis, pp. 52–54. Calgary, Alberta, Canada: University of Calgary Press.

Lorde, A. 1981. "The Master's Tools Will Never Dismantle the Master's House." In *This Bridge Called My Back: Radical Writings by Women of Color*, ed. C. B. Cherríe Moraga and G. Anzaldúa, pp. 98–101. New York: Kitchen Table, Women of Color Press.

Loring, Stephen. 1996. Community Anthropology at the Smithsonian. American Anthropological Association. *Anthropology Newsletter*, October: 23–24.

———. 1998. "Stubborn Independence: An Essay on the Innu and Archaeology." In *Bringing Back the Past, Historical Perspectives on Canadian Archaeology*, ed. Pamela Jane Smith and Donald Mitchell, pp. 259–276. Mercury Series Archaeological Survey of Canada Paper 158. Hull, Quebec: Canadian Museum of Civilization.

———. 2001a. "Introduction to Lucien M. Turner and the Beginnings of Smithsonian Anthropology in the North." In *Ethnology of the Ungava District, Hudson Bay Territory* by Lucien Turner, pp. vii–xxxii. Washington, D.C.: Smithsonian Institution Press.

———. 2001b. "Repatriation and Community Anthropology: The Smithsonian Institution's Arctic Studies Center." In *The Future of* the Past: Archaeologists, Native Americans, and Repatriation, ed. Tamara Bray, pp. 185–200. New York: Garland.

———. 2008. "The Wind Blows Everything Off the Ground: New Provisions and New Directions in Archaeological Research in the North." In Opening Archaeology: the Impact of Repatriation on the Discipline, ed. Thomas Killion, pp. 181–194. Santa Fe, N.Mex.: School of American Research.

Loring, Stephen, and Leah Rosenmeier, eds. 2005. Angutiup ânguanga/ Anguti's Amulet. Truro, Nova Scotia: Eastern Woodland Publishing, Milbrook First Nation.

Lyons, Natasha. 2007. "Quliaq tohongniaq tuunga" (Making Histories): Towards a Critical Inuvialuit Archaeology in the Canadian Western Arctic. Ph.D. diss., Department of Anthropology, University of Calgary.

McGhee, Robert. 2007. The Last Imaginary Place: A Human History of the Arctic World. Chicago: University of Chicago Press.

Murdoch, John. 1892. Ethnological Results of the Point Barrow Expedition. Ninth Annual Report of the Bureau of American Ethnology for the Years 1887–1888, pp. 19–441. Washington, D.C.: Government Printing Office.

Nadasdy, Paul. 1999. Politics of TEK: Power and the "Integration" of Knowledge. Arctic Anthropology, 36(1–2):1–18.

Nicholas, George. 2006. Decolonizing the Archaeological Landscape: The Practice and Politics of Archaeology in British Columbia. American Indian Quarterly, 30(3–4):350–380.

Nicholas, G., and T. D. Andrews, eds. 1997. At a Crossroads: Archaeology and First People in Canada. Burnaby, British Columbia, Canada: Simon Fraser University Archaeology Press.

Nelson, Edward William. 1899. The Eskimo about Bering Strait. Eighteenth Annual Report of the Bureau of American Ethnology for the Years 1896–1897, pp. 3–518. Washington, D.C.: Government Printing Office.

Parry, William Edward. 1821. Journal of a voyage for the discovery of a North-West Passage from the Atlantic to the Pacific; performed in the years 1819–20, in His Majesty's Ships Hecla and Griper with an appendix, containing the scientific and other observations. London: John Murray.

———. 1824. Journal of a second voyage for the discovery of a North-West Passage from the Atlantic to the Pacific; performed in the years 1821–22–23, in His Majesty's Ships Fury and Hecla, under the orders of Captain William Edward Parry. London: John Murray.

Rasmussen, Knud. 1929. Intellectual Culture of the Iglulik Eskimos. Report of the Fifth Thule Expedition, 1921–24, Volume 7(1). Copenhagen: Nordisk.

Rink, Hinrich. 1875. Tales and Traditions of the Eskimo: With a Sketch of Their Habits, Religion, Language and Other Peculiarities, ed. Robert Brown. Edinburgh: W. Blackwood and Sons.

Samson, Colin. 2003. A Way of Life That Does Not Exist. London: Verso.

Samson, Colin, James Wilson, and Jonathan Mazower. 1999. Canada's Tibet: The Killing of the Innu. London: Survival International.

Shkilnyk, Anastasia M. 1985. A Poison Stronger Than Love: The Destruction of an Ojibwa Community. New Haven, Conn.: Yale University Press.

Stevenson, M. G. 1996. Indigenous Knowledge in Environmental Assessment. Arctic, 49(3):278–291.

Swidler, Nina, Kurt Dongoske, Roger Anyon, and Alan Downer, eds. 1997. Native Americans and Archaeologists: Stepping Stones to Common Ground. Walnut Creek, Calif.: AltaMira Press.

Thomas, David H. 2000. Skull Wars: Kennewick Man, Archaeology, and the Battle for Native American Identity. New York: Basic Books.

Tonkin, E. 1992. Narrating Our Pasts: The Social Construction of Oral History. Cambridge, U.K.: Cambridge University Press.

Turner, Lucien M. n.d. Descriptive Catalogue of Ethnological Specimens Collected by Lucien M. Turner in Alaska. Lucien M. Turner papers, Bureau of American Ethnology collection, National Anthropological Archives, National Museum of Natural History, Smithsonian Institution, Washington, D.C.

———. 1886. Contributions to the Natural History of Alaska. Washington, D.C.: Government Printing Office.

———. 1888. On the Indians and Eskimos of the Ungava District, Labrador. Proceedings and Transactions of the Royal Society of Canada for the Year 1887, sect. II, vol. 5:99–119.

———. 1894. Ethnology of the Ungava District, Hudson Bay Territory. Eleventh Annual Report of the Bureau of American Ethnology for the Years 1889–1890, pp. 159–350. Washington, D.C.: Government Printing Office.

Watkins, Joe 2003. Archaeological Ethics and American Indians. In Ethical Issues in Archaeology, ed. Larry Zimmerman, Karen D. Vitelli, and Julie Hollowell-Zimmer, pp. 129–142. Walnut Creek, Calif.: AltaMira Press.

———. 2005. Through Wary Eyes: Indigenous Perspectives on Archaeology. Annual Review of Anthropology, 34:429–449.

Wood, Kevin R., and James E. Overland. 2006. Climate Lessons from the First International Polar Year. Bulletin of the American Meteorological Society, 86(12):1685–1697.

Woodman, David. 1991. Unraveling the Franklin Mystery: Inuit Testimony. Montreal: McGill-Queen's.

Zimmerman, Larry J., Karen D. Vitelli, and Julie Hollowell-Zimmer, eds. 2003. Ethical Issues in Archaeology. Walnut Creek, Calif.: AltaMira Press.

"The Way We See It Coming": Building the Legacy of Indigenous Observations in IPY 2007–2008

Igor Krupnik

ABSTRACT. All early International Polar Year/International Geophysical Year (IPY/IGY) initiatives were primarily geophysical programs and were exemplary products of the long-established paradigm of "polar science." Under that paradigm, scholarly data to be used in academic publications were to be collected by professional scientists and/or by specially trained observers. Arctic indigenous residents had hardly any documented voice in the early IPY/IGY ventures, except by serving as "subjects" for museum collecting or while working as dog-drivers, guides, and unskilled assistants to research expeditions. Natural scientists with strong interest in Native cultures were the first to break that pattern and to seek polar residents as a valuable source of expertise on the Arctic environment. The Smithsonian has a distinguished tradition in working with indigenous experts and documenting their knowledge, from the days of the First IPY 1882–1883 to the most recent projects on indigenous observations on Arctic climate change. The paper explores the unique role of IPY 2007–2008 and of recent efforts focused on the documentation of indigenous knowledge of Arctic environment and climate change, by using the experience of one IPY project, SIKU—Sea Ice Knowledge and Use—and research collaboration with local Yupik Eskimo experts from St. Lawrence Island, Alaska.

INTRODUCTION

This paper explores the emerging links among Arctic people's ecological knowledge, climate change research, and cultural (or "social science") studies in the polar regions. Residents of the Arctic are no strangers to today's debates about climate change and global warming (Kusugak, 2002; Watt-Cloutier, 2005). Their knowledge on the Arctic environment is being increasingly sought as a source of valuable data for documenting and modeling Arctic climate change (ACIA, 2005). Still, such a rapprochement is not yet an established practice, as many scientists still view Arctic people's perspectives on climate change as merely "anecdotal evidence."

Social science's interest in Arctic people's observations of climate change is, similarly, a rather recent phenomenon, barely 10 years old (McDonald et al., 1997). Of course, Arctic residents have been observing changes and reflecting upon fluctuations in their environment since time immemorial. Their knowledge, however, has been "archived" within northern communities and was transmitted in indigenous languages via elders' stories, personal observations,

Igor Krupnik, Department of Anthropology, National Museum of Natural History, Smithsonian Institution, P.O. Box 37012, MRC 112, Washington, DC 20013-7012, USA (krupniki@si.edu). Accepted 9 May 2008.

and information shared among hunters. As scientists became increasingly attentive to indigenous perspectives on Arctic climate change, several barriers to productive dialog and communication had to be overcome (see discussion in Krupnik, 2002; Laidler, 2006; Oakes and Riewe, 2006). Over the past decade, this new emerging collaboration produced numerous papers, volumes, collections, documentaries, interactive CD-ROMs, and museum exhibits (Figure 1; Ford et al., 2007; Herlander and Mustonen, 2004; Gearheard et al., 2006; Huntington and Fox, 2005; Krupnik and Jolly, 2002; Laidler, 2006; Laidler and Elee, 2006; Oakes and Riewe, 2006).

One of the key tasks of the International Polar Year (IPY) 2007–2008, articulated in its many documents, is to explore how data generated by polar residents can be matched with the observations and models used by polar scientists (Allison et al., 2007:51–52; International Council for Science, 2004:18). For the fist time, the IPY science program includes a special research theme with a goal

to investigate the cultural, historical, and social processes that shape the sustainability of circumpolar human societies, and to identify their unique contributions to global cultural diversity and citizenship. (International Council for Science, 2004:15; Krupnik et al., 2005:91–92)

The new IPY includes scores of science projects focused on the documentation of indigenous environmental knowledge and observations of climate change (Hovelsrud and Krupnik, 2006:344–345; Krupnik, 2007); it serves as an important driver to the growing partnership between Arctic residents and polar researchers. Many Arctic people also see IPY 2007–2008 as the first international science venture to which they have been invited and one in which

FIGURE 1. New public face of polar science, the exhibit *Arctic: A Friend Acting Strangely* at the National Museum of Natural History, 2006. (Photograph by Chip Clark, NMNH)

their environmental expertise is valued and promoted. This growing partnership in the documentation of polar residents' observations of climate change is widely viewed as a cutting edge of today's Arctic social and cultural research.

SOCIAL SCIENCES IN EARLIER INTERNATIONAL POLAR YEARS

All previous International Polar Year initiatives in 1882–1883, 1932–1933, and, particularly, the International Geophysical Year (IGY) in 1957–1958, were framed primarily, if not exclusively, as geophysical programs focused on meteorology, atmospheric and geomagnetic research, and later, glaciology, geology, space studies, oceanography, and sea ice circulation studies (Fleming and Seitchek, 2009, this volume). We have hardly any record of Arctic residents' involvement in previous IPYs, other than serving as guides, manual laborers, unskilled assistants, or being prospects for ethnographic collecting. None of these earlier IPY ventures organized primarily by meteorologists, geophysicists, and oceanographers considered the documentation of indigenous perspectives on Arctic environment a valid topic for scholarly research.

Nevertheless, social scientists and polar residents can justly claim a solid IPY legacy of their own that goes back to the first IPY of 1882–1883. Half of the 12 IPY-1 observational stations and four "auxiliary" missions that operated in the Arctic produced substantial, often extensive, accounts on local populations and their cultures (Barr, 1985; Krupnik et al., 2005:89–90). Four seminal ethnographic monographs, including three on Arctic indigenous people, were published as direct outcomes of the First IPY (Boas, 1888; Murdoch 1892; Turner 1894), in addition to several chapters in expedition reports, scores of scholarly articles, and popular accounts (Barr 1985; Burch, 2009, this volume). Some of these contributions—like those by Murdoch and Ray on Barrow; Tromholt (1885) on Kautokeino, Norway; and Bunge (1895) on the Lena River Delta—were illustrated by photographs and drawings of local communities, people, and cultural landscapes (Wood and Overland, 2007). Today, such records are treasures to museum curators, anthropologists, and historians, but even more so to local communities as resources to their heritage education programs (Crowell, 2009, this volume; Jensen, 2005).

Perhaps the most influential social science contribution to IPY-1 was the research of Franz Boas, a German-born physicist and, later, the founding figure of American anthropology. In 1883, Boas volunteered to do a post-doc study in human geography among the Canadian Inuit as a follow-up to the German IPY-1 observation mission on Baffin Island (Cole and Müller-Wille, 1984; Müller-Wille, 1998). Boas' research among the Baffin Island Inuit in 1883–1884 introduced to polar science much of what constitutes today the core of the "human agenda" of IPY 2007–2008: the study of indigenous knowledge, adaptation, culture change, and Arctic people's views on the environment. There is no wonder that Boas' monograph on the Central Inuit of Arctic Canada (1888/1964), as well as books by Murdoch on the people of Barrow (1892/1988) and by Turner on the Inuit and Innu of Ungava Bay (1894/2001), remain, perhaps, the most widely cited publications of the entire IPY-1 program. It is also no accident that these IPY-1 monographs on Arctic indigenous people and their cultures were published by the Smithsonian Institution. They also remain the only science writings from the First IPY that were ever read and used by Arctic indigenous people, prior to the recent "rediscovery" by the Norwegian Sámi of Sophus Tromholt's photographs of Kautokeino in 1882–1883.[1]

SMITHSONIAN AT THE POLES

The Smithsonian Institution has a distinguished record of pioneering cultural research and collecting in the Arctic (see Fitzhugh 2002; 2009, this volume). By the time of the first IPY 1882–1883, the Smithsonian had established productive partnerships with many federal agencies, private parties, and individual explorers (Fitzhugh, 1988b; Loring 2001). The connection to the Signal Office of the War Department was essential to the Smithsonian involvement in the first IPY, since the Office was put in charge of the preparation for two U.S. IPY expeditions to Barrow and Lady Franklin Bay in 1881. Dr. Spencer Baird, then Smithsonian Secretary, immediately seized the opportunity to advance the foremost role of the institution in national polar research and to expand its Arctic collections. The Smithsonian was instrumental in selecting natural scientists for both U.S. missions and in training them in conducting observations and collecting specimens.[2] According to the Secretary's Annual Reports for 1883 and 1884, the Smithsonian assumed responsibility for the natural history component of both U.S. IPY missions and of their collections (Baird 1885a:15–16; 1885b:15). Baird's relationship with John Murdoch, one of two natural scientists of the Point Barrow IPY team, is very well documented (Fitzhugh 1988a, xiv–xxix; Murdoch 1892:19–20). Lucien Turner's one-man mission to Ungava

Bay was primarily a Smithsonian (i.e., Baird's) initiative (Barr, 1985:204; Loring, 2001:xv).

To the returning IPY missions, the Smithsonian Institution offered its facilities, libraries, and the expertise of its curators for processing the records and specimens; for these and other efforts the Institution was designated to receive all of the collections brought from the north. The Barrow natural history collections were monumental, as were Turner's from Labrador.[3] The ethnological portion of the Barrow collection (1,189 specimens upon the original count[4]—see Crowell, 2009, this volume) is the second largest in the National Museum of Natural History (NMNH) Alaska ethnology collections, and Turner's IPY collection (530 objects) is the second largest among the ethnology acquisitions from Canada. Even most of the ill-fated Greely mission's natural history specimens, including some 100 ethnological objects (Greely, 1888:301–317) and personal memorabilia, ended up in the Smithsonian collections (Neighbors, 2005). All three U.S. IPY missions also produced several dozen photographs that are among the earliest from their respective areas.[5]

By the very scope of their assignments, early IPY scientists combined instrumental meteorological observations with natural history research and collecting; hence, the changes in local climate and natural environment may have been on their minds as well. We know that Boas was deeply interested in Inuit perspectives on their environment. He had been systematically documenting Inuit knowledge of sea ice, snow, weather, place-names, and navigation across the snow/ice covered terrain as part of his research program (Cole and Müller-Wille, 1984:51–53), very much like many IPY scientists are doing today.

In 1912, 30 years after Murdoch and Turner, Smithsonian anthropologist Riley Moore visited St. Lawrence Island, Alaska, and worked with a young hunter named Paul Silook (Figure 2). Silook assisted Moore in translating elders' stories about the famine of 1878–1879 that killed hundreds of island residents (Moore, 1923:356–358). Some scientists believe that the famine was caused by extraordinary sea ice and weather conditions that disrupted the islanders' hunting cycle (Crowell and Oozevaseuk, 2006). In the late 1920s, another Smithsonian scientist, Henry Collins, partnered with Silook in search for local knowledge about the early history of island's population. Collins also asked Silook to maintain a personal diary with the records of weather conditions; this diary has been preserved at the Smithsonian National Anthropological Archives (Jolles, 1995). Silook may have told Collins about the catastrophic storms that destroyed his native village of Gambell in 1913 and other extraordinary events, which he

FIGURE 2. Paul Silook, *Siluk* (1892–1946), worked with many scientists who came to his home village of Gambell over more than three decades, between 1912 and 1949. (Photograph by Riley D. Moore, 1912, Smithsonian Institution. NAA, Neg. # SI 2000-693)

described to other scholars in later years (Krupnik et al., 2002:161–163).

CONVERTING LOCAL OBSERVATIONS INTO "IPY SCIENCE"

If partnership between Arctic residents and polar researchers in IPY 2007–2008 is to bring tangible benefits to both sides, each party has to understand how the other observational system works. This implies certain steps needed to make the two systems compatible or, at least, open to data exchange. Local knowledge, very much like science, is based upon long-term observation and monitoring of dozens of environmental parameters, in other words, upon multifaceted data collection. By and large, indigenous experts follow many of the same analytical steps, though in their specific ways (Berkes 1999:9–12). Much like scientists, local hunters exchange individual observations and convert them into a shared body of data. They analyze the signals of change and seek explanations to the phenomena they observe (Krupnik 2002; Huntington et al., 2004).

When the first projects in the documentation of indigenous observations of Arctic climate change were started, scientists were literally overwhelmed by the sheer wealth of local records. As a result, much of the early work on indigenous observations, up to 2003–2005, focused on the mere documentation of various evidence of change coming from different areas.[6] Next, scientists tried to apply certain tools, such as typologies, maps, and matrix tables arranged by ecosystem component, to compare reports from different areas (McDonald et al., 1997:46–47; Krupnik and Jolly, 2002; Huntington and Fox, 2005). These first applications of scientific tools illustrated that Arctic residents observe a consistent pattern of change and that they interpret the phenomena they observe in a comprehensive, integrated manner. It also became clear that local people have documented rapid change in the Arctic environment in a profound and unequivocal way.

The next step in scientists' approach to indigenous records is to look for cases and areas where indigenous and scientific data *disagree* and offer differing, often conflicting interpretations (Huntington et al., 2004; Krupnik and Ray, 2007; Norton, 2002). This approach reveals certain features of indigenous versus scientific observation processes, such as differences in scaling, in the use of prime indicators, and in causes and linkages cited as explanations in two knowledge systems. It also offers a much more systemic vision that goes beyond a popular dichotomy that contrasts *local* or *traditional ecological knowledge* (TEK) and the scientific knowledge. Under such vision, the former is usually labeled "intuitive, holistic, consensual, and qualitative," whereas the latter is perceived as analytical, quantitative, and compartmentalized (Bielawski, 1992; Krupnik, 2002:184). While these labels contain some truth, Native experts have demonstrated repeatedly that they can effectively operate with both types of records and that they often match them more skillfully than scientists do (Aporta and Higgs, 2005; Bogoslovskaya, 2003; Krupnik and Ray, 2007; Noongwook et al., 2007).

Scientists commonly argue that Arctic people's records of climate change would be a valuable contribution to IPY 2007–2008 (Allison et al., 2007). Still, such accommodation requires substantial mutual adjustment of observa-tional and analytical practices. Scientists have to accept that data generated by local observers are crucial to cover certain gaps in instrumental or satellite records, despite some reservations with regard to how local observations are collected and transmitted. From their side, Native experts participating in joint projects have to acknowledge certain standards of science data collection, like consistency, transparency, and independent verification. Here the gap is indeed serious, since indigenous observations are mostly non-numerical, are freely and widely shared within the community, and are rarely if ever reported in writing (Bates, 2007:89–91). Because of these and other factors, indigenous records can rarely be tested by scientists' analytical procedures, like long-term series, statistical averaging, correlation, and trend verification, among others.

Also, indigenous observers have their specific "terms of references" when assessing the validity of their data, such as individual life experience, community-based memory, or verification by elders or individual experts (Noongwook et al., 2007:48; Gearheard et al., 2006). Nevertheless, the sheer volume of data to be generated by many participatory projects in IPY 2007–2008 has already triggered efforts to develop procedures and standards for local observations and for management of indigenous records.[7]

SIKU—SEA ICE KNOWLEDGE AND USE

The experience of one such project illustrates what scientists can learn from local experts and how indigenous knowledge may advance IPY science. "Sea Ice Knowledge and Use: Assessing Arctic Environmental and Social Change" (SIKU, IPY #166) is an IPY project aimed at the documentation of indigenous observations of Arctic climate change, with its focus on sea ice and the use of ice-covered habitats by polar residents. The project's acronym SIKU is also the most common word for sea ice (*siku*) in all Eskimo languages, from Bering Strait to Greenland. As a collaborative initiative, SIKU relies on partnership among anthropologists, geographers, and marine and ice scientists from the United States, Canada, Russia, Greenland, and France, and indigenous communities in Alaska, Canada, Greenland, and Russian Chukotka. SIKU is organized as a consortium of several research initiatives supported by funds from various national agencies. The project was started in winter 2006–2007 and it will continue through 2008 and 2009. The Alaska-Chukotka portion of SIKU has its three hubs at the Smithsonian Arctic Studies Center (managed by Igor Krupnik), the Russian Institute of Cultural and Natural Heritage in Moscow (Lyudmila Bogoslovskaya), and the University of Alaska, Fairbanks (Hajo Eicken). The Canadian portion of SIKU is called Inuit Sea Ice Use and Occupancy Project (ISIUOP); it is co-ordinated by Claudio Aporta and Gita Laidler at Carleton University, Ottawa (see http://gcrc.carleton.ca/isiuop).

Research under the SIKU-Alaska and SIKU-Chukotka program takes place in several local communities, such as Gambell, Shaktoolik, Wales, Shishmaref, Barrow, Tununak, Uelen, Lavrentiya, Sireniki, and so on (Figure 3). It includes daily ice and weather observations, collections of Native terms for sea ice and weather phenomena, docu-mentation of ecological knowledge related to sea ice and ice use from elders and hunters, and searches for historical records of ice and climate conditions (see http://www.ipy .org/index.php?ipy/detail/sea_ice_knowledge_and_use/).

This paper examines the contribution of one of such lo-cal SIKU observers, Leonard Apangalook Sr., a hunter and community leader from the Yupik village of Gambell on St. Lawrence Island, Alaska. Apangalook, 69, is a nephew of Paul Silook and he continues an almost 100-year tra-dition of his family's collaboration with Smithsonian scientists (Figure 4). Since spring 2006, Apangalook has produced daily logs on sea ice, weather, and local subsis-tence activities in his native community of Gambell. His personal contribution to the IPY 2007–2008 now covers two full "ice years," 2006–2007 and 2007–2008, and will hopefully extend into 2008–2009.

St. Lawrence Island residents' knowledge of sea ice has been extensively documented in recent years via sev-eral collaborative projects with two local Yupik communi-ties of Gambell and Savoonga (Huntington, 2000; Jolles,

FIGURE 3. The Yupik village of Gambell on St. Lawrence Island, Alaska, is one of the key research "sites" for the SIKU project. (Photo, Igor Krupnik, February 2008)

FIGURE 4. Leonard Apangalook Sr., SIKU participant and local observer in the village of Gambell, St. Lawrence Island (courtesy of Leonard Apangalook).

1995; 2003; Krupnik, 2000; 2002; Krupnik and Ray, 2007; Metcalf and Krupnik, 2003; Noongwook et al., 2007; Oozeva et al., 2004). The island people have long voiced concerns about shifts in the local environment they observed and about the growing impact of climate change upon their economy and way of living. Apangalook's observations help convert these statements into a written record open to scientific scrutiny and analysis.

New Patterns of Fall Ice Formation

St. Lawrence Islanders have a highly nuanced vision on how the new sea ice is being formed in their area or, rather, how it *used to be* formed in the old days. Their native Yupik language has more than 20 terms for various types of young ice and freezing conditions. Winds and currents would drive small chunks of floating ice (*kulusiit*) from the north in October or even in late September (Oozeva et al., 2004:133–134). Most would melt or would be washed ashore; but some would freeze into the locally formed slush or frazil ice. Around the time the first local ice is established (in late October or early November), the prevailing winds would shift direction, from primarily southerly to northerly, followed by a drop in daily temperatures. Depending upon year-to-year variability, but usually by late November, the thick Arctic ice pack, *sikupik*, would arrive from the Chukchi Sea, often smashing the young locally formed ice. Crashing, breaking, and refreezing would continue through December, until a more solid winter ice was formed to last until spring (Oozeva et al., 2004:136–137).

Since the 1980s, hunters started to observe changes to this pattern, which had until then been seen as normal. First, drifting ice floes, *kulusiit*, were late to arrive, often by a full month, and by the late 1990s, they have stopped coming altogether. The new ice is now being formed entirely out of local frozen slush or frazil ice, via its thickening, consolidation, repeated break-ups, and refreezing. Then the main pack ice ceased to arrive until January or even February; and in the last few years it did not arrive at all. Even when the pack ice finally comes from the north, it is not a solid thick ice, *sikupik*, but rather thin new ice that was formed further to the north. Because of this new set of dynamics, the onset of winter ice conditions on St. Lawrence Island is now delayed by six to eight weeks, that is, until late December or even January.[8]

Apangalook's observations during two IPY winters of 2006–2007 and 2007–2008 help document this new pattern in great detail. In addition, his daily records may be matched with the logbooks of early teachers from his village of Gambell that covered three subsequent winters of 1898–1899, 1899–1900, and 1900–1901 (Doty, 1900:224–256; Lerrigo, 1901:114–132; 1902:97–123; see Oozeva et al., 2004:168–191). According to Apangalook's logs, no drifting ice floes were seen in winter 2006–2007 and none in the month of November 2007. Although in 2007–2008 the formation of slush ice started more than two weeks earlier than in 2006–2007, the ice was quickly broken up by a warming spell, so that on 22 November 2007, Apangalook reported: "Thanksgiving Day with no ice in the ocean; normally [we] would have ice and hunt walrus on Thanksgiving Day but not anymore." In both 2006 and 2007, the temperature dropped solidly below freezing on the first week of December—and that was two to four weeks later than a century ago. The change of wind regime, from southerly to predominately northerly winds, also occurred in early December, that is, two to four weeks later than in 1898–1901 (Oozeva et al., 2004:185). Due to shift in wind and temperature, local slush ice solidified rapidly. On 16 December 2006, Apangalook reported that "when locally formed ice gets thick and encompasses the entire Bering Sea around our island, our elders used to say that we have a winter that is locally formed" (Figure 5).

Winter Weather and Ice Regimes

Apangalook's daily logs substantiate statements of other St. Lawrence hunters about the profound change in winter weather and ice regime over the past decades (cf. Oozeva et al., 2004; Noongwook et al., 2007). With the

FIGURE 5. The new ice is being formed from the pieces of floating icebergs and newly formed young ice. There are terms for every single piece of ice in this picture and many more in the local language ("Watching Ice and Weather Our Way," 2004, p. 114; original photo by Chester Noongwook, 2000).

FIGURE 7. Hunters rarely venture onto young unstable ice and they usually prefer to be accompanied by an experienced senior person. (Photo, Hiroko Ikuta, 2006)

absence of solid pack ice, people have to adapt to a far less stable local new ice that can be easily broken by heavy winds, storms, and even strong currents (Figure 6). According to the elders, this ice is "no good," as it is very dangerous for walking and winter hunting on foot or with skin boats being dragged over it, as used to be a common practice in the "old days" (Oozeva et al., 2004:137–138, 142–143, 163–166). As a result, few hunters dare to go hunting on ice in front of the village in wintertime (Figure 7). Instead,

they have to rely upon shooting the animals from the shore or from ice pressure ridges (Figure 8) or upon hunting in boats in the dense floating ice, a technique that is now the norm in Gambell during winter months (Figure 9). In the early teachers' era of 100 years ago, boat hunting for walruses did not start in Gambell until early or even late March (Oozeva et al., 2004:187–188).

Winter conditions in Gambell, with the prevailing northerly winds, are often interrupted by a few days of vi-

FIGURE 6. "Winter that is locally formed." Thin young ice solidifies along the shores of St. Lawrence Island, February 2008. Leonard Apangalook stands to the right, next to his sled. (Photo, Igor Krupnik, 2008)

FIGURE 8. Two Gambell hunters are looking for seals from ice pressure ridges. The ridges look high and solid, but they can be quickly destroyed under the impact of strong wind or storms. (Photo, Igor Krupnik, February 2008)

FIGURE 9. Hunting in boats in dense floating ice is now a common practice in Gambell during the wintertime. (Photo, G. Carleton Ray)

olent storms and warm spells brought by southerly winds. This happened twice in the winters of 1899–1900 and 1900–1901, and three times in the winter of 1898–1899 (Oozeva et al., 2004:185). According to Conrad Oozeva, an elderly hunter from Gambell, the warm spells have been also typical in his early days:

We commonly have three waves of warm weather and thawing during the wintertime. After these warmings, we love to go hunting in boats on water opening, before it covers again with the new ice. The only difference I see is that these warm waves were not long enough, just a few days only. We now have longer warming waves during the winter, often for several days. (Oozeva et al., 2004:186)

These days, violent winter storms often lead to numerous episodes of ice breakups and new ice formation every winter. Apangalook's record indicates at least four episodes of complete ice disintegration in Gambell in the period from December 2006 until March 2007. On 10 January 2007, he wrote in his log, "It is unusual to have swells and to lose ice in January compared to normal years in the past. Locally formed ice that covered our area to 9/10 easily disappears with rising temperatures and storm generated swells." Then on 31 January 2007, he reported again:

What a twist we have in our weather situation at the end of January! Wind driven waves cleared away pressure ridges on west side with open water west of the Island. Part of the shore-

fast ice broke away on the north side beach also from the swells. Unusual to have so many low pressures channel up the Bering Straits from the south in a sequence that brought in high winds and rain. Much of the snow melted, especially along the top of the beach where we now have bare gravel. Undeniably, the climate change has accelerated over the past five years where severity of winds and erratic temperatures occur more frequently every year.

Elders on St. Lawrence Island and in other northern communities unanimously point toward another big change in winter conditions. In the "old days," despite episodic snowstorms and warm spells, there were always extended periods of quiet, cold weather, with no winds. These long cold stretches were good for hunting and traveling; they also allowed hunters to predict the weather and ice conditions in advance. In the teachers' records of more than a century ago, those stretches of calm cold weather often covered two to three weeks. This pattern does not occur today. According to Apangalook's logs, there were a few periods of relatively quiet weather during the winter of 2006–2007; but they lasted for a few days only. December 2006 was particularly unstable and windy, with just one calm day. In comparison, during December 1899, the weather was quiet for 18 days, in two long stretches. In December 1900, quiet and calm weather persisted for almost 10 days in a row (Oozeva et al., 2004:185–186). No wonder Arctic elders claim that "the earth is faster now" (cf. Krupnik and Jolly, 2002:7).

CHANGES IN MARINE MAMMAL BEHAVIOR AND HABITATS

Local hunters' observations are naturally filled with the references to wildlife and subsistence activities. When seen upon a broader historical timeframe, those records provide compelling evidence of a dramatic shift that is taking place in the northern marine ecosystems. Apangalook reported (6 March 2007):

A few years back when the polar pack ice did not reach our area anymore, we sighted bowhead whales in our area sporadically in the middle of winter. Back when our seasons were normal, we saw whales in the fall going south for the winter and didn't see any in mid-winter, until they start coming back in mid-March-April and May. Now, with more whales in our area in mid-winter we know that they are (mostly) wintering in our area. Without polar pack ice we had suspected that some of the whales stopped that migration north of our island and are not going further south anymore. . . . We know today that their wintering area is further north.

Many local hunters, like Apangalook, argue that whale migrations have been deeply affected by climate change. Hunters started observing bowhead whales off St. Lawrence Island in December (usually, a few animals) since 1962. Since 1995, winter whaling has become a common practice in both Gambell and the other island community of Savoonga, so that some 40 percent of bowhead whales are now being taken in wintertime (Noongwook et al., 2007:51). The difference is indeed remarkable compared to the conditions of a century ago, when the bowhead whales were not hunted in Gambell until early April (as in 1899) or even early May, as in 1900 and 1901 (Oozeva et al., 2004:189). To the contrary, in early 2007, Apangalook reported sightings of bowhead whales on February 6, and the hunters first tried to pursue them on 10 February 2007. The whales were then seen off Gambell repeatedly for the entire month. Local hunters in Barrow have also spotted bowhead whales in mid-February 2007; recent underwater acoustic recording off Barrow documented the presence of gray whales (*Eschrichtius robustus*) during the winter of 2003/2004 (Stafford et al., 2007:170). If whales have become frequent in the northern Bering Sea and southern Chukchi Sea in mid-winter, that would be a strong indicator to the dramatic shift in their migration and distribution pattern across the North Pacific–Western Arctic region.

Pacific walrus, another marine mammal species of critical importance to St. Lawrence Island hunters is also becoming more common in wintertime. Back in the "olden days," walrus used to come to the island in great numbers in late October or early November, ahead of the moving polar pack ice (Krupnik and Ray, 2007:2950). The bulk of the herd usually moved south of the island in December; but a small number of bull walruses commonly remained around Gambell in wintertime, mostly in offshore leads and polynyas. Still, the main hunting season for walrus did not start until late April or May. According to Apangalook's records, the fall arrival of walrus in both 2006 and 2007 was delayed by several weeks, so that the first walruses were not seen until mid-December. After that, walruses have been hunted in Gambell on almost daily basis throughout the winter of 2006–2007, which indicates that, like bowhead whales, they are also staying in growing numbers during the winter months.

Besides "wintering" walruses, Gambell hunters in winter 2007–2008 have observed several ribbon seals (*Phoca fasciata*) that are normally not seen in the area until late April or May. In February 2007, SIKU observers in Wales, some 200 miles to the north of Gambell, have spotted belugas (white whales); in the "old days," beluga whales had not been seen in the Bering Strait area until mid-April.

Whereas some species are becoming more common in winter, others are moving out. Apangalook reports:

One species of birds we used to hunt ever since I was a young child was the old squaw [*Clangula hyemalis*—IK]. Flocks of these birds in the thousands would fly north every morning at daybreak and return in the evening to [the] leeward side of the island. This pattern of movement daily I have seen every day in the sixty plus years of my life; but within the past five years the numbers have dwindled to near zero. [. . .] Are their food sources moving to a different area or is [it] getting depleted? (1 February 2007)

CONCLUSIONS: MESSAGES FROM INDIGENOUS OBSERVATION

The evidence from the first systematic monitoring by local IPY observers confirms a substantial shift in sea ice and weather regime over that past decade, as has been claimed by polar scientists and indigenous experts alike. It is characterized by a much shorter presence of sea ice, often by several weeks. Many types of ice are becoming rare or have completely disappeared from the area, such as solid pack ice or forms of multi-layered ice built of old and new ice. Most of the ice formations are now built of young and fragile first-year ice. The ice is also becoming increasingly unstable and dangerous for hunters.[9] In Apangalook's words, "Even marine mammals avoid this kind of ice condition, as it is hazardous to the animals too. It looks like game animal are taking refuge in more solid ice elsewhere."

Hunters' observations also confirm the profound northward shift in the Bering Sea marine ecosystem, which is also detected by scientists (Grebmeier et al., 2006; Litzow, 2007). Arctic residents refer to such shift in many of their descriptions of climate change, although they use their own "flagship species" as prime indicators. Indigenous hunters, naturally, pay most attention to large marine mammal and bird species as opposed to fish, invertebrates, and benthic communities that are popular indicators of change among marine biologists and oceanographers (Grebmeier et al., 2006; Ray et al., 2006; Sarmiento et al., 2004).

Arctic residents are extremely worried about the impact of ecosystem change on their economies, culture, and lifestyles. As Apangalook put it,

Predictability of our game animals of the sea are inconsistent and erratic compared (to) how it used to be back in the normal seasons. We, the hunters, along with the marine mammals we hunt, are truly at the mercy of our rapidly changing environment. (Apangalook, 2 March 2007)

The last message from indigenous records is that local observations could be a valuable component of any instrumental observation network built for IPY 2007–2008 and beyond. Many hunters in small Alaskan villages are trained to keep daily weather logs and are very familiar with the practices of instrumental observation and forecasting. Also, their daily records can be matched with historical instrumental data from the same areas that sometimes go back to the years of the First IPY of 1882–1883 (Wood and Overland 2006), as well as with the readings of today's weather stations and ice satellite imagery. Such cross-reference with the long-term instrumental series would create the needed comparative context to indigenous observations and would help introduce analytical scholarly tools to the analysis of indigenous data. Arctic residents' observations are too precious a record to be discounted as "anecdotal evidence" in today's search for the documentation and explanation of environmental change.

Besides, local observations in places like Gambell, with the now-shortened ice season and thinned first-year ice, may offer a valuable insight into the future status of the Arctic sea ice of many climate models. Those models predict the shrinking, thinning, and eventual loss of multi-year ice over almost the entire Arctic Ocean by the middle of this century (Bancroft, 2007; Johannessen et al., 2004:336–338; Overland, 2007; Richter-Menge et al., 2006). Arctic residents' integrative vision of their environment can be invaluable to our understanding of this new Arctic system in the decades to come.

Acknowledgments

This paper is a tribute to the long-term partnership with local experts in the documentation of their observations of sea ice and climate change in the Bering Strait region. Collaboration with Herbert Anungazuk, Leonard Apangalook Sr., George Noongwook, Chester Noongwook, Conrad Oozeva, Willis Walunga, Winton Weyapuk Jr., and others turned into the bonds of friendship and gained new momentum under the SIKU project in 2006–2008. I am grateful to Leonard Apangalook Sr.; also to Hiroko Ikuta, Chester Noongwook, and G. Carleton Ray, who shared their photos for illustrations to this paper. My colleagues Ernest S. Burch Jr., Aron Crowell, William Fitzhugh, Molly Lee, G. Carleton Ray, Cara Seitchek, Dennis Stanford, and Kevin Wood offered helpful comments to the first drafts of this paper. I thank them all.

NOTES

1. Sophus Tromholt's photographs taken in 1882–1883 have been displayed at the "Indigenous Opening" of IPY 2007–2008 and used in a special trilingual calendar produced for the event. See http://www.ip-py.org/news_cms/2007/january/tromholt_exhibit_at_the_opening_ceremony/6 (accessed 30 March 2008).

2. Point no. 51 in Hazen's instructions, "Observations and collections in the realms of zoology, botany, geology, &c." (Ray, 1885:13; Greely, 1888:104).

3. The Barrow collections included "497 bird-skins, comprising about 50 species, and 177 sets of eggs; [. . .] a small collection of skins, skulls, and skeletons of mammals; 11 or 12 species of fishes; a very few insects; and some marine and fresh-water invertebrates. The plants of the region were carefully collected. A considerable number of Eskimo vocabularies were obtained, together with a large collection of implements, clothing, &c" (Baird, 1885a:15). Turner's collections from Labrador were described as "[. . .] of birds, 1,800 specimens; eggs, 1,800 specimens; fishes, 1,000 specimens; mammals, 200 specimens; ethnological, 600 artifacts; plants, a great number; insects, over 200,000; geological specimens, a great variety; Eskimo linguistics, over 500 pages of manuscript, embracing thousands of words and over 800 sentences" (Baird, 1885b:17).

4. In fact, there are 1,068 ethnological objects, according to today's electronic catalog, with Lt. P. Ray recorded as *donor*; plus 6 objects donated by Capt. Herendeen, another member of the Barrow mission.

5. Barrow team also conducted a census of the residents of Barrow, with 137 names of men, women, and children (Ray, 1885:49); that makes it one of the earliest samples of personal Inuit names from Arctic Alaska.

6. See reviews of several individual documentation projects on indigenous observations in Krupnik and Jolly, 2002; also Herlander and Mustonen, 2004; Huntington and Fox, 2005.

7. One of such projects, ELOKA (Exchange for Local Observations and Knowledge of the Arctic, IPY # 187) works "to provide data management tools and appropriate means of recording, preserving, and sharing data and information" from Arctic communities—See http://nsidc.org/eloka/ (accessed 30 March 2008).

8. This pattern has been consistently reported by indigenous observers across the Arctic area—see Gearheard et al., 2006; Laidler, 2006; Laidler and Elee, 2006; Laidler and Ikummaq, 2008; McDonald et al., 1997; Metcalf and Krupnik, 2003.

9. See similar conclusions from other projects in the documentation of indigenous knowledge on sea ice change (Gearheard et al., 2006; Laidler, 2006; Laidler and Elee, 2006; Norton, 2002). Murdoch's work in Barrow even inspired a special IPY 2007–2008 project aimed at replicating his ethnological collections by today's specimens (Jensen, 2005)

LITERATURE CITED

ACIA. 2005. *Arctic Climate Impact Assessment (ACIA)*. Cambridge, U.K.: Cambridge University Press.

Allison, I., M. Béland, K. Alverson, R. Bell, D. Carlson, K. Darnell, C. Ellis-Evans, E. Fahrbach, E. Fanta, Y. Fujii, G. Glasser, L. Goldfarb, G. Hovelsrud, J. Huber, V. Kotlyakov, I. Krupnik, J. Lopez-Martinez, T. Mohr, D. Qin, V. Rachold, C. Rapley, O. Rogne, E. Sarukhanian, C. Summerhayes, and C. Xiao. 2007. The Scope of Science for the International Polar Year 2007–2008. *World Meteorological Organization, Technical Documents* 1364. Geneva.

Aporta, C., and E. Higgs. 2005. Satellite Culture: Global Positioning Systems, Inuit Wayfinding, and the Need for a New Account of Technology. *Current Anthropology*, 46(5):729–753.

Baird, S. F. 1885a. Report of Professor Baird, Secretary of the Smithsonian Institution, for 1883. *Annual Report of the Board of Regents of the Smithsonian Institution, Showing the Operations, Expenditures, and Condition of the Institution for the Year 1883.* Washington, D.C.: Government Printing Office.

———. 1885b. Report of Professor Baird, Secretary of the Smithsonian Institution, for 1884. *Annual Report of the Board of Regents of the Smithsonian Institution, Showing the Operations, Expenditures, and Condition of the Institution for the Year 1884.* Washington, D.C.: Government Printing Office.

Bancroft, D. 2007. Ice in the Canadian Arctic—Canadian Ice Service (CIS) Perspective on the Future. Paper presented at the Symposium "Impact of an Ice-Diminishing Arctic on Naval and Maritime Operations," Washington, D.C., 10 July. http://www.orbit.nesdis.noaa.gov/star/IceSymposiumProgram.php (accessed 3 September 2007).

Barr, William. 1985. The Expeditions of the First International Polar Year, 1882–83. *The Arctic Institute of North America, Technical Paper* 29. Calgary, Alberta, Canada: University of Calgary.

Bates, Peter. 2007. Inuit and Scientific Philosophies about Planning, Prediction, and Uncertainty. *Arctic Anthropology*, 44(2):87–100.

Berkes, F. 1999. *Sacred Ecology: Traditional Ecological Knowledge and Resource Management.* London: Taylor and Francis.

Bielawski, E. 1992. Inuit Indigenous Knowledge and Science in the Arctic. *Northern Perspectives*, 20(1). http://www.carc.org/pubs/v20no1/index.html, (accessed 30 March 2008).

Boas, F. 1888. "The Central Eskimo." In *Sixth Annual Report of the Bureau of Ethnology for the Years 1884–1885*, pp. 399–669. Washington, D.C.: Government Printing Office. (Second edition, 1964, University of Nebraska Press.)

Bogoslovskaya, L. S. 2003. "The Bowhead Whale of Chukotka: Integration of Scientific and Traditional Knowledge." In *Indigenous Ways to the Present: Native Whaling in the Western Arctic*, ed. A. P. McCartney, pp. 209–254. Canadian Circumpolar Institute, Studies in Whaling 6, Occasional Publications 54. Edmonton: Canadian Circumpolar Institute, University of Alberta.

Bunge, A. 1895. "Opisanie puteshestviia k ustiu r. Leny 1881–1884" [Description of the Voyage to the Mouth of the Lena River, 1881–1884]. In *Trudy Russkoi Poliarnoi stantsii na ust'ie Leny*, ed. A. Tillo, vol. 1, appendix 1, pp. 1–96. St. Petersburg: Russian Geographical Society.

Burch, Ernest S., Jr. 2009. "Smithsonian Contributions to Alaskan Ethnography: The IPY Expedition to Barrow, 1881–1883." In *Smithsonian at the Poles: Contributions to International Polar Year Science*, ed. I. Krupnik, M. A. Lang, and S. E. Miller, pp. 89–98. Washington, D.C.: Smithsonian Institution Scholarly Press.

Cole, D., and L. Müller-Wille. 1984. Franz Boas' Expedition to Baffin Island, 1883–1884. *Études/Inuit/Studies*, 8(1):37–63.

Crowell, A. L., and E. Oozevaseuk. 2006. The St. Lawrence Island Famine and Epidemic, 1878–1880: A Yupik Narrative in Cultural and Historical Context. *Arctic Anthropology*, 43(1):1–19.

Crowell, Aron L. 2009. "The Art of Iñupiaq Whaling: Elders' Interpretations of International Polar Year Ethnological Collections." In *Smithsonian at the Poles: Contributions to International Polar Year Science*, ed. I. Krupnik, M. A. Lang, and S. E. Miller, pp. 99–114. Washington, D.C.: Smithsonian Institution Scholarly Press.

Doty, W. F. 1900. Log Book, St. Lawrence Island. *Ninth Annual Report on Introduction of Domestic Reindeer into Alaska 1899.* Washington, D.C.: Government Printing Office.

Fleming, James R., and Cara Seitchek. 2009. "Advancing Polar Research and Communicating Its Wonders: Quests, Questions, and Capabilities of Weather and Climate Studies in International Polar Years." In *Smithsonian at the Poles: Contributions to International Polar Year Science*, ed. I. Krupnik, M. A. Lang, and S. E. Miller, pp. 1–12. Washington, D.C.: Smithsonian Institution Scholarly Press.

Fitzhugh, William. 1988a. "Introduction to the 1987 Edition." In *Ethnological Results of the Point Barrow Expedition*, by John Murdoch. Washington, D.C.: Smithsonian Institution Press.

———. 1988b. "Baird's Naturalists: Smithsonian Collectors in Alaska." In *Crossroads of Continents: Cultures of Siberia and Alaska*, ed. W. W. Fitzhugh and A. Crowell, pp. 89–96. Washington, D.C.: Smithsonian Institution Press.

———. 2002. "Origins of Museum Anthropology at the Smithsonian and Beyond." In *Anthropology, History, and American Indians: Essays in Honor of William Curtis Sturtevant*, ed. W. L. Merrill and I. Goddard, pp. 179–200. Smithsonian Contributions to Anthropology, No. 44. Washington, D.C.: Smithsonian Institution Press.

———. 2009. "'Of No Ordinary Importance': Reversing Polarities in Smithsonian Arctic Studies." In *Smithsonian at the Poles: Contributions to International Polar Year Science*, ed. I. Krupnik, M. A. Lang, and S. E. Miller, pp. 61–78. Washington, D.C.: Smithsonian Institution Scholarly Press.

Ford, J., T. Pierce, B. Smit, J. Wandel, M. Allurut, K. Shappa, H. Ittusujurat, and K. Qrunnut. 2007. Reducing Vulnerability to Climate Change in the Arctic: The Case of Nunavut. *Arctic*, 60(2): 150–166.

Gearheard, S., W. Matumeak, I. Angutikjuaq, J. Maslanik, H. P. Huntington, J. Leavitt, D. Matumeak Kagak, G. Tigullaraq, and R. G. Barry. 2006. "It's Not That Simple": A Collaborative Comparison of Sea Ice Environments, Their Uses, Observed Changes, and Adaptations in Barrow, Alaska, USA, and Clyde River, Nunavut, Canada. *Ambio*, 35(4):203–211.

Grebmeier, J. M., J. E. Overland, S. E. Moore, E. V. Farley, E. C. Carmack, L. W. Cooper, K. E. Frey, J. H. Helle, F. A. McLaughlin, and S. L. McNutt. 2006. A Major Ecosystem Shift in the Northern Bering Sea. *Science*, 311:1461–1464.

Greely, A. W. 1888. Report on the Proceedings of the United States Expedition to Lady Franklin Bay, Grinnell Land. U.S. House of Representatives, 49th Congress, 1st Session, Misc. Document No. 393. Washington, D.C.: Government Printing Office.

Herlander, Elina, and Tero Mustonen, eds. 2004. "Snowscapes, Dreamscapes." *Snowchange Book on Community Voices of Change* Study Materials 12. Tampere, Finland: Tampere Polytechnic Publications.

Hovelsrud, G., and I. Krupnik. 2006. IPY 2007–08 and Social/Human Sciences: An Update. *Arctic*, 59(3):341–348.

Huntington, H. P., ed. 2000. *Impact of Changes in Sea Ice and Other Environmental Parameters in the Arctic.* Report of the Marine Mammal Commission Workshop. Girdwood, Alaska, 15–17 February 2000. Bethesda, Md.: Marine Mammal Commission.

Huntington, H. P., T. Callaghan, S. Fox, and I. Krupnik. 2004. Matching Traditional and Scientific Observations to Detect Environmental Change: A Discussion on Arctic Terrestrial Ecosystems. *Ambio*, 33(7):18–23.

Huntington, H. P., and S. Fox.. 2005. "The Changing Arctic: Indigenous Perspectives." In *Arctic Climate Impact Assessment*, ed. C. Symon, L. Arris, and B. Heal, pp. 61–98. New York: Cambridge University Press.

International Council for Science. 2004. *A Framework for the International Polar Year 2007–2008.* Produced by the ICSU IPY 2007–2008 Planning Group. http://www.icsu.org/Gestion/img/ICSU_DOC_DOWNLOAD/562_DD_FILE_IPY_web_version.pdf (accessed 30 March 2008).

Jensen, A. 2005. Northern Material Culture through International Polar Year Collections, Then and Now: In the Footsteps of Murdoch and Turner. http://www.uaf.edu/anthro/iassa/ipyjensen.htm (accessed 3 September 2007).

Johannessen, O. M., L. Bengtsson, M. W. Miles, S. I. Kuzmina, V. A. Semenov, G. A. Alekseev, A. P. Nagurnyi, V. F. Zakharov, L. B.

Bobylev, L. H. Pettersson, K. Hasselmann, and H. P. Cattle. 2004. Arctic Climate Change: Observed and Modeled Temperature and Sea-Ice Variability. *Tellus*, 56A:328–341.

Jolles, C. Z. 1995. "Paul Silook's Legacy: The Ethnohistory of Whaling on St. Lawrence Island." In *Hunting the Largest Animals: Native Whaling in the Western Arctic and Subarctic*, ed. A. P. McCartney, pp. 221–252. Canadian Circumpolar Institute, Studies in Whaling 6, Occasional Publications 36. Edmonton: Canadian Circumpolar Institute, University of Alberta.

———. 2003. "When Whaling Folks Celebrate: A Comparison of Tradition and Experience in Two Bering Sea Whaling Communities." In *Indigenous Ways to the Present: Native Whaling in the Western Arctic*, ed. A. P. McCartney, pp. 209–254. Canadian Circumpolar Institute, Studies in Whaling 6, Occasional Publications 54. Edmonton: Canadian Circumpolar Institute, University of Alberta.

Krupnik, I. 2000. "Native Perspectives on Climate and Sea Ice Changes." In *Impact of Changes in Sea Ice and Other Environmental Parameters in the Arctic*, ed. H. P. Huntington, pp. 25–39. Bethesda, Md.: Marine Mammal Commission.

———. 2002. "Watching Ice and Weather Our Way: Some Lessons from Yupik Observations of Sea Ice and Weather on St. Lawrence Island, Alaska." In *The Earth Is Faster Now: Indigenous Observations of Arctic Environmental Change*, ed. I. Krupnik and D. Jolly, pp. 156–197. Fairbanks, Alaska: ARCUS.

———. 2007. Progress Report on International Polar Year 2007–2008: How Are We Doing? *Northern Notes*, Summer: 4–9. http://www.iassa.gl/newsletter/news07_1.pdf (accessed 9 August 2008).

Krupnik, I., M. Bravo, Y. Csonka, G. Hovelsrude-Broda, L. Müller-Wille, B. Poppel, P. Schweitzer, and S. Sörlin. 2005. Social Sciences and Humanities in the International Polar Year 2007–2008: An Integrating Mission. *Arctic*, 58(1):89–95.

Krupnik, I., and D. Jolly, eds. 2002. *The Earth Is Faster Now: Indigenous Observations of Arctic Environmental Change*. Fairbanks, Alaska: ARCUS.

Krupnik, I., and G. Carleton Ray. 2007. Pacific Walruses, Indigenous Hunters, and Climate Change: Bridging Scientific and Indigenous Knowledge. *Deep-Sea Research Part II*, 54:2946–2957.

Krupnik, I., W. Walunga, and V. Metcalf, eds. 2002. *Akuzilleput Igaqullghet. Our Words Put to Paper. Sourcebook in St. Lawrence Island Yupik Heritage and History*. Contributions to Circumpolar Anthropology, 3. Washington, D.C.: Arctic Studies Center, Smithsonian Institution.

Kusugak, J. A. 2002. "Foreword: Where a Storm Is a Symphony and Land and Ice Are One." In *The Earth Is Faster Now: Indigenous Observations of Arctic Environmental Change*, ed. I. Krupnik and D. Jolly, pp. v–vii. Fairbanks, Alaska: ARCUS.

Laidler, G. 2006. Inuit and Scientific Perspectives on the Relationship between Sea Ice and Climate Change: The Ideal Complement? *Climatic Change*, 78 (2–4):407–444.

Laidler, G. J., and P. Elee. 2006. "Sea Ice Processes and Change: Exposure and Risk in Cape Dorset, Nunavut." In *Climate Change: Linking Traditional and Scientific Knowledge*, ed. J. Oakes and R. Riewe, pp. 155–175. Winnipeg, Manitoba, Canada: Aboriginal Issues Press.

Laidler, G. J., and T. Ikummaq. 2008. Human Geographies of Sea Ice: Freeze/Thaw Processes around Igloolik, Nunavut, Canada. *Polar Record*, 44 (229):127–153.

Lerrigo, P. H. J. 1901. Abstract of Journal, Gambell, St. Lawrence Island. Kept by P. H. J. Lerrigo, M.D. *Tenth Annual Report on Introduction of Domestic Reindeer into Alaska 1899*. Washington, D.C.: Government Printing Office.

———.1902. Abstract of Daily Journal on St. Lawrence Island. Kept by P. H. J. Lerrigo, M.D. Log Book, St. Lawrence Island. *Eleventh Annual Report on Introduction of Domestic Reindeer into Alaska 1899*. Washington, D.C.: Government Printing Office.

Litzow, M. 2007. Warming Climate Reorganizes Bering Sea Biogeography. http://www.afsc.noaa.gov/quarterly/jfm2007/divrptsRACE4.htm (accessed 9 December 2007).

Loring, S. 2001. "Introduction to Lucien M. Turner and the Beginning of Smithsonian Anthropology in the North." In *Ethnology of the Ungava District, Hudson Bay Territory*, by L. M. Turner, pp. vii–xxxii. Washington, D.C.: Smithsonian Institution Press.

McDonald, M., L. Arragutainaq, and Z. Novalinga, comps. 1997. *Voices from the Bay: Traditional Ecological Knowledge of Inuit and Cree in the Hudson Bay Bioregion*. Ottawa, Ontario: Canadian Arctic Resources Committee.

Metcalf, V., and I. Krupnik, eds. 2003. *Pacific Walrus: Conserving Our Culture through Traditional Management*. Report produced by Eskimo Walrus Commission, Kawerak, Inc. under the grant from the U.S. Fish and Wildlife Service, Section 119, Cooperative Agreement #701813J506.

Moore, R. D. 1923. Social Life of the Eskimo of St. Lawrence Island. *American Anthropologist*, n.s. 25(3):339–375.

Müller-Wille, L., ed. 1998. *Franz Boas among the Inuit of Baffin Island, 1883–1884*. Toronto: University of Toronto Press.

Murdoch, J. 1892. Ethnological Results of the Point Barrow Expedition. *Ninth Annual Report of the Bureau of Ethnology for the Years 1887–88*. Washington, D.C.: Government Printing Office. (Second edition, 1988, Smithsonian Institution Press.)

Neighbors, A. 2005. Smithsonian Institution—International Polar Year Arctic Expeditions' Collections Survey. Unpublished manuscript in possession of the Arctic Studies Center, Smithsonian Institution.

Noongwook, G., The Native Village of Savoonga, H. P. Huntington, and J. C. George. 2007. Traditional Knowledge of the Bowhead Whale (*Balaena mysticetus*) around St. Lawrence Island, Alaska. *Arctic*, 60(1):47–54.

Norton, D. 2002. "Coastal Sea Ice Watch: Private Confessions of a Convert to Indigenous Knowledge." In *The Earth Is Faster Now: Indigenous Observations of Arctic Environmental Change*, ed. I. Krupnik and D. Jolly, pp. 126–155. Fairbanks, Alaska: ARCUS.

Oakes, J., and R. Riewe, eds. 2006. *Climate Change: Linking Traditional and Scientific Knowledge*. Winnipeg, Manitoba, Canada: Aboriginal Issues Press.

Oozeva, C., C. Noongwook, G. Noongwook, C. Alowa, and I. Krupnik. 2004. *Watching Ice and Weather Our Way*. Washington, D.C.: Arctic Studies Center, Smithsonian Institution.

Overland, J. 2007. "IPCC Arctic Climate and Ice Projections." Paper presented at "Impact of an Ice-Diminishing Arctic on Naval and Maritime Operations" Symposium, Washington, D.C., 10 July. http://www.orbit.nesdis.noaa.gov/star/IceSymposiumProgram.php (accessed 3 September 2007).

Ray, G. C., J. McCormick-Ray, P. Berg, and H. E. Epstein. 2006. Pacific Walrus: Benthic Bioturbator of Beringia. *Journal of Experimental Marine Biology and Ecology*, 330:403–419.

Ray, P. H. 1885. *Report of the International Polar Expedition to Point Barrow, Alaska*. Washington, D.C.: Government Printing Office.

Richter-Menge, J., J. Overland, A. Proshutinsky, V. Romanovsky, L. Bengtsson, L. Bringham, M. Dyurgerov, J. C. Gascard, S. Gerland, R. Graversen, C. Haas, M. Karcher, P. Kuhry, J. Maslanik, H. Melling, W. Maslowski, J. Morison, D. Perovich, R. Przybylak, V. Rachold, I. Rigor, A. Shiklomanov, J. Stroeve, D. Walker, and J. Walsh. 2006. State of the Arctic Report. NOAA OAR Special Report. NOAA/OAR/PMEL. Seattle, Wash. http://www.pmel.noaa.gov/pubs/PDF/rich2952/rich2952.pdf (accessed 5 September 2007).

Sarmiento, J. L., R. Slater, R. Barber, L. Bopp, S. C. Doney, A. C. Hirst, J. Kleypas, R. Matear, U. Mikolajewicz. P. Monfray, V. Soldatov, S. A. Spall, and R. Stouffer. 2004. Response of Ocean Ecosystems to Climate Warming. *Global Biogeochemical Cycles*, 18(GB3003): 1–23.

Stafford, K. M., S. E. Moore, M. Spillane, and S. Wiggins. 2007. Gray Whale Calls Recorded near Barrow, Alaska, throughout the Winter of 2003–04. *Arctic*, 60(2):167–172.

Tromholt, S. 1885. *Under the Rays of the Aurora Borealis: In the Land of the Lapps and Kvaens*. Boston: Houghton, Mifflin and Co.

Turner, L. 1894. Ethnology of the Ungava District, Hudson Bay Territory. *Eleventh Annual Report of the Bureau of American Ethnology for the Years 1889–1890*, ed. Stephen Loring, pp.159–350. Washington, D.C.: Government Printing Office. (Second edition, 2001, Smithsonian Institution Press.)

Watt-Cloutier, Sheila. 2005. Connectivity: The Arctic–The Planet. *Silarjualiriniq/Inuit in Global* Issues, 20:1–4.

Wood, K., and J. E. Overland. 2006. Climate Lessons from the First International Polar Year. *Bulletin of the American Meteorological Society*, 87(12):1685–1697.

———. 2007. Documentary Image Collection from the First International Polar Year, 1881–1884. http://www.arctic.noaa.gov/aro/ipy-1/Frontpage.htm (accessed 3 September 2007).

Species Diversity and Distributions of Pelagic Calanoid Copepods from the Southern Ocean

E. Taisoo Park and Frank D. Ferrari

ABSTRACT. In the Southern Ocean, 205 species of pelagic calanoid copepods have been reported from 57 genera and 21 families. Eight species are found in the coastal zone; 13 are epipelagic, and 184 are restricted to deepwater. All 8 coastal species and eight of 13 epipelagic species are endemic, with epipelagic species restricted to one water mass. Of the 184 deepwater species, 50 are endemic, and 24 occur south of the Antarctic Convergence. Most of the remaining 134 deepwater species are found throughout the oceans with 86% percent reported as far as the north temperate region. The deepwater genus *Paraeuchaeta* has the largest number of species in the Southern Ocean, 21; all are carnivores. *Scolecithricella* is also speciose with 16 species, and more specimens of these detritivores were collected. Species with a bipolar distribution are not as common as bipolar species pairs. A bipolar distribution may result from continuous extinction in middle and low latitudes of a wide spread deepwater species with shallow polar populations. Subsequent morphological divergence results in a bipolar species pair. Most of the numerically abundant calanoids in the Southern Ocean are endemics. Their closest relative usually is a rare species found in oligotrophic habitats throughout the oceans. Abundant endemics appear adapted to high primary and secondary productivity of the Southern Ocean. Pelagic endemicity may have resulted from splitting a widespread, oligotrophic species into a Southern Ocean population adapted to productive habitats, and a population, associated with low productivity that remains rare. The families Euchaetidae and Heterorhabdidae have a greater number of their endemic species in the Southern Ocean. A phylogeny of these families suggests that independent colonization by species from different genera was common. Thus, two building blocks for the evolution of the Southern Ocean pelagic fauna are independent colonization and adaptation to high productivity.

INTRODUCTION

Copepods often are referred to as the insects of the seas. They certainly are comparable to insects in survival through deep time, ecological dominance, geographic range, and breadth of adaptive radiation (Schminke, 2007). However, they are not comparable to insects in numbers of species. Only 11,302 species of copepods were known to science toward the end of the last century (Humes, 1994), and 1,559 have been added since then. In contrast, the number of described insects approaches one million (Grimaldi and Engel, 2005). In terms of the number of individuals alive at any one time, however, copepods undoubtedly

E. Taisoo Park, Texas A&M University, 29421 Vista Valley Drive, Vista, CA 92084, USA. Frank D. Ferrari, Invertebrate Zoology, National Museum of Natural History, Smithsonian Institution, 4210 Silver Hill Road, Suitland, MD 20746, USA. Corresponding author: F. D. Ferrari (ferrarif@si.edu). Accepted 27 June 2008.

surpass the insects. Among the copepod orders, calanoid copepods contribute more numbers of individuals to the Earth's biomass, primarily because of their unique success in exploiting pelagic aquatic habitats. Calanoid copepods also are speciose; Bowman and Abele (1982) estimated 2,300 species of calanoids, and as of this writing, 525 species have been added. These calanoid species are placed in 313 nominal genera belonging to 45 families (F. D. Ferrari, personal database).

Knowledge about the distribution and diversity of calanoid copepods in the Southern Ocean has increased significantly over the past century (Razouls et al., 2000). Most of the calanoid copepods reported from the Southern Ocean have been collected from pelagic waters. However, more species new to science are now being described from waters immediately over the deep-sea floor of the Southern Ocean (Bradford and Wells, 1983; Hulsemann, 1985b; Schulz and Markhaseva, 2000; Schulz, 2004, 2006; Markhaseva and Schulz, 2006a; Markhaseva and Schulz, 2006b, 2007a, 2007b). The diversity of this benthopelagic calanoid fauna from other oceans (Grice, 1973; Markhaseva and Ferrari, 2006) suggests that the total calanoid diversity from this habitat of the Southern Ocean is significantly underestimated, and many new species are expected to be described. The present review then is restricted to pelagic calanoid copepods because the benthopelagic fauna has not been well surveyed and their species not as well known as pelagic calanoids.

Pelagic calanoid copepods are numerically the dominant species of the zooplankton community in the Southern Ocean (Foxton, 1956; Longhurst, 1985). Beginning with the *Challenger* expedition (1873–1876), many expeditions to the Southern Ocean have provided specimens for taxonomic studies of the calanoids. Early works by Brady (1883), based on the *Challenger* collections, Giesbrecht (1902), based on *Belgica* collections, Wolfenden (1905, 1906, 1911), based on the *Gauss* (German deepsea expedition) collections, and Farran (1929), based on the British *Terra Nova* collections, led to the discovery of most of the numerically dominant and widespread pelagic calanoid species in the Southern Ocean. Several major national expeditions followed, such as the *Meteor* expedition, 1925–1927, the SS *Vikingen* expedition, 1929–1930, and the *Norvegia* expedition, 1930–1931. However, collections obtained by these expeditions were studied mainly to understand the vertical or seasonal distribution or other aspects of the biology of pelagic animals. Significant publications resulting from these studies include Hentschel (1936), Steuer and Hentschel (1937), and Ottestad (1932, 1936). In 1925 the British

Discovery Committee launched a program of extensive oceanographic research in the Southern Ocean, including intensive studies of the zooplankton fauna. Publications by Mackintosh (1934, 1937), Hardy and Gunther (1935), and Ommanney (1936) based on the *Discovery* collections are notable for their valuable contributions to the population biology of the numerically dominant calanoid copepods. Continued studies of the *Discovery* collections led to the publication of additional papers, such as Foxton (1956) about the zooplankton community and Andrew (1966) on the biology of *Calanoides acutus*, the dominant herbivore of the Southern Ocean.

Southern Ocean copepods became the subject of taxonomic studies once again toward the middle of the last century with two important monographs (Vervoort, 1951, 1957). These were the most comprehensive treatments published on pelagic calanoids, to that time, and began a new era of taxonomic analyses of Southern Ocean copepods. In these two studies, many previously known species of the Southern Ocean calanoids were completely and carefully redescribed, confusion regarding their identity was clarified, and occurrences of these species in other oceans were noted from the published literature. Two papers by Tanaka (1960, 1964) appeared soon afterward, reporting on the copepods collected by the Japanese Antarctic Expedition in 1957 and 1959. On the basis of collections made by the Soviet Antarctic expeditions, 1955–1958, Brodsky (1958, 1962, 1964, 1967) published several studies of the important herbivorous genus *Calanus*. More recently, important contributions to taxonomy of the Southern Ocean calanoids have been made by Bradford (1971, 1981) and Bradford and Wells (1983), reporting on calanoids found in the Ross Sea. Additionally, invaluable contributions have been made to the taxonomy of the important inshore genus *Drepanopus* by Bayly (1982) and Hulsemann (1985a, 1991).

Beginning in 1962, the U.S. Antarctic Research Program funded many oceanographic cruises to the Southern Ocean utilizing the USNS *Eltanin*. Samples taken with opening-closing Bé plankton nets and Isaacs-Kidd midwater trawls on these cruises were made available by the Smithsonian Institution for study through the Smithsonian Oceanographic Sorting Center. The exhaustive taxonomic works by Park (1978, 1980, 1982, 1983a, 1983b, 1988, 1993) are based almost exclusively on the midwater trawl samples collected during the *Eltanin* cruises, and these results significantly increased taxonomic understanding of most species of pelagic calanoids. Other studies based on the *Eltanin* samples include the following: Björnberg's (1968) work on the Megacalanidae; Heron and Bowman's

(1971) on postnaupliar developmental stages of three species belonging to the genera *Clausocalanus* and *Ctenocalanus*; Björnberg's (1973) survey of some copepods from the southeastern Pacific Ocean; Yamanaka's (1976) work on the distribution of some Eucalanidae, Aetideidae, and Euchaetidae; Fontaine's (1988) on the *antarctica* species group of the genus *Paraeuchaeta*; Markhaseva's (2001) on the genus *Metridia*; and Markhaseva and Ferrari's (2005) work on Southern Ocean species of *Lucicutia*. In addition, four exhaustive monographs have treated the taxonomy of a pelagic calanoid family throughout the world's oceans, and these also have contributed further to an understanding of the Southern Ocean fauna: Damkaer's (1975) work on the Spinocalanidae, Park's (1995) on the Euchaetidae, Markhaseva's (1996) on the Aetideidae, and Park's (2000) on the Heterorhabdidae. These monographs were based on specimens from an extensive set of samples from the world's oceans. As a result, the taxonomy and geographical range of most of the widespread species of these families are now well known.

Recently described new species of Southern Ocean calanoids are either pelagic species that previous authors failed to recognize as distinct from similar relatives, e.g., *Pleuromamma antarctica* Steuer, 1931 (see Ferrari and Saltzman, 1998), or species inhabiting extraordinary habitats seldom explored previously, like the water immediately above the seafloor. Bradford and Wells (1983) described the first benthopelagic calanoid copepods of the Southern Ocean, *Tharybis magna* and *Xanthocalanus harpagatus*, from a bait bottle. *Neoscolecithrix antarctica* was collected in small numbers in the Antarctic Sound adjacent to the Antarctic Peninsula by Hulsemann (1985b), who believed the species lived in close proximity to the seafloor. More recent additions to the benthopelagic calanoid fauna include *Parabradyidius angelikae* Schulz and Markhaseva, 2000, *Paraxantharus brittae* Schulz, 2006, and *Sensiava longiseta* Markhaseva and Schulz, 2006, each belonging to a new genus, and *Brachycalanus antarcticus* Schulz, 2005, *Scolecitrichopsis elenae* Schulz, 2005, *Byrathis arnei* Schulz, 2006, *Pseudeuchaeta arcuticornis* Markhaseva and Schulz, 2006, *Bradyetes curvicornis* Markhaseva and Schulz, 2006, *Brodskius abyssalis* Markhaseva and Schulz, 2007, *Rythabis assymmetrica* Markhaseva and Schulz, 2007, and *Omorius curvispinus* Markhaseva and Schulz, 2007. These latter species were collected from the Weddell Sea, an arm of the Southern Ocean, and from the Scotia Sea.

In this paper, all relevant studies of the taxonomy of pelagic Southern Ocean calanoid copepods are reviewed. Lists are compiled of species, genera, and families, and the geographical range within the Southern Ocean and relative abundance of each species are noted. Morphological differences are used to suggest evolutionary relationships among species. The distribution of all species is reviewed, and several generalized patterns are hypothesized. Of particular interest here are the species for which fewer than 50 specimens have been collected during the extensive history of surveys of the Southern Ocean pelagic fauna. The distribution of these rare, pelagic calanoids, almost all deepwater species, contributes favorably to an understanding of patterns of distribution and of speciation in the Southern Ocean.

METHODS

Traditionally, the Southern Ocean has been described physiographically as including the ocean basins adjacent to the continent of Antarctica plus the following adjoining seas: Amundsen Sea, Bellingshausen Sea, Ross Sea, Weddell Sea, and the southern part of the Scotia Sea. In this review of pelagic calanoid copepods, the southern boundary of the Southern Ocean is defined physiographically by the Antarctic continent, but the northern boundary is defined hydrographically, by the average position of the Subtropical Convergence. The Subtropical Convergence is located around 40°S (Deacon 1934, 1937), where the surface temperature of the sea drops sharply from about 18°C to 10°C. In this review, then, the Southern Ocean includes both the Antarctic region and the subantarctic region. Antarctic and subantarctic regions are separated by the Antarctic Convergence, which is located around 55°S, where the sea surface temperature drops 3°C to 5°C over about 30 miles (48.3 km). Although the latitudinal positions of both the Subtropical Convergence, among the Atlantic, Pacific and Indian oceans, and the Antarctic Convergence, among the Atlantic, Pacific and Indian sectors of the Southern Ocean, may vary significantly, locally, these convergences seldom vary more than a degree of latitude from their mean position.

Studies of the distribution of organisms are one of the primary purposes of the discipline of taxonomy, and the scope and effectiveness of taxonomic studies is dictated by the availability of specimens. Like most pelagic organisms, calanoid copepods in the Southern Ocean have been collected mainly with tow nets operated aboard oceangoing ships, which usually sail to a preselected set of geographic positions in the ocean. Because of the physical isolation of the Southern Ocean, studies of its pelagic calanoid copepods have depended primarily on efforts of national oceanographic expeditions, many of which routinely carried out sampling protocols for pelagic organisms.

The Isaacs-Kidd midwater trawls employed by the U.S. Antarctic Research Program were particularly effective in collecting large, pelagic copepods and significantly increased knowledge about the calanoid fauna. More than 1,000 midwater trawl samples were taken, and these samples are believed to have collected nearly all of the pelagic calanoid copepods in the water column; most of these species have been described (Park, 1978, 1980, 1982, 1983a, 1983b, 1988, 1993). The trawls were not fitted with a device to measure water flow through the mouth of the trawl, so no quantitative measure of the amount of water filtered by the trawl can be calculated for these samples. Sampling times, ranging from one to four hours, have allowed a calculation of the number of animals collected per unit time of trawl operation for the more abundant species, e.g., *Paraeuchaeta antarctica* (see Ferrari and Dojiri, 1987, as *Euchaeta antarctica*), but this measure is too coarse for the rare species that are the primary focus of this study.

The Isaacs-Kidd midwater trawls were quickly lowered to a specified deepest depth, obliquely towed at 3-5 knots to a specified shallowest depth, and then quickly retrieved to the surface again. It is not possible to determine the depth of collection for the specimens captured in a sample with this protocol. Furthermore, normally, only one trawl sample was collected at a station, and therefore, only one depth range was sampled at a particular location. As a result of these constraints, studies based on these samples cannot provide direct information about the vertical distribution of the calanoid species. However, by comparing the presence or absence of a species in samples taken to different greatest depths at different locations here or by calculating a frequency of occurrence for each sampled depth range relative to all trawls at that depth range (Yamanaka, 1976), it is possible to make a first-order determination of how deep a trawl has to be towed in order to collect a certain species.

Southern Ocean pelagic calanoids are categorized here in several different ways. Species collected in the vicinity of continental or insular land masses are inshore species, while species collected away from continental or insular land masses have been categorized to vertical zones as follows: epipelagic (0–200m), mesopelagic (200–1,000m), and bathypelagic (1,000–4,000). The term "deepwater" refers to the mesopelagic and bathypelagic zones together. In terms of abundance, species are categorized by the number of specimens collected or known from other expeditions: CC, very common (over 100 specimens found); C, common (between 99 and 50 specimens found); R, rare

(between 49 and 10); and RR, very rare (less than 10 specimens found). These are not counts per sample, but are all specimens known to science.

A large number of endemic species are found in the Southern Ocean, and these discoveries are placed within the context of endemicity throughout the world's oceans for two well-studied families, Euchaetidae and Heterorhabdidae. To facilitate comparisons, four noncontiguous areas of interest were defined among the world's oceans: the Southern Ocean, the Arctic (including adjacent boreal seas of the Atlantic and Pacific oceans), the eastern Pacific Ocean (along the Pacific coasts of the Americas, including the boundary currents), and the Indo-West Pacific Ocean (in and around the Malay Archipelago). The latter three were chosen as areas of interest because most of the endemic species of Euchaetidae and Heterorhabdidae not found in the Southern Ocean occur in one of them. So, for example, the Atlantic Ocean was not considered an area of interest because its endemic species occur mainly toward its northern and southern boundaries, and these endemic species could be included in the Arctic Ocean and Southern Ocean areas, respectively. There are no a priori biological hypotheses that support these utilitarian areas of interest, although endemicity is discussed in the context of high primary and secondary productivity.

Three broad feeding categories, herbivory, carnivory, and detritivory, are recognized for many pelagic calanoids. Food preferences of calanoid copepods have not been studied systematically, but the following publications supported the general feeding categories of these taxa: Mullin's (1967) work on the herbivory of Calanidae and Eucalanidae, Yen's (1983) on the carnivory of Euchaetidae, Ohtsuka et al.'s (1997) on the carnivory of derived Heterorhabdidae, Nishida and Ohtsuka's (1997) on the detritivory of Scolecitrichidae, and Itoh's (1970) and Matsuura and Nishida's (2000) on the carnivory of Augaptilidae. Studies of a few species of the large family Aetideidae (Robertson and Frost, 1977; Auel, 1999) have suggested that these species may be omnivores, but on the basis of the morphology of their mouthparts, they are considered carnivores here. Feeding is connected to environment through areas of high primary and secondary productivity, and here high primary and secondary productivity is equated with permanent, annually episodic upwelling areas. These areas of upwelling are associated with western boundary currents adjacent to all continents or are associated with three oceanic bands: trans-Southern Ocean, worldwide equatorial, and boreal Pacific (LaFond, 1966; Huber, 2002).

Descriptions of the geographical distribution of a species beyond the Southern Ocean were initiated by dividing the world's oceans into the following regions, generally following Backus (1986): Antarctic (south of the Antarctic Convergence), subantarctic (between the Antarctic and Subtropical convergences), south temperate (Subtropical Convergence to Tropic of Capricorn, about 20°S), tropical (Tropic of Capricorn to Tropic of Cancer, about 20°N), north temperate (Tropic of Cancer to about 50°N), subarctic (boreal seas adjacent to the Arctic Ocean to the Arctic Circle at 66°N), and the region of the Arctic basin. Some of the boundaries of these areas correspond to hydrographic features, e.g., they are the surface manifestations of the boundaries of water masses. However, these boundaries have not been shown to describe the generalized distribution of deepwater animals, and, in fact, two other ways of explaining the distribution of deepwater animals are proposed here. Distribution records for the regions outside of the Southern Ocean are derived from the latest reference given to each species in Appendix 1. There has been no attempt to correct for differences in sampling intensity among these regions, although the south temperate region has been sampled least (only mentioned in reports by Grice and Hulsemann, 1968, and Björnberg, 1973), and the north temperate, subarctic, and Arctic have been sampled the most.

Most of the very common pelagic calanoids are usually widespread within the Southern Ocean and were discovered during the early expeditions that ended in the first part of the twentieth century. These species originally were described from specimens collected in the Southern Ocean rather than being inferred from descriptions of specimens from other oceans, and most of these species have been redescribed once or twice since their original description. As a result, their taxonomy is stable, and their morphology and distribution within the Southern Ocean are relatively well known. Many deepwater calanoids also originally have been described from the Southern Ocean. Their morphology is well known, but most of these deepwater species are rare. As a result, information about their distribution, particularly beyond the Southern Ocean, remains limited. Occurrences of these rare deepwater calanoids are based on only a few specimens captured at only a small number of locations, but at least some of the occurrences beyond the Southern Ocean have been confirmed by direct comparison of specimens. In contrast, other rare deepwater species originally were described from oceans other than the Southern Ocean and only subsequently were recorded from the Southern Ocean. Because specimens of these rare species from the Southern Ocean have not been compared

to specimens from the type locality, their nominal attribution has yet to be verified.

In this study, the distribution ranges of many species outside the Southern Ocean are determined from information available in the literature. Observations about distributions that are accompanied by species descriptions are the usual source for these data. However, not all species descriptions in the literature are equally informative, and in some cases, it is not easy to determine the identity of all species reported under the same name. In the present study, the distribution range assigned for many of the rare or very rare species, especially for those reports of a few specimens from several localities, should be considered provisional. The definitive answer to the geographical distribution for these rare species must wait until their potential distribution range has been more extensively sampled.

For rare and, particularly, very rare species, specimens may not have been reported from all of the regions between the Southern Ocean and the region farthest north from which a species has been collected. Initially, a continuous deepwater distribution is assumed if a species is present in more than one nonadjacent region, although a possible origin for disjunct distributions is considered here within a larger context of the evolution of bipolar species pairs.

Because the northern boundary of the Southern Ocean is defined hydrographically, certain warm-water species have been reported as penetrating for a relatively short distance south into the subantarctic region, while some typically subantarctic species have often been found to extend north of 40°S in small numbers. If the number of these reports is small, an extension of the species range is not considered here. In this study, warm-water species included in the list as subantarctic species are those that have been reported several times, south of the Subtropical Convergence and close to the Antarctic Convergence. Problems have been resolved in a similar manner for range extensions of species between the Antarctic and subantarctic regions. The identification of a species as having an Antarctic distribution as opposed to a subantarctic distribution is based on the number of reports in one water mass relative to the number in the other water mass.

In this study, the morphological divergence of the exoskeleton among species is used as a first approximation to the degree of relatedness among species, with the understanding that allopatric sibling species may not undergo significant morphological divergence in the absence of a strong adaptive pressure and that secondary sex characters of the exoskeleton are likely to diverge over a shorter period of time than the rest of the exoskeleton. Specimens from the wider geographical regions are reexamined for information regarding the morphological variation and distribution ranges of some of the species (T. Park, unpublished data).

The abundances found in Tables 1–7 are derived from Park (1978, 1980, 1982, 1983a, 1983b, 1988, 1993), who examined samples selected mainly from the *Eltanin* midwater trawl collections available from the Smithsonian Oceanographic Sorting Center. The selection was made to cover as wide an area as possible, but only an aliquot of the original sample was examined systemically and consistently so that the sorted specimens reflect the relative abundance of the species in the sample in a general way. In this paper's introduction, counts of the number of species of copepods and of calanoid copepods were determined by using an online species database (The World of Copepods, National Museum of Natural History) to extend the counts of Humes (1994), beginning with the year 1993, and Bowman and Abele (1982), beginning with the year 1982.

NUMBER SPECIES OF PELAGIC CALANOIDS FROM THE SOUTHERN OCEAN

Two hundred and five species of pelagic calanoid copepods (Appendix 1) in 57 genera from 21 families (Appendix 2) have been reported from the Southern Ocean. Among these, 8 (3.9%) species are coastal or inshore, 13 (6.3%) are epipelagic species, and 184 (89.8%) are deepwater species. Of the 57 genera of pelagic calanoids reported from the Southern Ocean, *Paraeuchaeta* is the most speciose genus with 21 species, followed by *Scolecithricella* (16 species), *Euaugaptilus* (14 species), *Scaphocalanus* (10 species), *Metridia* (9 species), *Pseudochirella* (9 species), *Gaetanus* (8 species), *Onchocalanus* (7 species), and *Lucicutia* (6 species). The 16 species included in the genus *Scolecithricella* are morphologically diverse, and recently, Vyshkvartzeva (2000) proposed to place the species of *Scolecithricella* in one of three genera. Although we are not comfortable with this proposal because the analysis was not exhaustive, acceptance would result in the following numbers from the Southern Ocean: *Scolecithricella* (9 species) and *Pseudoamallothrix* (6 species), with *S. pseudopropinqua* being moved to the genus *Amallothrix*.

Species of *Paraeuchaeta* (Euchaetidae) are deepwater calanoids, and some of them can be collected in large numbers in the Southern Ocean, e.g., *Paraeuchaeta antarctica*

(see Park, 1978; Ferrari and Dojiri, 1987) or *P. barbata, P. rasa,* and *P. biloba* (see Park, 1978). Feeding of a few species of *Paraeuchaeta* has been studied (Yen, 1983, 1991), and these species are known to be carnivores. On the basis of the similarity of feeding appendages among species, this feeding mode is assumed for all species of the genus. In the Southern Ocean, species of *Euaugaptilus* (Augaptilidae) are typically bathypelagic and thought to be carnivores on the basis of the structure of their feeding appendages (Itoh, 1970; Matsuura and Nishida, 2000); they have not been reported in large numbers. The family Aetideidae has the largest number of species (45) in the Southern Ocean, with almost 40% of its species belonging to two genera, *Pseudochirella* and *Gaetanus*; these species also are considered to be carnivores. The combined 80 species of *Paraeuchaeta, Euaugaptilus,* and Aetideidae, then, represent a significant contribution to carnivory in the Southern Ocean and so are believed to play a major role in the dynamics of the deepwater plankton community.

The Scolecitrichidae is the next most speciose family after Aetideidae. Among the 35 species of Scolecitrichidae, those in the genera *Scolecithricella* and *Scaphocalanus* make up 45% of the family in the Southern Ocean. Although the feeding niche of most species of Scolecitrichidae is not well known, derived chemosensory setae on maxilla 2 and maxilliped (Nishida and Ohtsuka, 1997) suggest that species of Scolecitrichidae are the major detritivores in the Southern Ocean. In contrast to carnivory and detritivory, herbivory in the Southern Ocean has been studied more extensively (Hardy and Gunther, 1935; Andrews, 1966). The herbivore fauna is structured by large numbers of individuals belonging to a few species in genera of two families: *Calanus* (three species) and *Calanoides* (one species) in Calanidae and *Eucalanus* (one species) and *Rhincalanus* (one species) in Eucalanidae.

Phylogenetic relationships among the congeneric species of the Southern Ocean have been proposed for two families that have been studied worldwide, Euchaetididae and Heterorhabdidae. Six monophyletic groups of species (species groups) of *Paraeuchaeta* have been identified (Park, 1995). One or more species in five of the six species groups of *Paraeuchaeta* are found in the Southern Ocean. One species group, the *antarctica* species group, consists of five species, and all of its species are limited to waters south of the Antarctic Convergence; this is the only species group of either family that is found only in the Southern Ocean. Three species in the *antarctica* species group of *Paraeuchaeta* appear to be restricted to waters along the edge of ice shelf of Antarctica, and all five may share this same inshore habitat (Fontaine, 1988). Species of the *antarctica* species group are assumed to have evolved after the colonization of the Southern Ocean by a common ancestor (see the Evolution of the Pelagic Calanoid Fauna within the Southern Ocean section). Each species of *Paraeuchaeta* in the remaining four species groups represented in the Southern Ocean has its closest relative in other oceans, rather than the Southern Ocean, suggesting that the remaining species of *Paraeuchaeta* may have colonized the Antarctic region independently.

The family Heterorhabdidae is represented in the Southern Ocean by three genera, *Heterorhabdus*, *Heterostylites*, and *Paraheterorhabdus*. There are five species in the first genus; a single species in each of the last two genera is found in the Southern Ocean (Park, 2000). Four of the five species of *Heterorhabdus* belong to the same species group, the *abyssalis* species group, with 17 species. Two of the four species of this group, *H. spinosus* and *H. paraspinosus*, are morphologically quite similar, suggesting a recent speciation event within the Southern Ocean. The remaining two *Heterorhabdus* species of the *abyssalis* species group, *H. austrinus* and *H. pustulifer*, are morphologically dissimilar; they may have colonized the Southern Ocean independently from one another and from the pair *H. spinosus* and *H. paraspinosus*. The fifth species, *H. lobatus*, belongs to the *papilliger* species group along with five other species found in other oceans; along with *Paraheterorhabdus farrani* and *Heterostylites nigrotinctus*, *H. lobatus* represents an independent colonization.

INSHORE CALANOIDS ALONG CONTINENTAL AND INSULAR COASTS OF THE SOUTHERN OCEAN

Eight species of pelagic calanoids have been found exclusively in waters close to a land mass of the Southern Ocean (Table 1): three species of *Drepanopus* (*D. bispinosus*, *D. forcipatus*, and *D. pectinatus*), three species of *Paralabidocera* (*P. antarctica*, *P. grandispina*, and *P. separabilis*), and two species of *Stephos* (*S. longipes* and *S. antarcticus*). The three species of *Drepanopus* have been collected several times, and all three occasionally have been collected in very large numbers, so their distribution is well known. *Drepanopus bispinosus* has been reported, often as abundant, from inshore waters adjacent to the Vestfold Hills region of Antarctica (Bayly, 1982), and its population structure has been established (Bayly, 1986). *Drepanopus pectinatus* occurs close to shores of Crozet Island, Kerguelen Island, and

TABLE 1. Inshore pelagic calanoid copepods of the southern ocean. Ant, waters south of the Antarctic Convergence; S-Ant, waters between the Antarctic Convergence and the Subantarctic Convergence; CC, very common (over 100 specimens found); C, common (between 99 and 50 specimens found); R, rare (between 49 and 10 specimens found).

Species name	Distribution	Abundance
Drepanopus bispinosus	Ant	CC
Drepanopus forcipatus	S-Ant	CC
Drepanopus pectinatus	S-Ant	CC
Paralabidocera antarctica	Ant	C
Paralabidocera grandispina	Ant	R
Paralabidocera separabilis	Ant	R
Stephos longipes	Ant	C
Stephos antarcticus	Ant	R

Heard Island in the Indian Ocean sector of the Southern Ocean (Hulsemann, 1985a); some aspects of its biology also have been elucidated (Razouls and Razouls, 1990). *Drepanopus forcipatus* is restricted to Atlantic and Pacific coastal and shelf areas along southern South America, including the Falkland Islands, and around South Georgia Island (Hulsemann, 1985a); its copepodid stages have been described (Hulsemann, 1991).

The distributions of the remaining five inshore species are not as well known, and only *Paralabidocera antarctica* and *Stephos longipes* have been reported from more than one locality. *Paralabidocera antarctica* is now known to occur in small numbers in waters close to the shoreline at several locations, including the South Shetland Islands, the extreme south of the Ross Sea, two localities in the Atlantic Ocean sector of Antarctica, and one locality in the Indian Ocean sector of Antarctica (Vervoort, 1957). The species is believed to inhabit the surface water layers and is occasionally captured under the ice (Vervoort, 1951); development of its marine and lacustrine populations has been described (Swadling et al., 2004). *Paralabidocera grandispina* Waghorn, 1979 and *P. separabilis* Brodsky and Zvereva, 1976 are known only from their type localities, beneath the ice along the Pacific Ocean sector of Antarctica and near the shore of Antarctica in the Indian Ocean sector, respectively.

Of the two species of *Stephos*, *S. longipes* has been found close to or under the ice shelf in the Pacific and Indian ocean sectors of Antarctica including the Ross Sea, where it can be very abundant (Giesbrecht, 1902; Farran, 1929; Tanaka, 1960). Its associations with the ice and the open water have been described (Kurbjeweit et al., 1993;

Schnack-Schiel et al., 1995). *Stephos antarcticus* is known only from its type locality, McMurdo Sound of the Ross Sea (Wolfenden, 1908). Most species of the genus *Stephos* are closely associated with the water immediately above the seafloor (Bradford-Grieve, 1999).

Among these eight species, the three species of *Drepanopus* and the three species of *Paralabidocera* clearly seem to be pelagic. The two species of *Stephos* appear to be ice oriented but are considered pelagic here. All of these inshore species are characteristically small in size, ranging from 0.85 to 2.80 mm in body length.

EPIPELAGIC FAUNA OF THE SOUTHERN OCEAN

The epipelagic calanoid fauna of the Southern Ocean south of the Antarctic Convergence (Table 2) is relatively simple in species composition. There are five species, all are very common, and their combined biomass is unsurpassed by the epipelagic calanoid fauna of any other region of the world's oceans (Foxton, 1956). These five epipelagic species are, in order of abundance, *Calanoides acutus*, *Rhincalanus gigas*, *Calanus propinquus*, *Metridia gerlachei*,

and *Clausocalanus laticeps*. These are the copepods most often associated by planktonologists with the Southern Ocean. All were discovered during the early expeditions, and their taxonomy and distribution have been clearly and carefully defined. Although these five species are more abundant in waters south of the Antarctic Convergence, they also may be collected north of the convergence, but here they appear to be associated with the deeper Antarctic Intermediate Water. *Calanoides acutus* and, to a lesser extent, *Rhincalanus gigas* and *Calanus propinquus* are the dominant herbivores south of the Antarctic Convergence, and their role in that ecosystem is well known (Chiba et al., 2002; Pasternak and Schnack-Schiel, 2001).

The analogous epipelagic calanoids of the subantarctic region, between the Antarctic and Subtropical convergences, are *Calanus simillimus*, *Clausocalanus brevipes*, and *Ctenocalanus citer*. These three herbivores are very common in the subantarctic region, but they are not as numerous in these waters as the previous five epipelagic calanoids are south of the Antarctic Convergence. Furthermore, the Antarctic Convergence does not limit the southern boundary of the range of these three species as precisely as it limits the northern boundary of the previous five epipelagic calanoids. The population structure and life histories of the three have been described (Atkinson, 1991; Schnack-Schiel and Mizdalski, 1994).

There are three additional large-sized, epipelagic herbivores that may be collected in the subantarctic region as well as in the south temperate midlatitudes: *Calanus australis*, *Neocalanus tonsus*, and *Subeucalanus longiceps*. *Calanus australis* is known to be distributed along the southern coast of Chile, off Argentina, in New Zealand waters, and in southeastern Australian waters (Bradford-Grieve, 1994). Its distribution during summer has been investigated (Sabatini et al., 2000). *Neocalanus tonsus* is widely distributed in subantarctic waters but also may be found in the deepwater of the south temperate region; some aspects of its life history are known (Ohman et al., 1989). *Subeucalanus longiceps* (Subeucalanidae) occurs circumglobally in the subantarctic and temperate regions of the Southern Hemisphere. These three species are important herbivores in the subantarctic as well as the south temperate region.

Two small-sized, epipelagic herbivores, *Clausocalanus parapergens* and *Ctenocalanus vanus*, are found in subantarctic waters. *Clausocalanus parapergens* has been reported as far north as the subtropical convergence (Frost and Fleminger, 1968). Specimens referred to as *Ctenocalanus vanus* from the Southern Ocean by Farran (1929) and Vervoort (1951, 1957) are *Ctenocalanus citer* (T. Park,

TABLE 2. Epipelagic calanoid copepods of the Southern Ocean. CC, very common (over 100 specimens found); C, common (between 99 and 50 specimens found).

Species name	Abundance
Species endemic to Antarctic waters	
Calanoides acutus	CC
Calanus propinquus	CC
Clausocalanus laticeps	CC
Metridia gerlachei	CC
Rhincalanus gigas	CC
Species endemic to subantarctic waters	
Calanus simillimus	CC
Clausocalanus brevipes	CC
Ctenocalanus citer	C
Species ranging from subantarctic water to south temperate region	
Calanus australis	C
Neocalanus tonsus	C
Subeucalanus longiceps	C
Species ranging from subantarctic waters to north temperate region	
Eucalanus hyalinus	C
Rhincalanus nasutus	C

unpublished observations); this species is restricted to the Southern Ocean.

Calanids like *Calanoides acutus, Calanus propinquus, Calanus simillimus, Calanus australis,* and *Neocalanus tonsus* as well as eucalanids like *Rhincalanus gigas* and subeucalanids like *Subeucalanus longiceps* are considered epipelagic here because they spend their juvenile and adult life in near-surface waters. However, during seasonal episodes of low primary productivity, some late juvenile stages of the populations of each of these species descend to mesopelagic depths (Vervoort, 1957) to diapause.

Two epipelagic calanoid species, *Eucalanus hyalinus* and *Rhincalanus nasutus,* do not occur in large numbers in the subantarctic region. North of the Subtropical Convergence, they often are encountered in warmer waters, and they have been collected in the north temperate region. Their taxonomy and distribution are well understood. Usually, only a few specimens are collected in pelagic samples from the Southern Ocean, and here these species are considered to be associated with habitats of low primary productivity.

In summary, 13 calanoid species contribute to the epipelagic fauna of the Southern Ocean. Five of them are endemic south of the Antarctic Convergence and are very common throughout this region. Three species are endemic to the subantarctic region and occur throughout that region. However, the subantarctic endemics are not as numerous as the five species endemic to the Antarctic region in midwater trawl samples. Three more epipelagic calanoid species occur widely in the subantarctic and temperate regions of the Southern Hemisphere. They are either common in productive coastal upwelling areas or are circumglobal in the West Wind Drift of the Southern Hemisphere. The broadest latitudinal range exhibited by subantarctic epipelagic calanoids is that of the two species of Eucalanidae that have been collected from the subantarctic region to the north temperate region.

DEEPWATER CALANOIDS RESTRICTED TO THE SOUTHERN OCEAN

Among the 184 species of deepwater calanoids found in the Southern Ocean, 50 species were originally described from the Southern Ocean and, to date, are known exclusively from there (Table 3). Twenty-four of these deepwater calanoids originally were described from waters south of the Antarctic Convergence and subsequently have been found exclusively in those waters; they are endemics of the Antarctic region. Of these 24 Antarctic endemics, six

species have a distinctly localized distribution, occurring almost exclusively along the ice edge of Antarctica. There are four closely related species of the *antarctica* species group of *Paraeuchaeta,* plus one species each of *Aetideopsis* and *Chiridiella.* All six species have strongly built bodies and limbs and a well-sclerotized exoskeleton; they are presumed to be carnivores. *Chiridiella megadactyla* was described from a single female collected close to the edge of the Ross Ice Shelf and has not been found again. *Aetideopsis antarctica,* a rare species, was collected initially from waters beneath the edge of the Ross Ice Shelf (Wolfenden, 1908); it subsequently has been found several other times from the same habitat. Three of the four species of the *antarctica* species group of *Paraeuchaeta, P. austrina, P. erebi,* and *P. tycodesma,* have also been reported only a few times and collected only in small numbers. *Paraeuchaeta similis,* the fourth species of the group, has occasionally been reported to be quite common under the ice (Bradford, 1981), unlike the above three congeners of its species group, which are rare. However, *P. similis* also may be collected in the deeper layer of warm water (Vervoort, 1965b), well away from the ice edge. Here it occasionally may co-occur with *P. antarctica* (see Ferrari and Dojiri, 1987), the fifth species of the group (Fontaine, 1988; Park, 1995). The three ice edge species of *Paraeuchaeta,* together with *P. similis* and *P. antarctica,* a species endemic to and abundant throughout Antarctic and the subantarctic regions (Park, 1978; Marín and Antezana, 1985; Ferrari and Dojiri, 1987), form the group of closely related species. Despite this close relationship, all five of these species have been collected a number of times in the same midwater trawl from waters adjacent to the ice edge.

Four other species, *Batheuchaeta antarctica, B. pubescens, Pseudochirella formosa,* and *Onchocalanus subcristatus,* were initially described from deep water south of the Antarctic Convergence. All have been collected only once, and each is known only from one or two specimens. The first three are aetideids and are presumed to be carnivores; the last belongs to Phaennidae, a family of detritivores related to the Scolecitrichidae. These four species and the earlier mentioned *Chiridiella megadactyla* remain so poorly known that their taxonomic status and distribution cannot be confirmed.

Among the 24 species endemic to the Antarctic region, the remaining 14 species have been collected widely south of the Antarctic Convergence and, except for *Euaugaptilus austrinus* and *Landrumius antarcticus,* are either common or very common, so their taxonomy and distribution have been well established. Among them are three species of small calanoid copepods, *Scaphocalanus vervoorti,*

TABLE 3. Abundances of deepwater calanoid species endemic to the Southern Ocean. CC, very common; C, common; R, rare; RR, very rare.

Species name	Abundance	Species name	Abundance
Species occurring along the ice edge of Antarctica (6 spp.)		Species occurring in both Antarctic and subantarctic waters (19 spp.)	
Aetideopsis antarctica	R	*Aetideus australis*	C
Chiridiella megadactyla	R	*Candacia maxima*	R
Paraeuchaeta austrina	R	*Cephalophanes frigidus*	C
Paraeuchaeta erebi	R	*Heterorhabdus pustulifer*	C
Paraeuchaeta similis	C	*Heterorhabdus austrinus*	C
Paraeuchaeta tycodesma	R	*Heterostylites nigrotinctus*	R
		Metridia pseudoasymmetrica	R
Species occurring widely in Antarctic waters (14 spp.)		*Paraeuchaeta antarctica*	CC
Euaugaptilus antarcticus	CC	*Paraeuchaeta biloba*	CC
Euaugaptilus austrinus	R	*Paraeuchaeta dactylifera*	C
Euchirella rostromagna	CC	*Paraeuchaeta parvula*	C
Haloptilus ocellatus	CC	*Paraeuchaeta rasa*	CC
Landrumius antarcticus	R	*Paraheterorhabdus farrani*	C
Onchocalanus magnus	C	*Pleuromamma antarctica*	C
Onchocalanus wolfendeni	C	*Pseudochirella mawsoni*	C
Paraeuchaeta eltaninae	C	*Scaphocalanus farrani*	CC
Scaphocalanus antarcticus	CC	*Scaphocalanus parantarcticus*	CC
Scaphocalanus subbrevicornis	CC	*Scolecithricella dentipes*	CC
Scaphocalanus vervoorti	CC	*Scolecithricella schizosoma*	CC
Scolecithricella cenotelis	CC		
Scolecithricella vervoorti	C	Species endemic to subantarctic waters (7 spp.)	
Spinocalanus terranovae	C	*Aetideopsis tumorosa*	R
		Bathycalanus eltaninae	R
Species known from 1 or 2 specimens in Antarctic waters (4 spp.)		*Bathycalanus unicornis*	R
Batheuchaeta antarctica	RR	*Bradycalanus enormis*	R
Batheuchaeta pubescens	RR	*Bathycalanus inflatus*	R
Onchocalanus subcristatus	RR	*Bradycalanus pseudotypicus*	R
Pseudochirella formosa	RR	*Candacia cheirura*	C

Scolecithricella cenotelis, and *Scaphocalanus subbrevicornis*, that may occur in particularly large numbers in waters close to continent, where they may be encountered in relatively shallow water (Park, 1980, 1982). These small, abundant species all belong to the family Scolecitrichidae and are presumed to be detritivores. Two other small, common, pelagic calanoids, *Scolecithricella vervoorti* and *Spinocalanus terranovae*, are found exclusively in the Antarctic region but in relatively smaller numbers than the first three. The former is a scolecitrichid. *Spinocalanus terranovae* belongs to the Spinocalanidae; its trophic niche is not known.

Of the remaining nine deepwater species restricted to waters south of the Antarctic Convergence, all are relatively large calanoids. They can be divided into two groups. Four species are very common; in order of the number of specimens collected they are *Euchirella rostromagna*, *Haloptilus ocellatus*, *Scaphocalanus antarcticus*, and *Euaugaptilus antarcticus*. Three species are common, *Onchocalanus wolfendeni*, *Paraeuchaeta eltaninae*, and *Onchocalanus*

magnus, and two species are rare, *Euaugaptilus austrinus* and *Landrumius antarcticus*. These large species are taxonomically diverse and belong to five calanoid families (Appendix 2).

There are 19 endemic species of calanoid copepods that have been found in both the Antarctic and the subantarctic regions, i.e., south of the Subtropical Convergence. Most prominent among them are five species of *Paraeuchaeta*: *P. antarctica*, *P. biloba*, *P. rasa*, *P. parvula*, and *P. dactylifera*. *Paraeuchaeta antarctica* and *P. rasa* are among the most abundant carnivorous calanoids of the Southern Ocean. They are usually encountered south of the Antarctic Convergence but may be collected in small numbers to the north in open waters; *P. antarctica* has also been reported as far north as the Chilean fjords (Marín and Antezana, 1985). *Paraeuchaeta biloba* can be collected immediately adjacent to, and on either side of, the Antarctic Convergence. A unique record of the co-occurrence of these three species of *Paraeuchaeta* is from a deep midwater trawl sample (0–1,295 m) taken off Uruguay (34°43′S, 49°28′W to 34°51′S, 49°44′W) in the southwestern Atlantic north of the Subtropical Convergence (Park, 1978).

Paraeuchaeta parvula, like *P. biloba*, has also been collected both north and south of the Antarctic Convergence. *Paraeuchaeta dactylifera* has only been found in relatively small numbers and usually in the subantarctic region; two specimens captured well south of the Antarctic Convergence (Park, 1978) are exceptions. Two aetideid species, *Aetideus australis* and *Pseudochirella mawsoni*, can also be found both north and south of the Antarctic Convergence. *Aetideus australis* has been collected more often in waters north of the convergence than south. *Pseudochirella mawsoni* has been reported from numerous localities in the Southern Ocean and has been collected in large numbers in midwater trawls immediately north of convergence. Both species are presumed to be carnivores.

Four very common scolecitrichid species are endemic to the Southern Ocean. *Scolecithricella dentipes* and *Scaphocalanus farrani* are found throughout the Antarctic and subantarctic regions, where they may be numerous in some samples. *Scaphocalanus parantarcticus* and *Scolecithricella schizosoma* are also distributed throughout the Southern Ocean and may be very common but are found in smaller numbers than the first two.

There are four species of the family Heterorhabdidae that are well-known endemics of the Southern Ocean: *Heterorhabdus pustulifer*, *H. austrinus*, *Heterostylites nigrotinctus*, and *Paraheterorhabdus farrani*. *Paraheterorhabdus farrani* is common and has been collected throughout the Southern Ocean; *Heterorhabdus pustulifer* and *H. austrinus* are also common, while *Heterostylites nigrotinctus* is rare. Among the remaining 4 of the 19 endemic species reported from both Antarctic and subantarctic regions, three rare species, *Candacia maxima*, *Cephalophanes frigidus*, and *Metridia pseudoasymmetrica*, and the common *Pleuromamma antarctica* are not often encountered in samples. However, there are enough records to suggest that these species are limited to the Southern Ocean.

There are seven deepwater species that have been found only in the subantarctic region (Table 3). Six of them, *Aetideopsis tumerosa*, *Bathycalanus eltaninae*, *B. unicornis*, *Bradycalanus enormis*, *B. inflatus*, and *B. pseudotypicus*, are known from a few localities and only a few specimens; their distribution cannot be determined with certainty. Of these six species, the latter five belong to the family Megacalanidae; *Aetideopsis tumerosa* is an aetideid. The seventh species, *Candacia cheirura*, has been collected often enough to be considered the only species of Candaciidae restricted to the subantarctic region. It is

common and has been hypothesized to be restricted to mesopelagic waters of the West Wind Drift (Vervoort, 1957), also called the Antarctic Circumpolar Current, which is the dominant circulation feature of the Southern Ocean.

In summary, among the 50 deepwater calanoid copepod species found exclusively in the Southern Ocean, six species occur close to the continent. Although these species have been captured in relatively small numbers, they may have been undersampled due to the difficulty in collecting with a midwater trawl in deepwater close to the continent. Among these six species, the closely related *Paraeuchaeta austrina*, *P. erebi*, and *P. tycodesma*, all members of the *antarctica* species group, appear to be restricted to the same habitat. Of the 18 species found in open waters south of the Antarctic Convergence, four were originally described from one or two specimens collected in a single sample, have not been rediscovered, and remain poorly known. The remaining 14 species can be regarded as typical endemics of the Antarctic deep water. Except for two relatively rare species, they are common or very common in waters south of the Antarctic Convergence. Nineteen of the 50 Southern Ocean deepwater species are typical endemics of the region as a whole, and most of them have been collected from many localities throughout the Southern Ocean. Seven of these species have only been found in the subantarctic region. Their distributions are based on a small number of specimens and therefore are insufficiently known. *Candacia cheirura* is an exception; it is a common endemic of the subantarctic region.

DEEPWATER CALANOIDS FROM ANTARCTIC WATERS REPORTED NORTH OF THE SUBTROPICAL CONVERGENCE

A total of 127 deepwater species of pelagic calanoid copepods have been reported from the Southern Ocean south of the Antarctic Convergence. Twenty-four of those species are limited to this region (see the Deepwater Calanoids Restricted to the Southern Ocean section), and 19 species have been found northward, into the subantarctic region, with their distribution terminating at the Subtropical Convergence. Thus, 43 of these 127 deepwater species collected south of the Antarctic Convergence are endemic to the Southern Ocean.

The remaining 84 species have been reported beyond the Subtropical Convergence to varying degrees. Seven (8%) of these species have been collected in the south temperate region, adjacent to the Southern Ocean (Table 4), and five (6%) species have been collected as far north as

TABLE 4. Abundances and locations of deepwater calanoid species collected south of the Antarctic Convergence that occur north of the Subtropical Convergence. 1, south temperate; 2, tropical; 3, north temperate; 4, subarctic; 5, Arctic basin. Abundance in Southern Ocean: CC, very common; C, common; R, rare; RR, very rare. A "+" indicates presence.

Species name	Abundance	Region				
		1	2	3	4	5
Species ranging from Antarctic waters to the south temperate region (7 spp.)						
Euaugaptilus hadrocephalus	RR	+				
Euaugaptilus perasetosus	R	+				
Onchocalanus paratrigoniceps	R	+				
Paraeuchaeta regalis	CC	+				
Pseudochirella hirsuta	C	+				
Scolecithricella hadrosoma	R	+				
Scolecithricella parafalcifer	R	+				
Species ranging from Antarctic waters to tropical region (5 spp.)						
Cornucalanus robustus	CC	+	+			
Farrania frigida	R	+	+			
Lucicutia bradyana	R	+	+			
Paraeuchaeta abbreviata	R	+	+			
Scaphocalanus major	R	+	+			
Species ranging from Antarctic waters to north temperate region (29 spp.)						
Batheuchaeta lamellata	R	+	+	+		
Batheuchaeta peculiaris	R	+		+		
Bathycalanus bradyi	R	+	+	+		
Chiridiella subaequalis	R			+		
Chiridius polaris	R			+		
Cornucalanus chelifer	CC	+		+		
Cornucalanus simplex	R	+		+		
Euaugaptilus bullifer	R			+		
Euaugaptilus magna	C	+		+		
Euaugaptilus maxillaris	R	+		+		
Euaugaptilus nodifrons	C	+		+		
Gaetanus antarcticus	R	+		+		
Gaetanus paracurvicornis	R	+		+		
Haloptilus fons	R	+	+	+		
Haloptilus oxycephalus	CC		+	+		
Lophothrix humilifrons	R	+		+		
Metridia ferrarii	R	+		+		
Onchocalanus cristatus	R	+		+		
Onchocalanus hirtipes	R	+		+		
Onchocalanus trigoniceps	R	+		+		
Scaphocalanus elongatus	C		+	+		
Scolecithricella altera	R			+		
Scolecithricella emarginata	CC	+	+	+		
Scolecithricella obtusifrons	R			+		
Scolecithricella ovata	C	+		+		
Talacalanus greeni	R			+		
Valdiviella oligarthra	R	+		+		
Valdiviella brevicornis	R	+		+		
Valdiviella insignis	R	+	+	+		

Species name	Abundance	Region 1	Region 2	Region 3	Region 4	Region 5
Species ranging from Antarctic waters to the subarctic region (30 spp.)						
Aetideopsis multiserrata	R	+	+	+	+	
Arietellus simplex	R	+	+	+	+	
Candacia falcifera	R		+	+	+	
Chiridius gracilis	R		+	+	+	
Haloptilus longicirrus	R	+	+	+	+	
Lucicutia curta	R	+	+	+	+	
Lucicutia macrocera	R	+	+	+	+	
Lucicutia magna	R	+	+	+	+	
Lucicutia ovalis	R	+	+	+	+	
Lucicutia wolfendeni	R	+	+	+	+	
Megacalanus princeps	R	+	+	+	+	
Metridia curticauda	R	+	+	+	+	
Metridia ornata	R			+	+	
Metridia princeps	R	+	+	+	+	
Mimocalanus cultrifer	R	+	+	+	+	
Nullosetigera bidentatus	R	+		+	+	
Pachyptilus eurygnathus	R	+		+	+	
Paraeuchaeta kurilensis	R	+		+	+	
Paraeuchaeta tumidula	R	+		+	+	
Pseudeuchaeta brevicauda	R	+	+	+	+	
Pseudochirella dubia	R	+	+	+	+	
Pseudochirella notacantha	R	+	+	+	+	
Pseudochirella obtusa	C	+	+	+		
Pseudochirella pustulifera	R	+	+	+		
Racovitzanus antarcticus	CC	+		+	+	
Scolecithricella minor	CC	+		+	+	
Scolecithricella valida	C	+		+	+	
Spinocalanus abyssalis	R	+		+	+	
Spinocalanus magnus	R	+		+	+	
Undeuchaeta incisa	R	+	+	+	+	
Species ranging from Antarctic waters to the Arctic Ocean (13 spp.)						
Aetideopsis minor	R				+	+
Aetideopsis rostrata	R				+	+
Augaptilus glacialis	R	+	+	+	+	+
Gaetanus brevispinus	CC	+	+	+	+	+
Gaetanus tenuispinus	CC	+	+	+	+	+
Microcalanus pygmaeus	R	+		+	+	+
Paraeuchaeta barbata	CC	+	+	+	+	+
Pseudaugaptilus longiremis	R			+	+	+
Pseudochirella batillipa	R			+		+
Pseudochirella spectabilis	R				+	+
Spinocalanus antarcticus	R					+
Spinocalanus horridus	R	+	+	+	+	+
Temorites brevis	R		+	+	+	+

the tropical region. There are records of 29 species (35%) from the Southern Ocean as far north as the north temperate region and reports of 30 species (36%) as far north as the subarctic seas (Table 5). Thirteen species (15%) have been collected as far north as the Arctic Ocean.

Five (71%) of the seven species ranging from the Antarctic region to the south temperate region are rare or very rare (Table 4). *Euaugaptilus hadrocephalus*, *E. perasetosus*, *Onchocalanus paratrigoniceps*, *Scolecithricella hadrosoma*, and *S. parafalcifer* originally were described from a few specimens and have not been collected again; they are poorly known. Two species, *Paraeuchaeta regalis* and *Pseudochirella hirsuta*, have been collected from many localities throughout the subantarctic region, and specimens have been found in small numbers from samples both northward in the south temperate region and southward into Antarctic regions. *Paraeuchaeta regalis*, like its euchaetid congeners, is probably a carnivore; *Pseudochirella hirsuta*, an aetideid, is also presumed to be carnivorous on the basis of the size and structure of its feeding appendages.

Of the five Southern Ocean species that have been collected into the deepwater of the tropical region (Table 4), *Farrania frigida*, *Lucicutia bradyana*, *Paraeuchaeta abbreviata*, and *Scaphocalanus major* are rare (80%) and remain poorly known; their records are based on a small number of specimens collected from a few widely separated localities. Only one of the five species, *Cornucalanus robustus*, occurs throughout the Southern Ocean; Park (1983b) recovered it from 37 deepwater stations in the Antarctic and subantarctic regions. Vervoort (1965a) identified five specimens, including two juvenile copepodids in the deep water of the Gulf of Guinea in the tropical Atlantic, and this remained the only record from outside the Southern Ocean until Björnberg (1973) reported it in the southeastern Pacific Ocean.

All 29 Southern Ocean species collected as far north as the north temperate region (Table 4) appear to be bathypelagic, found between 1,000 and 4,000 m. Twenty-two (76%) of these are rare in the Southern Ocean. Among the remaining seven species, six are either common or very common (number in the parenthesis is the number of specimens found in the Southern Ocean): *Haloptilus oxycephalus* (388), *Scolecithricella emarginata* (226), *Cornucalanus chelifer* (111), *Scolecithricella ovata* (76), *Euaugaptilus nodifrons* (71), and *Scaphocalanus elongatus* (63). *Scolecithricella emarginata* and *Cornucalanus chelifer* are very common in the Southern Ocean. *Haloptilus oxycephalus* is very common and *Euaugaptilus nodifrons* is common in the Southern Ocean, but only a few specimens of either species have been collected in the subantarctic, south temperate, or tropical regions. *Scolecithricella ovata* and *Scapho-*

calanus elongatus are common in the subantarctic region. Forty-four specimens of the seventh species, *Euaugaptilus magnus*, have been recovered from the Southern Ocean, but most of these are from the subantarctic region. It is categorized here as rare but is still better represented than the other 22 rare species.

Thirty species reported from Antarctic region also have been collected in the subarctic region (Table 4). All of them are bathypelagic, and 87% are rare. The remaining four species are common or very common in the Southern Ocean (number in the parenthesis is the number of specimens found in the Southern Ocean by T. Park): *Scolecithricella minor* (1,728), *Racovitzanus antarcticus* (1,077), *Scolecithricella valida* (74), and *Pseudochirella obtusa* (52). A greater number of specimens of *Scolecithricella minor* than any other species of this genus was encountered in the Southern Ocean. Specimens were more likely to be collected in water close to the continent, where the species occasionally has been reported from the epipelagic zone. *Racovitzanus antarcticus* is more likely to be encountered in the Antarctic region although it also occurs in waters immediately north of the Antarctic Convergence and beyond. *Scolecithricella valida* was found widely throughout the Southern Ocean. *Pseudochirella obtusa* was recorded from the Antarctic region by Park (1978) as *Pseudochirella polyspina*.

Thirteen species (Table 4) from the Antarctic region have also been collected in the Arctic region (Arctic Ocean basin). They are all bathypelagic, and 77% are rare except for the following three very common species (number in parenthesis is the number of specimens found in the Southern Ocean by T. Park): *Paraeuchaeta barbata* (462), *Gaetanus tenuispinus* (414), and *Gaetanus brevispinus* (150). The northern and southern polar populations of the species now known as *Paraeuchaeta barbata* at one time were considered to be a bipolar species, *Euchaeta farrani* (see Farran, 1929; Vervoort, 1957). Later, *Euchaeta farrani* was synonymized with *Euchaeta barbata* by Park (1978). *Euchaeta barbata* was then considered to have a wide distribution throughout the deep water of the world's oceans, as recorded under that name by Mauchline (1992) and later as *Paraeuchaeta barbata* by Park (1995). Throughout the Southern Ocean, *P. barbata* is very common in deep water. *Gaetanus tenuispinus* is very common south of the Antarctic Convergence. Specimens of the third very common species, *Gaetanus brevispinus* Sars, 1900, were initially described from the Southern Ocean as *Gaidius intermedius* Wolfenden, 1905, but specimens of this species now are considered to belong to *Gaetanus brevispinus* (see Markhaseva, 1996). *Gaetanus brevispinus* is most often encountered in large numbers south of the Antarctic Convergence.

TABLE 5. Abundances and locations of subantarctic deepwater calanoid species absent south of the Antarctic Convergence that occur north of the Subtropical Convergence. 1, south temperate; 2, tropical; 3, north temperate; 4, subarctic; 5, Arctic basin. Abundance in Southern Ocean: CC, very common; C, common; R, rare. A "+" indicates presence.

Species name	Abundance	Region 1	2	3	4	5
Species ranging from subantarctic to south temperate region (6 spp.)						
Euaugaptilus aliquantus	R	+				
Euaugaptilus brevirostratus	R	+				
Heterorhabdus spinosus	CC	+				
Heterorhabdus paraspinosus	C	+				
Paraeuchaeta exigua	C	+				
Scolecithricella pseudopropinqua	R	+				
Species ranging from subantarctic to tropical region (2 spp.)						
Euchirella similis	R	+	+			
Landrumius gigas	R	+	+			
Species ranging from subantarctic to north temperate region (31 spp.)						
Aetideus arcuatus	R	+	+	+		
Euaugaptilus angustus	R		+	+		
Euaugaptilus gibbus	R		+	+		
Euaugaptilus laticeps	R	+	+	+		
Euaugaptilus oblongus	R			+		
Euchirella rostrata	R	+	+	+		
Gaetanus minor	R	+	+	+		
Gaetanus pileatus	R	+	+	+		
Heterorhabdus lobatus	C	+	+	+		
Lophothrix frontalis	C	+	+	+		
Metridia lucens	R	+	+	+		
Metridia venusta	R	+	+	+		
Paraeuchaeta comosa	R	+	+	+		
Paraeuchaeta pseudotonsa	C	+	+	+		
Paraeuchaeta sarsi	R	+	+	+		
Paraeuchaeta scotti	R	+	+	+		
Pleuromamma abdominalis	R	+	+	+		
Pleuromamma peseki	R	+	+	+		
Pleuromamma quadrungulata	R	+	+	+		
Pleuromamma xiphias	R	+	+	+		
Scaphocalanus cristatus	R			+		
Scaphocalanus echinatus	CC	+	+	+		
Scaphocalanus medius	C		+	+		
Scolecithricella dentata	R	+	+	+		
Scolecithricella profunda	R	+	+	+		
Scolecithricella vittata	R	+	+	+		
Scottocalanus securifrons	C	+	+	+		
Scottocalanus helenae	R	+	+	+		
Undeuchaeta major	R	+	+	+		
Undeuchaeta plumosa	R	+	+	+		
Valdiviella minor	R	+	+	+		
Species ranging from subantarctic to subarctic waters (10 spp.)						
Centraugaptilus rattrayi	R	+	+	+	+	
Chirundina streetsii	R	+	+	+	+	
Disseta palumbii	R	+	+	+	+	
Euchirella maxima	R	+	+	+	+	
Gaetanus kruppii	R	+	+	+	+	
Gaetanus latifrons	R	+	+	+	+	
Metridia brevicauda	R	+	+	+	+	
Paraeuchaeta hansenii	R	+	+	+	+	
Scottocalanus thorii	R			+	+	
Undinella brevipes	R			+	+	
Species ranging from subantarctic to Arctic basin (1 sp.)						
Paraheterorhabdus compactus	R	+	+	+		+

In summary, there are 84 species of deepwater calanoid copepods that occur south of the Antarctic Convergence and have also been reported northward to different degrees; 86% of these species have been reported at least as far north as the north temperate region. Two of the seven species occurring from the Antarctic region to the south temperate region are common or very common in the Southern Ocean, while one of the five species found from the Antarctic region north to the tropical region is very common in the Southern Ocean. Seven of the 29 species reported from the Antarctic region and the north temperate region are common or very common in the Southern Ocean. Four of the 30 species from the Antarctic region and reported as far north as the subarctic region are common or very common in the Southern Ocean. Only 3 of the 13 species found in the Arctic Ocean are common or very common in the Southern Ocean. These observations suggest that most (80%) of the rare or very rare deepwater species occurring in the Antarctic region appear to be distributed widely throughout the world's oceans, where they also are rare or very rare deepwater species. However, there are a small number (17) of deepwater species that may be collected in large numbers in the Southern Ocean that are widely distributed and rare or very rare outside of the Southern Ocean.

In contrast to the epipelagic calanoid community, the deepwater pelagic calanoid community of the Southern Ocean is represented by a very diverse group of species. Many of the endemic species collected in the Southern Ocean are common or very common there, apparently having adapted to the high primary and secondary productivity (Park, 1994). Interestingly, a few of the species collected in other regions are also very common in the Southern Ocean, although they are known from only a few specimens throughout the rest of their range. These species appear to be capable of surviving in habitats of low productivity, and yet they can maintain larger populations in some eutrophic habitats like the Southern Ocean. This small number of deepwater species of pelagic calanoid copepods may also be well adapted to high primary and secondary productivity of the Southern Ocean, and this adaptation may result in relatively larger numbers of specimens (Park, 1994).

SUBANTARCTIC DEEPWATER CALANOIDS REPORTED NORTH OF THE SUBTROPICAL CONVERGENCE

Of the 167 deepwater calanoid species found in the subantarctic region, between the Antarctic Convergence and Subtropical Convergence, seven are endemic to that region; 110 species were also collected south of the Antarctic Convergence. The remaining 50 species are not collected south of the Antarctic Convergence, but their distribution does extend north of the Subtropical Convergence (Table 5). Six species (12%) can be found in the south temperate region, and two (4%) have been collected in the tropical region. There are records of 31 species (62%) in the north temperate region, 10 species (20%) in the subarctic region, and 1 species (2%) from the Arctic basin.

Of the six species ranging from the subantarctic to the south temperate regions, *Heterorhabdus spinosus* is very common, and *H. paraspinosus* and *Paraeuchaeta exigua* are common in the subantarctic region. The two species of *Heterorhabdus* occur together and have been collected from only three other widely separated areas: off the west coast of South Africa, off the southern west coast of Chile, and off the east coast of New Zealand and in the Tasman Sea. *Paraeuchaeta exigua* has been found in four widely separated areas: the eastern and the western parts of the South Atlantic Ocean, the Tasman Sea, and the western Indian Ocean, where it is very common (Park, 1995). These three species apparently are associated with habitats of high secondary productivity, especially coastal upwelling systems. The remaining three species have been found only once and remain poorly known.

Only two species, *Euchirella similis* and *Landrumius gigas*, have been reported from the subantarctic region to the tropical region. They are very rare in the subantarctic region and remain poorly known. All 31 species ranging from the subantarctic region to the north temperate region were originally described from the low or middle latitudes and subsequently have been reported from the subantarctic region. All are believed to be mesopelagic or bathypelagic except for two relatively shallow living species, *Scolecithricella dentata* and *Scolecithricella vittata*. Twenty-five of the species are rare in the subantarctic region, and five species, *Scottocalanus securifrons*, *Paraeuchaeta pseudotonsa*, *Lophothrix frontalis*, *Scaphocalanus medius*, and *Heterorhabdus lobatus*, are common. Only *Scaphocalanus echinatus* is very common in the subantarctic region.

Ten of the subantarctic species have been found as far north as the subarctic region. They are all rare deepwater calanoids. *Paraheterorhabdus compactus* is the only species known to occur from the subantarctic region north to the Arctic basin; it is bathypelagic and occurs in small numbers throughout its range (Park, 2000).

In summary, there are 50 species that are absent south of the Antarctic Convergence but are found in the subantarctic region and northward to varying degrees. Eighty-four percent of these species have been reported to at least the north temperate region. Eighty-two percent are rare; the exceptions are three of six species occurring in the subantarctic and south temperate regions, where they are common in the productive coastal waters, and 6 of 31 species found from the subantarctic to the north temperate regions. These latter six are common or very common in productive the subantarctic region.

SOUTHERN OCEAN CALANOIDS WITH A BIPOLAR DISTRIBUTION

There are nine pelagic calanoids whose distribution can be described as bipolar (Table 6). *Aetideopsis minor*, *Pseudochirella spectabilis*, and *Spinocalanus antarcticus* are found south of the Antarctic Convergence and in the Arctic basin (Table 4); *Aetideopsis rostrata* and *Pseudochirella batillipa* are found south of the Antarctic Convergence, in the Arctic basin and its adjacent boreal seas (Table 4); *Metridia ornata* and *Racovitzanus antarcticus* are found south of the Antarctic Convergence and in boreal seas adjacent to the Arctic basin (Table 4); *Batheuchaeta peculiaris* and *Chiridius polaris* are found both north and south of the Antarctic Convergence and in boreal seas adjacent to the Arctic basin. Eight of these nine species are rare or very rare deepwater species in both polar areas, and three of those eight have been found in the subarctic region but not in the Arctic Ocean basin. The ninth species, *Racovitzanus antarcticus*, is very common in the waters south of the Antarctic Convergence and has been described as common in the boreal seas adjacent to the Arctic basin (Brodsky, 1950).

TABLE 6. Nine Calanoid species with a bipolar distribution.

Species name	Distribution
Aetideopsis minor	Antarctic (61°–69°S), Arctic basin
Aetideopsis rostrata	Antarctic, Arctic and boreal seas
Batheuchaeta peculiaris	Antarctic (63°S), boreal region (45°–46°N)
Chiridius polaris	Antarctic (53°–68°S), boreal region (44°–46°N)
Metridia ornata	Antarctic (55°–70°S), boreal region (38°–57°N)
Pseudochirella batillipa	Antarctic (53°–66°S), 86°N and 44°–46°N
Pseudochirella spectabilis	Antarctic (61°–68°S), Arctic basin
Racovitzanus antarcticus	Southern Ocean, boreal seas
Spinocalanus antarcticus	Antarctic, Arctic basin

Park (1983a) examined specimens of *R. antarcticus* from the northern Pacific Ocean and found that they are identical to those from the Southern Ocean in anatomical details of the exoskeleton. In the Southern Ocean, the number of *R. antarcticus* collected appears to decrease rather abruptly with distance northward from the Antarctic Convergence, and there is some evidence that the species may be found in deeper waters north of the convergence but within the Southern Ocean (Park, 1983a). In the Northern Hemisphere, *R. antarcticus* seems to inhabit the mesopelagic zone (200–1,000 m).

Two hypotheses can be suggested to explain the distribution of *R. antarcticus*. The polar populations may be connected through very deep living populations in the north temperate, tropical, and south temperate regions at depths not adequately sampled to date. This connection would mediate gene flow through the undetected deepwater populations in the temperate and tropical regions and would result in the stable morphological similarity between specimens from the Southern and Northern hemispheres. A similar scenario may explain the apparent bipolar distribution of remaining eight deepwater calanoid copepods that are rare or very rare: at high latitudes they inhabit shallower depths, where individuals can be captured more easily, perhaps because secondary productivity is higher. At lower latitudes, populations are found much deeper and are not as readily collected. The alternate hypothesis is of incipient speciation from a previously more broadly distributed deepwater species that is no longer connected through temperate and tropical deepwater populations (see the Comparative Endemicity of the Southern Ocean Fauna section). Morphological similarity in this case is transitory because the absence of gene flow between the polar populations is expected to result in morphological divergence.

The remaining eight rare species have come to be recognized as having a bipolar distribution in one of three ways. *Aetideopsis minor*, *Chiridius polaris*, *Pseudochirella batillipa*, and *Spinocalanus antarcticus* originally were described from the Southern Ocean and subsequently reported from the Northern Hemisphere. *Spinocalanus antarcticus* was discovered in the Arctic Ocean (Damkaer, 1975), while *Aetideopsis minor*, *Chiridius polaris*, and *Pseudochirella batillipa* recently have been recorded for the first time beyond their type locality, in the Arctic Ocean and adjacent boreal seas (Markhaseva, 1996). Two species, *Batheuchaeta peculiaris* and *Metridia ornata*, originally were described from localities adjacent to the Arctic Ocean; subsequently, they were reported from the Southern Ocean, for the first time outside their type locality, by Markhaseva (1996, 2001). Finally, two species were recognized to be bipolar when specimens from southern and northern localities, originally considered different species, subsequently were proposed to be identical. *Aetideopsis inflata*, originally described from the Antarctic region, was synonymized with the subarctic species *Aetideopsis rostrata* (see Markhaseva, 1996), so *Aetideopsis rostrata* is now a bipolar species. Similarly, *Pseudochirella elongata*, also originally described from the Antarctic region, was synonymized with the Arctic species *Pseudochirella spectabilis* (see Markhaseva, 1996); the latter species now has a bipolar distribution. The geographical distribution of these rare species, as inferred from a small number of specimens and from a limited number of localities, however, may not be completely understood.

It is worth noting that some species of pelagic calanoid copepods previously regarded as having disjunct populations in the Southern and Arctic oceans have not subsequently been found to be bipolar. Rather, the northern and southern populations have been recognized as two separate species. As examples, the southern population previously referred to as *Calanus finmarchicus* is now *Calanus australis*; the northern population previously known as *Neocalanus tonsus* is now *Neocalanus plumchrus*; the southern population originally known as *Scaphocalanus brevicornis* is now *Scaphocalanus farrani*. The first two species are epipelagic herbivores; the third is a deepwater detritivore. The taxonomic history of *Paraeuchaeta barbata* is informative but more complex (see the Deepwater Calanoids from Antarctic Waters Reported North of the Antarctic Convergence section). This species originally was described as *Euchaeta farrani* from the Norwegian Sea by With (1915); subsequently, it was recorded from the Antarctic region by Farran (1929) and Vervoort (1957) and proposed by them to be a species with a bipolar distribution. As described more completely above (see the Deepwater Calanoids from Antarctic Waters Reported North of the Antarctic Convergence section), these specimens have been recognized by Park (1995) as belonging to *P. barbata*, a deepwater carnivore, now understood to be distributed throughout the world's oceans.

In summary, taxonomic analyses have reversed initial inferences of a bipolar distribution for *Calanus finmarchicus*, *Neocalanus tonsus*, and *Scaphocalanus brevicornis*. However, taxonomic analyses have established a bipolar distribution for the rare and very rare deepwater species *Aetideopsis rostrata*, *Aetideopsis minor*, *Chiridius polaris*, *Pseudochirella spectabilis*, and *Pseudochirella batillipa*. The distribution of the very common *P. barbata* offers reasons for caution in hypothesizing a bipolar distribution for rare and very rare deepwater species.

VERY COMMON PELAGIC CALANOIDS AND AREAS OF HIGH PRODUCTIVITY

All of the very common epipelagic calanoids of the Southern Ocean are herbivores (Table 2). In order of abundance, they are *Calanoides acutus*, *Rhincalanus gigas*, *Calanus propinquus*, *Calanus simillimus*, *Metridia gerlachei*, *Clausocalanus laticeps*, and *Clausocalanus brevipes*. These epipelagic calanoids are endemic to the Southern Ocean and appear to have successfully adapted to the high primary productivity there. The eutrophic conditions there may also be responsible for the high numbers of individuals of these endemic herbivores. The seven epipelagic species together make up the enormous secondary biomass of the Southern Ocean, a secondary biomass that is unsurpassed in any other region of the world's oceans (Foxton, 1956).

Among the deepwater calanoids of the Southern Ocean, there are 26 species (Table 7) from the studies of Park (1978, 1980, 1982, 1983a, 1983b, 1988, 1993) that are represented by more than 100 individuals and are considered very common. A majority, 14 of 26 species, of these very common deepwater calanoids are limited in their distribution to the Southern Ocean. Among the 14 very common deepwater endemic species, eight belong to two genera in the family Scolecitrichidae (five species of *Scaphocalanus* and three of *Scolecithricella*); all are detritivores. These are followed, in order of abundance, by three species of *Paraeuchaeta* in the Euchaetidae.

Twelve very common species are more widely distributed, found northward at varying distances beyond the Subtropical Convergence. Four species have been found as far north as the north temperate region, one has been found in the subarctic region, and three other deepwater species have a range extending into the Arctic Ocean. *Racovitzanus antarcticus* has a bipolar distribution. Most of these very common species, then, are either endemic to the Southern Ocean (14 species) or have a broad distribution extending north of the tropical region (9 species).

Among the 26 common deepwater calanoids of the Southern Ocean, 12 species belong to the family Scolecitrichidae (six species of *Scaphocalanus*, five species of *Scolecithricella*, and one species of *Racovitzanus*). The family is followed, in order of number of species, by the families Euchaetidae, with five species all belonging to the genus *Paraeuchaeta*; Aetideidae, with three species (two of *Gaetanus* and one *Euchirella*); Augaptilidae, also with three species (two *Haloptilus* and one *Euaugaptilus*); Phaennidae, with two species (both *Cornucalanus*); and Heterorhabdidae, with one species belonging to the genus *Heterorhabdus*.

TABLE 7. Very common deepwater calanoid species of the Southern Ocean (26 spp.).

Species name	Number of of specimens
Species endemic to the Southern Ocean (14 spp.)	
Euaugaptilus antarcticus	136
Euchirella rostromagna	182
Haloptilus ocellatus	152
Paraeuchaeta antarctica	602
Paraeuchaeta biloba	370
Paraeuchaeta rasa	546
Scaphocalanus antarcticus	130
Scaphocalanus farrani	1,271
Scaphocalanus parantarcticus	289
Scaphocalanus subbrevicornis	188
Scaphocalanus vervoorti	1,936
Scolecithricella cenotelis	929
Scolecithricella dentipes	1,603
Scolecithricella schizosoma	151
Species ranging from the Southern Ocean to south temperate region (2 spp.)	
Paraeuchaeta regalis	109
Heterorhabdus spinosus	243
Species ranging from the Southern Ocean to the tropical region (1 sp.)	
Cornucalanus robustus	161
Species ranging from the Southern Ocean to the north temperate region (4 spp.)	
Haloptilus oxycephalus	388
Scolecithricella emarginata	226
Cornucalanus chelifer	111
Scaphocalanus echinatus	114
Species ranging from the Southern Ocean to the subarctic region (1 sp.)	
Scolecithricella minor	1,728
Species ranging from the Southern Ocean to the Arctic basin (3 spp.)	
Gaetanus brevispinus	150
Gaetanus tenuispinus	414
Paraeuchaeta barbata	462
Species with a bipolar distribution (1 sp.)	
Racovitzanus antarcticus	1,077

The 12 scolecitrichid species together were represented by 9,642 individuals from the Southern Ocean, and the five *Paraeuchaeta* species were represented by 2,089 individuals. Three aetideid species and three augaptilids were represented by 746 and 676 individuals, respectively.

On the basis of the relatively large number of specimens of *Paraeuchaeta*, Aetideidae, Heterorhabdidae, and Augaptilidae that are carnivores, all of these species are presumed to be well adapted to the high secondary productivity resulting from the large populations of epipelagic

herbivores in the Southern Ocean. Species of Scolecitrichidae play a major ecological role as pelagic detritivores in the Southern Ocean, just as species of Scolecitrichidae and related bradfordian families of calanoids play a similar role (detritivory) in the deepwater benthopelagic habitat of other oceans (Markhaseva and Ferrari, 2006). Because of their relatively small body size, scolecitrichids may also serve as a food source for carnivorous calanoids like species of *Paraeuchaeta*, the aetideids, and the augaptilids during periods when the juvenile stages of herbivores are unavailable as prey for these carnivores.

These conclusions are reinforced by restricting observations to the 10 species represented in the Southern Ocean by more than 400 individuals (with number of individuals in parenthesis): *Scaphocalanus vervoorti* (1,936), *Scolecithricella minor* (1,728), *S. dentipes* (1,603), *Scaphocalanus farrani* (1,271), *Racovitzanus antarcticus* (1,077), *Scolecithricella cenotelis* (929), *Paraeuchaeta antarctica* (602), *Paraeuchaeta rasa* (546), *Paraeuchaeta barbata* (462), and *Gaetanus tenuispinus* (414). Four of the scolecitrichid species, *Scaphocalanus vervoorti*, *S. farrani*, *Scolecithricella dentipes*, and *S. cenotelis*, and two of the euchaetid species, *Paraeuchaeta antarctica* and *P. rasa*, are endemic to the Southern Ocean. The range of the very common *Scolecithricella minor* extends into the subarctic region, while *Paraeuchaeta barbata* and *Gaetanus tenuispinus* have been collected as far north as the Arctic basin. The scolecitrichid *Racovitzanus antarcticus* is also among the most common species in the Southern Ocean but exhibits a bipolar distribution, occurring in boreal waters adjacent to the Arctic basin. These 10 very common species either are endemic to the Southern Ocean (*Scaphocalanus vervoorti*, *Scolecithricella dentipes*, *Scaphocalanus farrani*, *Scolecithricella cenotelis*, *Paraeuchaeta antarctica*, and *Paraeuchaeta rasa*) or have a distribution that extends as far north as the subarctic region or Arctic basin (*Scolecithricella minor*, *Racovitzanus antarcticus*, *Paraeuchaeta barbata*, and *Gaetanus tenuispinus*). None of the very common deepwater Southern Ocean pelagic calanoids have distributions that extend only to the south temperate region to the tropical region.

Within the Southern Ocean the abundance and distribution of deepwater calanoids are believed to be determined, for the most part, by the availability of food rather than their adaptation to nonbiological environmental parameters such as water temperature (Park, 1994). Whether these eutrophic species are endemics or not, they are restricted to water of high primary and secondary productivity. They can be expected to be common or very common due to their adaptations for exploiting the available food sources associated with that habitat. In contrast, oligotrophic species in the Southern Ocean are not presumed to be adapted to waters of high productivity. Their distribution is expected to be worldwide because they are capable of surviving at most levels of food resources anywhere in the world's oceans. However, oligotrophic species are expected to be rare or very rare in most regions of the world's oceans. With these constraints, a distribution of common or very common species is expected to be limited to the highly productive Southern Ocean; this is observed about half the time. Fourteen of the 26 common or very common species of the Southern Ocean are endemic.

As noted, among the 10 most numerous of the very common species found in the Southern Ocean, six are endemic. Of the remaining four species represented by more than 400 specimens in the Southern Ocean, *Scolecithricella minor*, *Gaetanus tenuispinus*, and *Paraeuchaeta barbata* have been reported throughout the world's oceans, while *Racovitzanus antarctica* appears to have a bipolar distribution, restricted to the Southern Ocean and to the subarctic region (boreal seas adjacent to the Arctic Ocean). The distribution of *Scolecithricella minor* and *Gaetanus tenuispinus* outside the Southern Ocean is based on literature records. Until these records can be verified by direct comparison of specimens, the relationship of the Southern Ocean specimens to specimens collected elsewhere remains tentative, and we are unable to contribute more to the nature of these distributions.

The distribution of *Paraeuchaeta barbata* has become clearer in recent years and can also be understood within the context of the association of this abundant species with areas of high primary and secondary productivity. The polar populations of *Paraeuchaeta barbata* were once regarded as a separate, bipolar species (see the Deepwater Calanoids from Antarctic Waters Reported north of the Antarctic Convergence section). When Park (1995) restudied the various populations by analyzing a large number of specimens collected throughout the world's oceans, he found that specimens exhibited a considerable but continuous variation in size. As a result of this analysis and an earlier restricted analysis (Mauchline, 1992), body size was rejected as species-specific character state for *P. barbata*.

This considerable and continuous variation in body size of *P. barbata* was subsequently reexamined in association with the distribution of this species (T. Park, unpublished observations). Large-sized individuals occur not only at the high latitudes of both hemispheres but also along the west coast of the Americas in areas associated with significant coastal upwelling systems. Large individuals also were recorded in the Malay Archipelago and along the east coast of Japan up to Kuril and Kamchatka; these are also seasonally episodic areas of upwelling. Coastal upwelling systems along the west coast of the Americas and the east coast of Japan result in high primary and secondary productivity, which, in turn, may explain the larger-size individuals of *P. barbata* in these areas. The smallest individuals of *P. barbata* are found in the middle of the North Atlantic, an oligotrophic habitat.

Species like *P. barbata*, which are distributed throughout the world's oceans, may have become very common in the Southern Ocean and other areas of seasonally episodic upwelling by taking advantage of the high secondary productivity of eutrophic habitats; individuals of this species are also larger in these habitats as a result of the availability of prey. In contrast, away from areas of high productivity, few specimens are collected, and individuals are smaller in size.

COMPARATIVE ENDEMICITY OF THE SOUTHERN OCEAN FAUNA

The pelagic calanoid families Euchaetidae and Heterorhabdidae have been studied throughout the world's oceans (Park, 1995, 2000). From these publications, the number of endemic species belonging to these two families from the Southern Ocean can be compared to the number of endemics from three other areas of interest of the world's oceans: Arctic-boreal (including the adjacent boreal seas of the Atlantic and Pacific Oceans), Indo-West Pacific, and eastern Pacific. The Southern Ocean, with 10 endemic species of *Paraeuchaeta*, has the highest number for that genus (Table 8), followed by the Arctic Ocean, with seven endemic species of *Paraeuchaeta*, and the Indo-West Pacific and the eastern Pacific, each with four endemic species. Twenty-three of the 25 endemic species of *Paraeuchaeta* referred to above are bathypelagic; the exceptions are the Indo-West Pacific epipelagic species *Paraeuchaeta russelli* and *P. simplex*.

Six of the 10 Southern Ocean endemics, *P. antarctica*, *P. biloba*, *P. dactylifera*, *P. eltaninae*, *P. parvula*, and *P. rasa*, have been found in large numbers. *Paraeuchaeta austrina*, *P. erebi*, and *P. tycodesma* have not been collected in large numbers, but they appear to be restricted to the ice edge along Antarctica. This habitat may not have been adequately sampled with midwater trawls, and as a result, these species may be underrepresented in trawl samples. *Paraeuchaeta similis* and *P. antarctica* have a broader dis-

TABLE 8. Endemic species of *Paraeuchaeta* and Heterorhabdidae found in four different areas of interest. A "+" indicates presence.

Species	Area of interest			
	Southern Ocean	Arctic-boreal	Eastern Pacific	Indo-West Pacific
Paraeuchaeta antarctica	+			
P. austrina	+			
P. biloba	+			
P. dactylifera	+			
P. eltaninae	+			
P. erebi	+			
P. parvula	+			
P. rasa	+			
P. similis	+			
P. tycodesma	+			
P. birostrata		+		
P. brevirostris		+		
P. elongata		+		
P. glacialis		+		
P. norvegica		+		
P. polaris		+		
P. rubra		+		
P. californica			+	
P. copleyae			+	
P. grandiremis			+	
P. papilliger			+	
P. eminens				+
P. investigatoris				+
P. russelli				+
P. simplex				+
Heterorhabdus austrinus	+			
H. pustulifer	+			
H. spinosus	+			
H. paraspinosus	+			
Heterostylites nigrotinctus	+			
Paraheterorhabdus farrani	+			
Heterorhabdus fistulosus		+		
H. norvegicus		+		
H. tanneri		+		
Paraheterorhabdus longispinus		+		
Heterorhabdus abyssalis			+	
H. americanus			+	
H. prolixus			+	
H. quadrilobus			+	
Heterostylites echinatus			+	

tribution within the Southern Ocean, but only *P. antarctica* has been collected in large numbers.

The endemic species of the Arctic Ocean, including adjacent boreal waters, and the endemics of the eastern Pacific have also been found in large numbers. These species are all believed to inhabit waters of high primary and secondary productivity, where endemism may have developed as an adaptation to these eutrophic habitats (Park, 1994). Of the four endemics of the Indo-West Pacific, *Paraeuchaeta russelli* and *P. simplex* are neritic, inhabit-

ing relatively shallow water. *Paraeuchaeta eminens* and *P. investigatoris* are deepwater species. All four species are common in waters of the Malay Archipelago, an area with relatively high primary and secondary productivity. High primary and secondary productivity, rather than a habitats abiological attributes, appears to have been the primary determinant for the evolution of endemicity among these species of *Paraeuchaeta*.

Within the family Heterorhabdidae, six species are endemic to the Southern Ocean as compared to five endemic species in the eastern Pacific. Four species are restricted to the Arctic-boreal area, including three species endemic to the boreal Pacific and one endemic species found in the boreal Atlantic. No endemic species of Heterorhabdidae is found in the Indo-West Pacific. All of the heterorhabdid species discussed here are assumed to be carnivores, with the exception of *Heterostylites echinatus* (see Ohtsuka et al., 1997), and carnivory is assumed to have arisen from suspension feeding within the Heterorhabdidae only once (Ohtsuka et al., 1997).

The highest number of endemic heterorhabdid species, like the number of endemics of *Paraeuchaeta*, is found in the Southern Ocean. However, in contrast to species of *Paraeuchaeta*, of the six Southern Ocean endemic heterorhabdids, only *Heterorhabdus spinosus* is found in large numbers; it is common in coastal waters. Beyond the Southern Ocean, among the four endemic species of the Arctic and boreal seas, *Heterorhabdus norvegicus* is very common in the boreal Atlantic. *Heterorhabdus fistulosus*, *H. tanneri*, and *Paraheterorhabdus longispinus* are very common along the coasts of the boreal Pacific, and all occur in large numbers in some localities. Among the five endemic species of Heterorhabdidae in the eastern Pacific, all are limited in their distribution to waters close to the coasts of Americas, in areas of coastal upwelling, where they have been found in large numbers. One explanation for the different occurrences of *Paraeuchaeta* and heterorhabdid endemics in the Southern Ocean is that the heterorhabdids may be relatively late colonizers of the Southern Ocean; species of *Paraeuchaeta* may already have established themselves as the dominant carnivores before colonization of the Southern Ocean by species of Heterorhabdidae.

In summary, within the two families of pelagic calanoids that have been studied worldwide, the highest number of endemic species is found in the Southern Ocean. All Southern Ocean endemics of *Paraeuchaeta* are found in large numbers, except for *P. similis* and three species found near the ice edge adjacent to Antarctica where these ice edge species may have been undersampled. In contrast, the six endemic species of Heterorhabdidae found in the Southern Ocean are rare. However, beyond the Southern Ocean the endemics of both families of carnivores are associated with the waters of high primary and secondary productivity, where they may be collected in large numbers. On the basis of these observations, the endemicity of many of the very common bathypelagic calanoids of the Southern Ocean, like the endemicity of Southern Ocean epipelagic calanoids, is suggested to have resulted from the adaptation to conditions of high primary and secondary productivity.

EVOLUTION OF THE PELAGIC CALANOID FAUNA WITHIN THE SOUTHERN OCEAN

Among the 184 deepwater calanoid species found in the Southern Ocean, 50 species (27%) occur exclusively in the Southern Ocean; 20 of those species (40%) are rare or very rare (Table 3). Several factors may be responsible for the evolution of the deepwater pelagic calanoid fauna, restraining their dispersal throughout the deepwater of the world's oceans and selecting for this endemicity. Water temperature, as represented by the rather abrupt changes at the Antarctic Convergence or the Subtropical Convergence, is unlikely to affect the structure or the distribution of the deepwater calanoids because water temperatures below 1,000 m are uniformly cold within the Southern Ocean, and this uniformly cold deepwater is continuous with the deepwater of the adjacent Pacific, Atlantic, and Indian oceans. The proposed relationship between habitat productivity and endemism may be a more useful initial condition. The majority (60%) of deepwater endemic species of the Southern Ocean are common or very common. As mentioned earlier, this may be the product of the high primary and secondary productivity of the Southern Ocean, especially south of the Antarctic Convergence, resulting in the evolution and adaptation of an oligotrophic species to this eutrophic habitat. Endemism of deepwater pelagic calanoids in the Southern Ocean, therefore, is hypothesized to have evolved as rare species that are widely distributed in oligotrophic habitats throughout the world's oceans became adapted to exploit high primary and secondary productive habitats (Park, 1994); these adaptations have resulted in an increased population size of the eutrophic species.

A second explanatory condition for the evolution of the pelagic, marine calanoid fauna in the Southern Ocean depends on whether polar species within a single genus are monophyletic, having evolved from a single ancestral species that initially colonized the Southern Ocean, or polyphyletic, with each species having evolved independently from an ancestor distributed outside of the Southern Ocean or by evolving from more than one initially colonized ancestral species. There is evidence that supports this latter model of independent colonizations for Southern Ocean endemic species of the families Euchaetidae and Heterorhabdidae (see the Comparative Endemicity of the Southern Ocean Fauna section), although the situation is more complex for the *antarctica* species group of *Paraeuchaeta*.

Further evidence can be found in the phenomenon of sibling species pairs. When morphological details are closely compared, one species often can be found outside the Southern Ocean that is very similar to each Southern

Ocean endemic. These two species, the Southern Ocean endemic and its closest relative outside of the Southern Ocean, are referred to here as a sibling species pair. Fifteen endemics among the 17 sibling species pairs (Figure 1) have an allopatric distribution, rather than being sympat-

ric with its closest relative. In addition, the *antarctica* species group of *Paraeuchaeta* is also allopatric with its most closely related congener, *P. bisinuata*. The only exception is the pair *Haloptilus ocellatus* and *H. oxycephalus*; these two species may be considered allopatric but with a narrow

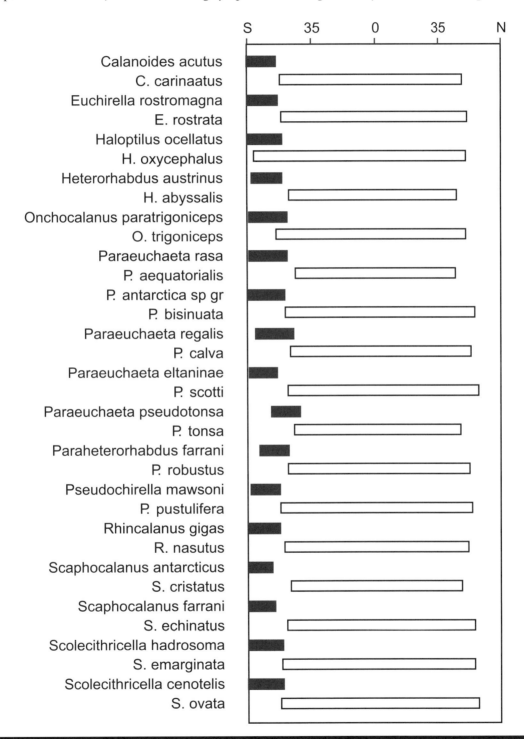

FIGURE 1. Distribution of selected pelagic calanoids of the Southern Ocean and their closest relatives.

zone of overlap. For many common or very common deep-water calanoid species that are endemic to the Southern Ocean (Figure 1, Tables 4, 5), the closest relative is not found in the Southern Ocean, is widely distributed, is rare, and is usually associated with oligotrophic habitats. Examples of these deepwater sibling species pairs (Southern Ocean species first) include (Figure 1) *Euchirella rostromagna* and *E. rostrata*, *Paraeuchaeta pseudotonsa* and *P. tonsa*, *P. antarctica* and *P. bisinuata*, *Scaphocalanus cristatus* and *S. antarcticus*, and *Paraheterorhabdus farrani* and *P. robustus*. The members of some sibling species pairs are so similar to each other morphologically that, originally, they were regarded as the same species, e.g., *Paraeuchaeta tonsa* and *P. pseudotonsa* or *Euchirella rostrata* and *E. rostromagna*. In addition to being more numerous, the Southern Ocean endemics are usually larger in size than their smaller, rare, cosmopolitan counterparts. Between members of the deepwater pairs, the common or very common endemics adapted to the eutrophic habitat of the Southern Ocean are hypothesized to have evolved from a rare widespread species adapted to oligotrophic habitats (Park, 1994). This evolutionary event has resulted in two closely related species, a sibling species pair with the species outside of the Southern Ocean remaining adapted to an oligotrophic environment and the Southern Ocean species adapted to high-productivity habitats. In view of the close morphological similarity between the species of a sibling species pair, this process seems to have a relatively short evolutionary history. However, this hypothesis does not imply that all pairs evolved about the same time.

The situation for *Paraeuchaeta antarctica* appears to be more complicated than a case of a simple sibling species pair. *Paraeuchaeta antarctica* is a very common predator and is morphologically similar to four other endemic species, *P. similis*, *P. austrina*, *P. erebi*, and *P. tycodesma*. These five endemic species make up the *antarctica* species group (Fontaine, 1988). All five of these species can be found to occur sympatrically adjacent to the ice edge of Antarctica. *Paraeuchaeta austrina*, *P. erebi*, and *P. tycodesma* are restricted to this habitat, while *P. antarctica* and *P. similis* may be found throughout the Southern Ocean. The most similar congener, and presumed closest relative, of the *antarctica* species group is *P. bisinuata*. *Paraeuchaeta bisinuata* is a rare deepwater species found in all the world's oceans except the Southern Ocean. *Paraeuchaeta bisinuata* and the common ancestor of the *antarctica* species group are hypothesized to have been a sibling species pair. The common ancestor of the *antarctica* species group is assumed to have colonized the Southern Ocean, eventually adapting and being confined to the eutrophic habitat.

All of its descendants, including *P. austrina*, *P. erebi*, and *P. tycodesma*, which are associated with waters adjacent to the ice edge, and the more broadly distributed *P. similis* and *P. antarctica*, are restricted to the Southern Ocean. *Paraeuchaeta bisinuata*, the cosmopolitan species of the original pair, remains associated with oligotrophic habitats throughout the world's oceans.

To summarize, the evolution of deepwater endemic species of the Southern Ocean can be hypothesized from an ordered set of changes in distribution and subsequent morphological divergence in the following way: (1) beginning with a rare, widely distributed species adapted to oligotrophic habitats, e.g., *Augaptilus glacialis*, (2) a Southern Ocean population becomes associated with its eutrophic habitat and becomes separated from the rare, widely distributed, oligotrophic species; (3) the Southern Ocean endemic population adapts to this eutrophic habitat, and its population size increases. It diverges from the rare, widely distributed, oligotrophic species, resulting in a sibling species pair, e.g., *Scolecithricella farrani* and *S. echinates*.

Another type of species pair identified in this study requires different explanatory conditions about the evolution of the Southern Ocean fauna. A bipolar species pair consists of two morphologically similar species, presumed closest relatives, one that is endemic to the Southern Ocean and a second that is endemic to the Arctic Ocean and adjacent boreal waters. Several endemic species of the Southern Ocean have a morphologically similar congener in the Arctic region (Table 7, Figure 2). The morphological similarities between the members are so close that some of the pairs were recognized as separate species only recently, e.g., the Southern Ocean *Scaphocalanus farrani* was separated from *S. brevicornis* by Park (1982). In general, the number of morphological differences is few and the degree of the morphological divergence is slight between members of these southern and northern oceanic pairs, e.g., *Paraheterorhabdus farrani* and *P. longispinus*, *Scaphocalanus parantarcticus* and *S. acrocephalus*, and *Paraeuchaeta regalis* and *P. polaris*. The extent of the morphological similarity between these polar species suggests that they may have been derived from a common ancestor (see below), although this does not imply that all pairs have evolved about the same time.

The evolution of deepwater bipolar species pairs can be hypothesized from an ordered set of changes in distribution and subsequent morphological divergence in the following way. Beginning with a widely distributed deepwater species with shallow populations in the Southern Ocean and Arctic Ocean, e.g., *Paraeuchaeta barbata*, (1)

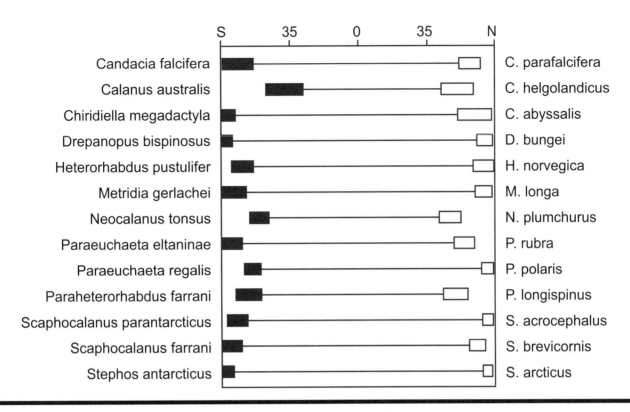

FIGURE 2. Distribution of selected pelagic calanoids of the Southern Ocean and their closest relatives in the subarctic region or the Arctic Ocean.

deepwater middle- and low-latitude populations become extinct over varying periods of time, resulting in a non-uniform distribution, e.g., *Batheuchaeta peculiaris*, (2) complete middle- and low-latitude extinctions eventually result in a species with a bipolar distribution, e.g., *Pseudochirella spectabilis*, and (3) subsequent morphological divergence of the bipolar populations results in a bipolar pair of species, e.g., *Paraeuchaeta regalis* and *P. polaris*.

The evolution of epipelagic calanoids of the Southern Ocean differs in some respects from deepwater pelagic calanoids. Throughout the world's oceans, there are many epipelagic marine calanoids whose distribution is confined to a water mass or current system within an ocean basin and sometimes very narrowly within that basin. Often, such distributions appear to be restricted to a zone of latitudes, although the causes may be related to specific nutrient and temperature regimes (Reid et al., 1978). Epipelagic species from the low or middle latitudes provide many examples of zonally distributed species (Frost and Fleminger, 1968). The circumpolar distributions of the epipelagic endemics of the Southern Ocean, *Calanoides acutus*, *Rhincalanus gigas*, *Calanus propinquus*, *Metridia gerlachei*, *Clausocalanus laticeps*, *Calanus simillimus*, *Clausocalanus bre-*

vipes, and *Ctenocalanus citer*, can be interpreted as zonal distributions. The first five are restricted to waters south of the Antarctic Convergence; the last three are restricted to waters south of the Subtropical Convergence and north of the Antarctic Convergence (Table 2). These two sets of epipelagic species may be adapted to the two different zones of cold water bounded by Antarctic Convergence and Subtropical Convergence, as well as by the unique primary productivity of the Southern Ocean.

In the Southern Ocean, the evolution of epipelagic calanoids shares some common attributes with deepwater pelagic calanoids. High primary productivity may have enabled the evolution of epipelagic species; all five endemic epipelagic species found south of the Antarctic Convergence are endemic herbivores utilizing the region's high primary productivity; all are very common. Three of the eight subantarctic epipelagic species are also endemic herbivores and are common or very common. Sibling species pairs can be found among epipelagic species as well as deepwater species, e.g., *Calanoides acutus* and *C. carinatus* or *Rhincalanus gigas* and *R. nasutus*. In contrast to deepwater sibling species pairs, both members of an epipelagic pair often are common or very common (Figure 1).

Epipelagic, bipolar species pairs have also been identified, e.g., *Calanus australis* and *C. helgolandicus* and *Neocalanus tonsus* and *N. plumchrus*.

The evolution of coastal species in the Southern Ocean may reflect processes similar to the model for the deepwater bipolar species pairs. Several species of coastal genera, such as *Drepanopus* and *Stephos*, are present in the Southern Ocean and the Arctic Ocean. However, the morphological differences between the Southern Ocean and the Arctic Ocean members are more extensive than those found between members of the oceanic genera of bipolar species pairs. The Southern Ocean coastal species *Drepanopus pectinatus*, *D. bispinosus*, and *D. forcipatus* and *Stephos longipes* and *S. antarcticus* are readily distinguished from their congeners *D. bungei* and *D. furcatus* and *S. arcticus* and its six relatives in the Arctic Ocean. In contrast, the Southern Ocean species of oceanic genera are difficult to distinguish from their Arctic and boreal congeners because they are very similar morphologically. Apparently, the species of these coastal pelagic genera may have had a different evolutionary history and perhaps a different biogeographical history than the oceanic pelagic calanoid species, although similar processes may have affected both groups. High productivity may have played an important role in the structure of the nearshore fauna because five of eight coastal species endemic to the Southern Ocean (Table 1) are common or very common.

The situation for *Paralabidocera antarctica*, *P. grandispina*, and *P. separabilis* requires further consideration. The genus *Paralabidocera*, an acartiid restricted to the Southern Hemisphere, is one of only five pelagic marine genera that are limited to one of the two hemispheres. The others are *Epilabidocera*, a pontellid, *Eurytemora*, a temorid, *Jashnovia*, an aetideid, and *Pseudocalanus*, a clausocalanid, and these four are limited to the Northern Hemisphere. Species of these genera are found in estuarine or inshore waters or in the neritic zone of the oceans. Each of these genera has a morphologically similar genus, and presumed closest relative (T. Park, unpublished data), distributed broadly throughout the world: species of *Paralabidocera* are similar to those of *Acartia*, species of *Epilabidocera* to *Labidocera*, *Eurytemora* to *Temora*, *Jashnovia* to *Gaetanus*, and *Pseudocalanus* to *Clausocalanus*. As a result, it seems reasonable to assume that the species of *Paralabidocera* have evolved from a cosmopolitan acartiid ancestor. In general, morphological differences between each limited genus and its cosmopolitan relative are not as great as between each limited genus and its remaining confamilial relatives, so that morphological

differences between species of *Paralabidocera* and *Acartia* are not as great as between *Paralabidocera* and species of *Acartiella* and *Paracartia*. The evolution of *Paralabidocera*, then, may be a relatively recent event within the Southern Ocean.

In summary, most genera of pelagic marine calanoid copepods found in the Southern Ocean are also found north of the Southern Ocean; *Paralabidocera*, restricted to the Southern Hemisphere, may be an exception. Many species of pelagic calanoid copepods endemic to the Southern Ocean are common or very common, reflecting their adaptation to the eutrophic environment there. The closest relative of many Southern Ocean species is usually a widely distributed congener adapted to waters of low primary and secondary productivity whose range does not extend into the Southern Ocean. These observations suggest that Southern Ocean endemics evolved from a common oligotrophic ancestor that split into two populations. The widely distributed daughter species retained its adaptation to oligotrophic habitats; the Southern Ocean endemic daughter became adapted to the eutrophic environment of the Southern Ocean. The *antarctica* species group of *Paraeuchaeta* appears to be monophyletic and may have subsequently evolved from a common Southern Ocean eutrophic daughter population after its initial split from an ancestor, similar to *P. bisinuata*, which is associated with oligotrophic habitats. Therefore, most Southern Ocean endemic species appear to have evolved after the Southern Ocean became an area of high primary and secondary productivity. High productivity is assumed to have developed with a strong circumpolar current following the separation of Antarctica from Australia. A hypothesis structuring the benthopelagic calanoid fauna from the divergence in feeding appendages differentially adapted for detritivory (Markhaseva and Ferrari, 2006) shares the same phenomenon, adaptation to diversity in food availability as an evolutionary cause of species diversity.

Another hypothesis to explain the endemicity of the Southern Ocean involves species that contribute to bipolar species pairs. These may have evolved from a widely distributed deepwater species with shallow polar populations whose intervening deepwater populations subsequently became extinct, leaving a species with a bipolar distribution. The two populations then diverged. In this model, bipolar species are transient natural phenomena. Finally, this review provides no unequivocal support for zonal distributions for mesopelagic or bathypelagic calanoid species. In general, mesopelagic or bathypelagic calanoids appear to occur broadly throughout the world's oceans and are unrestricted latitudinally or longitudinally.

FUTURE CONSIDERATIONS

Seventy-seven pelagic, marine calanoid copepods had been reported from the Southern Ocean prior to 1950. Vervoort (1951, 1957) added 26 species, bringing the total number to 103. A total of 117 calanoid species were known before Park (1978, 1980, 1982, 1983a, 1983b, 1988, 1993, 2000) added 73 species. During this period, a few other authors added several species, so that the total reached 201 species by the end of the century. Recently, three species of *Metridia* and one species of *Lucicutia* have been added (Markhaseva, 2001; Markhaseva and Ferrari, 2005), bringing the total to 205 species.

The midwater trawls employed by the U.S. Antarctic Research Program have been very effective in sampling the large pelagic copepods of the Southern Ocean. There can be very few pelagic species left to be collected with sampling gear of this kind of device. However, fine-mesh samples, less than 100 micrometers, taken with traditional sampling gear like the conical plankton net may add new pelagic species or new records of pelagic species already known from other areas of the world's oceans.

With new sampling methods capable of reaching unexplored habitats, more species of calanoids, many expected to be new to science, can be anticipated to increase the Southern Ocean fauna of calanoid copepods. Waters immediately above the seabed, where new benthopelagic calanoid copepods have only recently been collected and studied carefully, are an example. The diverse fauna of this habitat has been very poorly sampled, and lists of new species and new records are in a growth phase. However, new species and new records of benthopelagic copepods are not expected to effect the conclusions drawn here about pelagic calanoids.

Beginning with the studies by Vervoort (1950, 1951, 1957), the species descriptions available in the literature for the Southern Ocean calanoids have been based on the complete morphology of the exoskeleton. Generally, these descriptions are of excellent quality, and the observations are easily repeatable with newly collected specimens. Most of the species discovered earlier have been redescribed in detail by subsequent authors, making the identification of specimens of those species reliable. However, the zoogeographic distribution of most species, particularly in areas outside of the Southern Ocean, needs significant attention. Information about the vertical distribution of many species, except for the very common ones, remains insufficient. Finally, the population structure, particularly for nauplii, remains poorly known. These problems can be addressed with contemporary sampling gear but will require the kind of intellectual curiosity which drove the early exploration of the Southern Ocean by the U.S. Antarctic Research Program.

ACKNOWLEDGMENTS

We would like to thank former Under Secretary for Science Dr. David Evans and the Office of the Under Secretary for Science at the Smithsonian Institution for sponsoring the International Polar Year Symposium on 3 and 4 May 2007 in Washington, D.C. Rafael Lemaitre, Chairman of the Department of Invertebrate Zoology, kindly invited one of us (TP) to participate in the symposium. Scott Miller, Senior Program Officer, Office of Under Secretary for Science, edited this contribution.

LITERATURE CITED

Andrews, K. J. H. 1966. The Distribution and Life History of *Calanoides actus* (Giesbrecht). *Discovery Reports*, 34:117–162.

Atkinson, A. 1991. Life Cycles of *Calanoides acutus*, *Calanus simillimus* and *Rhincalanus gigas* (Copepoda: Calanoida) within the Scotia Sea. *Marine Biology*, 109(1):79–91.

Auel, H. 1999. The Ecology of Arctic Deep-Sea Copepods (Euchaetidae and Aetideidae). Aspects of Their Distribution, Trophodynamics and Effect on the Carbon Flux. *Berichte zur Polarforschung*, 319: 1–97.

Backus. R. H. 1986. Biogeographic Boundaries in the Open Ocean. *UNESCO Technical Papers in Marine Science*, 49:9–13.

Bayly, I. A. E. 1982. The Genus *Drepanopus* (Copepoda: Calanoida): A Review of Species in Antarctic and Subantarctic Waters, with a Description of *D. bispinosus*, sp. nov. *Australian Journal of Marine and Freshwater Research*, 33:161–172.

———. 1986. Ecology of the Zooplankton of a Meromictic Antarctic Lagoon with Special Reference to *Drepanopus bispinosus* (Copepoda: Calanoida). *Hydrobiologia*, 140(3):199–231.

Björnberg, T. K. S. 1968. "Four New Species of Megacalanidae (Crustacea: Copepoda)." In *Biology of the Antarctic Seas III*, ed. G. A. Llano, W. L. Schmitt, pp. 73–90. Antarctic Research Series, No. 11. Washington, D.C.: American Geophysical Union.

———. 1973. The Planktonic Copepods of the Marchile I Expedition and of the "Eltanin" Cruises 3–6 Taken in the SE Pacific. *Zoologia, Biologia e Marinha*, 30:245–394.

Boeck, A. 1864. Oversigt over de ved Norges Kyster iagttagne Copepoder, herhörende til Calanidernes, Cyclopidernes og Harpactidernes Familier. *Forhandlinger i Videnskabs-Selskabet i Christiania*, 1864:226–282.

Bowman, T. E., and L. G. Abele. 1982. "Classification of the Recent Crustacea." In *The Biology of Crustacea*. Volume 1, ed. D. E. Bliss, pp. 1–27. New York: Academic Press.

Bradford, J. M. 1969. New Species of *Aetideopsis* Sars and *Bradyidius* Giesbrecht (Copepoda; Calanoida) from the Southern Hemisphere. *New Zealand Journal of Marine and Freshwatater Research*, 3(1): 73–97.

———. 1971. The Fauna of the Ross Sea. 8. Pelagic Copepoda. *Bulletin of the New Zealand Department of Scientific and Industrial Research*, 206:9–31.

———. 1981. Records of *Paraeuchaeta* (Copepoda: Calanoida) from McMurdo Sound, Antarctica, with a Description of Three Hitherto Unknown Males. *New Zealand Journal of Marine and Freshwater Research*, 15:391–402.

Bradford, J. M., and J. B. J. Wells. 1983. New Calanoid and Harpacticoid Copepods from beneath the Ross Ice Shelf, Antarctica. *Polar Biology*, 2:1–15.

Bradford-Grieve, J. M. 1994. The Marine Fauna of New Zealand: Pelagic Calanoid Copepoda: Megacalanidae, Calanidae, Paracalanidae, Mecynoceridae, Eucalanidae, Spinocalanidae, Clausocalanidae. *New Zealand Oceanographic Institute Memoir*, 102:1–160.

———. 1999. New Species of Benthopelagic Copepods of the Genus *Stephos* (Calanoida: Stephidae) from Wellington Harbour, New Zealand. *New Zealand Journal of Marine and Freshwater Research*, 33(1):13–27.

Brady, G. S. 1883. "Report on the Copepoda Collected by H.M.S. *Challenger* during the Years 1873–76." In Report of Scientific Research on Voyage of H.M.S. *Challenger* during the Years 1873–76. *Zoology*, 8(23):1–142.

———. 1918. Copepoda. *Scientific Reports of the Australian Antarctic Expedition 1911–1914*, Series C, 5(3):1–48.

Brodsky, K. A. 1950. Calanoida of the Far Eastern Seas and Polar Basin of the USSR. *Opredeliteli po Faune SSSR*, 35:1–442. [In Russian]

———. 1958. Plankton Studies by the Soviet Antarctic Expedition (1955–1958). *Informatsionnyi Byulleten' Sovetskoi antarkticheskoi ekspeditsii, 1955–1958*, 3:25–30. [In Russian; English trans., Elsevier, Amsterdam, 1964]

———. 1959. On Phylogenetic Relations of Some *Calanus* (Copepoda) Species of Northern and Southern Hemispheres. *Zoologicheskii Zhurnal*, 38:1537–1553. [In Russian]

———. 1962. Distribution of Mass Species of the Genus *Calanus* in the Southern Hemisphere. *Doklady Akademii Nauk SSSR*, 143:709–712. [In Russian]

———. 1964. Distribution and Morphological Features of the Antarctic Species of *Calanus* (Copepoda). *Issledovaniya Fauny Morei*, 2: 189–251. [In Russian; English trans. , Israel Program for Scientific Translations, Jerusalem, 1966]

———. 1967. Distribution and Size Variability of Calanidae (Copepoda) in the Southern Hemisphere (from the Collections of the Soviet Antarctic Expedition 1955–1958). *Issledovaniya Fauny Morei*, 4(2): 190–219. [In Russian; English trans., Israel Program for Scientific Translations, Jerusalem, 1968]

Brodsky, K. A., and J. A. Zvereva. 1976. *Paralabidocera separabilis* sp. n. and *P. antarctica* (J. C. Thompson) (Copepoda, Calanoida) from Antarctica. *Crustaceana*, 31(3):233–240.

Campaner, A. F. 1978. On Some New Planktobenthic Aetideidae and Phaennidae (Copepoda, Calanoida) from the Brazilian Continental Shelf. II. Phaennidae. *Ciência e Cultura*, 30(8):966–982.

Chiba, S., T. Ishimaru, G. W. Hosie, and M. Fukuchi. 2002. Spatiotemporal Variability in Life Cycle Strategy of Four Pelagic Antarctic Copepods: *Rhincalanus gigas, Calanoides acutus, Calanus propinquus* and *Metridia gerlachei*. *Polar Bioscience*, 15:27–44.

Claus, C. 1866. Die Copepoden-Fauna von Nizza. Ein Beitrag zur Charakteristik der Formen und deren Abanderungen "im Sinne Darwin's." *Schriften der Gesellschaft zur Beförderung der Gesamten Naturwissenschaften zu Marburg*, Suppl., 1:1–34.

Cleve, P. T. 1904. The Plankton of the South African Seas. 1. Copepoda. *Marine Investigations in South Africa*, 3:177–210.

Dahl, F. 1893. Pleuromma, ein Krebs mit Leuchtorgen. *Zoologisches Anzeiger*, 16:104–109.

Damkaer, D. M. 1975. Calanoid Copepods of the Genus Spinocalanus and Mimocalanus from Central Arctic Ocean, with a Review of the Spinocalanidae. *NOAA Technical Reports, National Marine Fisheries Service, Circular*, 391:1–88.

Deacon, G. E. R. 1934. Die Nordgrenzen antarktischen und subantarktischen Wassers im Weltmeer. *Annalen de Hydrographie un Meritimen Meteorologie*, 4:129–136.

———. 1937. The Hydrology of the Southern Ocean. *Discovery Reports*, 15:1–124.

Esterly, C. O. 1911. Third Report on the Copepoda of the San Diego Region. *University of California Publications in Zoology*, 6(14): 313–352.

Farran, G. P. 1903. Record of the Copepoda Taken on the Mackerel Fishing Ground off Cleggan, Co. Galway, in 1901. *Scientific Investigations of the Fisheries Branch of Ireland*, 1901, part 2, appendix 7, 1–18, pls. 16, 17.

———. 1905. Report on the Copepoda of the Atlantic Slope off Counties Mayo and Galway. *Scientific Investigations of the Fisheries Branch of Ireland*, 1902–1903, part 2, appendix 2, 23–52, pls. 3–13.

———. 1908. Second Report on the Copepoda of the Irish Atlantic Slope. *Scientific Investigations of the Fisheries Branch of Ireland*, 1906, part 2, 1–104, 11 pls.

———. 1929. "Crustacea. 10. Copepoda." In Natural History Reports, British Antarctica "Terra Nova" Expedition, 1910. *Zoology*, 8(3): 203–306.

Ferrari, F. D., and M. Dojiri. 1987. The Calanoid Copepod *Euchaeta antarctica* from Southern Ocean Atlantic Sector Midwater Trawls, with Observations on Spermatophore Dimorphism. *Journal of Crustacean Biology*, 7:458–480.

Ferrari, F. D., and J. Saltzman. 1998. *Pleuromamma johnsoni*, a New Looking-Glass Copepod from the Pacific Ocean with Redescriptions of *P. robusta* (Dahl, 1893), *P. antarctica* Steuer, 1931 New Rank, and *P. scutullata* Brodsky, 1950 (Crustacea: Calanoida: Metridinidae). *Plankton Biology and Ecology*, 45:203–223.

Fontaine, M. 1967. Two New Species of Euchaeta (Copepoda, Calanoida). *Crustaceana*, 12(2):193–213.

———. 1988. "Taxonomy and Distribution of the Antarctica Species Group of the Genus Euchaeta (Copepoda, Calanoida)." In *Biology of the Antarctic Seas XIX*, ed. L. S. Kornicker, pp. 27–57. Antarctic Research Series, No. 47. Washington, D.C.: American Geophysical Union.

Foxton, P. 1956. The Distribution of the Standing Crop of Zooplankton in the Southern Ocean. *Discovery Reports*, 28:191–236.

Frost, B., and A. Fleminger. 1968. A Revision of the Genus Clausocalanus (Copepoda: Calanoida) with Remarks on Distributional Patterns in Diagnostic Characters. *Bulletin of the Scripps Institution of Oceanography*, 12:1–235.

Giesbrecht, W. 1888. Elenco dei Copepodi pelagici raccolti dal tenente di vascello Gaetano Chierchia durante il viaggio della R. Corvetta 'Vettor Pisani' negli anni 1882–1885, e dal tenente di vascello Francesco Orsini nel Mar Rosso, nel 1884. *Rendiconti Accademia dei Lincei*, 4(2):284–287, 330–338.

———. 1889a. Zoologia—Elenco dei Copepodi pelagici raccolti dal tenente di vascello Gaetano Chierchia durante il viaggio della R. Corvetta 'Vettor Pisani' negli anni 1882–1885, e dal tenente di vascello Francesco Orsini nel Mar Rosso, nel 1884. *Rendiconti Accademia dei Lince*, (4)5(1):811–815.

———. 1889b. Zoologia—Elenco dei Copepodi pelagici raccolti dal tenente di vascello Gaetano Chierchia durante il viaggio della R. Corvetta 'Vettor Pisani' negli anni 1882–1885, e dal tenente di vascello Francesco Orsini nel Mar Rosso, nel 1884. *Rendiconti Accademia dei Lince*, (4)5(2):24–29.

———. 1893. Systematik und Faunistik der pelagischen Copepoden des Golfes von Neapel und der angrenzenden Meeres-abschnitte. *Neapel Zoologischen Station, Fauna and Flora*, 19:1–831.

———. 1895. Reports on the Dredging Operations off the West Coast of Central America to the Galapagos, to the West Coast of Mexico, and in the Gulf of California, in Charge of Alexander Agassiz, Carried on by the U.S. Fish Commission Steamer Albatross, during 1891. Lieut.-Commander Z. L. Tanner, U.S.N., Commanding. 16. Die pelagischen Copepoden. *Bulletin of the Museum of Comparative Zoology at Harvard College*, 25(12):243–263.

———. 1902. "Copepoden." In *Resultats du voyage du S.Y. Belgica en 1897-1898-1899*, pp. 1–49. Rapports Scientifiques, Expédition Antarctique Belge, Zoologie.

———. 1903. Le pesche abissali eseguite da F. A. Krupp col yacht Puritan nelle adiacenze di Capri ed in altre località del Mediterraneo. *Mitteilungen aus dem Zoologisches Station Neapel*, 16:202–203.

Grice, G. D. 1973. The Existence of a Bottom-Living Calanoid Copepod Fauna in Deep Water with Descriptions of Five New Species. *Crustaceana*, 23(3):219–242.

Grice, G. D., and K. Hulsemann. 1965. Abundance, Vertical Distribution and Taxonomy of Calanoid Copepods at Selected Stations in the Northeast Atlantic. *Journal of Zoology*, 146(2):213–262.

———. 1968. Calanoid Copepods from Midwater Trawl Collections Made in the Southeastern Pacific Ocean. *Pacific Science*, 22(3): 322–335.

Grimaldi, D., and M. S. Engel. 2005. *Evolution of the Insects*. Cambridge: Cambridge University Press.

Hardy, A. C., and E. R. Gunther. 1935. The Plankton of the South Georgia Whaling Grounds and Adjacent Waters, 1926–1927. *Discovery Reports*, 11:1–456.

Hentschel, E. 1936. Allgemeine Biologie der südatlantischen Ozeans. *Wissenschaftliche Ergebnisse der Deutschen Atlantic Expedition 'Meteor,'* 11:1–344.

Heptner, M. V. 1971. On the copepod fauna of the Kurile-Kamchatka Trench. The Families Euchaetidae, Lucicutiidae, Heterorhabdidae. *Trudy Instituta Okeanologii im P. P. Shirshova*, 92:73–161. [In Russian]

Heron, G. A., and T. E. Bowman. 1971. "Postnaupliar Developmental Stages of the Copepod Crustaceans *Clausocalanus laticeps, C. brevipes*, and *Ctenocalanus citer* (Calanoida: Pseudocalanidae)." In *Biology of the Antarctic Seas IV*, ed. G. A. Llano and I. E. Wallen, pp. 141–165. Antarctic Research Series, no. 17. Washington, D.C.: American Geophysical Union.

Huber, M. 2002. Straw Man 1: A Preliminary View of the Tropical Pacific from a Global Coupled Climate Model Simulation of the Early Paleogene. *Proceedings of the Ocean Drilling Program, Initial Reports*, 199:1–30.

Hulsemann, K. 1966. A Revision of the Genus *Lucicutia* (Copepoda: Calanoida) with a Key to Its Species. *Bulletin of Marine Science*, 16(4):702–747.

———. 1985a. Two Species of *Drepanopus* Brady (Copepoda Calanoida) with Discrete Ranges in the Southern Hemisphere. *Journal of Plankton Research*, 7(6):909–925.

———. 1985b. A New Species of *Neoscolecithrix* Canu (Copepoda Calanoida) in Antarctic Waters with Remarks on the Genus. *Polar Biology*, 5:55–62.

———. 1991. The Copepodid Stages of *Drepanopus forcipatus* Giesbrecht, with Notes on the Genus and a Comparison with Other Members of the Family Clausocalanidae (Copepoda Calanoida). *Helgoländer Meeresunters*, 45:199–224.

Humes, A. G. 1994. How Many Copepods? *Hydrobiologia*, 292/293: 1–7.

Itoh, K. 1970. A Consideration on Feeding Habits of Planktonic Copepods in Relation to the Structure of Their Oral Parts. *Bulletin of the Plankton Society of Japan*, 17:1–10.

Kurbjeweit, F., R. Gradinger, and J. Weissenberger. 1993. The Life Cycle of *Stephos longipes*—An Example of Cryopelagic Coupling in the Weddell Sea (Antarctica). *Marine Ecology Progress Series*, 98(3): 255–262.

LaFond, E. C. 1966. "Upwelling." In *The Encyclopedia of Oceanography*, ed. R. W. Fairbridge, pp. 957–959. Stroudsburg, Pa.: Dowden, Hutchinson & Ross, Inc.

Longhurst, A. R. 1985. The Structure and Evolution of Plankton Communities. *Progress in Oceanography*, 15:1–35.

Lubbock, J. 1856. On Some Entomostraca Collected by D. Sutherland in the Atlantic Ocean. *Transactions of the Royal Entomological Society of London*, 4:8–39.

Mackintosh, N. A. 1934. Distribution of the Macroplankton in the Atlantic Sector of the Antarctic. *Discovery Reports*, 9:65–160.

———. 1937. The Seasonal Circulation of the Antarctic Macroplankton. *Discovery Reports*, 16:365–412.

Marín, V. H., and T. Antezana. 1985. Species Composition and Relative Abundance of Copepods in Chilean Fjords. *Journal of Plankton Research*, 7(6):961–966.

Markhaseva, E. L. 1983. New Deep-Water Species of *Batheuchaeta* (Copepoda, Calanoida). *Zoologicheskii Zhurnal*, 62(11):1740–1743. [In Russian]

———. 1986. Revision of the Genus *Batheuchaeta* (Calanoida, Aetideidae). *Zoologicheskii Zhurnal*, 65(6):837–850. [In Russian]

———. 1989. Review of the Genus *Pseudochirella* (Copepoda, Calanoida). *Issledovaniya Fauny Morei*, 41(49):33–60. [In Russian]

———. 1996. Calanoid Copepods of the Family Aetideide of the World Ocean. *Proceedings of the Zoological Institute of the Russian Academy of Sciences*, 268:1–331.

———. 2001. New and Rare Metridia from Antarctic and Subantarctic Waters (Copepoda, Calanoida: Metridinidae). *Zoosystematic Rossica*, 9:43–75.

Markhaseva, E. L., and F. D. Ferrari. 2005. New Species of *Lucicutia* and Taxonomic Status of *L. grandis* (Copepoda, Calanoida, Lucicutiidae). *Journal of Natural History*, 39(15):1077–1100.

———. 2006. New Benthopelagic Bradfordian Calanoids (Crustacea: Copepoda) From the Pacific Ocean with Comments on Generic Relationships. *Invertebrate Zoology*, 2:111–168.

Markhaseva, E. L., and K. Schulz. 2006a. *Sensiava longiseta* (Copepoda, Calanoida): A New Genus and Species from the Abyss of the Weddell Sea. *Zootaxa*, 1368:1–18.

———. 2006b. New Benthopelagic Aetideids (Crustacea: Copepoda: Calanoida) from Deep Antarctic Waters. *Invertebrate Zoology*, 3(2):137–155.

———. 2007a. New Species of *Brodskius, Rythabis*, and *Omorius* (Crustacea: Calanoida) from Deep Antarctic Waters. *Journal of Natural History*, 41:731–750.

———. 2007b. *Lamiantennula* gen. n. (Copepoda: Calanoida): A New Deep-Water Benthopelagic Genus of Arietelloidea. *Arthropoda Selecta*, 15(3):203–210.

Matsuura, H., and S. Nishida. 2000. Fine Structure of the "Button Setae" in the Deep-Sea Pelagic Copepods of the Genus *Euaugaptilus* (Calanoida: Augaptilidae). *Marine Biology*, 137(2):339–345.

Matthews, L. 1925. A New Antarctic Copepod Belonging to the Genus *Eucalanus*. *Annals and Magazine of Natural History*, 9:15, 127–129.

Mauchline, J. 1992. Taxonomy, Distribution and Biology of *Euchaeta barbata* (= E. farrani) (Copepoda: Calanoida). *Sarsia*, 77(2):131–142.

Mullin, M. M. 1967. On the Feeding Behaviour of Planktonic Marine Copepods and the Separation of Their Ecological Niches. *Marine Biological Association of India, Symposium Series*, 2(3):956–964.

National Museum of Natural History. The World of Copepods, http:// invertebrates.si.edu/copepod/index.htm (accessed 1 March 2008).

Nishida, S., and S. Ohtsuka. 1997. Ultrastructure of the Mouthpart Sensory Setae in Mesopelagic Copepods of the Family Scolecitrichidae. *Plankton Biology and Ecology*, 44(1/2):81–90.

Ohman, M. D., J. M. Bradford, and J. B. Jillett. 1989. Seasonal Growth and Lipid Storage of the Circumglobal, Subantarctic Copepod, *Neocalanus tonsus* (Brady). *Deep-Sea Research*, Part A, 36(9): 1309–1326.

Ohtsuka, S., H. Y. Soh, and S. Nishida. 1997. Evolutionary Switching from Suspension Feeding to Carnivory in the Calanoid Family Heterorhabdidae (Copepoda). *Journal of Crustacean Biology*, 17(4): 577–595.

Ommanney, F. D. 1936. *Rhincalanus gigas* (Brady). A Copepod of the Southern Macroplankton. *Discovery Reports*, 13:227–384.

Ottestad, P. 1932. On the Biology of Some Southern Copepoda. *Hvalrådets Skrifter*, 5:1–61.

———. 1936. On Antarctic Copepods from the Norvegia Expedition 1930–1931. *Scientific Results of the Norwegian Antarctic Expedition*, 15:1–44.

Park, T. 1978. "Calanoid Copepods (Aetideidae and Euchaetidae) from Antarctic and Subantarctic Waters." In *Biology of the Antarctic Seas VII*, ed. D. L. Pawson, pp. 91–290. Antarctic Research Series, no. 27. Washington, D.C.: American Geophysical Union.

———. 1980. "Calanoid Copepods of the Genus *Scolecithricella* from Antarctic and Subantarctic Waters." In *Biology of the Antarctic Seas IX*, ed. L. S. Kornicker, pp. 25–79. Antarctic Research Series, no. 31. Washington, D.C.: American Geophysical Union.

———. 1982. "Calanoid Copepods of the Genus *Scaphocalanus* from Antarctic and Subantarctic Waters." In *Biology of the Antarctic Seas XI*, ed. L. S. Kornicker, pp. 75–127. Antarctic Research Series, no. 34. Washington, D.C.: American Geophysical Union.

———. 1983a. "Calanoid Copepods of Some Scolecithricid Genera from Antarctic and Subantarctic Waters." In *Biology of the Antarctic Seas XIII*, ed. L. S. Kornicker, pp. 165–213. Antarctic Research Series, no. 38. Washington, D.C.: American Geophysical Union.

———. 1983b. "Calanoid Copepods of the Family Phaennidae from Antarctic and Subantarctic Waters." In *Biology of the Antarctic Seas XIV*, ed. L. S. Kornicker, pp. 317–368. Antarctic Research Series, no. 39. Washington, D.C.: American Geophysical Union.

———. 1988. "Calanoid Copepods of the Genus *Haloptilus* from Antarctic and Subantarctic Waters." In *Biology of the Antarctic Seas XIX*, ed. L. S. Kornicker, pp. 1–25. Antarctic Research Series, no. 47. Washington, D.C.: American Geophysical Union.

———. 1993. "Calanoid Copepods of the Genus *Euaugaptilus* from Antarctic and Subantarctic Waters." In *Biology of the Antarctic Seas XXII*, ed. S. Cairns, pp. 1–48. Antarctic Research Series, no. 58. Washington, D.C.: American Geophysical Union.

———. 1994. Geographical Distribution of the Bathypelagic Genus *Paraeuchaeta* (Copepoda, Calanoida). *Hydrobiologia*, 292/293: 317–332.

———. 1995. Taxonomy and Distribution of the Marine Calanoid Copepod Family Euchaetidae. *Bulletin of the Scripps Institution of Oceanography*, 29:1–203.

———. 2000. Taxonomy and Distribution of the Calanoid Copepod Family Heterorhabdidae. *Bulletin of the Scripps Institution of Oceanography*, 31:1–269.

Pasternak, A. F., and S. B. Schnack-Schiel. 2001. Seasonal Feeding Patterns of the Dominant Antarctic Copepods *Calanus propinquus* and *Calanoides acutus* in the Weddell Sea. *Polar Biology*, 24:771–784.

Razouls, C., and S. Razouls. 1990. Biological Cycle of a Population of Subantarctic Copepod, *Drepanopus pectinatus* (Clausocalanidae), Kerguelen Archipelago. *Polar Biology*, 10(7):541–543.

Razouls, S., C. Razouls, and F. de Bovee. 2000. Biodiversity and Biogeography of Antarctic Copepods. *Antarctic Science*, 12(3):343–362.

Reid, J. L., E. Brinton, A. Fleminger, E. Venrick, and J. A. McGowan. 1978. "Ocean Circulation and Marine Life." In *Advances in Ocean-*

ography, ed. H. Charnock and G. Deacon, pp. 63–130. London: Plenum Publishing Corporation.

Robertson, S. B., and B. W. Frost. 1977. Feeding by an Omnivorous Planktonic Copepod *Aetideus divergens* Bradford. *Journal of Experimental Marine Biology and Ecology*, 29:231–244.

Sabatini, M. E., F. C. Ramirez, and P. Martos. 2000. Distribution Pattern and Population Structure of *Calanus australis* Brodsky, 1959 over the Southern Patagonian Shelf off Argentina in Summer. *Journal of Marine Science*, 57(6):1856–1866.

Sars, G. O. 1900. *Crustacea*. The Norwegian North Polar Expedition 1893–1896. Scientific Results, ed. Fridtjof Nansen, Volume 1(5), pp. 1–141.

———. 1903. "Copepoda Calanoida." In *An Account of the Crustacea of Norway*, Volume 4(13, 14), pp. 145–171. Bergen, Norway: Bergen Museum.

———. 1905a. Liste Préliminaire des Calanoïdés Recueillis pendant les Campagnes de S. A. S. le Prince Albert de Monaco, avec Diagnoses des Genres et Espéces Nouvelles (1re Partie). *Bulletin du Musée Oceanographique de Monaco*, 26:1–22.

———. 1905b. Liste Préliminaire des Calanoïdés Recueillis pendant les Campagnes de S. A. S. le Prince Albert de Monaco, avec Diagnoses des Genres et Espéces Nouvelles (2e Partie). *Bulletin du Musée Oceanographique de Monaco*, 40:1–24.

———. 1907. Notes Supplémentaires sur les Calanoïdés de la Princesse-Alice. *Bulletin du Musée Oceanographique de Monaco*, 101:1–27.

———. 1920. Calanoïdés Recueillis pendant les Campagnes de S. A. S. le Prince Albert de Monaco. *Bulletin du Musée Oceanographique de Monaco*, 337:1–20.

———. 1925. Copépodes Particuliérement Bathypélagique Provenant des Campagnes Scientifiques du Prince Albert 1er de Monaco. *Resultats des Campagnes Scientifiques Prince Albert I*, 69:1–408.

Schminke, H.-K. 2007. Entomology for the Copepodologist. *Journal of Plankton Research*, 29(Suppl. 1):149–162.

Schnack-Schiel, S. B., and E. Mizdalski. 1994. Seasonal Variations in Distribution and Population Structure of *Microcalantis pygmaeus* and *Ctenocalanus citer* (Copepoda: Calanoida) in the Eastern Weddell Sea, Antarctica. *Marine Biology*, 119(3):357–366.

Schnack-Schiel, S. B., D. Thomas, G. S. Dieckmann, H. Eicken, R. Gradinger, M. Spindler, J. Weissenberger, E. Mizdalski, and K. Beyer. 1995. Life Cycle Strategy of the Antarctic Calanoid Copepod *Stephos longipes*. *Progress in Oceanography*, 36:45–75.

Schulz, K. 2004. New Species of Benthopelagic Copepods (Crustacea, Calanoida) from the Deep Southern Ocean. *Mitteilungen aus dem Hamburgischen Zoologischen Museum und Institut*, 102:51–70.

———. 2006. New Species and Genus of Calanoid Copepods (Crustacea) from Benthopelagic Collections of the Deep Weddell Sea, Southern Ocean. *Mitteilungen aus dem Hamburgischen Zoologischen Museum und Institut*, 103:47–68.

Schulz, K., and E. L. Markhaseva. 2000. *Parabradyidius angelikae*, a New Genus and Species of Benthopelagic Copepod (Calanoida; Aetideidae) from the Deep Weddell Sea (Antarctica). *Mitteilungen aus dem Hamburgischen Zoologischen Museum und Institut*, 97: 77–89.

Scott, A. 1909. The Copepoda of the Siboga Expedition. 1. Free-Swimming, Littoral and Semiparasitic Copepoda. *Siboga-Expeditie*, 29a:1–323.

Scott, T. 1894. Report on Entomostraca from the Gulf of Guinea. *Transactions of the Linnaean Society of London, Zoology Series*, 6(1): 1–161.

Sewell, R. B. S. 1932. The Copepoda of Indian Seas. Calanoida. *Memoirs of the Zoological Survey of India*, 10:223–407.

Steuer, A. 1904. Copepoden der Valdivia Expedition. *Zoologisches Anzeiger*, 27:593–598.

———. 1932. Copepoda (6). *Pleuromamma* Giesbr. 1898 der Deutschen Tiefsee Expedition. *Wissenschaftliche Ergebnisse der Deutschen Tiefsee-Expedition 'Valdivia,'* 24:1–119.

Steuer, A., and E. Hentschel. 1937. Die Verbreitung der copepodengattungen *Sapphirina, Copilia, Miracia, Pleuromamma, Rhincalanus* and *Cephalophanes* im südatlantischen Ozean. Nachtrag über die Verbreitung von *Pleuromamma* und *Rhincalanus* auf Vertikalschnitten. *Wissenschaftliche Ergebnisse der Deutschen Atlantic Expedition 'Meteor,'* 12:101–163.

Swadling, K. M., A. D. McKinnon, G. De'ath, and J. A. E. Gibson. 2004. Life Cycle Plasticity and Differential Growth and Development in Marine and Lacustrine Populations of an Antarctic Copepod. *Limnology and Oceanography*, 49(3):644–655.

Tanaka, O. 1958. The Pelagic Copepods of the Izu Region, Middle Japan. Systematic Account. 5. Family Euchaetidae. *Publications of the Seto Marine Biological Laboratory*, 6(3):327–367.

———. 1960. Biological Results of the Japanese Antarctic Research Expedition. Pelagic Copepoda. *Special Publications from the Seto Marine Biological Laboratory*, 10:1–177.

———. 1964. Two Small Collections of Copepods from the Antarctic. *Special Publications from the Seto Marine Biological Laboratory*, 22:1–20.

Thompson, I. C. 1898. Report on a Small Collection of Antarctic Plankton from the Neighbourhood of the South Shetland Islands, Collected by the Staff of the Dundee Whaler in 1892–3. *Proceedings and Transactions of the Liverpool Biological Society*, 12:291–297.

———. 1903. Report on the Copepoda Obtained by Mr. George Murray, F. R. S., during the Cruise of the Oceana in 1898. *Annals and Magazine of Natural History*, 12:1–36.

Vervoort, W. 1949. Some New and Rare Copepoda Calanoida from East Indian Seas. *Zoologische Verhandelingen*, 5:1–53.

———. 1950. The Genus *Onchocalanus* G. O. Sars, 1905 (Crustacea Copepoda). *Zoologische Verhandelingen*, 10:1–35.

———. 1951. Plankton Copepods from the Atlantic Sector of the Antarctic. *Verhandelingen der Koninklijke Nederlandse Akademie van Wetenschappen, Afd. Natuurkunde*, Section 2, 47(4):1–156.

———. 1957. Copepods from Antarctic and Sub-Antarctic Plankton Samples. The British-Australian-New Zealand Antarctic Research Expedition, 1929–1931, Reports. Under the Command of Sir Douglas Mawson, Kt, O.B.E., B.E., D.Sc., F.R.S. Series B, 3:1–160, figs. 1–138.

———. 1965a. Pelagic Copepoda. Part II. Copepoda Calanoida of the Families Phaennidae up to and Including Acartiidae, Containing the Description of a New Species of Aetideidae. *Atlantide Report*, 8:9–216.

———. 1965b. Notes on the Biogeography and Ecology of Free-Living, Marine Copepoda. *Monographiae Biologicae*, 15:381–400.

Vyshkvartzeva, N. V. 2000. Two New Genera of Scolecithrichidae and Redefinition of *Scolecithricella* Sars and *Amallothrix* Sars (Copepoda, Calanoida). *Zoosystematic Rossica*, 8(2), 1999:217–241.

Waghorn, E. J. 1979. Two New Species of Copepoda from White Island, Antarctica. *New Zealand Journal of Marine and Freshwater Research*, 13(3):459–470.

With, C. 1915. Copepoda. 1. Calanoida Amphascandria. *Danish Ingolf Expedition*, 3(4):1–260.

Wolfenden, R. N. 1903. Copepoda. *Proceedings of the Zoological Society of London*, Part 1:117–132.

———. 1904. Notes on the Copepoda of the North Atlantic Sea and the Faröe Channel. *Journal of the Marine Biological Association of the United Kingdom*, 7:110–146.

———. 1905. Plankton Studies: Preliminary Notes upon New or Interesting Species. *Copepoda*, Part 1, pp. 1–24. London: Rebman Limited.

———. 1906. Plankton Studies: Preliminary Notes upon New or Interesting Species. *Copepoda*, Part 2, pp. 25–44. London: Rebman Limited.

———. 1908. "Crustacea. 8. Copepoda." In *National Antarctic Expedition, 1901–1904*. Natural History. Volume 4. Zoology (Various invertebrata), pp. 1–46.

———. 1911. Die marinen Copepoden der deutschen Südpolar-Expedition 1901-1903. 2. Die pelagischen Copepoden der Westwinddrift und des südlichen Eismeers. *Deutsche Südpolar-Expedition, 1901–1903*, 12(2):181–380, pls. 22–41.

Yamanaka, N. 1976. The Distribution of Some Copepods (Crustacea) in the Southern Ocean and Adjacent Regions from 40E to 81EW Long. *Boletim de Zoologia, Universidade de Sao Paulo*, 1:161–196.

Yen, J. 1983. Effects of Prey Concentration, Prey Size, Predator Life Stage, Predator Starvation, and Season on Predation Rates of the Carnivorous Copepod *Euchaeta elongata*. *Marine Biology*, 75(1): 69–77.

———. 1991. Predatory Feeding Behaviour of an Antarctic Marine Copepod, *Euchaeta antarctica*. *Polar Research*, 10(2):433–442.

APPENDIX 1

This appendix contains a list of pelagic calanoid copepod species, alphabetical by genus and then species, reported from the Southern Ocean. Each species name includes the author and date of publication of the original species description. The author and date entry listed below a species name is the latest taxonomic reference to the species. Abbreviations for distributions are as follows: Ant, Antarctic; sAnt, subantarctic; Stemp, south temperate; Trop, tropical; Ntemp, north temperate; sArc, subarctic; Arc, Arctic.

Aetideopsis antarctica (Wolfenden, 1908): Ant
 Faroella antarctica Wolfenden, 1908:39, pl. 2, figs. 1–4.
 Aetideopsis antarctica Bradford, 1971:18, figs. 31–48.
Aetideopsis minor (Wolfenden, 1911): Ant, Arc
 Faroella minor Wolfenden, 1911:214.
 Aetideopsis minor Park, 1978:115–118, figs. 8–9; Markhaseva, 1996:32, figs. 20–21.
Aetideopsis multiserrata (Wolfenden, 1904): Ant, sArc
 Faroella multiserrata Wolfenden, 1904:117, pl. 9, figs. 26–28.
 Aetideopsis multiserrata Park, 1978:111–115, figs. 6–7; Markhaseva, 1996:37, figs. 22–23.
Aetideopsis rostrata Sars, 1903: Ant, sArc, Arc
 Aetideopsis rostrata Sars, 1903:160, pls. 4, 5; Markhaseva, 1996:42, figs. 26–28.
 Aetideopsis inflata Park, 1978:118–122, figs. 11–12.
Aetideopsis tumorosa Bradford, 1969: sAnt
 Aetideopsis tumorosa Bradford, 1969:74, figs. 1–28; Park, 1978:118, fig. 10; Markhaseva, 1996:42, fig. 29.
Aetideus arcuatus (Vervoort, 1949): sAnt, Ntemp
 Snelliaetideus arcuatus Vervoort, 1949:4, fig. 1; Park, 1978:108–111, figs. 4–5.
 Aetideus arcuatus Markhaseva, 1996:14, fig. 3.
Aetideus australis (Vervoort, 1957): Ant, sAnt
 Euaetideus australis Vervoort, 1957:46, figs. 16–19, 20a; Park, 1978:105–108, figs. 2–3.
Arietellus simplex Sars, 1905: Ant, sArc
 Arietellus simplex Sars, 1905:5, 22; 1925:334, pl. 120, figs. 7–12; Vervoort, 1957:141.
Augaptilus glacialis Sars, 1900: Ant, Arc
 Augaptilus glacialis Sars, 1900:88, pl.s 26, 27; 1925:254, pl. 76, figs.1–6; Vervoort, 1951:144, figs. 80, 81.
Batheuchaeta antarctica Markhaseva, 1986: Ant
 Batheuchaeta antarctica Markhaseva, 1986:848, fig. 6; 1996:53, fig. 34.

Batheuchaeta lamellata Brodsky, 1950: Ant-Ntemp
  Batheuchaeta lamellata Brodsky, 1950:189, figs. 106–107; Markhaseva, 1996:57–58.
Batheuchaeta peculiaris Markhaseva, 1983: Ant-Ntemp
  Batheuchaeta peculiaris Markhaseva, 1983:1740, fig. 1; 1996:58, figs. 41–42.
Batheuchaeta pubescens Markhaseva, 1986: Ant
  Batheuchaeta pubescens Markhaseva, 1986:846, fig. 5; 1996:58, fig. 43.
Bathycalanus bradyi (Wolfenden, 1905): Ant-Ntemp
  Megacalanus bradyi Wolfenden, 1905:1–3, pl. 1, figs. 1–6.
  Bathycalanus maximus Wolfenden, 1911:198, pl. 23, figs. 1–7, text fig. 2.
  Bathycalanus bradyi Vervoort, 1957:32, fig. 7.
Bathycalanus eltaninae Björnberg, 1968: sAnt
  Bathycalanus eltaninae Björnberg, 1968:75, figs. 15–41.
Bathycalanus inflatus Björnberg, 1968: sAnt
  Bathycalanus inflatus Björnberg, 1968:81, figs. 42–54.
Bathycalanus unicornis Björnberg, 1968: sAnt
  Bathycalanus unicornis Björnberg, 1968:73, figs. 1–14.
Bradycalanus enormis Björnberg, 1968: sAnt
  Bradycalanus enormis Björnberg, 1968:85, figs. 64–77.
Bradycalanus pseudotypicus Björnberg, 1968: sAnt
  Bradycalanus pseudotypicus Björnberg, 1968:82, figs. 55–63, 78.
Calanoides acutus (Giesbrecht, 1902): Ant
  Calanoides acutus Giesbrecht, 1902:17, pl. 1, figs. 10–14; Vervoort, 1951:42, figs. 25–33.
Calanus australis Brodsky, 1959: sAnt-Stemp
  Calanus australis Brodsky, 1959:1539–1542, pl. 1, figs. 9–12; pl. 2, figs. 4, 8, 10, 11; pl. 3, figs. 11, 13, 14; pl. 4, figs. 8, 9.
Calanus propinquus Brady, 1883: Ant
  Calanus propinquus Brady, 1883:34, pl. 2, figs. 1–7; pl. 14, figs. 10–11; Vervoort, 1951:27, figs. 14–24.
Calanus simillimus Giesbrecht, 1902: sAnt
  Calanus simillimus Giesbrecht, 1902:16, fig. 9; Vervoort, 1951:11, figs. 3–14.
Candacia cheirura Cleve, 1904: sAnt
  Candacia cheirura Cleve, 1904:180, 186, 198, pl. 1, figs. 1–6; pl. 2, figs. 7–10; Farran, 1929:273, fig. 29; Vervoort, 1957:142.
Candacia falcifera Farran, 1929: Ant-sArc
  Candacia falcifera Farran, 1929:270, fig. 28; Vervoort, 1957:142, fig. 132.
Candacia maxima Vervoort, 1957: Ant-sAnt
  Candacia maxima Vervoort, 1957:142–144, figs.132–138.
Centraugaptilus rattrayi (Scott, 1894): sAnt-sArc
  Augapatilus rattrayi Scott, 1894:36, pl. 2, figs. 25–37.
  Centraugaptilus rattrayi Sars, 1925:304, pl. 106; Hardy and Gunther, 1935:183.
Cephalophanes frigidus Wolfenden, 1911: Ant-sAnt
  Cephalophanes frigidus Wolfenden, 1911:284–285, fig. 46; Park, 1983b:321–325, figs. 3–4.
Chiridiella megadactyla Bradford, 1971: Ant
  Chiridiella megadactyla Bradford, 1971:19–20, figs. 49–60.
Chiridiella subaequalis Grice and Hulsemann, 1965: Ant-Ntemp
  Chiridiella subaequalis Grice and Hulsemann, 1965:231–235, fig. 10a–l; Markhaseva, 1996:108, fig. 82.
Chiridius gracilis Farran, 1908: Ant-sArc
  Chiridius gracilis Farran, 1908:30, pl. 2, figs. 1–3; Park, 1978:122–124, fig. 13; Markhaseva, 1996:111, figs. 83–84.
Chiridius polaris Wolfenden, 1911: Ant, Ntemp
  Chiridius polaris Wolfenden, 1911:211, text fig. 6, pl. 24, figs. 9–12; Markhaseva, 1996:119, figs. 94–97.
  Chiridius subantarcticus Park, 1978:125–127, fig. 14.
Chirundina streetsii Giesbrecht, 1895: sAnt-sArc
  Chirundina streetsii Giesbrecht, 1895:249, pl. 1, figs. 5–10; Park, 1978:179, figs. 52–53.

Clausocalanus brevipes Frost and Fleminger, 1968: sAnt
  Clausocalanus brevipes Frost and Fleminger, 1968:70, figs. 56–59.
Clausocalanus brevipes Farran, 1929: Ant
  Clausocalanus laticeps Farran, 1929:224, fig. 4; Frost and Fleminger, 1968:42, figs. 24–28.
Cornucalanus chelifer (Thompson, 1903): Ant-Ntemp
  Scolecithrix chelifer Thompson, 1903:21, pl. 5, figs. 1–9; Park, 1983b:352–357, figs. 23–26.
Cornucalanus robustus Vervoort, 1957: Ant-Trop
  Cornucalanus robustus Vervoort, 1957:88–91, figs. 71–76; Park, 1983:358–363, figs. 27–30.
Cornucalanus simplex Wolfenden, 1905: Ant-Ntemp
  Cornucalanus simplex Wolfenden, 1905:22; Park, 1983b:364–365, fig. 31.
Ctenocalanus citer Heron and Bowman, 1971: sAnt
  Ctenocalanus citer Heron and Bowman, 1971:142, figs. 1, 16–18, 31–36, 54–58, 71–77, 94–99, 130–150.
  Ctenocalanus vanus Vervoort, 1951:59–61; 1957:37.
Disseta palumbii Giesbrecht, 1889: sAnt-sArc
  Disseta palumbii Giesbrecht, 1889a:812; 1893:369, pl. 29, figs. 2, 8, 14, 19, 23–25, 27; pl. 38, fig. 44; Park, 2000:14–18, figs. 1–3.
Drepanopus bispinosus Bayly, 1982; Ant
  Drepanopus bispinosus Bayly, 1982:165, figs. 2a–2h, 3a–3f.
Drepanopus forcipatus Giesbrecht, 1888: sAnt
  Drepanopus forcipatus Giesbrecht, 1888:335; Hulsemann, 1985:911, figs. 2–4, 6–8, 10, 12, 14, 16–20, 23, 24, 27–29, 32–33.
Drepanopus pectinatus Brady, 1883: sAnt
  Drepanopus pectinatus Brady, 1883:77, pl. 24, figs. 1–11; Hulsemann, 1985a:910, figs. 1, 5, 9, 11, 13, 15, 21, 22, 25, 26, 30, 31.
Euaugaptilus aliquantus Park, 1993: sAnt-Stemp
  Euaugaptilus aliquantus Park, 1993:13–14, figs. 7–8.
Euaugaptilus angustus (Sars, 1905): sAnt-Ntemp
  Augaptilus angustus Sars, 1905:10–11.
  Euaugaptilus angustus Sars, 1925:281–282, pl. 91; Park, 1993:27–30, figs. 19–20.
Euaugaptilus antarcticus Wolfenden, 1911: Ant
  Euaugaptilus antarcticus Wolfenden, 1911:334–336, fig. 70, pl. 36, figs. 6–7; Park, 1993:32–37, figs. 23–25.
Euaugaptilus austrinus Park, 1993: Ant
  Euaugaptilus austrinus Park, 1993:37–41, figs. 26–28.
Euaugaptilus brevirostratus Park, 1993: sAnt-Stemp
  Euaugaptilus brevirostratus Park, 1993:19–22, figs. 12–14.
Euaugaptilus bullifer (Giesbrecht, 1889): Ant-Ntemp
  Augaptilus bullifer Giesbrecht, 1889a:813; 1893:400, pl. 28, figs. 6, 21, 24; pl. 39, fig. 46.
  Euaugaptilus bullifer (Giesbrecht, 1889); Park, 1993:22–25, figs. 15–16.
Euaugaptilus gibbus (Wolfenden, 1904): sAnt-Ntemp
  Augaptilus gibbus Wolfenden, 1904:122; 1911:337–339, fig. 72, pl. 37, figs. 2–3.
  Euaugaptilus gibbus (Wolfenden, 1904); Park, 1993:25–27, figs. 17–18.
Euaugaptilus hadrocephalus Park, 1993: Ant-Stemp
  Euaugaptilus hadrocephalus Park, 1993:6–9, figs. 3, 4.
Euaugaptilus laticeps (Sars, 1905): sAnt-Ntemp
  Augaptilus laticeps Sars, 1905b:11.
  Euaugaptilus laticeps Sars, 1925:264–265, pl. 80; Park, 1993:30–32, figs. 21–22.
Euaugaptilus magnus (Wolfenden, 1904): Ant-Ntemp
  Augaptilus magnus Wolfenden, 1904:111, 122, 142, 145; Wolfenden 1911:341–343, fig. 74, pl. 37, figs. 4–9.
  Euaugaptilus magnus Park, 1993:41–44, figs. 29–30.
Euaugaptilus maxillaris Sars, 1920: Ant-Ntemp
  Euaugaptilus maxillaris Sars, 1920:15; 1925:287–288, pl. 95; Park, 1993:5–6, figs. 1–2.

Euaugaptilus nodifrons (Sars, 1905): Ant-Ntemp
    Augaptilus nodifrons Sars, 1905b:13–14.
    Euaugaptilus nodifrons Sars, 1925:267–269, pl. 82; Park, 1993:14–19, figs. 9–11.
Euaugaptilus oblongus (Sars, 1905): sAnt-Ntemp
    Augaptilus oblongus Sars, 1905b:11.
    Euaugaptilus oblongus Sars, 1925:266–267, pl. 81; Park, 1993:44–47, figs. 31–32.
Euaugaptilus perasetosus Park, 1993: Ant-Stemp
    Euaugaptilus perasetosus Park, 1993:9–13, figs. 5–6.
Eucalanus hyalinus (Claus, 1866): sAnt-Ntemp
    Calanella hyaline Claus, 1866:8.
    Eucalanus hyalinus Bradford–Grieve, 1994:76, figs. 42, 88.
Euchirella maxima Wolfenden, 1905: sAnt-sArc
    Euchirella maxima Wolfenden, 1905:18, pl. 6, figs. 9–11; Park, 1978:149–151, fig. 30.
Euchirella rostrata (Claus, 1866): sAnt-Ntemp
    Undina rostrata Claus, 1866:11, pl. 1, fig. 2.
    Euchirella rostrata Park, 1978:147–149, fig. 29.
Euchirella rostromagna Wolfenden, 1911: Ant
    Euchirella rostromagna Wolfenden, 1911:235; Park, 1978:151–155, figs. 31–34.
Euchirella similis Wolfenden, 1911: sAnt-Trop
    Euchirella similis Wolfenden, 1911:238, text fig. 23, pl. 28, figs. 1–2; Park, 1978:155–158, figs. 35–36.
Farrania frigida (Wolfenden, 1911): Ant-Trop
    Drepanopsis frigida Wolfenden, 1911:245, text fig. 29; Vervoort, 1951:61, figs. 34–39.
    Farrania frigida Vervoort, 1957:38–39.
Gaetanus antarcticus Wolfenden, 1905: Ant-Ntemp
    Gaetanus antarcticus Wolfenden, 1905:7, pl. 3, fig. 1; Park, 1978:141–144, figs. 25, 26; Markhaseva, 1996:178, figs. 138–139.
Gaetanus brevispinus (Sars, 1900): Ant-Arc
    Chiridius brevispinus Sars, 1900:68, pl. 19; Markhaseva, 1996:187–195, figs. 149–152.
    Gaidius intermedius Wolfenden, 1905:6, pl. 3, figs. 4–5; Park, 1978:131–136, figs. 18–20.
Gaetanus kruppii Giesbrecht, 1903: sAnt-sArc
    Gaetanus kruppii Giesbrecht, 1903:22; Park, 1978:136–139, figs. 21–22; Markhaseva, 1996:196–201, figs. 157–158.
Gaetanus latifrons Sars, 1905: sAnt-sArc
    Gaetanus latifrons Sars, 1905a: 4, 11; Vervoort, 1957:61–62; Markhaseva, 1996, p.201–204, figs. 159–160.
Gaetanus minor Farran, 1905: sAnt-Ntemp
    Gaetanus minor Farran, 1905:34, pl. 5; Park, 1978:144–147, figs. 27–28; Markhaseva, 1996:205–206, fig. 164.
Gaetanus paracurvicornis Brodsky, 1950: Ant-Ntemp
    Gaetanus paracurvicornis Brodsky, 1950:167, fig. 84; Markhaseva, 1996:211, fig. 167.
Gaetanus pileatus Farran, 1903: sAnt-Ntemp
    Gaetanus pileatus Farran, 1903:16, pl. 17, figs. 1–11; Park, 1978:139–141, figs. 23–24; Markhaseva, 1996:211–212, figs. 168–169.
Gaetanus tenuispinus (Sars, 1900): Ant-Arc
    Chiridius tenuispinus Sars, 1900:67, pl. 18.
    Gaidius tenuispinus Park, 1978, pp.127–131, figs. 15–17.
    Gaetanus tenuispinus Markhaseva, 1996:221–225, figs. 177–178.
Haloptilus fons Farran, 1908: Ant-Ntemp
    Haloptilus fons Farran, 1908:69–71, pl. 7, figs. 11–15; Park, 1988:3–4, figs. 1–2.
Haloptilus longicirrus Brodsky, 1950: Ant-sArc
    Haloptilus longicirrus Brodsky, 1950:363–364, fig. 254; Park, 1988:21–22, fig. 13.
Haloptilus ocellatus Wolfenden, 1905: Ant
    Haloptilus ocellatus Wolfenden, 1905:14–15, pl. 5; Park, 1988:4–9, figs. 3–4.

Haloptilus oxycephalus (Giesbrecht, 1889): Ant-Ntemp
    Hemicalanus oxycephalus Giesbrecht, 1889a:813; Giesbrecht, 1893:384, pl. 42, figs. 16, 23.
    Haloptilus oxycephalus Park, 1988:9–14, figs. 5–6.
Heterorhabdus austrinus Giesbrecht, 1902: Ant-sAnt
    Heterorhabdus austrinus Giesbrecht, 1902:28, pl. 6, figs. 1–9; Park, 2000:132–133, figs. 104–105.
Heterorhabdus lobatus Bradford, 1971: sAnt-Ntemp
    Heterorhabdus lobatus Bradford, 1971:131, figs. 9, 10a–c; Park, 2000:105–106, fig. 74.
Heterorhabdus paraspinosus Park, 2000: sAnt-Stemp
    Heterorhabdus paraspinosus Park, 2000:131–132, figs. 102–103.
Heterorhabdus pustulifer Farran, 1929: Ant-sAnt
    Heterorhabdus pustulifer Farran, 1929:266, fig. 27; Park, 2000:124–125, figs. 92–93.
Heterorhabdus spinosus Bradford, 1971: sAnt-Stemp
    Heterorhabdus spinosus Bradford, 1971:121, figs.1, 2g–k, 3c, 4c; Park, 2000:130–131, figs. 100–101.
Heterostylites nigrotinctus Brady, 1918: Ant-sAnt
    Heterostylites nigrotinctus Brady, 1918:27, pl. 6, figs. 1–8; Park, 2000:44–45, figs. 22–23.
Landrumius antarcticus Park, 1983a: Ant
    Landrumius antarcticus Park, 1983a:192–195, figs. 15–16.
Landrumius gigas (Scott, 1909): sAnt-Trop
    Brachycalanus gigas Scott, 1909:81–82, pl. 35, figs. 10–18.
    Lophothrix gigas Grice and Hulsemann, 1968:332–334, figs. 63–74.
    Landrumius gigas Park, 1983:195–197, figs. 17–18.
Lophothrix frontalis Giesbrecht, 1895: sAnt-Ntemp
    Lophothrix frontalis Giesbrecht, 1895:254–255, pl. 2, figs. 1–5, 9–12; Park, 1983a:178–184, figs. 7–10.
Lophothrix humilifrons Sars, 1905: Ant-Ntemp
    Lophothrix humilifrons Sars, 1905a:22; 1925:166–167, pl. 46, figs. 15–22; Park, 1983a:184–188, figs. 11–12.
Lucicutia bradyana Cleve, 1904: Ant-Trop
    Lucicutia bradyana Cleve, 1904:204–206, pl. 6, figs. 33, 34; Markhaseva and Ferrari, 2005:1084–1091, figs. 3–7.
Lucicutia curta Farran, 1905: Ant-sArc
    Lucicutia curta Farran, 1905:44, pl. 12, figs. 1–7; Vervoort, 1957:128–129, figs. 114–117.
Lucicutia macrocera Sars, 1920: Ant-sArc
    Lucicutia macrocera Sars, 1920:10; 1925:213, pl. 57, figs. 12–15; Vervoort, 1957:130, figs. 118, 119.
Lucicutia magna Wolfenden, 1903: Ant-sArc
    Lucicutia magna Wolfenden, 1903:124; Wolfenden, 1911:316–317, text fig. 59; Hulsemann, 1966:727, fig. 119.
Lucicutia ovalis (Giesbrecht, 1889): Ant-sArc
    Isochaeta ovalis Giesbrecht, 1889a:812.
    Lucicutia frigida Wolfenden, 1911:320, text fig. 62; Vervoort, 1957:126–128, figs. 111–114.
Lucicutia wolfendeni Sewell, 1932: Ant-sArc
    Lucicutia wolfendeni Sewell, 1932:289; Markhaseva and Ferrari, 2005:1091–1094, figs. 8–9.
Megacalanus princeps Wolfenden, 1904: Ant-sArc
    Megacalanus princeps Wolfenden, 1904:49, fig. 4; Vervoort, 1957: 32, fig. 7.
Metridia brevicauda Giesbrecht, 1889: sAnt-sArc
    Metridia brevicauda Giesbrecht, 1889b:24; 1893:340, pl. 33, figs. 5, 10–11, 14, 21, 32; Vervoort, 1957:122.
Metridia curticauda Giesbrecht, 1889: Ant-sArc
    Metridia curticauda Giesbrecht, 1889b:24; 1893:340, pl. 33, figs. 4, 15, 33; Vervoort, 1951:121, figs. 65–67; 1957:122.
Metridia ferrarii Markhaseva, 2001: Ant-Ntemp
    Metridia ferrarii Markhaseva, 2001:44–46, figs. 1–59.
Metridia gerlachei Giesbrecht, 1902: Ant
    Metridia gerlachei Giesbrecht, 1902:27, pl. 5, figs. 6–14; Vervoort, 1951:120; 1957:120–121, figs. 109, 110.

Metridia lucens Boeck, 1864: sAnt-Ntemp
   Metridia lucens Boeck, 1864:238; Vervoort, 1957:119.
   Metridia hibernica Giesbrecht, 1893:345, pl. 32, fig. 11; pl. 35, figs. 2, 12, 16, 22, 28, 36, 39.
Metridia ornata Brodsky, 1950: Ant-sArc
   Metridia ornata Brodsky, 1950:303–305, fig. 210; Markhaseva, 2001:48–49, figs. 184–243.
Metridia princeps Giesbrecht, 1889: Ant-sArc
   Metridia princeps Giesbrecht, 1889b:24; Markhaseva, 2001:47–48, figs. 148–183.
Metridia pseudoasymmetrica Markhaseva, 2001: Ant-sAnt
   Metridia pseudoasymmetrica Markhaseva, 2001:46–47, figs. 60–110.
Metridia venusta Giesbrecht, 1889: sAnt-Ntemp
   Metridia venusta Giesbrecht, 1889b:24; 1893:340, pl. 33, figs. 7, 17, 29; Vervoort, 1957:121–122.
Microcalanus pygmaeus (Sars, 1900): Ant-Arc
   Pseudocalanus pygmaeus Sars, 1900:73, pl. 21.
   Microcalanus pygmaeus Vervoort, 1957:36–37, fig. 9; Bradford-Grieve, 1994:130, fig. 75.
Mimocalanus cultrifer Farran, 1908: Ant-sArc
   Mimocalanus cultrifer Farran, 1908:23, pl. 1, figs. 5–9; Damkaer, 1975:68–69, figs. 164–168.
Neocalanus tonsus (Brady, 1883): sAnt-Stemp
   Calanus tonsus Brady, 1883:34, pl. 4, figs. 8, 9; Vervoort, 1957:27, figs. 3–6.
   Neocalanus tonsus Bradford-Grieve, 1994:42, figs. 17, 82.
Nullosetigera bidentatus (Brady, 1883): Ant-sArc
   Phyllopus bidentatus Brady, 1883:78, pl. 5, figs. 7–16; Vervoort, 1957:141.
Onchocalanus cristatus (Wolfenden, 1904): Ant-Ntemp
   Xanthocalanus cristatus Wolfenden, 1904:119, pl. 9, figs. 18–19.
   Onchocalanus cristatus Park, 1983b:335–343, figs. 13–15.
Onchocalanus hirtipes Sars, 1905: Ant-Ntemp
   Onchocalanus hirtipes Sars, 1905a:20–21; 1925:148–149, pl. 41, figs. 6–11; Park, 1983b:351, fig. 22.
Onchocalanus magnus (Wolfenden, 1906): Ant
   Xanthoclanus magnus Wolfenden, 1906:32–33, pl. 10, figs. 7–9.
   Onchocalanus magnus Park, 1983:343–347, figs. 16–19.
Onchocalanus paratrigoniceps Park, 1983b: Ant-Stemp
   Onchocalanus paratrigoniceps Park, 1983b:333–335, figs. 10–12.
Onchocalanus subcristatus (Wolfenden, 1906): Ant
   Xanthocalanus subcristatus Wolfenden, 1906:31–32, pl. 10, figs. 4–6.
   Onchocalanus subcristatus Wolfenden, 1911:278, pl. 31, figs. 6–8.
Onchocalanus trigoniceps Sars, 1905: Ant-Ntemp
   Onchocalanus trigoniceps Sars, 1905a:20; 1925:144–147, pl. 40, figs. 1–15; Park, 1983b:329–333, figs. 7–9.
Onchocalanus wolfendeni Vervoort, 1950: Ant
   Onchocalanus wolfendeni Vervoort, 1950:22–26, figs. 9–11; Park, 1983b:347–351, figs. 20–21.
Pachyptilus eurygnathus Sars, 1920: Ant-sArc
   Pachyptilus eurygnathus Sars, 1920:18; 1925:321, pl. 114; Vervoort, 1957:140.
Paraeuchaeta abbreviata (Park, 1978): Ant-Trop
   Euchaeta abbreviata Park, 1978:240–244, figs. 92, 93.
   Paraeuchaeta abbreviata Park, 1995:63–64, figs. 58–59.
Paraeuchaeta antarctica (Giesbrecht, 1902): Ant-sAnt
   Euchaeta antarctica Giesbrecht, 1902:21, pl. 3, figs. 1–8; Fontaine, 1988:32–38, figs. 3–8.
   Paraeuchaeta antarctica Park, 1995:88–89, figs. 84–85.
Paraeuchaeta austrina (Giesbrecht, 1902): Ant
   Euchaeta austrina Giesbrecht, 1902:22, pl. 3, figs. 9–16; Fontaine, 1988:46–49, figs. 6, 13, 16, 17.

Paraeuchaeta barbata (Brady, 1883): Ant-Arc
   Euchaeta barbata Brady, 1883:66, pl. 22, figs. 6–12.
   Paraeuchaeta barbata Park, 1995:37–38, fig. 23.
Paraeuchaeta biloba Farran, 1929: Ant-sAnt
   Paraeuchaeta biloba Farran, 1929:242, fig. 11.
   Euchaeta biloba Park, 1978:217–220, figs. 74–76.
Paraeuchaeta comosa Tanaka, 1958: sAnt-Ntemp
   Paraeuchaeta comosa Tanaka, 1958:363, fig. 79a–g; Park, 1995:56–57, fig. 50.
Paraeuchaeta dactylifera (Park, 1978) Ant-sAnt
   Euchaeta dactylifera Park, 1978:240, fig. 91.
   Paraeuchaeta dactylifera Park, 1995:70, fig. 67.
Paraeuchaeta eltaninae (Park, 1978): Ant
   Euchaeta eltaninae Park, 1978:280–283, figs. 118–120.
   Paraeuchaeta eltaninae Park, 1995:39, fig. 25.
Paraeuchaeta erebi Farran, 1929: Ant
   Paraeuchaeta erebi Farran, 1929:239, fig. 9.
   Euchaeta erebi Fontaine, 1988:41–45, figs. 11–13.
Paraeuchaeta exigua (Wolfenden, 1911): sAnt-Stemp
   Euchaeta exigua Wolfenden, 1911:300, text fig. 52.
   Paraeuchaeta exigua Park, 1995:77–78, fig. 74.
Paraeuchaeta hansenii (With, 1915): sAnt-sArc
   Euchaeta hansenii With, 1915:181, text fig. 52.
   Paraeuchaeta hansenii Park, 1995:57–58, fig. 51.
Paraeuchaeta kurilensis Heptner, 1971: Ant-sArc
   Paraeuchaeta kurilensis Heptner, 1971:83, fig. 4; Park, 1995:62–63, fig. 57.
Paraeuchaeta parvula (Park, 1978): Ant-sAnt
   Euchaeta parvula Park, 1978:256–259, figs. 102–104.
   Paraeuchaeta parvula Park, 1995:38, fig. 24.
Paraeuchaeta pseudotonsa (Fontaine, 1967): sAnt-Ntemp
   Euchaeta pseudotonsa Fontaine, 1967:204, figs. 1B, 2B, 3B, 3E, 6B, 6E, 7B, 8B, E, 9A, 9C, 10, 12.
   Paraeuchaeta pseudotonsa Park, 1995:74–75, fig. 71.
Paraeuchaeta rasa Farran, 1929: Ant-sAnt
   Paraeuchaeta rasa Farran, 1929:240, fig. 10; Park, 1995:46, fig. 35.
Paraeuchaeta regalis (Grice and Hulsemann, 1968): Ant-Stemp
   Euchaeta regalis Grice and Hulsemann, 1968:329, figs. 34–40.
   Paraeuchaeta regalis Park, 1995:50, fig. 41.
Paraeuchaeta sarsi (Farran, 1908): sAnt-Ntemp
   Euchaeta sarsi Farran, 1908:41, pl. 3, figs. 15–16.
   Paraeuchaeta sarsi Park, 1995:47–48, figs. 37–38.
Paraeuchaeta scotti (Farran, 1908): sAnt-Ntemp
   Euchaeta scotti Farran, 1908:42, pl. 3, figs. 11–12.
   Paraeuchaeta scotti Park, 1995:40–41, fig. 27.
Paraeuchaeta similis (Wolfenden, 1908): Ant
   Euchaeta similis Wolfenden, 1908:19, pl. 4, figs. 1–4; Park, 1978:227–229, fig. 82; Fontaine, 1988:38–41, figs. 6, 9, 10.
Paraeuchaeta tumidula (Sars, 1905): Ant-sArc
   Euchaeta tumidula Sars, 1905a:15.
   Paraeuchaeta tumidula Park, 1995:82–83, fig. 79.
   Euchaeta biconvexa Park, 1978:264–267, figs. 108, 109.
Paraeuchaeta tycodesma (Park, 1978): Ant
   Euchaeta tycodesma Park, 1978:229–231, fig. 83; Fontaine, 1988:45–46, figs. 13–15.
Paraheterorhabdus compactus (Sars, 1900): sAnt-Arc
   Heterorhabdus compactus Sars, 1900:83, pls. 24, 25.
   Paraheterorhabdus compactus Park, 2000:85–88, figs. 56–58.
Paraheterorhabdus farrani (Brady, 1918): Ant-sAnt
   Heterorhabdus farrani Brady, 1918:27, pl. 4, figs.10–18.
   Paraheterorhabdus farrani Park, 2000:78–80, figs. 48, 49.
Paralabidocera antarctica (Thompson, 1898): Ant
   Paracartia antarctica Thompson, 1898:295, pl. 18, figs. 1–12.

Paralabidocera hodgsoni Wolfenden, 1908:26, pl. 6, figs. 1–13.
Paralabidocera antarctica Farran, 1929:280; Vervoort, 1951:148.
Paralabidocera grandispina Waghorn, 1979: Ant
    Paralabidocera grandispina Waghorn, 1979:465, figs. 5–8.
Paralabidocera separabilis Brodsky and Zvereva, 1976: Ant
    Paralabidocera separabilis Brodsky and Zvereva, 1976:234, figs. 1–4.
Pleuromamma abdominalis (Lubbock, 1856): sAnt-Ntemp
    Diaptomus abdominalis Lubbock, 1856:22, pl. 10.
    Pleuromamma abdominalis Steuer, 1932:9–17, kartes 3–7; Vervoort, 1957:123–124.
Pleuromamma antarctica Steuer, 1931: Ant-sAnt
    Pleuromamma robusta forma *antarctica* Steuer, 1932:24–25, karte 10; Vervoort, 1951:123–126, figs. 68, 69; Vervoort, 1957:125.
    Pleuromamma antarctica Ferrari and Saltzman, 1998:217–220, fig. 8.
Pleuromamma peseki Farran, 1929: sAnt-Ntemp
    Pleuromamma gracilis forma *peseki* Steuer, 1932:34–36.
    Pleuromamma peseki Farran, 1929:260, figs. 23, 24; Vervoort, 1957:124.
Pleuromamma quadrungulata (Dahl, 1893): sAnt-Ntemp
    Pleuromma quadrungulata Dahl, 1893:105.
    Pleuromamma quadrungulata Steuer, 1932:26–30, karte 12–13; Vervoort, 1957:124.
Pleuromamma xiphias (Giesbrecht, 1889): sAnt-Ntemp
    Pleuromma xiphias Giesbrecht, 1889b:25; 1893:347, pl. 32, fig. 14; pl. 33, figs. 42, 45, 50.
    Pleuromamma xiphias Steuer, 1932:1–9, karte 1–2; Vervoort, 1957:124.
Pseudaugaptilus longiremis Sars, 1907: Ant-Arc
    Pseudaugaptilus longiremis Sars, 1907:24; 1925:310, pl. 109; Vervoort, 1951:144–147, fig. 82; 1957:140.
Pseudeuchaeta brevicauda Sars, 1905: Ant-sArc
    Pseudeuchaeta brevicauda Sars, 1905a:5, 18; Park, 1978:187–191, figs. 57, 58.
Pseudochirella batillipa Park, 1978: Ant, Ntemp, Arc
    Pseudochirella batillipa Park, 1978:176, figs. 50, 51; Markhaseva, 1996:255–256, fig. 203.
Pseudochirella dubia (Sars, 1905): Ant-sArc
    Undeuchaeta dubia Sars, 1905a:15.
    Pseudochirella dubia Markhaseva, 1996:262, figs. 208–209.
Pseudochirella formosa Markhaseva, 1989: Ant
    Pseudochirella formosa Markhaseva, 1989:33, figs. 1, 7; 1996:264, fig. 212.
Pseudochirella hirsuta (Wolfenden, 1905): Ant-Stemp
    Euchirella hirsuta Wolfenden, 1905:17, pl. 6, figs. 7–8.
    Pseudochirella hirsuta Park, 1978:163–165, figs. 41, 42; Markhaseva, 1996:266, figs. 214–215.
Pseudochirella mawsoni Vervoort, 1957: Ant-sAnt
    Pseudochirella mawsoni Vervoort, 1957:64, figs. 44–48; Park, 1978:172–176, figs. 48, 49; Markhaseva, 1996:272–275, figs. 219–220.
Pseudochirella notacantha (Sars, 1905): Ant-sArc
    Gaidius notacanthus Sars, 1905a:9.
    Pseudochirella notacantha Markhaseva, 1996:275–276, figs. 221–222.
Pseudochirella obtusa (Sars, 1905): Ant-sArc
    Undeuchaeta obtusa Sars, 1905a:4, 13.
    Pseudochirella obtusa Markhaseva, 1996:278, figs. 225–226.
    Pseudochirella polyspina Park, 1978:169–172, figs. 45–47.
Pseudochirella pustulifera (Sars, 1905): Ant-sArc
    Undeuchaeta pustulifera Sars, 1905a:14.
    Pseudochirella pustulifera Park, 1978:165–169, figs. 43–44.

Pseudochirella spectabilis (Sars, 1900): Ant, Arc
    Undeuchaeta spectabilis Sars, 1900:59, pls. 15, 16.
    Pseudochirella spectabilis Markhaseva, 1996:289–290, figs. 233–235.
    Euchirella elongata Wolfenden, 1905:19, pl. 6, figs. 12–13.
    Pseudochirella elongata Park, 1978:159–163, figs. 37–40.
Racovitzanus antarcticus Giesbrecht, 1902: Ant, sAnt, sArc
    Racovitzanus antarcticus Giesbrecht, 1902:26–27, pl. 4, figs. 8–13; pl. 5, figs.1–5; Park, 1983:172–177, figs. 4–6.
Rhincalanus gigas Brady, 1883: Ant
    Rhincalanus gigas Brady, 1883:42, pl. 8, figs. 1–11; Vervoort, 1951:57; 1957:34.
Rhincalanus nasutus Giesbrecht, 1888: sAnt-Ntemp
    Rhincalanus nasutus Giesbrecht, 1888:334; 1893:152–154, 761, pl. 3, fig. 6; pl. 9, figs. 6, 14; pl. 12, figs. 9–12, 14, 16, 17; pl. 35, figs. 46, 47, 49; Vervoort 1957:33.
Scaphocalanus antarcticus Park, 1982: Ant
    Scaphocalanus antarcticus Park, 1982:83–89, figs. 3–7.
Scaphocalanus cristatus (Giesbrecht, 1895): sAnt-Ntemp
    Scolecithrix cristata Giesbrecht, 1895:252–253, pl. 2, figs. 6–8; pl. 3, figs. 1–5.
    Scaphocalanus cristatus Park, 1982:92–95, fig. 10.
Scaphocalanus echinatus (Farran, 1905): sAnt-Ntemp
    Scolecithrix echinata Farran, 1905:37–38, pl. 4, figs. 15–18; pl. 5, figs. 12–17.
    Scaphocalanus echinatus Park, 1982:101–104, figs. 15–16.
Scaphocalanus elongatus Scott, 1909: Ant-Ntemp
    Scaphocalanus elongatus A. Scott, 1909:98, pl. 32, figs. 10–16; Park, 1982:106–108, figs. 18–19.
Scaphocalanus farrani Park, 1982: Ant-sAnt
    Scaphocalanus farrani Park, 1982:95–101, figs. 11–14.
Scaphocalanus major (Scott, 1894): Ant-Trop
    Scolecithrix major Scott, 1894:52, pl. 3, figs. 24–26; pl. 5, figs. 44–45.
    Scaphocalanus major Park, 1982:108–110, fig. 20.
Scaphocalanus medius (Sars, 1907): sAnt-Ntemp
    Amallophora media Sars, 1907:16.
    Scaphocalanus medius Sars, 1925:173–174, pl. 49, figs. 1–8; Park, 1982:110–112, fig. 21.
Scaphocalanus parantarcticus Park, 1982: Ant-sAnt
    Scaphocalanus parantarcticus Park, 1982:89–92, figs. 8–9.
Scaphocalanus subbrevicornis (Wolfenden, 1911): Ant
    Amallophora subbrevicornis Wolfenden, 1911:262–263, text fig. 37.
    Scaphocalanus subbrevicornis Park, 1982:117–121, fig. 26.
Scaphocalanus vervoorti Park, 1982: Ant
    Scaphocalanus vervoorti Park, 1982:112–117, figs. 22–25.
Scolecithricella altera (Farran, 1929): Ant-Ntemp
    Amallophora altera Farran, 1929:252, fig. 19.
    Scolecithricella altera Park, 1980:70–72, fig. 22.
Scolecithricella cenotelis Park, 1980: Ant
    Scolecithricella cenotelis Park, 1980:59–60, fig. 18.
Scolecithricella dentata (Giesbrecht, 1893): sAnt-Ntemp
    Scolecithrix dentata Giesbrecht, 1893:266, pl.13, figs. 12, 20, 33, pl. 37, figs. 13–14.
    Scolecithricella dentata Park, 1980:42–43, fig. 7.
Scolecithricella dentipes Vervoort, 1951: Ant-sAnt
    Scolecithricella dentipes Vervoort, 1951:108, figs. 55–59; Park, 1980:46–50, figs. 10–11.
Scolecithricella emarginata (Farran, 1905): Ant-Ntemp
    Scolecithrix emarginata Farran, 1905:36, pl. 7, figs. 6–17.
    Scolecithricella emarginata Park, 1980:61–66, fig. 19.
    Scolecithrix polaris Wolfenden, 1911:252–253, pl. 30, figs. 1–2, text fig. 31a–e.

Scolecithricella hadrosoma Park, 1980: Ant-Stemp
　Scolecithricella hadrosoma Park, 1980:66, fig. 20.
Scolecithricella minor (Brady, 1883): Ant-sArc
　Scolecithrix minor Brady, 1883:58, pl. 16, figs. 15–16.
　Scolecithricella minor Park, 1980:31–36, figs. 2–3.
　Scolecithrix glacialis Giesbrecht, 1902:25, pl. 4, figs. 1–7.
Scolecithricella obtusifrons (Sars, 1905): Ant-Ntemp
　Amallophora obtusifrons Sars, 1905a:22.
　Scolecithricella obtusifrons Park, 1980:66–70, fig. 21.
Scolecithricella ovata (Farran, 1905): Ant-Ntemp
　Scolecithrix ovata Farran, 1905:37, pl. 6, figs. 13–18; pl. 7, figs. 1–5.
　Scolecithricella ovata Park, 1980:58–59, fig. 17.
Scolecithricella parafalcifer Park, 1980: Ant-Stemp
　Scolecithricella parafalcifer Park, 1980:50–51, fig. 12.
Scolecithricella profunda (Giesbrecht, 1893): sAnt-Ntemp
　Scolecithrix profunda Giesbrecht, 1893:266, pl. 13, figs. 5, 26.
　Scolecithricella profunda Park, 1980:36–37, fig. 4.
Scolecithricella pseudopropinqua Park, 1980: sAnt-Stemp
　Scolecithricella pseudopropinqua Park, 1980:51–55, figs. 13–14.
Scolecithricella schizosoma Park, 1980: Ant-sAnt
　Scolecithricella schizosoma Park, 1980:43–46, figs. 8–9.
Scolecithricella valida (Farran, 1908): Ant-sArc
　Scolecithrix valida Farran, 1908:55, pl. 5, figs. 14–17; pl. 6, fig. 7.
　Scolecithricella valida Park, 1980:55–58, figs. 15–16.
Scolecithricella vervoorti Park, 1980: Ant
　Scolecithricella vervoorti Park, 1980:72–74, figs. 23–24.
Scolecithricella vittata (Giesbrecht, 1893): sAnt-Ntemp
　Scolecithrix vittata Giesbrecht, 1893:266, pl. 13, figs. 2, 23, 32, 34; pl. 37, figs. 5, 8.
　Scolecithricella vittata Park, 1980:37–42, figs. 5–6.
Scottocalanus helenae (Lubbock, 1856): sAnt-Ntemp
　Undina helenae Lubbock, 1856:25–26, pl. 4, fig. 4; pl. 7, figs. 1–5.
　Scottocalanus helenae Park, 1983:205–208, figs. 23–24.
Scottocalanus securifrons (Scott, 1894): sAnt-Ntemp
　Scolecithrix securifrons Scott, 1894:47–48, figs. 41, 43–47, 49–52, 54, 56, pl. 5, fig. 1.
　Scottocalanus securifrons Park, 1983:200–205, figs. 19–22.
Scottocalanus thorii With, 1915: sAnt-sArc
　Scottocalanus thorii With, 1915:215–219, pl. 6, figs. 14a–14c; pl. 8, figs. 14a–14b, text figs. 68–70; Park, 1983:208–210, fig. 25.
Spinocalanus abyssalis Giesbrecht, 1888: Ant-sArc
　Spinocalanus abyssalis Giesbrecht, 1888:355; 1893:209, pl. 13, figs. 42–48; Damkaer, 1975:17–20, figs. 4–10, 148.
Spinocalanus antarcticus Wolfenden, 1906: Ant, Arc
　Spinocalanus antarcticus Wolfenden, 1906:43, pl. 14, figs. 6–9; Damkaer, 1975:30–35, figs. 43–68, 152; Bradford-Grieve, 1994:101, 103, fig. 57.
Spinocalanus horridus Wolfenden, 1911: Ant-Arc
　Spinocalanus horridus Wolfenden, 1911:216, text fig. 7, pl. 25, figs. 1–2; Damkaer, 1975:37–41, figs. 69–83, 153.
Spinocalanus magnus Wolfenden, 1904: Ant-sArc
　Spinocalanus magnus Wolfenden, 1904:118; Damkaer, 1975: 26–30, figs. 35–42, 150.
Spinocalanus terranovae Damkaer, 1975: Ant
　Spinocalanus terranovae Damkaer, 1975:60–62, figs. 141–147, 159.
Stephos longipes Giesbrecht, 1902: Ant
　Stephos longipes Giesbrecht, 1902:20, pl. 2, 6–14; Tanaka, 1960:37, pl. 14, figs. 1–10.
Stephos antarcticus Wolfenden, 1908: Ant
　Stephos antarcticus Wolfenden, 1908:24, pl. 5, figs. 4–8.

Subeucalanus longiceps (Matthews, 1925): sAnt-Stemp
　Eucalanus longiceps Matthews, 1925:127, pl. 9; Vervoort, 1957:33, fig. 8.
　Subeucalanus longiceps Bradford-Grieve, 1994:88, figs. 40, 41, 91.
Talacalanus greeni (Farran, 1905): Ant-Ntemp
　Xanthocalanus greeni Farran, 1905:39, pl. 8, figs. 1–13; Park, 1983:325–327, figs. 5–6.
　Talacalanus calaminus Wolfenden, 1906, pl. 11, figs. 3–5.
　Talacalanus greeni (Farran, 1905); Campaner, 1978:976.
Temorites brevis Sars, 1900: Ant-Arc
　Temorites brevis Sars, 1900:100, pls. 30, 31; Vervoort, 1957:115–118, figs. 102–108.
Undeuchaeta incisa Esterly, 1911: Ant-sArc
　Undeuchaeta incisa Esterly, 1911:319, pl. 27, figs. 12, 19; pl. 28, fig. 28; pl. 29, fig. 59; Park, 1978:183–187, figs. 54–56; Markhaseva, 1996:302, figs. 243–244.
Undeuchaeta major Giesbrecht, 1888: sAnt-Ntemp
　Undeuchaeta major Giesbrecht, 1888, p.336; Markhaseva, 1996:305, figs. 246–247.
Undeuchaeta plumosa (Lubbock, 1856): sAnt-Ntemp
　Undina plumosa Lubbock, 1856:24, pl. 9, figs. 3–5; Markhaseva, 1996:310, figs. 248–249.
Undinella brevipes Farran, 1908: sAnt-sArc
　Undinella brevipes Farran, 1908:12, 50, pl. 5, figs. 1–4; Vervoort, 1957:95–96.
Valdiviella brevicornis Sars, 1905: Ant-Ntemp
　Valdiviella brevicornis Sars, 1905a:17; 1925:101, pl. 28, figs. 11–17; Park, 1978:195–197, fig. 61.
Valdiviella insignis Farran, 1908: Ant-Ntemp
　Valdiviella insignis Farran, 1908:45, pl. 3, figs. 1–6; Park, 1978:197–199, fig. 62.
Valdiviella minor Wolfenden, 1911: sAnt-Ntemp
　Valdiviella minor Wolfenden, 1911:249, pl. 29, figs. 8–11; Park, 1978:199, figs. 63, 64.
Valdiviella oligarthra Steuer, 1904: Ant-Ntemp
　Valdiviella oligarthra Steuer, 1904:593, figs. 1–3; Park, 1978:191–195, figs. 59–60.

APPENDIX 2

This appendix lists families, alphabetically, and genera within families, alphabetically, with species reported from the Southern Ocean.

Acartiidae
　Paralabidocera
Aetideidae
　Aetideopsis
　Aetideus
　Batheuchaeta
　Chiridiella
　Chiridius
　Chirundina
　Gaetanus
　Euchirella
　Pseudeuchaeta
　Pseudochirella
　Undeuchaeta
　Valdiviella
Arietellidae
　Arietellus

Augaptilidae
    Augaptilus
    Centraugaptilus
    Euaugaptilus
    Haloptilus
    Pachyptilus
    Pseudaugaptilus
Bathypontiidae
    Temorites
Calanidae
    Calanoides
    Calanus
    Neocalanus
Candaciidae
    Candacia
Clausocalanidae
    Clausocalanus
    Ctenocalanus
    Drepanopus
    Farrania
    Microcalanus
Eucalanidae
    Eucalanus
    Rhincalanus
Euchaetidae
    Paraeuchaeta
Heterorhabdidae
    Disseta
    Heterorhabdus
    Heterostylites
    Paraheterorhabdus
Lucicutiidae
    Lucicutia
Megacalanidae
    Bathycalanus
    Bradycalanus
    Megacalanus
Metridinidae
    Metridia
    Pleuromamma
Nullosetigeridae
    Nullosetigera
Phaennidae
    Cornucalanus
    Onchocalanus
    Talacalanus
Scolecitrichidae
    Cephalophanes
    Landrumius
    Lophothrix
    Racovitzanus
    Scaphocalanus
    Scolecithricella
    Scottocalanus
Spinocalanidae
    Spinocalanus
Stephidae
    Stephos
Subeucalanidae
    Subeucalanus
Tharybidae
    Undinella

Brooding and Species Diversity in the Southern Ocean: Selection for Brooders or Speciation within Brooding Clades?

John S. Pearse, Richard Mooi, Susanne J. Lockhart, and Angelika Brandt

ABSTRACT. We summarize and evaluate explanations that have been proposed to account for the unusually high number of benthic marine invertebrate species in the Southern Ocean with nonpelagic development. These explanations are divided between those involving adaptation to current conditions in this cold-water environment, selecting for nonpelagic larval development, and those involving vicariant events that either exterminated a high proportion of species with pelagic development (the extinction hypothesis) or enhanced speciation in taxa that already had nonpelagic development. In the latter case, glacial maxima over the Antarctic Continental Shelf in the Pliocene/Pleistocene glacial cycles could have created refuges where speciation occurred (the ACS hypothesis), or the powerful Antarctic Circumpolar Current passing through Drake Passage for over 30 million years could have transported species with nonpelagic development to new habitats to create new species (the ACC hypothesis). We examine the distribution and phylogenetic history of echinoderms and crustaceans in the Southern Ocean to evaluate these different explanations. We could find little or no evidence that nonpelagic development is a direct adaptation to conditions in the Southern Ocean. Some evidence supports the three vicariant hypotheses, with the ACC hypothesis perhaps the best predictor of observed patterns, both the unusual number of species with nonpelagic development and the notably high biodiversity found in the Southern Ocean.

INTRODUCTION

John S. Pearse, Department of Ecology and Evolutionary Biology, Long Marine Laboratory, University of California, Santa Cruz, 100 Shaffer Road, Santa Cruz, CA 95060, USA. Richard Mooi and Susanne J. Lockhart, Department of Invertebrate Zoology and Geology, California Academy of Sciences, 55 Music Concourse Drive, San Francisco, CA 94118-4503, USA. Angelika Brandt, Zoologisches Institut und Zoologisches Museum, Martin-Luther-King-Platz 3, 20146 Hamburg, Germany. Corresponding author: J. S. Pearse (pearse@biology .ucsc.edu). Accepted 19 May 2008.

The unusually high incidence of parental care displayed by marine benthic invertebrates in the Southern Ocean was first noted by members of the pioneering nineteenth century expedition of the R/V *Challenger* (Thomson, 1876, 1885). Examples were found in four of the five classes of echinoderms as well as in molluscs, polychaetes, and other groups. By the end of the century, the idea was widely accepted: nonpelagic development by brooding or viviparity or within egg capsules was the dominant mode of reproduction by benthic marine animals, not only for Antarctic and subantarctic forms but also for cold-water species in general (Thomson, 1885; Murray, 1895; beautifully reviewed by Young, 1994). This notion was persuasively reinforced by Thorson (1936, 1950), who focused on gastropods in the Northern Hemisphere, and Mileikovsky (1971), who termed it "Thorson's rule." Both Thorson (1936) and Mileikovsky (1971), however, recognized many exceptions, and subsequently, with more information and reanalyses of earlier data, the generality of Thorson's rule weakened substantially (Pearse et al., 1991; Clarke, 1992; Hain and Arnaud, 1992; Pearse, 1994; Young, 1994; Stanwell-Smith et al., 1999; Arntz and Gili, 2001; Schluter and Rachor, 2001; Absher et al., 2003; Sewell, 2005; Vázquez et al., 2007; Fetzer and Arntz, 2008). We now know that many of the most abundant species in Antarctic waters, especially those in shallow water, have pelagic larvae as in other areas of the world. Moreover, taxa in the Arctic (Dell, 1972; Fetzer and Arntz, 2008) and the deep sea (Gage and Tyler, 1991) do not have the unusually high numbers of brooding species found in the Antarctic, with the exception of peracarids, all of which brood and are abundant in the Arctic and deep sea, though less diverse than in the Antarctic. Indeed, as shown by Gallardo and Penchaszadeh (2001), the incidence of brooding species of gastropods depends at least as much on the clades present in an area as on location.

Although Thorson's rule no longer applies in general terms, it was originally based on solid observations of some unusual taxa that brood in the Southern Ocean (reviewed by Pearse and Lockhart, 2004). Initially, the finding of species with nonpelagic development was attributed to adaptation to conditions peculiar to polar seas (Murray, 1895; Thorson, 1936, 1950; Hardy, 1960: Pearse, 1969; Mileikovsky, 1971). However, because high incidences of brooding occur mainly in Antarctic waters and not in the Arctic (Ludwig, 1904; Östergren, 1912; Dell, 1972), it became clear that something besides adaptation to "harsh" polar conditions had to be involved. Thorson (1936), recognizing the difference between the two polar seas, suggested that the Arctic fauna, being younger than those around the Antarctic, had not had as much time to adapt; this explanation was accepted by others (e.g., Arnaud, 1974; Picken, 1980). Nevertheless, as recognized by Dell (1972), the discrepancy between the two polar seas meant that the unusual incidence of nonpelagic development in the Southern Ocean was not likely to be the consequence of simple adaptation to some general polar conditions.

While there can be little doubt that developmental mode is influenced by, and at least initially determined by, natural selection, the adaptive nature of one particular mode over another has been subject to considerable speculation and debate (Strathmann, 1993; Havenhand, 1995; Wray, 1995; Gillespie and McClintock, 2007). Pelagic development, either with feeding or nonfeeding larvae, has usually been assumed to be plesiomorphic, and benthic development has been assumed to be derived (Jägersten, 1972; Villinski et al., 2002; Gillespie and McClintock, 2007). Moreover, once lost, planktotrophic development is rarely reacquired (Strathmann, 1978; Reid,

1990; Levin and Bridges, 1995; but see Collin et al., 2007), and this generalization probably applies to pelagic development in general. Consequently, the occurrence of benthic development in a taxon may be an adaptation to particular conditions (e.g., oligotrophic water or offshore currents), or it may be a phyletic constraint reflecting earlier adaptations that no longer apply. Paleontological evidence suggests that species of marine molluscs with nonpelagic development had smaller distributions and were more susceptible to extinction than those with pelagic development (Jablonski and Lutz, 1983; Jablonski and Roy, 2003); presumably, these had more genetically fragmented populations as well.

An alternative explanation to the unusually numerous brooding species in the Southern Ocean is that their high numbers are the consequence of populations being repeatedly fragmented, with isolated units forming new species. That is, nonpelagic development in the Southern Ocean might not reflect adaptation scattered among several clades, as it does elsewhere (e.g., Byrne et al., 2003; Collin, 2003), but rather, it may occur mainly in relatively few clades in which species proliferated. Moreover, some of these species-rich, brooding clades could contribute substantially to the unexpected high species diversity found in the Southern Ocean (Brandt et al., 2007a, 2007b; Rogers, 2007). Indeed, in some taxa, species-rich clades of brooders constitute most of the species (e.g., echinoids: Poulin and Féral, 1996; David et al., 2003, 2005; crustaceans: Brandt, 2000; Brandt et al., 2007a, 2007b). Consequently, the occurrence of many species with nonpelagic development may not be due to specific adaptations to conditions in the Antarctic but, instead, may be a consequence of isolation after vicariant events that now or in the past led to their proliferation. In this paper we evaluate and compare several adaptation versus vicariant explanations for the occurrence of species-rich clades in the high latitudes of the Southern Ocean.

PROPOSED EXPLANATIONS

Adaptation

Although some aspect of the current polar environment has usually been assumed to have led to the selection of nonpelagic development in the Southern Ocean, identification of the responsible agents has been elusive. The problem is compounded because unusually high numbers of brooding species are found in Antarctic and subantarctic waters but not in either the Arctic or deep sea, the other areas of the world ocean with cold water year-round. We briefly consider below some of the ideas that have been proposed, including those that apply to cold-water environments in general.

Low Temperature

Murray (1895:1459) suggested simply that "animals with pelagic larvae would be killed out or be forced to migrate towards the warmer tropics" when temperatures cooled, to be replaced by animals without larvae existing below the "mud-line" where he thought very few animals had pelagic larvae. Similarly, Thatje et al. (2005b) argue that the predominance of developmental lecithotrophy in the Antarctic is the consequence of the near-complete extinction of benthic communities during glacial maxima and recolonization from deeper waters where species had undergone an "evolutionary temperature adaptation" that led to lecithotrophy. However, no evidence supports the idea that either nonpelagic development or lecithotrophy is an adaptation to low temperature, and the fact that a wide variety of both planktotrophic and lecithotrophic pelagic larvae have been found in both Antarctic and Arctic waters (e.g., Thorson, 1936; Stanwell-Smith et al., 1999; Sewell, 2005; Palma et al., 2007; Vázquez, 2007; Fetzer and Arntz, 2008) persuasively indicates that marine invertebrate larvae are able to survive and grow at freezing temperatures—even under high pressures found in the deep sea (Tyler et al., 2000), where many species have pelagic, planktotrophic larvae (Gage and Tyler, 1991; however, see below).

Low Temperature and Slow Development

Many studies have shown that larval development is greatly slowed at very low temperatures (e.g., Hoegh-Guldberg and Pearse, 1995; Peck et al., 2007), and the metabolic basis of this effect is gradually being sorted out (e.g., Peck, 2002; Clarke, 2003; Peck et al. 2006; Pace and Manahan, 2007). The longer larvae are in the plankton, the greater the chance that they will perish by predation or be swept away from suitable settling sites. Indeed, Smith et al. (2007) argued that lecithotrophic development might be selected because eliminating the feeding stage substantially shortens the time larvae spend in the plankton, a particular advantage for polar areas where development is slow. Going one step further, nonpelagic development eliminates loss in the plankton altogether. However, not only would this explanation apply to the cold-water environment of the Arctic and deep sea as well as to the Antarctic, but as mentioned above, many particularly abundant polar species do have slow-developing planktotrophic pe-

lagic larvae; long periods of feeding in the plankton do not necessarily appear to be selected against.

Low Temperature, Slow Development, and Limited Larval Food

Thorson (1936, 1950) developed the idea that planktotrophic larvae would be food limited in polar seas because phytoplanktonic food is available only during the summer plankton bloom, too briefly for such larvae to complete their slow development. This durable hypothesis remains current (e.g., Arntz and Gili, 2001; Thatje et al., 2003, 2005b), although little or no evidence supports it. Indeed, planktotrophic larvae of a wide range of taxa are well known in polar seas (see above). Moreover, extremely low metabolic rates of gastropod and echinoid larvae, indicative of very low food requirements, have been demonstrated by Peck et al. (2006) and Pace and Manahan (2007), respectively. There is no evidence that other planktotrophic larvae of polar seas are food limited either. In addition, this proposal is not specific to the Southern Ocean. Finally, it applies only to planktotrophic larval development, not lecithotrophic pelagic development; our concern here is pelagic and nonpelagic development, not mode of nutrition for developing embryos or larvae.

Low Adult Food Supply

Chia (1974) suggested that poor nutritional conditions for adults might favor nonpelagic development on the assumption that adults require more energy to produce the multitude of pelagic larvae needed to overcome high larval mortality in the plankton than to produce a few protected offspring. Such conditions do prevail in polar seas, where primary production is extremely seasonal (Clarke, 1988), or especially during periods of maximal multiyear sea ice and glacial expansion during the Pliocene/Pleistocene ice ages (see below). However, studies on a poecilogonous species of polychaete indicate that nutritional investment is higher in the form that produces lecithotrophic larvae than in one that produces planktotrophic larvae (Bridges, 1993), countering Chia's (1974) assumption. Moreover, even if true, the argument applies to both polar seas and is not specific to the Southern Ocean. Finally, there is little evidence that polar species are food limited over an entire year.

Large Egg Sizes

It has long been known that egg size and, presumably, energy investment into individual eggs increase with increasing latitude (reviewed by Laptikhovsky, 2006). If more energy is allocated to each egg, fecundity is lowered. Moreover, larger eggs require more time to complete the nonfeeding phase of development than smaller eggs (Marshall and Bolton, 2007), increasing the risk of embryonic/larval mortality while in the plankton. With lower fecundity and increased risk of mortality, there could be strong selection for nonpelagic development, eliminating mortality in the plankton altogether. While the underlying reason why egg size increases with latitude remains to be understood, it could be a factor leading to nonpelagic development. However, this explanation also applies to both polar regions and not solely to the Southern Ocean.

Small Adult Size

It is also well known that taxa composed of smaller individuals tend to have nonpelagic development, while those with larger individuals tend to have planktotrophic, pelagic development (reviewed by Strathmann and Strathmann, 1982). This observation is also based on fecundity: small animals cannot produce enough offspring for any of them to have much chance of surviving the high mortality faced in the plankton. However, there are many examples of species comprised of very small individuals producing planktotrophic larvae, making generalization difficult. Nevertheless, most species in some major taxa (e.g., bivalves: Clarke, 1992, 1993) in the Southern Ocean are composed of very small individuals, so this explanation could apply to them, at least in terms of factors originally selecting for nonpelagic development.

Low Salinity

Östergren (1912) suggested that melting ice during the summer would create a freshwater layer unfavorable to pelagic larvae and therefore could be a factor selecting against them. Thorson (1936), Hardy (1960), Pearse (1969), and Picken (1980) also considered low salinity to be a factor selecting against pelagic development in polar seas. The large rivers flowing into the Arctic Ocean should make low salinity an even greater problem there than around the Antarctic. Yet, as with most of the adaptationist explanations focusing on polar conditions, the fact that nonpelagic development is less prevalent in the Arctic than in the Antarctic undermines this explanation. Thus, low salinity is not likely to be an important factor selecting for nonpelagic development in the Southern Ocean.

Narrow Shelf

Recognizing that the presence of unusually high numbers of species with nonpelagic development is mainly a feature of the Antarctic, especially the subantarctic, rather than the Arctic, Östergren (1912) also proposed that the narrow shelf and the strong winds blowing off the continent would drive larvae offshore, away from suitable settling sites. Consequently, there would be strong selection against pelagic larvae in the Antarctic but not in the Arctic. This was the first attempt to explain the high number of brooding species specifically for the Southern Ocean. However, the idea was quickly discounted by Mortensen (1913), who pointed out that it should apply as well to remote oceanic islands in the tropics, where pelagic development was already well known.

SELECTIVE EXTINCTION

Another possibility is that events in the past led to the extinction of many or most species with pelagic development in the Antarctic, leaving a disproportionate number of species with nonpelagic development. This proposal by Poulin and Féral (1994) argues that pelagic development was not adaptive, while nonpelagic development was neutral at certain times in the past in the Southern Ocean. It was developed further by Poulin and Féral (1996), Poulin et al. (2002), and Thatje et al. (2005b) and is based on the finding that during the glacial maxima of the late Quaternary ice ages, grounded ice extended to the edge of the Antarctic shelf (Clarke and Crame, 1989), obliterating most life on the shelf. During such times, thick, multiyear sea ice probably occurred year-round and extended far into the Southern Ocean surrounding the Antarctic, blocking sunlight and photosynthesis beneath it. Consequently, there would be little (only laterally advected) phytoplanktonic food to support planktotrophic larvae, and selection would be strong for lecithotrophic development, whether pelagic or benthic. Of course, primary production is necessary to support populations of juveniles and adults as well, and although massive extinction would be expected during the glacial maxima of the Pliocene/Pleistocene regardless of developmental mode, this apparently did not happen (Clarke, 1993).

Poulin and Féral (1994, 1996) suggested that selective extinction of species with planktotrophic larvae during the glacial maxima would leave behind species with nonpelagic development, but as Pearse and Lockhart (2004) pointed out, such selective extinction would leave species with both pelagic and nonpelagic lecithotrophic development. Consequently, the selective extinction hypothesis is inadequate to explain the unusual abundance of species with nonpelagic development. However, in the case of echinoids (the taxon of concern for Poulin and Féral, 1994, 1996), there are very few species anywhere with lecithotrophic pelagic larvae—and none in the Antarctic—so the selective extinction hypothesis applies at least partly to echinoids. Similarly, the high diversity of peracarid crustaceans, most of which brood, and the paucity of decapod crustaceans, most of which have planktotrophic larvae, also may be the consequence, at least in part, of selective extinction (Thatje et al., 2003, 2005b).

Recognizing that brooding might have originated outside the Antarctic, Dell (1972), Arnaud (1974), and Picken (1980) suggested that brooding species could have colonized the Southern Ocean from elsewhere after massive extinctions, perhaps by rafting (see Thiel and Gutow, 2005). On the other hand, polar emergence from the deep sea following the retreat of multiyear sea ice in interglacial periods might have taken place for some taxa, which subsequently speciated on the Antarctic shelf (e.g., isopod families Munnopsidae, Desmosomatidae, Ischnomesidae, e.g., Brökeland, 2004; Raupach et al., 2007).

ENHANCED SPECIATION

In contrast to enhanced extinction of species with pelagic development, which would leave behind a disproportionate number of species with nonpelagic development, speciation could be enhanced by conditions in the Southern Ocean, in the past or persisting to the present, to produce species-rich clades of taxa with nonpelagic development. Nonpelagic development could have developed well before the Southern Ocean cooled, or even elsewhere altogether, but spread via a founding species to the Southern Ocean and then undergone radiation. Regardless of where or how nonpelagic development originated, if this is the case, we have not only an explanation of the unusually high number of species with nonpelagic development but also, perhaps, an explanation for the unexpected high species diversity in the Southern Ocean (Brandt et al., 2007a, 2007b; Rogers, 2007). At least two different scenarios about how this might occur are specific to the Southern Ocean.

Isolation and Speciation on the Antarctic Continental Shelf (the ACS Hypothesis)

Clarke and Crame (1989, 1992, 1997), Brandt (1991, 2000), and Thatje et al. (2005b) pointed out that during the glacial maxima, grounded ice probably did not completely cover the shelf areas around the Antarctic continent. Instead, some isolated areas would likely be open and habitable under the ice, as seen today under ice shelves (e.g., Littlepage and Pearse, 1962; Post et al., 2007). These areas could behave as "islands" with remnants of the previously more widespread shelf fauna. Species with nonpelagic development would be effectively isolated. With the retreat of the grounded glaciers, the shelf fauna would reconnect, mixing the newly formed species as they expanded around the continent. Similar phenomena might be happening now after the disintegration of the Larsen A and B ice shelves in 2002. During the height of interglacial periods, when there was a minimum of ice cover, the Weddell and Ross seas could have been connected (Scherer et al., 1998; Thomson, 2004), further mixing species, which would be fragmented again during the subsequent glacial cycle. Clarke and Crame (1989) proposed that such repeated cycles of glacial advances and retreats over the shelf could favor speciation, and Clarke and Crame (1992, 1997) further developed this idea and suggested that such oscillation would act as a "species diversity pump." It would be most effective, however, for species having limited dispersal capabilities, such as those with nonpelagic development.

Isolation during glacial maxima is not the only possibility for fragmenting populations on the Antarctic Continental Shelf. At present, most shallow-water habitats (<150 m) around the Antarctic continent are covered by grounded ice or floating ice shelves, and only scattered fragments of suitable habitats remain. Raguá-Gil et al. (2004) found that three such habitats, one on the west side of the Antarctic Peninsula and two others on the eastern coast of the Weddell Sea, support very different faunas. The biotas in the two habitats in the Weddell Sea differ as much from each other as they do from the one on the Antarctic Peninsula. According to Raguá-Gil et al. (2004), these differences indicate limited exchange due at least in part to a predominance of species with nonpelagic larvae. Similar differences were detected for isopod composition at sites around the Antarctic Peninsula and in the Weddell Sea (Brandt et al., 2007c). Such isolation could lead to speciation, particularly of cryptic species formed by nonselective processes (e.g., genetic drift).

Speciation of fragmented populations on the Antarctic Continental Shelf, the ACS hypothesis, would result in an increase of shelf species, so that the greatest species richness would be expected on the shelf, with decreasing richness down the slope into deeper depths. That was found to be the case for amphipods (Brandt, 2000), polychaetes (but not isopods or bivalves) (Ellingsen et al., 2007), and many other taxa (Brandt et al., 2007a) sampled in the Atlantic sector of the Southern Ocean. In addition, because most of the glacial cycles occurred during the Pliocene and Pleistocene over only the past few million years, genetic divergence of these fragmented populations would be relatively slight, and very similar or cryptic sister species would be predicted. Molecular analyses have revealed cryptic species in isopods, which brood (Held, 2003; Held and Wägele, 2005), and a bivalve that broods (Linse et al., 2007) as well as in a crinoid, which has pelagic, lecithotrophic larvae (Wilson et al., 2007).

Isolation and Speciation via the Antarctic Circumpolar Current (the ACC Hypothesis)

Pearse and Bosch (1994) analyzed available data for mode of development in shallow-water Antarctic and subantarctic echinoderms (128 species) and found the highest proportion of species with nonpelagic development in the region of the Scotia Arc (65%), not the Antarctic continent or subantarctic islands (42% each). This pattern led them to focus on Drake Passage and the powerful Antarctic Circumpolar Current (ACC) that has been flowing through it for more than 30 million years (Thomson, 2004). They proposed that individuals of species with nonpelagic development could be rafted *infrequently* to other downstream habitats and could become established to form new isolated populations, i.e., new species. Moreover, tectonic activity in the Scotia Arc region has continually formed new habitats as crustal plates shifted, which also influenced complex eddies as water flowed through Drake Passage (Thomson, 2004). With more than 30 million years since the ACC broke through Drake Passage, many new species could form and accumulate. Pearse and Lockhart (2004) reviewed these ideas, found further support for them, and suggested ways to test them using cidaroids.

The ACC hypothesis predicts that species richness would consist of species-rich clades of taxa with nonpelagic development and would not be an accumulation of many species-poor clades with a variety of reproductive modes, including nonpelagic development, which appears to be the case (see below). Moreover, species richness would be greatest within and east of the Scotia Arc, downstream from Drake Passage. The Scotia Arc region, in fact, appears to be unusually diverse (Barnes, 2005; Barnes et al., 2006; Linse et al., 2007). Conversely, species diversity should be lower upstream, on the western side of the Antarctic Peninsula, and that is exactly the pattern Raguá-Gil et al. (2004) found in their analysis of three

shallow-water communities. Similar differences in species richness between the eastern Weddell Sea and the western coast of the Antarctic Peninsula were reported by Starmans and Gutt (2002). On a different scale, Linse et al. (2006) likewise found the highest diversity of molluscs to be in the Weddell Sea, east of the Scotia Arc, and the lowest on the western side of the Antarctic Peninsula (although this might have been due to sampling discrepancies). It can also be predicted that because the ACC hits the Antarctic Peninsula as it flows around the continent, it could carry species to the western side of the peninsula, where they might accumulate (A. Mahon, Auburn University, personal communication).

In addition, because the ACC is funneled through the whole of Drake Passage, the ACC hypothesis does not necessarily predict a depth gradient of species richness, in contrast to the ACS hypothesis. No depth gradient is seen for isopods and bivalves (Ellingsen et al., 2007). Indeed, the ACC hypothesis may account for the unexpected high species diversity recently documented for some deep-sea taxa in the Atlantic portion of the Southern Ocean (Brandt et al., 2007a, 2007b).

Finally, because the ACC continues to this day, it would not be unexpected for species to have formed, as described above, at any time over the past 30 million years, including within the past few million years, so that closely related cryptic species would be found as well as more distantly related species, all in the same clade. Unlike the ACS hypothesis, the ACC hypothesis predicts the existence of a spectrum of variously diverged species within the clades. That result is what has been found in Lockhart's (2006) analysis of brooding cidaroids, the first thorough phylogenetic analysis of a major clade of brooders within the Southern Ocean (see below).

Species with nonpelagic development are thought to be prone to high extinction rates because they typically have small population sizes and limited distributions, which make them particularly susceptible to environmental change (Jablonski and Lutz, 1983). Poulin and Féral (1994) suggested that because of such susceptibility, any enhanced speciation rate in the Southern Ocean would be countered by a high extinction rate. Consequently, they rejected an enhanced speciation model for explaining high species diversity in clades with nonpelagic development. However, with the ACC in effect for over 30 million years, the Southern Ocean has been an extraordinarily stable marine environment. Jeffery et al. (2003) proposed an idea similar to the ACC hypothesis to explain the high proportion of brooding early Cenozoic echinoids that occurred on the southern coast of Australia after Australia separated from the Antarctic. Strong currents swept through the Tasmanian Gateway then and could have swept individuals with nonpelagic development to new habitats, where they would have potentially formed new species. McNamara (1994) earlier recognized the importance of the stability provided by the strong, constant current through the Tasmanian Gateway for favoring the accumulation of brooding echinoids; he suggested that their later disappearance was a result of the widening of the gateway and a decrease in the environmental stability. Similarly, we suggest that the ACC flowing through Drake Passage provides conditions both for enhancing speciation and for tempering extinction.

EVALUATING THE EXPLANATIONS

The proposed explanations above for the unusual abundance of species with nonpelagic development in the Southern Ocean are not mutually exclusive of each other, and one or more may apply to one or more taxa. However, with recent advances in molecular phylogenetic analyses (Rogers, 2007), these proposed explanations may be better evaluated than was possible earlier. For example, (1) if nonpelagic development is scattered within taxa found in widely distributed clades and these taxa are found both within and outside the Southern Ocean, such a mode of development is not likely to be an adaptation to conditions in the Southern Ocean. (2) If taxa with nonpelagic development in widely distributed clades are restricted to both polar environments and the deep sea, nonpelagic development might be an adaptation to cold water; if they are only in the Southern Ocean, specific conditions around the Antarctic would more likely be involved. (3) If nonpelagic development is found in all the taxa of clades found in both the Southern Ocean and elsewhere, where the basal taxa are found may indicate where the trait originated, and conditions there might be involved in the selection of nonpelagic development. (4) If nonpelagic development is found disproportionately more in Southern Ocean taxa of clades than elsewhere, either this development is a consequence of adaptation to conditions specific to the Southern Ocean, or it is the result of extinction of taxa with pelagic development. (5) If nonpelagic development is found in many taxa of clades in the Southern Ocean but only in a few taxa of basal clades found elsewhere, the Southern Ocean taxa may have proliferated because of unusual conditions there (not necessarily because nonpelagic development was adaptive). (6) If most taxa with nonpelagic development appeared only over the past few

million years, when massive glacial advances and retreats occurred, they may have been generated on the Antarctic Continental Shelf when the glacial advances separated and fragmented populations (the ACS hypothesis). (7) If the taxa appeared more or less steadily since Antarctica separated from South America, about 30 million years ago, and are most abundant in and east of the Scotia Arc, they may have been generated by infrequently rafting with the ACC to new locations (the ACC hypothesis).

SELECTED TAXA

Below we review some of the information now available for taxa of two major groups in the Southern Ocean: echinoderms and crustaceans. Species in these taxa are major components of the Southern Ocean biota, and they are relatively well known. Moreover, phylogenetic analyses are now available for some groups within them, including speciose, brooding clades. Other taxa could also be evaluated for a stronger comparative analysis, in particular, molluscs, pycnogonids, and teleosts; we hope that research is done by others.

ECHINODERMS

Nonpelagic development in echinoderms caught the attention of naturalists with the *Challenger* expedition in the nineteenth century (Thomson, 1876, 1885; Murray, 1895), setting the foundation for what became "Thorson's rule." Echinoderms now are among the first groups of animals in the Antarctic to have their phylogenetic relationships documented. Echinoids, in particular, are revealing. Only four major clades are present in the Southern Ocean, echinids, cidaroids, holasteroids, and schizasterids (David et al., 2003, 2005). The near absence of other clades suggests either that major extinctions have occurred or that other taxa did not find a foothold in the Southern Ocean. It is interesting to note that there are presently no clypeasteroids (sand dollars and allies) in Antarctica today, in spite of their ubiquity in cold waters both in the past and present, and that at least one species has been recorded from the Paleogene of Black Island, McMurdo Sound (Hotchkiss and Fell, 1972). Hotchkiss (1982) used this and other fossil evidence to call into question the supposed slow rate of evolution in cidaroids and any connection between the fossil Eocene faunas of Australasia and those of the so-called "Weddellian Province" of the Southern Ocean. Hotchkiss (1982:682) pointed out that any supposed "shallow-marine connection had disappeared by middle Oligocene time because there is evidence for the deep-flowing Antarctic Circumpolar Current south of the South Tasman Rise at that time."

Of the three major clades, there are only seven presently recognized species of echinids, all in the genus *Sterechinus*. Phylogenetic analysis using mitochondrial DNA sequences indicates that the genus diverged from *Loxechinus* in South America 24–35 million years ago, when the Antarctic separated from South America (Lee et al., 2004). Two species, *Sterechinus neumayeri* and *S. antarcticus*, are abundant and widespread around the continental shelf (Brey and Gutt, 1991). The former is known to have typical echinoid planktotrophic development (Bosch et al., 1987). The other species are less well known and are taxonomically questionable but almost certainly also have pelagic development.

Although an extensive revision is pending (see Lockhart, 2006), as of 2005, there were more than 20 recognized cidaroid taxa, and the vast majority of those have been recorded to be brooders—and present evidence (Lockhart, 2006) strongly suggests that all of them are brooders. A recent phylogenetic cladogram developed by Lockhart (2006) used fossils and a penalized likelihood analysis of CO_1, Cytochrome *b* (Cyt*b*), and 18-s mitochondrial sequences to establish divergence times for the taxa of cidarids (see Smith et al., 2006, for an evaluation of using fossils for dating cladograms). The dated cladogram revealed that Southern Ocean cidaroids are monophyletic with the most likely sister taxon being the subfamily Goniocidarinae, now found in the southwest Pacific, including New Zealand and Australia, but not in the Southern Ocean. A few species of goniocidarines are known to brood, but it is not yet known whether these are sister species to the Southern Ocean clade (making goniocidarines paraphyletic). The oldest fossil goniocidarine, from the Perth Basin of Western Australia when Australia and Antarctica were connected, is more than 65 million years old, and the oldest cidaroid in the Southern Ocean clade is *Austrocidaris seymourensis*, from Eocene deposits on Seymour Island in the Scotia Arc, dated at 51 million years ago. *Austrocidaris seymourensis* had distinctive aboral brood chambers, showing that brooding was established in this clade long before cooling began. Consequently, brooding in these animals is not an adaptation to present-day conditions in the Southern Ocean.

Lockhart (2006) also showed that there are two sister clades of Southern Ocean cidaroids: the subfamily Astrocidarinae with two to three recently diverged species in a single genus (*Austrocidaris*) found in subantarctic waters on the northern edge of the Scotia Arc and the subfamily Ctenocidarinae with more than 20 species in at least five genera found in the southern and eastern portions of the Scotia Arc and around the Antarctic Continent. Moreover, clades within the ctenocidarines diverged more or less steadily over the last 30 million years, that is, since the Antarctic Circumpolar Current was established. This pattern is precisely what the ACC hypothesis predicts.

Among the 16 species of Holasteroida found south of the convergence, very few are found at depths less than 2000 m. Only three genera occur in relatively shallow waters: *Pourtalesia*, *Plexechinus*, and two of the three known species of *Antrechinus*. With the exception of the latter two genera, all holasteroids belong to widespread deep-sea clades that occur well north of the Southern Ocean, and none are known to have nonpelagic, lecithotrophic development. However, within *Antrechinus*, we find the most extreme form of brooding known in the Echinoidea—species that brood their young internally and "give birth" (David and Mooi, 1990; Mooi and David, 1993). The two species known to brood are found no deeper than 1500 m. The third species ascribed to *Antrechinus*, *A. drygalskii*, was only provisionally considered a plesiomorphic sister group to these remarkable brooders (Mooi and David, 1996) and occurs below 3000 m. There are no known fossil holasteroids from the Antarctic region.

There are 30 recognized species of schizasterid Spatangoida recorded by David et al. (2003, 2005) to occur in the Antarctic region. These are distributed in seven genera: *Abatus* with 11 species, *Amphipneustes* with 9, *Tripylus* with 4, *Brisaster* with 2, and *Brachysternaster*, *Delopatagus*, *Genicopatagus*, and *Tripylaster* each with a single species. Most phylogenetic analyses recognize *Brisaster* and *Tripylaster* as a monophyletic assemblage that is, at best, a sister taxon to the rest of the Antarctic Schizasteridae (Féral, et al., 1994; Hood and Mooi, 1998; Madon-Senez, 1998; David et al., 2005; Stockley et al., 2005). The ranges of *Brisaster* and *Tripylaster* are best considered subantarctic, as there is only a single record from south of 55°S, and none have been recorded in the shelf regions of the Antarctic continent. Interestingly, these genera are the only species not known to brood. All other schizasterids have nonpelagic development, brooding the young in well-developed marsupia in the aboral, ambulacral petaloid areas (Magniez, 1980; Schatt, 1988; Pearse and McClintock, 1990; Poulin and Féral, 1994; David et al., 2005; Galley et al., 2005).

The brooding schizasterids almost undoubtedly constitute a single clade (Madon-Senez, 1998; David et al., 2005). Recognizing early on the need for understanding evolutionary history to understand their phylogenies, Féral et al. (1994) compared RNA sequences in species of the four main genera of brooding schizasterids then recognized in the Southern Ocean, supporting the monophyly of the brooding genera but partially undermining the monophyly of some of the constituent genera and therefore reinforcing the later morphological work of Madon-Senez (1998).

Fossils assigned to *Abatus*, with distinctive brood chambers, are known from the Eocene of Seymour Island on the Scotia Arc (McKinney et al., 1988). Consequently, as with the cidaroids, brooding appeared in these animals well before the Southern Seas cooled, and that mode of development cannot be attributed to polar conditions.

Poulin and Féral (1994) showed that populations of the brooding schizasterid echinoid *Abatus cordatus* in embayments around Kerguelen Island are genetically distinct, presumably because of limited gene flow. Consequently, there is genetic differentiation in these populations of brooding echinoids, and it is likely to be occurring with other brooding species with limited dispersal elsewhere in the Southern Ocean, leading to many shallow divergences in genetic structure. This is also borne out by morphological variation among specimens from different regions (Madon-Senez, 1998) and the small amounts of morphological divergence among the species themselves (David et al., 2005).

Among the brooding schizasterids, very few have ranges west of the Antarctic Peninsula. Most are distributed east of Drake Passage, along the South Shetlands and eastward through the Weddell region. For example, the genus *Amphipneustes* does not seem to occur immediately to the west of the peninsula but has abundant representation to the east of the Drake Passage, with major centers of diversity in the South Shetlands and in the region of the Weddell Sea (Figure 1). This pattern is repeated for *Abatus* and the other brooding schizasterid genera. Although sampling bias could remain a mitigating factor in the accuracy of these distributions, we do not believe that is the case for echinoids because David et al. (2003) shows that forms such as the echinids are well represented to the west of the peninsula. Even the most difficult taxa to sample, the abyssal holasteroids, are almost evenly distributed around Antarctica, with no obvious gaps in the overall distribution of this clade.

The implication is that the ranges of these brooding forms are being influenced by the prevailing ACC, which tends to force the ranges "downstream" of the Drake Passage. The precise mechanism by which brooding schizasterids are redistributed and then speciate remains unknown, but it does not overextend present data to suggest that once established, new populations of brooding forms can rapidly diverge from the originating population.

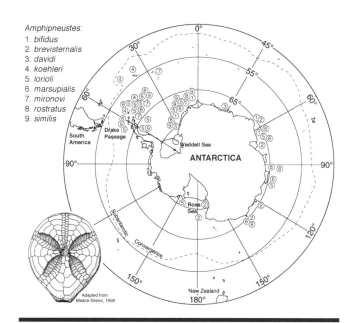

FIGURE 1. Distribution of nine species of *Amphipneustes* around Antarctica. Data were compiled from David et al. (2003) and *Polarstern* and Antarctic Marine Living Resources expeditions.

In addition to echinids, cidaroids, holasteroids, and schizasterids, there are a few other echinoid taxa known from the deeper portions of the Southern Ocean. One species of echinothurioid is known (Mooi et al., 2004); all species so far studied in this monophyletic, widespread, mostly deep-water clade have pelagic, lecithotrophic development, and the Antarctic species presumably does as well.

Unusual brooding in the Southern Ocean was also highlighted in the *Challenger* expedition reports for the other classes of echinoderms (Thomson, 1885). However, to date, there has been no phylogenetic analysis examining whether brooders belong to a few speciose clades in these classes, as is becoming evident for echinoids. In addition, members of these other classes do not have as good a fossil record, and they do not have fossilizable structures indicative of brooding, as do many echinoids. Nevertheless, if the major taxonomic groups of these classes are monophyletic, the brooding species do belong to a few speciose clades.

The majority of Southern Ocean asteroids, for example, are forcipulates in the family Asteriidae. Brooding is rare in asteriids in most of the world, limited to the speciose genus *Leptasterias* in north temperate/polar waters (Foltz et al., 2008) and several species in genera that are mainly Antarctic/subantarctic but are also found in southern South America (e.g., *Anasterias*, Gil and Zaixso,

2007; *Diplasterias*, Kim and Thurber, 2007) and southern Australia (*Smilasterias,* Rowe and Gates, 1995; Komatsu et al, 2006). However, most if not all species of asteriids in the Southern Ocean are brooders. Arnaud (1974) lists 22 species, Pearse and Bosch (1994) list 25 species, and Clarke and Johnston (2003) report that there are approximately 37 species of asteriids in the Southern Ocean. Foltz et al. (2007) analyzed 31 species of forcipulates using mitochondrial and nuclear sequences and found that 30 formed a clade. Only three were Southern Ocean species (*Psalidaster mordax, Cryptasterias turqueti,* and *Notasterias pedicellaris),* but they formed a clade within the forcipulate clade. There are 11 brooding species of asteroids on the subantarctic islands; seven of them are in the asteriid genus *Anasterias* (Pearse and Bosch, 1994). Of the 24 species of brooding asteroids known from Antarctic waters, 18 are asteriids, and 13 of these are in two genera, *Diplasterias* and *Lyasterias* (Pearse and Bosch, 1994). Moreover, 19 of the 24 brooding asteroids in Antarctic waters are found in the Scotia Arc region, as would be expected from the ACC hypothesis. On the other hand, most of the genera with brooding species are circumpolar (Clark, 1962; C. Mah, Smithsonian Institution, personal communication), and it may be too early to conclude that there is a disproportional number of species in the Scotia Arc region, which has been most heavily sampled to date.

There is evidence that even brooding species of asteroids are capable of wide dispersal. *Diplasterias brucei,* for example, is not only found around the Antarctic continent and in the southern portion of the Scotia Arc but also north of the polar front on Burdwood Bank and in the Falklands Island (Kim and Thurber, 2007). Such a wide distribution by a brooding species suggests unusual capabilities of dispersal, such as by rafting. Moreover, genetic analyses would be expected to show considerable genetic differentiation, as found for *Abatus cordatus* at Kerguelen Islands (Poulin and Féral, 1994). Such analyses would be most welcome.

Although some of the asteriid species with nonpelagic development are commonly found in the Southern Ocean, the most frequently encountered asteroids on the Antarctic shelf are species of Odontasteridae, especially *Odontaster validus,* which like the echinid echinoid *Sterechinus neumayeri,* is found around the Antarctic continent, often in very high numbers. There are about 11 species of odontasterids in the Southern Ocean (Clarke and Johnston, 2003), two or three in the genus *Odontaster.* All, including *O. validus* (Pearse and Bosch, 1986), have pelagic development as far as is known. Consequently, as with echinoids, asteroid clades with nonpelagic development

are speciose, but most individuals are not very abundant; those with pelagic development have few species, but individuals of some species can be very abundant. Pearse et al. (1991) and Poulin et al. (2002) suggest that this difference in abundance patterns is due to ecological factors: species with pelagic development colonize and thrive in shallow areas disturbed by ice, while those with nonpelagic development occur in more stable, deeper habitats, where interspecific competition is more intense. Comparing two shallow-water habitats, Palma et al. (2007) found that an ice-disturbed habitat is dominated by *O. validus* and *S. neumayeri,* species with planktotrophic development, while a less disturbed habitat is dominated by brooding *Abatus agassizii.*

Brooding is widespread among holothurians in the Southern Ocean. Seventeen of the 41 brooding species of holothurians listed worldwide by Smiley et al. (1991) are found in Antarctic and subantarctic waters. Moreover, 15 of those species are in the order Dendrochirotida, with six each in the genera *Cucumaria* and *Psolus,* and brooding by an addition species of *Psolus* was described by Gutt (1991). In addition, 12 of the brooding species of holothuroids are found in the Scotia Arc area (Pearse and Bosch, 1994). These patterns mirror those seen in echinoids and asteroids.

Brooding is also widespread among ophiuroids in the Southern Ocean; Mortensen (1936) estimated that about 50% of the species in Antarctic and subantarctic waters are brooders. Pearse and Bosch (1994) list 33 species of brooding ophiuroids, 21 of which are found in the Scotia Arc area. Moreover, most of these species are in the most diverse families in these waters, amphiurids, ophiacanthids, and ophiurids (Hendler, 1991). In contrast to the relatively few speciose genera with brooders in the Southern Ocean, brooding species at lower latitudes are scattered among different genera; Hendler (1991:477) suggests from this difference that there "may be selection for brooding within clades, rather than a propensity for certain clades to evolve brooding" in the Antarctic ophiuroid fauna. That is, once brooding is established in a clade, speciation is likely to occur.

There has been no phylogenetic analysis of the 12 species of Southern Ocean crinoids reported to brood, all of them occurring in the Scotia Arc region (Pearse and Bosch, 1994). However, phylogenetic analyses of *Promachocrinus kerguelensis* in the Atlantic section of the Southern Ocean revealed at least five "species-level" clades (Wilson et al., 2007). *P. kerguelensis* is found throughout Antarctic and subantarctic waters, and the one population studied, in McMurdo Sound, produces large numbers of pelagic, lecithotrophic larvae (McClintock and Pearse, 1987). Finding such cryptic speciation suggests that other populations might brood or have other means of reducing dispersal.

CRUSTACEANS

Peracarid crustaceans, especially amphipods and isopods, are among the most diverse taxa in the Southern Ocean (Held, 2003; Raupach et al., 2004, 2007; Lörz et al., 2007) and are the major contributor to the high species diversity in those waters. Indeed, the extraordinary species richness of peracarids documented by recent Antarctic deep-sea benthic biodiversity (ANDEEP) cruises (Brandt et al., 2004, 2007a, 2007b) in the Atlantic sector of the deep Southern Ocean challenges the idea that a latitudinal gradient exists in the Southern Hemisphere. Moreover, molecular analyses have revealed additional cryptic species in isopods (Held, 2003; Held and Wägele, 2005; Raupach et al., 2007). All peracarids brood embryos, and most release juveniles that remain close to their parents after being released (the exceptions include exoparasitic isopods, e.g., Dajidae and Bopyridae, and pelagic forms such as mysids and hyperiid amphipods).

In contrast to the peracarids, species of decapod crustaceans, almost all of which release pelagic larvae after brooding embryos, are remarkably few in today's Southern Ocean. Only a few species of caridean shrimps inhabit the Southern Ocean, and all produce pelagic larvae, even those in the deep sea (Thatje et al., 2005a). Brachyuran crabs are important components of Patagonian benthic ecosystems (Arntz et al., 1999; Gorny, 1999), yet they are entirely absent from the Scotia Arc and Antarctic waters. Recent records of lithodid anomuran crabs in the Southern Ocean indicate a return of these crabs to the Antarctic, perhaps as a consequence of global warming, after their extinction in the lower Miocene ((15 Ma) (Thatje et al., 2005b).

The dichotomy in the Southern Ocean between a scarcity of decapods, which have pelagic larvae, and a richness of peracarids, which do not have pelagic larvae, fits the extinction hypothesis (Thatje et al., 2005b). Peracarids constitute an important part of the prey of lithodid crabs (Comoglio and Amin, 1999). After the climate deteriorated in the Eocene/Oligocene and benthic decapods became extinct, the absence or scarcity of these top predators may well have created new adaptive zones, leading to a selective advantage for peracarids and favoring their diversification. Indeed, free ecological niches may have opened opportunities for spectacular adaptive radiations, as seen in some peracarid taxa (Brandt, 1999, 2005; Held, 2000; Lörz and Brandt, 2004; Lörz and Held, 2004), which were also favored because of their brooding biology.

The exceptionally high species diversity of peracarids, especially isopods in the Southern Ocean and its deep environment, cannot, however, be due simply to the fact that they are brooders without pelagic larvae. Peracarids are found throughout the world's oceans, including the Arctic. However, the Southern Ocean deep-sea samples revealed a strikingly high biodiversity (Brandt et al., 2007a, 2007b). Rather, the high diversity of peracarids in the Southern Ocean may better be accounted for by the unusual oceanographic and topographic conditions there, namely, the ACC that has been sweeping through Drake Passage for 30 million years or more. If brooding individuals have been continually displaced by that current and survive downstream in isolation from the parent population, a major "species diversity pump" would result, producing many species over time. The distribution of species in the well-studied isopod genus *Antarcturus* reveals the pattern predicted by the ACC hypothesis (Figure 2); 7 of the 15 species are found in the Scotia Arc–Weddell Sea sector, and an additional 6 are found on the coast of eastern Antarctica. Considering the extensive amount of work that has been done in the Ross Sea during the twentieth century, the bias in species richness toward the Scotia Arc–Weddell Sea and eastern Antarctic coast is unlikely to be a sampling artifact. Several other conditions may have contributed to the high diversity of peracarids in the Southern Ocean. Gaston (2000), for example, correlated high habitat heterogeneity with high diversity, and high levels of tectonic activity in

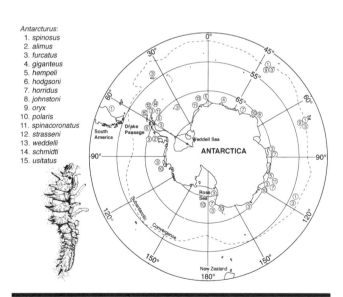

FIGURE 2. Distribution of 15 species of *Antarcturus* around Antarctica. Data were compiled from Brandt (1991), Brandt et al. (2007c), and unpublished records from *Polarstern* expeditions.

the Scotia Arc region could have produced relatively high habitat heterogeneity, although not as high as coral reef areas in lower latitudes (Crame, 2000).

Mitochondrial gene sequence analyses of iphimediid amphipods, endemic to the Antarctic, indicate that the age of the last common ancestor of this group is approximately 34 million years (Lörz and Held, 2004), after the Southern Ocean was isolated from other fragments of Gondwanaland but well before the Pliocene-Pleistocene glacial sheets extended over the Antarctic Continental Shelf. Speciation, therefore, has probably taken place throughout the time since the ACC became established with the breakthrough of Drake Passage.

In summary, crustaceans appear to have patterns of diversity similar to those seen in echinoderms: relatively few major taxa, which are likely monophyletic clades. Some of the peracarid clades are extremely diverse and speciose, while the decapod clades present, which have pelagic development, are relatively depauperate in terms of species richness. This pattern indicates that brooding is not so much an adaptation to conditions in the Antarctic but that exceptional conditions in Antarctic waters enhance speciation of brooders.

CONCLUSIONS

1. While nonpelagic development is certainly an adaptation resulting from natural selection, it may not be an adaptation to any condition in the present-day Southern Ocean. There is no evidence that nonpelagic development is adaptive to polar conditions or, in particular, to conditions in the Southern Ocean. Instead, it may have developed in other environments long ago and is now phylogenetically constrained.

2. It is possible that most species with lecithotrophic development (pelagic as well as nonpelagic) survived periods when the Antarctic Continental Shelf was largely covered with glacial ice and the Southern Ocean was largely covered with multiyear sea ice, while most species with planktotrophic larvae went extinct because of severely reduced primary production of food for the larvae. The net effect would be (1) an increase in the proportion of species with lecithotrophic development (both pelagic and nonpelagic) and (2) an overall decrease in species richness/biodiversity. However, the Southern Ocean is notable for its high species richness/diversity.

3. Speciation could be enhanced in taxa with nonpelagic development when the following occur: (1) Refuges form on the Antarctic Continental Shelf during the glacial maxima, fragmenting populations into small isolated units that could undergo speciation. If these formed repeatedly during the glacial-interglacial cycles of the Pliocene-Pleistocene, a "species diversity pump" would be created. This idea, termed ACS hypothesis, predicts the presence of many closely related cryptic species around the Antarctic continent, mainly at shelf and slope depths. (2) Individuals of species with nonpelagic development are infrequently carried to new habitats by the ACC flowing through the Drake Passage and over the Scotia Arc, where, if established, they form new species. Over more than 30 million years, such a process could generate many species. This idea, termed the ACC hypothesis, predicts the existence of many species in clades of varied divergence times, at a wide range of depths but with highest diversity downstream of Drake Passage, in the Scotia Arc and Weddell Sea.

4. All these possibilities appear to be important, depending on the taxon of concern, for explaining the unusual abundance of species with nonpelagic development in the Southern Ocean, but emerging data are giving most support for the ACC hypothesis. In addition, the ACC hypothesis may help account for the relatively high diversity found for many taxa in the Southern Ocean, especially in the area of the Scotia Arc and Weddell Sea.

ACKNOWLEDGMENTS

We are indebted to the superb library of Stanford University's Hopkins Marine Station for making accessible most of the literature reviewed in this paper. Katrin Linse, British Antarctic Survey, Cambridge, provided useful suggestions when the manuscript was being developed, and Vicki Pearse, University of California, Santa Cruz, added substantially both to the thinking and content that went into the work as well as with her editorial skills. We thank Andy Clarke, British Antarctic Survey, Cambridge; Ingo Fetzer, UFZ-Center for Environmental Research, Leipzig; Andy Mahon, Auburn University; Chris Mah, Smithsonian Institution; Jim McClintock, University of Alabama at Birmingham, and anonymous reviewers for comments and information that greatly improved the manuscript. We also thank Rafael Lemaitre, Smithsonian Institution, for inviting us to participate in the Smithsonian International Polar Year Symposium, where the ideas for this synthesis came together. Support for this work was provided by the National Science Foundation (grant OPP-0124131 to JSP) and the German Science Foundation. This is ANDEEP publication number 112.

LITERATURE CITED

Absher, T. M., G. Boehs, A. R. Feijo, and A. C. Da Cruz. 2003. Pelagic Larvae of Benthic Gastropods from Shallow Antarctic Waters of Admiralty Bay, King George Island. *Polar Biology*, 26:359–364.

Arnaud P. M. 1974. Contribution à la Bionomie Marine Benthique des Régions Antarctiques et Subantarctiques. *Téthys*, 6:465–656.

Arntz, W. E., and J.-M. Gili. 2001. A Case for Tolerance in Marine Ecology: Let Us Not Put out the Baby with the Bathwater. *Scientia Marina*, 65(Suppl. 2):283–299.

Arntz, W. E., M. Gorny, I. S. Wertmann, R. Soto, M. A. Lardies, and M. Retamal. 1999. Species Composition and Distribution of Decapod Crustaceans in the Waters off Patagonia and Tierra del Fuego, South America. *Scientia Marina*, 63(Suppl. 1):303–314.

Barnes, D. K. A. 2005. Changing Chain: Past, Present and Future of the Scotia Arc's and Antarctica's Shallow Benthic Communities. *Scientia Marina*, 69(Suppl. 2):65–89.

Barnes, D. K. A., D. A. Hodgson, P. Convey, C. S. Allen, and A. Clarke. 2006. Incursion and Excursion of Antarctic Biota: Past, Present and Future. *Global Ecology and Biogeography*, 15(2):121–142.

Bosch, I., K. A. Beauchamp, M. E. Steele, and J. S. Pearse. 1987. Development, Metamorphosis, and Seasonal Abundance of Embryos and Larvae of the Antarctic Sea Urchin *Sterechinus neumayeri*. *Biological Bulletin*, 173:126–135.

Brandt, A. 1991. Zur Besiedlungsgeschichte des antarktischen Schelfes am Beispiel der Isopoda (Crustacea, Malacostraca). *Berichte zur Polarforschung*, 98:1–240.

———. 1999. On the Origin and Evolution of Antarctic Peracarida (Crustacea, Malacostraca). *Scientia Marina*, 63 (Suppl. 1):261–274.

———. 2000. Hypotheses on Southern Ocean Peracarid Evolution and Radiation (Crustacea, Malacostrasca). *Antarctic Science*, 12:269–275.

———. 2005. Evolution of Antarctic Biodiversity in the Context of the Past: The Importance of the Southern Ocean Deep Sea. *Antarctic Science*, 17(4):509–521.

Brandt, A., W. Brökeland, S. Brix, and M. Malyutina. 2004. Diversity of Antarctic Deep-Sea Isopoda (Crustacea, Malacostraca)—A Comparison with Shelf Data. *Deep-Sea Research, Part II*, 51(14–16):1753–1769.

Brandt, A., C. De Broyer, I. De Mesel, K. E. Ellingsen, A. J. Gooday, B. Hilbig, K., Linse, M. R. A. Thomson, and P. A. Tyler. 2007a. The Biodiversity of the Deep Southern Ocean Benthos. *Philosophical Transactions of the Royal Society, Series B*, 362:39–66.

Brandt, A., A. J. Gooday, S. N. Brandão, S. Brix, W. Brökeland, T. Cedhagen, M. Choudhury, N. Cornelius, B. Danis, I. De Mesel, R. J. Diaz, D. C. Gillan, B. Ebbe, J. A. Howe, D. Janussen, S. Kaiser, K. Linse, M. Malyutina, J. Pawlowski, M. Raupach, and A. Vanreusel. 2007b. First Insights into the Biodiversity and Biogeography of the Southern Ocean Deep Sea. *Nature*, 447:307–311.

Brandt, A., S. Brix, W. Brökeland, M. Choudhury, S. Kaiser, and M. Malyutina. 2007c. Deep-Sea Isopod Biodiversity, Abundance and Endemism in the Atlantic Sector of the Southern Ocean—Results from the ANDEEP I–III Expeditions. *Deep-Sea Research, Part II*, 54:1760–1775.

Brey, T., and J. Gutt. 1991. The Genus *Sterechinus* (Echinodermata: Echinoidea) on the Weddell Sea Shelf and Slope (Antarctica): Distribution, Abundance and Biomass. *Polar Biology*, 11:227–232.

Bridges, T. S. 1993. Reproductive Investment in Four Developmental Morphs of *Streblospio* (Polychaeta: Spionidae). *Biological Bulletin*, 184:144–152,

Brökeland, W. 2004. Systematics, Zoogeography, Evolution and Biodiversity of Antarctic Deep-Sea Isopoda (Crustacea: Malacostraca). Ph.D. diss., University of Hamburg, Germany.

Byrne, M., M. W. Hart, A. Cerra, and P. Cisternas. 2003. Reproduction and Larval Morphology of Broadcasting and Viviparous Species in the *Cryptasterina* Species Complex. *Biological Bulletin*, 205:285–294.

Chia, F.-S. 1974. Classification and Adaptive Significance of Developmental Patterns in Marine Invertebrates. *Thalassia Jugoslavia*, 10:121–130.

Clark, A. M. 1962. Asteroidea. *Reports of the British-Australian-New Zealand Antarctic Research Expedition, 1929–1931, Series B*, 9:1–104.

Clarke, A. 1988. Seasonality in the Antarctic Marine Environment. *Comparative Biochemistry and Physiology*, 90B:461–473.

———. 1992. Reproduction in the Cold: Thorson Revisited. *Invertebrate Reproduction and Development*, 22:175–184.

———. 1993. Temperature and Extinction in the Sea: A Physiologist's View. *Paleobiology*, 19:499–518.

———. 2003. Costs and Consequences of Evolutionary Temperature Adaptation. *Trends in Ecology and Evolution*, 18:573–581.

Clarke, A., and J. A. Crame 1989. "The Origin of the Southern Ocean Marine Fauna." In *Origins and Evolution of the Antarctic Biota*, ed. J. A. Crame, pp. 253–268. Special Publication, No. 47. London: Geological Society.

———. 1992. The Southern Ocean Benthic Fauna and Climate Change: A Historical Perspective. *Philosophical Transactions of the Royal Society of London, Series B*, 339:299–309.

———. 1997. "Diversity, Latitude and Time: Patterns in the Shallow Sea." In *Marine Biodiversity: Causes and Consequences*, ed. R. F. G. Ormond, pp. 122–147. Cambridge, U.K.: Cambridge University Press.

Clarke, A., and N. M. Johnston. 2003. Antarctic Marine Benthic Diversity. *Oceanography and Marine Biology—An Annual Review*, 41:47–114

Collin, R. 2003. World-wide Patterns of Development in Calyptraeid Gastropods. *Marine Ecology Progress Series*, 247:103–122.

Collin, R., O. R. Chaparro, F. Winkler, and D. Véliz. 2007. Molecular Phylogenetic and Embryological Evidence That Feeding Larvae Have Been Reacquired in a Marine Gastropod. *Biological Bulletin*, 212:83–92.

Comoglio, L. I., and O. A. Amin. 1999. Feeding Habits of the False Southern King Crab *Paralomis granulosa* (Lithodidae) in the Beagle Channel, Tierra del Fuego, Argentina. *Scientia Marina*, 63 (Suppl. 1):361–366.

Crame, J. A. 2000. Evolution of Taxonomic Diversity Gradients in the Marine Realm: Evidence from the Composition of Recent Bivalve Faunas. *Palaeontology*, 26(2):188–214.

David, B., and R. Mooi. 1990. An Echinoid That "Gives Birth": Morphology and Systematics of a New Antarctic Species, *Urechinus mortenseni* (Echinodermata, Holasteroida). *Zoomorphology*, 110:75–89.

David, B., T. Choné, A. Festeau, R. Mooi, and C. De Ridder. 2003. *Antarctic Echinoids. An Interactive Database on CD-ROM. Version 2.0*. Dijon: Biogeosciences Publisher, University of Burgundy.

David, B., T. Choné, C. De Ridder, and A. Festeau. 2005. *Antarctic Echinoidea*. Ruggell, Liechtenstein: A.R.G. Gantner Verlag.

Dell, R. K. 1972. Antarctic Benthos. *Advances in Marine Biology*, 10:1–216.

Ellingsen, K. E., A. Brandt, B. Ebbe, and K. Linse. 2007. Diversity and Species Distribution of Polychaetes, Isopods and Bivalves in the Atlantic Sector of the Deep Southern Ocean. *Polar Biology*, 30:1265–1273.

Féral, J.-P., E. Derelle, and H. Philippe. 1994. "Inferred Phylogenetic Trees of Antarctic Brood-Protecting Schizasterid Echinoids from Partial 28S Ribosomal RNA Sequences." In *Genetics and Evolution of Aquatic Organisms*, ed. A. R. Beaumont, pp. 199–207. London: Chapman & Hall.

Fetzer, I., and W. E. Arntz. 2008. Reproductive Strategies of Benthic Invertebrates in the Kara Sea (Russian Arctic): Adaptation of Reproduction Modes to Cold Waters. *Marine Ecology Progress Series*, 356:189–202.

Foltz, D. W., M. T. Bolton, S. P. Kelley, B. D. Kelley, and A. T. Nguyen. 2007. Combined Mitochondrial and Nuclear Sequences Support the Monophyly of Forcipulatacean Sea Stars. *Molecular Phylogenetics and Evolution*, 43:627–634.

Foltz, D. W., A. T. Nguyen, J. R. Kiger, and C. L. Mah. 2008. Pleistocene Speciation of Sister Taxa in a North Pacific Clade of Brooding Sea Stars (*Leptasterias*). *Marine Biology*, 154:593–602.

Gage, J. D., and P. A. Tyler. 1991. *Deep-Sea Biology: A Natural History of Organisms at the Deep-Sea Floor.* Cambridge, U.K.: Cambridge University Press.

Gallardo, C. S., and P. E. Penchaszadeh. 2001. Hatching Mode and Latitude in Marine Gastropods: Revisiting Thorson's Paradigm in the Southern Hemisphere. *Marine Biology*, 138:547–552.

Galley, E. A., P. A. Tyler, A. Clarke, and C. R. Smith. 2005. Reproductive Biology and Biochemical Composition of the Brooding Echinoid *Amphipneustes lorioli* on the Antarctic Continental Shelf. *Marine Biology*, 148:59–71.

Gaston, K. J. 2000. Global Patterns in Biodiversity. *Nature*, 405:220–227.

Gil, D. G., and H. E. Zaixso. 2007. The Relation between Feeding and Reproduction in *Anasterias minuta* (Asteroidea: Forcipulata). *Marine Biology Research*, 3:256–264.

Gillespie, J. M., and J. B. McClintock. 2007. Brooding in Echinoderms: How Can Modern Experimental Techniques Add to Our Historical Perspective? *Journal of Experimental Marine Biology and Ecology*, 342:191–201.

Gorny, M. 1999. On the Biogeography and Ecology of the Southern Ocean Decapod Fauna. *Scientia Marina*, 63(1):367–382.

Gutt, J. 1991. Investigations on Brood Protection in *Psolus dubiosus* (Echinodermata: Holothuroidea) from Antarctica in Spring and Autumn. *Marine Biology*, 111:281–186.

Hain, S., and P. M. Arnaud. 1992. Notes on the Reproduction of High-Antarctic Molluscs from the Weddell Sea. *Polar Biology*, 12:303–312.

Hardy, A. 1960. "Remarks." In *Dispersal and Endemism among Southern Marine Faunas. Proceedings of the Royal Society of London, Series B*, 152:641–642.

Havenhand, J. N. 1995. "Evolutionary Ecology of Larval Types." In *Ecology of Marine Invertebrate Larvae,* ed. L. McEdward, pp. 79–122. London: CRC Press.

Held, C. 2000. Phylogeny and Biogeography of Serolid Isopods (Crustacea, Isopoda, Serolidae) and the Use of Ribosomal Expansion Segments in Molecular Systematics. *Molecular Phylogenetics and Evolution*, 15(2):165–178.

Held, C. 2003. "Molecular Evidence for Cryptic Speciation within the Widespread Antarctic Crustacean *Ceratoserolis trilobitoides* (Crustacea, Isopoda)." In *Antarctic Biology in a Global Context*, eds. A. H. K. Huiskes, W. W. C. Giekes, J. Rozema, R. M. L. Schorno, S. M. van der Vies, and W. J. Wolv, pp. 135–139. Leiden, Netherlands: Backhuys.

Held, C., and J.-W. Wägele. 2005. Cryptic Speciation in the Giant Antarctic Isopod *Glyptonotus antarcticus* (Isopoda: Valvifera: Chaetiliidae). *Scientia Marina*, 69:175–181.

Hendler, G. 1991. Echinodermata: Ophiuroidea. In *Reproduction of Marine Invertebrates*. Volume VI. *Echinoderms and Lophophorates,* eds. A. C. Giese, J. S. Pearse, and V. B. Pearse, pp. 355–511. New York: Academic Press.

Hoegh-Guldberg, O., and J. S. Pearse. 1995. Temperature, Food Availability, and the Development of Marine Invertebrate Larvae. *American Zoologist*, 35:415–425.

Hood, S., and R. Mooi. 1998. "Taxonomy and Phylogenetics of Extant *Brisaster* (Echinoidea: Spatangoida)." In *Echinoderms: San Francisco. Proceedings of the Ninth International Echinoderm Conference*, eds. R. Mooi and M. Telford, pp. 681–686. Rotterdam: A. A. Balkema.

Hotchkiss, F. H. C. 1982. "Antarctic Fossil Echinoids: Review and Current Research." In *Antarctic Geoscience*, ed. C. Craddock, pp. 679–684. Madison: University of Wisconsin Press.

Hotchkiss, F. H. C., and H. B. Fell. 1972. Zoogeographical Implications of a Paleogene Echinoid from East Antarctica. *Journal of the Royal Society of New Zealand*, 2:369–372.

Jablonski, D., and R. A. Lutz. 1983. Larval Ecology of Marine Benthic Invertebrates: Paleobiological Implications. *Biological Reviews*, 58:21–89.

Jablonski, D., and K. Roy. 2003. Geographic Range and Speciation in Fossil and Living Molluscs. *Proceedings of the Royal Society, Series B*, 270:401–406.

Jägersten, G. 1972. *Evolution of the Metazoan Life Cycle.* New York: Academic Press.

Jeffery, C. H., R. B. Emlet, D. T. J. Littlewood. 2003. Phylogeny and Evolution of Developmental Mode in Temnopleurid Echinoids. *Molecular Phylogenetics and Evolution*, 28:99–118.

Kim, S., and A. Thurber. 2007. Comparison of Seastar (Asteroidea) Fauna across Island Groups of the Scotia Arc. Polar Biology, 30: 415–425.

Komatsu, M., P. M. O'Loughlin, B. Bruce, H. Yoshizawa, K. Tanaka, and C. Murakami. 2006. A Gastric Brooding Asteroid, *Smilasterias multipara. Zoological Science*, 23:699–705.

Laptikhovsky, V. 2006. Latitudinal and Bathymetric Trends in Egg Size Variation: A New Look at Thorson's and Rass's Rules. *Marine Ecology*, 27:7–14.

Lee, Y.-H., M. Song, S. Lee, R. Leon, S. O. Godoy, and I. Canete. 2004. Molecular Phylogeny and Divergence Time of the Antarctic Sea Urchin (*Sterechinus neumayeri*) in Relation to the South American Sea Urchins. *Antarctic Science*, 16:29–36.

Levin, L. A., and T. S. Bridges. 1995. "Pattern and Diversity in the Reproduction and Development." In *Ecology of Marine Invertebrate Larvae*, ed. L. McEdward, pp. 1–48. London: CRC Press.

Linse, K., H. J. Griffiths, D. K. A. Barnes, and A. Clarke. 2006. Biodiversity and Biogeography of Antarctic and Sub-Antarctic Mollusca. *Deep-Sea Research, Part II*, 53:985–1008.

Linse, K., T. Cope, A.-N. Lörz, and C. Sands. 2007. Is the Scotia Sea a Centre of Antarctic Marine Diversification? Some Evidence of Cryptic Speciation in the Circum-Antarctic Bivalve *Lissarca notorcadensis* (Arcoidea: Philobryidae). *Polar Biology*, 30:1059–1068.

Littlepage, J. L., and J. S. Pearse. 1962. Biological and Oceanographic Observations under an Antarctic Ice Shelf. *Science*, 137:679–681.

Lockhart, S. J. 2006. Molecular Evolution, Phylogenetics, and Parasitism in Antarctic Cidaroid Echinoids. Ph.D. diss., University of California, Santa Cruz.

Lörz, A., and A. Brandt. 2004. Phylogeny of Antarctic *Epimeria* (Epimeriidae: Amphipoda). *Journal of the Marine Biological Association of the United Kingdom*, 84:179–190.

Lörz, A. N., and C. Held. 2004. A Preliminary Molecular and Morphological Phylogeny of the Antarctic Epimeriidae and Iphimediidae (Crustacea, Amphipoda). *Molecular Phylogenetics and Evolution*, 31:4–15.

Lörz, A.-N., E. W. Maas, K. Linse, and G. D. Fenwick. 2007. *Epimeria schiaparelli* sp. nov., an Amphipod Crustacean (Family Epimeriidae) from the Ross Sea, Antarctica, with Molecular Characterization of the Species Complex. *Zootaxa*, 1402:23–37.

Ludwig, H. 1904. Brutpflege bei Echinodermen. *Zoologisch Jahrbuch, Jena*, Suppl. 7:217–219.

Madon-Senez, C. 1998. Disparité Morphologique et Architecturale des Schizasteridae Incubants (Echinoidea, Spatangoida) de Régions Australes. Ph.D. diss., University of Burgundy, Dijon, France.

Magniez, P. 1980. "Modalitiés de l'Incubation chez *Abatus cordatus* (Verrill), Oursin Endémique des Îles Kerguelen." In *Echinoderms Present and Past,* ed. M. Jangoux, pp. 399–403. Rotterdam: A. A. Balkema.

Marshall, D. J., and T. F. Bolton. 2007. Effects of Egg Size on the Development Time of Non-feeding Larvae. *Biological Bulletin,* 212: 6–11.

McClintock, J. B., and J. S. Pearse. 1987. Reproductive Biology of the Common Antarctic Crinoid *Promachocrinus kerguelensis* (Echinodermata: Crinoidea). *Marine Biology,* 96:375–383.

McKinney, M. L., K. J. McNamara, and L. A. Wiedman. 1988. Echinoids from the La Meseta Formation (Eocene), Seymour Island, Antarctica. *Geological Society of America Memoirs,* 169:499–503.

McNamara, K. J. 1994. Diversity of Cenozoic Marsupiate Echinoids as an Environmental Indicator. *Lethaia,* 27:257–268.

Mileikovsky, S. A. 1971. Types of Larval Development in Marine Bottom Invertebrates, Their Distribution and Ecological Significance: A Re-evaluation. *Marine Biology,* 10:193–213.

Mooi, R., and B. David. 1993. Ontogeny and Origin of the Brooding System in Antarctic Urechinid Sea Urchins (Holasteroida). *Zoomorphology,* 113:69–78.

Mooi, R., and B. David. 1996. Phylogenetic Analysis of Extreme Morphologies: Deep-Sea Holasteroid Echinoids. *Journal of Natural History,* 30:915–953.

Mooi, R., H. Constable, S. Lockhart, and J. Pearse. 2004. Echinothurioid Phylogeny and the Phylogenetic Significance of *Kamptosoma* (Echinoidea: Echinodermata). *Deep-Sea Research, Part II,* 51: 1903–1919.

Mortensen, T. 1913. Die Echinodermenlarven der Deutschen Süd-Polar Expedition 1901–1903. *Deutschen Südpolar Expedition,* 14(Zool. 6):69–111.

———. 1936. Echinoidea and Ophiuroidea. *Discovery Reports,* 12: 199–348.

Murray, J. 1895. "General Observations on the Distribution of Marine Organisms." In *Report on Scientific Research, Voyage H.M.S. Challenger 1873–1876. A Summary of the Scientific Results,* Second Part, pp. 1431–1462. London: Published by Order of Her Majesty's Government.

Östergren, H. 1912. Über dieBrutpflege der Echinodermen in den Südpolaren Küstengebieten. *Zeitschrift Wissenschaften Zoologie,* 101: 325–341.

Pace, D. A., and D. T. Manahan. 2007. Cost of Protein Synthesis and Energy Allocation During Development of Antarctic Sea Urchin Embryos and Larvae. *Biological Bulletin,* 212:104–129

Palma, A. T., E. Poulin, M. G. Silva, R. B. San Martín, C. A. Muñoz, and A. D. Díaz. 2007. Antarctic Shallow Subtidal Echinoderms: Is the Ecological Success of Broadcasters Related to Ice Disturbance? *Polar Biology,* 30:343–350.

Pearse, J. S. 1969. Slow Developing Demersal Embryos and Larvae of the Antarctic Sea Star *Odontaster validus. Marine Biology,* 3:110–116.

———. 1994. "Cold-Water Echinoderms Break 'Thorson's Rule.'" In *Reproduction, Larval Biology, and Recruitment in the Deep-Sea Benthos,* eds. K. J. Eckelbarger and C. M. Young, pp. 26–39. New York: Columbia University Press.

Pearse, J. S., and I. Bosch. 1986. Are the Feeding Larvae of the Commonest Antarctic Asteroid Really Demersal? *Bulletin of Marine Science,* 39:477–484.

———. 1994. "Brooding in the Antarctic: Östergren Had It Nearly Right." In *Echinoderms Through Time,* eds. B. David, A. Guille, J.-P. Féral, and M. Roux, pp. 111–120. Rotterdam: A. A. Balkema.

Pearse, J. S., and S. J. Lockhart. 2004. Reproduction in Cold Water: Paradigm Changes in the 20th Century and a Role for Cidaroid Sea Urchins. *Deep-Sea Research, Part II,* 51:1533–1549.

Pearse, J. S., and J. B. McClintock. 1990. A Comparison of Reproduction by the Brooding Spatangoid Echinoids *Abatus shackletoni* and *A. nimrodi* in McMurdo Sound, Antarctica. *Invertebrate Reproduction and Development,* 17:181–191.

Pearse, J. S., J. B. McClintock, and I. Bosch. 1991. Reproduction of Antarctic Benthic Marine Invertebrates: Tempos, Modes, and Timing. *American Zoologist,* 31:65–80.

Peck, L. S. 2002. Ecophysiology of Antarctic Marine Ectotherms: Limits to Life. *Polar Biology,* 25:31–40.

Peck, L. S., A. Clarke, and A. L. Chapman. 2006. Metabolism and Development of Pelagic Larvae of Antarctic Gastropods with Mixed Reproductive Strategies. *Marine Ecology Progress Series,* 318:213–220.

Peck, L. S., D. K. Powell, and P. A. Tyler. 2007. Very Slow Development in Two Antarctic Bivalve Molluscs, the Infaunal Clam *Laternula elliptica* and the Scallop *Adamussium colbecki. Marine Biology,* 150:1191–1197.

Picken, G. B. 1980. Reproductive Adaptations of Antarctic Benthic Invertebrates. *Biological Journal of the Linnean Society,* 14:67–75.

Post, A. L., M. A. Hemer, P. E. O'Brien, D. Roberts, and M. Craven. 2007. History of Benthic Colonisation beneath the Amery Ice Shelf, East Antarctica. *Marine Ecology Progress Series,* 344:29–37.

Poulin, E., and J.-P. Féral. 1994. "The Fiction and the Facts of Antarctic Brood Protecting: Population Genetics and Evolution of Schizasterid Echinoids." In *Echinoderms Through Time,* eds. B. David, A. Guille, J.-P. Féral, and M. Roux, pp. 837–843. Rotterdam: A. A. Balkema.

———. 1996. Why Are There So Many Species of Brooding Antarctic Echinoids? *Evolution,* 50:820–830.

Poulin, E., A. T. Palma, and J.-P. Féral. 2002. Evolutionary Versus Ecological Success in Antarctic Benthic Invertebrates. *Trends in Ecology and Evolution,* 17:218–222.

Raguá-Gil, J. M., J. Gutt, A. Clarke, and W. E. Arntz. 2004. Antarctic Shallow-Water Mega-epibenthos: Shaped by Circumpolar Dispersion or Local Conditions? *Marine Biology,* 144:829–839.

Raupach, M. J., C. Held, and J.-W. Wägele. 2004. Multiple Colonization of the Deep Sea by the Asellota (Crustacea: Peracarida: Isopoda). *Deep-Sea Research, Part II,* 51:1787–1797.

Raupach, M., M. Malyutina, A. Brandt, and J. W. Wägele. 2007. Molecular Data Reveal a Highly Diverse Species Flock within the Munnopsoid Deep-Sea Isopod *Betamorpha fusiformis* (Barnard, 1920) (Crustacea: Isopoda: Asellota) in the Southern Ocean. *Deep-Sea Research, Part II,* 54:1820–1830.

Reid, D. G. 1990. A cladistic phylogeny of the genus *Littorina* (Gastropods): Implications for Evolution of Reproductive Strategies and for Classification. *Hydrobiologia,* 193:1–19.

Rogers, A. D. 2007. Evolution and Biodiversity of Antarctic Organisms: A Molecular Perspective. *Philosophical Transactions of the Royal Society, Series B,* 362:39–88

Rowe, F. W. E., and J. Gates. 1995. "Echinodermata." In *Zoological Catalogue of Australia.* Volume 33. Melbourne: CSIRO Australia.

Schatt, P. 1988. "Embryonic Growth of the Brooding Sea Urchin *Abatus cordatus.*" In *Echinoderm Biology,* eds. R.D. Burke, P. V. Mladenov, P. Lambert, and R. L. Parsley, pp. 225–228. Rotterdam: A. A. Balkema.

Scherer, R. P., A. Aldahan, S. Tulaczyk, G. Possnert, H. Engelhardt, and B. Kamb. 1998. Pleistocene Collapse of the West Antarctic Ice Sheet. *Science,* 281:82–85.

Schluter, M., and E. Rachor. 2001. Meroplankton Distribution in the Central Barents Sea in Relation to Local Oceanographic Patterns. *Polar Biology,* 24:582–592.

Sewell, M. 2005. Examination of the Meroplankton Community in the South-western Ross Sea, Antarctica, Using a Collapsible Plankton Net. *Polar Biology*, 28:119–131.

Smiley, S., F. S. McEuen, C. Chaffee, and S. Krishnan. 1991. "Echinodermata: Holothuroidea." In *Reproduction of Marine Invertebrates*. Volume VI. *Echinoderms and Lophophorates*, ed. A. C. Giese, J. S. Pearse, and V. B. Pearse, pp. 663–750. Pacific Grove, Calif.: Boxwood Press.

Smith, A. B., D. Pisani, J. A. Mackenzie-Dodds, B. Stockley, B. L. Webstger, and T. J. Littlewood. 2006. Testing the Molecular Clock: Molecular and Paleontological Estimates of Divergence Times in the Echinoidea (Echinodermata). *Molecular Biology and Evolution*, 23:1832–1851.

Smith, M. S., K. S. Zigler, and R. A. Raff. 2007. Evolution of Direct-Developing Larvae: Selection Versus Loss. *BioEssays*, 29:566–571.

Stanwell-Smith, D., L. S. Peck, A. Clarke, A. W. A Murray, and C. D. Todd. 1999. The Distribution, Abundance and Seasonality of Pelagic Marine Invertebrate Larvae in the Maritime Antarctic. *Philosophical Transactions of the Royal Society, London, Series B*, 354: 471–484.

Starmans, A., and J. Gutt. 2002. Mega-epibenthic Diversity: A Polar Comparison. *Marine Ecology Progress Series*, 225:45–52.

Stockley, B., A. B. Smith, T. Littlewood, H. A. Lessios, and J. A. Mackenzie-Dodds. 2005. Phylogenetic Relationships of Spatangoid Sea Urchins (Echinoidea): Taxon Sampling Density and Congruence between Morphological and Molecular Estimates. *Zoologica Scripta*, 34:447–468.

Strathmann, R. R. 1978. The Evolution and Loss of Feeding Larval Stages of Marine Invertebrates. *Evolution*, 32:894–906.

———. 1993. Hypotheses on the Origins of Marine Larvae. *Annual Review of Ecology and Systematics*, 24:89–117.

Strathmann, R. R., and M. F. Strathmann. 1982. The Relationship between Adult Size and Brooding in Marine Invertebrates. *American Naturalist*, 119:91–101.

Thatje, S., S. Schnack-Schiel, and W. E. Arntz. 2003. Developmental Trade-Offs in Sub-Antarctic Meroplankton Communities and the Enigma of Low Decapod Diversity in High Southern Latitudes. *Marine Ecology Progress Series*, 260:195–207.

Thatje, S., R. Bacardit, and W. Arntz. 2005a. Larvae of the Deep-Sea Nematocarcinidae (Crustacea: Decapoda: Caridea) from the Southern Ocean. *Polar Biology*, 28:290–302.

Thatje, S., C. Hillenbrand, and R. Larter. 2005b. On the Origin of Antarctic Marine Benthic Community Structure. *Trends in Ecology and Evolution*, 20:534–540.

Thiel, M., and L. Gutow. 2005. The Ecology of Rafting in the Marine Environment. II. The Rafting Organisms and Community. *Oceanography and Marine Biology—An Annual Review*, 43:279–418.

Thomson, C. W. 1876. Notice of Some Peculiarities in the Mode of Propagation of Certain Echinoderms of the Southern Sea. *Journal of the Linnean Society of London, Zoology*, 13:55–79.

———. 1885. "Notes on the Reproduction of Certain Echinoderms from the Southern Ocean." In *Report of Scientific Research, Voyage H.M.S. Challenger 1873–1876. Narrative*, Volume I, First Part, pp. 379–396. London: Published by Order of Her Majesty's Government.

Thomson, M. R. A. 2004. Geological and Paleoenvironmental History of the Scotia Sea Region as a Basis for Biological Interpretation. *Deep-Sea Research, Part II*, 51:1467–1487.

Thorson, G. 1936. The Larval Development, Growth, and Metabolism of Arctic Marine Bottom Invertebrates Compared with Those of Other Seas. *Meddelelser om Grønland*, 100 (6):1–155.

———. 1950. Reproduction and Larval Ecology of Marine Bottom Invertebrates. *Biological Reviews of the Cambridge Philosophical Society*, 25:1–45.

Tyler, P. A., C. M. Young, and A. Clarke. 2000. Temperature and Pressure Tolerances of Embryos and Larvae of the Antarctic Sea Urchin *Sterechinus neumayeri* (Echinodermata: Echinoidea): Potential for Deep-Sea Invasion from High Latitudes. *Marine Ecology Progress Series*, 192:173–180.

Vázquez, E., J. Ameneiro, S. Putzeys, C. Gordo, and P. Sangrà. 2007. Distribution of Meroplankton Communities in the Bransfield Strait, Antarctica. *Marine Ecology Progress Series*, 338:119–129.

Villinski, J. T., J. C. Villinski, M. Byrne, and R. A. Raff. 2002. Convergent Maternal Provisioning and Life-History Evolution in Echinoderms. *Evolution*, 56:1764–1775.

Wilson, N. G., R. L. Hunter, S. J. Lockhart, and K. M. Halanych. 2007. Multiple Lineages and Absence of Panmixia in the "Circumpolar" Crinoid *Promachocrinus kerguelensis* from the Atlantic Sector of Antarctica. *Marine Biology*, 152:895–904.

Wray, G. A. 1995. "Evolution of Larvae and Developmental Modes." In *Ecology of Marine Invertebrate Larvae*, ed. L. McEdward, pp. 413–447. London: CRC Press.

Young, C. M. 1994. "A Tale of Two Dogmas: The Early History of Deep-Sea Reproductive Biology." In *Reproduction, Larval Biology, and Recruitment in the Deep-Sea Benthos*, ed. K. J. Eckelbarger and C. M. Young, pp. 1–25. New York: Columbia University Press.

Persistent Elevated Abundance of Octopods in an Overfished Antarctic Area

Michael Vecchione, Louise Allcock, Uwe Piatkowski, Elaina Jorgensen, and Iain Barratt

Michael Vecchione, National Marine Fisheries Service, Systematics Laboratory, National Museum of Natural History, P.O. Box 37012, MRC 153, Washington, DC 20013-7012, USA. Louise Allcock, Martin Ryan Marine Science Institute, National University of Ireland, Galway, University Road, Galway, Ireland. Uwe Piatkowski, Institute for Marine Research, Universitat Kiel, Dusternbrooker Weg 20, D-24105, Kiel, Germany. Elaina Jorgensen, National Marine Fisheries Service, Alaska Fisheries Science Center, 7600 Sand Point Way N.E., Seattle, WA 98115, USA. Iain Barratt, Ecology and Evolutionary Biology, School of Biological Sciences, Queen's University Belfast, 97 Lisburn Road, Belfast BT9 7BL, UK. Corresponding author: M. Vecchione (vecchiom@ si.edu). Accepted 19 May 2008.

ABSTRACT. Trawl surveys conducted between 1996 and 2007 show that populations of octopods have significantly higher abundances around Elephant Island, off the Antarctic Peninsula, than in similar areas nearby. This elevated abundance was first detected following the cessation of commercial fishing and has persisted for many years beyond, possibly indicating an enduring shift in the structure of the ecosystem.

INTRODUCTION

Concern about the effects of overfishing on marine ecosystems has increased substantially in recent years (e.g., Jackson et al., 2001). One of these potential effects is a shift in the suite of dominant predators in the ecosystem (Fogarty and Murawski, 1998; Choi et al., 2004). Unusually high abundances of squids and octopods in some areas have been related to man's removal of their finfish predators and competitors (Caddy and Rodhouse, 1998). Furthermore, anthropogenic changes in polar regions are of particular conservation concern (e.g., Smith et al., 2002). In Antarctica, a bottom-trawl fishery primarily targeting mackerel icefish (*Champsocephalus gunnari*) and marbled notothenia (*Notothenia rossii*) developed in 1978 around Elephant Island, in the South Shetland Archipelago off the Antarctic Peninsula. The fishery continued until 1988/1989 but rapidly depleted the populations of the target species (Kock and Stransky, 2000). We report here that in this overfished area, populations of octopods have significantly higher abundances than in similar areas nearby. This elevated abundance has persisted for years beyond the cessation of commercial fishing, possibly indicating an enduring shift in the structure of the ecosystem.

MATERIALS AND METHODS

R/V *Polarstern* cruises ANT XIV/2 (November–December 1996), ANT XIX/3 (January–February 2002), and ANT XXIII/8 (December 2006 to January 2007) were conducted to assess the status of fish stocks in the region around Elephant Island monitored internationally under the Convention on Conservation of Antarctic Marine Living Resources. Sampling stations were selected randomly from depth strata between 50 and 500 m. These stations were sampled by 30-min tows with a large double-warp otter trawl. The 2002 cruise also conducted similar sampling off the southern South Shetland Islands and off Joinville Island across the Bransfield Strait (both areas with shelves of similar widths and depths to the Elephant Island area), as well as an intensive sampling series of 20 tows in a shallow-water grid near Elephant Island. The 2006–2007 cruise similarly sampled additional stations across the Bransfield Strait close to the peninsula and in the western Weddell Sea (Figure 1). We identified and counted all cephalopods collected on these cruises, including both the cod end sample and specimens entangled in the net mesh. The material included many more species than were recognized previous to this work (Allcock,

2005). We first noticed the abundance patterns reported here during the 2002 cruise and have since examined the 2006–2007 cruise as a test of our unpublished 2002 hypothesis. Because the sample sizes, depths, etc., were balanced between the Elephant Island area and the out-groups in 2002, we emphasize these results and present the 1996 and 2006–2007 results for temporal comparisons.

For some of the comparisons presented below, we have eliminated the shallow-grid samples and pooled the observations from the southern South Shetland Islands, close to the Antarctic Peninsula, Joinville Island, and Weddell Sea (termed "out-groups" below) because this created similar-sized sets of samples with similar ranges and variances in depth, a controlling factor in the abundance and diversity of Antarctic octopods (Figure 2). Intensive shallow-grid sampling was not conducted in the out-group areas. A

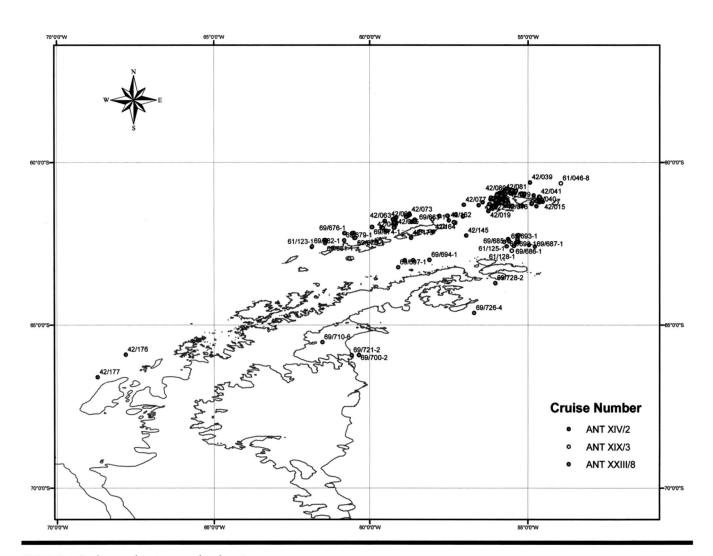

FIGURE 1. Study area showing sampling locations.

a.

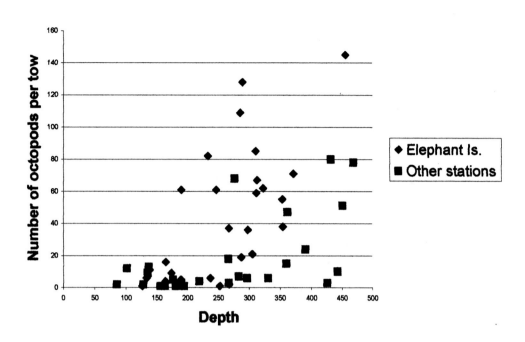

b.

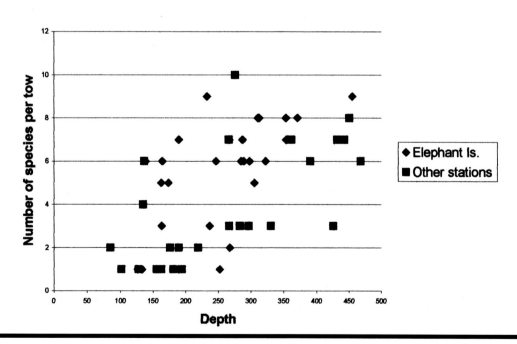

FIGURE 2. Relationship between mean depth of tow and octopod catch in 2002 trawl samples from around Elephant Island and similar nearby areas: (a.) total number of octopods per tow, (b.) approximate number of octopod species per tow.

TABLE 1. Summary of octopod collections by cruise year and location.

Year	Location	Number of stations	Parameter[a]	Maximum	Mean	95% confidence interval	Minimum
2006–2007	Elephant Island	51	Depth (m)	486	208	26	62
			catch	169	18	8	0
			no. spp.	8	3	0.5	0
2006–2007	out-group	38	depth (m)	490	275	35	87
			catch	35	7	2	0
			no. spp.	5	2	0.5	0
2002	Elephant Island	28	depth (m)	455	257	32	127
			catch	145	42	16	1
			no. spp.	9	6	1	1
2002	shallow grid	20	depth (m)	209	146	18	74
			catch	306	37	15	4
			no. spp.	7	4	1	2
2002	out-group	26	depth (m)	468	266	49	85
			catch	80	18	10	1
			no. spp.	10	4	1	1
1996	Elephant Island	38	depth (m)	477	243	33	89
			catch	135	52	10	9

[a]Depth is based on mean depth of each tow, catch is the number of octopods per tow, and no. spp. is the approximate number of species per tow; no. spp. is not included for 1996 cruise because identifications have not yet been revised based on updated taxonomy resulting from 2002 cruise.

summary of the collections is presented in Table 1. Statistical comparisons used two-sample t-tests assuming unequal variances, with the a priori confidence level for significance at $\alpha = 0.05$ (two tailed). Depths presented are based on the mean depth of each tow, calculated as the average of the depth at the beginning and at the end of the tow.

RESULTS

Although the depths of the 28 Elephant Island stations sampled in 2002 were slightly shallower than the 26 out-group stations, the difference was not statistically significant. However, the total number of octopods collected per tow at Elephant Island averaged over twice as high (Table 2) as that at the out-group stations (significant, $p < 0.001$). Had we included the 20 shallow-grid stations, the difference in catch between the areas would have been even greater (Table 1) because these tows included two catches that were anomalously high (98 and 306 octopods) for that depth range and strongly dominated by one shallow-dwelling species, *Pareledone charcoti* (Joubin, 1905). Although the difference between areas in number of species collected was not great, it was statistically significant. This is likely because an increased number of specimens in the catch generally includes a higher number of species (Figure 3) rather than because of a difference in species richness in the two areas. Depths of the 38 stations sampled around Elephant Island in 1996 were not significantly different from those sampled in 2002, nor was the average catch significantly different from the 2002 catch in the same area. Only three samples were collected in 1996 from the southern South Shetland Islands (in the same area as the out-groups in 2002) with the same net at similar depths; the catches in these samples were very low (12, 7, and 5 octopods). The few samples that were collected from Joinville Island in 2002 included the lowest numbers of octopods caught that year, but those were qualitatively similar to the octopod fauna of the Weddell Sea (Allcock et al., 2001).

In 2006–2007, both the mean depth and number of octopods per sample around Elephant Island were less than in 2002. The mean depth at the out-group stations in 2006–2007 was somewhat greater than in 2002 and significantly greater than the Elephant Island stations in 2006–2007. However, the number of octopods per sample around Elephant Island was >2.5 times higher than in the out-group samples, a statistically significant difference (Table 3). As in

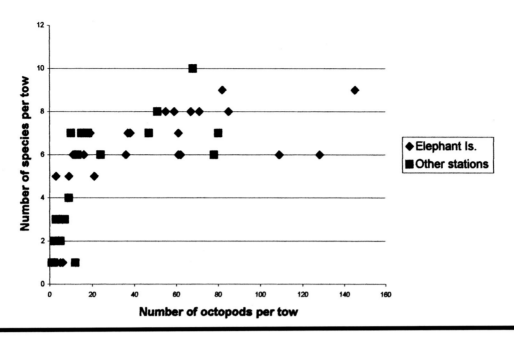

FIGURE 3. Relationship between number of octopods collected and approximate number of species collected in 2002.

2002, the larger catches of octopods around Elephant Island included a significantly greater number of species than in the smaller out-group samples.

DISCUSSION

We have no quantitative information about the abundance of octopods in the area of Elephant Island prior to the onset of commercial fishing in the area. Therefore, some unknown natural factor in that location could have resulted in high octopod abundances relative to levels in similar areas nearby. However, at least eight bottom-trawl surveys of the fish fauna around Elephant Island were conducted between 1976 and 1987 (Kock and Stransky, 2000), and we know of no indication of elevated octopod abundance in those surveys. Conversely, during a U.S. trawl survey in 1998, octopod abundance was higher around Elephant Island than off the South Shetland Islands (C. Jones, NMFS Antarctic Program, Southwest Fisheries Science Center, personal communications, 2002). These sampling efforts, together with the present surveys, revealed that bycatch fish species had recovered by the early 1990s but populations of target species had not fully recovered (Kock and Stransky, 2000; K.-H. Kock, Institute for Sea Fisheries, personal communication, 2002). The abun-

dance of octopods may have increased coincidently with the recovery of populations of finfish bycatch.

We are not sure why the overall abundance of octopods around Elephant Island was lower in 2006–2007 than during previous surveys. Perhaps this is because the sampling was concentrated at somewhat shallower depths, which resulted in fewer catches with very high numbers of octopods (Figure 2). However, details of the configuration of the trawl, such as height of the footrope above the rollers and the presence of a "tickler" chain, were modified during this cruise to reduce the bycatch of sessile megafauna (e.g., sponges and cnidarians). It seems quite likely that these modifications affected the net's sampling characteristics for benthic octopods. An indication that high numbers of octopods remained around Elephant Island during 2006–2007 is found in the very high numbers of small specimens caught at three stations (59 specimens at station 614-3, 24 at 642-1, and 15 at 654-6) using a different gear type, an Agassiz beam trawl, not included in the comparisons presented here.

The pattern reported here is consistent with other reports from around the world of elevated cephalopod abundances coincident with reduction of finfish populations by commercial harvesting. As the inferred increase in octopod abundance appears to be coincident with recovery of bycatch fish populations, release from predation pressure

TABLE 2. Two-sample t-test assuming unequal variances comparing areas in February 2002.[a]

Parameter	Elephant Island	Out-groups
Station depths		
Mean	256.9892857	265.8461538
Variance	6694.207844	14457.90058
Observations	28	26
df	44	
t statistic	−0.314090727	
$P(T \le t)$ one-tail	0.377468272	
t critical one-tail	1.680230071	
$P(T \le t)$ two-tail	0.754936545	
t critical two-tail	2.0153675	
Number of octopods per tow		
Mean	42.85714286	18.07692308
Variance	1652.941799	609.6738462
Observations	28	26
df	45	
t statistic	2.728499663	
$P(T \le t)$ one-tail	0.004521735	
t critical one-tail	1.679427442	
$P(T \le t)$ two-tail	0.009043469	
t critical two-tail	2.014103302	
Number of species per tow		
Mean	5.535714286	4
Variance	6.406084656	7.36
Observations	28	26
df	51	
t statistic	2.146507581	
$P(T \le t)$ one-tail	0.018305786	
t critical one-tail	1.675284693	
$P(T \le t)$ two-tail	0.036611573	
t critical two-tail	2.007582225	

[a]Out-groups are pooled samples from southern South Shetland Islands plus Joinville Island. On the basis of these analyses, the depths of the stations sampled do not differ significantly between the areas, but both the number of octopods per tow and the number of octopod species per tow were significantly higher in the area around Elephant Island than in other areas.

rather than competitive processes seems to be responsible for the good fortune of the octopods. Because ecological processes in polar regions tend to be comparatively slow, such ecosystem-level impacts of fishing may take longer to become apparent than at lower latitudes but also may be very persistent.

ACKNOWLEDGMENTS

We thank Karl-Hermann Kock and the Institute for Sea Fisheries in Hamburg, Germany, for allowing us to participate in these cruises, which were conducted by the Alfred Wegener Institute for Polar Research in Bremerhaven, Germany. Silke Stiemer (Universitat Kiel) assisted with the field work, and R. E. Young (University of Hawaii) and C. F. E. Roper (Smithsonian Institution) provided helpful comments on an early draft of the manuscript.

LITERATURE CITED

Allcock, A. L. 2005. On the Confusion Surrounding *Pareledone charcoti*: Endemic Radiation in the Southern Ocean. *Zoological Journal of the Linnean Society,* 143(1):75–108.

Allcock, A. L., U. Piatkowski, P. K. G. Rodhouse, and J. P. Thorpe. 2001. A Study on Octopodids from the Eastern Weddell Sea, Antarctica. *Polar Biology,* 24:832–838.

Caddy, J. F., and P. G. Rodhouse. 1998. Cephalopod and Groundfish Landings: Evidence for Ecological Change in Global Fisheries? *Reviews in Fish Biology and Fisheries,* 8:431–444.

Choi, J. S., K. T. Frank, W. C. Leggett, and K. Drinkwater. 2004. Transition to an Alternate State in a Continental Shelf Ecosystem. *Canadian Journal of Fisheries and Aquatic Sciences,* 61:505–510.

TABLE 3. Two-sample t-test assuming unequal variances comparing areas in December 2006 to January 2007.[a]

Parameter	Elephant Island	Out-groups
Station depths		
Mean	208.2411765	274.6736842
Variance	8640.174871	11619.0328
Observations	51	38
df	73	
t statistic	−3.047557645	
$P(T \leq t)$ one-tail	0.001605534	
t critical one-tail	1.665996224	
$P(T \leq t)$ two-tail	0.003211069	
t critical two-tail	1.992997097	
Number of octopods per tow		
Mean	18.23529412	7.184210526
Variance	733.5835294	45.66785206
Observations	51	38
df	58	
t statistic	2.799243278	
$P(T \leq t)$ one-tail	0.003472082	
t critical one-tail	1.671552763	
$P(T \leq t)$ two-tail	0.006944163	
t critical two-tail	2.001717468	
Number of species per tow		
Mean	3.215686275	2.473684211
Variance	3.77254902	1.877667141
Observations	51	38
Hypothesized mean difference	0	
df	87	
t statistic	2.11239907	
$P(T \leq t)$ one-tail	0.018759109	
t critical one-tail	1.66255735	
$P(T \leq t)$ two-tail	0.037518218	

[a]Out-groups are pooled samples from areas other than Elephant Island. In these analyses, the number of octopods per tow and the number of octopod species per tow were significantly higher in the area around Elephant Island than in other areas, but the sampled depths around Elephant Island were shallower, which could be a confounding factor.

Fogarty, M. J., and S. A. Murawski. 1998. Large-Scale Disturbance and the Structure of Marine Systems: Fishery Impacts on Georges Bank. *Ecological Applications*, 8(S1):S6–S22.

Jackson, J., M. X. Kirby, W. H. Berger, K. A. Bjorndal, L. W. Botsford, B. J. Bourque, R. H. Bradbury, R. Cooke, J. Erlandson, J. A. Estes, T. P. Hughes, S. Kidwell, C. B. Lange, H. S. Lenihan, J. M. Pandolfi, C. H. Peterson, R. S. Steneck, M. J. Tegner, and R. R. Warner. 2001.

Historical Overfishing and the Recent Collapse of Coastal Ecosystems. *Science*, 293:629–638.

Kock, K.-H., and C. Stransky. 2000. The Composition of the Coastal Fish Fauna around Elephant Island (South Shetland Islands, Antarctica). *Polar Biology*, 23:825–832.

Smith, J., R. Stone, and J. Fahrenkamp-Uppenbrink. 2002. Trouble in Polar Paradise. *Science* 297:1489.

Cold Comfort: Systematics and Biology of Antarctic Bryozoans

Judith E. Winston

ABSTRACT. Antarctic bryozoans are spectacular. They are often larger and more colorful than their temperate relatives. Antarctic bryozoans are also outstanding in their diversity. Well over 300 species have been described, and new descriptions continue to appear. In the U.S. Antarctic Research Program (USARP) collections we have identified 389 species so far, mostly belonging to the Cheilostomata, the dominant order in Recent seas. Much about their ecology can be learned from study of the abundant material preserved in the USARP collections. Yearly growth bands demonstrate that colonies may live for decades and that growth rates are very close to those of related temperate species. The presence of embryos in the brood chambers of many species allows determination of seasonality of reproduction and fecundity of colonies of different sizes. A large proportion of Antarctic bryozoan species (81% for cheilostomes) are endemic. Endemic groups include bizarre and unusual forms in which polymorphism, the occurrence of individuals specialized to perform different tasks, is highly developed. Behavioral studies carried out with living colonies in the Antarctic have shown how different polymorphs function in cleaning and protecting colonies from trespassers or predators: capturing motile animals such as amphipods, polychaetes, and nematodes and sweeping colonies free of debris.

INTRODUCTION

The more than 5,000 members of the phylum Bryozoa, belonging to the Lophotrochozoa group of protostome invertebrates, are found in marine and freshwater habitats worldwide, including the seas that surround Antarctica. Bryozoans are colonial, benthic, sessile animals. They reproduce asexually by budding new members of a colony or, in some cases, by fragmentation of an existing colony. Colonies also reproduce sexually. Embryos, often brooded, develop into free-swimming larvae that settle and metamorphose to begin a new colony. Although individual bryozoan zooids are microscopic (ranging from about 0.30 to 2.0 mm in length), colonies can be quite large, consisting of many thousands of individuals and, in some places, creating three-dimensional benthic habitats that serve as shelter, feeding, and nursery grounds for other organisms. Bryozoans are suspension feeders, part of the benthic biological filter system made up of sessile filter-feeding animals. Bryozoans also produce physical and chemical defenses against their enemies. Many members of the dominant Recent order of bryozoans, the cheilostomes, have developed a high degree of polymorphism,

Judith E. Winston, Department of Marine Biology, Virginia Museum of Natural History, 21 Starling Avenue, Martinsville, VA 24112, USA (judith.winston@vmnh.virginia.gov). Accepted 19 May 2008.

with heterozooids specialized for reproduction, attachment, cleaning, and defense. Their chemical defenses consist of natural products such as alkaloids or terpenoids, which are toxic or discouraging to predators or disease agents (Sharp et al., 2007).

The chilly Antarctic seafloor, where seawater temperatures are near or below freezing year-round, might not seem like an ideal habitat for benthic organisms. Food is plentiful for only part of the year, and, in shallow water, icebergs may scour the seafloor, destroying everything they touch. Yet more than 300 species of bryozoans have been found there, including a large number of distinctive endemic taxa. This paper will discuss some results from more than 20 years of study of the U.S. Antarctic Research Program (USARP) bryozoan collections by the author and collaborators A. E. Bernheimer, P. J. Hayward, and B. F. Heimberg.

TAXONOMY AND DISTRIBUTION OF USARP BRYOZOANS

BRYOZOAN COLLECTION IN THE ANTARCTIC

The beginning of bryozoan collecting in the Antarctic dates from the last part of the nineteenth century and the early part of the twentieth, the era of the national expeditions for the exploration of the continent. Although a few species from Cape Adare in the Ross Sea were recorded by Kirkpatrick (1902), the first major report on the bryozoan fauna was by Waters (1904) on the 89 taxa collected in the Bellingshausen Sea by the *Belgica* Expedition. Analysis of collections from other expeditions followed (Calvet, 1904a, 1904b, 1909; Kluge, 1914; Thornely, 1924; Livingstone, 1928). A second wave of collecting began with a series of voyages carried out by the British Discovery Investigations (of which some of the bryozoans appeared in Hastings, 1943). The first U.S. specialist to study Antarctic bryozoans was Mary Rogick, who published 13 papers on the taxonomy of the bryozoans collected during the U.S. Navy's 1947–1948 Antarctic Expedition between 1955 and 1965 (summarized in Rogick, 1965).

THE USARP BRYOZOAN COLLECTIONS

The International Geophysical Year of 1957–1958 marked a new era of marine research and benthic collecting in the Antarctic. The USARP bryozoan collections consist of more than 5,000 lots collected by various U.S. research groups between 1958 and 1982. The earliest lots in the collection were obtained during benthic studies by Stanford University researchers working in the McMurdo

Sound and the Ross Sea. Later systematic collections of all benthos, including bryozoans, were made by scientists and technicians during oceanographic cruises of USNS *Eltanin* (1962–1968) and R/V *Hero* (1968–1982). These collections were returned to the United States to be processed by technicians at the Smithsonian Oceanographic Sorting Center (SOSC) and were distributed to taxonomic specialists on each group. The stations from which bryozoans were collected ranged from 10°W to 70°E but were concentrated in the following Antarctic and subantarctic areas: the Ross Sea, the Antarctic Peninsula, off the islands of the Scotia Arc, and from Tierra del Fuego to the Falkland Islands (Figure 1).

My involvement with the collections included training SOSC technicians in bryozoan identification and working with technicians and volunteers at SOSC, the American Museum of Natural History, and the Virginia Museum of Natural History to sort and identify those lots, now separated into almost 8,000 vials and jars. It also led to a 1985 NSF grant to work at Palmer Station to study ecology and behavior of living colonies of some Antarctic species. In spite of the large amount of marine biology carried out in Antarctica, relatively little attention had been paid to benthic community structure or to the ecology of benthic organisms. For this reason, as part of the project on behavioral and chemical ecology of Antarctic bryozoans,

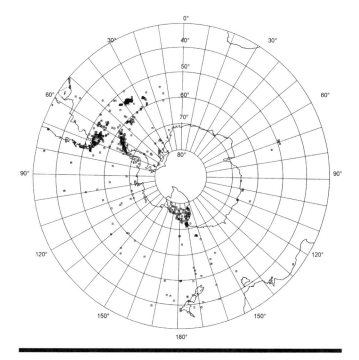

FIGURE 1. Location of USARP stations containing bryozoans processed by the Smithsonian Oceanographic Sorting Center.

we attempted to learn more about the role these animals played in one particular benthic community, that off the southern end of Low Island, South Shetland Islands. Finally, as a lecturer on the American Museum's Discovery tours, I made three additional trips to the Antarctic Peninsula and South Shetland Islands, where I was able to observe beach drift organisms and intertidal bryozoan habitats at a number of locations.

TAXONOMIC DISTRIBUTION OF USARP BRYOZOANS

Two classes, Gymnolaemata and Stenolaemata, and three orders of bryozoans are recorded from the Antarctic. The Gymnolaemata include the orders Ctenostomata and Cheilostomata. The Cyclostomata are the only living order of the Stenolaemata.

The dominant bryozoans in Recent oceans are the cheilostomes, a group whose diversity and abundance has increased greatly since its origin in the Cretaceous. Cheilostomes have box-like zooids, variously reinforced with calcium carbonate skeletons, a hinged operculum protecting the orifice through which the polypide extends to feed, and colonies often displaying a high degree of polymorphism. Most cheilostomes brood their embryos to the larval stage in variously formed reproductive structures called ovicells.

Of the 389 species so far recorded in the sorted and identified USARP collections, 344 (88.5%) are cheilostomes. Four new species have been described so far from the collection (Hayward and Winston, 1994) with more to follow. Although most of the major groups of cheilostomes are represented in the Antarctic and subantarctic, several groups have undergone a good deal of radiation with numerous species, most of them endemic. Families especially well represented (10 or more species) include the Flustridae, Calloporidae, Bugulidae, Cabereidae, Cellariidae, Arachnopusiidae, Exochellidae, Sclerodomidae, Smittinidae, Microporellidae, Celleporidae, and Reteporidae (Hayward, 1995). This pattern is reflected in the USARP collections. Some representative species are shown in Figure 2.

Although cyclostome bryozoans rank well below cheilostomes in terms of species diversity, they are abundant in the Antarctic, forming large colonies, easily recognizable as cyclostomes, although often difficult or impossible to determine to species level because colonies lack gonozooids, a vital taxonomic character in the group. Like cheilostomes, cyclostome bryozoans have calcified walls. Their zooids are tubular. The zooid orifice, at the distal end of the tube, has no operculum but closes by a sphinc-

ter instead. Polymorphism is much less common, but some species have nanozooids. They brood embryos in one or more brood chambers or gonozooids, and sexual reproduction is unusual, involving polyembryony: larval fission in which the original fertilized egg results in many genetically identical larvae. Thirty-seven cyclostomes (9.55% of the total USARP bryozoan fauna) were found in USARP collections. Figure 3 (left) shows an erect branching cyclostome of the genus *Hornera*.

Members of the order Ctenostomata have chitinous and/or gelatinous walls. Some form encrusting or massive colonies. Others form delicate vine-like colonies consisting of single or clumps of tubular zooids along stolons or with zooid bases constricting into stolonate tubes that join adjacent zooids. They have no operculum but close the orifice by muscular constriction. Sexual reproduction may involve brooding embryos in body cavities of maternal zooids or broadcasting fertilized eggs into seawater, where development into larvae takes place. Although the first bryozoan described from the Antarctic continent was a ctenostome, *Alcyonidium flabelliforme* (Kirkpatrick, 1902), in terms of species diversity the group is less well represented there than in some other environments. Only eight species (2%) of the total bryozoan fauna were found in the USARP collections, but three of them represented new species (Winston and Hayward, 1994), one encrusting on other bryozoans and the other two boring into live bryozoan colonies or living in dead zooids or crevices (e.g., *Bowerbankia antarctica*, Figure 3).

The most abundant species in the Antarctic Peninsula and South Shetland Islands form foliaceous, lightly calcified colonies (*Carbasea ovoidea, Kymella polaris, Flustra astrovae, Himantozoum antarcticum,* and *Nematoflustra flagellata*), delicate jointed branching colonies (*Cellaria divisa*), or encrusting colonies (e.g., *Micropora brevissima, Inversiula nutrix, Celleporella antarctica, Ellisina antarctica, Harpecia spinosissima, Lacerna hosteensis, Escharoides tridens,* and *Lichenopora canaliculata*). From the Ross Sea, the most abundant species in the USARP collections in shallow water (less than 50 m) is *Eminoecia carsonae*, with rigidly branching erect colonies. In deeper water, erect forms are also common, including *Cellaria monilorata, Arachnopusia latiavicularis, Antarcticaetos bubeccata, Thryptocirrus phylactellooides, Melicerita obliqua*, species of Cellarinellidae, *Reteporella antarctica* and other Reteporidae, with well-calcified branching or reticulate colony forms (see Figure 4), as well as some of the same epizoic species found in the Antarctic Peninsula area: *Celleporella antarctica, Ellisina antarctica,* and *Harpecia spinosissima.*

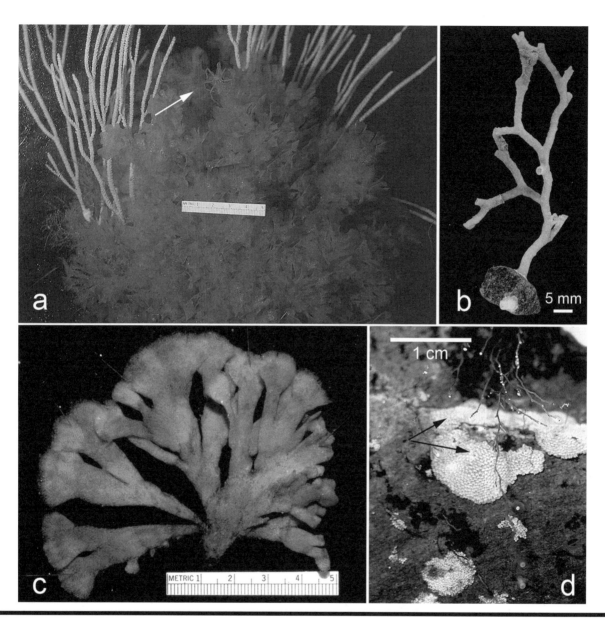

FIGURE 2. Morphologies common in bryozoans from USARP collections. (a) Large foliaceous colony of *Carbasea ovoidea* from Low Island. Scale = 5 cm. Arrow points to pycnogonid. (b) Rigid branching colony of *Cellarinella foveolata* attached to glacial pebble. (c) Living colony of *Kymella polaris* pinned out for study of reproduction and fouling. (d) Encrusting colonies of *Inversiula nutrix* on underside of an intertidal rock, shown by arrows. Branching hydroid above colonies and crustose algae (dark patches) are also visible.

The Antarctic intertidal zone has been considered to be almost barren due to scouring by seasonal sea ice (Barnes, 1994a; Knox, 2007). This is not the case, however, in many localities along the Antarctic Peninsula and in the South Shetlands. Sheltered intertidal sites, often with plankton-rich eutrophic water due to runoff from adjacent colonies of birds or marine mammals, contain tide pools and crevices whose inhabitants include calcareous and macroalgae, limpets, amphipods, *Glyptonotus*, brittle stars, starfish, and sea urchins. A number of bryozoans, of which *Inversiula nutrix* (Figure 2d) was most common, encrust intertidal rocks or attach to seaweed in intertidal to shallow subtidal habitats (Winston and Hayward, 1994).

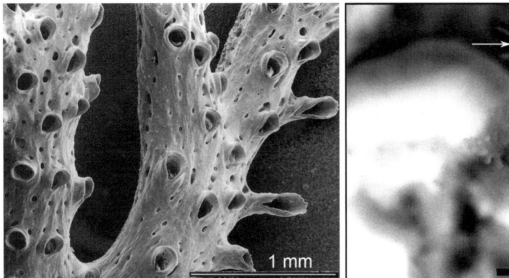
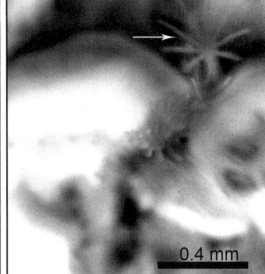

FIGURE 3. (left) An Antarctic cyclostome, *Hornera* sp. (scanning electron microscope image). (right) Living colony of an Antarctic ctenostome, *Bowerbankia antarctica*. Arrow points to lophophore emerging from crevice between two spirorbid tubes. Tentacle crown of spirorbid is visible below that of bryozoan.

BIOLOGY AND ECOLOGY OF ANTARCTIC BRYOZOANS

STUDY AREAS, METHODS, AND MATERIALS

In addition to long-term taxonomic projects, other studies using preserved USARP material, ecological and behavioral work on living Antarctic bryozoans, were carried out during the austral summer and fall of 1985 at Palmer Station and off the southernmost of the South Shetland Islands. Low Island (latitude 63°25′S, longitude 62°10′W) lies off the western coast of the Antarctic Peninsula. The Low Island area was a favorite collecting site for fish biologists working out of Palmer Station during our stay. It was close enough to the station (within 12 hours' cruise time) that fish could be maintained in good condition, and the sea bottom off its southern side slopes off to a relatively flat surface, free of projecting ledges or pinnacles that would tear the trawls used to collect specimens. By sharing cruise time with fish and krill biologists we were able to return to the site several times during the summer and fall. A 4 × 10 ft (1.2 × 3 m) otter trawl was used to collect both fish and bryozoans. Proportionate biomass of benthic organisms was determined on shipboard by averaging the blotted wet weights of different groups of organisms taken in three timed trawls of equal length. For studies of the food of the bryozoans we froze a number of freshly trawled colonies of the most common species in the ultracold freezer on the ship. They were later defrosted in the lab, and polypides were dissected and gut contents were examined by light and epifluorescence microscopy. For other studies of living material the bryozoans collected were maintained in holding tanks with running seawater until the ship returned to Palmer Station. On return to the lab they were placed in running seawater tanks and examined as soon as possible. Specimens for behavioral studies were collected both from Low Island by trawling and from Arthur Harbor, using a hand dredge from an inflatable boat. Autozooid feeding and behavior of avicularian polymorphs was recorded using a macrovideo setup in the lab at Palmer Station. Freshly collected material was maintained at close to normal seawater temperature during behavioral observations by an ice bath surrounding the observation dish.

To analyze growth and injury, colonies were pinned out in seawater in a shallow dissecting tray. A piece of clear Mylar film was then placed over them, and the colony outline, including growth checks, was traced with a waterproof marking pen. The traced version was immediately copied and used as a map to record areas of injury and fouling. Each colony was examined under the dissecting microscope, and all injuries, discoloration, bites, rips, empty zooids, and fouling organisms were recorded.

Growth of individual colonies was analyzed by measuring the distance between yearly growth checks.

For the reproductive study five colonies (if possible) were examined after each collection. Each colony was pinned out flat in a dissecting tray filled with seawater. It was then examined under a dissecting microscope for the following: developing ovicells, developing embryos, mature embryos, and empty ovicells. The colonies were also photographed and finally preserved in 70% ethanol.

BIOLOGICAL CHARACTERISTICS

Outstanding characteristics of invertebrates occurring in Antarctic benthic communities include a high degree of endemism, large body size in comparison with temperate or tropical relatives, and the prevalence of suspension feeding organisms (Hedgpeth, 1969, 1970; Dell, 1972; Arnaud, 1974; White, 1984; Gallardo, 1987; Arntz et al., 1994, 1997; Clarke and Johnston, 2003; Knox, 2007).

Many Antarctic bryozoans are large in size. Figure 2a shows a large colony of *Carbasea ovoidea*, a flexible, lightly calcified, foliaceous species collected at Low Island, South Shetland Islands. The size of the colony is approximately 20 cm in width by 15 cm in height. Individual zooids of many Antarctic species also are large in size, many of them between 1 and 2 mm long, versus the more common 0.4–0.9 mm zooid length of species found in warmer waters.

Figures 2 and 3 show some of the range of colony morphology found in species in the USARP collections. Branching colonies consisting of rooted seaweed-like fronds, wide or narrow, are abundant, especially in the Antarctic Peninsula and South Shetland Islands. Jointed and rigid erect forms, branching, unbranched, or anastomosing and reticulate, may be attached to other substrata, such as glacial pebbles (Figure 2b), vertical walls, or the dead colonies of other bryozoans or rooted in sediment (Figure 2c). Encrusting species are also abundant and diverse. Some form massive or nodular colonies consisting of several layers of frontally budded zooids. Other species form single-layered crusts, loosely or tightly attached to other bryozoans, other organisms, or hard substrata (Figure 2d).

Many Antarctic bryozoans are also more colorful than their temperate relatives. Bryozoans derive their pigment from the carotenoids in their phytoplankton food or, in some cases, from coloration present in symbiotic bacteria inhabiting zooids (Sharp et al., 2007). Colors of living colonies range from dark red (e.g., *Carbasea curva*) to orange brown (e.g., *Nematoflustra flagellata*), to yellow orange (e.g., *Kymella polaris*), to peach (e.g., *Orthoporidra* spp.), purple, pink (e.g., chaperiids and reteporids), and tan to white. The one *Bugula* species known, *Bugula longissima*, has dark green coloration when living, apparently derived from bacterial symbionts (Lebar et al., 2007).

The dark red *Carbasea curva*, which lacks the physical defense of avicularia, was found to show moderate haemolytic activity, killing 60% of human and 50% of dog erythrocytes (Winston and Bernheimer, 1986). Some of the species from Low Island were also tested for antibiotic activity. *Kymella polaris* and *Himantozoum antarcticum* both strongly inhibited the growth of *Staphylococcus aureus*. *Nematoflustra flagellata*, *Caberea darwinii*, and *Austroflustra vulgaris* moderately inhibited growth. Only *Beania livingstonei* was noninhibitory (Colon-Urban et al., 1985).

STUDIES OF BRYOZOANS FROM THE LOW ISLAND BENTHIC COMMUNITY

Shallow shelf environments (less than 500 m) in many areas of the Antarctic are dominated by communities made up largely of sessile suspension feeders like sponges, bryozoans, hydroids, gorgonians, and tunicates, whose colonies may form dense thicket-like growths spreading over large areas of the sea bottom (Belyaev, 1958; Uschakov, 1963; Propp, 1970; White and Robins, 1972; Barnes, 1995b, 1995c; Saíz-Salinas et al., 1997; Saíz-Salinas and Ramos, 1999; San Vincente et al., 2007). In contrast to epifaunal communities elsewhere, which are mostly limited to hard substrata, such communities in Antarctica commonly rest on or are rooted in soft sediments or are attached to scattered rocks and pebbles. Gallardo (1987) first called attention to the need to for recognizing the distinctiveness of this epi-infaunal or soft-bottom epifaunal community as a prerequisite to the study of its structure. The community we studied fit this epi-infaunal pattern.

Biomass

Inshore, in depths of 70 m or less, benthic biomass consisted primarily of macroalgae and echinoderms, a community similar to that reported at a number of localities along the peninsula (Gruzov and Pushkin, 1970; Delaca and Lipps, 1976; Moe and Delaca, 1976) and in the South Orkney Islands as well (White and Robins, 1972).

Between about 80 and 110 m a soft-bottom epi-infaunal community of the type discussed by Gallardo (1987) occurred. By wet weight (Figure 4) the dominant components of this community were sponges (31.4%); echinoderms, chiefly holothurians (24.6%); ascidians (18.7%);

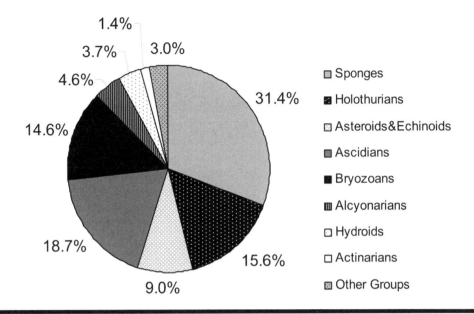

FIGURE 4. Biomass of organisms from three trawl collections at 100 m, Low Island, Antarctic Peninsula.

bryozoans (14.6%) and coelenterates, mostly gorgonians, especially *Ophidogorgia paradoxa* and *Thouarella* spp.; and hydroids (10.0%) (Winston and Heimberg, 1988). Over 30 species of bryozoans occurred. The five most abundant species (*Carbasea ovoidea, Nematoflustra flagellata, Austroflustra vulgaris, Kymella polaris,* and *Himantozoum antarcticum*) all have flexible, foliaceous, lightly calcified colonies (e.g., Figure 2a,c). Therefore, in terms of volume or area of sea bottom covered, bryozoans are an even more important component of the community than would be indicated by biomass alone. Although not the highest bryozoan biomass reported from Antarctic benthic communities (Starmans et al., 1999, reported 22% bryozoan biomass in Amundsen and Bellingshausen seas), the biomass of bryozoans is typical of the multilayered, microhabitat-rich, filter-feeding community reported from many areas of the Antarctic shelf from the Ross Sea (e.g., Bullivant, 1959:488, fig. 3; Dayton et al., 1974; Dayton, 1990), to King George Island (e.g., Rauschert, 1991:67, fig. 23), to Signy Island (Barnes, 1995b), to the Weddell Sea (Starmans et al., 1999).

Large motile invertebrates found in this habitat included the isopods *Glyptonotus antarcticus* and *Serolis* sp., the echinoid *Sterechinus neumayeri,* and various asteroids, e.g., *Odontaster validus* and *Labidaster annulatus.* Demersal fish species included nototheniids (*Notothenia gibberifrons, N. larseni, N. nudifrons,* and *N. coriiceps*) and the icefish *Chaenocephalus aceratus.*

Growth and Longevity of Most Abundant Species

Life history characteristics of Antarctic bryozoans are amenable to analysis for the following three reasons: (1) Growth is in discrete modules (zooids), making increments of growth easy to measure. (2) Colony fronds of perennial Antarctic species, like those of some temperate species, show yearly growth checks where growth stops during winter months, making it possible to determine the age of fronds as well as their yearly growth rate by back measurement (Stebbing, 1971b; Winston, 1983; Pätzold et al., 1987; Barnes, 1995c; Brey et al., 1998). (3) Embryos, usually brooded in zooid cavities or in ovicells, are easily detectable in living colonies, making it possible to quantify reproductive effort.

Carbasea ovoidea was the most abundant bryozoan species in the Low Island community, often comprising more than half the bryozoan biomass in a trawl sample. The delicate, tan, unilaminar fronds of *Carbasea* colonies showed no growth checks, indicating that all the growth of a particular frond took place during one season, although basal rhizoids and stolons (of this and the other species) might be perennial, producing new fronds yearly. The mean increase in height for *Carbasea* fronds was 8.6 cm per year.

In the other dominant species, both colonies and fronds were perennial. The narrow, curling fronds of *Himantzoum* could not be accurately measured and so were excluded from this part of the study. The other three perennial species grew much more slowly than *Carbasea*. Figure 5 compares growth in height for individual colonies of all three species as determined by back measurement. Two of them, *Austroflustra vulgaris* and *Nematoflustra flagellata* are related to *Carbasea* (family Flustridae). *Nematoflustra* fronds showed a mean increase in height of only 0.92 cm per year, whereas *Austroflustra* fronds increased 1.2 cm per year. The ascophoran cheilostome *Kymella polaris* is not closely related to the other species but grew at a similar rate. On average, *Kymella* fronds increased 1.3 cm in height per year.

The oldest fronds of *Kymella* were at least six years in age, and those of *Austroflustra* and *Nematoflustra* were seven years. As none were complete colonies, the genetic individuals they represented may have persisted much longer. The life spans of these species appear somewhat shorter than the 10–50+ year life spans of some of the rigid erect bryozoan species found in deeper Antarctic shelf habitats (Winston, 1983; Brey et al., 1998). However, both growth rates and life spans for both *Austroflustra* and *Nematoflustra* were in the same range as those of temperate perennials like *Flustra foliacea* (12 years) (Stebbing, 1971b). Barnes (1995c) also studied growth of *Nematoflustra* in shallow water at Signy Island. He found an average yearly increase in height of 0.7 cm and estimated that the oldest colonies at that location were 26 years old.

Reproduction

Three methods of protecting developing embryos were represented among the dominant species. *Austroflustra vulgaris* and *Nematoflustra flagellata* brood eggs internally in zooid body cavities, while *Kymella polaris* broods eggs in ovicells of maternal zooids. In contrast, *Carbasea ovoidea* broods developing embryos externally in embryo sacs attached in clusters of four or five to the orifice of each fertile zooid.

The reproductive pattern of *Carbasea* also contrasted with that of the other common species. Reproductive effort in *Carbasea* was very high (averaging 2953 embryos per colony) at the time of our first census in late austral summer (1 March) and may have peaked earlier in the summer. By the next sampling period, reproduction had ceased entirely, although zooids, like those of other species, continued to contain actively feeding polypides throughout the study period.

The mean number of embryos per colony was lower in the other species studied: *Nematoflustra, Austroflustra,*

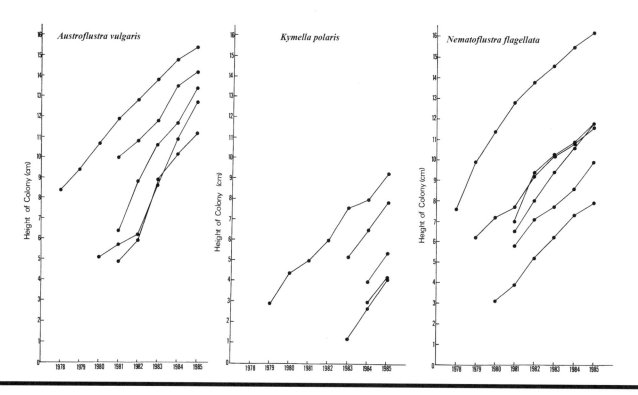

FIGURE 5. Annual growth of individual colonies of three species of Low Island bryozoans determined by back measurement.

Himantozoum, and *Kymella,* averaging a few hundred per colony at any one census (Table 1). In these species, sexual reproduction was still occurring at the last date sampled. For *Kymella* and *Himantozoum,* the two species in which embryos were brooded in ovicells, we could determine the percentage of ovicells brooding embryos versus empty ovicells over the course of the season (Table 2). The percentage of empty ovicells gradually increased until by 20 April, 72% of all *Kymella* ovicells and 95% of all *Himantozoum* ovicells were empty, indicating that the end of the reproductive season was approaching for at least these two species. In *Nematoflustra* the number of embryos fluctuated slightly from census to census but showed no significant decline as of 20 April. *Austroflustra vulgaris* colonies contained mature embryos at the 7 March census (mean of 258 per colony), while colonies collected on 20 April had an average of 227 embryos per colony. Although there was no way for us to tell how long the embryos present in late April would be brooded, it may well be as later workers (e.g., Barnes and Clarke, 1995; Bowden, 2005; Knox, 2007) have suggested, that "winter" may not be as long for the benthos as predicted on the basis of light and phytoplankton abundance.

TABLE 1. Mean number of embryos produced per colony for most abundant Low Island species.

Species	Total number of embryos	Mean number per colony	Number of colonies
Carbasea	15,355	1536	10
Austroflustra	5920	321	20
Himantozoum	6326	452	14
Kymella	3698	247	15
Nematoflustra	19,277	741	26

TABLE 2. Percent of ovicells empty for two Low Island species at three census periods.

Species	1 March	2 April	20 April
Kymella	19%	40%	75%
Himantozoum	46%	62%	95%

Partial Mortality and Predation

Like most clonal organisms, bryozoans have retained extensive powers of regeneration and can tolerate a high degree of injury or death of portions of the colony without death of the entire colony. Such partial mortality may be caused by physical disturbance of the environment or by predators or grazers. A few invertebrates, including some pycnogonids and nudibranchs, are specialized as single-zooid predators of bryozoans. These animals pierce a zooid with proboscis or radula and suck out body fluids and tissues, leaving an empty or broken zooid behind. Single or small patches of empty zooids were probably the result of such predators. The grazing or browsing activities of fish, echinoids, and mollusks leave larger scrapes, rips, and bites on colony fronds. We examined colonies for injuries of the different types and noted where they occurred on the fronds. Table 3 shows that all species sustained a considerable amount of damage. *Carbasea* colonies showed the least amount of injury to growing tips (the most delicate and accessible portion of the frond). This is most likely due to their much higher growth rate.

Evidence from studies of gut contents of associated macrobenthic organisms also suggested that most of the injuries observed were not due to feeding by specialized bryozoan predators. A search of the literature revealed that small quantities (from less than 1% to about 3%) of bryozoans had been found in gut contents of several Antarctic fish and echinoderms (Dayton et al., 1974; Dearborn, 1977). We examined gut contents of a number of invertebrates from Low Island trawls (including polychaetes, echinoderms, and crustaceans) to learn whether any of them were feeding on bryozoans. Two Low Island invertebrates, the echinoid *Sterechinus neumayeri* and the isopod *Glyptonotus antarcticus,* did contain bryozoan fragments. But our results, like those of later workers, indicated that gut contents of invertebrate carnivores and scavengers, like those of the demersal fish, consisted primarily of small motile invertebrates: amphipods, isopods, polychaetes, and mollusks (Schwartzbach, 1988; Ekau and Gutt, 1991: McClintock, 1994).

Another source of damage to colonies is caused by fouling of colonies by other organisms. Table 4 shows the most common organisms found attached to frontal surfaces of colonies of the five most abundant Low Island species. Some of them, such as the stalked barnacles found in branch bifurcations or the colonies of the bryozoan *Beania livingstonei,* which attach loosely to the host colony, may benefit the host, augmenting colony water currents by their own feeding activities. Others, such as

TABLE 3. Mean number of injuries per colony and percent of branch tips injured.

Species	Number of rips torn in branches	Number of injuries to branch tip (growing edge)	Number of bites to branch edges (sides of branches)	Number of injuries to center of a branch	Number of empty zooids	Percentage of branch tips injured
Carbasea	1.7	3.4	1.1	1.4	130	4.4%
Nematoflustra	4.0	3.5	5.0	7.2	41	23.5%
Austroflustra	1.4	2.8	3.0	3.8	81	52%
Kymella	1.2	4.1	0.5	0.2	50	53%

encrusting bryozoans like *Ellisina* and *Harpecia*, disable the host zooids they overgrow. Table 5 shows the diversity and density of fouling on Low Island species compared with that on NE Atlantic *Flustra foliacea*, as studied by Stebbing (1971a). The overall number of taxa and number of epizoans per colony was lower for all the Low Island species studied than for *Flustra*. However, when the number of epizoans per square centimeter was calculated, two species, *Austroflustra* (1.10/cm²) and *Kymella* (1.2/cm²), were in the same range as *Flustra foliacea* (1.0/cm²). Barnes (1994) studied the epibiota of two erect species, *Alleoflustra tenuis* and *Nematoflustra flagellata,* from shallow (36–40 m) and deeper (150 m) habitats at Signy Island. The frontal surface of *Nematoflustra* showed fewer colonizers than the abfrontal surface, and for both species the amount of fouling decreased to almost zero at 150 m. The number of taxa encrusting both species was also low (median = 3.0 for *Alleoflustra* and 2.0 for *Nematoflustra*). Our methods were somewhat different, but it appears that overall diversity of epibiotic taxa was higher at Low Island, but the diversity of epibiotic bryozoan taxa was much higher at Signy Island.

Food Sources

Gut contents of the bryozoans studied are summarized in Table 6. Each autozooid polypide has a mouth at the base of the lophophore funnel. Mouth size is slightly variable, as the mouth expands and contracts slightly with particle swallowing, but it is closely correlated with zooid size (Winston, 1977). These Antarctic species had large mouths compared to species from warmer water but, somewhat surprisingly, were still feeding primarily on very small plankton cells, mostly tiny diatoms and dark, rough-walled cysts less than 20 μm in size, probably resting stages of either choanoflagellates (Marchant, 1985; Marchant and McEldowny, 1986) or diatoms (Bodungen et al., 1986). Most of the phytoplankton component of their diet was thus within the nanoplankton, a size range which has been shown to account for much of the primary productivity in some areas of Antarctic seas (Bracher, 1999; Knox, 2007). The Bransfield Strait area is an important breeding ground for krill, which feed on larger plankton. Nanoplankton and picoplankton populations increase as microplankton blooms diminish (Varela et al., 2002). Some studies have found

TABLE 4. Dominant epizoans attached to dominant Low Island bryozoan species; a "+" indicates their presence on a particular bryozoan species.

Epizoan organisms	*Carbasea*	*Nematoflustra*	*Flustra*	*Himantozoum*	*Kymella*
Foraminiferans	+	+		+	
Diatoms				+	
Hydroids		+	+		
Stalked barnacles		+			+
Beania livingstonei		+			+
Harpecia spinosissima				+	
Ellisina antarctica			+	+	
Osthimosia sp.	+				
Cyclostome bryozoans				+	

TABLE 5. Diversity and density of epizoans fouling Low Island bryozoans compared with fouling on northeast Atlantic *Flustra foliacea*.

Species	Number of epizoic taxa	Mean number of epizoans/colony	Mean number/cm² of colony surface
Carbasea ovoidea	9	28	0.56
Nematoflustra flagellata	13	14	0.24
Austroflustra vulgaris	12	36	1.10
Himantozoum antarcticum	9	9	—
Kymella polaris	9	28	1.2
Flustra foliacea	42	558	1.0

TABLE 6. Gut contents of Low Island bryozoans.

Species	Mean mouth size (μm)	Dominant particle types[a]	Particle size range (μm)
Carbasea ovoidea	59	BPM, diatoms, cysts	3–66
Austroflustra vulgaris	96	BPM, cysts	3–45
Kymella polaris	94	BPM, sediment grains	6–60
Nematoflustra flagellata	87	Cysts, diatoms	9–69
Beania livingstonei	114	BPM, diatoms, cysts, sediment grains	3–93

[a]BPM = brown particulate material.

nanoplankton making up 83% of phytoplankton carbon in February and March (Kang and Lee, 1995). Sediments in the peninsula are also rich in organic matter (Bodungen et al., 1989). Benthic microalgae (Vincent, 1988; Gilbert, 1991) may also be important in areas reached by light.

The bryozoans studied also ingested large amounts of "brown particulate material." This material contained chlorophyll and may have been derived from the fecal pellets of zooplankton or those of other benthos. Fecal material could also have derived from benthos (Nöthig and von Bodungen, 1989; Tatián et al., 2004). Feeding on dead organisms or fecal material has been shown to occur in other Antarctic animals and may aid them in surviving seasons of low food supply. Sediment particles may indicate the importance of an advected food supply, as Gutt (2007) has speculated, which might explain the sediment grains found in bryozoan gut contents.

Some food resource besides phytoplankton seems likely to be part of Antarctic bryozoan life histories. Polypides of colonies of all species we observed were still actively feeding at the end of our stay in late April. This is in keeping with the observations made by Barnes and Clarke (1994), who monitored colony activity every month for a two-year period at Signy Island. Most bryozoans they observed stopped feeding for only a two- to three-month period in mid–austral winter.

Habitat and Ecosystem Role

The primary role of bryozoans in the Low Island ecosystem appeared to be that of habitat and foraging ground for demersal fish and motile invertebrates. To assess their importance in that regard, we selected three large clusters of *Carbasea ovoidea* from a single trawl and immediately immersed them in large jars of seawater formalin to kill and preserve their inhabitants for later analysis. Table 7 shows the results. When living, these clumps contained about 0.09 m³ of habitat space (in overall volume, not counting areas of each frond) and held almost 500 individual invertebrates. Most were arthropods (81.6%), of which amphipods comprised the majority: 345 individuals (69.6%). Nematodes were the next largest group present, with 54 individuals (10.8%). Other motile and sessile groups made up the remainder of the inhabitants. Most of them figure in the diets of demersal fishes and benthic invertebrates of the Antarctic Peninsula region (Targett, 1981; Daniels, 1982).

Figure 6 is a diagrammatic representation of a Low Island food web, placing the bryozoans within it as part of the link to the benthos. The major role of bryozoans within the Low Island ecosystem is as a three-dimensional, layered habitat and shelter for the small invertebrates on which larger demersal fish and benthic invertebrates feed

TABLE 7. Animals inhabiting three *Carbasea ovoidea* colonies collected at Low Island.

Group	Number of specimens
Amphipods	345
Nematodes	54
Isopods	41
Pycnogonids	19
Ascidians	17
Bivalves	12
Holothurians	4
Sponges	2
Sipunculans	1
Asteroids	1
Total	496

and a part of the epibenthic nursery ground for juveniles of demersal fish and motile invertebrates. Along with other sessile epifauna, they may also provide large epibiotic filter-feeding invertebrates with a higher perch and better access to food (Gutt and Shickan, 1998). The bryozoans themselves are suspension-feeding consumers of microplankton and nanoplankton, as well as fecal material or detritus supplied from above their colonies. They may also play a minor role as a food source for single-zooid predators and a few fish and invertebrates.

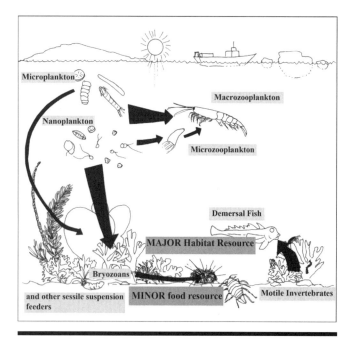

FIGURE 6. Low Island food web. Diagrammatic representation of links between benthic and pelagic communities.

BEHAVIOR OF ANTARCTIC BRYOZOANS

Morphological studies of avicularia and vibracula (Winston, 1984) and behavioral studies carried out with living colonies (Winston, 1991) have shown how different polymorphs, including those of Antarctic species, function within colonies. These functions include sweeping debris from zooids and colonies, protecting the colony from trespassers, and capturing motile organisms and possible predators.

NEMATOFLUSTRA—VIBRACULA

Distal to each autozooid of *Nematoflustra flagellata* is a vibraculum zooid with a long, curved, bristle-like mandible (Figure 7a). Mechanical stimulation or the vibration of a small organism, such as a pycnogonid or polychaete, triggered a wave of vibracular movement over a part or all of the colony surface. The circumrotary reversal of the vibracula mandibles was sequentially synchronized at first, traveling proximally from the branch tip, but later waves became less synchronous. The waves of moving setae effectively carried organisms or debris from the branches (Figure 7b) (Winston, 1991).

BEANIA—BIRD'S HEAD AVICULARIA

Unlike sessile avicularia and vibracula, the pedunculate (bird's head) avicularia found in the cellularine group of bryozoans close and open mandibles frequently, even when undisturbed, showing a species-specific pattern of ongoing activity. For example, in *Beania livingstonei* (Figure 7c) the avicularium bends forward on its peduncle, then snaps back into an upright position, while the mandible closes. Once the avicularium is upright, the mandible slowly reopens. Although the avicularian movements did not increase in the presence of trespassers, their activity was still effective as organisms caught by one avicularium were usually captured by the mandibles of several more in their struggles to free themselves (e.g., Figure 7d). Some were eventually able to pull free, detaching the avicularia from their peduncles in the process (Winston, 1991).

CAMPTOPLITES—LONG-STALKED BIRD'S HEAD AVICULARIA

The long-stalked avicularia of *Camptoplites* species (Figure 7e) show an even more complex pattern. The long, slender peduncles of these avicularia sway slowly back and forth across the frontal surface of colony branches. As they sway, the mandibles of the avicularia snap open and

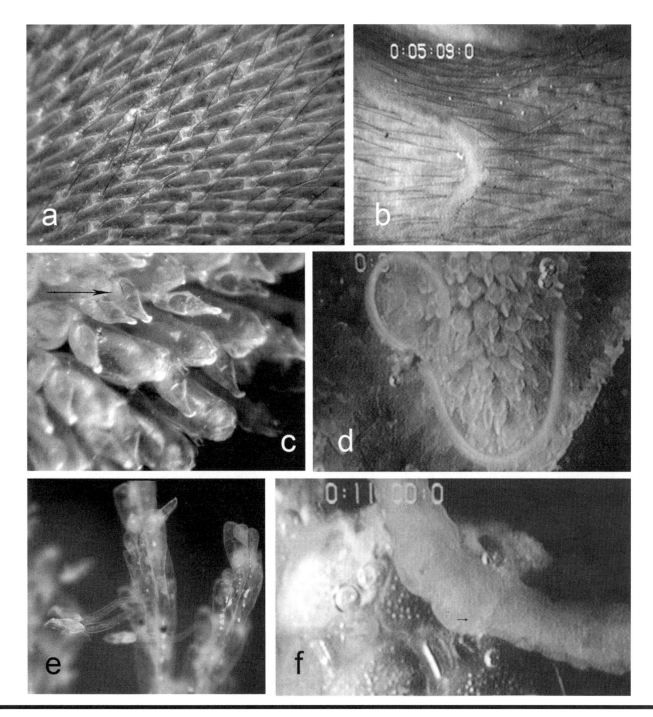

FIGURE 7. Avicularia and vibracula of some Antarctic bryozoan species studied. (a) Living branch of *Nematoflustra* with vibracula in undisturbed position. (b) Vibracula-sweeping polychaete from colony surface (still photo from video). (c) *Beania livingstonei*. Arrow points to one of the bird's head avicularia. (d) Nematode caught by several avicularia (still photo from video). (e) Long-stalked bird's head avicularia of *Camptoplites* colony. (f) Worm speared by one of the sharp-pointed mandibles of *Micropora brevissima*. Tiny arrow points to mandible inside worm's translucent body.

shut. They show no increase in activity when a trespassing organism touches the branches, but when a mandible intercepts an object soft and narrow enough to grasp (such as a polychaete chaeta or arthropod appendage), it snaps shut upon it. The swaying activity then carries the organism toward the edge of the colony (Winston, 1991).

MICROPORA—SESSILE AVICULARIA

Micropora brevissima (Figure 7f) has sessile avicularia with sharply pointed mandibles. In avicularia of this type, the bodies of the avicularia are fixed on the colony, and their mandibles close rarely, remaining in an open position even when zooid opercula are shut. The mandible shuts in response to physical stimuli, probing, jarring, or vibration of palate or mandible. Despite their small size, such avicularia are able to capture and hold relatively large trespassers by their appendages, e.g., cirri of polychaetes or legs of amphipods or pycnogonids. During observations of living colonies of this species carried out at Palmer Station, avicularia of *Micropora* captured several annelids and held them despite their much greater size (Winston, 1991).

CONCLUSIONS

Antarctic bryozoans are taxonomically rich and, like many other Antarctic organisms, show a high degree of endemism. Preliminary analysis of USARP bryozoan collections from the Ross Sea and Antarctic Peninsula yielded 222 species from all three marine orders: five ctenostomes, 28 cyclostomes, and 189 cheilostomes. Hayward (1995) studied Antarctic cheilostomes, primarily from British Antarctic research programs but also including some information from USARP collections. He listed 264 species of cheilostomes, of which 215 (81%) were endemic. Moyano (2005) took a different approach in summarizing taxonomic research on Antarctic bryozoans through 2004. He included taxa from all three orders, but some of his totals included subantarctic species. His list totaled 315 species, 250 (79%) of which were endemic.

Antarctic bryozoans are abundant. It is hard to find a published underwater benthic photograph from the Antarctic in which a bryozoan colony cannot be seen, and in many areas, their skeletons, along with sponge spicules and glacial pebbles, make up a significant component of the sediment. As shown in results from work at Low Island and elsewhere, bryozoans play a significant role in benthic ecosystems, providing habitat and foraging ground as well as a minor food resource for fish and motile invertebrates.

Many of the erect, branching, and foliose bryozoans which form such three-dimensional habitats are perennial, with life spans lasting several years, perhaps several decades. Their growth rates are slow and their fecundity low. *Carbasea ovoidea*, the exception to this pattern at Low Island, is a species whose northernmost range extends into the subantarctic and probably reaches the southernmost extent of its range somewhere along the peninsula (Hayward, 1995).

Most of the Antarctic fish and many other benthic invertebrates that feed among the bryozoans are similarly slow growing and long-lived. Their survival has depended on long-term stability of their environment. Two factors, trawling (illegal fishing), which has already decimated stocks of the most desirable fish species, and global climate change, could have severe consequences for such communities.

The impact of climate change will differ depending on the temperature scenario. As pointed out by Thatje et al. (2005), the lowering of temperatures, leading to a glacial period, could almost completely eliminate the benthic fauna of the Antarctic shelf and slope. Increasing temperatures (as seen today, especially in the West Antarctic) will probably lead to enhanced diversity in a few habitats (e.g., the intertidal zone of the peninsula) but also to a change in present-day communities due to human impact and temperature stress. Human impact, including increased travel, both scientific and touristic, will increase the likelihood of ship fouling (Lewis et al., 2005; Barnes and Conlan, 2007). In addition, an increase in growth rate with higher temperatures has already been detected in one bryozoan, *Cellarinella nutti* (Barnes et al., 2006).

As Collie et al. (2000) noted in their analysis of the impacts of fishing on shelf benthos, there are large gaps in our knowledge of the effects of trawling on three-dimensional epifaunal communities. Reduction in habitat complexity caused by intensive bottom fishing may have long-term negative consequences for fish communities (loss of nest sites and nursery and breeding grounds).

Although benthic habitats with a high degree of structural heterogeneity occur in areas besides Antarctica, such as New Zealand (Bradstock and Gordon, 1983; Batson and Probert, 2000) and Helgoland (de Kluijver, 1991), they are rare. In only one (Tasman Bay, New Zealand) have erect bryozoan communities been protected in an attempt to restore a fishery (Bradstock and Gordon, 1983).

Finally, despite all the biological work that has occurred in the Antarctic since the 1980s, we still have a very poor idea of the link between what happens in pelagic communities and the benthos. A solid understanding of benthic-pelagic coupling, factoring in life histories of structural epibenthos and their epibionts as well as resting stages of phytoplankton, importance of fecal pellets, and the role of benthic meiofauna in food chains and shelf ecosystems, has hardly begun (Marcus and Boero, 1998).

ACKNOWLEDGMENTS

Thanks go to the staff members of SOSC and staff and volunteers at American Museum of Natural History and Virginia Museum of Natural History, who sorted thousands of specimens, and to my colleagues Peter J. Hayward, University of Wales, Swansea, for making several trips to the United States to work on the collections with me, sorting, identifying, and verifying preliminary identification, and Beverly Heimberg, American Museum of Natural History, for her work with me at Palmer Station and American Museum of Natural History. Thanks also go to the Smithsonian Institution for the loan of the specimens and several SOSC and Invertebrate Biology contracts that helped support the sorting, identification, and cataloging of results and to the National Science Foundation for NSF grant DPP-8318457 (1984), which supported the work on ecology and behavior of living Antarctic bryozoans. Thanks to support staff and other scientists at the station in late summer and fall of 1985 and to the crew of the *Polar Duke* for their logistical support and entertainment.

LITERATURE CITED

Arnaud, P. M. 1974. Contribution à la Bionomie Marine Benthic des Regions Antarctiques et Subantarctiques. *Téthys*, 6:467–653.

Arntz, W. E., T. Brey, and V. A. Gallardo. 1994. Antarctic Zoobenthos. *Oceanography and Marine Biology Annual Review*, 32:241–304.

Arntz, W. E., J. Gutt, and M. Klages. 1997. "Antarctic Marine Biodiversity: An Overview." In *Antarctic Communities: Species, Structure and Survival,* ed. W. E. Arntz, J. Gutt, and M. Klages, pp. 3–13. Cambridge: Cambridge University Press.

Barnes, D. K. A. 1994. Communities of Epibiota on Two Species of Erect Antarctic Bryozoa. *Journal of the Marine Biological Association of the United Kingdom*, 47:863–872.

———. 1995a. Sublittoral Epifaunal Communities at Signy Island, Antarctica. I. The Ice-Foot Zone. *Marine Biology*, 121:555–563.

———. 1995b. Sublittoral Epifaunal Communities at Signy Island, Antarctica. II. Below the Ice-Foot Zone. *Marine Biology*, 121:565–572.

———. 1995c. Seasonal and Annual Growth in Erect Species of Antarctic Bryozoans. *Journal of Experimental Marine Biology and Ecology*, 188:181–198.

Barnes, D. K. A., and A. Clarke. 1994. Seasonal Variation in the Feeding Activity of Four Species of Antarctic Bryozoan in Relation to Environmental Factors. *Journal of Experimental Marine Biology and Ecology*, 181:117–133.

———. 1995. Seasonality of Feeding Activity in Antarctic Suspension Feeders. *Polar Biology*, 15:335–340.

Barnes, D. K. A., and K. E. Conlan. 2007. Disturbance, Colonization and Development of Antarctic Benthic Communities. *Philosophical Transactions of the Royal Society*, Series B, 362:11–38.

Barnes, D. K. A., K. Webb, and K. Linse. 2006. Slow Growth of Antarctic Bryozoans Increases over 20 Years and Is Anomalously High in 2003. *Marine Ecology Progress Series*, 314:187–195.

Batson, P. B., and P. K. Probert. 2000. Bryozoan Thickets off Otago Peninsula, New Zealand. *New Zealand Fisheries Assessment Report*, 2000/46.

Belyaev, G. M. 1958. Some Patterns in the Qualitative Distribution of Bottom Fauna in the Antarctic. *Soviet Antarctic Information Bulletin*, 1:119–121.

Bodungen, B. v., V. S. Smetacek, M. M. Tilzer, and B. Zeitzschel. 1986. Primary Production and Sedimentation during Spring in the Antarctic Peninsula Region. *Deep-Sea Research*, Part A, 33:177–194.

Bowden, D. A. 2005. Seasonality of Recruitment in Antarctic Sessile Marine Benthos. *Marine Ecology Progress Series*, 297:101–118.

Bracher, A. 1999. Photoacclimation of Phytoplankton in Different Biogeochemical Provinces of the Southern Ocean and Its Significance for Estimating Primary Production. *Berichte zur Polarforschung*, 341:1–88.

Bradstock, M., and D. P. Gordon. 1983. Coral-like Bryozoan Growths in Tasman Bay, and Their Protection to Conserve Commercial Fish Stocks. *New Zealand Journal of Marine and Freshwater Research*, 17:159–163.

Brey, T., J. Gutt, A. Mackensen, and A. Starmans. 1998. Growth and Productivity of the High Antarctic Bryozoan *Melicerita obliqua*. *Marine Biology*, 132:327–333.

Bullivant, J. S. 1959. Photographs of the Bottom Fauna in the Ross Sea. *New Zealand Journal of Science*, 2:485–497.

Calvet, L. 1904a. Diagnoses de Quelques Espèces de Bryozoaires Nouvelles ou Oncomplètement de la Région Sub-antarctique de l'Océan Atlantique. *Bulletin de la Société zoologique de France*, 29:50–59.

———. 1904b. Bryozoen. *Hamburger Magalhaensische Sammelreise.* Hamburg: L. Friedrichsen & Co.

———. 1909. *Bryozoaires. Expedition Antarctique Française (1903–1905) Commandée par le Dr. Jean Charcot.* Paris: Masson et Cie.

Clarke, A., and N. M. Johnston. 2003. Antarctic Marine Biodiversity. *Oceanography and Marine Biology: An Annual Review*, 41:47–114.

Collie, J. S., S. J. Hall, M. J. Kaiser, and I. R. Poiner. 2000. A Quantitative Analysis of Fishing Impacts on Shelf-Sea Benthos. *Journal of Animal Ecology*, 69:785–798.

Colon-Urban, R., L. Reyes, and J. E. Winston. 1985. Antibiotic Substances from Several Antarctic Bryozoans. *American Zoologist*, 25(4):52A.

Daniels, R. A. 1982. Feeding Ecology of Some Fishes of the Antarctic Peninsula. *Fishery Bulletin*, 80:575–588.

Dayton, P. K. 1990. "Polar Benthos." In *Polar Oceanography*. Part B. *Chemistry, Biology and Geology*, ed. W. O. Smith, Jr., pp. 631–685. San Diego: Academic Press.

Dayton, P. K., G. A. Robilliard, R. T. Paine, and L. B. Dayton. 1974. Biological Accommodation in the Benthic Community at McMurdo Sound, Antarctica. *Ecological Monographs*, 44:105–128.

Dearborn, J. H. 1977. "Foods and Feeding Characteristics of Antarctic Asteroids and Ophiuroids." In *Adaptations within Antarctic Ecosystems*, ed. G. Llano, pp. 293–326. Houston: Gulf Publishing Company.

Delaca, T. E., and J. H. Lipps. 1976. Shallow-Water Marine Associations, Antarctic Peninsula. *Antarctic Journal of the United States*, 11:12–20.

Dell, R. K. 1972. Antarctic Benthos. *Advances in Marine Biology*, 10:1–216.

de Kluijver, M. J. 1991. Sublittoral Hard Substrate Communities off Helgoland. *Helgoländer Meeresuntersuchungen*, 45:317–344.

Ekau, W., and J. Gutt. 1991. Notothenioid Fishes from the Weddell Sea and Their Habitat, Observed by Underwater Photography and Television. *Proceedings of the NIPR Symposium on Polar Biology*, 4: 36–49.

Gallardo, V. A. 1987. The Sublittoral Macrofaunal Benthos of the Antarctic Shelf. *Environment International*, 13:71–81.

Gilbert, N. S. 1991. Primary Production by Benthic Microalgae in Nearshore Marine Sediments of Signy Island, Antarctica. *Polar Biology*, 11:339–346.

Gruzov, E. N. and A. F. Pushkin.1970. "Bottom Communities of the Upper Sublittoral of Enderby Land and the South Shetland Islands." In *Antarctic Ecology*, ed. M. Holdgate, pp.235–238. London: Academic Press.

Gutt, J. 2007. Antarctic Macro-zoobenthic Communities: A Review and an Ecological Classification. *Antarctic Science*, 19:165–182.

Gutt, J., and T. Shickan. 1998. Epibiotic Relationships in the Antarctic Benthos. *Antarctic Science*, 10:398–405.

Hastings, A. B. 1943. Polyzoa (Bryozoa) 1. Scrupcellariidae, Epistomiidae, Fraciminariidae, Bicellariidae, Aeteidae, Scrupariidae. *Discovery Reports*, 32:301–510.

Hayward, P. J. 1995. *Antarctic Cheilostomatous Bryozoa*. Oxford: Oxford University Press.

Hayward, P. J., and J. E. Winston. 1994. New Species of Cheilostomate Bryozoa Collected by the US Antarctic Research Program. *Journal of Natural History*, 28:237–246.

Hedgpeth, J. W. 1969. Introduction to Antarctic Zoogeography. *Antarctic Map Folio Series*, 2:1–9.

———. 1970. "Marine Biogeography of the Antarctic Regions." In *Antarctic Ecology*. Volume 1, ed. M. Holdgate, pp.97–104. London: Academic Press.

Kang, S.-H., and S. H. Lee. 1995. Antarctic Phytoplankton Assemblage in the Western Bransfield Strait Region, February 1993: Composition, Biomass, and Mesoscale Variations. *Marine Ecology Progress Series*, 129:253–267.

Kirkpatrick, R. 1902. "Polyzoa." In *Report on the Collections of Natural History Made in the Antarctic Regions during the Voyage of the "Southern Cross."* XVI, Polyzoa, pp. 286–289. London: Trustees of the British Museum (Natural History).

Kluge, H. 1914. "Die Bryozoen der Deutschen Südpolar-Expeditionen 1901–1903. 1." In *Deutsche Südpolar-Expeditionen*, Volume 15. *Zoologie*, 7:601–678.

Knox, G. A. 2007. *Biology of the Southern Ocean*. 2nd ed. Boca Raton, Fla.: CRC Press.

Lebar, M. D., J. L. Heimbegner, and B. J. Baker. 2007. Cold-Water Marine Natural Products. *Natural Product Reports*, 24:774–797.

Lewis, P. N., M. J. Riddle, and S. D. A. Smith. 2005. Assisted Passage or Passive Drift: A Comparison of Alternative Transport Mechanisms for Non-indigenous Coastal Species into the Southern Ocean. *Antarctic Science*, 17:183–191.

Livingstone, A. A. 1928. The Bryozoa, Supplementary Report. *Scientific Reports, Australasian Antarctic Expedition 1911–1914, Series C, Zoology and Botany*, 9:1–93.

Marchant, H. J. 1985. "Choanoflagellates in the Antarctic Marine Food Chain." In *Antarctic Nutrient Cycles and Food Webs*, ed. W. R. Siegfriend, P. R. Condy, and R. M. Laws, pp. 271–276. Berlin: Springer-Verlag.

Marchant, H. J., and A. McEldowney. 1986. Nanoplankton Siliceous Cysts from Antarctic Are Algae. *Marine Biology*, 92:53–57.

Marcus, N. H., and F. Boero. 1998. Minireview: The Importance of Benthic-Pelagic Coupling and the Forgotten Role of Life Cycles in Coastal Aquatic Systems. *Limnology and Oceanography*, 43:763–768.

McClintock, J. B. 1994. Trophic Biology of Shallow Water Echinoderms. *Marine Ecology Progress Series*, 111:191–202.

Moe, R. L., and T. E. Delaca. 1976. Occurrence of Macroscopic Algae Along the Antarctic Peninsula. *Antarctic Journal of the United States*, 11:20–24.

Moyano, H. I. 2005. 100 Años de Briozoologia Antarctica: Desde la Expedición Antarctica Belga, 1904, hasta la 13ª Conferencia International de Bryzoologia, Concepción, Chile 2004. *Gayana*, 69:122–138.

Nöthig, E.-M., and B. von Bodungen. 1989. Occurrence and Vertical Flux of Faecal Pellets of Probably Protozoan Origin in the Southeastern Weddell Sea (Antarctica). *Marine Ecology Progress Series*, 56:281–289.

Pätzold, J., H. Ristedt, and G. Wefer. 1987. Rate of Growth and Longevity of a Large Colony of *Pentapora foliacea* (Bryozoa) Recorded in Their Oxygen Isotope Profiles. *Marine Biology*, 96:535–538.

Propp, M. B. 1970. "The Study of the Sandy Bottom at Halswell Islands by Scuba Diving." In *Antarctic Ecology*. Volume 1, ed. M. Holdgate, pp. 239–241. London: Academic Press.

Rauschert, M. 1991. Ergebnisse der faunistischen Arbeiten im Benthal von King George Island (Südshetlandinseln, Antarktis). *Berichte zur Polarforschung*, 76:1–75.

Rogick, M. D. 1965. "Bryozoa of the Antarctic." In *Biogeography and Ecology in Antarctica*, ed. J. Van Mieghem and P. Van Oye, pp. 401–403. Monographiae Biologicae, No. 15. The Hague: W. Junk..

Saíz-Salinas, J. I., and A. Ramos. 1999. Biomass Size-Spectra of Macrobenthic Assemblages along Water Depth in Antarctica. *Marine Ecology Progress Series*, 178:221–227.

Saíz-Salinas, J. I., A. Ramos, F. J. Garcìa, J. S. Troncoso, G. San Martin, C. Sanz, and C. Palacín. 1997. Quantitative Analysis of Macrobenthic Soft-Bottom Assemblages in South Shetland Waters (Antarctica). *Polar Biology*, 17:393–400.

San Vincente, C., J. Castelló, J. Corbera, A. Jimeno, T. Munilla, M. C. Sanz, J. C. Sorbe, and A. Ramos. 2007. Biodiversity and Structure of the Suprabenthic Assemblages from South Shetland Islands and Bransfield Strait, Southern Ocean. *Polar Biology*, 30:477–486.

Schwartzbach, W. 1988. Die Fischfauna des östlichen und südlichen Weddellmeeres: geographische Verbreitung, Nahrung und tropische Stellung der Fischarten. *Berichte zur Polarforschung*, 54:1–87.

Sharp, J. H., M. K. Winson, and J. S. Porter. 2007. Bryozoan Metabolites: An Ecological Perspective. *Natural Product Reports*, 24:659–673.

Starmans, A., J. Gutt, and W. E. Arntz. 1999. Mega-epibenthic Communities in Arctic and Antarctic Shelf Areas. *Polar Biology*, 269–280.

Stebbing, A. R. S. 1971a. Growth of *Flustra foliacea* (Bryozoa). *Marine Biology*, 9:267–273.

———. 1971b. The Epizoic Fauna of *Flustra foliacea* (Bryozoa). *Journal of the Marine Biological Association of the United Kingdom*, 51: 283–300.

Targett, T. E. 1981. Trophic Ecology and Structure of Coastal Antarctic Fish Communities. *Marine Ecology Progress Series*, 4:243–263.

Tatián, M., R. Sahade, and G. B. Esnal. 2004. Diet Components in the Food of Antarctic Ascidians Living at Low Levels of Primary Productivity. *Antarctic Science*, 16:123–128.

Thatje, S., C.-D. Hillenbrand, and R. Larter. 2005. On the Origin of Antarctic Benthic Community Structure. *Trends in Ecology and Evolution*, 20:534–540.

Thornely, L. 1924. Polyzoa. *Scientific Reports, Australasian Antarctic Expedition 1911-1914, Series C, Zoology and Botany*, 6:1–23.

Uschakov, P. V. 1963. Quelques Particularités de la Bionomie Benthique de l'Antarctique de l'Est. *Cahiers de Biologie Marine*, 4:81–89.

Varela, M., E. Fernandez, and P. Serret. 2002. Size-Fractionated Phytoplankton Biomass and Primary Production in the Gerlache and South Branfield Straits (Antarctic Peninsula) in Austral Summer 1995–1996. *Deep-Sea Research, Part II*, 49:7409–768.

Vincent, W. F. 1988. *Microbial Ecosystems of Antarctica*. Cambridge: Cambridge University Press.

Waters, A. W. 1904. Bryozoa. Resultats du Voyage du S. Y. 'Belgica' en 1897–99. *Zoologie*, 4:1–114.

White, M. G. 1984. "Marine Benthos." In *Antarctic Ecology.* Volume 2, ed. R. M. Laws, pp. 421–461. London: Academic Press.

White, M. G., and M. W. Robins. 1972. Biomass Estimates from Borge Bay, South Orkney Islands. *Bulletin of the British Antarctic Survey*, 3:45–56.

Winston, J. E. 1977. "Feeding in Marine Bryozoans." In *Biology of Bryozoans*, ed. R. M. Woollacott and R. L. Zimmer, pp. 233–271. New York: Academic Press.

———. 1983. Patterns of Growth, Reproduction and Mortality in Bryozoans from the Ross Sea, Antarctica. *Bulletin of Marine Science*, 33:688–702.

———. 1984. Why Bryozoans Have Avicularia—A Review of the Evidence. *American Museum Novitates*, 2789:1–26.

———. 1991. Avicularian Behavior—A Progress Report. *Bulletin de la Société des Sciences Naturelles de l'Ouest de la France, Mémoire*, HS 1:531–540.

Winston, J. E., and A. W. Bernheimer. 1986. Haemolytic Activity in an Antarctic Bryozoan. *Journal of Natural History*, 20:69–374.

Winston, J. E., and P. J. Hayward. 1994. "Bryozoa of the U.S. Antarctic Research Program: A Preliminary Report." In *Biology and Paleobiology of Bryozoans*, ed. P. J. Hayward, J. S. Ryland, and P. D. Taylor, pp. 205–210. Fredensborg, Denmark: Olsen & Olsen.

Winston, J. E., and B. F. Heimberg. 1988. The Role of Bryozoans in the Benthic Community at Low Island, Antarctica. *Antarctic Journal of the United States*, 21:188–189.

Considerations of Anatomy, Morphology, Evolution, and Function for Narwhal Dentition

Martin T. Nweeia, Frederick C. Eichmiller, Cornelius Nutarak, Naomi Eidelman, Anthony A. Giuseppetti, Janet Quinn, James G. Mead, Kaviqanguak K'issuk, Peter V. Hauschka, Ethan M. Tyler, Charles Potter, Jack R. Orr, Rasmus Avike, Pavia Nielsen, and David Angnatsiak

Martin T. Nweeia, Harvard University, School of Dental Medicine, Boston, MA, USA. Cornelius Nutarak and David Angnatsiak, Community of Mittimatilik, Nunavut, Canada. Frederick C. Eichmiller, Delta Dental of Wisconsin, Stevens Point, WI, USA. Naomi Eidelman, Anthony A. Giuseppetti, and Janet Quinn, ADAF Paffenbarger Research Center, National Institute of Standards and Technology, Gaithersburg, MD, USA. James G. Mead and Charles Potter, Smithsonian Institution, Division of Mammals, Department of Zoology, Washington, DC, USA. Kaviqanguak K'issuk and Rasmus Avike, Community of Qaanaaq, Greenland. Peter V. Hauschka, Smithsonian Institution, Division of Mammals, Department of Zoology, Washington, DC, USA. Ethan M. Tyler, National Institutes of Health, Clinical Center, Bethesda, MD, USA. Jack R. Orr, Fisheries and Oceans Canada, Arctic Research Division, Winnipeg, MB, Canada. Pavia Nielsen, Community of Uummannaq, Greenland. Corresponding author: M. T. Nweeia (martin_nweeia@hsdm.harvard.edu). Accepted 19 May 2008.

ABSTRACT. Interdisciplinary studies of narwhal cranial and tooth anatomy are combined with Inuit traditional knowledge to render a more complete description of tooth-related structures and to propose a new hypothesis for tusk function in the adult male. Gross anatomy findings from computed tomography (CT) and magnetic resonance (MR) imaging and dissections of an adult male and female and one fetus, four to six months in development, were documented. Computed tomography scans rendered images of the tusks and vestigial teeth and their shared sources of innervation at the base of the tusks. Paired and asymmetrical tusks and vestigial teeth were observed in all three samples, and their relative positions reversed during development. Vestigial teeth shifted anteriorly during growth, and the developing tusks moved posteriorly as they developed. Examination of tusk microanatomy revealed the presence of a dentinal tubule network with lumena approximately 2 micrometers in diameter and 10–20 micrometers apart over the pulpal and erupted tusk surfaces. Orifices were present on the cementum surface indicating direct communication and sensory capability from the environment to the inner pulpal wall. Flexural strength of 95 MPa at mid tusk and 165 MPa at the base indicated resistance to high flexural stresses. Inuit knowledge describes a tusk with remarkable and combined strength and flexibility. Elder observations of anatomy are described by variable phenotypes and classified by skin coloration, sex, and tusk expression. Behavioral observations of males leading seasonal migration groups, nonaggressive tusk encounters, and frequent sightings of smaller groups separated by sex add to the discussion of tusk function.

INTRODUCTION

The narwhal is unique among toothed marine mammals and exhibits unusual features, which are described in the literature (Figure 1). A single 2–3 m tusk is characteristic of adult males (Tomlin, 1967). Tusks are horizontally imbedded in the upper jaw and erupt through the left side of the maxillary bone, while the smaller tusk on the right side, usually not longer than 30 cm, remains embedded in the bone. Narwhal thus exhibit an extreme form of dental asymmetry (Hay and Mansfield, 1989; Harrison and King, 1965). One and a half percent of narwhal exhibit double tusks. Such expression is marked by a right tusk that is slightly shorter than the left (Fraser, 1938) and has the same left-handed helix surface morphology (Clark, 1871; Gervais, 1873; Thompson, 1952). An expected tusk antemere would be equal in size and have a mirror-imaged morphology. Thus, narwhal dental asymmetry is uncharacteristic in size and shape. Only in rare instances, such as the fossil record of *Odobenoceptops peruvianus*, a walrus-like cetacean hypothesized to be in the Delphinoidae family and possibly related to Monodontidae, does such tusk asymmetry exist (de Muizon et al., 1999; de Muizon and Domning, 2002). Thus, narwhal dental asymmetry is uncharacteristic in size and shape.

Erupted tusks pierce through the lip, while the embedded tusk remains in bone. Tusk surface morphology is distinguished by a characteristic left-handed helix (Kingsley and Ramsay, 1988; Brear et al., 1990) rarely seen in other tusked mammals, with the exception of unusual examples like elephants that undergo trauma shortly after birth and develop spiraled tusks (Busch, 1890; Colyer, 1915; Goethe, 1949). Most male narwhal have a tusk, while only 15% of females have a tusk (Roberge and Dunn, 1990). When exhibited, female tusks are shorter and narrower than male tusks (Clark, 1871; Pedersen, 1931). Narwhal tusk expression is thus an unusual example of sexual dimorphism in mammalian teeth. Comparative findings are limited for other beaked whales that exhibit sexually dimorphic teeth (Heyning, 1984; Mead, 1989). Fetal narwhal develop six pairs of maxillary teeth and two pairs of mandibular teeth. Only two pairs of upper teeth form in the adult narwhal, the second pair being vestigial and serving no known function.

FIGURE 1. Male narwhal whales with their characteristic tusks.

Many theories have been hypothesized to explain the purpose and function of the erupted tusk. Proposed explanations include a weapon of aggression between males (Brown, 1868; Beddard, 1900; Lowe, 1906; Geist et al., 1960), a secondary sexual characteristic to establish social hierarchy among males (Scoresby, 1820; Hartwig,1874; Mansfield et al., 1975; Silverman and Dunbar, 1980), an instrument for breaking ice (Scoresby, 1820; Tomlin, 1967), a spear for hunting (Vibe, 1950; Harrison and King, 1965; Bruemmer, 1993:64; Ellis, 1980), a breathing organ, a thermal regulator, a swimming rudder (Kingsley and Ramsay, 1988), a tool for digging (Freuchen, 1935; Pederson, 1960; Newman, 1971), and an acoustic organ or sound probe (Best, 1981; Reeves and Mitchell, 1981).

Examination of tusk anatomy, histology, and biomechanics combined with traditional knowledge of Inuit elders and hunters has revealed features that support a new sensory hypothesis for tusk function (Nweeia et al., 2005). Narwhal tusk reaction and response to varying salinity gradients introduced during field experiments support this.

GROSS CRANIAL AND TOOTH ANATOMY

Three narwhal head samples, obtained during legal Inuit harvests in 2003 and 2005 were examined by computerized axial tomography and magnetic resonance imaging and then dissected. They included one adult male, one adult female, and one fetal specimen between four and six months in its development. The department of radiology at Johns Hopkins Hospital conducted computed tomography (CT) scans on all three specimens using a Siemens Medical Solutions SOMATOM Sensation Cardiac 64. The scanner generated 0.5-mm-thick slices on each of the three specimens. Original data from these scans has been archived at the Smithsonian Institution. Materialize Mimics 8.0 and Discreet 3D Studio Max 7 was used to create digital 3-D models of narwhal dental anatomy. Magnetic resonance imaging (MRI) was also used to investigate and visualize narwhal dental anatomy. Scientists at the National Institutes of Health MRI Research Facility conducted MRI on the thawed narwhal heads. Data from MRI assisted verification of known cranial anatomy and enabled examination of tooth vasculature. The narwhal heads were dissected at the Osteo-Prep Laboratory at the Smithsonian Institution, and digital photographs were taken to record anatomical landmarks and features of gross anatomy.

The skull of the fetus was 6.23 cm in length and 4.96 cm in width at the most distal points on its frontal bones (Figure 2). Computed tomography data were collected for the entire body of the fetus, though only the head was investigated for the purpose of this research. The total length of the specimen was 31.68 cm. Calcification of major bones of the skull was incomplete in the fetal narwhal specimen. The top of the skull was smoothly rounded, with a large anterior fontanelle, and there were lateral vacuities where ossification was incomplete. Most of the main membrane bones were present at this stage. The nasal bones were small elliptical bones positioned on the summit of the head dorsal to the tectum nasi; they did not make medial contact. The premaxillae were long, narrow shafts of bone medial to maxillae. The maxillae were large bones that were excavated anteroventrally to form two conspicuous pairs of tooth sockets, or alveoli. The maxillae overlapped the frontal bones. Pre- and postorbital processes were well developed. The parietal bones were small lateral bones that made contact with frontal

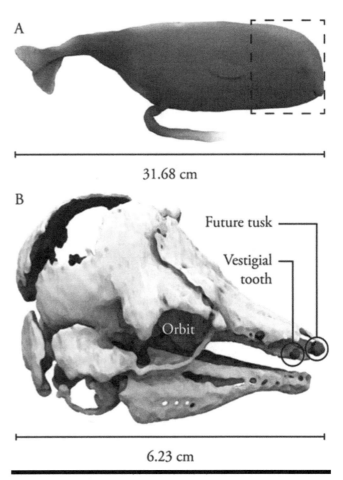

FIGURE 2. A drawing made from CT scans of the skull and teeth of a narwhal fetus showing the positions of the teeth.

bones on their anterior borders. As some of the bone was very thin and articulated with cartilage, digital models of the specimen had some minor artifacts.

Two pairs of teeth were evident in the upper jaw of the fetal narwhal specimen. Future tusks and vestigial teeth were located in their respective sockets in the maxillary bones. The future tusks were located anteromedially to the vestigial pair of teeth. These moved in a posterior direction during development, forming the two large tusks in the adult narwhal (Figure 3). In the male, the left future tusk usually becomes the erupted tusk, and the right tusk typically remains embedded in the maxilla. The future tusks exhibited asymmetry, with the right being 0.44 cm

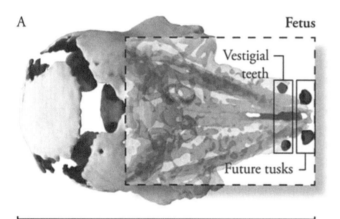

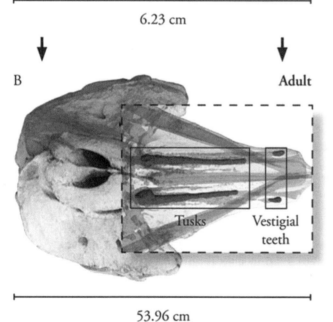

FIGURE 3. A drawing showing the migration and reversal of position of the teeth from fetus to adult that occurs during development.

in length and 0.38 cm in width at its widest point and the left being 0.36 cm length and 0.36 cm in width at its widest point.

The vestigial pair of teeth also exhibited asymmetry. The right vestigial tooth was 0.26 cm in length and 0.25 cm in width at its widest point, and the left vestigial tooth was 0.32 cm in length and 0.25 cm in width at its widest point. No teeth were evident in the mandible of this fetus, though dental papillae in the lower jaw have been documented in a report that describes up to six pairs of teeth in the upper jaw and two pairs in the lower jaw (Eales, 1950). The vestigial pair of teeth and their shared blood and nerve supply with the tusks suggest that the narwhal may have exhibited at least two well-developed pairs of teeth at some point in its evolution.

The head of the adult female narwhal was 55.82 cm in length and 47.90 cm in width at its base. The skull of the specimen was 53.96 cm in length and 35.08 cm in width at the level of the bases of the embedded tusks. Like most cetaceans in the family Odontoceti, the skull of the narwhal was asymmetrical, with bony structures skewed toward the left side of the head.

Two pairs of teeth were visible in the upper jaw of the female narwhal specimen (Figures 4 and 5). Both pairs, tusks and vestigial, were found in their respective sockets in the maxillae. The tusks were located posteromedially to the vestigial pair. In the female, the paired tusks typically remain embedded in the maxillae, as was the case for this specimen. The tusks exhibited asymmetry. The right tusk was 17.47 cm in length, 2.39 cm in width at its base, and 0.80 cm in width at its distal end. The left tusk was 18.33 cm in length, 2.06 cm in width at its base, and 1.07 cm in width at its distal end. In rare cases, the left tusk of the female erupts from the maxilla. Sockets for the tusks in the skull begin at the bases of the teeth and terminate in the most distal part of each respective maxillary bone.

The vestigial pair of teeth also exhibited asymmetry. The right vestigial tooth was 2.39 cm in length and 0.98 cm in width at its widest point. The left vestigial tooth was 1.90 cm in length and 0.98 cm in width at its widest point. Sockets for the vestigial teeth began near the bases of the tusks and, like the tusks, terminated in the most distal part of each maxillary bone. The right vestigial tooth slightly protruded from the bone. During dissection and preparation, vestigial teeth may be lost because they are not securely embedded in the bone. There is limited documentation on the presence and morphology of vestigial teeth. Evidence of developed sockets for the vestigial teeth in the narwhal is significant, as it suggests that this species may have exhibited at least two well-developed pairs of teeth

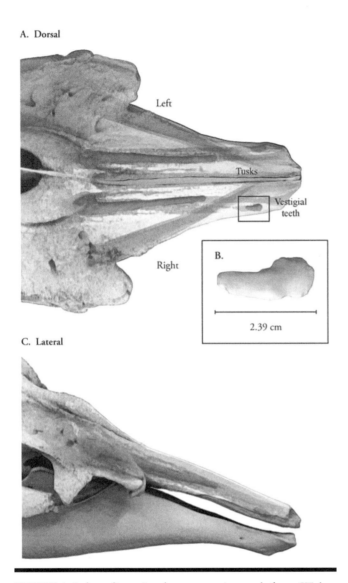

A. Dorsal

Left

Tusks

Vestigial
teeth

Right

B.

2.39 cm

C. Lateral

FIGURE 4. A three dimensional reconstruction made from CT data of the adult female dentition of *M. monoceros* showing (A) the dorsal view and (C) lateral view of the unerupted tusks with (B) detail of left vestigial tooth.

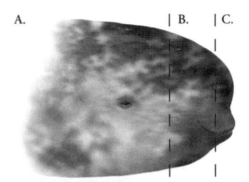

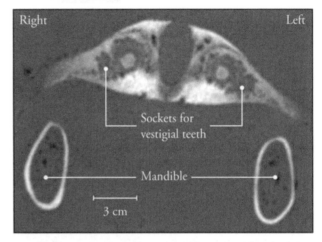

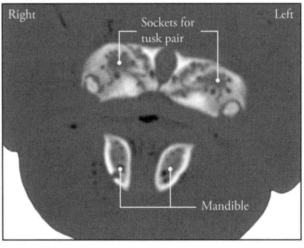

FIGURE 5. (A) Lateral view of the complete female head with coronal cuts (B) and (C). (B) shows the embedded tusks and vestigial teeth and (C) shows vestigial teeth with vascularized tusk sockets.

at some point in its evolution. The two pairs of teeth also effectively reverse positions during development.

On the basis of intracranial dissection of the trigeminal or fifth cranial nerve, the optic nerve branch passed through the superior orbital fissure (Figure 6). The maxillary branch, a sensory nerve, passed through the foramen rotundum, and the mandibular nerve branch, a motor and sensory nerve, passed through the foramen ovale.

The head of the male narwhal was 62.33 cm in length and 49.70 cm in width at its base. The skull of the speci-

men was 57.24 cm in length and 35.01 cm in width at the level of the base of the left tusk. Like the female narwhal, the skull of the male narwhal was asymmetrical, and bony structures skewed toward the left side of the head.

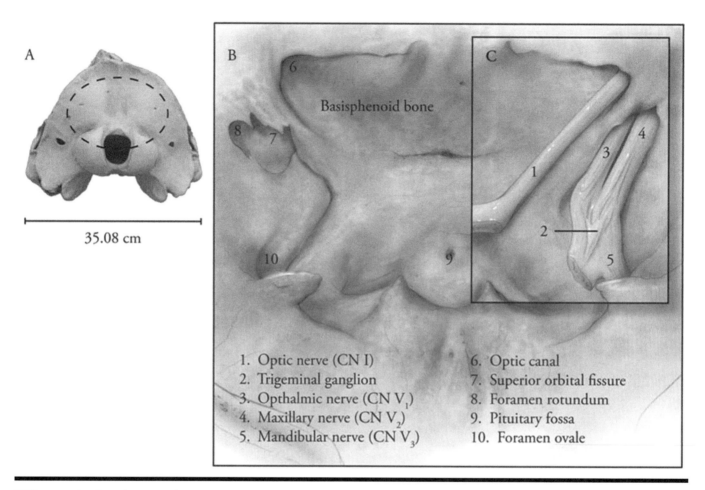

FIGURE 6. (A) Three dimensional reconstruction made from CT data showing the posterior view of the adult female *M. monoceros* skull with the access opening for intracranial dissection, and (B, C) a drawing from photographs taken during dissection showing the nerves and foramen at the cranial base.

Two pairs of teeth were visible in the upper jaw of the male narwhal specimen (Figure 7). The paired tusks were located posteromedially to the vestigial pair of teeth. As is typical with the species, the right tusk remained embedded in the skull, and the left tusk erupted from the maxilla. The right tusk was 20.81 cm in length and 2.51 cm at its base; it was 0.96 cm in width at its distal end. The left tusk was 89.62 cm in length and 4.33 cm in width at its base. It was 4.36 cm in width as it exited the maxilla, and 2.96 cm in width at the termination of CT data at 56.45 cm distal to the maxilla. Bony sockets for the tusks began at the bases of the teeth and terminated in the most distal part of each respective maxillary bone. The vestigial pair of teeth also exhibited asymmetry. Unlike the vestigial teeth of the female specimen, the vestigial teeth of the male narwhal were not embedded in bone; they were suspended in the tissue lateral to the maxillae. The right vestigial tooth was 0.59 cm in length and 0.21 cm in width at its widest point; the left vestigial tooth was 0.67 cm in length and 0.20 cm in width at its widest point.

The Inuit classify narwhal with separate names on the basis of skin color and tusk expression. For example, a male with black coloration is ᕿᓂᕐᑐᖅ, and a male with white coloration is ᖃᑯᕐᑐᖅ. Males with a shorter and wider tusk are called ᑐᒡᐱᑐᖃ, and those with a longer, narrower tusk and black skin coloration are ᑐᒡᓕᖕᓂᖅᐃ. Several Inuit from High Arctic communities in northwestern Greenland are able to recognize and differentiate narwhal populations from Canada and Greenland by their body form and their behavior. They describe Canadian narwhal as being narrower through the length of their bodies and more curious and social, while the Greenlandic narwhal

A

B

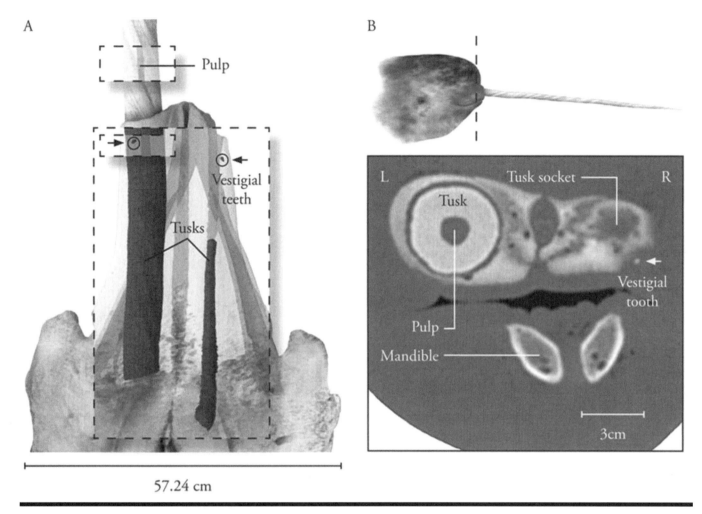

57.24 cm

FIGURE 7. (A) Three dimensional reconstruction made from CT data of the adult male dentition of *M. monoceros* showing the dorsal view of the fully developed tusk, the unerupted tusk, and the vestigial teeth, and (B) a lateral view of the complete head illustrating the location of the coronal slice at the level of the right vestigial tooth.

are wider and more bulbous in the anterior two thirds of their bodies and taper at the tail. Their personalities are described as being shyer, and thus they are more elusive.

GROSS TUSK MORPHOLOGY

A 220-cm-long tusk harvested in 2003 at Pond Inlet, Nunavut, Canada, during the Inuit hunting season was sectioned in the field using a reciprocating saw into transverse slices averaging approximately 5 cm in length. Sectioning was started approximately 40 cm inside the skull from the point of tusk eruption and as close to the devel-

oping base as possible. The sections were immersed in an aqueous solution of 0.2% sodium azide and frozen in individual serially identified containers. The sections were first evaluated for gross features and dimensions while intact, and selected specimens were further sectioned for more detailed microscopy.

Gross section measurements revealed an outer diameter tapering evenly from approximately 6 cm at the base to 1.6 cm at the tip (Figure 8). The tusk diameter increased evenly to the point of eruption at approximately 175 cm from the tip and then decreased rapidly within the skull. A regression of average outer diameter to distance from the tip for the length of tusk starting at the point of eruption

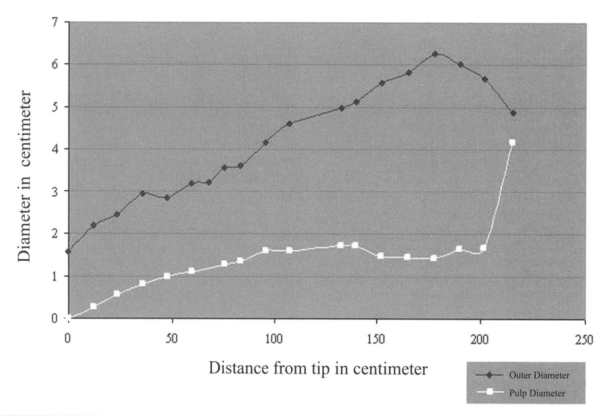

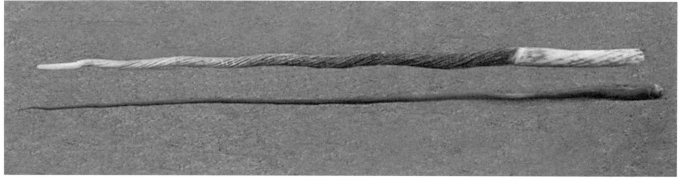

FIGURE 8. (top) A plot of the average cross sectional diameter in cm of the outer surface and pulp chambers of the sectioned tusk as a function of distance from the tip. (bottom) Photograph shows pulpal tissue removed from an intact tusk.

resulted in an equation yielding the average diameter in centimeters as follows: Diameter = 1.75 + 0.025 × (distance from tip), with an R^2 value of 0.989.

The average pulp chamber diameter is shown in lower plot of the graph in Figure 8 and does not mirror the linear trend of the outer diameter. The chamber tapers evenly for the first 100 cm from the tip and then reaches a plateau of approximately 1.75 cm for the next 50 cm and decreases in diameter slightly at 150 to 175 cm from the tip. The

pulp diameter increases dramatically over the last 10 cm at base of the tusk. Soft tissue remnants were visible in the pulp chamber of all the frozen sections. A photo of an intact tusk with the entire body of pulp tissue removed is shown in the photograph in Figure 8.

The cross sections of the tusk were often not symmetric, but rather slightly oblong, with a major diameter in many sections being several millimeters larger than the minor diameter. The shape of the pulp chamber generally mimicked the shape and profile of the outer surface. The walls of the inner pulp chamber were very smooth when observed after removing the soft tissue remnants.

The outer surface of the tusk demonstrated a series of major and minor ridges and valleys that progressed down the length of the tusk following a left-hand helix. The major ridges were anywhere from 2 to 10 mm in width and 1 to 2 mm in depth, while the minor ridges were approximately 0.1 mm in width and depth. Brown and green deposits covered the major valleys, while the tops of the highest and broadest ridges were clean and white, accentuating the helical pattern of these features (Figure 9).

The tip section was relatively smooth with an oblique, slightly concave facet approximately 3 cm in length extending backward from the rounded end (Figure 10). A small stained deposit was present in the deepest depression of the facet. Higher magnification did not reveal surface scratches indicating abrasive wear, and a small occluded remnant of the pulp chamber could be seen at the tip. The surface of the facet had what appeared to be many small grooves and smooth indentations on the surface that may be due to the exposure of softer areas in the layered tissue described later in the microanalysis. The lack of abrasion scratches, the concave profile, and these small depressions

indicate that the facet is more likely due to a combination of abrasion and erosion from abrasive slurry, such as sand, rather than being caused by rubbing against a hard abrasive surface. Facets were found on many but not all tusks observed during the hunting season, while all exhibit the smoothly polished or clean tip section of approximately 10 cm in length. It was not possible to determine the anatomical orientation of the facet in the sectioned tusk, but field observations describe it as varying in orientation from right, left, and downward, with an upward orientation rarely being reported.

Inuit descriptions of gross tusk morphology are described by variations of form within each sex and dimorphic traits that differentiate tusk expression in females. Most hunters note that the blood and nerve supply in the pulp extends to the tip, and indeed, some hunters are experienced in the extirpation of the pulp to its entire length. They describe a receding pulpal chamber for older narwhal, which is a consistent finding with the increased age of most mammalian teeth. However, the female tusk is quite different in morphology. Female tusks are shorter, narrower, and evenly spiraled and denser, with little or no pulp chamber, even at an early age. Such an observation suggests a difference in functional adaptation as females

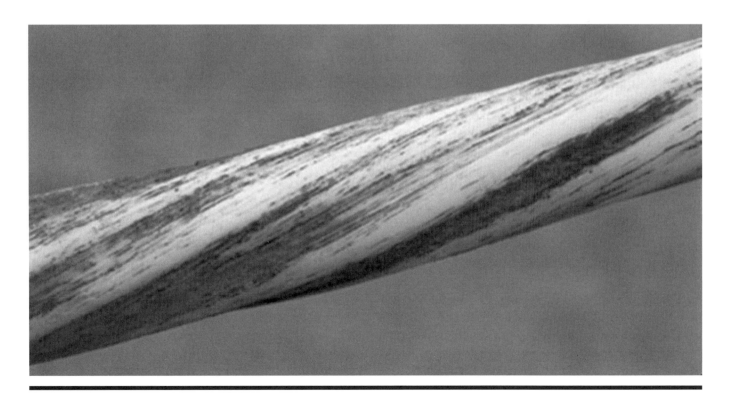

FIGURE 9. A photograph showing the helical staining due to surface deposits of algae that remain in the deeper grooves of the tusk.

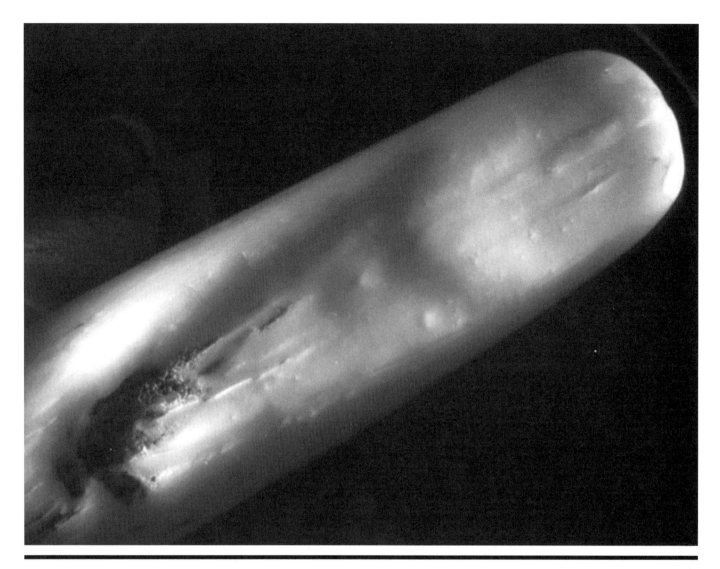

FIGURE 10. A close-up photograph of the flat facet on the tip of the tusk. A translucent remnant of the pulp chamber can be seen at the tip as well as many minor grooves and indentations.

would lack substantial tusk innervation to sense their environment.

TUSK MICROMORPHOLOGY

A mid-length section was chosen for visible and scanning electron microscopy (SEM). A 1-mm-thick slice was cut from the end of a section and polished using a metallographic polishing wheel and a series of abrasives down to 4000 grit size. Care was taken to retain the hydration of the section during processing and observation. The cross-sectional visual observation of this slice showed the tusk to be composed of several distinct layers (Figure 11). An outermost layer described as cementum was more translucent and approximately 1.5 to 2 mm thick. There was a distinct boarder between this outermost layer and the underlying dentin. The bulk of the section was made up of a relatively homogenous dentin that had numerous distinct rings, appearing much like the growth rings in a tree. The outermost rings were slightly whiter in color while the innermost ring adjacent to the pulp chamber appeared slightly darker opaque than the surrounding dentin rings. The dark lines radiating outward from the pulp chamber to the surface were associated with microtubules observable under SEM and are described later.

An additional pie-shaped section was cut from this polished slice to include both the pulpal and outer sur-

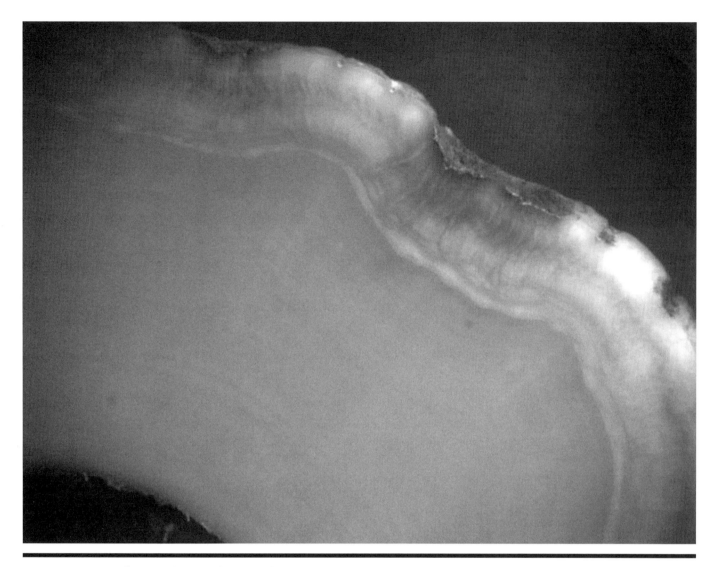

FIGURE 11. A transilluminated corner of a polished cross section showing the many distinct layer or rings within the tissue. The wide band of tissue making up the outer surface is described as "cementum."

faces for SEM observation. The specimen was cleaned to remove surface debris using a mild HCL acid etch followed by rinsing in dilute sodium hypochlorite. This piece was then dried in a vacuum dessicator and gold sputter coated for conductivity. The SEM images of the outer surface showed that the dark stain material found at the base of the grooves was made up of microscopic diatoms from algae deposits adhering in multiple layers to the surface (Figure 12).

The smooth white ridge areas were regions where these deposits were either very sparse or completely missing. The level of artifacts and debris on the surface made it difficult to observe the underlying tooth surface as cleaning did not remove the tightly adhered deposits in the grooves

but did occasionally expose the ends of small tubule-like canals opening to the tusk surface. A more thorough cleaning removed more of the deposits and exposed the outer openings with regular frequency (Figure 13). These openings were approximately one to two micrometers in diameter and were similar in appearance to those found on the pulpal surface of the dentin.

Scanning electron microscopy observation of the pulpal surface of the section revealed the openings of multiple dentin tubules. These dentin tubules ranged from 0.5 to several micrometers in diameter and were evenly distributed with spacing of approximately 10 to 20 micrometers between tubules (Figure 14). This spacing was less dense than that observed on the pulpal surfaces of human or bovine teeth,

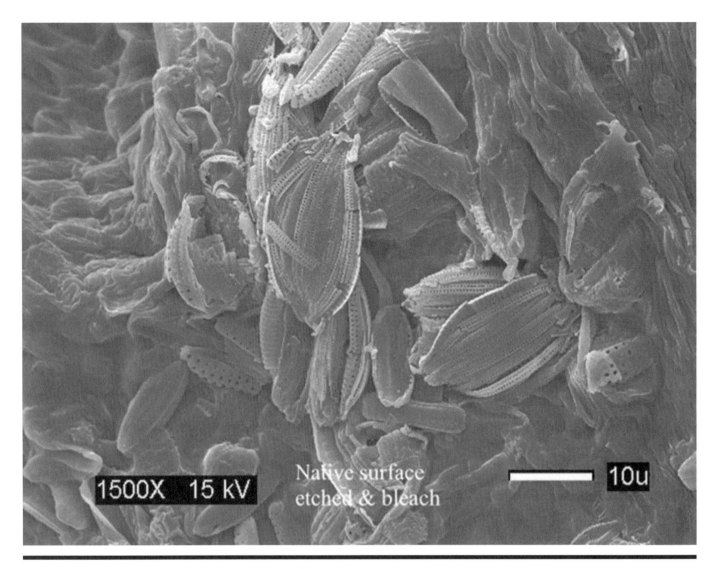

FIGURE 12. A scanning electron micrograph of the outside tusk surface showing stain deposits composed of diatoms and algae.

where spacing is approximately 3 to 5 micrometers between tubules. The appearance of the bell-shaped openings and lumen of the tubules was similar to that observed in the teeth of other mammals. The cross-sectional surface of one pie-shaped piece was acid etched to remove the collagen smear layer that forms as an artifact of polishing. This section and other serial sections taken across the tubules revealed that the tubules radiated outward from the pulpal surface through the entire thickness of the dentin and appeared to communicate into the outermost cementum surface layer (Figure 15). This observation is in contrast to what is found in masticating teeth of mammals, where tubules radiate through the body of the dentin but terminate within dentin or at the base of the outer enamel layer.

The flexural strength of the dentin from two fresh sections, one close to the base and one mid length down the tusk, was measured using $2 \times 2 \times 15$ mm rectangular bars cut longitudinally down the length of the tusk. These bars were loaded to fracture in a three-point bending mode over a 10-mm span using a universal testing machine. Nine specimens were cut from the midsection of the tusk and four from the base section. The transverse rupture strength at the midsection was 94.6 ± 7.0 MPa (mean $\pm$ standard deviation) and 165.0 ± 11.7 MPa near the base. The bars from near the base underwent much more deformation prior to fracture than those from the midsection with approximately twice the amount of strain occurring at fracture.

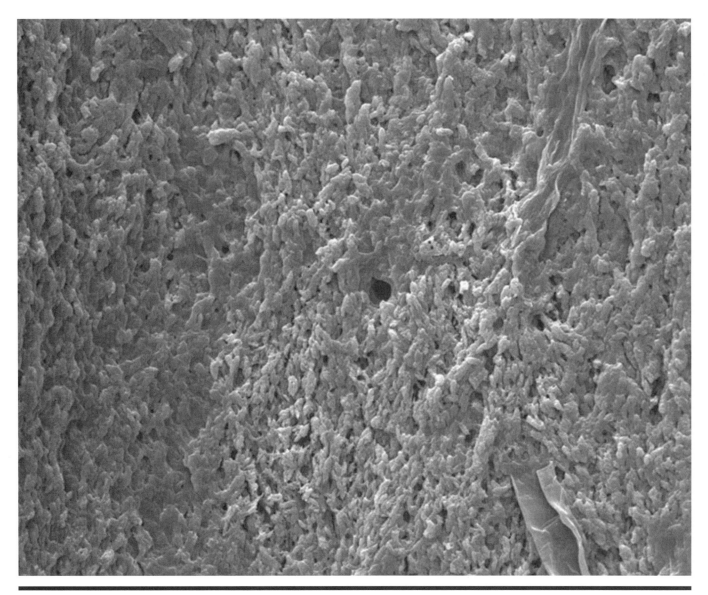

FIGURE 13. A scanning electron micrograph at 1000X magnification of the outer surface of the tusk after cleaning deposits from the surface. Tubule openings can be observed on the surface at a regular frequency. The large center orifice is approximately two micrometers in diameter.

DISCUSSION

Imaging and dissection of adult male, adult female, and fetal narwhal specimens recorded a detailed visual record of the cranial and dental anatomy. Among the findings were three new discoveries of the dental anatomy and one observation of growth and development for the tusks. The first major finding was the presence of paired vestigial teeth in all three specimens. Although a previous report in the literature found single vestigial teeth in a small collection of narwhal skulls (Fraser, 1938), this is the first study to document paired vestigial teeth. The lack of prior documentation on vestigial teeth may be due to their location, as they were embedded in bone in the female specimen and suspended in the tissue located lateral to the anterior third of the maxillary bone plate. Radiography and digital imaging provided an undisturbed view of these teeth in situ. The second discovery was linked to the anatomical location of all four maxillary teeth and their relative locations during growth and development as the two pairs of teeth reverse positions. In the fetus, the future tusks are located anteromedially to the vestigial teeth pair of teeth at four to

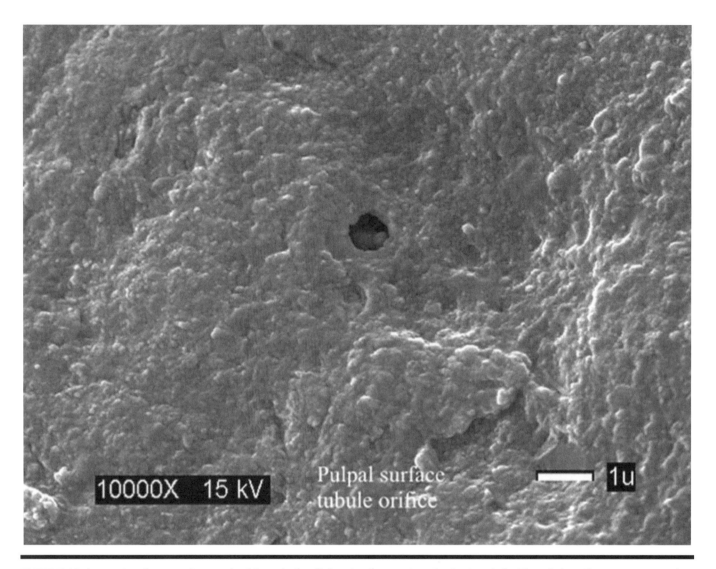

FIGURE 14. A scanning electron micrograph of the pulpal wall showing the opening of a dentin tubule. The tubule orifice is approximately 1 micrometer in diameter. The size and shape of the tubules is similar to those found in human and other mammalian teeth.

six months in development. The fully developed tusks are located posteromedially to the vestigial pair of teeth in the adult narwhal. The third finding was evidence of developed sockets for the vestigial teeth that extend posteriorly to the base of the developed tusks and communicate with their nerve and blood supply. Evidence of these developed vestigial tooth sockets suggests that this species may have exhibited at least two pairs of well-developed teeth at some point in its evolution. Likewise, if the vestigial teeth never existed beyond their current state, then well-developed sockets for these structures would not be expected as visualized in the fetal and adult female specimen. Intracranial dissection revealed fifth cranial nerve pathways that were consistent with other mammals, though there were some expected modifications based on the skull asymmetry.

The gross morphology of the male narwhal tusk showed a surprisingly unique feature by having a nearly full length pulp chamber. This observation is confirmed by most of the Inuit interviewed, though this feature has dimorphic characteristics, as traditional knowledge describes females with little to no pulp chamber, even at younger ages. This is much different from other tusked mammals, where the pulp chamber is often only a small proportion of the tusk length. It would also seem counterintuitive for a tooth evolving in a harsh and cold environment to contain vital vascular and nervous tissue through-

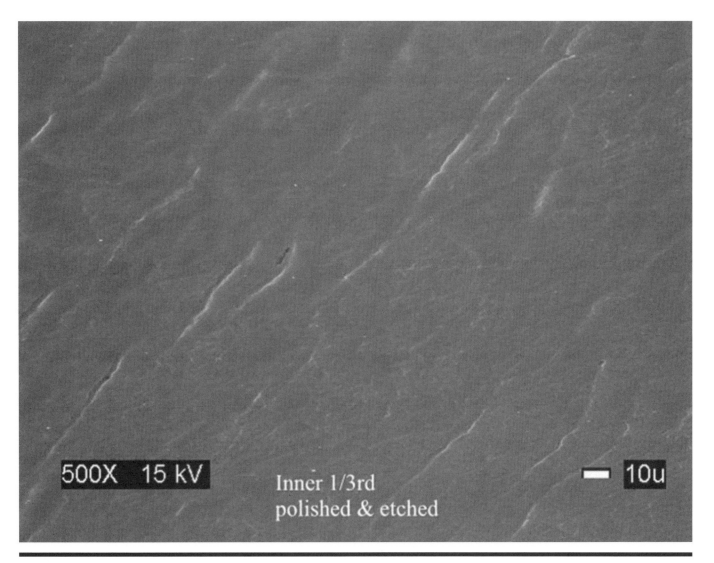

FIGURE 15. A scanning electron micrograph of a polished section of dentin shows the radiating and continuous nature of the tubules. Serial cross sections of tubules confirmed their presence throughout the tusk wall.

out its length. The pulp chamber also compromises the strength of this long and seemingly fragile tooth. The residual chamber seen at the tip of the tusk indicates that the chamber forms throughout tusk growth and development. One conversation with a broker of harvested tusks revealed that occasionally, a tusk is seen where the pulp chamber is very small and narrow and this usually occurs in larger and older tusks. It was not possible to verify the order or timing of dentin deposition using the methods of this study, but the possibility exists that the inner pulpal layer of dentin may be a feature of dentin formed at a later stage of tooth development or as a process of aging.

The left-hand helical nature of tooth development has been hypothesized to be a functional adaptation to main-tain the overall concentric center of mass during growth. This hypothesis certainly makes a great deal of sense when one considers the hydrodynamic loads that would develop if the tooth were curved or skewed to one side. The clean smooth tip and facet observed in this specimen appears to be a secondary feature resulting from some form of abrasion and/or erosion. The lack of scratch patterns and the presence of large and small concavities across the facet indicate it is not formed by abrasion against a hard surface, but rather could result from gradual attrition by an abrasive slurry, such as sand or sediment. This cleanly polished tip appears on every tusk observed, regardless of the presence or absence of the facet. The behavior that causes this feature must be almost universal and is likely to be continuous, as the algae deposits that stain the surface would likely reappear if not continually removed. Water turbulence alone would probably not account for removal of these deposits from the tip and ridge areas of the tusk. The cleaned ridges are also smoothed, indicating that they could be cleaned by physically rubbing against a surface such as ice. There have also been traditional knowledge descriptions of "tusking," where males will gather in small groups and rub tusks in a nonaggressive manner. Hunters clean harvested tusks by rubbing them with sand to remove these deposits. Perhaps tusks come in contact with sand and sediment when narwhal feed close to the bottom.

The cementum layer on the outer surface of the tusk is also a rare feature for an erupted tooth. Cementum is generally found as a transitional layer between dentin and the periodontal ligaments that hold teeth into bone. These ligaments are able to attach to the cementum with small fibers, tying it to the surrounding bone. This appears to be consistent with the cementum observed in sections from the tusk base that were attached to segments of bone. In human teeth, however, if cementum becomes exposed to the oral environment, it is rapidly worn away, exposing the root dentin. In the tusk, the cementum layer appears to remain intact, even after long exposure to the ocean

FIGURE 16. A section (2.0 cm corresponding to the third plotted point in Figure 8) cut near the tusk tip showing multiple dentin rings under transillumination.

environment. The thickness of the cementum layer also appears to increase as the tooth increases in diameter. Cementum in mammalian teeth is generally a more proteinaceous tissue with greater toughness than enamel or dentin. A toughened outer layer that increases in thickness toward the tusk base would be consistent with the mechanics of fracture resistance, where tensile stresses would also be highest at the tusk surface and base. This toughened layer of tissue would resist cracking under functional stresses that could lead to tusk fracture.

It is impossible to tell from these studies what causes color changes that distinguish the rings observed within the dentin, but one possibility would be a change in developmental growth conditions, such as nutrition (Nweeia et al., in press) (Figure 16). The flexural strength and work of fracture both increased for dentin when comparing the tusk base to the midsection. The flexural strengths of 95 MPa at mid tusk and 165 MPa at the base compare to approximately 100 MPa for human dentin. These are adaptations for a tooth that must withstand high flexural stresses and deformation rather than the compressive loads of chewing.

The microanatomy of the tusk also provides insight into potential function. Scanning electron micrographs of the pulpal surface revealed tubule features that are similar in size and shape to the dentin tubules found in masticating teeth. The tubule diameters are similar to those observed in human teeth, but the spacing of these tubules across the pulpal wall is three to five times wider than that seen in human dentin. The polished cross sections show that these tubules run continuously throughout the entire thickness of dentin, just as they do in human dentin. A surprising finding, however, was the presence of tubule orifices on the outer surface of the cementum. This indicates that the dentin tubules communicate entirely through the wall of the tusk with the ocean environment. It is well established that dentin tubules in human and animal teeth provide sensory capabilities. Exposure of these tubules to the oral environment in human teeth is responsible for sensing temperature changes, air movement, and the presence of chemicals, such as sugar. An example of this phenomenon would be the pain one senses in a cavity when the tooth is exposed to sugar or cold air. The decay from the cavity removes the overlying protective enamel and exposes the underlying dentin, allowing the dentin tubules to communicate directly with the oral cavity. Changes in temperature, air movement, or osmotic gradient set up by the sugar cause movement of fluid within these tubules. This movement is detected by neurons at the pulpal end of the tubule, and these neurons send the pain signal to our brains. Narwhal teeth have similar physiology to human teeth, having both pulpal neurons and dentin tubules. The most distinguishing difference is that the tubules in the narwhal tusk are not protected by an overlying layer of enamel. This raises the distinct possibility that the tusk could provide a variety of sensory capabilities. Any stimulus that would result in movement of fluid within these tubules could possibly elicit a response (Figure 17). These include ion gradients, such as water salinity, pressure gradients caused by dive depth or atmospheric pressure changes, air temperature and movement, or possibly other chemical stimuli specific to food sources or environment. Field experiments on three captive male narwhal completed during August 2007 in the Canadian High Arctic provided evidence that water salinity is one stimulus that can be sensed by this tusk. Introduction of a high salt ion solution (approximately 42 psu), immediately after freshwater exposure, within a fixed gasket isolating a 35-cm portion of tusk surface, produced a marked movement of the head region and coordinated respiratory response. Two separate salt ion solution stimuli in two males and one stimulus in the third

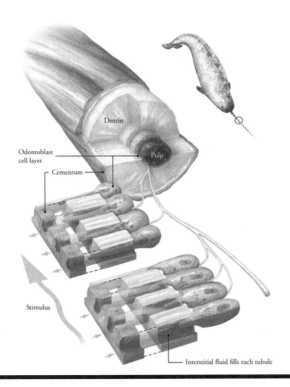

FIGURE 17. Tusk of male *M. monoceros* as a hydrodynamic sensor. The anatomic features of the narwhal tusk provide the potential for sensing stimuli that would result in movement of interstitial fluid within the dentin tubules. This fluid movement stimulates neurons located at cellular odontoblastic layer found at the base of each tubule.

male were witnessed by twelve team members. Responses subsided immediately after freshwater was reintroduced to the tusk gasket. Though monitoring equipment was attached to the whale during experimentation, physiologic data recordings (EEG and ECG) were hindered by difficult field conditions.

ACKNOWLEDGMENTS

Our sincere and kind thanks, *qujanamik*, to the Inuit High Arctic communities of Nunavut and northwestern Greenland and the 55 elders and hunters who gave their time and *Inuit Qaujimajatuqangit*, knowledge to add to the understanding for this extraordinary marine mammal and its unique tusk. We also wish to acknowledge the support of the National Science Foundation; Astromed's Grass Telefactor Division for their gracious support in loaning electroencephalographic equipment; Arctic Research Division, Fisheries and Oceans, Canada; the National Geographic Society, The Explorers Club, World Center for Exploration, the National Institutes of Health's (NIH) Imaging Department, and the Johns Hopkins University's Integrated Imaging Center, as well as individuals, including Leslee Parr, San Jose State University; Sam Ridgway, Judith St. Ledger, and Keith Yip, Sea World, San Diego; Joseph Meehan; Jim (Wolverine) Orr; Giuseppe Grande; Glenn Williams, Director of Wildlife, Nunavut Tunngavik, Inc.; Doug Morris and John Butman, NIH MRI Research Facility; Sandie Black, Head of Veterinary Services, Calgary Zoo Animal Care Centre; Rune Dietz, Department of Arctic Environment, National Environmental Research Institute; Mosesie Kenainak; Mogens Andersen, Assistant Curator, Vertebrate Department, Zoological Museum of Copenhagen; Michel Gosselin and Natalia Rybczynski, Canadian Museum of Nature; Judith Chupasko and Mark Omura, Museum of Comparative Zoology, Harvard University; Lisa Marie Leclerc, University of Quebec at Rimouski; Kevin Hand, Newsweek Corporation; Bruce Crumley, Hawk Enterprises; and William Fitzhugh, Daryl Domning, and Dee Allen, National Museum of Natural History, Smithsonian Institution.

EXPANDED AUTHOR INFORMATION

Martin T. Nweeia, Harvard University, School of Dental Medicine, 188 Longwood Ave, Boston, MA 02115, USA; also Smithsonian Institution, Division of Mammals, Department of Zoology, 100 Constitution Avenue, Washington, DC 20056, USA. Cornelius Nutarak and David Angnatsiak, Community of Mittimatilik, Nunavut X0A

0S0, Canada. Frederick C. Eichmiller, Delta Dental of Wisconsin, 2801 Hoover Road, Stevens Point, WI 54481, USA. Naomi Eidelman, Anthony A. Giuseppetti, and Janet Quinn, ADAF Paffenbarger Research Center, National Institute of Standards and Technology, 100 Bureau Drive, Gaithersburg, MD 20899-8546, USA. James G. Mead and Charles Potter, Smithsonian Institution, Division of Mammals, Department of Zoology, 100 Constitution Avenue, Washington, DC 20056, USA. Kaviqanguak K'issuk and Rasmus Avike, Community of Qaanaaq, Greenland 3980. Peter V. Hauschka, Children's Hospital, Department of Orthopaedic Surgery, Boston, MA 02115, USA. Ethan M. Tyler, National Institutes of Health, Clinical Center, 9000 Rockville Pike, Bethesda, MD 20892, USA. Jack R. Orr, Fisheries and Oceans, Canada, Arctic Research Division, 501 University Crescent, Winnipeg, MB, R3T 2N6, Canada. Pavia Nielsen, Community of Uummannaq, Greenland 3962.

LITERATURE CITED

Beddard, F. E. 1900. *A Book of Whales.* New York: Putnam and Sons.

Best, R. C. 1981. The Tusk of the Narwhal (L.): Interpretation of Its Function (Mammalia: Cetacea). *Canadian Journal of Zoology,* 59: 2386–2393.

Brear, K., J. D. Curry, C. M. Pond, and M. A. Ramsay. 1990. The Mechanical Properties of the Dentine and Cement of the Tusk of the Narwhal *Monodon monoceros* Compared with Those of Other Mineralized Tissues. *Archives of Oral Biology,* 35(8):615–621.

Brown, R. 1868. Cetaceans of the Greenland Seas. *Proceedings of the Zoological Society of London,* 35:552–554.

Bruemmer, F. 1993. *The Narwhal Unicorn of the Sea.* Emeryville: Publishers Group West.

Busch, F. 1890. Zur physiologie und pathologie der zahne des elefanten. *Verhandlungen der Deutschen Odontologischen, Gesellschaft,* 1: 246–315.

Clark, J. W. 1871. On the Skeleton of a Narwhal (*Monodon monoceros*) with Two Fully Developed Tusks. *Proceedings of the Zoological Society of London,* VI(2):41–53.

Colyer, J. F. 1915. Injuries of the Jaws and Teeth in Animals. *The Dental Record,* 35:61–92, 157–168.

de Muizon, C., and D. P. Domning. 2002. The Anatomy of *Obobenocetops* (Delphinoidea, Mammalia), the Walrus-Like Dolphin from the Pliocene of Peru and Its Palaeobiological Implications. *Zoological Journal of the Linnaean Society,* 134:423–452.

de Muizon, C., D. P. Domning, and M. Parrish. 1999. Dimorphic Tusks and Adaptive Strategies in a New Species of Walrus-Like Dolphin (Odobenocetopsidae) from the Pliocene of Peru. *Earth and Planetary Sciences,* 329:449–455.

Eales, N. B. 1950. The Skull of the Foetal Narwhal, *Monodon monoceros* L. *Philosophical Transactions of the Royal Society of London, Series B, Biological Sciences,* 235(621):1–33.

Ellis, R. 1980. *The Book of Whales.* New York: Alfred A. Knopf.

Fraser, F. C. 1938. Vestigial Teeth in the Narwhal. *Proceedings of the Linnaean Society of London,* 150:155–162.

Freuchen, P. 1935. Mammals. Part II. Field Notes and Biological Observations. *Report of the Fifth Thule Expedition, 1921–24,* 2(4–5): 68–278.

Gervais, P. 1873. Remarques sur la Dentition du Narval. *Journal de Zoologie,* 2:498–500.

Geist, O. W., J. W. Manley, and R. H. Manville. 1960. Alaskan Records of the Narwhal. *Journal of Mammalogy,* 41(2):250–253.

Goethe, J. W. 1949. *Gedenkausgabe der Werke, Brief und Gespräche.* Volume 11. Zürich: Artemis-Verlag.

Harrison, R. J., and J. E. King. 1965. "Family Monodontidae." In *Marine Mammals,* ed. R. J. Harrison and J. E. King, pp. 36–39. London: Hutchison University Library.

Hartwig, G. 1874. *The Polar and Tropical Worlds.* Ottawa: J. W. Lyon.

Hay, K. A., and A. W. Mansfield. 1989. "Narwhal—*Monodon monoceros* Linnaeus, 1758." In *Handbook of Marine Mammals,* ed. S. H. Ridgeway and R. Harrison, Volume 4, pp. 145–159. London: Academic Press.

Heyning, J. E. 1984. Functional Morphology Involved in Interspecific Fighting of the Beaked Whale, *Mesoplodon carlhubbsi. Canadian Journal of Zoology,* 645:59–60.

Kingsley, M., and M. A. Ramsay. 1988. The Spiral in the Tusk of the Narwhal. *Arctic,* 41(3):236–238.

Lowe, A. P. 1906. *The Cruise of the Neptune. Report on the Dominion Government Expedition to Hudson Bay and the Arctic Islands, 1903–1904.* Ottawa: Government Printing Bureau.

Mansfield, A. W., T. G. Smith, and B. Beck.1975. The Narwhal (*Monodon monoceros*) in Eastern Canadian Waters. *Journal of the Fisheries Research Board of Canada,* 32(7):1041–1046.

Mead, J. G. 1989. "Beaked Whales of the Genus *Mesoplodon.*" In *Handbook of Marine Mammals.* Volume 4. *River Dolphins and Larger Toothed Whales,* ed. S. H. Ridgeway and R. Harrison, pp. 349–430. London: Academic Press.

Newman, M. A. 1971. Capturing Narwhals for the Vancouver Public Aquarium, 1970. *Polar Record,* 15.922–923.

Nweeia, M. T., J. F. Thackeray, F. C. Eichmiller, P. Richard, L.-M. Leclerc, J. Lanham, and I. Newton. In press. A Note on Isotopic Analysis of Sectioned Tusks of Narwhal (*Monodon monoceros*) and Tusk Growth Rates. Annals of the *Transvaal Museum.*

Nweeia, M. T., N. Eidelman, F. C. Eichmiller, A. A. Giuseppetti, Y. G. Jung, and Y. Zhang. 2005. Hydrodynamic Sensor Capabilities and Structural Resilience of the Male Narwhal Tusk. Abstract presented at the 16th Biennial Conference on the Biology of Marine Mammals, San Diego, Calif., 13 December 2005.

Pederson, A. 1931. Mammals and Birds along the East Coast of Greenland. *Fisheries Research Board of Canada Translation Series,* 1206: 412–417.

Reeves, R. R., and E. Mitchell. 1981. The Whale behind the Tusk. *Natural History,* 90(8):50–57.

Roberge, M. M., and J. B. Dunn. 1990. Assessment of the Subsistence Harvest and Biology of Narwhal (*Monodon monoceros* L.) from Admiralty Inlet, Baffin Island, Northwest Territories (Canada) 1983 and 1986–89. *Canadian Technical Report of Fisheries and Aquatic Sciences,* 1947:1–32.

Scoresby, W., Jr. 1820. *An Account of the Arctic Regions, with a History and Description of the Northern Whale-Fishery.* Volumes 1–2. London: Archibald Constable and Co.

Silverman, H. B., and M. J. Dunbar. 1980. Aggressive Tusk Use by the Narwhal (*Monodon monoceros* L.). *Nature,* 284:57.

Thompson, D. W. 1952. On *Growth and Form.* Volume 2. 2nd ed. London: Cambridge University Press.

Tomlin, A. G. 1967. *Mammals of the U.S.S.R.* Volume 9. *Cetacea.* Jerusalem: Israel Program for Scientific Translation.

Vibe, C. 1950. The Marine Mammals and Marine Fauna in the Thule District (N.W. Greenland) with Observations on Ice Conditions in 1939, 1940, and 1941. *Meddelelser om Grønland,* 150(6):117.

Scientific Diving Under Ice: A 40-Year Bipolar Research Tool

Michael A. Lang and Rob Robbins

ABSTRACT. Approximately four decades ago, scientists were first able to enter the undersea polar environment to make biological observations for a nominal period of time. The conduct of underwater research in extreme environments requires special consideration of diving physiology, equipment design, diver training, and operational procedures, all of which enable this under-ice approach. Since those first ice dives in wetsuits and double-hose regulators without buoyancy compensators or submersible pressure gauges, novel ice diving techniques have expanded the working envelope based on scientific need to include the use of dive computers, oxygen-enriched air, rebreather units, blue-water diving, and drysuit systems. The 2007 International Polar Diving Workshop in Svalbard promulgated consensus polar diving recommendations through the combined international, interdisciplinary expertise of participating polar diving scientists, equipment manufacturers, physiologists and decompression experts, and diving safety officers. The National Science Foundation U.S. Antarctic Program scientific diving exposures, in support of underwater research, enjoy a remarkable safety record and high scientific productivity due to a significant allocation of logistical support and resources to ensure personnel safety.

INTRODUCTION

Milestones of U.S. Antarctic diving activities (Table 1) start with the first dive by Americans in Antarctic waters made just after New Year's Day in 1947 as part of Operation Highjump, the United States' first major postwar Antarctic venture. Lieutenant Commander Tommy Thompson and a Chief Dixon used "Jack Brown" masks and Desco® oxygen rebreathers. Early scuba divers braved McMurdo Sound's −1.8°C water with wetsuits and double-hose regulators. Equipment advances since then have led to the use of variable volume drysuits, buoyancy compensators (BCs), and dive computers. Because of their resistance to freezing, however, double-hose regulators were used almost exclusively in the McMurdo area from 1963 until 1990. Since then, single-hose regulators that also resist freeze-up failure have been used. From 1947 to 1967, research diving operations fell under the control of the U.S. Naval Support Force Antarctica and divers adhered to established U.S. Navy diving regulations. In 1967, James R. Stewart, Scripps Institution of Oceanography diving officer, established guidelines for the conduct of research diving in the polar

Michael A. Lang, Smithsonian Institution, Office of the Under Secretary for Science, P.O. Box 37102, MRC 009, Washington, DC 20013-7012, USA. Rob Robbins, Raytheon Polar Services Company, 7400 South Tucson Way, Centennial, CO 80112, USA. Corresponding author: M. Lang (langm@si.edu). Accepted 28 May 2008.

TABLE 1. Milestones of USAP Dive Program (adapted from Brueggeman, 2003).

Date(s)	Milestone
1947	First dive by Americans in Antarctic waters, LCDR Thompson and Chief Dixon, as part of Operation Highjump, using Jack Brown masks and Desco oxygen rebreathers
1951	First Antarctic open-circuit scuba dive
1947–1967	Research diving operations under USN Support Force, Antarctica
1961–1962	Verne E. Peckham (Donald E. Wohlschlag project, Stanford University) logged 35 science dives tended topside on occasion by Arthur Devries and Gerry Kooyman
1962–1963	John S. Bunt (Donald E. Wohlschlag project, Stanford University) logged 7 science dives
1963–1964	G. Carleton Ray (New York Zoological Society), Elmer T. Feltz and David O. Lavallee logged 10 scuba dives
1963–1964	Gerald Kooyman started diving under ice with Weddell Seals with Paul K. Dayton tending topside
1963–1964	Willard I. Simmonds (Jacques S. Zaneveld project, Old Dominion University) logged 45 tethered science dives
1964–1965	Gerry Kooyman, Jack K. Fletcher and James M. Curtis logged 71 science dives
1965–1966	David M. Bresnahan (NSF OPP) and Leonard L. Nero dived on Zaneveld's project
1965–1966	G. Carleton Ray, Michael A. deCamp, and David O. Lavallee diving with Weddell seals
1967	NSF-SIO agreement for polar research diving (James R. Stewart)
1968	Paul K. Dayton benthic ecology project divers Charles Gault, Gerry Kooyman, Gordon Robilliard. Dayton has logged over 500 hundred dives under McMurdo ice
1978–1979	Dry Valley Lake diving: George F. Simmons, Bruce C. Parker and Dale T. Andersen
1987	USAP Guidelines for Conduct of Research Diving
1990	Double-hose regulators phased out in favor of single-hose regulators.
1992	AAUS Polar Diving Workshop (Lang, M.A and J.R. Stewart, eds.)
1995	RPSC on-site Scientific Diving Coordinator (Rob Robbins)
2001	NSF-Smithsonian Interagency Agreement for polar research diving (Michael A. Lang)
2003–2007	Svalbard ice diving courses (Michael A. Lang)
2007	International Polar Diving Workshop, Svalbard (M.A. Lang and M.D.J. Sayer, eds.)
2008	Smithsonian/NSF ice-diving regulator evaluation project, McMurdo (Michael A. Lang, P. I.)

regions for the National Science Foundation (NSF) Office of Polar Programs (OPP). Since 1995, Rob Robbins, Raytheon Polar Services Company, has served as onsite scientific diving coordinator. In 2001, Michael A. Lang, director of the Smithsonian Scientific Diving Program, enacted an Interagency Agreement between the Smithsonian Institution and the NSF for the management of the U.S. Antarctic Program (USAP) scientific diving program. As NSF OPP Diving Safety Officer (DSO), these responsibilities include, with the USAP Diving Control Board, promulgation of diving safety standards and procedures, evaluation and training of prospective divers, and authorization of dive plans. The USAP *Standards for the Conduct of Scientific Diving* (USAP, 1991) references the scientific diving standards published by the American Academy of Underwater Sciences (AAUS). Approximately half of the Principal Investigators (Table 2) are employees of AAUS organizational member institutions. The USAP researchers understand that polar diving demands the acceptance of responsibility for an increased level of risk and diver preparation. Polar conditions are more rigorous and de-

manding of scientific divers and their equipment than most other diving environments.

Approximately 36 scientists dive each year through USAP and have logged more than 11,400 scientific ice dives since 1989 (Figure 1). Average dive times are 45 minutes; generally, no more than two dives are made per day within the no-decompression limits. The USAP scientific diving authorization process requires submission of information on diver training and history, depth certification, diving first aid training (Lang et al., 2007) and drysuit experience. Minimum qualification criteria for NSF diving authorization include: (a) a one-year diving certification; (b) 50 logged open-water dives; (c) 15 logged drysuit dives; and, (d) 10 logged drysuit dives in the past six months. Somers (1988) described ice diver training curricula considerations. A pre-dive orientation and checkout dive(s) are done on site to ensure that the diver exhibits a satisfactory level of comfort under the ice with their equipment. Divers new to the Antarctic program are usually accompanying experienced Antarctic research teams and are thus mentored in an "apprentice" mode. However, divers must

TABLE 2. Principal Investigators and Co-PIs of USAP diving projects (1989–2006).

Investigator	Project
Amsler, C.	University of Alabama, Birmingham*
Baker, W.	Florida Institute of Technology/University of South Florida*
Barry, J.	Monterey Bay Aquarium Research Institute*
Bosch, I.	SUNY-Geneseo
Bowser, S.	NY Dept. of Health-Wadsworth Center
Conlan, K.	Canadian Museum of Natural History
Davis, R.	Texas A&M University*
Dayton, P.	Scripps Institution of Oceanography*
DeVries, A.	University of Illinois-Urbana
Doran, P.	University of Illinois-Chicago
Dunton, K.	University of Texas-Austin*
Harbison, R.	Woods Hole Oceanographic Institution*
Kaiser, H.	N/A
Kennicutt, M.	University of Texas-Austin*
Kim, S.	Moss Landing Marine Laboratories*
Kooyman, G.	Scripps Institution of Oceanography*
Kvitek, R.	California State University, Monterey Bay
Lang, M.	Smithsonian Institution*
Lenihan, H.	University of North Carolina*
Madin, L.	Woods Hole Oceanographic Institution*
Manahan, D.	University of Southern California*
Marsh, A.	University of Delaware
McClintock, J.	University of Alabama, Birmingham*
McFeters, G.	Montana State University
Miller, M.	Exploratorium, San Francisco
Moran, A.	Clemson University
Oliver, J.	Moss Landing Marine Laboratories*
Pearse, J.	University of California, Santa Cruz*
Ponganis, P.	Scripps Institution of Oceanography*
Quetin, L.	University of California, Santa Barbara*
Torres, J.	University of South Florida*
Wharton, R.	University of Nevada-Desert Research Institute
Wu, N.	Mo Yung Productions

*AAUS organizational member institution.

become proficient with the gear and techniques they will be using prior to deployment.

THE POLAR DIVING ENVIRONMENT

ICE FORMATION

Ice crystallization begins at the air-sea interface where the temperature differential is greatest. Because the air may be as much as 50°C colder than the water, heat conduction to the air from the water promotes the formation of ice. Under calm conditions, this *congelation* ice is composed of needles, small disks, and dendritic stars and will form a smooth sheet over the sea. When the freezing sea is sub-

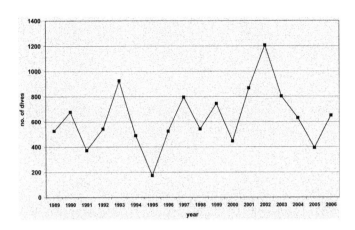

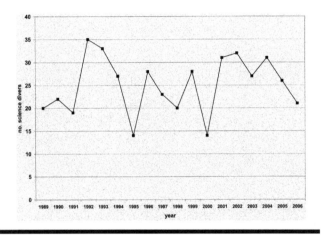

FIGURE 1. (top) USAP dive summary, 1989–2006. (bottom) USAP authorized diver summary, 1989–2006.

jected to wind and wave action, frazil ice crystals clump together into *pancake ice* (0.5 m to 2 m in diameter) that consists of roughly circular, porous slabs with upturned edges. If the water between them freezes, the "pancakes" may solidify and join together. Otherwise, pancake ice continually interacts with wind, waves, and other ice to create complex, many-layered floes of pack ice. When the ice sheet, whether congelation or frazil ice in origin, becomes a solid surface joined to the shoreline, it forms *fast ice*. Once the ice sheet is established, it continues to grow from beneath. Low-density seawater emanating from beneath ice shelves and floating glaciers undergoes adiabatic supercooling. *Platelet* ice crystals form in this supercooled water and float upward, accumulating in an initially loose and porous layer at the bottom of the surface ice sheet. This unfrozen platelet layer (1 cm to several m thick) continually solidifies by freezing, increasing the thickness of the ice sheet. The platelet layer forms a substrate for the growth of microbial communities dominated by microalgae fed upon by amphipods and ice fish. Ice may also crystallize on the benthos. This *anchor ice* generally forms at depths of 15 m or less, attaching to rocks and debris—and even to live invertebrates. If enough ice forms on these objects, they will float up and may become incorporated into the ice sheet.

FAST ICE

Diving conditions are usually associated with solid fast-ice cover for most of the austral diving season at McMurdo Station (annual average thickness 2 m, multiyear 4 m), limited freezing at Palmer Station (under 30 cm), periodically in the Svalbard fjords (average 1 m), and the perennially ice-covered Dry Valley lakes (greater than 6 m; Andersen, 2007). A solid fast-ice cover provides a calm, surge-free diving environment and offers a stable working platform with no surface wave action. Fast-ice strength and thickness varies with time of year and ambient temperature affecting diving operational support. The under-ice topography varies dramatically at dive site, time of year, microalgal activity, ocean current, age of ice, and other oceanographic and physical factors. When viewed from below, a fast-ice sheet may appear relatively homogenous as a hard, flat surface but in places can be punctuated by cracks and openings that appear as bright lines in an otherwise dark roof. If platelet ice is present, the underside of the ice appears rough and uneven. Areas of multiyear ice and thick snow cover are darker. Where pressure ridges and tidal cracks are present, the under-ice topography has more relief. Large and small chunks of broken ice may jut down into the water column in profusion, creating an environment reminiscent of cave diving. *Brine channels* or *ice stalactites* form as seawater cools and freezes and salt is excluded. This salt forms a supercooled brine solution that sinks because of its increased density and freezes the seawater around it resulting in a thin, hollow tube of ice stretching down from the underside of the ice sheet. These brine channels can reach several m in length and may appear singly or in clusters.

PACK ICE

Fast-ice diving differs from pack-ice diving (Quetin and Ross, 2009, this volume), where broken ice cover usually eliminates the need to cut access holes for diving because of easy access to the surface. The pack-ice environment tends to be more heterogeneous than that of fast ice. Ice may be present in all stages of development and the floes themselves may vary in size, age, structure, and integrity. Pack-ice divers will find themselves under an ever-shifting and dynamic surface and wave action and currents must be considered. At sites where the pack ice is forced against the shore and is solid but unstable, an access hole will have to be opened near shore in shallow water. Tidal fluctuations may alter the size of dive holes or vary the water depth under the holes.

UNDERWATER VISIBILITY

In August and September in the McMurdo region, underwater visibility may range up to a record 300 m. As solar radiation increases during the austral summer, an annual plankton bloom develops and quickly diminishes visibility to as little as 1 m by late December. Other water visibility factors influencing the polar regions include glacial melt and wind and temperature conditions. Visibility in the open waters of the Antarctic Peninsula may vary from 300 m to less than 3 m, depending on plankton densities and sea state. As glacial or sea ice melts, the resulting water may form a brackish water lens over the seawater. Visibility within these lenses is markedly reduced, even when the visibility in the water is still good otherwise. It may be possible to lose sight of the entry hole even when divers are near the surface.

POLAR DIVING OPERATIONS

DIVE ACCESS THROUGH ICE

Tidal action, currents, and other forces produce open cracks and leads that divers may use to enter the water. Divers working from USAP research vessels often use the leads cut by the vessel for their access to the water (Quetin and Ross, 2009, this volume). A hydraulically operated mobile drill can be used to cut 1.3 m diameter holes in ice that is over 5 m in thickness. In addition to the primary dive hole, at least one safety hole is required. Hole melters consisting of coiled copper tubing filled with hot circulating glycol or alcohol are used to open a clean, 1 m diameter hole in the thick ice cap that covers the freshwater Dry Valley Lakes (Andersen, 2007), taking from several hours to several days. Chain saws can also be used to cut an access hole through ice that is 15 to 60 cm thick. Access holes are cut into square or triangular shapes and made large enough to accommodate two divers in the water simultaneously. Another method is to use Jiffy drills that bore pilot holes in ice 15 to 30 cm thick and then saws can be used to cut a large dive hole between them;

attaching ice anchors to the chunks of ice allows for easy removal once they are sawed free. For ice from 15 to 25 cm thick, ice saws and breaker bars (2 m lengths of steel pipe or solid bar with a sharpened tip) are used to cut and break away the ice to form a hole. Divers enter the water through pack ice from shore, from an inflatable boat launched from shore or a research vessel, or from large ice floes or a fast-ice edge.

If dive holes are required in ice thicker than 5 m or in ice out of range of the mobile drill, explosives may be necessary. However, the use of explosives is generally discouraged for environmental reasons and requires several hours of clearing ice from the hole before a dive can be made.

Fast-ice diving requires one or more safety holes in addition to the primary dive hole. During times of the year when air temperatures are extremely cold, dive holes freeze over quickly. Positioning a heated hut or other portable shelter over a dive hole will delay the freezing process. Solar powered electric muffin fans are used to blow warm air from near the ceiling of the hut to the ice hole through a plastic tube. Down lines must mark all holes available for use on each dive because safety holes that are allowed to freeze at the surface are hard to distinguish from viable holes while diving under the ice.

DOWN LINES AND TETHERS

A down line is required on all untethered dives conducted from fast ice or any other stable overhead environment with limited surface access. Specific down line characteristics and components are described by Lang and Robbins (2007).

A minimum of one supervisor/tender per dive is required. Because they are a critical part of the diving operation and the first responders in case of accident, tenders receive training in diving first aid (Lang et al., 2007), radio use and communication procedures, scuba gear assembly, tether management, and vehicle or boat operation.

Dives conducted under fast ice where there is a current, reduced visibility or open blue water, or where the water is too shallow to maintain visual contact with the dive hole, require individual diver tethers that are securely attached at the surface. Use of the T- or L-shaped tether system is not ideal, making line-pull communication signals difficult and tether entanglement a possibility. Surface tender training is necessary to maintain enough positive tension on the tether line to immediately recognize line-pull signals from the safety diver, without impeding the activity or motion of the scientists working under the ice. The safety diver's function is to keep tethers untangled, watch for large predators

and communicate via line-pull signals to the surface and other working divers.

Other hole-marking techniques to further protect against loss of the dive hole are snow removal (straight lines radiating outward from the dive hole that are very visible from under water) and benthic ropes which consist of 30 m lines laid out by divers when they first reach the benthos, radiating outward like the spokes of a wheel from a spot directly beneath the dive hole and marked so that the direction to the dive hole is clearly discernible.

POLAR DIVING EQUIPMENT

Members of the dive team take particular care in the selection and maintenance of polar diving equipment (Lang and Stewart, 1992; Lang and Sayer, 2007). Antarctic waters are among the coldest a research diver can expect to experience (−1.8°C in McMurdo Sound). In these temperatures, not all diving equipment can be expected to operate properly and freeze-ups may be more frequent. Diving under total ice cover also imposes safety considerations that are reflected in the choice of gear. We have developed specific care and maintenance procedures to ensure the reliability of life support equipment.

Divers are required to have two fully independent regulators attached to their air supply whenever they are diving under a ceiling. Modified Sherwood Maximus regulators (SRB3600 models, Figure 2) have been used successfully through the installation of a heat retention plate and adjustment of the intermediate pressure to 125

FIGURE 2. Sherwood Maximus SRB3600 second stage with heat retention plate.

psi. These units are rebuilt at the beginning of each season and with more than 7,000 dives have a freeze-up incident rate of 0.3 percent. Proper use and pre- and post-dive care substantially improves the reliability of ice diving regulators, which must be kept warm and dry before a dive. Divers should not breathe through the regulator before submersion except to briefly ensure that the regulator is functioning because of ice crystallization on the air delivery mechanism from breath moisture. This is particularly important if the dive is being conducted outside in very cold air temperatures. During a dive, a regulator is never used to fill a lift bag (small "pony bottles" are available for this purpose) because large volumes of air exhausted rapidly through a regulator will almost certainly result in a free-flow failure. Inflator hoses are attached to the backup regulator in case the air supply to the primary regulator must be turned off to stem a free flow. The backup regulator second stage is attached to the cylinder harness or buoyancy compensator (BC) such that it is readily accessible and easily detached. If the second stage is allowed to hang loosely from the cylinder and drag on the bottom, it will become contaminated with mud and sediment and may not function properly when required. After the dive, the regulators are rinsed and allowed to dry. During rinsing, care is taken to exclude water from the interior regulator mechanism. The diver ensures that the regulator cap is seated tightly, that the hoses and plugs on the first stage are secure, and that the purge on the second stage is not accidentally depressed during the rinse. The primary cause of regulator free-flow failure is from water entry within the mechanism that freezes once the regulator is used (Clarke and Rainone, 1995). Freshwater in the regulator may freeze simply with submersion of the regulator in seawater or upon exposure to extremely cold surface air temperatures. If multiple dives are planned, it is recommended to postpone a freshwater rinse of the regulator until all dives are completed for the day.

Inflator valves are also subject to free-flow failure, because of water entry into the inflation mechanism. Drysuit and BC inflators must be kept completely dry and hose connectors blown free of water and snow before attachment to the valve. When inflating a drysuit or a BC, frequent short bursts of air are used. Inflator buttons must never be depressed for longer than one second at a time because rapid air expansion, adiabatic cooling (5°C drop), and subsequent condensation and freezing may cause a free flow.

Buoyancy compensators need to allow unimpeded access to drysuit inflator and exhaust valves. Water must be removed from the BC bladder after diving and rinsing be-

cause freshwater in the bladder may freeze upon submersion of the BC in ambient seawater. In the McMurdo area, BC use is not currently required when the dive is conducted under a fast-ice ceiling because of the lack of need for surface flotation. A BC must never be used to compensate for excess hand-carried weight. Because of their buoyancy characteristics and durability in cold temperatures, steel, instead of aluminum, scuba cylinders are used.

Divers must wear sufficient weight, without overweighting, to allow for maintenance of neutral buoyancy with a certain amount of air in the drysuit. Runaway negative buoyancy is as great a safety problem to recover from as out-of-control ascent. Because of the amount of weight (30 to 40 lbs) and potential for accidental release, weight belts are not used. Diving Unlimited International (DUI) has developed weight and trim systems (Fig. 3) that retain the benefits of a harness while still allowing full or partial

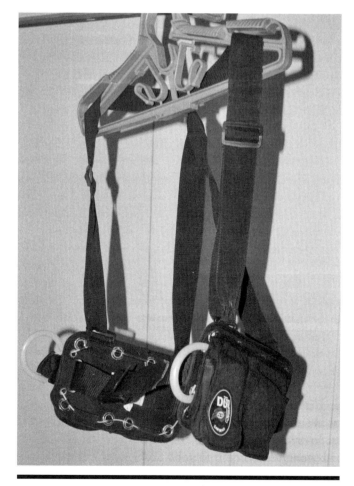

FIGURE 3. DUI weight and trim system with bilaterally removable weight pockets (by pulling surgical tubing loops) and shoulder harness.

dumping of weight under water. The weight system prevents accidental release and improves comfort by shifting the weight load from the diver's hips to the shoulders.

Drysuit choice depends on the diver's preference, the requirement for range and ease of motion, and the options available with each suit. Vulcanized rubber suits must be used when diving in contaminated water because of post-dive suit decontamination requirements. Drysuits must be equipped with hands-free, automatic exhaust valves. Over-inflation of the drysuit should never be used as a means to compensate for excess hand-carried weight. The choice of drysuit underwear is perhaps more important than the choice of drysuit construction material, because it is the underwear that provides most of the thermal protection. Many divers wear an underlayer of expedition-weight polypropylene with an outer layer of 400 g Thinsulate®. Dry gloves or mitts with an inner liner instead of wet gloves are now used with the drysuit. The DUI zipseal dry gloves enjoy widespread use and are effective at warm air equalization from the drysuit into the glove at depth. A disadvantage of these dry-glove systems is the complete lack of thermal protection if the gloves flood or are punctured, and the related inevitability of flooding the entire drysuit.

Severe cold can damage o-ring seals exposed to the environment requiring frequent cleaning and lubrication. Compressor care and adequate pre-operation warming are necessary to ensure a reliable supply of clean air checked by air-quality tests conducted at six-month intervals. Air filters and crankcase oil are scheduled to be changed on a regular basis. The filtering capacity of portable compressors is usually limited, necessitating air intake hose positioning upwind and well away from compressor engine exhaust. Manual condensate drains are purged frequently to prevent moisture contamination and freezing of the filter.

Each diver conducts a functional check of all equipment before each dive. Particular attention is paid to regulators and inflator valves. If leakage or free flow is detected at the surface, the dive is postponed and the gear serviced because it will certainly free flow at depth. All divers must be able to disconnect, with gloved hands, the low-pressure hose from a free-flowing drysuit inflator valve to avoid an uncontrolled ascent.

Because a drysuit must be inflated to prevent "suit squeeze" with increasing pressure, it is most efficient to regulate buoyancy at depth by the amount of air in the drysuit. Drysuits must be equipped with a hands-free exhaust valve (Lang and Egstrom, 1990). The BCs are considered emergency equipment, to be used only in the event of a drysuit failure. This procedure eliminates the need to vent two air sources during ascent, reduces the chance of BC inflator free-flow, and simplifies the maintenance of neutral buoyancy during the dive. The main purpose of air in a drysuit is to provide thermal insulation as a low-conductivity gas. Buoyancy compensators and drysuits must never be used as lift bags. When heavy items must be moved underwater, separate lift bags designed specifically for that purpose are used. Lang and Stewart (1992) concluded that there may be occasions when the drysuit diver is more at risk with a BC than without one. Accordingly, BCs are not required for dives under fast ice where a down line is deployed and the dive is not a blue-water dive.

SURFACE-SUPPLIED DIVING UNDER ICE

Robbins (2006) described USAP's surface-supplied diving activities, history, equipment, training, operations, and costs. By taking advantage of the equipment and expertise brought to the USAP program by commercial divers, scientific diving has benefited from the use of surface-supplied diving techniques. Safety, comfort, and efficiency are enhanced in some applications by using this mode long associated with industry but rarely used in the scientific arena. Since 1992, USAP has supported surface-supplied diving. In that period, 459 surface-supplied dives (of 8,441 total dives) were logged by 32 divers (of 107 total divers). The vast majority of surface-supplied dives were performed by 8 divers.

The USAP's experience with EXO-26 masks has been 11 free-flows in 106 dives (10.4 percent failure rate). AGA masks have had 2 free-flows in 26 dives (7.7 percent failure rate). These data come from dives in the Dry Valley Lakes where water temperatures range between 0°C and 2°C. The failure rate would be even higher in −1.8°C water of McMurdo Sound.

A minimum of two familiarization dives are made by each new surface-supplied diver over two days in addition to topside and underwater training. A three-person crew is the minimum personnel requirement including a supervisor/tender, a diver, and a suited standby diver using either scuba or surface supply.

Currently, the majority of surface-supplied diving is done utilizing 2-m tall high-pressure gas cylinders as an air source. A large 35 cfm/150 psi diesel compressor and smaller 14 cfm/125 psi gas compressor are available but used rarely for scientific diving operations. The USAP uses Kirby-Morgan Heliox-18 bandmasks and Superlite-17 helmets. While these units have a greater propensity to freeze and free-flow than Sherwood Maximus scuba regulators, their track record is as good as either the EXO-26 or AGA Divator full-face masks.

POLAR DIVING HAZARDS AND EMERGENCIES

FAST-ICE DIVING HAZARDS

Lighting is often dim under a solid ice cover, particularly early in the austral spring when the sun is low on the horizon. The amount of snow cover and ice thickness will also attenuate light transmission. Microalgal blooms and increasing zooplankton during the austral summer reduces available light, making it difficult for divers to locate buddies, down lines, and underwater landmarks. High visibility early in the austral summer season may make under-ice or benthic objects seem closer than they are. This illusion may entice divers to travel farther from the access hole than is prudent.

The greatest hazard associated with fast-ice diving is the potential loss of the dive hole or lead. Access holes, leads, and cracks in the ice are often highly visible from below because of downwelling daylight streaming through them. However, dive holes may be difficult to see due to conditions of darkness or of covering the holes with portable shelters. Therefore, a well-marked down line is required for fast-ice dives. Divers maintain positive visual contact with the down line during the dive and avoid becoming so distracted by their work that they fail to take frequent note of their position in relation to the access hole or lead. Problems requiring an emergency ascent are serious, since a vertical ascent is impossible except when a diver is directly under the dive hole or lead. Additional safety holes ameliorate the danger of losing the primary dive hole but former dive holes that have frozen over may still look like safety holes from below. To eliminate confusion in a frequently drilled area, all active holes are marked with a down line.

PACK-ICE DIVING HAZARDS

Pack ice is inherently unstable and its conditions can change rapidly, primarily from surface wind conditions. An offshore wind may blow pack ice away from the shoreline and loosen the pack, whereas an onshore wind may move significant quantities of pack ice against shorelines or fast-ice edges, obstructing what may have been clear access areas when divers entered the water. Similarly, increased wind pressure on pack ice may make driving and maneuvering an inflatable Zodiac more difficult or impossible. Under a jumble of pack ice, the topography is reminiscent of cave diving. The condition of the pack must be continually monitored by divers and tenders for changes that may affect dive safety and the entry area must be kept clear. Down lines and tethers can be disturbed by shifting pack ice, forcing dive tenders to be alert in keeping these lines free of moving ice.

Surface swells, even if only light to moderate, may cause pack ice to oscillate up and down. In shallow water, it is possible for a diver to be crushed between rising and falling pack ice and the benthos. At Palmer Station, surges from the calving glacier in Arthur Harbor may create a similar hazard. Divers avoid diving under pack ice if the clearance between the ice and the benthos is 3 m or less. In addition, lighting may be dim under a heavy pack-ice cover.

Open water develops in McMurdo Sound when the fast ice breaks up in late December or early January. In the Palmer region, any existing fast ice usually breaks up by the end of October. Pack ice may be present for another month or two, and intermittently after that, but open water generally characterizes the diving environment after early December. Kongsfjorden in Svalbard has not formed a substantial ice cover since 2005. Climatic conditions will cause variation in annual ice conditions.

Divers operating in open water and from small boats fly a "diver down" or "Alpha" flag to warn other boat traffic in the area. When diving from small boats a rapid exit from the water into the boat may be necessary. Because this can be difficult when fully laden with gear, lines with clips hang over the side of the boat to temporarily secure gear and a ladder facilitates diver exit.

When diving in blue water (a deep open water environment devoid of visual cues as to the diver's vertical position in the water column) blue water diving guidelines generally apply (Haddock and Heine, 2005). Divers are tethered and wear buoyancy compensators and a down line is deployed if conditions warrant. Divers operating under pack ice in blue water often perceive current increases. Wind action causes the pack to move, which in turn moves the water directly below it. This effect decreases with depth, such that divers in still water at 10 m will have the illusion of movement as the pack ice above them drifts.

Ice-edge diving is usually conducted in blue water, and it tends to be shallow (less than 10 m). The underside of the ice sheet provides a depth reference lacking in ice-free blue water dives. Divers watch continuously for leopard seals known to lunge out of the water to attack people at the ice edge. They may also lurk under the ice waiting for a penguin, or a diver, to enter the water. If penguins in the area demonstrate a reluctance to enter the water, it may be an indication that a leopard seal is nearby.

MARINE LIFE HAZARDS

Few polar animal species are considered dangerous to the diver. Southern elephant seals (*Mirounga leonina*) and Antarctic fur seals (*Arctocephalus gazelli*) may become aggressive during the late spring/early summer breeding season. Crabeater seals (*Lobodon carcinophagus*) have demonstrated curiosity toward divers and aggression to humans on the surface. Leopard seals (*Hydrurga leptonyx*) have been known to attack humans on the surface and have threatened divers in the water. A case report of the single known in-water fatality caused by a leopard seal is described by Muir et al. (2006). Should any aggressive seal approach divers in the water, similar techniques to those protecting against sharks are applied. Polar bears (*Ursus maritimus*) and walrus (*Odobenus rosmarus*) in the Arctic are considered predatory mammals against which diving personnel must be safeguarded. Encounters with all of the aforementioned mammals are usually restricted to areas of open water, ice edges, or pack ice.

Divers in the fast ice around McMurdo may encounter Weddell seals (*Leptonychotes weddelli*) in the water. Occasionally a Weddell seal returning from a dive may surface to breathe in a dive hole to replenish its oxygen stores after a hypoxic diving exposure (Kooyman, 2009, this volume). Usually the seal will vacate the hole once it has taken a few breaths particularly if divers are approaching from below and preparing to surface. Divers must approach such a seal with caution, since an oxygen-hungry seal may aggressively protect its air supply. Weddell seals protecting their surface access will often invert into a head-down, tail-up posture to watch for rivals. Divers entering or exiting the water are particularly vulnerable to aggressive male Weddells, who tend to bite each other in the flipper and genital regions. There are no recorded incidents of killer whale (*Orcinus orca*) attacks on divers.

POLAR DIVING EMERGENCIES

The best method to mitigate scuba diving emergencies is through prevention. Divers must halt operations any time they become unduly stressed because of cold, fatigue, nervousness, or any other physiological reason. Similarly, diving is terminated if equipment difficulties occur, such as free-flowing regulators, tether-system entanglements, leaking drysuits, or buoyancy problems. Emergency situations and accidents stem rarely from a single major cause and they generally result from the accumulation of several minor problems. Maintaining the ability to not panic and to think clearly is the best preparation for the unexpected. Most diving emergencies can be mitigated by assistance from the dive buddy, reinforcing the importance of maintaining contact between two comparably equipped scientific divers while in the water.

Loss of contact with the dive hole may require divers to retrace their path. Scanning the water column for the down line is done slowly and deliberately because the strobe light flash rate is reduced in the cold water. If the hole cannot be found, an alternate access to the surface may have to be located. Often there will be open cracks at the point where fast ice touches a shoreline. Lost divers will have to constantly balance a desirable lower air consumption rate in shallow water with the need for the wider field of vision available from deeper water. Maintaining a safe proximity to the surface access point has made losing the dive hole an extremely unlikely occurrence.

Loss of the tether on a fast-ice dive that requires its use is one of the most serious polar diving emergencies. Lost diver search procedures are initiated immediately (i.e., assumption of a vertical position under the ice where the tethered buddy will swim a circular search pattern just under the ceiling to catch the untethered diver). The danger associated with the loss of a tether in low visibility is mitigated if the divers have previously deployed a series of benthic lines. If a diver becomes disconnected from the tether down current under fast ice, it may be necessary to crawl along the bottom to the down line. To clearly mark the access hole divers deploy a well-marked down line, establish recognizable "landmarks" (such as specific ice formations) under the hole at the outset of the dive, leave a strobe light, a flag, or other highly visible object on the substrate just below the hole or shovel surface snow off the ice in a radiating spoke pattern that points the way to the dive hole.

The under-ice platelet layer can be several meters thick and can become a safety concern if positively buoyant divers become trapped within this layer, become disoriented, and experience difficulty extricating themselves. The most obvious solution is to exhaust air from the drysuit to achieve negative buoyancy. If this is not possible and the platelet layer is not too thick, the diver may stand upside down on the hard under surface of the ice so that the head is out of the platelet ice to orient to the position of the dive hole and buddy. Another concern is that abundant platelet ice dislodged by divers will float up and plug a dive hole.

Fire is one of the greatest hazards to any scientific operation in polar environments. The low humidity ultimately renders any wooden structure susceptible to combustion and once a fire has started, it spreads quickly. Dive teams must always exercise the utmost care when using heat or open flame in a dive hut. If divers recognize during the dive that the dive hut is burning they must terminate the dive and ascend to a safety hole or to the under surface of the ice next to the hole (but not below it) in order to conserve air.

ENVIRONMENTAL PROTECTION

There are research diving sites in Antarctica (e.g., Palmer sewage outfall, McMurdo sewage outfall, and Winter Quarters Bay) that must be treated as contaminated water environments because of the high levels of *E. coli* bacteria (that have been measured up to 100,000/100 ml) or the presence of a hydrogen-sulfide layer (e.g., Lake Vanda). Diving with standard scuba or bandmask, where a diver may be exposed to the water, is prohibited in these areas. Surface-supplied/contaminated-water diving equipment is used at these sites ranging from Heliox-18 bandmasks for use with a vulcanized rubber drysuit to Superlite-17 helmets that mate to special Viking suits.

All researchers must avoid degrading the integrity of the environment in which they work. In particular, polar divers should avoid over-collecting, to not deplete an organism's abundance and alter the ecology of a research site; unduly disturbing the benthos; mixing of water layers such as haloclines; using explosives for opening dive holes; and, spilling oil, gasoline, or other chemicals used with machinery or in research. Increased attention to Antarctic Treaty protocols on environmental protection and implementation of the Antarctic Conservation Act have made human–seal interactions a more sensitive issue. Dive groups should avoid Weddell seal breeding areas during the breeding season and their breathing holes in particular.

PHYSIOLOGICAL CONSIDERATIONS

COLD

Cold ambient temperature is the overriding limiting factor on dive operations, especially for the thermal protection and dexterity of hands. Dives are terminated before a diver's hands become too cold to effectively operate the dive gear or grasp a down line. This loss of dexterity can occur quickly (5–10 min if hands are inadequately protected). Grasping a camera, net, or other experimental apparatus

will increase the rate at which a hand becomes cold. Switching the object from hand to hand or attaching it to the down line may allow hands to rewarm. Dry glove systems have greatly improved thermal protection of the hands.

The cold environment can also cause chilling of the diver, resulting in a reduced cognitive ability with progressive cooling. Monitoring the progression of the following symptoms to avoid life-threatening hypothermia is important: cold hands or feet, shivering, increased air consumption, fatigue, confusion, inability to think clearly or perform simple tasks, loss of memory, reduced strength, cessation of shivering while still cold, and finally hypothermia.

Heat loss occurs through inadequate insulation, exposed areas (such as the head under an inadequate hood arrangement), and from breathing cold air. Scuba cylinder air is initially at ambient temperature and chills from expansion as it passes through the regulator. Air consumption increases as the diver cools, resulting in additional cooling with increased ventilation. Significant chilling also occurs during safety stops while the diver is not moving. Polar diving requires greater insulation, which results in decreasing general mobility and increasing the potential for buoyancy problems. This also means that an increased drag and swimming effort, along with the donning and doffing of equipment, all increase fatigue.

SURFACE COLD EXPOSURE

Dive teams are aware that the weather can change quickly in polar environments. While they are in the field, all divers and tenders have in their possession sufficient cold-weather clothing for protection in any circumstance. Possible circumstances include loss of vehicle power or loss of fish hut caused by fire. Boat motor failure may strand dive teams away from the base station. Supervisors/tenders on dives conducted outside must also be prepared for the cooling effects of inactivity while waiting for the divers to surface. In addition, some food and water is a part of every dive team's basic equipment. Besides serving as emergency rations, water is important for diver rehydration after the dive.

HYDRATION

Besides the dehydrating effect of breathing filtered, dry, compressed air on a dive, Antarctica and the Arctic are extremely low-humidity environments where dehydration can be rapid and insidious. Continuous effort is advised to stay hydrated and maintain proper fluid balance.

Urine should be copious and clear and diuretics (coffee, tea, and alcohol) should be avoided before a dive.

DECOMPRESSION

Mueller (2007) reviewed the effect of cold on decompression stress. The relative contributions of tissue N_2 solubility and tissue perfusion to the etiology of decompression sickness (DCS) are not resolved completely. Over-warming of divers, especially active warming of cold divers following a dive, may induce DCS. Divers in polar environments should, therefore, avoid getting cold during decompression and/or after the dive and if they feel hypothermic, wait before taking hot showers until they have rewarmed themselves, for example, by walking. The effect of cold on bubble grades (as measured by Doppler scores) may be the same for a diver who is only slightly cold as for one who is severely hypothermic. Long-term health effects for divers with a high proportion of coldwater dives should be considered in the future.

Dive computers were examined for use by scientific divers (Lang and Hamilton, 1989) and have now been effectively used in scientific diving programs for almost two decades in lieu of U.S. Navy or other dive tables. Currently, the decompression status of all USAP divers is monitored through the use of dive computers (UWATEC Aladin Pro) and data loggers (Sensus Pro). Battery changes may be needed more frequently because of higher discharge rates in extreme cold. Advantages of dive computers over tables include their display of ascent rates, no-decompression time remaining at depth, and their dive profile downloading function. Generally, no more than two repetitive dives are conducted to depths less than 130fsw (40msw) and reverse dive profiles for no-decompression dives less than 40msw (130fsw) and depth differentials less than 12 msw (40fsw) are authorized (Lang and Lehner, 2000). Oxygen-enriched air (nitrox) capability (Lang, 2006) and rebreather use have, to date, not been requested nor implemented by the USAP Diving Program. Cold and the physical exertion required to deal with heavy gear in polar diving can increase the risk of DCS. Furthermore, because of the polar atmospheric effect, the mean annual pressure altitude at McMurdo Station is 200 meters. Under certain conditions, pressure altitude may be as low as 335 meters at sea level. Surfacing from a long, deep dive (on dive computer sea level settings) to an equivalent altitude of 335 meters may increase the probability of DCS. Safety stops of three to five minutes between 10- to 30-foot (3.3 to 10 m) depths are required for all dives (Lang and Egstrom, 1990).

ACKNOWLEDGMENTS

The authors wish to thank the Smithsonian Office of the Under Secretary for Science, the National Science Foundation Office of Polar Programs, the U.K. NERC Facility for Scientific Diving, Diving Unlimited International, Inc., and Raytheon Polar Services Company.

LITERATURE CITED

Andersen, D. T. 2007. "Antarctic Inland Waters: Scientific Diving in the Perennially Ice-Covered Lakes of the McMurdo Dry Valleys and Bunger Hills." In *Proceedings of the International Polar Diving Workshop*. ed. M. A. Lang and M. D. J. Sayer, pp. 163–170. Washington, D.C.: Smithsonian Institution.

Brueggeman, P. 2003. *Diving under Antarctic Ice: A History*. Scripps Institution of Oceanography Technical Report. http://repositories.cdlib.org/sio/techreport/22 (accessed 8 August 2008).

Clarke, J. R., and M. Rainone. 1995. Evaluation of Sherwood Scuba Regulators for Use in Cold Water. U.S. Navy Experimental Diving Unit Technical Report 9–95. Panama City: U.S. Navy.

Haddock, S. H. D., and J. N. Heine. 2005. *Scientific Blue-Water Diving*. California Sea Grant College Program. La Jolla, Calif.: University of California.

Kooyman, G. 2009. "Milestones in the Study of Diving Physiology: Antarctic Emperor Penguins and Weddell Seals." In *Smithsonian at the Poles: Contributions to International Polar Year Science*, ed. I. Krupnik, M. A. Lang, and S. E. Miller, pp. 265–270. Washington, D.C.: Smithsonian Institution Scholarly Press.

Lang, M. A. 2006. The State of Oxygen-Enriched Air (Nitrox). *Journal of Diving and Hyperbaric Medicine*, 36(2):87–93.

Lang, M. A., and G. H. Egstrom, eds. 1990. *Proceedings of the Biomechanics of Safe Ascents Workshop*. Costa Mesa, Calif.: American Academy of Underwater Sciences.

Lang, M. A., and R. W. Hamilton, eds. 1989. *Proceedings of the Dive Computer Workshop*. Costa Mesa, Calif.: American Academy of Underwater Sciences and California Sea Grant College Program.

Lang, M. A., and C. E. Lehner, eds. 2000. *Proceedings of the Reverse Dive Profiles Workshop* Washington, D.C.: Smithsonian Institution

Lang, M. A., A. G. Marsh, C. McDonald, E. Ochoa, and L. Penland. 2007. "Diving First Aid Training for Scientists." In *Diving for Science: Proceedings of the AAUS 25th Symposium*, ed. J. M. Godfrey and N. W. Pollock., pp. 85–102. Dauphin Island, Ala.: American Academy of Underwater Sciences.

Lang, M. A., and R. Robbins. 2007. "USAP Scientific Diving Program." In *Proceedings of the International Polar Diving Workshop*, ed. M. A. Lang and M. D. J. Sayer, pp. 133–155. Washington, D.C.: Smithsonian Institution.

Lang, M. A., and M. D. J. Sayer, eds. 2007. *Proceedings of the International Polar Diving Workshop*. Washington, D.C.: Smithsonian Institution.

Lang, M. A., and J. R. Stewart, eds. 1992. *Proceedings of the Polar Diving Workshop*. Costa Mesa, Calif.: American Academy of Underwater Sciences.

Mueller, P. H. J. 2007. "Cold Stress as Decompression Sickness Factor." In *Proceedings of the International Polar Diving Workshop*, ed. M. A. Lang and M. D. J. Sayer, pp. 63–72. Washington, D.C.: Smithsonian Institution.

Muir, S. F., D. K. A. Barnes, and K. Reid. 2006. *Interactions between Humans and Leopard Seals*. British Antarctic Survey Technical Report. Cambridge, U.K.: British Antarctic Survey.

Quetin, L. B., and R. M. Ross. 2009. "Life under Antarctic Pack Ice: A Krill Perspective." In *Smithsonian at the Poles: Contributions to International Polar Year Science*, ed. I. Krupnik, M. A. Lang, and S. E. Miller, pp. 285–298. Washington, D.C.: Smithsonian Institution Scholarly Press.

Robbins, R. 2006. "USAP Surface-Supplied Diving." In *Proceedings of the Advanced Scientific Diving Workshop,* ed. M. A. Lang and N. E. Smith, pp. 187–191. Washington, D.C.: Smithsonian Institution.

Somers, L. H. 1988. "Training Scientific Divers for Work in Cold Water and Polar Environments." In *Proceedings of Special Session on Coldwater Diving*, ed. M. A. Lang and C. T. Mitchell, pp. 13–28. Costa Mesa, Calif.: American Academy of Underwater Sciences.

USAP. 1991. *Standards for the Conduct of Scientific Diving*. Arlington, Va.: National Science Foundation, Office of Polar Programs.

Environmental and Molecular Mechanisms of Cold Adaptation in Polar Marine Invertebrates

Adam G. Marsh

ABSTRACT. The under-ice environment places extreme selective pressures on polar marine invertebrates (sea urchins, starfish, clams, worms) in terms of the low temperature, oligotrophic waters, and limited light availability. Free-swimming embryos and larvae face inordinate challenges of survival with almost nonexistent food supplies establishing near starvation conditions at the thermal limits of cellular stress that would appear to require large energy reserves to overcome. Yet, despite the long developmental periods for which these embryos and larvae are adrift in the water column, the coastal under-ice habitats of the polar regions support a surprising degree of vibrant marine life. How can so many animals be adapted to live in such an extreme environment? We all recognize that environmental adaptations are coded in the DNA sequences that comprise a species genome. The field of polar molecular ecology attempts to unravel the specific imprint that adaptations to life in a polar habitat have left in the genes and genomes of these animals. This work requires a unique integration of both field studies (under ice scuba diving and experiments) and laboratory work (genome sequencing and gene expression studies). Understanding the molecular mechanisms of cold adaptation is critical to our understanding of how these organisms will respond to potential future changes in their polar environments associated with global climate warming.

INTRODUCTION: THE NECESSITY OF SCIENCE DIVING

Looking across the coastal margins of most polar habitats, one is immediately struck by the stark, frozen wasteland that hides the transition from land to sea beneath a thick layer of snow and ice. Standing on the sea ice surface along any shore line above 70° latitude, it is hard to imagine that there is fluid ocean anywhere nearby, and even harder to think that there is even a remote possibility of animal life in such an environment. Yet under the five meters of solid sea ice, a rich and active community of marine organisms exists. The real challenge is getting to them.

Scientists studying how these organisms are adapted to survive and persist near the poles are limited by the logistical constraints in getting access under the ice to collect animals and plants for study. The sea ice cover establishes an effective barrier to using most of the common collection techniques that marine biologists employ from vessel-based sampling operations. The time and effort that is invested in opening a hole in the ice greatly precludes the number of sampling sites

Adam G. Marsh, Professor, College of Marine and Earth Studies, University of Delaware, 700 Pilottown Road, Smith Laboratory 104, Lewes, DE 19958, USA (amarsh@udel.edu). Accepted 28 May 2008.

that one can establish. Thus, from one ice hole, we need to be able to collect or observe as many animals as possible. To this end, scuba diving is an invaluable tool for the marine biologist because the ability to move away from the dive hole after entering the water greatly expands the effective sampling area that can be accessed from each individual hole. There is just no way to drill or blast a hole in the ice and drop a "collection-device" down the hole and get more than one good sample. The first deployment would collect what is under the hole, and after that, there is little left to collect. At present, there is still no better method (in terms of observational data, reliability, and cost effectiveness) than scuba diving for providing a scientist the necessary access to collect and study benthic marine invertebrates living along the coastal zones of polar seas.

Although scuba diving under harsh, polar conditions is difficult and strenuous and not without risks, it is an absolute necessity for scientists to work in the water under the ice. We need to be able to collect, observe, manipulate, and study these unique polar marine invertebrates in their own environment. This is especially true for the developing field of environmental genomics, where scientists are attempting to decipher the molecular and genetic level changes in these organisms that make them so successful at surviving under extreme conditions of cold, dark and limited food. This paper will describe how important it is to ultimately understand how these adaptations work in the very sensitive early life stages of embryos and larvae, and how efforts to begin culturing these embryos and larvae under *in situ* conditions under the sea ice will contribute to this greater understanding.

ADAPTATIONS IN POLAR MARINE INVERTEBRATES

Antarctic marine organisms have faced unique challenges for survival and persistence in polar oceans and seas. The impacts of low temperatures and seasonally limited food availability have long been recognized as primary selective forces driving the adaptational processes that have led to the evolution of many endemic species in Antarctica (Clarke, 1991; Peck et al., 2004; Portner 2006; Clarke et al., 2007). Many elegant studies have demonstrated a wide-array of specific molecular adaptations that have been fixed in specific genera or families of Antarctic fish, including chaperonins (Pucciarelli et al., 2006), heat shock proteins (Buckley et al., 2004; Hofmann et al., 2005), red blood cells (O'Brien and Sidell,

2000; Sidell and O'Brien, 2006), tubulin kinetics (Detrich et al., 2000), and anti-freeze proteins (Devries and Cheng, 2000; Cheng et al., 2006). In contrast, the work with invertebrates has been less molecular and more focused on physiology and ecology, in terms of identifying adaptations in life-history strategies (Pearse et al., 1991; Poulin and Feral, 1996; Pearse and Lockhart, 2004; Peck et al., 2007), secondary metabolites (McClintock et al., 2005), energy budgets and aging (Philipp et al., 2005a; Philipp et al., 2005b; Portner et al., 2005, Portner, 2006), and an ongoing controversy over the ATP costs of protein synthesis (Marsh et al., 2001b; Storch and Portner, 2003; Fraser et al., 2004; Fraser and Rogers, 2007; Pace and Manahan, 2007).

Although much progress has been made over the last decade, we still barely have a glimmer as to the full set of adaptations at all levels of organization that have guided species evolution in polar environments. Each genetic description, each physiological summary provides a snapshot of a component of the process, but we are still much in the dark as to how all the expressed phenotypes of an organism are integrated into one functional whole, upon which selection is active. The survival of any one individual will depend upon the integrated effectiveness of "millions" of phenotypic character states ranging from molecular to organismal level processes. *How do you apply one snap shot to such a broad continuum spanning different organizational scales?* At present, there is a daunting lack of any specific indications of the "key" genetic adaptations in single gene loci of any marine invertebrate. This is in stark contrast to the literature that exists for adaptations in fish genes and microbial genomes (Peck et al., 2005). Without the guidance of knowing "where to look," we are faced with identifying the best strategy for surveying an entire genome to pinpoint any possible genetic adaptations to survival in polar environments.

The unique feature of cold-adaptation in polar marine invertebrates is that they are always exposed to a near-freezing temperature. Their entire lifecycle must be successfully completed at $-1.8°C$ (from embryo development to adult gametogenesis). Cold water (-2 to $2°C$) is an extreme environmental condition because of the complexity of the hydrogen bonding interactions between water molecules at the transition between liquid and solid phases. For a simple three atom molecule, the structure of water near freezing is very complex, with over four solid phases and the potential for two different liquid phases at low temperatures. In polar marine invertebrates, significant changes in the molecular activity of water at the liquid-solid interface (-1.8°C) are likely to pose a strong selective force on biochemical and molecular function. Understanding how some organisms have adapted to this level of natural selection will provide information about the essential set of genetic components necessary for survival at low temperature margins of our biosphere.

EMBRYOS IN THE COLD

The fact that polar marine invertebrates can maintain a complex program of embryological development at low temperatures has received much discussion in the literature in terms of life-history adaptations. Of these ecological studies, Thorson's rule has provided a focal point for numerous considerations of why development is so prolonged in marine invertebrates at high latitudes (Pearse et al., 1991; Pearse and Lockhart, 2004). The limited availability of food in polar oceans has lead to uncertainty regarding the relative importance of low food availability compared with low temperatures as the primary selective force limiting developmental rates (Clarke, 1991; Clarke et al., 2007). Overall, limits on metabolism have now received considerable attention in the literature and a general synthesis of the physiological constraints on organismal function in polar environments now appears to primarily involve cellular energetics at molecular and biochemical levels (Peck et al., 2004; Peck et al., 2006a; Peck et al., 2006b; Clarke et al., 2007). Recent work with the planktotrophic larvae of the Antarctic sea urchin, *Sterechinus neumayeri*, has demonstrated that changes in the nutritional state of this feeding larvae do not alter its rate of early larval development (Marsh and Manahan, 1999; 2000). Low temperatures are likely a primary selective force and these larvae exhibit unique molecular adaptations to conserve cellular energy (Marsh et al., 2001b). This may be a general characteristic of polar invertebrate larvae, and could account for the predominance of nonfeeding developmental modes found among benthic, macrofaunal invertebrates in Antarctica, particularly among echinoderms.

EMBRYO ENERGY METABOLISM

One of the most striking characteristics of embryonic development in Antarctic marine invertebrates is the slow rate of cell division. In the sea urchin *S. neumayeri*, early cleavage has a cell cycle period of 12 h, which is an order of magnitude slower than in a temperate sea urchin embryo at 15°C. In the Antarctic asteroid *Odontaster validus* the embryonic cell cycle period is just as long, and in the Antarctic mollusk *Tritonia antarctica*, it is extended to almost 48 h (Marsh, University of Delware, unpublished data). In general we assume that cell division is linked or coordinated to metabolic rates and that the increase in cell cycle period results from an overall decrease in metabolic rate processing at low temperatures. Embryos of *S. neumayeri* are sensitive to changes in temperatures around 0°C. Between -1.5°C and $+0.5$°C, cell division exhibits a large change in the cycle period that is equivalent to a Q10 value of 6.2 (*i.e.*, a 6.2-fold increase in cell division rates if extrapolated to a $\Delta 10$°C temperature difference, Figure 1A). A Q10 greater than 3 indicates the long cell division cycles are determined by processes other than just the simple kinetic effects of temperature on biochemical reaction rates. In contrast, metabolic rates in *S. neumayeri* do not evidence a change over this same temperature gradient ($\Delta 2$°C; Figure 1B). There is no difference in oxygen consumption rates in embryos at the hatching blastula stage between $+0.5$°C and -1.5°C, despite large differences in cell division rates. This directly implies that the cell cycle period is not determined by a functional control or coordination to metabolic rates. The *S. neumayeri* results suggest that embryo development is not tied to metabolism at these low temperatures and the current notions of a selective mechanism that could favor patterns of protracted development by direct coordination to metabolic rates (ATP turnover) remain to be investigated.

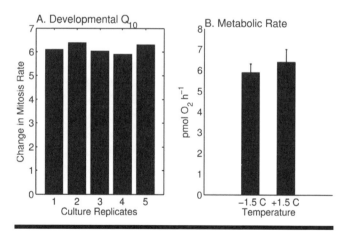

FIGURE 1. Temperature Q10 for developmental rates and energy utilization in the Antarctic sea urchin *Sterechinus neumayeri*. (A) Embryogenesis at $+1.5$°C was much faster than at -1.5°C and was equivalent to a 6-fold rate change per 10°C (i.e., Q10 estimate). (B) The metabolic rates of hatching blastulae at these two temperatures did not reveal any impact of temperature (i.e., Q10 $\sim$ 0).

EMBRYO MOLECULAR PHYSIOLOGY

Some embryos of polar marine invertebrates appear to have specialized programs of gene expression that suggest a coordinated system of activity as a component of metabolic cold-adaptation. Most notable are the recent findings in *S. neumayeri* embryos that mRNA synthesis rates are ~5-fold higher than in temperate urchin embryos (Marsh et al., 2001b). These data were determined from a time course study of whole-embryo RNA turnover rates and show that despite a large difference in environmental temperatures (~ $\Delta 25°C$) rates of total RNA synthesis are nearly equivalent. In comparing the rate constants for the synthesis of the mRNA fraction there is a clear 5x upregulation of transcriptional activity in the *S. neumayeri* embryos. What we need to know about this increased transcriptional activity is whether or not the upregulation of expression is limited to a discrete set of genes, or represents a unilateral increase in expression of all genes. In order to perform these kinds of studies, we need to be able to work with embryos and larvae in their natural environment under the sea ice.

In addition to deciphering the magnitude of changes in transcriptional activities, we are now just beginning to realize the importance of how transcript levels may vary among individuals within a cohort. Variation is a necessity of biological systems. We generally think in terms of point mutations when we conceptualize the underlying basis of how individual organisms differ from one another within a species, and how novel phenotypes arise through the slow incremental accumulation of changes in nucleotide sequence (evolution). At odds with this ideology is the observation that human and chimpanzee genes are too identical in DNA sequence to account for the phenotypic differences between them. This lead A.C. Wilson (King and Wilson, 1975) to conclude that most phenotypic variation is derived from differences in gene expression rather than differences in gene sequence. Microarray studies are now revealing to us an inordinate amount of variation in gene expression patterns in natural populations, and we need to understand both the degree to which that variance may be determined by the environment, and the degree to which that variance may be significantly adaptive.

Although it is clear that interindividual variance in gene expression rates is a hallmark of adaptation and evolution in biological systems, at present, only a few studies have looked at this variation and the linkages to physiological function in field populations. For Antarctic marine invertebrates, most of the molecular and biochemical work looking at adaptations in developmental processes has focused on trying to find "extraordinary" physiological mechanisms to account for the adaptive success of these embryos and larvae. But what if the mechanism of adaptation is not extra-ordinary for polar environments? What if the mechanism is just "ordinary" environmental adaptation: natural selection of individual genotype fitness from a population distribution of expressed phenotypes. Understanding adaptive processes in early life-history stages of polar marine invertebrates will ultimately require an understanding of the contribution that interindividual variance in gene expression patterns plays in determining lifespan at an individual level, survival at a population level and adaptation at a species level in extreme environments.

THE PROCESS OF ADAPTATION

Natural selection operates at the level of an individual to remove less-fit phenotypes from subsequent generations. However, it is clear that a hallmark of biological systems is the "maintenance" of interindividual variance among individuals at both organismal (Eastman 2005) and molecular levels (Oleksiak et al., 2002; Oleksiak et al., 2005; Whitehead and Crawford, 2006). Although early life-history stages (embryos and larvae) are a very good system for looking at selective processes because there is a continual loss of genotypes/phenotypes during development, they are difficult to work with in terms of making individual measurements to describe a population (cohort) distribution. Their small size limits the amount of biomass per individual and consequently most of what we know about molecular and physiological processes in polar invertebrate larvae is derived from samples where hundreds to thousands of individuals have been pooled for a single measurement.

However, methodological advances have allowed for quantitative measurements of molecular and physiological rate processes at the level of individual larvae in terms metabolic rates (Szela and Marsh, 2005), enzyme activities (Marsh et al., 2001a), and transcriptome profiling (Marsh and Fielman, 2005). We are now beginning to understand the ecological importance of assessing the phenotypic variance of characteristics likely experiencing high selective pressures. In Figure 2, the phenotype distributions of two species are presented to illustrate the significant functional difference between how a change in the mean metabolic rate of a cohort (A) could be functionally equivalent to a change in the variance of metabolic rates within a cohort (B), where a decrease in metabolic rates (equivalent to an increase in potential larval lifespan) could arise from either

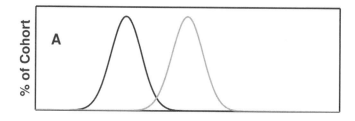

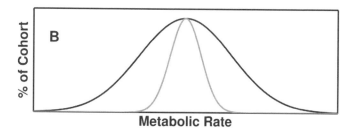

FIGURE 2. Illustrated selection shifts in the frequency distributions of larval metabolic rates in an environment favoring greater energy conservation (black) over one that does not (gray). A change in metabolic efficiency within a cohort could arises at either the level of: (A) the mean phenotype or (B) the interindividual variance around the same mean in the phenotype.

process. Natural selection acts at the level of the phenotype of an individual, not at the level of the mean phenotype of a population or cohort. Thus, in order to understand most of the fine-scale biological processes by which organisms are adapted to polar environments (integrated phenotypes from multiple gene loci), we must be able to describe the distribution of the potential phenotypic space encoded by a genome relative to the distribution of successful (surviving) phenotypes at a cohort (population) scale.

Hofmann et al.'s recent review (2005) of the application of genomics based techniques to problems in marine ecology clearly describes a new landscape of primary research in which it is possible to pursue the mechanistic linkages between an organism and its environment. One of the most interesting aspects of this revolution is the use of microarray hybridization studies for assessing gene expression profiles to identify the level of interindividual variance that does exist in gene expression activities within a population (Oleksiak et al., 2005; Whitehead and Crawford, 2006). Although there are clearly some primary responses that organisms exhibit following specific environmental stresses or cues in terms of gene up- or down-regulation (Giaever et al., 2002; Huening et al., 2006), the power of assessing the expression patterns of thousands of genes simultaneously has opened an intriguing avenue of biological research: *Why are gene expression patterns so*

variable, where is the source of that variation, what determines the adaptive significance of this variation? Although the mechanistic linkage between gene expression events and physiological rate changes may yet remain obscure, it is clear that a significant level of biological variance is introduced at the transcriptome level, and the degree to which that variance may be significantly adaptive requires exploration (Figure 2).

HYPOTHESIS

Overall, this research focus is attempting to describe a component of environmental adaptation as an integrative process to understand the mechanisms that may contribute to long lifespans of larvae in polar environments. *The over arching hypothesis is that embryos and larvae from the eggs of different females exhibit substantial variation in transcriptome expression patterns and consequently metabolic rates, and that these differences are an important determinant of the year-long survival of the few larvae that will successfully recruit to be juveniles.*

BIG PICTURE

Variation is an inherent property of biological systems. We know that genetic variation generates phenotypic variation within a population. However, we also know that there is more phenotypic variation evident within a population than can be accounted for by the underlying DNA sequence differences in genotypes. Much recent attention has been focused on the role of epigenetic information systems in regulating gene expression events, but there has been no consideration yet of the contribution of epigenetics to the level of variation in a phenotypic character, whether morphological, physiological, or molecular. This idea focuses on a potential genome-wide control that could serve as a primary gating mechanism for setting limits on cellular energy utilization within a specific individual, while at the same time allowing for greater potential interindividual variance in metabolic activities within a larval cohort. Understanding the sources of variation in gene transcription rates, metabolic energy utilization, and ultimately lifespans in polar larvae (i.e., the "potential" range in responses to the selection pressures in polar environments) is essential for our understanding of how populations are adapted to cold environments in the short-term, and ultimately how some endemic species have evolved in the long term.

Within a cohort of larvae, it is now likely show that the variance at the level of gene expression events is amplified to a greater level of expressed phenotypic variance. Thus, subtle changes in gene promoter methylation patterns (epigenetics) may have very pronounced impacts on downstream phenotypic processes (physiological energy utilization). Describing how genomic information is ultimately expressed at a phenotypic level is vital for our understanding of the processes of organismal adaptation and species evolution. Although phenotypic plasticity is documented in marine organisms (particularly with regard to metabolic pathways), what is absolutely novel in this idea is that we may be able to demonstrate how changes in the phenotype distribution within a cohort of a character such as metabolic rates can routinely arise independently of genetic mutations (*i.e.*, epigenetic controls). Conceptually, almost all studies of the regulation of gene expression events have been focused on a functional interpretation at the level of the fitness of an individual. Our work to describe the variance in the distribution of expression rates within a group of larvae opens up a new dimension of trying to describe adaptational mechanisms at the larger level of total cohort fitness.

INTERINDIVIDUAL VARIATION IN EMBRYOS AND LARVAE

DEVELOPMENT

Embryos and larvae are rarely considered as populations of individuals. They are normally just cultured in huge vats and mass sampled with the assumption that there is negligible interindividual variance among sibling cohorts. In *S. neumayeri*, we have observed substantial functional differences in the distribution of "rate" phenotypes when the effort is made to collect data at the level of individual embryos and larvae. In Figure 3, eggs from five females were fertilized and individual zygotes of each were scored for their rate of development to the morula stage (~4 days at −1.5°C). Even in this short span of time, there was clearly a difference in the embryo performance from different females with an almost two-fold variance in the mean cohort rates and an order of magnitude difference in the rates among all individuals. We normally think faster is better, at least in temperate and tropical marine environments, but is that the case in polar environments? *Are the fastest developing embryos and larvae the ones that are the most likely to survive and recruit 12 months later?*

ENERGY METABOLISM

A novel methodology for measuring respiration rates in individual embryos and larvae has been developed for

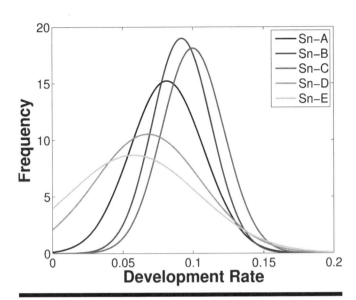

FIGURE 3. Normal Distributions of development rates in late morula embryos of *S. neumayeri* produced from different females. After fertilization, individual zygotes were transferred to 96-well plates and then scored individually for the time to reach 2-, 4-, 8-, 16-cell, and morula stages (n = 90 for each distribution).

measuring metabolism in many individual embryos or larvae simultaneously (Szela and Marsh, 2005). This high-throughput, optode-based technique has been successfully used to measure individual respiration rates in small volumes (5 ul) as low as 10 pmol O_2 x h^{-1}. The largest advantage of this technique is that hundreds of individuals can be separately monitored for continuous oxygen consumption in real-time. The most striking observations we have made so far with *S. neumayeri* embryos is that there are large differences in metabolic rates between individuals and that these differences appear to be influenced by the eggs produced by different females (Figure 4). Understanding the distribution of metabolic rates among individuals within a cohort of embryos or larvae is critical for understanding how metabolic rates may be "tuned" to polar environments.

In Figure 4, the most intriguing aspect of the distributions is the 2- to 3-fold difference in metabolic rates that can be found among individual embryos. Clearly there is a large degree of interindividual variance in the cellular rate processes that set total embryo metabolism, and we need to understand the mechanistic determinants of that variance. What we need to know now is how the biological variance at the level of the transcriptome (gene expression rates) impacts the variance at the level of physiological function (respiration rates). To date, the embryos and larvae of most polar invertebrates studied appear to evidence a strategy of metabolic down-regulation with the apparent

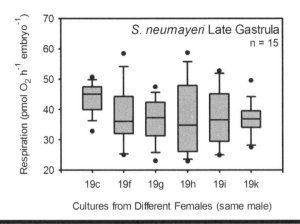

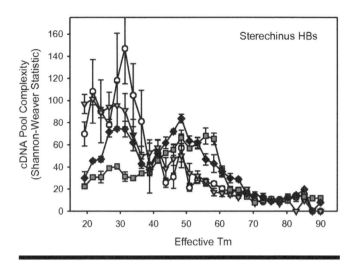

FIGURE 4. Distribution of respiration rates in late gastrula embryos of *S. neumayeri*. Eggs from 6 females were fertilized with the sperm from one male and maintained as separate cultures. The distribution of metabolic rates in these cultures is not equivalent (n = 15 for each culture; 90 individuals total).

FIGURE 5. Individual cDNA libraries were constructed for four embryos and profiled for sequence complexity using a novel approach to measuring reannealing kinetics. Large differences in the sequence distribution and abundance of the transcriptome pool are evident among these sibling embryos.

effect of extending larval lifespan (Peck et al., 2004; Peck et al., 2005; Peck et al., 2006a; Peck et al., 2006b). That is the observation at a population level. At an individual level this could be achieved by one of two mechanisms: (1) embryos in a cohort could maintain the same relative distribution of metabolic rates around a lower mean rate (as in Figure 1A), or (2) embryos in a cohort could express a larger degree of interindividual variance (stochastic regulation) in respiration rates such that a larger fraction of the cohort would have lower metabolic rates that might concomitantly contribute to extended larval lifespans (as in Figure 1B).

GENE EXPRESSION

Physiological changes in metabolic rates must have an underlying basis in molecular events associated with gene expression rates. In order to compare changes within embryos or larvae to changes in gene activities, a novel methodology based on reannealing kinetics is employed for the rapid, high-throughput, efficient, and economical profiling of the sequence complexity of a transcriptome (Marsh and Fielman, 2005; Hoover et al., 2007a; b; c). Measuring renaturation rates of cDNA along a temperature gradient can provide information about the transcript sequence complexity of a nucleic acid pool sample. In our assay, the reannealing curves at discrete temperature intervals can be described by a second-order rate function. A full kinetic profile can be constructed by analyzing all the curves using an informatics statistic (Shannon-Weaver entropy) for individual *S. neumayeri* embryos (hatching blastula stage). In Figure 5, each

point represents the total mRNA pool complexity at a given Tm class with a mean (sd) of 4 duplicate assays at each Tm. Our novel revelation is that these mRNA pools among embryos are not identical. We can detect discrete differences in the distribution and abundance of component transcripts at the level of these individuals, even though they are all apparently progressing through the same developmental program. Thus, there is a large variance component that arises at the level of gene expression within these Antarctic sea urchin embryos.

One of the most prominent mechanisms determining gene expression patterns is the system of chemical modifications on DNA that establish an epigenetic pattern of information. Epigenetic processes refer to heritable molecular structures that regulate gene expression events independent of any DNA nucleotide sequence within a genome. There is currently a clear recognition that a large component of gene regulation can operate at this level of local DNA structure and composition and that DNA methylation is one of the dominant mechanisms. Methylation of promoter domains is one of the key mechanisms that can account for temporal patterns of differential gene expression during embryological development (MacKay et al., 2007; Sasaki et al., 2005; Haaf, 2006). During cell division, this genome methylation pattern is re-established with high fidelity in daughter cells by a suite of methyl-transferases immediately after DNA synthesis. Consequently, an established regulatory "imprint" can be perpetuated during development and across generations. In this sense, methylation serves as a cell-based memory system for maintaining a pattern of gene expression regulation.

Methylation is also evident in invertebrate genomes, although the distribution of methylated sites appears to be more variable than in vertebrates, being mainly concentrated within areas of gene loci (Levenson and Sweatt, 2006; Schaefer and Lyko, 2007; Suzuki et al., 2007). Some invertebrates exhibit mammalian-type levels of DNA methylation (up to 15 percent of all cytosine residues methylated). In many invertebrates, DNA methylases appear to be very active during development (Meehan et al., 2005) and we can measure ~4 percent methyl-cytosine levels in *S. neumayeri* (Kendall et al., 2005). More importantly, the presence/absence of specific methylation sites within a genome can be rapidly assessed using an Amplified Fragment Length Polymorphism derived assay. The key observations here are that methylation fingerprints can be rapidly assessed following experimental treatments, and that methylated sites in gene promoters can be identified and scored separately (Kaminsk et al., 2006; Rauch et al. 2007). The number and diversity of methylation sites we can identify in early *S. neumayeri* embryos indicates an active DNA methylation system that could be generating the variance in metabolic rates and developmental rates that we have observed.

DIVING WITH EMBRYOS AND LARVAE UNDER THE ICE

The previous sections have documented the prevalence of a high component of interindividual variance among individual embryos of *S. neumayeri*. In order to fully understand the implications for this variance in terms of its impact on the survival of a cohort of larvae and the persistence of a sea urchin population through time, we need to study lots of individual larvae under natural conditions. This is absolutely impossible to do in a laboratory setting because of the large volumes of sea water that would have to be maintained. As an alternative, a pilot program is underway to investigate the success of culturing embryos and larvae in flow-through containers under the sea ice in McMurdo Sound. The concept is simple: Let the embryos and larvae grow naturally without investing much time or effort in their husbandry.

Current efforts to mass culture sea urchin larvae utilize 200-liter drums stocked at densities of ~10 per ml. At those densities, the water needs to be changed every two days. One water change on one 200 liter drum can take 2 hours in order to "gently" filter all the larvae out first

and then put them into another clean 200 liter drum. The word *gently* is emphasized here for irony, because there is nothing gentle about using a small-mesh screen to filter out all the embryos and larvae. It is a very physically stressful process, and mortality rates are significant.

An alternative approach utilizing in situ chambers could allow for the embryos and larvae to develop without human intervention. The under ice environment around McMurdo Station is very stable and the epiphytic fouling community of organisms is almost nonexistent. In Figure 6, photographs of under ice culture bags in use in McMurdo Sound are shown. These trial bags were fitted with two open ports having a 40 μm mesh Nytek screen coverings so that water could be freely exchanged through the bag. Low densities of embryos from different marine

FIGURE 6. Culture bags with embryos and larvae of different marine invertebrates are tethered to the bottom rubble of the McMurdo Jetty under 6 m of solid sea ice and 25 m total water depth (photos by Adam G. Marsh).

invertebrates were placed in the bag and sampled at different time intervals. We have been successful at culturing larvae of the clam *Laternula eliptica* for over 13 months under the ice, and recovering fully metamorphosed juveniles at the end of that time period.

The ability to place embryos and larvae under the ice in culture containers in the Austral summer, then leave them in place through the winter season, means that we now have the potential to work with the full lifecycle of some marine invertebrate larvae. Because of the slow developmental rates of these larvae and protracted lifespans, there are relatively few studies that have been able to collect any data on the later life-stage as they approach metamorphosis. However, divers can now establish cultures in situ under the ice, then return at any time point later on to sample individuals. This increase in the time span for which we can now study will fill in the large gap in our current knowledge of what happens at the end of the Austral winter period when the larvae are ready to become juveniles.

In order to understand how larvae are adapted to survive in polar environments, we really need to make our best measurements and execute our most exact experiments on the individuals that have survived for the complete developmental period and are now ready to become juveniles. If only 10 percent of a cohort survives to this stage (+12 months development), then making early measurements on the other 90% (at 1 month) that were destined to die would essentially just give you information about what *does not* work. It is the survivors that hold the key to understanding how these organisms are adapted to persist in a harsh polar environment. In essence, all the existing studies on adaptations in polar marine larvae that have made measurements from bulk cultures at early developmental time points could be grossly misleading. All of those individuals are not likely to survive the full year to recruitment. Consequently, we need an experimental culturing system that will allow scientists to work with larvae that have survived the harsh polar environment. Those are the individuals that have the key to understanding adaptive processes.

Overall, the *in situ* culturing approach offers us three main advantages:

1. Large numbers of individuals can be cultured with relatively little husbandry effort. Once the culture containers are setup and stocked, then the only effort necessary is for a dive team to periodically sample and remove individuals. There is no feeding and little maintenance required.

2. Larvae can be cultured under very natural conditions without laboratory artifacts. The most important variable to control is temperature and by not having open culture containers in an aquarium room, there is no worry about the temperature in the vessels changing because of problems with electricity supply, pumps breaking down and losing the cold sea water supply rate, or someone just changing the thermostat within the aquarium room. The second most important variable is food, and under in situ conditions, the feeding larvae will receive a diet of natural species and in a natural supply.

3. Long term cultures can be maintained across the entire developmental period, which in most polar marine invertebrates can easily extend upwards of a year. This approach will provide access to larvae that have successfully survived their full lifecycle in a harsh polar environment.

CONCLUSION

The *S. neumayeri* distributions in developmental rate (Figure 3), respiration distributions (Figure 4), transcriptome profiles (Figure 5), and gene methylation (data not shown) have focused our attention on trying to understand the functional significance of interindividual variability at these levels of biological organization. In a life-history model that selects for a prolonged larval lifespan, it is intriguing to ask whether or not it is a reduction in individual metabolic rates (Figure 2A) or an increase in the cohort variance in metabolic rates (Figure 2B) that could account for the adaptation in metabolic phenotypes. The metabolic lifespans of polar invertebrate larvae could be under the same genetic determinants as other temperate species, but changes in patterns of gene regulation could substantially alter the distribution of physiological phenotypes within a cohort. Being able to study long-lived larvae that are ready to become juveniles holds the key for deciphering the adaptive mechanism that may be operative at the level of a full cohort to ensure that some percentage is capable of surviving. Selection is surely not operating to force the survival function of all individuals within a cohort. Only enough need to survive to keep a population established and stable.

Scientific diving will be an important component of discovering how these animals are adapted to survive. The opportunity to now work *in situ* with embryos and larvae will open new avenues of research and understanding. Even though the under ice work is not complex, it is nonetheless rigorous and demanding. Any diver working on the bottom for more than 45 minutes will readily attest to the extreme nature of the cold that impacts all organisms in that environment. Being in the water gives one a unique perspective on the survival challenges that are facing the embryos and larvae of these polar marine invertebrates.

ACKNOWLEDGMENTS

This work was conducted with the help, collaboration, and participation of numerous students and postdoctoral associates in my lab and I am grateful for their efforts, energies and cold tolerance. The research was supported by a grant from the National Science Foundation, Office of Polar Programs (#02–38281 to AGM).

LITERATURE CITED

Buckley, B. A., S. P. Place, and G. E. Hofmann. 2004. Regulation of Heat Shock Genes in Isolated Hepatocytes from an Antarctic Fish, *Trematomus bernacchii*. *Journal of Experimental Biology*, 207: 3649–3656.

Cheng, C. H. C., P. A. Cziko, and E. W. Clive. 2006. Nonhepatic Origin of Notothenioid Antifreeze Reveals Pancreatic Synthesis as Common Mechanism in Polar Fish Freezing Avoidance. *Proceedings of the National Academies of Science*, 103:10491–10496.

Clarke, A. 1991. What Is Cold Adaptation and How Should We Measure It? *American Zoologist*, 31:81–92.

Clarke, A., N. M. Johnston, E. J. Murphy, and A. D. Rogers. 2007. Introduction: Antarctic Ecology from Genes to Ecosystems: The Impact of Climate Change and the Importance of Scale. *Philosophical Transactions of the Royal Society B-Biological Sciences,* 362:5–9.

Detrich, H. W., S. K. Parker, R. C. Williams, E. Nogales, and K. H. Downing. 2000. Cold Adaptation of Microtubule Assembly and Dynamics—Structural Interpretation of Primary Sequence Changes Present in the Alpha- and Beta-Tubulins of Antarctic Fishes. *Journal of Biological Chemistry*, 275:37038–37047.

Devries, A. L. and C. H. C. Cheng. 2000. Freezing Avoidance Strategies Differ in Antarctic And Arctic Fishes. *American Zoologist*, 40:997.

Eastman, J. T. 2005. The Nature of the Diversity of Antarctic Fishes. *Polar Biology*, 28:93–107.

Fraser, K. P. P., L. S. Peck, and A. Clarke. 2004. Protein Synthesis, RNA Concentrations, Nitrogen Excretion, and Metabolism Vary Seasonally in the Antarctic Holothurian *Heterocucumis steineni* (Ludwig 1898). *Physiological and Biochemical Zoology*, 77:556–569.

Fraser, K. P. P., and A. D. Rogers. 2007. Protein Metabolism in Marine Animals: The Underlying Mechanism of Growth. *Advances in Marine Biology*, 52:267–362.

Giaever, G., A. M. Chu, L. Ni, C. Connelly, L. Riles, S. Veronneau, S. Dow, A. Lucau-Danila, K. Anderson, B. Andre, A. P. Arkin, A. Astromoff, M. El Bakkoury, R. Bangham, R. Benito, S. Brachat, S. Campanaro, M. Curtiss, K. Davis, A. Deutschbauer, K. D. Entian, P. Flaherty, F. Foury, D. J. Garfinkel, M. Gerstein, D. Gotte, U. Guldener, J. H. Hegemann, S. Hempel, Z. Herman, D. F. Jaramillo, D. E. Kelly, S. L. Kelly, P. Kotter, D. LaBonte, D. C. Lamb, N. Lan, H. Liang, H. Liao, L. Liu, C. Y. Luo, M. Lussier, R. Mao, P. Menard, S. L. Ooi, J. L. Revuelta, C. J. Roberts, M. Rose, P. Ross-Macdonald, B. Scherens, G. Schimmack, B. Shafer, D. D. Shoemaker, S. Sookhai-Mahadeo, R. K. Storms, J. N. Strathern,

G. Valle, M. Voet, G. Volckaert, C. Y. Wang, T. R. Ward, J. Wilhelmy, E. A. Winzeler, Y. H. Yang, G. Yen, E. Youngman, K. X. Yu, H. Bussey, J. D. Boeke, M. Snyder, P. Philippsen, R. W. Davis, and M. Johnston. 2002. Functional Profiling of the *Saccharomyces cerevisiae* Genome. *Nature*, 418:387–391.

Haaf, T. 2006. Methylation Dynamics in the Early Mammalian Embryo: Implications of Genome Reprogramming Defects for Development. *Current Topics in Microbiology and Immunology*, 310:13–22.

Hofmann, G. E., S. G. Lund, S. P. Place, and A. C. Whitmer. 2005. Some Like It Hot, Some Like It Cold: The Heat Shock Response Is Found in New Zealand but Not Antarctic Notothenioid Fishes. *Journal of Experimental Marine Biology and Ecology*, 316:79–89.

Hoover, C. A., M. Slattery, and A. G. Marsh. 2007a. A Functional Approach to Transcriptome Profiling: Linking Gene Expression Patterns to Metabolites That Matter. *Marine Biotechnology*, doi:10.1007/s10126–007–9008–2.

———. 2007b. Comparing Gene Expression Profiles of Benthic Soft Coral Species, *Sinularia polydactyla, S. maxima,* and Their Putative Hybrid. *Comparative Biochemistry and Physiology (Part D)*, 2:135–143.

———. 2007c. Profiling Transcriptome Complexity during Secondary Metabolite Synthesis Induced by Wound Stress in a Benthic Soft Coral, *Sinularia polydactyla*. *Marine Biotechnology*, doi:10.1007/s10126–006–6048–y.

Huening, M. A., D. W. Sevilla, A. Potti, D. H. Harpole, J. R. Nevins, and M. B. Datto. 2006. A First Step towards Validating Microarray Gene Expression Profiling for Clinical Testing: Characterizing Biological Variance. *Journal of Molecular Diagnostics*, 8:660–665.

Kaminsk, Z., S. C. Wang, S. Ziegler, I. Gottesman, A. Wong, A. McRae, P. Visscher, N. Martin, and A. Petronis. 2006. Epigenomic Microarray Profiling of DNA Methylation Variability in Monozygotic and Dizygotic Twins. *American Journal of Medical Genetics Part B-Neuropsychiatric Genetics*, 141B:708–714.

Kendall, L. R., E. McMullin, and A. G. Marsh. 2005. Genome Methylation Patterns during Early Development in the Antarctic Sea Urchin, *Sterechinus neumayeri*. *Integrative and Comparative Biology*, 45:1153.

King, M. C., and A. C. Wilson. 1975. Evolution at 2 Levels in Humans and Chimpanzees. *Science*, 188:107–116.

Levenson, J. M., and J. D. Sweatt. 2006. Epigenetic Mechanisms: A Common Theme in Vertebrate and Invertebrate Memory Formation. *Cellular and Molecular Life Sciences*, 63:1009–1016.

MacKay, A. B., A. A. Mhanni, R. A. McGowan, and P. H. Krone. 2007. Immunological Detection of Changes in Genomic DNA Methylation during Early Zebrafish Development. *Genome*, 50:778–785.

Marsh, A. G., S. Cohen, and C. E. Epifanio. 2001a. Larval Energy Metabolism and Physiological Variability in the Shore Crab, *Hemigrapsus sanguineus*. *Marine Ecology Progress Series,* 218:303–309.

Marsh, A. G., and K. T. Fielman. 2005. Transcriptome Profiling of Individual Larvae of Two Different Developmental Modes in the Poecilogonous Polychaete *Streblospio benedicti* (Spionidae). *Journal of Experimental Zoology—Molecular Development and Evolution*, 304B:238–249.

Marsh, A. G., and D. T. Manahan. 1999. A Method for Accurate Measurements of the Respiration Rates of Marine Invertebrate Embryos and Larvae. *Marine Ecology Progress Series*, 184:1–10.

———. 2000. Metabolic Differences between "Demersal" and "Pelagic" Development of the Antarctic Sea Urchin *Sterechinus neumayeri*. *Marine Biology*, 137:215–221.

Marsh, A. G., R. E. Maxson, and D. T. Manahan. 2001b. High Macromolecular Synthesis with Low Metabolic Cost in Antarctic Sea Urchin Embryos. *Science*, 291:1950–1952.

McClintock, J. B., C. D. Amsler, B. J. Baker, and R. W. M. van Soest. 2005. Ecology of Antarctic Marine Sponges: An Overview. *Integrative and Comparative Biology*, 45:359–368.

Meehan, R. R., D. S. Dunican, A. Ruzov, and S. Pennings. 2005. Epigenetic Silencing in Embryogenesis. *Experimental Cell Research*, 309: 241–249.

O'Brien, K. M., and B. D. Sidell. 2000. The Interplay among Cardiac Ultrastructure, Metabolism and the Expression of Oxygen-Binding Proteins in Antarctic Fishes. *Journal of Experimental Biology.*, 203: 1287–1297.

Oleksiak, M. F., G. A. Churchill, and D. L. Crawford. 2002. Variation in Gene Expression within and among Natural Populations. *Nature Genetics*, 32:261–266.

Oleksiak, M. F., J. L. Roach, and D. L. Crawford. 2005. Natural Variation in Cardiac Metabolism and Gene Expression in *Fundulus heteroclitus*. *Nature Genetics*, 37:67–72.

Pace, D. A., and D. T. Manahan. 2007. Cost of Protein Synthesis and Energy Allocation during Development of Antarctic Sea Urchin Embryos and Larvae. *Biological Bulletin*, 212:115–129.

Pearse, J. S., and S. J. Lockhart. 2004. Reproduction in Cold Water: Paradigm Changes in the 20th Century and a Role for Cidaroid Sea Urchins. *Deep-Sea Research Part II-Topical Studies in Oceanography*, 51:1533–1549.

Pearse, J. S., J. B. McClintock, and I. Bosch. 1991. Reproduction of Antarctic Benthic Marine-Invertebrates—Tempos, Modes, and Timing. *American Zoologist*, 31:65–80.

Peck, L. S., M. S. Clark, A. Clarke, C. S. Cockell, P. Convey, H. W. Detrich, K. P. P. Fraser, I. A. Johnston, B. A. Methe, A. E. Murray, K. Romisch, and A. D. Rogers. 2005. Genomics: Applications to Antarctic Ecosystems. *Polar Biology*, 28:351–365.

Peck, L. S., A. Clarke, and A. L. Chapman. 2006a. Metabolism and Development of Pelagic Larvae of Antarctic Gastropods with Mixed Reproductive Strategies. *Marine Ecology Progress Series*, 318: 213–220.

Peck, L. S., P. Convey, and D. K. A. Barnes. 2006b. Environmental Constraints on Life Histories in Antarctic Ecosystems: Tempos, Timings and Predictability. *Biological Review*, 81:75–109.

Peck, L. S., D. K. Powell, and P. A. Tyler. 2007. Very Slow Development in Two Antarctic Bivalve Molluscs, the Infaunal Clam *Laternula elliptica* and the Scallop *Adamussium colbecki*. *Marine Biology*, 150: 1191–1197.

Peck, L. S., K. E. Webb, and D. M. Bailey. 2004. Extreme Sensitivity of Biological Function to Temperature in Antarctic Marine Species. *Functional Ecology*, 18:625–630.

Philipp, E., T. Brey, H. O. Portner, and D. Abele. 2005a. Chronological and Physiological Ageing in a Polar and a Temperate Mud Clam. *Mechanisms of Ageing and Development*, 126:598–609.

Philipp, E., H. O. Portner, and D. Abele. 2005b. Mitochondrial Ageing of a Polar and a Temperate Mud Clam. *Mechanisms of Ageing and Development*, 126:610–619.

Portner, H. O. 2006. Climate-Dependent Evolution of Antarctic Ectotherms: An Integrative Analysis. *Deep-Sea Research Part II-Topical Studies in Oceanography*, 53:1071–1104.

Portner, H. O., D. Storch, and O. Heilmayer. 2005. Constraints and Trade-Offs in Climate-Dependent Adaptation: Energy Budgets and Growth in a Latitudinal Cline. *Scientia Marina*, 69:271–285.

Poulin, E., and J. P. Feral. 1996. Why Are There So Many Species of Brooding Antarctic Echinoids? *Evolution*, 50:820–830.

Pucciarelli, S., S. K. Parker, H. W. Detrich, and R. Melki. 2006. Characterization of the Cytoplasmic Chaperonin Containing TCP-1 from the Antarctic Fish *Notothenia coriiceps*. *Extremophiles*, 10: 537–549.

Rauch, T., Z. D. Wang, X. M. Zhang, X. Y. Zhong, X. W. Wu, S. K. Lau, K. H. Kernstine, A. D. Riggs, and G. P. Pfeifer. 2007. Homeobox Gene Methylation in Lung Cancer Studied by Genome-Wide Analysis with a Microarray-Based Methylated CpG Island Recovery Assay. *Proceedings of the National Academies of Science*, 104:5527–5532.

Sasaki, A., N. Takatori, and N. Satoh. 2005. The Role of DNA Methylation in the Early Development of Ciona Intestinalis. *Zoological Science*, 22:1459–1463.

Schaefer, M. and F. Lyko. 2007. DNA Methylation with a Sting: An Active DNA Methylation System in the Honeybee. *Bioessays*, 29: 208–211.

Sidell, B. D. and K. M. O'Brien. 2006. When Bad Things Happen to Good Fish: The Loss of Hemoglobin and Myoglobin Expression in Antarctic Icefishes. *Journal of Experimental Biology*, 209:1791–1802.

Storch, D. and H. O. Portner. 2003. The Protein Synthesis Machinery Operates at the Same Expense in Eurythermal and Cold Stenothermal Pectinids. *Physiological and Biochemical Zoology*, 76:28–40.

Suzuki, M. M., A. R. W. Kerr, D. DeSousa, and A. Bird. 2007. CpG Methylation is Targeted to Transcription Units in an Invertebrate Genome. *Genome Research*, 17:625–631.

Szela, T. L. and A. G. Marsh. 2005. Microtiter Plate, Optrode Respirometry Reveals Large Interindividual Variance in Metabolic Rates among Individual Nauplii of *Artemia* sp. *Marine Ecology Progress Series*, 296:291–309.

Whitehead, A., and D. L. Crawford. 2006. Variation within and among Species in Gene Expression: Raw Material for Evolution. *Molecular Ecology*, 15:1197–1211.

Milestones in the Study of Diving Physiology: Antarctic Emperor Penguins and Weddell Seals

Gerald Kooyman

Gerald Kooyman, Research Professor, Scholander Hall, Scripps Institution of Oceanography, University of California–San Diego, 9500 Gilman Drive, La Jolla, CA 92093-0204, USA (gkooyman@ucsd.edu). Accepted 28 May 2008.

ABSTRACT. McMurdo Sound, Antarctica, is the best place to conduct diving physiology studies on marine birds and mammals under free-diving conditions. Both emperor penguins and Weddell seals live naturally in areas of extensive sea ice under which they dive and hunt for prey. The first experimental diving studies were conducted on Weddell seals in 1964 using the isolated breathing hole protocol for the first time. Sea ice, 2 m thick, covers McMurdo Sound until late December. Below the ice is the deepwater environment where Antarctic predators hunt their prey. Here in the Sound diving studies involve attachment of a recording device to a seal or bird and release of the animal into the hole cut in sea ice. This procedure sets the stage for a bird or mammal to hunt without competition, and the only restrictive condition is that they must return to the release hole to breathe. After the animal surfaces, the attached recording devices can be retrieved and the information downloaded. Results from using this experimental protocol range from determining the first foraging patterns of any diving mammal, to measuring the first blood and muscle chemistry fluctuations during the extended and unrestrained dives. These experiments are the standard for understanding the hypoxic tolerance of diving animals, their aerobic diving limits, and their strategies of foraging, to mention a few. The protocol will continue to be used in 2008 for studies of both emperor penguins and Weddell seals by several investigators.

INTRODUCTION

My goal in this presentation is to engender an understanding of the valuable resource we have next to McMurdo Station, the largest base in Antarctica. That asset is McMurdo Sound itself, which is covered by perhaps the largest and most southerly annual fast-ice sheet in Antarctica. The ice cover most commonly ranges in thickness from 1 to 4 m in thickness, and extends from the McMurdo Ice Shelf to Cape Royds to the north, and east to west from Ross Island to the continent (Figure 1). It covers an oceanic area reaching to depths of 600 m. It is also one of the most stable fast ice areas and it persists until late December. Like almost every first-time visitor, when I arrived in 1961, I was not impressed by the Sound's uniqueness. However, McMurdo Sound may have the only such *annual* fast-ice shelf anywhere in Antarctica where it can be used extensively for innumerable projects. Among the many uses are: (1) the largest and most active airport in Antarctica, (2) "at-sea" marine biological and oceanographic stations

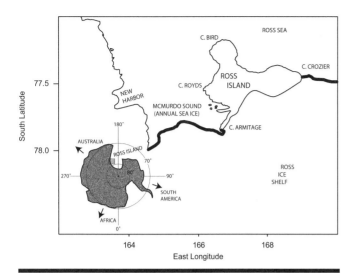

FIGURE 1. Location of McMurdo Sound. The annual sea ice northern limit is usually at Cape Royds, but occasionally extends to Cape Bird. The two major research stations of McMurdo Station (US) and Scott Base (NZ) are near the tip of Cape Armitage.

without the inconveniences and cost of research vessels, (3) scuba diving stations, and (4) at least three to four experimental laboratories for the study of marine organisms. These stations are scattered throughout the Sound in the spring and sometimes in the winter. As an example of the Sound's value as a scientific asset I will describe what is most familiar to me. For the past 43 years, the Sound has been the premier study site for the investigation of diving and behavioral physiology of birds and mammals, and the training of three generations of scientists. These kinds of studies began not long after the station was established in 1957, and there was a surge in scientific endeavor promoted by, and in celebration of the Second International Polar Year, or International Geophysical Year (IGY), as it was called then. The diving studies have been continuous ever since.

The crucial attributes that a plate of fast ice must have to make it useful year-round, is a large surface area of at least 10s of km². It must have an ice thickness that will support large vehicles such as Caterpillar D8's, substantial buildings, and large aircraft of at least the size of an LC 130. McMurdo Sound fast ice will support the Boeing C5, the largest aircraft known. Ross Island, where McMurdo Station resides, also provides protection for the Sound from ocean currents and storms so that the annual fast ice persists until early January. In fact, in the last few years, since about 2001 until 2006, little of the Sound ice broke up and departed. This was a result of the added

protection given to the Sound by the giant iceberg B15. As a consequence of the Sound's fast-ice stability, the largest airport in Antarctica was built in McMurdo Sound during the IGY (1957), and a new one has been built every spring since that first season. In addition, there is a large, local Weddell seal population in McMurdo Sound that has been the object of intensive ecology and physiology studies since the establishment of the two bases of McMurdo Station and Scott Base.

McMurdo Sound fulfills all the above requirements. It is about 64 km across the Sound from Ross Island to the mainland, and it is about 32 km from Cape Royds to the McMurdo Ice Shelf near Cape Armitage (Figure 1). The sea ice forms in April and decays in January, usually breaking out annually on the eastern half by mid to late February. The ice grows through October at which the maximum is usually about 2 m thick at its southern base next to the McMurdo Ice Shelf, and about 1.5 m thick near the edge at Cape Royds. It is noteworthy to illustrate the variability of the sea ice breakout, formation, and extent. In 1981 during the first overwintering study of Weddell seals, investigators were hampered by the late development of sea ice well into the winter after a previous extensive summer ice breakout to the McMurdo Ice Shelf. In contrast, in 2001 after the arrival of B15 at the northern edge of Ross Island, the annual fast ice became multi-year ice and extended well beyond Beaufort Island. This condition persisted until 2006 when the last remnants of this iceberg drifted north of the zone of influence on McMurdo Sound. Because of the numerous science programs at McMurdo Station and Scott Base, as well as McMurdo Station's function as the logistic center for supplying South Pole Station, the airport, that has hundreds of landings every season, is essential for this region of Antarctica. In addition, sea ice to land access for large vehicles to reach McMurdo Station and Scott Base is ideal with gently sloping land down to the sea ice edge. Finally, the Weddell seal population along the coast of Ross Island from Turtle Rock to Cape Royds (~15 km) harbors about 500 breeding females and it is one of the largest concentrations of seals in the Ross Sea.

The above-described attributes of McMurdo Sound are matchless. There are no other stations throughout Antarctica that have the air support or base size and support of McMurdo Station. Consider the rest of the Ross Sea. There are two possibilities: Terra Nova Bay (TNB) and Moubray Bay both of which have extensive fast ice sheets. In the southern end of Terra Nova Bay resides the Italian base of Zuchelli Station. The Campbell Ice Tongue bisects the bay. The small southern section would be feasible for only limited bird and mammal work. Here there is a small airstrip and a few offshore marine stations. The northern portion of TNB is much larger and has both a large population of Weddell seals, and one of the largest known emperor penguin colonies. This part of the bay is bordered by high ice cliffs and is not accessible from land. There is also a large perennial ice crack that bisects the eastern part of TNB from east to west that limits its usefulness for bird and mammal studies. There is also no access to land so that a shore station could not be established to support the kind of programs that are carried out from McMurdo Station and, at least for seals, it would be difficult to establish a functional sea ice station where the isolated hole protocol (IHP) would work. Wood Bay to the north of Cape Washington has no bases except for a small field camp at Edmonston Point for Adélie penguin research, and there is no good site for a station. Little is known about this area, but it appears to have a substantial seal population.

The only accessible land to sea ice in Moubray Bay is on Hallett Peninsula where a large Adélie penguin colony occupies the entire land surface area, and consequently is not an option for a research station now, although there was a research station there in the past. In the eastern Ross Sea adjacent to Cape Colbeck, Bartlett Inlet forms about a 15 km bight into an embayment of fast ice, which at the most southern extension is found a large emperor penguin colony. Little is known about this very isolated region that is notorious for foul weather and extensive pack ice. There is no easy access to land where a permanent station might be established. All of the described areas are small compared to McMurdo Sound and would provide a much more limited program of research than is possible at McMurdo Sound. These are the areas that I have first hand knowledge. As far as the rest of Antarctica is concerned, to my knowledge, there are no areas with air strips to handle routine air support from outside of Antarctica, with the exception of the Antarctic Peninsula, and none of those in the peninsula have extensive fast-ice sounds for the conduct of marine research. In short, there are no other places in the Antarctica or the world, where marine research, especially on birds and mammals can be conducted in the way I describe below.

METHODS

With a 2-meter-thick layer of ice over the Sound, the first objective is to pierce through it to reach the marine environment below. In the early days, this was a major, backbreaking task to cut a hole through the ice with a chainsaw and lift out the cut blocks from the developing hole with ice tongs. Depending upon the number of labor-

ers and the thickness of the ice, the task of penetration could take from a few hours to several days. Thankfully, soon after the cutting task was assisted by using explosives and the sea ice landscape began to be peppered with marine stations. However, this was not ideal for several reasons one of which was the potential harm to seals diving under the ice. By the early 1970s, a 1.2 m diameter augur was employed for hole cutting. Because the holes even in the thickest ice can be cut in about 20 min, this has become one of the most valuable assets in the toolbox of marine work in McMurdo Sound.

The sea ice stations have a range of functions. Some are platforms for setting fish and invertebrate traps to capture benthic specimens for ecology and physiology studies. Others are used for setting up a long-line to capture the large Antarctic cod, *Dissostichus mawsoni*, which may weigh greater than 100 kg. From these specimens much has been learned about anti-freeze properties of the body fluids, their physiology, and their natural history. My own personal experience has been to use the sea ice stations for conducting detailed diving studies on unrestrained Weddell seals and emperor penguins. For these kinds of experiments there is no match for the situation. In 1964 I established the isolated hole protocol wherein the dive hole was established a distance of 1 to 4 km from any other hole, either manmade or natural. Under these circumstances a penguin or seal released into the isolated hole had to return to this same breathing hole, and therefore, instruments could be deployed and recovered after each or a series of subsequent dives. Normally the diving seals would remain and use the hole for hours to days. During this period the hole was covered with a heated hut for the convenience of the investigators. The emperor penguins were peculiar because they would never surface in a hole covered with a hut if they had an option to go to a hole in the open. At the open air hole they would leave the water after almost every dive. The IHP has been used continuously by a variety of investigators over the past 43 years (as of 2007), and several projects are planned for the future. A great deal of information has been collected during these studies and the following are a few highlights most familiar to me.

RESULTS (BIRDS AND MAMMALS)

BEHAVIOR—WEDDELL SEALS

The first diving studies ever conducted on a diving animal, in which detailed diving information was obtained, occurred in 1964 in McMurdo Sound. Using time-depth recorders full advantage of the IHP was used to determine the behavior and physiology of Weddell seals (Kooyman, 1968). Investigations of this kind have been in progress ever since. The first results broke new ground in many ways, and one of the most significant was to show that we had been far too conservative in assumptions about marine mammal diving capacities. Indeed, even the first two publications on Weddell seals were too conservative on the estimates of what these animals could do (DeVries and Wohlschlag, 1964; Kooyman, 1966). In the latter report it was proposed that the maximum depths and durations were proposed to be 600 m and 46 min, respectively. At present the depth and duration records for Weddell seals now stand at 714 m (Testa, 1994), and 96 min (Zapol, Harvard Medical School, personal communication). Seals accomplished all of these exceptionally long dives while diving from an isolated hole. This procedure brings out the extremes in breath holding of these animals. Presumably they are responding to the trauma of capture and transport to the hole, and are trying to find an escape route from the new environment. However, within a few hours they settle in to routine hunting dives, and take advantage of the isolation and being away from competition with other seals. This provides to the investigator the best of both worlds. One is the discovery of some of the limits the seals may press themselves toward followed by the ordinary kind of effort that they do routinely. Both are of interest to the behaviorist and physiologist.

BEHAVIOR—EMPEROR PENGUINS

Emperor penguins have responded in a somewhat different way from Weddell seals to the IHP. They still achieve some of the longest dives recorded by emperor penguins and this record stands at 23 min (P. J. Ponganis, Scripps Institution of Oceanography, personal communication) compared to 21.8 min obtained from a free ranging bird (Wienecke et al., 2007). However, emperor penguins seldom make deep dives during the IHP compared to animals foraging under more natural conditions of the pack ice. The maximum depth of the IHP is 250 m (Ponganis et al., 2004), while that of the free ranging animals is 560 m (Wienecke et al., 2007). At least part of the reason for the shallow dives by emperor penguins during IHP is the lack of incentive. Free ranging birds feed primarily on Antarctic silver fish at mid-water depths in the Ross Sea. However, birds hunting under thick fast ice of the Sound switch from silver fish, even though these are abundant and the primary prey of Weddell seals, to another fish, *Pagothenia borchgrevinki*, which is present in large numbers just un-

der the ice. This has been a frustration to the physiologist who wants to explore the responses of the animals under extreme conditions. However, deep dives are so rare that it is purely by chance when physiological protocols are in place when the animals dive to extremes.

Indeed, in the many thousands of dives observed in Weddell seals only once were some of the responses made. In one case, a blood lactate sample was obtained after a 66 min dive (Kooyman et al., 1980), and pulmonary function measurements were obtained from a seal that made an 82 min dive (Kooyman et al., 1971). However, a benefit for the behaviorist and ecologist working in McMurdo Sound is that it has been possible to deploy "Crittercams" or "VDAPS" on emperor penguins and Weddell seals, respectively. These are animal borne imaging devices that have made it possible to observe their hunting tactics. With the Crittercam on emperor penguins taped images show how the birds catch *P. borchgrevinki* hiding in ice crystals attached to the fast ice undersurface (Ponganis et al., 2000). Similarly, with the VDAP Weddell seals' captures of Antarctic silverfish and Antarctic cod were documented (Davis et al., 1999). All of these imaging results proved exciting both to the scientific community and the media.

PHYSIOLOGY—WEDDELL SEALS

For the comparative physiologist working on diving physiology McMurdo Sound has been a magnet because of the IHP. This protocol has made possible the attachment of complex instruments to record heart rate, measure blood chemistry, and to determine oxygen and nitrogen tension in blood at known depths and times in the dive. Some of the results have been the generation of the lactate endurance curve from blood samplings of several different seals (Kooyman et al., 1980). This curve has defined the aerobic diving limit (ADL) of Weddell seals by the inflection area within the curve (Figure 2). The concept was defined by Kooyman (1985), and states that "The ADL is defined as the maximum breath hold that is possible without any increase in blood LA concentration during or after the dive." It was further explained that the calculated ADL (cADL) could be estimated if the body oxygen store and diving metabolic rate were known. This concept has motivated many research projects to make estimates of the ADL in a variety of diving animals. Several of these studies have been done on Antarctic divers including the emperor penguin using the IHP for the study in McMurdo Sound.

Another landmark study on Weddell seals, among the many that have occurred, was the determination of blood N_2 levels while Weddell seals were diving to depth

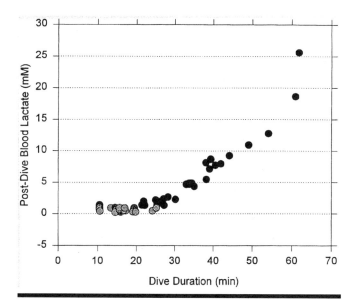

FIGURE 2. Lactate endurance curve of the Weddell seal. The gray dots are peak arterial post-dive lactic acid concentrations of aerobic dives. The black dots are the peak arterial post-dive lactic acid concentrations after dives with a lactate accumulation above resting levels (modified from Kooyman et al., 1980).

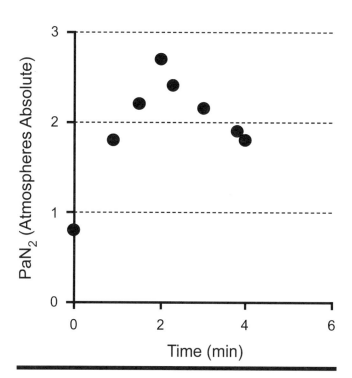

FIGURE 3. Arterial N_2 tensions in a Weddell seal. The seal made a free dive to 89 m under McMurdo Sound fast ice. The dive began at zero on the abscissa, reached a maximum depth at 5 min, and the dive ended after 8 min.

(Falke et al., 1985) (Figure 3). This result corroborated the more artificial studies conducted on elephant seals forcibly submerged and compressed in a hyperbaric chamber (Kooyman et al., 1971) a number of years earlier. The salient feature of these blood pN_2 results was that no matter the depth of the dive the N_2 tensions do not rise above a relatively low value that is unlikely to cause decompression sickness. The only similar measurements on other species diving under unrestrained conditions are those of the emperor penguin using the IHP in McMurdo Sound (Ponganis, personal communication).

PHYSIOLOGY—EMPEROR PENGUINS

Using the same procedures as applied to the Weddell seal, the ADL of emperor penguins has been determined (Ponganis et al., 1997), and it has equally important implications for diving birds as the studies of Weddell seals had for diving mammals. To probe this problem further a recent study has asked the question of how emperor penguins manage their oxygen stores. This question is of exceptional importance to understanding the physiological principles of how diving animals overcome the problems of limited oxygen and endure hypoxia on a routine basis. In the course of these studies the investigators have shown

that emperor penguins can tolerate exceptionally low arterial O_2 tensions in the range of 5–10 mmHg (Ponganis, personal communication). These values are at levels below what could maintain consciousness in most terrestrial birds and mammals, including humans. Indeed they are substantially below the expected arterial O_2 tension of a person standing on Mt. Everest (Chomolungma), and they raise a series of questions about how this diving bird overcomes such extreme hypoxia.

DISCUSSION

I have briefly mentioned several types of studies on birds and mammals that have had a significant impact on diving behavior and physiology of marine animals. If this were a comprehensive review of work accomplished in McMurdo Sound there would be many disciplines and investigators represented and the number of publications would be in the hundreds if not thousands. Many of the studies could not have been done anywhere other than in McMurdo Sound. As for the birds and mammals studies there are at least three generations of investigators, spanning 45 years that have found the greatest contributions to their field in McMurdo Sound. In regard to the diving studies mentioned above, many of the results are fundamental to the field of behavior and physiology of diving.

Reflecting on these accomplishments and many others such as the long-term works of Siniff's trends in Weddell seal populations (Siniff et al., 1977), DeVries's range of work on ecology to the molecular nature of antifreeze compounds in fish (DeVries, 1971) and long term catch data on the highly sought after Antarctic cod (DeVries, University of Illinois, unpublished data), and Dayton's cage exclusion studies of benthic organisms (Dayton et al., 1974; Dayton, 1985), I wonder if McMurdo Sound is not underappreciated. In the early days it was not coveted at all, and was used as a dumping ground for human waste and many harmful inorganic and organic products. Thankfully those "bad old days" ended a long time ago, and like Antarctica in general, it is treated by a much softer human footprint. Still, to recognize the distinct value of McMurdo Sound it should be given some sanctuary or museum status as the great contributor to biological sciences, because as I hoped to achieve in this review, there is no other place like it. We do not know what specific effects the changing climate in Antarctica will have on the seas that surround the continent, but with the long-term history of science in McMurdo Sound, it will be one of the areas invaluable in assessing some of the changes. Especially with the large modern laboratory of Crary Center adjacent to the Sound where researchers can study the animals with some of the most sophisticated techniques in the world.

ACKNOWLEDGMENTS

Thanks to Smithsonian for making this symposium possible and providing the travel funds to attend. All my work over the past 45 years at McMurdo Sound has been supported by numerous NSF OPP grants for which I will always be grateful. I give thanks, as well, to the many support contractors and their staff on land, sea, and air that have made the journeys such a fine experience. In the background always has been my wife Melba and my sons, Carsten and Tory. It was also an inestimable joy to see both sons become the best field assistants one could ever want.

LITERATURE CITED

Davis, R., L. Fuiman, T. Williams, S. Collier, W. Hagey, S. Kanatous, S. Kohin, and M. Horning. 1999. Hunting Behavior of a Marine Mammal beneath the Antarctic Fast Ice. *Science*, 283:993–996.

Dayton, P. K. 1985. Antarctica and Its Biota (A Review of Antarctic Ecology). *Science*, 229:157–158.

Dayton, P. K., G. A. Robilliard, R. T. Paine, and L. B. Dayton. 1974. Biological Accommodation in the Benthic Community at McMurdo Sound, Antarctica. *Ecology (Monograph)*, 44:105–128.

DeVries, A. L. 1971. Glycoproteins as Biological Antifreeze Agents in Antarctic Fishes. *Science*, 172:1152–1155.

DeVries, A. L., and D. E. Wohlschlag. 1964. Diving Depths of the Weddell Seal. *Science*, 145:292.

Falke, K. J., R. D. Hill, J. Qvist, R. C. Schneider, M. Guppy, G. C. Liggins, P. W. Hochachka, and Z. Elliot. 1985. Seal Lungs Collapse during Free Diving: Evidence from Arterial Nitrogen Tensions. *Science*, 229:556–558.

Kooyman, G. L. 1966. Maximum Diving Capacities of the Weddell Seal (*Leptonychotes weddelli*). *Science*, 151:1553–1554.

Kooyman, G. L. 1968. An Analysis of Some Behavioral and Physiological Characteristics Related to Diving in the Weddell Seal. In *Biology in the Antarctic Seas III*, ed. G. A. Llano and W. L. Schmitt. Antarctic Research Series, Vol. 11. Washington, D.C.: American Geophysical Union.

———. 1985. Physiology without Restraint in Diving Mammals. *Marine Mammal Science*, 1:166–178.

Kooyman, G. L., D. H. Kerem, W. B. Campbell, and J. J. Wright. 1971. Pulmonary Function in Freely Diving Weddell Seals (*Leptonychotes weddelli*). *Respiratory Physiology*, 12:271–282.

Kooyman, G. L., E. Wahrenbrock, M. Castellini, R. W. Davis, and E. Sinnett. 1980. Aerobic and Anaerobic Metabolism during Voluntary Diving in Weddell Seals: Evidence of Preferred Pathways from Blood Chemistry and Behavior. *Journal of Comparative Physiology*, 138:335–346.

Ponganis, P. J., G. L. Kooyman, L. N. Starke, C. A. Kooyman, and T. G. Kooyman. 1997. Post-Dive Blood Lactate Concentrations in Emperor Penguins, *Aptenodytes forsteri*. *Journal of Experimental Biology*, 200:1623–1626.

Ponganis, P. J., R. P. Van Dam, G. Marshall, T. Knower, and D. Levenson. 2000. Sub-Ice Foraging Behavior of Emperor Penguins. *Journal of Experimental Biology*, 203:3275–3278.

Ponganis, P. J., R. P. van Dam, D. H. Levenson, T. Knower, and K. V. Ponganis. 2004. Deep Dives and Aortic Temperatures of Emperor Penguins: New Directions for Biologging at the Isolated Dive Hole. Memoirs of National Institute of Polar Research Special Issue No. 58, Biologging Science, pp. 155–161.

Siniff, D. B., D. P. Demaster, R. J. Hofman, and L. L. Eberhart. 1977. An Analysis of the Dynamics of a Weddell Seal Population. *Ecological Monographs*, 47(3):319–335.

Testa, J. 1994. Over-Winter Movements and Diving Behaviour of Female Weddell Seals (*Leptonychotes weddellii*). *Canadian Journal of Zoology*, 72:1700–1710.

Wienecke, B., G. Robertson, R. Kirkwood, and K. Lawton. 2007. Extreme Dives by Free-Ranging Emperor Penguins. *Polar Biology*, 30:133–142.

Interannual and Spatial Variability in Light Attenuation: Evidence from Three Decades of Growth in the Arctic Kelp, *Laminaria solidungula*

Kenneth H. Dunton, Susan V. Schonberg, and Dale W. Funk

ABSTRACT. We examined long-term variations in kelp growth in coincidence with recent (2004–2006) measurements of underwater photosynthetically active radiation (PAR), light attenuation coefficients, chlorophyll concentrations, and total suspended solids (TSS) to determine the impact of sediment resuspension on the productivity of an isolated kelp bed community on the Alaskan Beaufort Sea coast. Attenuation coefficients exhibited distinct geographical patterns and interannual variations between 2004 and 2006 that were correlated with temporal and geographical patterns in TSS (range 3.5–23.8 mg L^{-1}). The low chlorophyll levels (<3.0 μg L^{-1}) in all three years were unlikely to have contributed significantly to periods of low summer water transparency. Blade elongation rates in the arctic kelp, *Laminaria solidungula*, are excellent integrators of water transparency since their annual growth is completely dependent on PAR received during the summer open-water period. We noted that blade growth at all sites steadily increased between 2004 and 2006, reflective of increased underwater PAR in each successive year. Mean blade growth at all sites was clearly lowest in 2003 (<8 cm) compared to 2006 (18–47 cm). We attribute the low growth in 2003 to reported intense storm activity that likely produced extremely turbid water conditions that resulted in low levels of ambient light. Examination of a 30-year record of annual growth at two sites revealed other periods of low annual growth that were likely related to summers characterized by exceptional strong storm activity. Although kelp growth is expected to be higher at shallower sites, the reverse occurs, since sediment re-suspension is greatest at shallower water depths. The exceptionally low growth of kelp in 2003 indicates that these plants are living near their physiological light limits, but represent excellent indicators of interannual changes in water transparency that result from variations in local climatology.

INTRODUCTION

Research studies conducted over the past two decades have clearly documented that kelp biomass, growth, and productivity in the Alaskan Beaufort Sea are strongly regulated by light availability (photosynthetically active radiation, PAR). Results from a variety of experimental studies, including the linear growth response of kelp plants to natural changes in the underwater light field (Dunton, 1984; 1990; Dunton and Schell, 1986;), carbon radioisotope tracer experiments (Dunton and Jodwalis, 1988), and laboratory and field physiological work (Henley and Dunton, 1995; 1997) have been used successfully to develop models of kelp productivity in relation to PAR. Yet, until recently, the relationship

Kenneth H. Dunton and Susan V. Schonberg, University of Texas Marine Science Institute, 750 Channel View Dr., Port Aransas, TX 78373, USA. Dale W. Funk, LGL Alaska Research Associates, Inc., 1101 East 76th Avenue, Suite B, Anchorage, AK 99516, USA. Corresponding author: K. Dunton (ken.dunton@mail.utexas.edu). Accepted 28 May 2008.

between water turbidity—as measured by total suspended solids (TSS) or optical instruments—and benthic algal production was unknown. Aumack et al. (2007) were the first to establish the quantitative link between water column turbidity, PAR and kelp production through a model that uses TSS data to predict estimates of kelp productivity in an area known as the Stefansson Sound Boulder Patch on the central Alaskan Beaufort Sea coast. This information is essential for evaluating how changes in water transparency are related to higher suspended sediment concentrations from anthropogenic activities near the Boulder Patch, coastal erosion, and increased freshwater inflow (McClelland et al., 2006). The quantitative measurements of TSS collected by Aumack et al. (2007) in summers 2001 and 2002 were a critical first step in the establishment of an accurate basin-wide production model for the Stefansson Sound Boulder Patch.

The productivity of *Laminaria solidungula* in subtidal coastal ecosystems is an important factor that regulates benthic biodiversity and ultimately, the intensity of biological interactions such as competition, facilitation, predation, recruitment, and system productivity (Petraitis et al., 1989; Worm et al., 1999; Mittelbach et al., 2001; Paine 2002). On a larger scale, biodiversity measurements can serve as an indicator of the balance between speciation and extinction (McKinney, 1998a; 1998b; Rosenzweig, 2001). The interesting biogeographic affinities of organisms in the Boulder Patch led Dunton (1992) to refer to the area as an "arctic benthic paradox," based on the Atlantic origin of many of the benthic algae (e.g. the red algae *Odonthalia dentata*, *Phycodrys rubens*, *Rhodomela confervoides*) in contrast to the Pacific orientation of many of the invertebrates (most polychaetes and gastropods). This unique character of the biological assemblage, combined with the Boulder Patch's isolated location (Dunton et al., 1982), suggests the potential of the area as a biogeographic stepping-stone. Thus, the Boulder Patch likely has large biological and ecological roles outside Stefansson Sound.

The overarching objective of our study was to use synoptic and long-term measurements of PAR, light attenuation coefficients, total suspended solids (TSS; mg L^{-1}), and indices of kelp biomass to determine the impact of sediment resuspension on kelp productivity and ecosystem status in the Stefansson Sound Boulder Patch. Between 2004 and 2006, we initiated studies to monitor water quality, light, kelp growth, and the associated invertebrate community in the Boulder Patch. This research program was designed to address ecosystem change as related to anthropogenic activities from oil and gas development. Our initial effort was focused on establishing a quantitative relationship between total suspended solids (TSS) and benthic kelp productivity (see Aumack, 2003; Aumack et al., 2007). Our current objectives included (1) defining the spatial variability in annual productivity and biomass of kelp, (2) monitoring incident and in situ ambient light (as PAR) and TSS, and (3) using historical datasets of kelp growth to establish a long-term record of kelp productivity.

MATERIALS AND METHODS

Our overall sampling strategy during summers 2004, 2005, and 2006 incorporated: (1) semi-synoptic maps of TSS and light attenuation parameters generated through sampling at 30 randomly-selected points in a 300 km^2 area that included the Boulder Patch and the region south of Narwhal Island to Point Brower on the Sagavanirktok Delta (Figure 1; 70°23'N; 147°50'W); (2) long-term variations in underwater PAR at three fixed sites and incident PAR at one coastal site during the summer open-water period; and (3) kelp growth at several monitoring stations established during the 1984–1991 Boulder Patch Monitoring Program (LGL Ecological Research Associates and Dunton, 1992). A majority of our study sites were located within the Stefansson Sound Boulder Patch, which is characterized by non-contiguous patches of >10% rock cover. These patches are depicted by gray contour lines in Figures 1–5.

SYNOPTIC SAMPLING

In order to describe the spatial extent and patterns of TSS, light attenuation, chlorophyll, nutrients, and physiochemical properties across Stefansson Sound, we sampled 30 sites across the monitoring area (Figure 1), which ranges in depth from 3 to 7 m. The location for each site was chosen by laying a probability-based grid over the area and randomly choosing a location within each grid cell. This method allowed sampling locations to be spaced quasi-evenly across the landscape while still maintaining assumptions required for a random sample (i.e., all locations have an equal chance of being sampled). All 30 sites were visited on three separate occasions during summers 2004, 2005, and 2006 using a high-speed vessel (*R/V Proteus*). We measured TSS, incident PAR, inorganic nutrients (ammonia, phosphate, silicate, nitrogen), water column chlorophyll, and physiochemical parameters (temperature, salinity, dissolved oxygen, and pH) during each synoptic sampling effort.

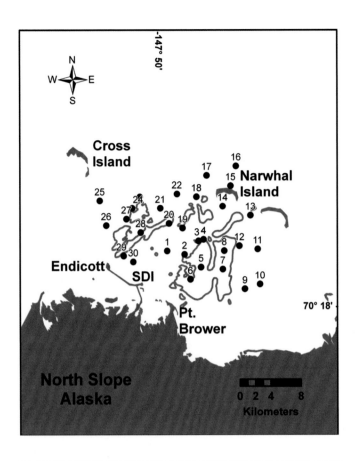

FIGURE 1. The project study area showing 30 synoptic collection sites used in summers 2004, 2005, and 2006. SDI: Satellite Drilling Island. Gray contour lines show >10% rock cover.

Replicate water samples were collected at 2 and 4 m depths using a van Dorn bottle. All samples were placed in pre-labeled plastic bottles, with sampling point geographic coordinates (Lat/Long) recorded using a handheld Garmin Global Positioning System, GPSMap 76S (Garmin International Inc., Olathe, Kansas, USA). In situ physiochemical measurements were made from the vessel. All other samples were stored in a dark cooler and transported to a laboratory on Endicott Island for processing.

Light Attenuation

Simultaneous surface and underwater measurements of PAR data were collected using LI-190SA and LI-192SA cosine sensors, respectively, connected to a LI-1000 datalogger (LI-COR Inc., Lincoln, Nebraska, USA). The LI-190SA sensor was placed at a 4 m height on the vessel mast. Coincident underwater measurements with the LI-192SA

sensor were made using a lowering frame deployed at 2 and 4 m depths. Care was taken to avoid interference from shading of the sensor by the vessel. The Brouger-Lambert Law describes light attenuation with water depth:

$$k = \frac{\ln(I_o/I_z)}{z} \qquad (a)$$

where I_o is incident (surface) light intensity, I_z is light intensity at depth z, and k is the light attenuation coefficient (m^{-1}).

TSS

A known volume of water from each sample was filtered through pre-weighed, pre-combusted glass fiber filters (Pall Corporation, Ann Arbor, Michigan, USA). Following a distilled water rinse filters were oven-dried to constant weight at 60°C. The net weight of particles collected in each sample was calculated by subtracting the filter's initial weight from the total weight following filtration.

Chlorophyll

For chlorophyll measurement, 100 ml of water from each replicate sample was filtered through a 0.45 μm cellulose nitrate membrane filter (Whatman, Maidstone, England) in darkness. After filtration, the filters and residue were placed in pre-labeled opaque vials and frozen. The frozen filters were transported to The University of Texas Marine Science Institute (UTMSI) in Port Aransas, Texas, for chlorophyll analysis. At UTMSI, filters were removed from the vials and placed in pre-labeled test tubes containing 5 ml of methanol for overnight extraction (Parsons et al., 1984:3–28). Chlorophyll *a* concentration, in μg L^{-1}, was determined using a Turner Designs 10-AU fluorometer (Turner Design, Sunnyvale, California, USA). Non-acidification techniques are used to account for the presence of chlorophyll *b* and phaeopigments (Welschmeyer, 1994).

Nutrients

Water samples were frozen and transferred to UTMSI for nutrient analysis. Nutrient concentrations for NH_4^+, PO_4^{3-}, SiO_4, and $NO_2^- + NO_3^-$ were determined by continuous flow injection analysis using colorimetric techniques on a Lachat QuikChem 8000 (Zellweger Analytics Inc., Milwaukee, Wisconsin, USA) with a minimum detection level of 0.03 μM.

Physiochemical Parameters

Temperature (°C), salinity (‰), dissolved oxygen (% and mg L^{-1}) pH, and water depth (m), were measured using a YSI Data Sonde (YSI Inc., Yellow Springs, Ohio, USA).

PERMANENT SITES

Underwater Irradiance

In addition to the synoptic sampling, we established eight permanent sites for collection of long-term data. Continuous underwater PAR measurements were collected at three sampling sites (DS-11, E-1, and W-1) in the Boulder Patch study area (Figure 2) and terrestrial PAR measurements at one coastal location (Endicott Island). These sites have been the focus of previous long-term monitoring efforts; measurements of PAR and kelp growth are reported in published literature (Dunton, 1990). Site DS-11, established as a reference site, has been a primary research site for the Boulder Patch since 1978. This site lies well outside the area most likely impacted by sediment plumes originating from the pro-

posed Liberty Project, including construction of a buried pipeline and Stockpile Zone 1 (Ban et al., 1999). All three Boulder Patch sites are located on seabed characterized by >25% rock cover. Sites were chosen based on either their southern-most location in the Boulder Patch (W-1, E-1), existence of historical PAR data (W-1, E-1, and DS-11), and their likelihood of being impacted by oil and gas development through dredging activities associated with pipeline or island construction.

Underwater data were collected using LI-193SA spherical quantum sensor (for scalar measurements) connected to a LI-1000 datalogger (LI-COR Inc., Lincoln, Nebraska, USA) at each site. Sensors were mounted on PVC poles and positioned just above the kelp canopy to prevent fouling or shading by kelp fronds. Instantaneous PAR measurements were taken at 1 min intervals and integrated over 1 h periods. Coincident surface PAR measurements were taken with LI-190SA terrestrial cosine sensor connected to LI-1000 datalogger located on Endicott Island.

Kelp Elongation

At each of the nine dive sites (depth range 5–7 m) within the Boulder Patch (DS-11, Brower-1, E-1, E-2, E-3, L-1, L-2, W-1, and W-3), SCUBA divers collected 15–30 individual specimens of *Laminaria solidungula* attached to large cobbles and boulders in summers 2004, 2005, and 2006. Samples were placed in pre-labeled black bags, transported to Endicott, and processed. Blade segments from every specimen, which corresponded to one year's growth (Dunton, 1985), were measured and recorded to produce a recent (3–4 yr) growth record of linear blade expansion at each site. Blades measured in summer reflect growth during both the present and previous calendar year since more than 90% of a kelp's frond expansion occurs between November and June under nearly complete darkness (Dunton and Schell, 1986). Linear growth in *L. solidungula* from the Boulder Patch is heavily dependent on photosynthetic carbon reserves that accumulate during the previous summer in proportion to the underwater light environment. A growth year (GWYR) is dictated by the formation of a new blade segment, which begins in mid-November every year and is defined by the summer that precedes new blade formation (e.g., basal blade growth measured in summer 2007 depicts GWYR 2006).

Kelp Biomass

Frond lengths of *Laminaria solidungula* plants were measured at W-3, E-1, E-3, and DS-11 along four 25 m

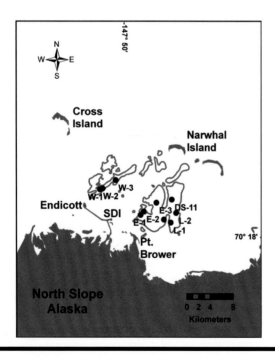

FIGURE 2. The project study area. The indicated sites are historical Boulder Patch stations that have been visited repeatedly since 1984. During summers 2004, 2005, and 2006, long-term light was measured at sites DS-11, E-1, and W-1; kelp blade length data were also collected at these sites.

transects. Transects radiated from a central point at random chosen directions at 280°, 80°, 260°, and 110°Magnetic.

Statistics and GIS

TSS concentrations, chlorophyll *a* concentrations, and the attenuation coefficient (*k*) were matched with their respective geographic coordinates and plotted using GIS software ArcMap 9.2 (ERSI, Redlands, California). Data were interpolated across a polygon of Stefansson Sound, including the Boulder Patch, using Geospatial Analyst extension and Kriging function in ArcMap following Aumack et al. (2007). Data were analyzed using standard parametric models. Spatial and interannual significance among *k*, TSS, and chlorophyll measurements were determined using a paired t-test to examine significant differences ($p < 0.05$) among treatment variables using Microsoft Excel. Significant differences in PAR among years and sites was tested using a two-way analysis of variance (ANOVA) using time as a block with a general linear models procedure (SAS Institute Inc, 1985) following Dunton (1990).

RESULTS

SYNOPTIC SAMPLING

Light attenuation (*k*) was derived from coincident in situ measurements of surface and underwater PAR at 2 and 4 m depths collected at 30 stations on three differ-

ent occasions each summer. Attenuation was consistently elevated in coastal zones with highest *k* values observed near Endicott Island and SDI (Satellite Drilling Island) indicating more turbid water closer to shore (Figure 3). Lower *k* values were recorded offshore along the eastern and northeastern sides of Stefansson Sound. In summer 2004, *k* ranged from 0.43–1.34 m^{-1} (mean 0.73 ± 0.14) throughout Stefansson Sound. In 2005 *k* ranged from 0.47–1.32 m^{-1} (mean 0.69 ± 0.03) and in 2006, *k* was 0.54–1.08 m^{-1} (mean 0.72 ± 0.01). The majority of the Boulder Patch, including areas with dense kelp populations (>25% rock cover), were found predominantly in offshore waters where attenuation measurements were consistently less than 1.0 m^{-1}.

The TSS concentrations were dramatically lower in summers 2004 and 2006 compared with 2005, yet the same general trends were observed (Figure 4). Since a paired t-test indicated that the TSS values measured at 2 and 4 m depths were not significantly different in either year (2004 p = 0.065; 2005 p = 0.156) the means of the two depths are displayed. In 2004, the highest concentrations (7.6–8.3 mg L^{-1}) were found near Endicott Island and SDI and in a turbid area just north of Narwhal Island (5.7–6.1 mg L^{-1}). The TSS ranged from 3.8–7.6 mg L^{-1} outside the Boulder Patch with a mean of 5.0 mg L^{-1}. Inside the Boulder Patch the data ranged from 4.0 to 8.3 mg L^{-1} (mean 5.0 mg L^{-1}); the overall site average was 5.0 ± 1.8 mg L^{-1}.

The TSS measurements were much higher and varied greatly throughout Stefansson Sound during summer

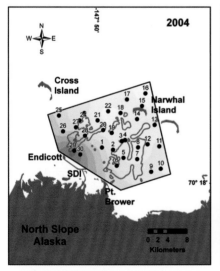
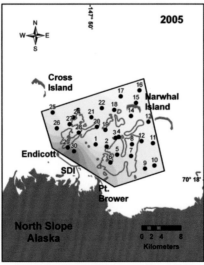
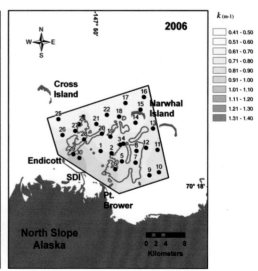

FIGURE 3. Combined mean attenuation coefficient (*k*) values calculated from measurements collected at 2 m and 4 m water depths in summers 2004, 2005, and 2006.

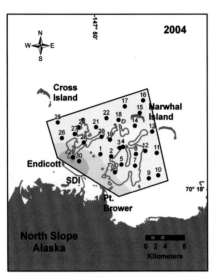 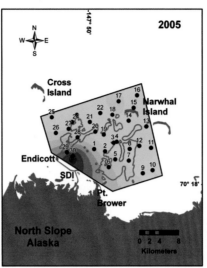 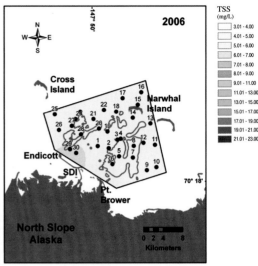

FIGURE 4. Combined mean total suspended solids (TSS) from samples collected at 2 m and 4 m water depths in 2004, 2005, and 2006.

2005 (7.5–23.8 mg L^{-1}; mean 11.1 ± 1.1 mg L^{-1}). The highest values (17.6–23.8 mg L^{-1}) were located nearshore, adjacent to Endicott Island, SDI, and Point Brower. Outside the Boulder Patch, TSS ranged from 7.5 to 23.8 mg L^{-1} (mean 11.2 mg L^{-1}). Inside the Boulder Patch, values ranged from 9.0 to 17.6 mg L^{-1} (mean 11.0 mg L^{-1}).

In 2006, TSS concentrations were similar to those measured in 2004 (range of 3.5–6.9 mg L^{-1}; mean of 4.7 ± 0.2 mg L^{-1}). The highest values were again adjacent to Endicott Island, SDI and Point Brower. Outside the Boulder Patch, TSS ranged from 3.6 to 6.9 mg L^{-1} (mean 4.6 ± 0.2 mg L^{-1}). The TSS values ranged from 3.5 to 5.9 mg L^{-1} inside the Boulder Patch with a mean of 4.6 ± 0.2 mg L^{-1}.

Chlorophyll *a* measurements from 2 and 4 m depths were relatively low but significantly different from each other in all years (p < 0.05). In all three years, 4 m chlorophyll values were higher than the 2 m measurements (Figure 5). The 2005 chlorophyll means were the highest followed by 2004 means, with the lowest values occurring in 2006. In 2004, chlorophyll measurements ranged from 0.11 to 2.63 µg L^{-1} (mean 0.39 ± 0.2 µg L^{-1}). In summer 2005, values ranged from 0.11 to 3.54 µg L^{-1} (mean 0.76 ± 0.08 µg L^{-1}) compared to 0.11–0.41 µg L^{-1} (mean 0.18 ± 0.01 µg L^{-1}) in 2006.

Ammonium concentrations (Table 1) were significantly different among samples collected at 2 and 4 m in all years (p < 0.05); all values were low (0.12 ± 0.06 µM at 2 m and 0.17 ± 0.07 µM at 4 m in 2004; 0.40 ± 0.04 µM at 2 m and 0.65 ± 0.04 µM at 4 m in 2005 and

0.25 ± 0.05 µM at 2 m and 0.12 ± 0.02 µM at 4 m). Ammonium ranged from 0.0–0.52 µM in 2006. Highest concentrations were noted at sites adjacent to barrier islands (Sites 13 and 15); lowest values were noted offshore (0.0–0.02 µM).

In general, phosphate concentrations were low. Mean values in 2004 were 0.24 ± 0.03 µM at 2 m and 0.19 ± 0.05 µM at 4 m. Phosphate values ranged from 0.11–0.39 µM with the highest concentrations collected at sites adjacent to Endicott. Several other random sites displayed higher values at either 2 or 4 m. The lowest values were observed at sites seaward of Narwhal Island (0.0–0.02) µM. In 2005, phosphate measurements were lower in 2 m samples (mean 0.29 ± 0.01 µM) versus the 4 m samples (mean 0.35 ± 0.01 µM). The same pattern held for the 2006 (2 m mean 0.17 ± 0.01 µM; 4 m mean 0.20 ± 0.01 µM).

Silicate values collected from 2 and 4 m in 2004 were not significantly different (p = 0.51), ranging from 0.07–4.90 µM; mean 1.84 ± 0.26 µM (Table 1). Silicate was quite low at 2 and 4 m in 2004 compared to 2005 (2 m mean 5.64 ± 0.19 µM; 4 m mean 5.19 ± 0.16 µM) and 2006 (2 m mean 7.05 ± 0.14 µM; 4 m mean 6.89 ± 0.16 µM).

$NO_2^- + NO_3^-$ measurements throughout Stefansson Sound were also generally low, with 2004 station means ranging from 0.0–0.29 µM at 2 m; 0.12 ± 0.21 µM at 4 m (Table 1). The 2005 station means ranged from 0.0–0.61 µM at 2 m; 0.03–1.98 µM at 4 m, and 2006 means were 0.03–0.33 µM at 2 m; 0.02–0.44 µM at 4 m. In all three

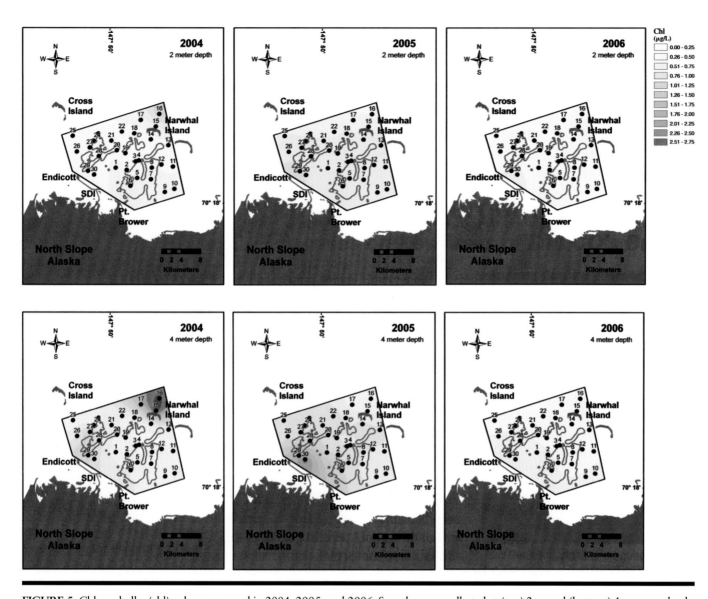

FIGURE 5. Chlorophyll *a* (chl) values measured in 2004, 2005, and 2006. Samples were collected at (top) 2 m and (bottom) 4 m water depth.

TABLE 1. Measurements of ammonium, phosphate, silicate, and nitrate + nitrite at 30 sites measured annually in July and August 2004, 2005, and 2006. Samples were collected at 2 and 4 m water column depths. Values are x ± SE.

YEAR μM	Ammonium (NH$_4^+$) 2 m	Ammonium (NH$_4^+$) 4 m	Phosphate (PO$_4^{3-}$) 2 m	Phosphate (PO$_4^{3-}$) 4 m	Silicate (SiO$_4$) 2 m	Silicate (SiO$_4$) 4 m	Nitrate + Nitrite (NO^{2-} + NO^{3-}) 2 m	Nitrate + Nitrite (NO^{2+} + NO^{3-}) 4 m
2004	0.12 ± 0.06	0.17 ± 0.07	0.24 ± 0.03	0.19 ± 0.05	1.76 ± 0.18	1.84 ± 0.26	0.14 ± 0.10	0.15 ± 0.01
2005	0.40 ± 0.04	0.65 ± 0.05	0.29 ± 0.01	0.35 ± 0.01	5.64 ± 0.19	5.19 ± 0.16	0.21 ± 0.04	0.29 ± 0.08
2006	0.25 ± 0.05	0.12 ± 0.02	0.17 ± 0.01	0.20 ± 0.01	7.05 ± 0.14	6.89 ± 0.16	0.07 ± 0.01	0.10 ± 0.02

sampling years, the 4 m nitrate concentrations were slightly higher than the 2 m but were not significantly different.

Mean sea surface temperature (2 m and 4 m) increased throughout the Boulder Patch each year between 2004 and 2006 (Table 2). Summer 2004 was characterized by frequent storm activity, which was reflected in depressed surface water temperatures that were negative at some sites. The 2006 mean 2 m temperature (4.6 ± 0.2°C) was more than double the value measured in 2004 (2.1 ± 0.6°C). The 4 m mean temperature increased more than fourfold between 2004 and 2006 (0.9 ± 0.7; 4.2 ± 0.2).

Salinity measurements were homogeneous across the Boulder Patch and means were consistent between summers 2004 and 2005 at both 2 m (23.8 ± 1.0‰; 23.8 ± 1.7 ‰) and 4 m (26.8 ± 1.2 ‰; 26.6± 1.4 ‰) depths, but values dropped precipitously in 2006 (2 m 16.9 ± 0.35‰; 4 m 20.7± 0.5‰; Table 2). In 2004, the salinity range at 2 m was 20.4–27.4‰; the 4 m 2004 range was 23.5 to 31.7‰. In summer 2005, measurements at 2 m ranged from 17.7 to 26.21‰ and at 4 m salinity varied from 24.9 to 30.8‰. During 2006, the 2 m salinity low was measured at 11.3 ‰ and the high was 23.5‰; the 4 m low was 12.3 ‰ and high 30.0‰. At 2 m, waters were slightly fresher than at 4 m during all three years.

We only report pH data from 2004 and 2006 since the probe malfunctioned during the 2005 field season (Table 2). In 2004, pH measurement means were remarkably constant at 8.2 ± 0.04 at both 2 and 4 m. The measurements in 2006 were also very consistent (7.9 ± 0.01 ‰) throughout the sampling area and between the 2 and 4 m depths, but were more acidic than the 2004 values. Measurements of dissolved oxygen revealed values at or near saturation in all years (Table 2). The range in values reflect differences in water temperature and wind induced turbulence of surface waters.

PERMANENT STATIONS

Blade elongation in *Laminaria solidungula* displayed large spatial and temporal variability as reflected in measurements from nine sites (Table 3). Mean site blade growth was lower at every site in GWYR 2003 compared to GWYRs 2004, 2005, and 2006, reflecting the exceptionally poor weather conditions in summer 2003 that produced extremely low levels of ambient PAR. Kelp collected in 2004 (GWYR 2003) had annual average growth rates ranging between 4.4 and 10.4 cm. In contrast, blade elongation ranged from 10 to 25.5 cm in GWYR 2004 and from 16.7 to 47.3 cm in GWYR in 2005 and 2006, comparable to previous studies (Dunton, 1990; Martin and Gallaway, 1994). Specimens from DS-11 showed the greatest annual growth of all sites in most years.

In conjunction with blade elongation rates, we collected PAR measurements during summers 2004, 2005, and 2006. Surface irradiance followed a typical cyclical pattern, peaking between 1200–1400 μmol photons m^{-2} s^{-1} in the afternoon before declining to nearly undetectable levels after midnight (Figure 6). Highest levels of underwater PAR were normally recorded by scalar sensors in the early afternoon (1400 hrs), which also corresponded to the period of maximum incident PAR. In 2004, from 31 July to 6 August, underwater irradiance dropped to near zero at all three sites (DS-11, E-1, and W-1). These low values were coincident with a series of intense storms that generated winds in excess of 10 m s^{-1} from the southwest and southeast. Extremely low underwater PAR concentrations continued through 9 August followed by four days of slightly higher values, at which point the dataloggers were removed. Prior to the storm, underwater scalar irradiance at DS-11 ranged from 180 to 200 μmol m^{-2} s^{-1} compared to less than 20 μmol m^{-2} s^{-1} during the storm,

TABLE 2. Average temperature, salinity, dissolved oxygen, and pH measurements for 30 sites measured annually in July and August 2004, 2005, and 2006. Samples were collected at 2 and 4 m water column depths. Values are means ± SE. ND indicates no data.

YEAR	Temp (°C) 2 m	Temp (°C) 4 m	Salinity (‰) 2 m	Salinity (‰) 4 m	Dissolved O$_2$ (mg L^{-1}) 2 m	Dissolved O$_2$ (mg L^{-1}) 4 m	pH (m^{-1}) 2 m	pH (m^{-1}) 4 m
2004	2.11 ± 0.55	0.88 ± 0.75	23.80 ± 0.99	26.81 ± 1.16	13.18 ± 0.35	14.22 ± 0.38	8.19 ± 0.05	8.22 ± 0.04
2005	2.62 ± 1.07	1.97 ± 1.32	23.85 ± 1.66	26.65 ± 1.36	11.48 ± 0.45	11.53 ± 0.39	ND	ND
2006	4.64 ± 0.16	4.21 ± 0.22	16.91 ± 0.35	20.67 ± 0.49	11.45 ± 0.02	11.57 ± 0.05	7.90 ± 0.01	7.88 ± 0.01

TABLE 3. Average *Laminaria solidungula* basal blade length from nine sites in Stefansson Sound. Blade lengths were measured during summers 2004–2007. A growth year (GWYR) is defined as the period beginning 15 November one year and ending 15 November the following year. Values are means ± SE. ND is no data.

GWYR	DS-11 cm	E-1 cm	E-2 cm	E-3 cm	L-1 cm	L-2 cm	B-1 cm	W-1 cm	W-3 cm
2003	7.20 ± 0.50	4.38 ± 0.36	7.85 ± 0.40	5.24 ± 0.40	6.56 ± 0.54	6.53 ± 0.86	7.16 ± 0.60	7.93 ± 0.51	10.45 ± 0.94
2004	25.46 ± 0.93	10.93 ± 0.37	9.98 ± 0.38	22.79 ± 0.76	18.03 ± 0.59	14.67 ± 0.59	18.59 ± 0.69	13.73 ± 0.53	20.88 ± 1.04
2005	27.65 ± 0.85	18.97 ± 0.53	19.10 ± 0.76	28.54 ± 0.93	23.77 ± 0.91	21.82 ± 0.84	24.76 ± 1.02	18.49 ± 0.71	24.94 ± 1.05
2006	47.32 ± 1.64	16.71 ± 0.71	18.04 ± 0.96	25.84 ± 1.07	18.85 ± 0.75	36.77 ± 1.72	20.70 ± 1.00	ND	ND

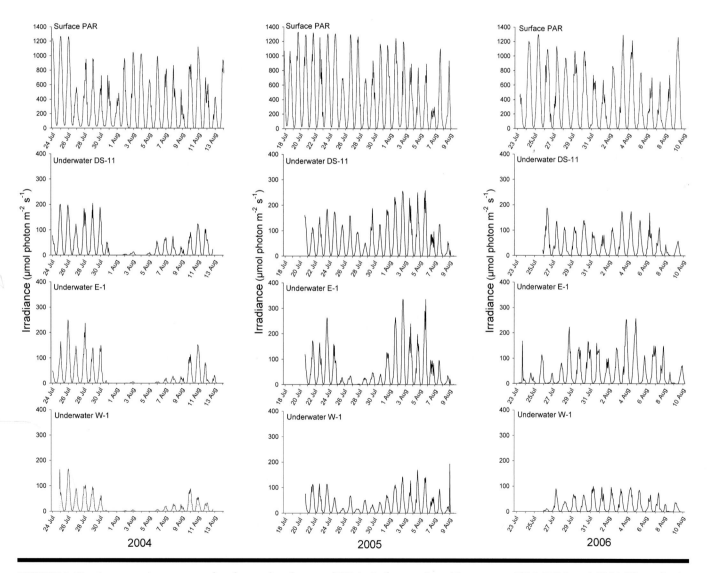

FIGURE 6. Continuous measurements of surface and underwater PAR in Stefansson Sound in summers 2004, 2005, and 2006. Water depths ranged from 5 m (E-1) to 6.5 m (DS-11 and W-1). Missing surface PAR data in 2004 and 2005 were obtained from an irradiance sensor maintained 5 km distant at SDI by Veltkamp and Wilcox (2007).

before rebounding to about 100 µmol m^{-2} s^{-1}. In 2005, underwater PAR was lowest at E-1 and W-1 from 26–31 July in response to a storm event that generated winds in excess of 9 m s^{-1} from the east-northeast but which had little effect on underwater PAR at DS-11.

Overall, water transparency, as reflected by consistently low k values (generally <1.0 m^{-1}) and high light transmission (>55% m^{-1}) at all three sites, was highest in 2006 as reflected by the absence of significant storm events during the study period (Figure 7). In all three years, mean irradiance was significantly ($p < 0.05$) lower at site W-1 compared to all other sites (Table 4) for the period 26 July to 10 August although the surface irradiance was high on most days. Values recorded from both surface and underwater PAR sensors are similar to irradiance measurements made in Stefansson Sound during previous studies (Dunton, 1990). Lowest light transmission (<10% m^{-1}) and highest k values (2–3 m^{-1}) were observed at all three sites in 2004. Conditions in 2005 improved considerably, with just one peak in water turbidity occurring in late July as noted earlier. The shallower depth at E-1, compared to W-1 and DS-11 amplifies the k values at this site for similar levels of underwater PAR recorded at all three sites.

DISCUSSION

The relatively uniform and low water column chlorophyll *a* concentrations measured across Stefansson Sound from 2004–2006 (Figure 5) agree well with earlier assessments made through the same area in 2001, but were lower than those recorded in 2002 by Aumack (2003). Chlorophyll was consistently lower at 2 m than at 4 m depths, which may reflect the consistently higher availability of inorganic nutrients at depth in all three years for silicate, ammonium, phosphate, and nitrate + nitrite (Table 1). Water

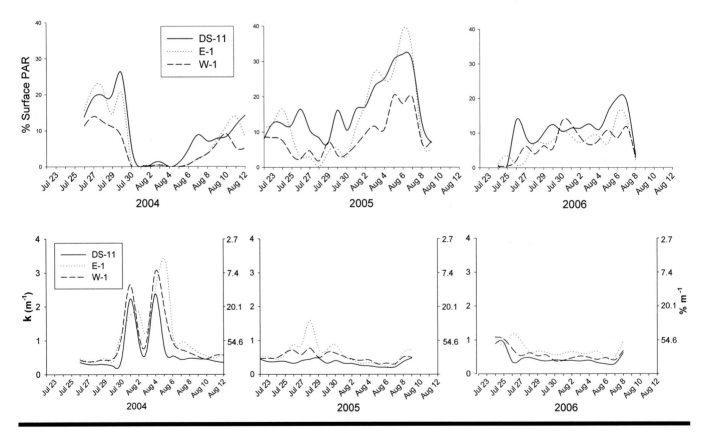

FIGURE 7. Measurements of water transparency at various sites in Stefansson Sound from 2004 to 2006. Top panel: percentage of surface irradiance (%SI). Bottom panel: diffuse attenuation coefficient expressed as k-values (left axis) and as % m^{-1} (right axis). Underwater measurements were made at kelp canopy levels at E-1 (4.6 m), W-1 (5.8 m), and DS-11 (6.1 m) with a spherical quantum sensor.

TABLE 4. Mean PAR for each site for the period 26 July–10 August (n = 1071 hourly measurements for each site) from 2004–2006. Asterisks denote site means that are significantly different (p < 0.05) within years. Average surface PAR for the same period is provided for reference.

| | Mean PAR (μmol m^{-2} s^{-1}) | | | |
Year	W-1	E-1	DS-11	Surface
2004	15.3*	23.3	28.0	314.9
2005	28.3*	45.1*	59.2*	356.0
2006	23.3*	48.1	42.0	347.9

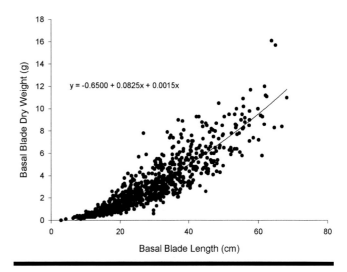

FIGURE 8. Correlation between basal blade dry weight (g) and basal blade length (cm) in *Laminaria solidungula*.

temperatures were about 2°C warmer in 2006 compared to 2004 and 2005, which was coincident with a 6–7‰ drop in surface and bottom water salinities in 2006. Decreased salinities and pH in 2006 likely reflect freshwater input from the nearby Sagavanirktok River, which produced a distinct brackish water layer to 4 m depths that was not evident in 2004 or 2005. Measurement of bottom salinity at depths exceeding 6 m at various sites (data not reported here) indicate that this brackish water layer seldom extended to the seafloor, sparing benthic organisms at depths greater than 5 m exposure to widely fluctuating salinities and temperatures. However, vertical gradients in temperature and/or salinity were apparent all three years, producing a clear pycnocline.

Based on in situ frond length measurements made on *Laminaria solidungula* plants in summers 2005 and 2006, we were able to make new calculations of kelp biomass at sites DS-11 (n = 226) and E-1 (n = 53). Areal biomass at each site was calculated using a correlation coefficient between basal blade dry weight (gdw) and basal blade length (cm) developed for the Stefansson Sound Boulder Patch using specimens collected between 1980 and 1984 (n = 912; Figure 8). Biomass at DS-11 (>25% rock cover) ranged from 5 to 45 gdw m^{-2} (mean 23 gdw m^{-2}) compared to a range of 0.5 to 2.7 gdw m^{-2} (mean 1.7 gdw m^{-2}) at site E-1 (10–25% rock cover). Intermediate levels of biomass were recorded at sites W-3 (10.1 gdw m^{-2}) and E-3 (14.8 gdw m^{-2}), both designated as sites with >25% rock cover by Toimil (1980). The range in biomass at DS-11 is within the estimates reported by Dunton et al. (1982). Estimates of benthic biomass at sites in Stefansson Sound are critical for calculation of realistic basin-wide benthic production models in relation to changes in PAR.

Blade elongation in *Laminaria solidungula* displays large spatial and temporal variability as reflected in mea-

surements from nine sites over the past decade (Figure 9). In addition, mean blade growth at two sites, DS-11 and E-1, made since 1977 and 1981, respectively, reveal some interesting long-term interannual variations (Figure 10). The two years of lowest growth (1999 and 2003) occurred relatively recently and coincide with summers characterized by intense storm activity that likely produced extremely turbid water conditions resulting in extremely

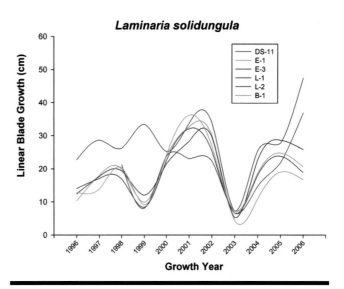

FIGURE 9. Variation in annual growth in *Laminaria solidungula* from 1996 to 2006 at sites occupied in the Stefansson Sound Boulder Patch. Measurements are based on blade lengths of plants collected between 2001 and 2006. Values are means ± SE.

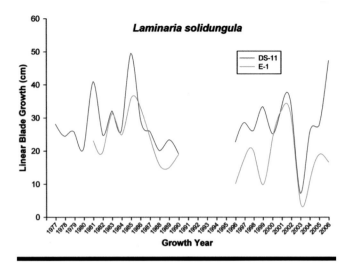

FIGURE 10. Mean annual linear growth of *Laminaria solidungula* from 1977 to 2006 at sites DS-11 (blue) and E-1 (green) in Stefansson Sound Boulder Patch.

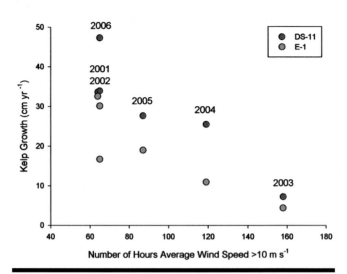

FIGURE 11. Annual mean linear growth of *Laminaria solidungula* as a function of the number of hours that wind speed exceeded 10 m s^{-1} at SDI in July and August, from 2001 to 2006. Wind speed data from Veltcamp and Wilcox, 2007. Sites DS-11 (blue) and E-1 (green) are located in the Stefansson Sound Boulder Patch.

low levels of ambient light. Wind speed data collected at SDI by Veltcamp and Wilcox (2007) from 2001 to 2006 revealed that 2003 was marked by the highest maximum wind speeds and lowest light levels in July and August when compared to all other years (Table 5). In addition, since light attenuation was lowest in offshore waters and increased with proximity to the coastline, kelp growth at site E-1 was consistently much less than at DS-11 (Table 3). Changes in local climatology clearly has an important role in regulating kelp growth as a consequence of increased cloud cover and sustained winds that negatively impact kelp growth (Figure 11).

The exceptionally low growth of kelp in 2003 (4–7 cm) indicates that kelp in the Boulder Patch are living close to their physiological light limits and might die if subjected to multiple years of low water transparency. Other factors

that could exacerbate light limitation include increases in temperature and lower salinities. As noted above, between 2004 and 2006 mean water temperature over the study area more than doubled and salinity measurements dropped significantly to depths of 4 m. Since much of the Boulder Patch occurs at depths less than 6 m, kelp could be exposed to periods of lower salinities and higher temperatures during periods of higher than normal precipitation and/or freshwater inflows. Thus, continuous monitoring of kelp growth in Stefansson Sound provides valuable insights into the role of local climate in affecting water transparency through processes that suspend and/or promote phytoplankton (chlorophyll) production.

TABLE 5. Open-water meteorological data collected at SDI from 2001–2006 for the period 10 July–9 September (from Veltkamp and Wilcox, 2007).

| Year | Wind Speed m s^{-1} | | Number of Hours | Average Wind Direction | Average Solar Radiation |
	Average	Maximum	>10 meters s^{-1}	°Mag	W m^{-2}
2001	5.10	7.18	64	157	133.7
2002	4.67	6.50	65	174	145.8
2003	5.62	7.98	158	172	123.3
2004	5.46	7.37	119	149	150.6
2005	5.57	7.47	87	125	145.8
2006	5.12	6.94	65	148	131.5

We derived measures of light attenuation from both synoptic measurements collected at the 30 survey sites, and continuously from dataloggers deployed on the seabed. These coincident measurements of surface and underwater light exhibited distinct geographical patterns and interannual variations between 2004 and 2006 (Figures 3 and 7). Attenuation was consistently elevated in coastal zones, with highest values observed near Endicott Island and SDI indicating more turbid water closer to shore. Lower values were recorded offshore along the eastern and northeastern sides of Stefansson Sound. Attenuation coefficients were also highest in shallower water depths as reflected by site E-1, compared to the lower k values at the deeper sites (W-1 and DS-11). The higher k values recorded at the permanent sites reflect the value of continuously recording instruments; during major storms it is virtually impossible to conduct field measurements, but these events are perhaps the most interesting and important in computing an accurate assessment of benthic production. We noted that k values were nearly three times higher at the three permanent sites than at any point during synoptic sampling at 30 sites, despite the use of a scalar sensor in the calculation of k at the permanent sites. The application of cosine measurements of PAR from the permanent sites would have resulted in still higher values for k.

Our data and that of Aumack et al. (2007) strongly suggest that both the spatial and interannual variations in water transparency are correlated with TSS. In general, the majority of the Boulder Patch, including areas with dense kelp populations (>25% rock cover), was found predominantly in clear offshore waters where attenuation measurements were consistently less than 1.0 m^{-1}. Our data show that years characterized by frequent storm activity are likely to have significant impacts on annual kelp growth and production. Local climatic change that results in more frequent storm events are thus likely to have a significant and detrimental impact on nearshore kelp bed community production, and could lead to large scale losses of these plants and their associated diverse epilithic and epiphytic fauna.

Acknowledgments

We thank Ted Dunton and John Dunton (University of Texas at Austin) for their mechanical expertise and piloting of the *R/V Proteus*. Special appreciation to Brenda Konar, Katrin Iken, and Nathan Stewart (all at University of Alaska Fairbanks) for their diving assistance and with kelp collection. We are grateful to Bill Streever (BP Exploration) for ocean access and the kindness and hospitality extended to us by the entire Endicott facility of BP Exploration. Constructive comments to the paper were kindly provided by Craig Aumack (University of Alabama) and Lanny Miller (Algenol Biofuels, Inc.). This study was funded by the U.S. Department of the Interior, Minerals Management Service (MMS), Alaska Outer Continental Shelf Region, Anchorage, Alaska under Contract Numbers 1435–01–99-CT-30998 and 1435-01-04-CT-32148 as part of the continuation (cANIMIDA) of the Arctic Nearshore Impact Monitoring in the Development Area (ANIMIDA) Project and the MMS Alaska Environmental Studies Program under the superb leadership of Richard Prentki (MMS COTR).

LITERATURE CITED

Aumack, C. F. 2003. Linking Water Turbidity and TSS Loading to Kelp Productivity within the Stefansson Sound Boulder Patch. M.S. thesis. University of Texas at Austin, Marine Science Institute, Port Aransas.

Aumack, C. F., K. H. Dunton, A. B. Burd, D. W. Funk, and R. A. Maffione. 2007. Linking Light Attenuation and Suspended Sediment Loading to Benthic Productivity within an Arctic Kelp Bed Community. *Journal of Phycology*, 43:853–863.

Ban, S. M., J. Colonell, K. H. Dunton, B. Gallaway, and L. Martin. 1999. Liberty Development: Construction Effects on Boulder Patch Kelp Production. Report to BP Exploration Alaska, Inc., Anchorage.

Dunton, K. H. 1984. "An Annual Carbon Budget for an Arctic Kelp Community." In *The Alaska Beaufort Sea—Ecosystems and Environment*, ed. P. Barnes, D. Schell, and E. Reimnitz, pp. 311–326. Orlando, Fla.: Academic Press.

———. 1985. Growth of Dark-Exposed *Laminaria saccharina* (L.) Lamour and *Laminaria solidungula* (J.) Ag. (Laminariales, Phaeophyta) in the Alaskan Beaufort Sea. *Journal of Experimental Marine Biology and Ecology*, 94:181–189.

———. 1990. Growth and Production in *Laminaria solidungula*: Relation to Continuous Underwater Light Levels in the Alaskan High Arctic. *Marine Biology*, 106:297–304.

———. 1992. Arctic Biogeography: The Paradox of the Marine Benthic Fauna and Flora. *Trends in Ecology and Evolution*, 7:183–189.

Dunton, K. H., and C. M. Jodwalis. 1988. Photosynthetic Performance of *Laminaria solidungula* Measured in situ in the Alaskan High Arctic. *Marine Biology*, 98:277–285.

Dunton, K. H., E. Reimnitz, and S. Schonberg. 1982. An Arctic Kelp Community in the Alaskan Beaufort Sea. *Arctic*, 35(4):465–484.

Dunton, K. H., and D. M. Schell. 1986. A Seasonal Carbon Budget for the Kelp *Laminaria solidungula* in the Alaskan High Arctic. *Marine Ecology Progress Series*, 31:57–66.

Dunton, K. H., and S. V. Schonberg. 2000. "The Benthic Faunal Assemblage of the Boulder Patch Kelp Community." In *The Natural History of an Arctic Oil Field*, ed. J. C. Truett and S. R. Johnson, pp. 338–359. *San Diego, Calif.*: Academic Press.

Henley, W. J., and K. H. Dunton. 1995. A Seasonal Comparison of Carbon, Nitrogen, and Pigment Content in *Laminaria solidungula* and *L. saccharina* (Laminariales, Phaeophyta) in the Alaskan Arctic. *Journal of Phycology*, 31:325–331.

———. 1997. Effects of Nitrogen Supply and Seven Months of Continuous Darkness on Growth and Photosynthesis of the Arctic Kelp,

Laminaria solidungula. Limnology and Oceanography, 42(2): 209–216.

LGL Ecological Research Associates, Inc., and K. H. Dunton. 1992. Endicott Beaufort Sea Boulder Patch Monitoring Program (1984–1991). Final Report to BP Exploration (Alaska) Inc., Anchorage, Alaska.

Martin, L. R., and B. J. Gallaway. 1994. The Effects of the Endicott Development Project on the Boulder Patch, an Arctic Kelp Community in Stefansson Sound, Alaska. *Arctic,* 47(1):54–64.

McClelland, J. W. 2006. A Pan-Arctic Evaluation of Changes in River Discharge during the Latter Half of the 20th Century. *Geophysical Research Letters,* 33:L06715, doi:10.1029.

McKinney, M. L. 1998a. On Predicting Biotic Homogenization: Species-Area Patterns in Marine Biota. *Global Ecology and Biogeography Letters,* 7:297–301.

———. 1998b. Is Marine Biodiversity at Less Risk? Evidence and Implications. *Diversity and Distributions,* 4:3–8.

Mittelbach, G. G., C. F. Steiner, S. M. Scheiner, K. L. Gross, H. L. Reynolds, R. B. Waide, M. R. Willig, S. I. Dodson, and L. Gough. 2001. What Is the Observed Relationship between Species Richness and Productivity? *Ecology,* 82:2381–2396.

Paine, R. T. 2002. Trophic Control of Production in a Rocky Intertidal Community. *Science,* 296(5568):736–739.

Parsons, T. R., Y. Maita, and C. M. Lalli. 1984. *A Manual of Chemical and Biological Methods for Seawater Analysis.* Oxford: Pergamon.

Petraitis, P. S., R. E. Latham, and R. A. Niesenbaum. 1989. The Maintenance of Species Diversity by Disturbance. *Quarterly Review of Biology,* 64:393–418.

Rosenzweig, M. L. 2001. Loss of Speciation Rate Will Impoverish Future Diversity. *Proceedings of the National Academy of Sciences,* 98: 5404–5410.

SAS Institute Inc. 1985. SAS/STAT Guide for Personal Computers. Version 6 ed. SAS Institute Inc., Cary, North Carolina.

Toimil, L. J. 1980. Investigation of Rock Habitats and Sub-Sea Conditions, Beaufort Sea, Alaska. Volume 2. Report to Exxon Company, USA, by Harding-Lawson Associates, Novato, California.

Veltkamp, B., and J. R. Wilcox. 2007. Nearshore Beaufort Sea Meteorological Monitoring and Data Synthesis Project. Final Report to U.S. Department of the Interior Minerals Management Service Alaska OCS Region, Anchorage, Alaska.

Welschmeyer, N. A. 1994. Fluorometric Analysis of Chlorophyll *a* in the Presence of Chlorophyll *b* and Pheopigments. *Limnology and Oceanography,* 39(8):1985–1992.

Worm, B., H. K. Lotze, C. Bostroem, R. Engkvist, V. Labanauskas, and U. Sommer. 1999. Marine Diversity Shift Linked to Interactions among Grazers, Nutrients and Propagule Banks. *Marine Ecology Progress Series,* 185:309–314.

Life under Antarctic Pack Ice: A Krill Perspective

Langdon B. Quetin and Robin M. Ross

ABSTRACT. The life cycle of the Antarctic krill, *Euphausia superba*, intersects in space and time with the expansion and contraction of annual pack ice. Consequently, the circumpolar distribution of krill has often been defined as generally limited to an area bounded by the maximum extent of pack ice. Pack ice has both direct and indirect effects on the life cycle of krill. During the austral winter, larval krill are found in direct association with the underside of the ice and feed on the small plants and animals that constitute the sea ice microbial community, a food source relatively abundant in winter compared to food sources in the water column. Indirectly, melting pack ice in late winter or early spring stabilizes the water column and promotes growth of the preferred food of krill, which, in turn, likely provides the fuel for egg production during the summer months. Thus, the warming trend west of the Antarctic Peninsula with attendant changes in both the timing and duration of winter ice has implications for the population dynamics of krill. Given the complexity of the habitat–life cycle interaction, research on Antarctic krill involves diverse sampling tools that are dependent on the size and habitat of krill during a particular stage of their life cycle, and the nature of the study itself. In particular, and pertinent to the topic of diving in polar research, the research has been greatly enhanced by diving techniques developed to allow both observation and sampling of krill in their winter pack-ice habitat.

INTRODUCTION

One of the reasons that Antarctic krill, *Euphausia superba*, has been a focus of international research in the Antarctic since the Discovery days, before World War II, is that it is viewed as a key species in the Southern Ocean ecosystem. Various investigators have referred to Antarctic krill, *Euphausia superba*, as a keystone (Moline et al., 2004) or core or key (Quetin and Ross, 2003) or dominant (Ju and Harvey, 2004) species in the pelagic ecosystem of the Southern Ocean. The rationale for the use of these terms has been based on the facts that it is among the world's most abundant metazoan species (Nicol, 1994) and that it is important in the diets of many of the species of the upper trophic levels (Everson, 2000). However, given the suggestion that the term *keystone species* only refers to those species exercising an effect on ecosystem function disproportionate to abundance and thus is almost always a predator (Power et al., 1996), Antarctic krill may be more accurately defined as a *foundation species* in the

Langdon B. Quetin and Robin M. Ross, University of California at Santa Barbara, Marine Science Institute-UCSB, Santa Barbara, CA 93106-6150, USA. Corresponding author: L. Quetin (Langdon@icess.ucsb.edu). Accepted 28 May 2008.

sense of Dayton (1972). A foundation species is one that controls community dynamics and modulates ecosystem processes such as energy flux, and whose loss would lead to system-wide changes in the structure and function of the ecosystem (Ellison et al., 2005). Understanding that Antarctic krill may be a foundation species in many regions of the pelagic Southern Ocean highlights the need to elucidate the factors affecting its population dynamics and its possible response to climate change. After introducing the concept of Antarctic krill as a foundation species, and the pack ice as a habitat, we focus on what has been learned about interactions between krill life history and the pack ice habitat, as well as the importance of viewing seasonal sea ice dynamics from a krill perspective.

FOUNDATION SPECIES

Distribution and Biomass

Several characteristics of the distribution and biomass of Antarctic krill suggest it is a foundation species. First, the distribution of Antarctic krill is circumpolar. However, abundance is patchy with highest abundances in the southeast Atlantic. Most krill are found within the area south of the northern extent of annual sea ice and within the boundaries of minimal and maximal sea ice, with the exception of krill around South Georgia (Marr, 1962; Laws, 1985; Siegel, 2005). This coherence led investigators to postulate a key role for seasonal pack ice in the life cycle and population dynamics of Antarctic krill.

Second, Antarctic krill often dominate the zooplankton biomass in the upper 200 m of the seasonal sea ice zone (Hopkins, 1985; Hopkins and Torres, 1988; Miller and Hampton, 1989; Ward et al., 2004; Siegel, 2005). Antarctic krill biomass was recently resurveyed in Area 48, the southwest Atlantic, during the CCAMLR 2000 Survey (Hewitt et al., 2004). From these results, acoustic estimates of the circumpolar krill biomass were estimated to be 60–155 million metric tones (Nicol et al., 2000), within the range estimated consumed by predators (Everson, 2000; Barrera-Oro, 2002). However, krill biomass in a region varies substantially—seasonally with shifts in population distribution, interannually due to variation in recruitment success during its lifespan, and within a season due to local oceanographic variables (Siegel, 2005; Ross et al., 2008).

Role in Ecosystem

Due in part to its high biomass and in part to the fact that there are no true prey substitutes in the seasonal sea-ice zone for upper-level predators, Antarctic krill dominate energy flow to upper trophic levels (Barrera-Oro, 2002). In a review of the diets of Southern Ocean birds, Croxall (1984) identified both (1) species highly dependent on Antarctic krill, for example, the brushtail penguins up to 98%, and (2) species whose diet was only 16–40% krill, namely, flying seabirds such as albatrosses and petrels. All Antarctic seals depend somewhat on Antarctic krill, with the exception of the elephant seal (Laws, 1984). The crab-eater seal is a specialist on these euphausiids whereas the diet of leopard seals is only about 50% krill. Baleen whales (minke, blue, fin, sei, and humpback) feed predominantly on Antarctic krill. Lastly, both fish and squid (Everson 2000) are known predators of krill. In particular, the mesopelagic myctophid *Electrona antarctica* is an important predator of krill (Hopkins and Torres, 1988; Lancraft et al., 1989; 1991; Barrera-Oro, 2002).

One aspect of the Southern Ocean ecosystem that lends support to the characterization of Antarctic krill as a foundation species is that there is little functional redundancy in prey items for the upper-trophic-level predators in the food web. Another large and sometimes biomass-dominant grazer in the zooplankton is the salp, *Salpa thompsoni*. However, although some fish are known to ingest *S. thompsoni*, its high water content and the variation in biomass by orders of magnitude during the spring/summer season due to its characteristic alternation of generations rends it a less desirable food item. The pelagic fish fauna in the Southern Ocean, a logical alternate source of food, is relatively scarce and only a minor component of the epiplankton of the Antarctic Ocean (Morales-Nin et al., 1995; Hoddell et al., 2000), except in the high latitude regions of the cold continental shelf (high Antarctic) such as the Ross Sea or the southern Weddell Sea, the habitat of the nototheniid *Pleuragramma antarcticum*. In deeper pelagic waters, (>500 m) the mesopelagic myctophid *E. antarctica* is the dominant fish (Barrera-Oro, 2002), and is available as prey to diving birds and seals when it migrates into the upper 0–300 m during the night (Robison, 2003; Loots et al., 2007). However, in many regions of the Southern Ocean neither of these two species would be available in high enough biomass as an alternate prey if *Euphausia superba* disappeared.

Although Antarctic krill themselves are omnivorous and do ingest both plant and animal matter (Atkinson and Snÿder, 1997; Schmidt et al., 2006), they are very important herbivorous grazers and their growth and reproduction rates appear to be tightly linked to phytoplankton concentrations, particularly diatoms (Ross et al., 2000; Schmidt et al., 2006; Atkinson et al., 2006). This short link between primary producers and the upper trophic levels creates a very efficient transfer of energy to the top-level predators.

The role of Antarctic krill as one of the dominant macrozooplanktonic grazers, particularly of the larger phytoplankton, suggests that grazing by krill affects phytoplankton community composition and is a significant loss term in some years (Ross et al., 1998; Garibotti et al., 2003; Daniels et al., 2006). Daniels et al. (2006), in a network analysis of the pelagic food web on the shelf west of the Antarctic Peninsula, found that in years of high primary production and high krill abundance, more than 50% of the large phytoplankton cells were ingested by Antarctic krill. In addition, its production of large fast-sinking fecal pellets (Ross et al., 1985; Fowler and Small, 1972; Cadée et al., 1992; González, 1992; Turner, 2002) enhances its contribution to carbon sequestration (Smetacek et al., 2004).

PACK ICE HABITAT FROM KRILL PERSPECTIVE

Three types of pack ice can be delineated: seasonal, perennial, and marginal (Eicken, 1992). During the annual growth and melt cycle, the proportion of each type varies, which in turn means that the ecological habitats provided by each vary in space and time. Seasonal pack ice is a circumpolar environment that grows each fall and shrinks each spring, covering a vast area at its greatest extent. In the winter and spring, seasonal pack ice has phytoplankton/ice algal standing stocks that are one to three orders of magnitude higher than in the water column immediately below. This annual phenomenon thus provides a source of food for grazers (microheterotrophs, copepods, euphausiids) during times in the annual cycle when food resources in the water column are low. The process of formation of seasonal pack ice involves frazil ice formation scavenging particles from the water column, congelation into pancake ice, and aggregation into ice floes. Once the floes are 0.5 to 0.7 m thick, the annual ice only thickens by processes of deformation, particularly over-rafting. The seasonal pack ice, particularly the zone of highly over-rafted ice, is a favored habitat of Antarctic krill (*Euphausia superba*) in winter (Marschall, 1988; Smetacek et al., 1990; Quetin et al., 1996; Frazer et al. 1997; 2002). The perennial pack ice, in contrast, is a mixture of annual and primarily second year sea ice, and the water column below perennial pack ice tends to have even lower phytoplankton concentrations than below seasonal sea ice due to the increased light attenuation.

In the main body of this contribution, we will illustrate how putting one's self into the winter habitat as a diver, or taking on the krill perspective, has allowed unique in-

sight into the physiological and behavioral adaptations of Antarctic krill to winter conditions. In turn, this insight allows us to further our understanding of the impact of climate change. We will focus on the increased understanding over the last 25 years of interactions between the krill life cycle and seasonal sea ice dynamics as gained from both long-term research conducted in the summer months and from cruises conducted during winter months. Lastly, we will put these results into the context of climate warming and its effect on seasonal sea ice dynamics west of the Antarctic Peninsula.

BACKGROUND OBSERVATIONS

LIFE HISTORY OF ANTARCTIC KRILL

Characteristics of Life Cycle

Antarctic krill is a relatively large (maximum length about 60 mm) and long-lived crustacean that occurs in schools, leading Hamner et al. (1983) to suggest that it has attributes more like small fish such as an anchovy or sardine than like a zooplankter. The life cycle of this euphausiid is complex, with 11 larval stages over the first 9 to 10 months, at least 1 year as a juvenile/subadult, and then 3 to 4 years as an adult. First reproduction can be as early as the third summer (Age Class 2+), but may be delayed if food resources are inadequate (Ross and Quetin, 2000). Ovarian development begins in the spring, fueled by food ingested during that time and not by stored reserves (Hagen et al., 2001). The embryos sink rapidly and hatch in deep water and the nauplii swim toward the surface (Marr, 1962; Quetin and Ross, 1984; Hofmann et al., 1992). The krill in their first feeding stage (Calyptopis 1) reach the surface approximately three weeks after hatching, and must find sufficient food for continued development within a few weeks or else they die (Ross and Quetin, 1989). The larvae spend their first winter in the late furcilia stages; they begin to metamorphosize into juveniles and then subadults at the end of winter and throughout the spring.

Critical Periods

Three facets of the influence of seasonal pack ice on the population dynamics of Antarctic krill have emerged from the research of multiple investigators. Here we briefly describe how two of the three critical periods interact with the seasonal cycles within the pack ice habitat (Figure 1).

First, in the austral spring as the ovary begins to develop, investigators postulate that the female must store lipid in the "fat body" from ongoing ingestion to reach a threshold or ovarian development cannot continue (Cuzin-Roudy, 1993; Cuzin-Roudy and Labat, 1992; Ross and Quetin, 2000; Quetin and Ross, 2001), as shown for another species of euphausiid (Cuzin-Roudy, 2000). Thus, an individual female will only reproduce during a summer following a spring with adequate food sources. Each austral spring, the retreat and melting of the seasonal pack ice sets up the conditions for marginal ice-edge blooms, providing an important and timely food resource for female krill for ovarian development and eventual spawning.

Second, the larva needs to feed within 10–14 days of the time of metamorphosis into the first feeding stage or it passes the point-of-no-return and will not survive even if food becomes available later (Ross and Quetin, 1989).

For this critical period, the effect of seasonal sea ice is indirect, through the impact of the seasonal sea ice cycle on annual primary production and the timing of blooms (Vernet et al., 2008).

Lastly, although adult krill tolerate prolonged starvation and could survive a winter without food (Ikeda and Dixon, 1982), larval krill have a much lower starvation tolerance (for furcilia 6, about 6 wks) (Ross and Quetin, 1991; Quetin et al., 1996; Meyer and Oettl, 2005). Sea-ice microbial communities (SIMCOs) provide larval krill an alternate food source in the winter when food in the water column is at an annual low. In winter, larval krill from the under-ice habitat are in better condition than those from open water, as measured by condition factor, lipid content and in situ growth rates (Ross and Quetin, 1991), supporting this concept.

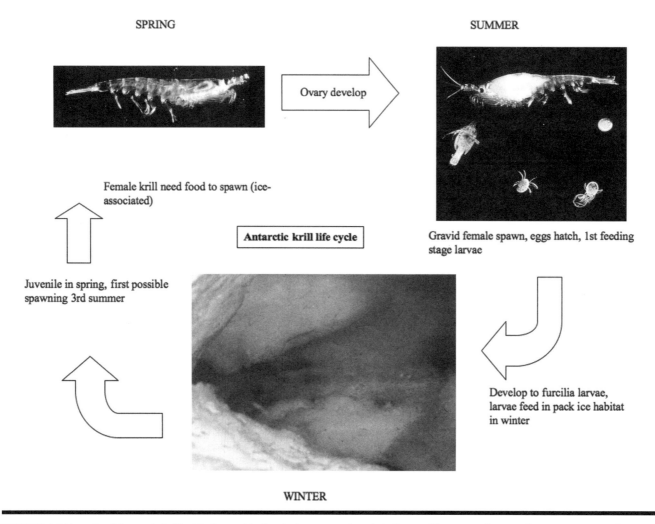

SPRING

SUMMER

Ovary develop

Female krill need food to spawn (ice-associated)

Antarctic krill life cycle

Gravid female spawn, eggs hatch, 1st feeding stage larvae

Juvenile in spring, first possible spawning 3rd summer

Develop to furcilia larvae, larvae feed in pack ice habitat in winter

WINTER

FIGURE 1. Life cycle of Antarctic krill with three critical periods; two are directly influenced by seasonal sea ice dynamics: ovarian development in the austral spring and survival during the first winter.

Variability in the environment, including seasonal sea ice dynamics, impacts food available to the Antarctic krill during these critical periods and is a primary factor driving variability in recruitment success or year class strength. Recruitment in this species shows high interannual variability as illustrated by two long-term research programs in the region of the Antarctic Peninsula—Antarctic Marine Living Resources (AMLR), Siegel and Loeb (1995), and Palmer Long Term Ecological Research (LTER), Quetin and Ross (2003)—and by shorter series in other regions (Watkins, 1999; Siegel 2000, 2005). Within the Palmer LTER study region, recruitment has been episodic with two sequential high years followed by two to three years of low or zero recruitment (Quetin and Ross, 2003), a 5–6 year cycle. Further north, with a longer time series, the frequency of high recruitment years has not been as repetitive (Siegel and Loeb, 1995; Siegel, 2005), although there is a rough correspondence between successful recruitment years between the two regions 800 km apart (Siegel et al., 2003; Ducklow et al., 2007). However, with several possible reproductive summers, Antarctic krill would not need successful recruitment every year, and models suggest that several years of low to zero recruitment would not preclude recovery of the stock (Priddle et al., 1988).

These results provide the opportunity to use correlations with environmental variability to formulate potential mechanisms that drive the variability (Siegel and Loeb, 1995; Quetin and Ross, 2003; Quetin and Ross, 2001). From these long-term studies, correlations have been found between both reproduction and recruitment success and various aspects of seasonal sea ice dynamics, including timing, duration, and maximum extent, with the dominant parameter varying with the study region and/or latitude. Evidence from two long-term studies suggests that timing and extent of sea ice in winter and/or spring impact the reproductive cycle (Siegel and Loeb, 1995; Loeb et al., 1997; Quetin and Ross, 2001). We will use examples from the Palmer LTER[1] as illustrations of the correlations found and potential mechanisms suggested.

Our first example illustrates the impact of the timing of sea ice retreat in the spring on the reproductive cycle. The most important factor in estimates of population fecundity (numbers of larvae produced in a region during the season) is the intensity of reproduction (percentage female krill in the reproductive cycle for a season), an index that can vary by a factor of 10 interannually (Quetin and Ross, 2001). The intensity of reproduction correlated with both dynamics of sea ice in spring and with annual primary production, which are both environmental factors associated with food availability, as seasonal sea ice dynamics mediates the availability of food in the austral spring. Intensity of reproduction was consistently low when sea ice retreat was either early (August) or late (November), and highest when retreat occurred around the climatological mean for the region (Quetin and Ross, 2001). We emphasize here that the timing of retreat influences the timing of the food available for ovarian development, critical for a successful reproductive season. As discussed by Cuzin-Roudy (1993), Cuzin-Roudy and Labat (1992), and Quetin and Ross (2001), accumulation of stores in the "fat body" by late spring is hypothesized to be necessary for continued ovarian development. If development does not or cannot continue because of lack of adequate food in the spring, then the intensity of reproduction is low.

In the second example, we examine recruitment success and timing of sea ice advance. Our measure of recruitment success, the recruitment index, R_1, is a consequence of both the numbers of larval krill entering the winter (reproductive output in the summer) and larval mortality during the winter (availability of winter food sources), and thus reflects two critical periods in the life cycle. From catches of krill from each station during the summer cruise, we calculate a recruitment index for the year, the proportion of one-year-old krill of the entire population one-year and older, as described in Quetin and Ross (2003). For the time series to date (Quetin and Ross, 2003; Ducklow et al., 2007) R_1 decreases exponentially with delay in sea ice advance. With advance in April, R_1 is greater than 0.4 (defined as a high recruitment year; Ducklow et al., 2007), but if advance is delayed until May or June, then R_1 is usually below 0.4. The suggestion is that if sea ice does not advance until late in the fall, that is, May, then recruitment tends to be low. However, the outliers or exceptions also provide insight into the mechanisms involved, in this instance the year classes of 1992 and 2001, as detailed in Quetin and Ross (2003). For the year class of 1992, although sea ice advanced early (March), retreat was also early (July), so SIMCOs were not available as an alternate food source in later winter, and presumably larval mortality was high. For the year class of 2001, sea ice did not advance until July, yet the R_1 (0.9) indicated a very successful year class. In this year, we had observed a strong reproductive output in the summer, leading to high numbers of larval krill entering the winter, so even with presumed high mortality due to a lack of SIMCOs early in the winter, enough larvae survived for a strong year class. This latter point emphasizes the importance of understanding the reproductive cycle and population fecundity, as well as mortality during the first year.

DIVING IN THE PACK ICE

The above examples illustrate how seasonal sea ice dynamics is correlated with the population dynamics of Antarctic krill. What have we learned about the interaction between Antarctic krill and the pack ice habitat from entering the habitat itself?

Historical Overview

The pack ice environment is dynamic—on both seasonal and shorter time scales—which creates challenges for investigators. In the early 1960s, biologists began to realize that sea ice presents a variety of different modes and contains distinct communities of plants and animals (Fogg, 2005). Scuba diving with observations of both the habitat and its inhabitants has played a key role in revealing the mysteries of the seasonal pack ice habitat, and scuba diving has become a key tool in investigations of the pack ice environment. Bunt (1963) used scuba diving to examine sea ice algal communities in situ and suggested ice algae could add appreciably to primary production in the Southern Ocean. He gave one of the earliest hints of the possible importance of sea ice algae as a food source for grazers. Early observations of the pack ice habitat were infrequent due to the lack of dedicated ice-capable research vessels. This limitation was relieved with the introduction of the RVIB *Polarstern*, commissioned in 1982 and operated by the Alfred Wegener Institute of Germany, and shortly thereafter, the MV *Polar Duke*, which began operations for the National Science Foundation of the USA in 1985. The advent of dedicated, ice-worthy research vessels led to a proliferation of studies in ice-covered waters (Ross and Quetin, 2003).

Some of the earliest observations of Antarctic krill under the pack ice were made by U.S. Coast Guard (USCG) scuba divers during spring (November 1983) and fall (March 1986) cruises in the Weddell Sea for the Antarctic Marine Ecosystem Ice Edge Zone (AMERIEZ) program (Daly and Macaulay, 1988; 1991). Subsequently, in late winter 1985 west of the Antarctic Peninsula during the first of a series of six winter cruises (WinCruise I, Quetin and Ross, 1986), divers investigating the SIMCOs associated with the underside of the ice (Kottmeier and Sullivan, 1987) observed larval krill in the under-ice habitat. Quetin and Ross (1988) began research on the physiology and distribution of larval krill found on the underside of the ice with WinCruise II in 1987; recently Quetin and Ross (2007) published detailed protocols, based on their experience, for diving in pack ice under various conditions that included a table of the year and month of their pack ice diving activities (Table 1). O'Brien (1987) observed both Antarctic krill and ice krill (*Euphausia crystallorophias*) in the under-ice habitat in austral spring of 1985. Hamner et al. (1989) found larval krill in austral fall 1986 associated with newly forming sea ice. In all cases, the investigators observed larval krill in higher abundance associated with the sea ice than with the water column, and observed larval krill feeding on the sea ice algae (Table 1). Investigators made complementary observations onboard ships both west of the Antarctic Peninsula (Guzman, 1983) and in the Weddell Sea in spring (Marschall, 1988).

Gains from Diving Activities

Distinct advances in our understanding of the interaction of Antarctic krill and the pack ice environment emerged from diving activities. Not only were larval krill observed directly feeding on sea ice algae (as detailed above), but scuba observations also documented that a clear habitat segregation existed between adult and larval krill in winter (Quetin et al., 1996), with adult krill away from the underside of the pack ice, and larval krill coupled to the underside of the pack ice. These observations led to the concept of "risk-balancing" as put forth by Pitcher et al. (1988) for these two life stages of krill in winter; for example, the degree of association with the under-ice surface and its SIMCOs (food source) is a balance between the need to acquire energy and the need to avoid predation. The two life stages differ in both starvation tolerance and vulnerability to predation. The smaller larvae appear to have a refuge in size (Hamner et al., 1989), as most vertebrate predators ingest primarily adults (Lowry et al., 1988; Croxall et al., 1985). Thus, the risk of predation for the adults is higher near the pack ice that is used as a platform for many upper-level predators. Quantitative surveys also revealed that larval krill occurred in over-rafted pack ice and not smooth fast ice, and that they were more commonly found on the floors of the "caves" formed by the over-rafting pack ice than the walls or ceilings (Frazer, 1995; Frazer et al., 1997; 2002). Not only were gains made in our understanding of the natural history and habitat use of Antarctic krill in winter, but also the ability to collect krill directly from the habitat has advantages over other collection methods such as towing through ice. First, the gentle collection of specimens by scuba divers with aquarium nets yields larval krill in excellent physiological conditions for experiments, for example, growth and grazing. Second, this method allows for immediate processing of larval krill for time-dependent indices such as pigment

TABLE 1. Diving projects at Palmer Station and on cruises in the Southern Ocean, 1983–2005.

Palmer Station	Year	Fall			Winter			Spring			Summer			Ship
		A	M	J	J	A	S	O	N	D	J	F	M	
	1983								AZ					
	1984													
	1985					W	W		O'B					*PD*
	1986	H	AZ											*PD (H)*
	1987			W	W									*PD*
	1988													
	1989				W									*PD*
	1990									K				*PD*
L	1991		K				W							*PD*
L	1992													
L	1993	L	L	W			L							*PD*
L	1994			W	W									*PD*
L	1995													
L	1996													
L	1997													
L	1998													
	1999		L											*LMG*
L	2000										A	A		*NBP*
L	2001				G	G	L	L						*LMG (G) NBP (L)*
L	2002					G	G							*LMG*
L	2003													
L	2004													
L	2005													

AZ–AMERIEZ, W–WinCruise krill studies to Ross and Quetin, K–krill studies to Ross and Quetin, H–krill studies to Hamner, O'B–krill studies to O'Brien, L–Palmer Long-Term Ecological Research project, A–Antarctic Pack Ice Seals research project, G–Southern Ocean GLOBEC, PD–M/V *Polar Duke*, LMG–ARSV *Laurence M Gould*, NBP–RVIB *Nathaniel B. Palmer*.

content, an index of feeding on ice algae in situ (Ross et al., 2004). Entry into the under-ice habitat also meant that larval krill and their food resource (SIMCOs on the bottom surface of the pack ice) could be collected simultaneously, allowing for close temporal/spatial linkages.

PROCESS CRUISES—SOUTHERN OCEAN GLOBEC

ICE CAMPS

With the correlations that suggested mechanisms and the scuba diving protocols in place, the next step was to move beyond the correlations and explore and test mechanisms consistent with the observations. The evolution of pack ice diving is far from complete, however. Although long-term ice camps have been occupied in the perennial ice of the Weddell Sea on floes of much greater dimension than we describe below (Melnikov and Spiridonov 1996),

shorter term ice camps on smaller floes west of the Antarctic Peninsula had not been attempted. On some recent cruises with both the Palmer LTER and U.S. Southern Ocean GLOBEC (Global Ocean Ecosystem Dynamics) programs, we pulled together many historical observations of ways to cope with the dynamics of the pack ice environment west of the Antarctic Peninsula, and developed the ability to dive from small (>50 m) consolidated floes west of the Antarctic Peninsula repeatedly for periods up to nine days (Ross et al., 2004; Quetin et al., 2007). These ice camps entailed sampling from consolidated pack ice floes occupied for periods of days using the research vessel to stage operations (Quetin and Ross, 2007). Diving on floes for days at a time enabled us to explore local variability in the pack ice community associated with an individual floe over time as the floe drifted within the pack ice. Scuba diving was not the only activity that occurred at these ice camps. In fact, the ability to do simultaneous sampling both from the topside and underside of the ice floes made for efficient sampling and better linkage between data sets.

During ice camps on two winter cruises for Southern Ocean GLOBEC west of the Antarctic peninsula in 2001 and 2002 (methods and results described in Quetin et al., 2007), total integrated chlorophyll a in multiple ice cores (Fritsen et al., 2008) was measured on the same ice floes where larval krill were collected by scuba divers. The amount of chlorophyll a in the ice cores was used as a proxy for the SIMCOs available as food to the larval krill living on the underside of the pack ice. Some of the larval krill were used immediately for an index of feeding (pigment content) (as described in Ross et al., 2004), while others were used in instantaneous growth rate experiments (in situ growth rate estimates as described in Ross and Quetin, 1991; Quetin et al., 2003; Ross et al., 2004). Growth of larval krill in their winter habitat reflects their feeding history over the past three weeks to one month, and may be an indicator of their ability to survive, that is, better growth indicates higher survivorship than lower growth. Evidence for similar linkages has been found for larval fish; larvae in better condition will have lower mortality rates and hence lead to stronger year classes, all else being equal (Pepin, 1991; Ottersen and Loeng, 2000; Takahashi and Watanabe, 2004).

CONTRAST TWO YEARS

The contrast in the results for total integrated chlorophyll a in ice cores, pigment content in larval krill, and the in situ growth rates of larvae for 2001 and 2002 was marked (Table 2) (fig. 5 in Quetin et al., 2007). Generally, in 2002 the ice cores contained an order of magnitude more chlorophyll a than in 2001 (Fritsen et al., 2008), leading us to suggest that more food was available to larval krill in 2002 than 2001. The median pigment content and in situ growth rates were also higher in larval krill in 2002 than in 2001. In both years, the distribution of pigment content was skewed to the left, but in 2002 more than 70% of the samples showed higher pigment content than those of larval krill collected from under the ice in 2001. A similar difference in distribution occurred for the in situ growth rates (Table 2). In 2002, more than 60% of the growth increments were positive, whereas in 2001 only 13% were positive.

The hypothesis that high concentrations of ice algae lead to higher growth rates is supported by a comparison of the in situ growth rates in the larvae and an index of feeding for larvae collected from the same place and at the same time. For this comparison, in situ growth rates

TABLE 2. Comparison of data from ice camps in 2001 and 2002 during two winter process cruises west of the Antarctic Peninsula near Marguerite Bay: median values of integrated chlorophyll a in ice cores, pigment content in larval krill, and in situ growth rates in larval krill. Ranges are in parentheses below median values; n = number of samples. Data in graph form in Quetin et al. (2007).

Data type (unit) and statistic	2001	2002
Integrated Chl a (mg m^{-3})	1	10
Pigment Content	0.148	2.594
(median μg chl a gwwt^{-1})	(0.074–0.226)	(0.088–16.615)
n	29	71
In situ Growth Rate	−1.31	1.54
(% intermolt period^{-1})	(−6.10–5.13)	(−3.23–11.69)
n	114	132

in units of percent per intermolt period (the growth increment) were converted to growth in units of mm d^{-1}. For larvae that molted we used the median intermolt period of 30 d found for both years (Quetin et al., 2007), and individual growth increments and total lengths to estimate growth in mm d^{-1}:

$$(\text{total length (mm)} \bullet \% \text{ IMP}^{-1})/(\text{IMP (d)}).$$

The relationship between growth and the index of feeding for the eight in situ growth experiments from both years for which we have complimentary pigment content data is exponential, similar to a functional response curve with a maximum growth rate above a threshold feeding intensity or pigment level (Figure 2). The different symbols for the two years illustrate that data from ice camps from one year alone would not have yielded as comprehensive an illustration of the relationship between the feeding index and growth rates. Larvae with very low pigment content and negative growth rates were those from 2001, whereas larvae with a range of pigment content above 0.2 μg chl a g wwt^{-1} and with positive growth rates were those from 2002. Thus, the combined data presents strong evidence that larval krill with a higher feeding index are growing at higher rates than those with lower feeding indices, and that the relationship holds at the large scale of the entire cruise (Table 2), and at the smaller scale of ice camps (Figure 2) with simultaneously collected data sets. This relationship and the difference between years in the chlorophyll a in the ice cores gives support to the infer-

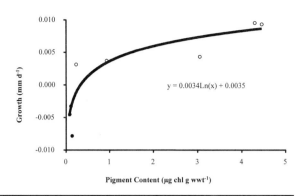

FIGURE 2. Growth rate (mm d^{-1}) of larval krill as a function of feeding index (pigment content, μg chl a g wwt $^{-1}$) of krill from same school. Growth rate is average for an experiment, with n = 3 to 14 individual measurements per experiment. Pigment content is average of 3 to 6 subsamples of larvae from same school, with 15–20 larvae per subsample. Filled circles = 2001, open circles = 2002. Exponential equation, r^2 = 0.81.

ence that larval krill have higher growth rates during years when there is more ice algae in the pack ice.

INTERACTION OF KRILL POPULATION DYNAMICS AND SEA ICE DYNAMICS

CONCEPTS DEVELOPED

One of the major concepts developed from these results and from the results of a diagnostic algal growth and ice dynamics model (Fritsen et al., 1998) is that not all pack ice has the same value as habitat for larval krill. Not only have we learned that larval krill appear to prefer over-rafted pack ice in preference to fast ice or un-rafted pack ice, but we have learned that there is significant variability in the quality of the habitat that the over-rafted pack ice habitat affords larval krill. What causes these differences in habitat quality for larval krill? The hypothesis is that the timing of ice formation in the austral fall impacts two aspects of production in SIMCOs and thus food available: (1) the amount of material in the water column to be scavenged and incorporated into the forming ice, or the base standing stock, and (2) the amount of photosynthetically available radiation (PAR) for in situ growth of the ice algae to take place integrated over the time between ice formation and mid-winter darkness. In general the rate of accumulation of SIMCO biomass slows during the transition from fall to winter as the daily PAR decreases (Hoshiai, 1985; Fritsen and Sullivan, 1997; Melnikov, 1998), following the decrease in day length.

Simulations predict that in winters when ice forms early, chlorophyll *a* will be higher in the pack ice due to both factors. Even a 10-day delay may cause an effect (C. H. Fritsen, unpublished data). Timing of ice formation is critical since the earlier ice forms, the higher the probability of incorporation of high abundances of phytoplankton from fall blooms into the ice lattice, and earlier ice formation also means more total light available for the ice algae to grow before mid-winter when light levels are too low for net primary production at most latitudes. The variation in PAR is significant, as illustrated by the decrease by more than 50% in the day length from March to April to May: 12.8 h to 9.2 h to 5.6 h at 66°S (Figure 3) and 12.8 h to 4.4 h at 68°S (Quetin et al. 2007). For our two-year comparison, the sea ice advance was a month earlier in 2002 than in 2001, April versus May. Thus, day length at the time of sea ice advance was about twice as long in 2002, 9 h versus 5 h, possibly one of the factors leading to the order of magnitude difference in the biomass of ice algae in the ice cores between the years (Table 2).

Thus, in mid-winter when larval krill need to feed, earlier forming ice will have higher concentrations of ice algae than later forming ice. Ultimately with later forming ice, lower food concentrations of ice algae leads to less food available for the larval krill, lower growth rates, and lower predicted survivorship rates (Figure 3). We suggest that this mechanism underlies the correlation seen between the timing of sea ice advance and recruitment success in the Palmer

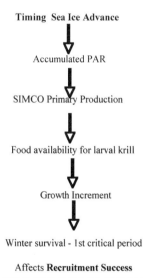

FIGURE 3. Concept of mechanism underlying the correlation found between timing of ice advance and recruitment in Antarctic krill (Siegel and Loeb, 1995; Quetin and Ross, 2003).

LTER study region (Quetin and Ross, 2003; Quetin et al., 2007). When ice does not form until May or June there is little in the water column to scavenge and PAR is near or at the minimum for the year. Thus, net primary production from ice formation to mid-winter will be low, and as a consequence so will food for larval krill.

POTENTIAL IMPACT OF CLIMATE CHANGE

The development of this conceptual view of the mechanism(s) underlying the correlation found between timing of sea ice advance and recruitment success in the Palmer LTER study region west of the Antarctic Peninsula underscores the importance of sea ice in the life cycle of Antarctic krill, and enhances our ability to predict how climate changes might impact krill population dynamics (Quetin et al., 2007). In a recent paper, Quetin et al. (2007) discuss the various scenarios and combinations of sea ice, light regime, and presence of Antarctic Circumpolar Deep Water that would create an optimal habitat for Antarctic krill.

The Palmer LTER study region is situated in one of the fastest warming regions of the world, with the other two in the northern hemisphere, the Svalbard Island group and the Bering Sea. The evidence of warming west of the Antarctic Peninsula comes from multiple studies: the air temperatures are rapidly warming, with an increase in winter temperatures over the last 50 years of about 6°C (Smith and Stammerjohn, 2001; Vaughan et al., 2003); there is a warming of ocean temperatures at both surface and sub-surface depths (Gille, 2002; Meredith and King, 2005); and ice shelves and marine glaciers are retreating (Scambos et al., 2003; Cook et al., 2005). With the warming climate, the duration of winter sea ice is shorter, but perhaps more importantly the timing is changing—sea ice advance is now later and retreat earlier (Parkinson, 2002; Smith et al., 2003; Stammerjohn et al., 2008). Sea ice advance west of the Antarctic Peninsula is now usually in April or May, whereas in the late 1970s sea ice advanced in March (Parkinson, 2002). In a recent analysis of the 25-year satellite record for sea ice, Stammerjohn found that the mean day of advance is 20–30 days later in the latter half of that period (1992–2004) than in the earlier half (1979–1991) (Stammerjohn et al., 2008). From the model simulations of Fritsen (1998), the impact of the 20- to 30-day delay in advance on accumulated SIMCO biomass in the sea ice between ice formation and mid-winter is likely to be substantial.

Do we have any evidence of changes in the Antarctic krill population concurrent with this regional warming?

Two studies to the north of the Palmer LTER study region suggest that populations of Antarctic krill are in decline. Atkinson et al. (2004) collated and compared trawl data from diverse studies in the Southern Ocean between 1926–2003, and concluded that stocks of Antarctic krill in the southwest Atlantic have declined since the 1970s by a factor of two. Shorter-term and smaller-space scale studies at the northern tip of the Antarctic Peninsula have included both net and bioacoustic data. The net data suggest a decline in krill stocks (Siegel, 2000) whereas the acoustic data suggest a cycle (Hewitt et al., 2003). One of the difficulties in the analysis of these time-series data is that detecting a linear trend in data that exhibit a repetitive cycle will take many years. In the Palmer LTER study region, where we have shown that the pattern of episodic recruitment leads to a five- to six-year cycle in the abundance of Antarctic krill (Quetin and Ross, 2003), a linear trend was not detectable in the 12-year time series (Ross et al., 2008). In this last section, we show the same data (methods and results in Quetin and Ross (2003) and Ross et al. (2008) from a different perspective, incorporating our understanding of the predictability of the cycle in the population dynamics and interannual variability in the pattern of abundance. With the five- to six-year cycle and two sequential years of successful recruitment followed by several years of low to no recruitment (Quetin and Ross 2003) in the LTER study region, the peak biomass in the cycle will appear in the January following the second good year class—in the time-series to date, in January of 1997 and 2003 (Figure 4). We can also look at the trend in the abundance during the fourth January: 1993, 1998 and 2004 (Figure 4). In both instances (year of maximum abundance, year 4 in cycle) the abundance

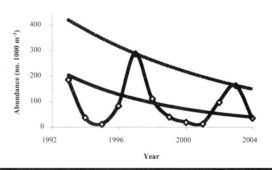

FIGURE 4. Mean abundance of Antarctic krill within the Palmer LTER study region from 1993 to 2004, calculated with equations of the delta distribution as detailed in Ross et al. (2008). The dotted line follows the year of maximum abundance within the 5–6 yr cycle, and the solid line follows the fourth year within the cycle.

has declined by 40%–45% (Figure 4). We suggest that this analysis provides preliminary evidence from the Palmer LTER study region that populations of Antarctic krill are declining in this region in concert with the change in timing of advance of sea ice. However, to date, the analysis only encompasses two full cycles; an additional cycle may yield a different trend.

SUMMARY

Scuba diving research during the past 30 years has enhanced our understanding of the linkages between Antarctic krill and sea ice. We have been able to make key observations and conduct experiments on the dependency of larval Antarctic krill on the SIMCOs in the pack ice habitat. Our conceptual understanding of the ecology of the pack ice habitat and the intricacies of the interactions has greatly increased due to these activities.

ACKNOWLEDGMENTS

We would like to gratefully acknowledge the captains, crews, and support teams (from the NSF contractor, technicians, and volunteers) that have made our research over the years both possible and enjoyable. Discussions with some of our colleagues have helped develop the concepts and ideas contained within this manuscript, and those from whom we have most benefited in recent years are C. H. Fritsen (Desert Research Institute), M. Vernet (Scripps Institution of Oceanography), and S. Stammerjohn (NASA Goddard Institute for Space Studies). This material is based upon work supported by the National Science Foundation, Office of Polar Programs, under Award Nos. OPP-9011927 and OPP-9632763, and OPP-0217282 for the Palmer LTER, OPP-9909933 for Southern Ocean GLOBEC, and ANT-0529087 for PIIAK, The Regents of the University of California, the University of California at Santa Barbara, and the Marine Science Institute, UCSB. This is Palmer LTER contribution no. 315.

NOTE

1. Since 1993 the Palmer LTER, a multidisciplinary program focused on the pelagic ecosystem west of the Antarctic Peninsula (Smith 1995), has conducted research cruises in January/February, sampling a geographical area from the southern end of Anvers Island to Marguerite Bay to the south. The sampling grid is composed of five transect lines extending approximately 200 km offshore, with stations every 20 km, and 100 km apart alongshore, and covers an area of nearly 80,000 km^2.

LITERATURE CITED

Atkinson, A., R. S. Shreeve, and A. G. Hirst. 2006. Natural Growth Rates in Antarctic Krill (*Euphausia superba*): II. Predictive Models Based on Food, Temperature, Body Length, Sex, and Maturity Stage. *Limnology and Oceanography*, 51:973–987.

Atkinson, A., V. Siegel, E. A. Pakhomov, and P. Rothery. 2004. Long-Term Decline in Krill Stock and Increase in Salps within the Southern Ocean. *Nature*, 432:100–103.

Atkinson, A., and R. Snӱder. 1997. Krill-Copepod Interactions at South Georgia, Antarctica, I. Omnivory by *Euphausia superba*. *Marine Ecology Progress Series*, 160:63–76.

Barrera-Oro, E. 2002. The Role of Fish in the Antarctic Marine Food Web: Differences between Inshore and Offshore Waters in the Southern Scotia Arc and West Antarctic Peninsula. *Antarctic Science*, 14:239–309.

Bunt, J. S. 1963. Diatoms of Antarctic Sea Ice as Agents of Primary Production. *Nature*, 199:1255–1257.

Cadée, G. C., H. González, and S. B. Schnack-Schiel. 1992. Krill Diet Affects Faecal String Settling. *Polar Biology*, 12:75–80.

Cook, A. J., A. J. Fox, D. G. Vaughan, and J. G. Ferrigno. 2005. Retreating Glacier Fronts on the Antarctic Peninsula over the Past Half-Century. *Science*, 308:541–544.

Croxall, J. P. 1984. "Seabirds." In *Antarctic Ecology*, ed. R. M. Laws, pp. 533–616. London: Academic Press.

Croxall, J. P., P. A. Prince, and C. Ricketts. 1985. "Relationships between Prey Life Cycles and the Extent, Nature, and Timing of Seal and Seabird Predation in the Scotia Sea." In *Antarctic Nutrient Cycling and Food Webs*, ed. W. R. Siegfried, P. R. Condy, and R. M. Laws, pp. 516–533. Berlin: Springer-Verlag.

Cuzin-Roudy, J. 1993. Reproductive Strategies of the Mediterranean Krill, *Meganyctiphanes norvegica* and the Antarctic Krill, *Euphausia superba* (Crustacea, Euphausiacea). *Invertebrate Reproduction and Development*, 23:105–114.

———. 2000. Seasonal Reproduction, Multiple Spawning and Fecundity in Northern Krill, *Meganyctiphanes norvegica*, and Antarctic Krill, *Euphausia superba*. Proceedings of the Second International Krill Symposium, Santa Cruz, California, August 1999. *Canadian Journal of Fisheries and Aquatic Sciences*, 57(Suppl. 3):6–15.

Cuzin-Roudy, J., and J. P. Labat. 1992. Early Summer Distribution of Antarctic Krill Sexual Development in the Scotia-Weddell Region: A Multivariate Approach. *Polar Biology*, 12:65–74.

Daly, K. L., and M. C. Macaulay. 1988. Abundance and Distribution of Krill in the Ice Edge Zone of the Weddell Sea, Austral Spring 1983. *Deep-Sea Research*, 35:21–41.

———. 1991. Influence of Physical and Biological Mesoscale Dynamics on the Seasonal Distribution and Behavior of *Euphausia superba* in the Antarctic Marginal Ice Zone. *Marine Ecology Progress Series*, 79:37–66.

Daniels, R. M., T. L. Richardson, and H. W. Ducklow. 2006. Food Web Structure and Biogeochemical Processes during Oceanic Phytoplankton Blooms: An Inverse Model Analysis. *Deep-Sea Research II*, 53:532–554.

Dayton, P. K. 1972. "Toward an Understanding of Community Resilience and the Potential Effects of Enrichments to the Benthos at McMurdo Sound, Antarctica." In *Proceedings of the Colloquium on Conservation Problems in Antarctica*, ed. B. C. Parker, 81–96. Lawrence, Kan.: Allen Press.

Ducklow, H. W., K. Baker, D. G. Martinson, L. B. Quetin, R. M. Ross, R. C. Smith, S. E. Stammerjohn, M. Vernet, and W. Fraser. 2007. Marine Pelagic Ecosystems: The West Antarctic Peninsula. *Philosophical Transactions of the Royal Society B*, 362:67–94.

Eicken, H. 1992. The Role of Sea Ice in Structuring Antarctic Ecosystems. *Polar Biology,* 12:3–13.

Ellison, A. M., M. S. Bank, B. D. Clinton, E. A. Colburn, K. Elliot, C. R. Ford, D. R. Foster, B. D. Kloeppel, J. D. Knoepp, G. M. Lovett, J. Mohan, D. A. Orwig, N. L. Rodenhouse, W. V. Sobczak, K. A. Stinson, J. K. Stone, C. M. Swan, J. Thompson, B. Von Holle, and J. R. Webster. 2005. Loss of Foundation Species: Consequences for the Structure and Dynamics of Forested Ecosystems. *Frontiers in Ecology and the Environment,* 3:479–486.

Everson, I. 2000. "Role of Krill in Marine Food Webs: The Southern Ocean." In *Krill: Biology, Ecology and Fisheries,* ed. I. Everson, pp. 194–201. Oxford: Blackwell Science Ltd.

Fogg, G. E. 2005. *A History of Antarctic Science.* Cambridge, U.K.: Cambridge University Press.

Fowler, S. W., and L. F. Small. 1972. Sinking Rates of Euphausiid Fecal Pellets. *Limnology and Oceanography,* 17:293–296.

Frazer, T. K. 1995. On the Ecology of Larval Krill, *Euphausia superba,* during Winter: Krill–Sea Ice Interactions. Ph.D. diss., University of California, Santa Barbara.

Frazer, T. K., L. B. Quetin, and R. M. Ross. 1997. "Abundance and Distribution of Larval Krill, *Euphausia superba,* Associated with Annual Sea Ice in Winter." In *Antarctic Communities: Species, Structure and Survival,* ed. B. Battaglia, J. Valencia, and D. W. H. Walton, pp. 107–111. Cambridge, U.K.: Cambridge University Press.

———. 2002. Abundance, Sizes and Developmental Stages of Larval Krill, *Euphausia superba,* during Winter in Ice-Covered Seas West of the Antarctic Peninsula. *Journal of Plankton Research,* 24:1067–1077.

Fritsen, C. H., S. F. Ackley, J. N. Kremer, and C. W. Sullivan. 1998. "Flood-Freeze Cycles and Microalgal Dynamics in Antarctic Pack Ice." In *Antarctic Sea Ice—Biological Processes, Interactions and Variability,* ed. M. P. Lizotte and K. R. Arrigo, pp. 1–21. Washington, D.C.: American Geophysical Union.

Fritsen, C. H., J. C. Memmott, and F. J. Steward. 2008. Interannual Sea Ice Dynamics and Micro-Algal Biomass in Winter Pact Ice: Marguerite Bay, Antarctica. *Deep-Sea Research, Part II,* 55, doi:10.1016/j.dsr2.2008.04.034.

Fritsen, C. H., and C. W. Sullivan. 1997. "Distributions and Dynamics of Microbial Communities in the Pack of the Western Weddell Sea, Antarctica." In *Antarctic Communities: Species, Structure and Survival,* ed. B. Battaglia, J. Valencia, and D. W. H. Walton, pp. 101–106. Cambridge, U.K.: Cambridge University Press.

Garibotti, I. A., M. Vernet, M. E. Ferrario, R. C. Smith, R. M. Ross, and L. B. Quetin. 2003. Phytoplankton Spatial Distribution Patterns along the Western Antarctic Peninsula (Southern Ocean). *Marine Ecology Progress Series,* 261:21–39.

Gille, S. T. 2002. Warming of the Southern Ocean since the 1950s. *Science,* 295:1275–1277.

González, H. E. 1992. The Distribution and Abundance of Krill Faecal Material and Oval Pellets in the Scotia and Weddell Seas (Antarctica) and Their Role in Particle Flux. *Polar Biology,* 12:81–91.

Guzman, O. 1983. "Distribution and Abundance of Antarctic Krill (*Euphausia superba*) in the Bransfield Strait." In *On the Biology of Krill* Euphausia superba, ed. S. B. Schnack, pp. 169–190. Bremerhaven, Germany: Alfred-Wegener-Institute for Polar Research.

Hagen, W., G. Kattner, A. Terbrüggen, and E. S. van Vleet. 2001. Lipid Metabolism of Antarctic Krill *Euphausia superba* and Its Ecological Implications. *Marine Biology,* 139:95–104.

Hamner, W. M., P. P. Hamner, B. S. Obst, and J. H. Carleton. 1989. Field Observations on the Ontogeny of Schooling of *Euphausia superba* Furciliae and Its Relationship to Ice in Antarctic Waters. *Limnology and Oceanography,* 34:451–456.

Hamner, W. M., P. P. Hamner, S. W. Strand, and R. W. Gilmer. 1983. Behavior of Antarctic Krill, *Euphausia superba*: Chemoreception, Feeding, Schooling, and Molting. *Science,* 220:433–435.

Hewitt, R., D. A. Demer, and J. H. Emery. 2003. An 8-Year Cycle in Krill Biomass Density Inferred from Acoustic Surveys Conducted in the Vicinity of the South Shetland Islands during the Austral Summers of 1991/1992 through 2001/2002. *Aquatic Living Resources,* 16: 205–213.

Hewitt, R. P., J. L. Watkins, M. Naganobu, V. Sushin, A. S. Brierley, D. Demer, S. Kasatkina, Y. Takao, C. Goss, A. Malyshko, M. Brandon, S. Kawaguchi, V. Siegel, P. Trathan, J. Emery, I. Everson, and D. Miller. 2004. Biomass of Antarctic Krill in the Scotia Sea in January/February 2000 and Its Use in Revising an Estimate of Precautionary Yield. *Deep-Sea Research II,* 51:1215–1236.

Hoddell, R. J., A. C. Crossley, R. Willimas, and G. W. Hosie. 2000. The Distribution of Antarctic Pelagic Fish and Larvae (CCAMLR division 58.4.1). *Deep-Sea Research II,* 47:2519–2541.

Hofmann, E. E., J. E. Capella, R. M. Ross, and L. B. Quetin. 1992. Models of the Early Life History of *Euphausia superba*—Part I: Time and Temperature Dependent Dependence during the Descent-Ascent Cycle. *Deep-Sea Research,* 39:1177–1200.

Hopkins, T. L. 1985. The Zooplankton Community of Croker Passage, Antarctic Peninsula. *Polar Biology,* 4:161–170.

Hopkins, T. L., and J. J. Torres. 1988. The Zooplankton Community in the Vicinity of the Ice Edge, Western Weddell Sea, March 1986. *Polar Biology,* 9:79–87.

Hoshiai, T. 1985. Autumnal Proliferation of Ice-Algae in Antarctic Sea Ice. In *Antarctic Nutrient Cycles and Food Webs,* ed. W. R. Siegfried, P. R. Condy, and R. M. Laws, pp. 89–92. Berlin: Springer.

Ikeda, T., and P. Dixon. 1982. Body Shrinkage as a Possible Over-Wintering Mechanism of the Antarctic Krill, *Euphausia superba. Journal of Experimental Marine Biology and Ecology,* 62:143–151.

Ju, S.-J., and H. R. Harvey. 2004. Lipids as Markers of Nutritional Condition and Diet in the Antarctic Krill *Euphausia superba* and *Euphausia crystallorophias* during Austral Winter. *Deep-Sea Research II,* 51:2199–2214.

Kottmeier, S. T., and C. W. Sullivan. 1987. Late Winter Primary Production and Bacterial Production in Sea Ice and Seawater West of the Antarctic Peninsula. *Marine Ecology Progress Series,* 36:287–298.

Lancraft, T. M., T. L. Hopkins, J. J. Torres, and J. Donnelly. 1991. Oceanic Micronektonic Macrozooplanktonic Community Structure and Feeding in Ice-Covered Antarctic Waters during the Winter (AMERIEZ 1988). *Polar Biology,* 11:157–167.

Lancraft, T. M., J. J. Torres, and T. L. Hopkins. 1989. Micronekton and Macrozooplankton in the Open Waters Near Antarctic Ice Edge Zones (AMERIEZ 1983 and 1986). *Polar Biology,* 9:225–233.

Laws, R. M. 1984. "Seals." In *Antarctic Ecology,* ed. R. M. Laws, pp. 621–716. London: Academic Press.

———. 1985. The Ecology of the Southern Ocean. *American Scientist,* 73:26–40.

Loeb, V., V. Siegel, O. Holm-Hansen, R. Hewitt, W. Fraser, W. Trivelpiece, and S. Trivelpiece. 1997. Effects of Sea-Ice Extent and Krill or Salp Dominance on the Antarctic Food Web. *Nature,* 387:897–900.

Loots, C., P. Koubbi, and G. Duhamel. 2007. Habitat Modeling of *Electrona antarctica* (Myctophidae, Pisces) in Kerguelen by Generalized Additive Models and Geographic Information Systems. *Polar Biology,* 30:951–959.

Lowry, F. F., J. W. Testa, and W. Calvert. 1988. Notes on Winter Feeding of Crabeater and Leopard Seals near the Antarctic Peninsula. *Polar Biology,* 8:475–478.

Marr, J. W. S. 1962. The Natural History and Geography of the Antarctic Krill (*Euphausia superba* Dana). *Discovery Reports,* 32:33–464.

Marschall, H.-P. 1988. The Overwintering Strategy of Antarctic Krill under the Pack Ice of the Weddell Sea. *Polar Biology,* 2:245–250.

Melnikov, A. A., and V. A. Spiridonov. 1996. Antarctic Krill under Perennial Sea Ice in the Western Weddell Sea. *Antarctic Science,* 8: 323–329.

Melnikov, I. 1998. Winter Production of Sea Ice Algae in the Western Weddell Sea. *Journal of Marine Systems,* 17:195–205.

Meredith, M. P., and J. C. King. 2005. Rapid Climate Change in the Ocean West of the Antarctic Peninsula during the Second Half of the 20th Century. *Geophysical Research Letters,* 32: L19604, doi: 10_1029/2005GL024042.

Meyer, B., and B. Oettl. 2005. Effects of Short-Term Starvation on Composition and Metabolism of Larval Antarctic Krill *Euphausia superba. Marine Ecology Progress Series,* 292:263–270.

Miller, D. G. M., and I. Hampton. 1989. *Biology and Ecology of the Antarctic Krill (Euphausia superba Dana): A Review.* Cambridge, U.K.: Scientific Committee on Antarctic Research and Scientific Committee on Oceanic Research of the International Council of Scientific Unions.

Moline, M. A., H. Claustre, T. K. Frazer, O. Schofields, and M. Vernet. 2004. Alterations of the food web along the Antarctic Peninsula in response to a regional warming trend. *Global Change Biology,* 10: 1973–1980.

Morales-Nin, B., I. Palomera, and S. Schadwinkel. 1995. Larval Fish Distribution and Abundance in the Antarctic Peninsula Region and Adjacent Waters. *Polar Biology,* 15:143–154.

Nicol, S. 1994. "Antarctic Krill: Changing Perceptions of Its Role in the Antarctic Ecosystem." In *Antarctic Science—Global Concerns,* ed. G. Hempel, pp. 144–166. Berlin: Springer-Verlag.

Nicol, S., A. J. Constable, and T. Pauly. 2000. Estimates of Circumpolar Abundance of Antarctic Krill Based on Recent Acoustic Density Measurements. *CCAMLR Science,* 7:87–99.

O'Brien, D. P. 1987. Direct Observations of the Behavior of *Euphausia superba* and *Euphausia crystallorophias* (Crustacea:Euphausiacea) under Pack Ice during the Antarctic Spring of 1985. *Journal of Crustacean Biology,* 7:437–448.

Ottersen, G. B., and L. H. Loeng. 2000. Covariability in Early Growth and Year-Class Strength of Barents Sea Cod, Haddock and Herring: The Environmental Link. *ICES Journal of Marine Science,* 57: 339–348.

Parkinson, C. L. 2002. Trends in the Length of the Southern Ocean Sea Ice Seasons, 1979–1999. *Annals of Glaciology,* 34:435–440.

Pepin, P. 1991. The Effect of Temperature and Size on Development and Mortality Rates of Pelagic Life History Stages of Marine Fish. *Canadian Journal of Fisheries and Aquatic Sciences,* 48:503–518.

Pitcher, T. J., S. H. Lang, and J. A. Turner. 1988. A Risk-Balancing Trade-Off between Foraging Rewards and Predation Hazard in a Shoaling Fish. *Behavioral Ecology and Sociobiology,* 22:225–228.

Power, M. E., D. Tilman, J. A. Estes, B. A. Menge, W. J. Bond, L. S. Mills, G. Daily, J. C. Castilla, J. Lubchenco, and R. T. Paine. 1996. Challenges in the Quest for Keystones. *BioScience,* 46:609–620.

Priddle, J., J. P. Croxall, I. Everson, R. B. Heywood, E. J. Murphy, P. A. Prince, and C. B. Sear. 1988. "Large-Scale Fluctuations in Distribution and Abundance of Krill—A Discussion of Possible Causes." In *Antarctic Resources and Variability,* ed. D. Sahrhage, pp. 169–182. Berlin: Springer-Verlag.

Quetin, L. B., and R. M. Ross. 1984. Depth Distribution of Developing *Euphausia superba* Embryos, Predicted from Sinking Rates. *Marine Biology,* 79:47–53.

———. 1986. Summary of Cruise 85–5 of the Polar Duke to the Antarctic Peninsula during August and September. *Antarctic Journal of the United States,* 21:192–193.

———. 1988. Summary of WinCruise II to the Antarctic Peninsula during June and July 1987. *Antarctic Journal of the United States,* 23: 149–151.

———. 2001. Environmental Variability and Its Impact on the Reproductive Cycle of Antarctic Krill. *American Zoologist,* 41:74–89.

———. 2003. Episodic Recruitment in Antarctic Krill, *Euphausia superba,* in the Palmer LTER Study Region. *Marine Ecology Progress Series,* 259:185–200.

———. 2007. "Pack Ice Diving." In *Proceedings of the International Polar Diving Workshop,* ed. M. A. Lang and M. D. J. Sayer, pp. 111–131. Washington, D.C.: Smithsonian Institution.

Quetin, L. B., R. M. Ross, T. K. Frazer, M. O. Amsler, C. Wyatt-Evens, and S. A. Oakes. 2003. Growth of Larval Krill, *Euphausia superba,* in Fall and Winter West of the Antarctic Peninsula. *Marine Biology,* 143:833–843.

Quetin, L. B., R. M. Ross, T. K. Frazer, and K. L. Haberman. 1996. "Factors Affecting Distribution and Abundance of Zooplankton, with an Emphasis on Antarctic Krill, *Euphausia superba.*" In *Foundations for Ecological Research West of the Antarctic Peninsula,* ed. R. M. Ross, E. E. Hofmann, and L. B. Quetin, pp. 357–371. Washington, D.C.: American Geophysical Union.

Quetin, L. B., R. M. Ross, C. H. Fritsen, and M. Vernet. 2007. Ecological Responses of Antarctic Krill to Environmental Variability: Can We Predict the Future? *Antarctic Science,* 19:1–14.

Robison, B. 2003. What Drives the Diel Vertical Migrations of Antarctic Midwater Fish? *Journal of the Marine Biological Association of the United Kingdom,* 83:639–642.

Ross, R. M., and L. B. Quetin. 1989. Energetic Cost to Develop to the First Feeding Stage of *Euphausia Superba* Dana and the Effect of Delays in Food Availability. *Journal of Experimental Marine Biology and Ecology,* 133:103–127.

———. 1991. Ecological Physiology of Larval Euphausiids, *Euphausia superba* (Euphausiacea). *Memoirs of the Queensland Museum,* 31: 321–333.

———. 2000. "Reproduction in Euphausiacea." In *Krill: Biology, Ecology and Fisheries,* ed. I. Everson, pp. 150–181. Cambridge, U.K.: Blackwell Science.

———. 2003. Working with Living Krill: The People and the Places. *Marine and Freshwater Behaviour and Physiology,* 36:207–228.

Ross, R. M., L. B. Quetin, and M. O. Amsler. 1985. *Euphausia superba*: A Preliminary Report on Three Areas of Investigation. *Antarctic Journal of the United States,* 19:153–155.

Ross, R. M., L. B. Quetin, K. S. Baker, M. Vernet, and R. C. Smith. 2000. Growth Limitation in Young *Euphausia superba* under Field Conditions. *Limnology and Oceanography,* 45:31–43.

Ross, R. M., L. B. Quetin, and K. L. Haberman. 1998. Interannual and Seasonal Variability in Short-Term Grazing Impact of *Euphausia superba* in Nearshore and Offshore Waters West of the Antarctic Peninsula. *Journal of Marine Systems,* 17:261–273.

Ross, R. M., L. B. Quetin, D. G. Martinson, R. Iannuzzi, S. S. Stammerjohn, and R. C. Smith. 2008. Palmer LTER: Patterns of Distribution of 5 Dominant Zooplankton Species in the Epipelagic Zone West of the Antarctic Peninsula, 1993–2004. *Deep-Sea Research, Part II,* 55, doi:10.1016/j.dsr2.2008.04.037.

Ross, R. M., L. B. Quetin, T. Newberger, and S. A. Oakes. 2004. Growth and Behavior of Larval Krill (*Euphausia superba*) under the Ice in Late Winter 2001 West of the Antarctic Peninsula. *Deep-Sea Research II,* 51:2169–2184.

Scambos, T., C. Hulbe, and M. Fahnestock. 2003. "Climate-Induced Ice Shelf Disintegration in the Antarctic Peninsula." In *Antarctic Peninsula Climate Variability: Historical and Paleoenvironmental Perspectives,* ed. E. Domack, A. Burnett, A. Leventer, P. Conley, M. Kirby, and R. Bindschadler, pp. 79–92. Washington, D.C.: American Geophysical Union.

Schmidt, K., A. Atkinson, K.-J. Petzke, M. Voss, and D. W. Pond. 2006. Protozoans as a Food Source for Antarctic Krill, *Euphausia superba*: Complementary Insights from Stomach Contents, Fatty Acids, and Stable Isotopes. *Limnology and Oceanography,* 51: 2409–2427.

Siegel, V. 2000. Krill (Euphausiacea) Life History and Aspects of Population Dynamics. Proceedings of the Second International Krill Symposium, Santa Cruz, California, August 1999. *Canadian Journal of Fisheries and Aquatic Sciences,* 57(Suppl. 3):130–150.

————. 2005. Distribution and Population Dynamics of *Euphausia superba*: Summary of Recent Findings. *Polar Biology*, 29:1–22.

Siegel, V., and V. Loeb. 1995. Recruitment of Antarctic Krill (*Euphausia superba*) and Possible Causes for Its Variability. *Marine Ecology Progress Series*, 123:45–56.

Siegel, V., R. M. Ross, and L. B. Quetin. 2003. Krill (*Euphausia superba*) Recruitment Indices from the Western Antarctic Peninsula: Are They Representative of Larger Regions? *Polar Biology*, 26: 672–679.

Smetacek, V., P. Assmy, and J. Henjes. 2004. The Role of Grazing in Structuring Southern Ocean Pelagic Ecosystems and Biogeochemical Cycles. *Antarctic Science*, 16:541–558.

Smetacek, V., R. Scharek, and E.-M. Nothig. 1990. "Seasonal and Regional Variation in the Pelagial and Its Relationship to the Life History Cycle of Krill." In *Antarctic Ecosystems: Ecological Change and Conservation*, ed. K. R. Kerry and G. Hempel, pp. 103–114. Berlin: Springer-Verlag.

Smith, R. C., W. R. Fraser, and S. E. Stammerjohn. 2003. "Climate Variability and Ecological Response of the Marine Ecosystem in the Western Antarctic Peninsula (WAP) region." In *Climate Variability and Ecosystem Response at Long-Term Ecological Research Site*, ed. D. Greenland, D. G. Goodin, and R. C. Smith, pp. 158–173. New York: Oxford University Press.

Smith, R. C., and S. E. Stammerjohn. 2001. Variations of Surface Air Temperature and Sea-Ice Extent in the Western Antarctic Peninsula Region. *Annals of Glaciology*, 33:493–500.

Stammerjohn S. E., D. G. Martinson, R. C. Smith, and R. A. Iannuzzi. 2008. Sea Ice in the Western Antarctic Peninsula Region: Spatio-Temporal Variability from Ecological and Climate Change Perspectives. *Deep-Sea Research, Part II*, 55, doi:10.106lj.dsr2.2008.04.026.

Takahashi, M., and Y. Watanabe. 2004. Growth Rate-Dependent Recruitment of Japanese Anchovy *Engraulis japonicus* in the Kuroshio-Oyashio Transitional Waters. *Marine Ecology Progress Series*, 266: 227–238.

Turner, J. T. 2002. Zooplankton Fecal Pellets, Marine Snow and Sinking Phytoplankton Blooms. *Aquatic Microbial Ecology*, 27:57–102.

Vaughan, D. G., G. J. Marshall, W. M. Connolley, C. Parkinson, R. Mulvaney, D. A. Hodgson, J. C. King, C. J. Pudsey, and J. Turner. 2003. Recent Rapid Regional Climate Warming on the Antarctic Peninsula. *Climatic Change*, 60:243–274.

Vernet, M., D. Martinson, R. Iannuzzi, S. Stammerjohn, W. Kozlowski, K. Sines, R. Smith, and I. Garibotti. 2008. Primary Production within the Sea-Ice Zone West of the Antarctic Peninsula: Sea Ice, Summer Mixed Layer, and Irradiance. *Deep-Sea Research, Part II*, 55, doi:10.1016/j.dsr2.2008.05.021.

Ward, P., S. Grant, M. Brandon, V. Siegel, V. Sushin, V. Loeb, and H. Griffiths. 2004. Mesozooplankton Community Structure in the Scotia Sea during the CCAMLR 2000 Survey: January–February 2000. *Deep-Sea Research II*, 51:1351–1367.

Watkins, J. 1999. A Composite Recruitment Index to Describe Interannual Changes in the Population Structure of Antarctic Krill at South Georgia. *CCAMLR Science*, 6:71–84.

Inhibition of Phytoplankton and Bacterial Productivity by Solar Radiation in the Ross Sea Polynya

Patrick J. Neale, Wade H. Jeffrey, Cristina Sobrino, J. Dean Pakulski, Jesse Phillips-Kress, Amy J. Baldwin, Linda A. Franklin, and Hae-Cheol Kim

Patrick J. Neale, Jesse Phillips-Kress, and Linda A. Franklin, Smithsonian Environmental Research Center, 647 Contees Wharf Road, Edgewater, MD 21037, USA. Wade H. Jeffrey and J. Dean Pakulski, Center for Environmental Diagnostics and Bioremediation, University of West Florida, 11000 University Parkway, Building 58, Pensacola, FL 32514, USA. Cristina Sobrino, Smithsonian Environmental Research Center; now at Departamento de Ecología y Biología Animal, University of Vigo, 36310 Vigo, Spain. Amy J. Baldwin, Center for Environmental Diagnostics and Bioremediation; now at Florida Department of Environmental Protection, 160 Governmental Center, Pensacola, FL 32502-5794, USA. Hae-Cheol Kim, Smithsonian Environmental Research Center; now at Harte Research Institute for Gulf of Mexico Studies, 6300 Ocean Drive, Corpus Christi, TX 78412, USA. Corresponding author: P. Neale (nealep@si.edu). Submitted 26 October 2007; revised 21 June 2008; accepted 28 May 2008.

ABSTRACT. The Ross Sea polynya is one of the most productive areas of the Southern Ocean; however, little is known about how plankton there respond to inhibitory solar exposure, particularly during the early-spring period of enhanced UVB (290–320 nm) due to ozone depletion. Responses to solar exposure of the phytoplankton and bacterial assemblages were studied aboard the research ice breaker *Nathaniel B. Palmer* during cruises NBP0409 and NBP0508. Photosynthesis and bacterial production (thymidine and leucine incorporation) were measured during in situ incubations in the upper 10 m at three stations, which were occupied before, during, and after the annual peak of a phytoplankton bloom dominated by *Phaeocystis antarctica*. Near-surface production was consistently inhibited down to 5–7 m, even when some surface ice was present. Relative inhibition of phytoplankton increased and productivity decreased with increasing severity of nutrient limitation as diagnosed using F_v/F_m, a measure of the maximum photosynthetic quantum yield. Relative inhibition of bacterial production was high for both the high-biomass and postbloom stations, but sensitivity of thymidine and leucine uptake differed between stations. These results provide the first direct evidence that solar exposure, in particular solar ultraviolet radiation, causes significant inhibition of Ross Sea productivity.

INTRODUCTION

Solar radiation, particularly that in the ultraviolet waveband (UV, 290–400 nm), affects planktonic processes in the surface layer of diverse aquatic environments (polar and elsewhere) and, in particular, the metabolism and survival of bacterioplankton, phytoplankton, and zooplankton. A subject of much recent work has been the extent to which these effects are augmented by enhanced UVB (290–320 nm) due to Antarctic ozone depletion, which is most severe during the springtime "ozone hole." UVB-induced DNA damage has been measured in a wide variety of environments and trophic levels, for example, planktonic communities from tropical (Visser et al., 1999) and subtropical waters (Jeffrey et al., 1996a, 1996b), coral reefs (Lyons et al., 1998), and the Southern Ocean (Kelley et al., 1999; Buma et al., 2001; Meador et al., 2002). DNA damage in zooplankton and fish larvae has been reported in the Southern Ocean (Malloy et al., 1997) and in anchovy eggs and larvae (Vetter et al., 1999).

The UV responses of Antarctic phytoplankton have been the focus of many studies (e.g., El-Sayed et al., 1990; Holm-Hansen and Mitchell, 1990; Mitchell, 1990; Helbling et al., 1992; Lubin et al., 1992; Smith et al., 1992; Boucher and Prézelin, 1996). However, there is little quantitative information on the photosynthetic response to UV in the Ross Sea and on the responses of natural assemblages of the colonial prymnesiophyte *Phaeocystis antarctica,* despite the important contribution of the Ross Sea to overall productivity of the Southern Ocean (see Smith and Comiso, 2009, and references therein). *P. antarctica* is the dominant phytoplankter in the Ross Sea, particularly during the early-spring period of ozone depletion. At this time of year most of the Ross Sea is covered by ice, so phytoplankton growth occurs in an open water area, or polynya, located just north of the Ross Ice Shelf (for more background, see DiTullio and Dunbar, 2004). Our lack of knowledge about responses to UV is not only for *P. antarctica* but also for other phytoplankton and the associated bacterioplankton community.

Bacterioplankton abundance can reach 3×10^9 cells/L in the Ross Sea, equal to bacterial blooms in other oceanic systems. Bacterioplankton do bloom in response to the *Phaeocystis* bloom, but with a delay of one or two months after the onset of the phytoplankton bloom (Ducklow et al., 2001). DOC release by *Phaeocystis* is low, but is believed to be labile (Carlson et al., 1998) and may limit bacterial production in the upper water layer (Ducklow et al., 2001). Bacterial production in deeper waters is relatively high (Ducklow et al., 2001) and may be related to sinking *Phaeocystis* POC (DiTullio et al., 2000).

There are many other measurements to suggest that enhanced UVB and environmental UV in general have effects on organismal physiology and survival (reviewed in de Mora et al., 2000). Direct measurements of quantitative in situ effects, on the other hand, are difficult to make for most cases. However, estimates can be made using mathematical models. The quantitative response to UV exposure is characterized well enough for some processes that statements can be made about integrated effects over the water column as a function of vertical mixing in the surface layer (Neale et al., 1998; Huot et al., 2000; Kuhn et al., 2000). These model results, together with profiles of UV-specific effects like DNA damage under qualitatively different mixing conditions (Jeffrey et al., 1996b; Huot et al., 2000), argue that mixing significantly modifies water column effects (Neale

et al., 2003). However, there are no instances where UV responses and vertical mixing have been quantitatively measured at the same time.

Here we present results from field work conducted in the Ross Sea polynya to assess the quantitative impact of UV on the phytoplankton and bacterioplankton communities. Both communities play a crucial role in carbon and nutrient cycling. They are also tightly coupled, so it is important to examine both communities simultaneously to understand UV impacts on the system as a whole. For example, a decrease in phytoplankton production may result in a decline in bacterial production that may be compounded by direct UVB effects on bacterioplankton. A primary physical factor controlling exposure of these communities to UV is vertical mixing. Thus, our work examined the effects of vertical mixing using a combination of field measurements and modeling approaches.

Our assessments of UV responses of Ross Sea plankton used three approaches: laboratory spectral incubations, surface (on deck) time series studies, and daylong in situ incubations. The first two approaches enable estimation of spectral response (biological weighting functions, Cullen and Neale, 1997) and kinetic response. From this information we are constructing general, time-dependent models of UV response to variable irradiance in the mixed layer. While providing less detail on specific responses, in situ incubations have the advantage of using natural irradiance regimes. However, they are not sufficient in themselves in measuring actual water column effects since they introduce the artifact of keeping samples at a constant depth throughout the day. For example, depending on the kinetics of UV inhibition, a static incubation may overestimate the response at the surface but underestimate the integrated response over the water column (Neale et al., 1998).

Nevertheless, in situ incubations still provide useful information on responses of natural plankton assemblages. They provide direct evidence that UV exposure is sufficiently high to cause some effect, in particular, inhibition of near-surface productivity. Moreover, in situ observations can be compared to predictions of laboratory-formulated models evaluated using measured irradiance at the incubation depths and thus provide an independent validation of the models.

Here we present measurements of phytoplankton productivity (^{14}C-HCO3$^-$ incorporation) and bacterial production (^{3}H-leucine and ^{3}H-thymidine incorporation) for daylong incubations conducted in the near surface (upper 10 m) of the Ross Sea polynya for three dates spanning the early-spring through summer period.

MATERIALS AND METHODS

IRRADIANCE MEASUREMENTS

Radiometers were mounted on top of a science mast (nominally 33 m above ocean surface). Photosynthetically available radiation (PAR, 400–700 nm) incident on a flat plane (2-π collector) was measured with a Biospherical Instruments (San Diego, California, USA) GUV 2511. Spectral UV irradiance was recorded with a Smithsonian-designed multifilter radiometer, the SR19, which measures between 290 and 324 nm with 2-nm bandwidth (FWHM) and resolution and at 330 nm with 10-nm bandwidth (technical description in Lantz et al., 2002). Broadband UV measurements (nominal 10 nm bandwidth) in the UV were also made by the GUV 2511. The transmission of downwelling irradiance ($E_d[\lambda]$) through the water column was measured by a free-fall, profiling radiometer, the Biospherical Instruments PUV 2500. Four to five casts were made near solar noon from 0 to 50 m, and attenuation coefficients ($k_d[\lambda]$) were computed from the regression of $\log(E_d[\lambda])$ versus depth. Profiles of E_d were recorded at 305, 313, 320, 340, and 395 nm (only $k_d[\lambda]$ are presented here) and for PAR.

PRODUCTIVITY ASSAYS

Sample water for the incubations was obtained with 30-L "Go-Flo" Niskin bottles (General Oceanics) mounted on a conductivity-temperature-depth (CTD) rosette. The CTD cast was made in open water at 5-m depth at approximately 0500 local time (LT) (GMT+13), ensuring minimal exposure to UV prior to incubation. The sample was immediately dispensed through wide-bore tubing and stored in the dark at 0°C until use. For photosynthesis assays, UV-transparent polyethylene sample bags (113-mL Whirl-Pak bag) were prepared by extensive rinsing with sample water. Then ^{14}C-bicarbonate was added to 700 mL of sample water (~1 μCi/mL), which was distributed into 14 sample bags in 50-mL aliquots. The unfilled portion of the bag was tightly rolled and twist sealed to prevent leakage. A second set of bags was prepared for measurements of bacterial productivity. Tritium (^{3}H) labeled thymidine (60 Ci/mmol) or ^{3}H-leucine (60 Ci/mmol) was added to 175 mL of seawater to a final concentration of 10 nM for 19 January and 21 November and 20 nM for 28 November. Five milliliters of the amended solution were added to each of three Whirl-Pak bags, as for photosynthesis, such that triplicates for each substrate were placed at each depth. After inoculation, the bags for both photosynthesis and bacterial productiv-

ity were secured with plastic ties to 25 × 25 cm "crosses" made of UV-transparent acrylic sheet (Plexiglas) (Figure 1). Each "arm" was 10 cm wide; one set of replicate photosynthesis bags was fastened to one set of opposing arms, and triplicate ^{3}H-thymidine incorporation and triplicate ^{3}H-leucine incorporation bags were attached to each of the other two arms. Crosses were kept at 0°C and in the dark until just before deployment. These Plexiglas pieces were then secured at 1-, 2-, 3-, 4-, 5-, 7.5- and 10-m depth to a weighted line which passed through the center of each cross. A primary float was attached at the surface along with a second float containing a radar reflector and a radio beacon. The array was hand deployed from the stern of the research vessel and followed for 12 h. Upon retrieval of the array, bags were quickly removed from the arms and transported to the laboratory in the dark. For photosynthesis, five replicate aliquots (5 mL) were removed from the bags and analyzed for incorporated organic ^{14}C-carbon by acidification, venting and scintillation counting. Replicate 1.5-mL samples for ^{3}H-thymidine or ^{3}H-leucine incorporation were removed from each Whirl-Pak bag and placed in 2-mL microfuge tubes containing 100 μL of 100% trichloroacetic acid (TCA). Samples were processed via the

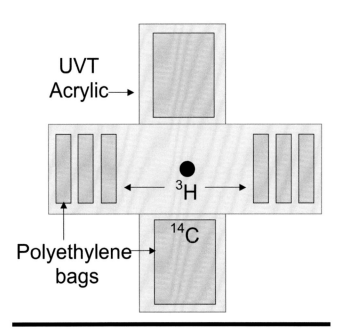

FIGURE 1. Schematic diagram of "cross" supports for the in situ array. The cross pieces are 25 cm in length. Darker shaded boxes indicate position of the UV-transparent polyethylene (Whirl-Pak) incubation bags. The center circle indicates where the support attached to the incubation line.

microcentrifugation method described by Smith and Azam (1992) as modified by Pakulski et al. (2007).

BIOMASS AND PHOTOSYNTHETIC QUANTUM YIELD

Chlorophyll concentration and bacterial cell abundance was measured on aliquots of the early-morning 5-m sample at all cruise stations (including the incubation stations). Samples for chlorophyll were concentrated on glass fiber filters (GF/F, Whatman Inc., Florham Park, New Jersey, USA) and extracted with 90% acetone overnight at 0°C. After extraction, chlorophyll concentration was measured as the fluorescence emission in a Turner 10-AU fluorometer calibrated with pure chlorophyll *a* (Sigma Chemical, St. Louis, Missouri, USA). Bacterial abundances were determined by epifluorescence microscopy of 5–10 mL of 4′, 6-diamidino-2-phenylindole (DAPI) stained samples collected on black 0.2-μm polycarbonate filters (Porter and Feig, 1980). A pulse-amplitude-modulated fluorometer (Walz Water PAM, Effeltrich, Germany) with red LED (650 nm) excitation was used to assess the maximum photosynthetic efficiency (quantum yield) of the samples. Measurements on the 5-m sample were made after at least one hour of dark incubation at 0°C. The data are expressed as the PSII quantum yield, $F_v/F_m = (F_m-F_0)/F_m$, which has been correlated with the maximum quantum yield of photosynthesis (Genty et al., 1989). F_0 is the steady-state yield of in vivo chlorophyll fluorescence in dark-adapted phytoplankton, and F_m is the maximum yield of fluorescence obtained from the same sample during application of a saturating light pulse (400-ms duration).

SITE DESCRIPTION

The Ross Sea polynya was sampled in two research cruises aboard the R/V *Nathaniel B. Palmer* taking place in December 2004 to January 2005 (NBP0409) and October through November 2005 (NBP0508). Overall trends in surface biomass are shown in Figure 2. During both years, this south central region of the Ross Sea supported a strong bloom of *P. antarctica* in November, peaking in early December (on the basis of Moderate Resolution Imaging Spectroradiometer (MODIS) satellite images). The bloom slowly declined through January, becoming mixed with other species, mostly diatoms. Bacterial biomass displayed a more complex pattern, with biomass peaks occurring during each of the cruise periods. Bacterioplankton

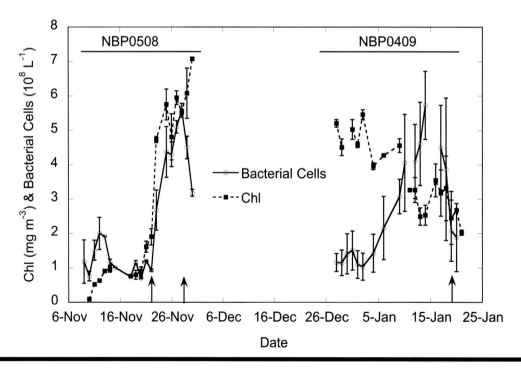

FIGURE 2. Time series of chlorophyll and bacterial cell concentration at 5 m for all stations in two cruises to the Ross Sea polynya. Bars indicate standard deviation of triplicate determinations. The two sampling periods for NBP0409 (December 2004 to January 2005) and NBP0508 (November 2005) are indicated by horizontal lines, and vertical arrows indicate dates of incubations.

are seen to increase along with the onset of the bloom followed by a second peak occurring in mid-January as the bloom receded. Our data from October–November is very similar to Ducklow et al. (2001), but this previous study and ours differ for the December–January period. We observed relatively low bacterial numbers at the end of December when the cruise began. Bacterioplankton then increased to a second peak occurring at approximately the same time as that reported by Ducklow et al. (2001) but at a maximum density of only 0.6×10^9 cells/L compared to the $\sim 2 \times 10^9$ cells/L reported in the previous study. These contrasting observations may be due to differences in specific bloom conditions between years or specific sampling locations within the Ross Sea. Deployment locations and times of the incubations are given in Table 1. During the early-spring (October–November) cruise, the surface was covered with moderate to heavy pack ice interspersed with leads until the last week in November. For the first incubation (21 November), samples were obtained and the array was deployed while the ship was in a lead. Shortly after deployment, the array became surrounded with a raft of "pancake" ice extending at least a 100 m in all directions (Figure 3), and this continued until retrieval. The 28 November and 19 January deployments were conducted in open water.

RESULTS

SOLAR IRRADIANCE

Surface UV and PAR were similar between all three days, with midday PAR in the range of 1000–1200 μmol m^{-2} s^{-1} and midday UV at 320 nm between 100 and 150 mW m^{-2} nm^{-1} (Figure 4). Transmission of UV and PAR varied between dates in inverse relation to phytoplankton biomass. Attenuation coefficients were similar for the prebloom and postbloom stations but were considerably higher in both UV and PAR for the station on 28 November near the peak of the bloom (Table 1).

FIGURE 3. Typical surface conditions during the 21 November incubation. The surface float of the array sitting on top of the ice is approximately 75 cm in diameter.

PHOTOSYNTHESIS

All in situ profiles exhibited lowest rates at the surface and higher rates with depth, with the near-surface "photoactive" zone of inhibitory effect extending to at least 5 m on all dates (Figure 5). The 21 November profile shows an inhibitory trend over the full profile, but differences below 4 m are not significant due to high sample variability. This high variability may be associated with ice-cover-generated heterogeneity in the underwater light field. Interestingly, relative inhibition at 1 m is only 10% less than in the 28 November profile, despite the presence of ice cover on 21 November (Figure 2). On 28 November, the depth maximum in productivity was observed at 5 m, which was much shallower than the other dates. This is consistent with the relatively low transparency to both PAR and UV on this date due to high phytoplankton biomass (5.5 mg m^{-3}), mostly

TABLE 1. Background information on the three stations where in situ incubations were conducted. LT = local time.

Date (LT)	Latitude	Longitude	Chl a (mg m^{-3})	$k_d[320]$ (m^{-1})	k_d PAR (m^{-1})
21 Nov 2005	−77°35.113′	178°23.435′	1.9	0.32	0.15
28 Nov 2005	−77°34.213′	−178°57.763′	5.5	0.54	0.27
19 Jan 2005	−74°30.033′	173°30.085′	2.8	0.32	0.17

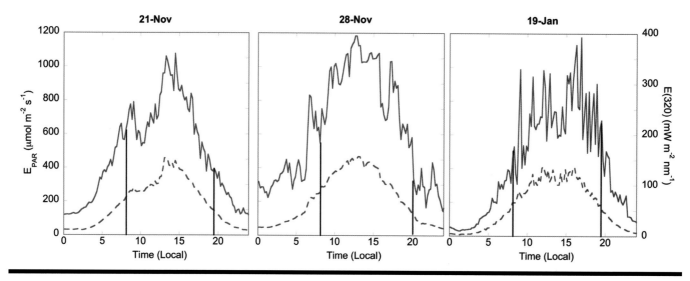

FIGURE 4. Daily variation in the surface quantum flux of photosynthetically available radiation (μmol m^{-2} s^{-1} PAR, 400–700 nm, solid line) and spectral irradiance at 320 nm (mW m^{-2} nm^{-1}, 2.0-nm bandwidth at half maximum, dashed line). Vertical lines indicate period of incubation on each date.

comprised of *P. antarctica* (data not shown). The presence of *P. antarctica* decreased not only PAR transparency because of absorbance by photosynthetic pigments but also UV transparency (Table 1). The decreased UV transparency is caused in part by the presence of UV screening pigments, the mycosporine-like amino acids, which are known to be accumulated by this species and were present in separate absorbance scans of particulates (data not shown). The 19 January incubation was at a postbloom station for which the depth of UV effects is comparable to the prebloom 21 November station and relative inhibition at 1 m was the highest of all profiles.

If the three profiles are regarded as showing the sequential development of the Ross Sea polynya bloom (despite the 19 January station being from the previous season), a couple of trends are apparent. One is the large increase in productivity associated with the high biomass on 28 November. Also, productivity was higher in the prebloom station compared to the postbloom station despite similar biomass. In other words, biomass-specific maximum productivity in the profile (P^B_{max}, at 5 m on 28 November and 10 m on 21 November and 19 January) was highest before the bloom and actually decreased with time (Figure 6). Parallel to this result was a decrease in the maximum quantum yield of photosynthesis as measured by PAM fluorometry (Figure 6). The most likely reason for the declining quantum yield, which has been observed previously for postbloom phytoplankton in the Ross Sea (e.g., Peloquin and Smith, 2007), is the depletion of dissolved

iron, the limiting nutrient for phytoplankton growth in most areas of the Ross Sea (Smith et al., 2000). An additional factor could be the cumulative effect of recurring inhibitory solar exposure on the functioning of the photosynthetic apparatus.

BACTERIOPLANKTON PRODUCTION

Similar to the pattern observed for photosynthetic rates, bacterial incorporation of either leucine or thymidine was most inhibited at the high-biomass and postbloom stations. For leucine incorporation, the lowest rates and least inhibition at 1 m were observed for the early-season sample, while the highest production rates were observed in the high-biomass sample. The pattern was similar for thymidine incorporation, although there was minimal difference between the high-biomass and postbloom samples. The pattern of dark leucine rates generally followed bacterial biomass (Figure 2), with minor variation in rates per cell (not shown). In contrast, thymidine rates remained high at the postbloom station.

DISCUSSION

The results presented here show some of the first observations of the effects of full-spectrum, near-surface solar exposure on plankton assemblages in the Ross Sea polynya from which we can already make several conclu-

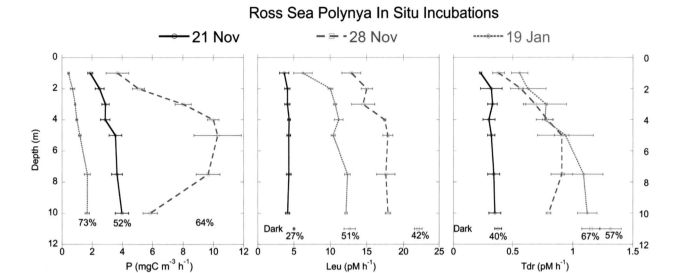

FIGURE 5. Hourly productivity rates for photosynthesis (P) and bacterial incorporation of leucine (Leu) and thymidine (Tdr) for the incubations on 21 November, 28 November, and 19 January (all in 2005). The bottom symbols for Leu and Tdr show rates for samples incubated in the dark. Horizontal bars indicate assay standard deviation (P, $n = 10$; Leu/Tdr, $n = 6$). The numbers below each profile show the percent inhibition at 1 m relative to the peak rate in the profile (photosynthesis) or rate in the dark (bacterial incorporation).

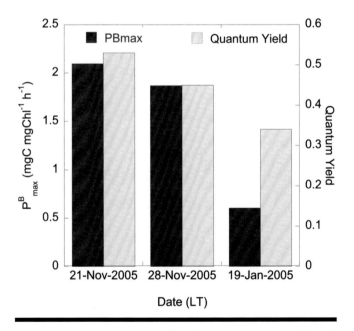

FIGURE 6. Measurements on the early-morning 5-m sample used for the in situ incubations. Maximum chlorophyll-specific rate of photosynthesis of the in situ incubation (black bars, left axis) and maximum photosynthetic quantum yield as measured with PAM fluorometry (gray bars, right axis). These are two independent approaches to indicate the relative variation in the overall photosynthetic capacity of the sampled phytoplankton assemblage.

sions. First, it is clear that incident solar exposure is sufficiently high and plankton assemblages are sufficiently sensitive that inhibition of near-surface algal and bacterial productivity is a regular occurrence during the spring–summer period in the southern Ross Sea. Photosynthesis was more strongly inhibited than bacterial productivity, such that effects on phytoplankton could even be observed below light ice cover (21 November). These effects were also observed even though UVB exposure was not significantly enhanced by ozone depletion. Although low ozone can occur throughout November in the Ross Sea region (Bernhard et al., 2006), the "ozone hole" was not present during the NBP0508 incubations.

Indeed, UV and PAR exposure in the Ross Sea polynya were not high compared to other observations in Antarctic waters (Kieber et al., 2007; Pakulski et al., 2007). Thus, the assemblages must be particularly sensitive to solar exposure in order for effects to be so pronounced despite moderate exposure levels. This conclusion is consistent with the preliminary results of our laboratory measurements of biological weighting functions for UV inhibition. These showed the highest sensitivity to UV yet recorded for Antarctic phytoplankton and modest sensitivity to UV for Ross Sea bacterioplankton (Neale et al., 2005; Jeffrey et al., 2006). They also showed that most of the inhibitory effect of near-surface irradiance on photosynthesis was due to UV, with PAR having only a small effect. Similarly, Smith et al. (2000) did not observe significant near-surface inhibition when they measured daily in situ primary productivity in the Ross Sea using UV-opaque enclosures, although PAR inhibition was observed in on-deck incubations receiving higher than in situ irradiance. This high sensitivity to UV may be a consequence of the acclimation to low-irradiance conditions in the early-season assemblage (before iron depletion) and iron limitation during the late season. The lower sensitivity of bacterioplankton to UVR may have been related to nutrient replete conditions. Three separate experiments over the course of the sampling period during November 2005 indicated that the bacterioplankton were not nutrient (Fe, N, C) limited (data not shown). Our previous work has suggested that alleviation of nutrient limitation often reduced UVR sensitivity (Jeffrey et al., 2003). Unfortunately, no data is available for the summer 2005 samples. Bacterioplankton abundance increased as did chl *a* during this period, in contrast to the lags reported by others. Our observation may be, in part, due to the apparent replete nutrient conditions we observed. Although Ducklow et al. (2001) reported low DOC production by the *Phaeocystis* bloom, it is labile (Carlson et al., 1998) and it has been hypothesized that macronutrient depletion seldom occurs in the Ross Sea (Ducklow et al., 2001).

Results have been combined for two years; however, the time course of phytoplankton biomass in the Ross Sea for both 2004–2005 and 2005–2006 followed the normal pattern of peak biomass at the end of November (Peloquin and Smith, 2007). Although species composition shifted between the cruises, inhibition was consistently high for all profiles. In contrast, bacterial response was less consistent between the cruises. The ratio between leucine and thymidine dark uptake was >10 in November 2005 but <10 in January 2005, suggesting basic metabolic differences between assemblages. The abundance patterns during the cruises also show separate growth "events" occurring during each cruise (though some of the variation may be due to spatial differences). These observations suggest that the two cruises sampled physiologically distinct bacterial assemblages, a conclusion that is consistent with differences in sample genetic composition as determined using terminal restriction fragment length polymorphisms (TRFLP) analysis (A. Baldwin, University of West Florida, and W. H. Jeffrey, University of West Florida, personal communication).

In summary, our results provide direct evidence that in situ UV irradiance in the Ross Sea is inhibitory for both phytoplankton photosynthesis and bacterioplankton production. In terms of the magnitude of the responses observed in the incubations, these should be conservative estimates of the effects of solar exposure on in situ planktonic production. Models of UV- and PAR-dependent photosynthetic response, when evaluated for the exposure occurring at each depth in the array, predict a comparable response as observed in situ (Neale et al., 2005). In contrast, vertical profiles of fluorescence-based photosynthetic quantum yield showed that inhibited phytoplankton are found deeper in the water column than the 5-7 m depth of the photoactive zone in the incubations. This enhancement of inhibition in the water column is consistent with vertical exchange due to both Langmuir ciculation and near-surface internal waves, both of which increase the proportion of surface layer phytoplankton exposed to inhibiting irradiance. The operation of these mechanisms was confirmed by physical measurements. Detailed comparisons of production estimates using these multiple approaches will be presented in subsequent reports.

ACKNOWLEDGMENTS

We thank the captain and crew of the R/V *Nathaniel B. Palmer* and Raytheon Polar Services Co. for the field support provided. The authors gratefully acknowledge Ronald Kiene, Dauphin Island Sea Lab, Chief Scientist on NBP0409, for providing the PAM fluorometer, and Hyakubun Harada, Dauphin Island Sea Lab, for assistance in its use. Support was provided by National Science Foundation Office of Polar Programs grant 0127037 to PJN and 0127022 to WHJ. CS was supported by an Asturias Fellowship from the Scientific Committee for Antarctic Research (SCAR) and by the Spanish Ministry of Education and Science (MEC).

LITERATURE CITED

Bernhard, G., C. R. Booth, J. C. Ehramjian, and S. E. Nichol. 2006. UV Climatology at McMurdo Station, Antarctica, Based on Version 2 Data of the National Science Foundation's Ultraviolet Radiation Monitoring Network. *Journal of Geophysical Research*, 111: D11201, doi:10.1029/2005JD005857.

Boucher, N. P., and B. B. Prézelin. 1996. Spectral Modeling of UV Inhibition of in situ Antarctic Primary Production Using a Field Derived Biological Weighting Function. *Photochemistry and Photobiology*, 64:407–418.

Buma, A. G. J., M. K. de Boer, and P. Boelen. 2001. Depth Distributions of DNA Damage in Antarctic Marine Phyto- and Bacterioplankton Exposed to Summertime UV Radiation. *Journal of Phycology*, 37: 200–208.

Carlson, C. A., H. Ducklow, D. Hansell, and W. O. Smith. 1998. Organic Carbon Partitioning during Spring Phytoplankton Blooms in the Ross Sea Polynya and the Sargasso Sea. *Limnology Oceanography*, 43:375–386.

Cullen, J. J., and P. J. Neale. 1997. "Biological Weighting Functions for Describing the Effects of Ultraviolet Radiation on Aquatic Systems." In *Effects of Ozone Depletion on Aquatic Ecosystems*, ed. D.-P. Häder, pp. 97–118. Austin, Tex.: R. G. Landes.

de Mora, S. J., S. Demers, and M. Vernet, eds. 2000. *The Effects of UV Radiation on Marine Ecosystems*. Cambridge: Cambridge University Press.

DiTullio, G. R., J. M. Grebmeier, K. R. Arrigo, M. P. Lizotte, D. H. Robinson, A. Leventer, J. P. Barry, M. L. VanWoert, and R. B. Dunbar. 2000. Rapid and Early Export of Phaeocystis Antarctica Blooms in the Ross Sea, Antarctica. *Nature*, 404:595–598.

DiTullio, G. R., and R. B. Dunbar, eds. 2004. *Biogeochemistry of the Ross Sea*. Washington, D.C.: AGU.

Ducklow, H., C. Carlson, M. Church, D. Kirchman, and G. Steward. 2001. The Seasonal Development of Bacterioplankton in the Ross Sea, Antarctica, 1994–97. *Deep Sea Research II: Topical Studies in Oceanography*, 48:4199–4221.

El-Sayed, S. Z., F. C. Stephens, R. R. Bidigare, and M. E. Ondrusek. 1990. "Effect of Ultraviolet Radiation on Antarctic Marine Phytoplankton." In *Antarctic Ecosystems: Ecological Changes and Conservation*, ed. K. R. Kerry and G. Hempel, pp. 379–385. New York: Springer-Verlag.

Genty, B., J. M. Briantais, and N. Baker. 1989. The Relationship between the Quantum Yield of Photosynthetic Electron Transport and Quenching of Chlorophyll Fluorescence. *Biochimica Biophysica Acta*, 990:87–92.

Helbling, E. W., V. Villafañe, M. Ferrario, and O. Holm-Hansen. 1992. Impact of Natural Ultraviolet Radiation on Rates of Photosynthesis and on Specific Marine Phytoplankton Species. *Marine Ecology Progress Series*, 80:89–100.

Holm-Hansen, O., and B. G. Mitchell. 1990. Effect of Solar UV Radiation on Photosynthetic Rates of Antarctic Marine Phytoplankton. *Eos, Transactions, American Geophysical Union*, 71:138.

Huot, Y., W. H. Jeffrey, R. F. Davis, and J. J. Cullen. 2000. Damage to DNA in Bacterioplankton: A Model of Damage by Ultraviolet Radiation and Its Repair as Influenced by Vertical Mixing. *Photochemistry and Photobiology*, 72:62–74.

Jeffrey, W. H., P. Aas, M. M. Lyons, R. Pledger, D. L. Mitchell, and R. B. Coffin. 1996a. Ambient Solar Radiation Induced Photodamage in Marine Bacterioplankton. *Photochemistry and Photobiology*, 64:419–427.

Jeffrey, W. H., R. J. Pledger, P. Aas, S. Hager, R. B. Coffin, R. Von Haven, and D. L. Mitchell. 1996b. Diel and Depth Profiles of DNA Photodamage in Bacterioplankton Exposed to Ambient Solar Ultraviolet Radiation. *Marine Ecology Progress Series*, 137:283–291.

Jeffrey, W. H., J. P. Kase, and J. D. Pakulski. 2003. The Effects of Temperature, Nutrients and Growth Rate on the Response to Ultraviolet Radiation by Marine Bacterioplankton. American Society for Limnology and Oceanography Meeting, Salt Lake City, Utah, 9–14 February.

Jeffrey, W. H., J. D. Pakulski, S. Connelly, A. J. Baldwin, D. Karentz, J. D. Phillips-Kress, C. Sobrino, L. A. Franklin, and P. J. Neale. 2006. Effects of Ultraviolet Radiation on Bacterioplankton Production in the Ross Sea, Antarctica. *Eos, Transactions, American Geophysical Union*, 87(36), Ocean Sciences Meeting Supplement: Abstract OS42L-04.

Kelley, C. A., J. D. Pakulski, S. L. H. Sandvik, R. B. Coffin, R. C. Downer, P. Aas, M. M. Lyons, and W. H. Jeffrey. 1999. Phytoplanktonic and Bacterial Carbon Pools and Productivities in the Gerlache Strait, Antarctica, During Early Austral Spring. *Microbial Ecology*, 38: 296–305.

Kieber, D. J., D. A. Toole, J. J. Jankowski, R. P. Kiene, G. R. Westby, D. A. del Valle, and D. Slezak. 2007. Chemical "Light Meters" for Photochemical and Photobiological DMS and DMSP Studies. *Aquatic Sciences*, 69:360–376.

Kuhn, P. S., H. I. Browman, R. F. Davis, J. J. Cullen, and B. McArthur. 2000. Modeling the Effects of Ultraviolet Radiation on Embryos of *Calanus finmarchicus* and Atlantic Cod (*Gadus morhua*) in a Mixing Environment. *Limnology and Oceanography*, 45:1797–1806.

Lantz, K., P. Disterhoft, E. Early, A. Thompson, J. DeLuisi, J. Berndt, L. Harrison, P. Kiedron, J. Ehramjian, G. Bernhard, L. Cabasug, J. Robertson, W. Mou, T. Taylor, J. Slusser, D. Bigelow, B. Durham, G. Janson, D. Hayes, M. Beaubien, and A. Beaubien. 2002. The 1997 North American Interagency Intercomparison of Ultraviolet Spectroradiometers Including Narrowband Filter Radiometers. *Journal of Research of the National Institute of Standards and Technology*, 107:19–62.

Lubin, D., B. G. Mitchell, J. E. Frederick, A. D. Alberts, C. R. Booth, T. Lucas, and D. Neuschuler. 1992. A Contribution toward Understanding the Biospherical Significance of Antarctic Ozone Depletion. *Journal of Geophysical Research*, 97:7817–7828.

Lyons, M. M., P. Aas, J. D. Pakulski, L. Van Waasbergen, R. V. Miller, D. L. Mitchell, and W. H. Jeffrey. 1998. DNA Damage Induced by Ultraviolet Radiation in Coral-Reef Microbial Communities. *Marine Biology*, 130:537–543.

Malloy, K. D., M. A. Holman, D. Mitchell, and H. W. Detrich III. 1997. Solar UVB-Induced DNA Damage and Photoenzymatic Repair in Antarctic Zooplankton. *Proceedings of the National Academy of Sciences of the United States of America*, 94:1258–1263.

Meador, J., W. H. Jeffrey, J. P. Kase, J. D. Pakulski, S. Chiarello, and D. L. Mitchell. 2002. Seasonal Fluctuation of DNA Photodamage in Marine Plankton Assemblages at Palmer Station, Antarctica. *Photochemistry and Photobiology*, 75:266–271.

Mitchell, B. G. 1990. "Action Spectra of Ultraviolet Photoinhibition of Antarctic Phytoplankton and a Model of Spectral Diffuse Attenuation Coefficients." In *Response of Marine Phytoplankton to Natural Variations in UV-B Flux*, ed. B. G. Mitchell, O. Holm-Hansen, and I. Sobolev, Appendix H, pp. 1–15. Washington, D.C.: Chemical Manufacturers Association.

Neale, P. J., R. F. Davis, and J. J. Cullen. 1998. Interactive Effects of Ozone Depletion and Vertical Mixing on Photosynthesis of Antarctic Phytoplankton. *Nature*, 392:585–589.

Neale, P. J., E. W. Helbling, and H. E. Zagarese. 2003. "Modulation of UV Exposure and Effects by Vertical Mixing and Advection." In *UV Effects in Aquatic Organisms and Ecosystems*, ed. E. W. Helbling and H. E. Zagarese, pp. 107–134. Cambridge: Royal Society of Chemistry.

Neale, P. J., C. Sobrino, L. A. Franklin, and J. D. Phillips-Kress. 2005. "Ultraviolet Radiation Effects on Diatoms and *Phaeocystis antarctica* in the Ross Sea Polynya." In *Phaeocystis, Major Link in the Biogeochemical Cycling of Elements*, p. 16. SCOR Working Group, No. 120. Groeningen, Netherlands: SCOR Working Group.

Pakulski, J. D., J. A. Meador, J. P. Kase, and W. H. Jeffrey. 2007. Effect of Stratospheric Ozone Depletion and Enhanced Ultraviolet Radiation on Marine Bacteria at Palmer Station, Antarctica in the Early Austral Spring. *Photochemistry and Photobiology*, 83:1–7.

Peloquin, J. A., and W. O. Smith. 2007. Phytoplankton Blooms in the Ross Sea, Antarctica: Interannual Variability in Magnitude, Temporal Patterns, and Composition. *Journal of Geophysical Research*, 112:C08013, doi:10.1029/2006JC003816.

Porter, K. G., and Y. S. Feig. 1980. The Use of DAPI for Identifying and Counting Aquatic Microflora. *Limnology and Oceanography*, 25: 243–248.

Smith, D. C., and F. A. Azam. 1992. A Simple, Economical Method for Measuring Bacterial Protein Synthesis Rates in Seawater Using 3h-Leucine. *Marine Microbial Food Webs*, 6:107–114.

Smith, R. C., B. B. Prézelin, K. S. Baker, R. R. Bidigare, N. P. Boucher, T. Coley, D. Karentz, S. MacIntyre, H. A. Matlick, D. Menzies, M. Ondrusek, Z. Wan, and K. J. Waters. 1992. Ozone Depletion:

Ultraviolet Radiation and Phytoplankton Biology in Antarctic Waters. *Science*, 255:952–959.

Smith, W. O., Jr., and J. C. Comiso. 2009. "Southern Ocean Primary Productivity: Variability and a View to the Future." In *Smithsonian at the Poles: Contributions to International Polar Year Science*, ed. I. Krupnik, M. A. Lang, and S. E. Miller, pp. 309–318. Washington, D.C.: Smithsonian Institution Scholarly Press.

Smith, W. O., Jr., J. Marra, M. R. Hiscock, and R. T. Barber. 2000. The Seasonal Cycle of Phytoplankton Biomass and Primary Productivity in the Ross Sea, Antarctica. *Deep-Sea Research, Part II*, 47: 3119–3140.

Vetter, R. D., A. Kurtzman, and T. Mori. 1999. Diel Cycles of DNA Damage and Repair in Eggs and Larvae of Northern Anchovy, *Engraulis mordax*, Exposed to Solar Ultraviolet Radiation. *Photochemistry and Photobiology*, 69:27–33.

Visser, P. M., E. Snelder, A. J. Kop, P. Boelen, A. G. J. Buma, and F. C. van Duyl. 1999. Effects of UV Radiation on DNA Photodamage and Production in Bacterioplankton in the Coastal Caribbean Sea. *Aquatic Microbial Ecology*, 20:49–58.

Southern Ocean Primary Productivity: Variability and a View to the Future

Walker O. Smith Jr. and Josefino C. Comiso

ABSTRACT. The primary productivity of the Southern Ocean south of 58°S is assessed using satellite data on ice concentrations, sea surface temperatures, and pigment concentrations, a vertically generalized production model, and modeled photosynthetically active radiation. Daily productivity is integrated by month and by year to provide an estimate of new production. The productivity of the Southern Ocean is extremely low relative to other oceanic regions, with annual net rates throughout the region of less than 10 g C m^{-2}. This low annual value is largely the result of negligible productivity throughout much of the year due to low irradiance and high ice cover. Despite the annual oligotrophic state, monthly productivity during the summer (December through February) is substantially greater, averaging from 100 to 1,500 mg C m^{-2} mo^{-1}. Substantial interannual variability occurs, and certain subregions within the Southern Ocean experience greater interannual variations than others. Those regions, like the West Antarctic Peninsula, the Ross Sea polynya region, and the Weddell Sea, are characterized as being continental shelf regions and/or those that are substantially impacted by ice. Despite this relationship, no significant changes in primary production were observed in regions where large trends in ice concentrations have been noted. The driving forces for this variability as well as the implications for long-term changes in regional and Southern Ocean productivity are discussed.

INTRODUCTION

The Southern Ocean is a vast region within the world's oceans that has presented some significant challenges to oceanographers. It is the site of large numbers of birds, marine mammals, and fishes and extensive sedimentary deposits of biogenic material, and is presently being impacted by physical forcing external to the region, such as ozone depletion (Neale et al., 1998, 2009, this volume) and climate change (e.g., Vaughan et al., 2003). However, because of its size and remoteness, it is difficult to conduct experimental programs to adequately assess the role of various environmental factors on biological processes in the region. In addition, a large fraction of the Southern Ocean is ice covered for much of the year, restricting access to many locations and making sampling of other regions nearly impossible. To assess the productivity of the entire Southern Ocean, it is necessary to "sample" using techniques that can quantify processes over large

Walker O. Smith Jr., Virginia Institute of Marine Sciences, College of William and Mary, Gloucester Point, VA 23062, USA. Josefino C. Comiso, NASA Goddard Space Flight Center, Code 614.1, Greenbelt, MD 27701, USA. Corresponding author: W. O. Smith (wos@vims.edu). Accepted 28 May 2008.

spatial scales through time. At present, the only means to accomplish this on the appropriate scales is via satellite oceanography.

Satellites presently have the capability to accurately map the distributions of ice (Comiso, 2004), sea surface temperature (SST; Comiso, 2000; Kwok and Comiso, 2002), and pigment concentrations (Moore and Abbott, 2000), as well as other parameters such as winds, bathymetry, cloud cover, and some gas concentrations such as ozone (Comiso, 2009). Some measurements use visible wavelengths and reflectance from the surface, and therefore the data returned are reduced in space and time because of clouds; others are either passively detected or use other wavelengths to determine the distribution of the variable. In biological oceanography a major variable of interest is ocean color, which is converted into quantitative estimates of pigment (chlorophyll) concentrations. While the estimates include significant error terms (because of the dependence of pigment estimates as a function of latitude, the limitation of reflectance to the optical surface layer rather than the entire euphotic zone, and the interference in some waters of dissolved organic matter), these estimates remain, and will remain, the only means to obtain synoptic assessments of phytoplankton distributions over large areas as well as their temporal changes over relatively short (e.g., days) periods.

Two satellites have provided nearly all of the data in the past three decades on pigment distributions in the Southern Ocean. The first was the Nimbus 7 satellite, launched in 1978, which carried the Coastal Zone Color Scanner (CZCS). While questions concerning the data quality and coverage from CZCS have been voiced, the data were used to investigate both the large-scale distributions of pigments in relation to oceanographic variables (Sullivan et al., 1993; Comiso et al., 1993) and also the specific processes and regions (e.g., Arrigo and McClain, 1994). However, given the orbit, the frequency of data collection in the Southern Ocean was quite restricted, and when compounded by the loss of data from cloud cover, the temporal frequency was far from optimal. In 1996 the ORBView-2 satellite was launched, which included the Sea-viewing Wide Field-of-view Sensor (SeaWiFS). This satellite proved to be an extremely useful tool for biological oceanographers, as the sampling frequency was much greater and the data return in polar regions was far greater. For example, Moore et al. (1999) were able to detect a short-lived bloom in the Pacific sector of the Southern Ocean that was only infrequently sampled by ships. Dierssen et al. (2002) assessed the variability of productivity in the West Antarctic Peninsula region and found (based on a model) that pigment concentrations

were the dominant variable creating variations in space and time. Smith and Comiso (2008) assessed the productivity of the entire Southern Ocean and found that the "hot spots" of production were limited to continental shelf regions, and suggested that this was a result of low iron concentrations coupled with deeper mixing in the offshore regions. The interaction of low iron and low irradiance (Sunda and Huntsman, 1997; Boyd and Abraham, 2001) gives rise to a large spatial limitation over broad areas.

It is the purpose of this manuscript to look at the scales of variability in the Southern Ocean as a whole and to determine where such variations are large by using primary production derived from SeaWiFS ocean color and advanced very high resolution radiometer (AVHRR) SST data in conjunction with a bio-optical model. We also will compare the modeled productivity with observed values, where those data are available to test the robustness of the model. Finally, some aspects of the temporal patterns of productivity in the Southern Ocean are reviewed.

MATERIALS AND METHODS

Primary productivity was estimated using various data derived from satellites and a bio-optical model. The model was a vertically generalized production model (Behrenfeld and Falkowski, 1997b), in which primary productivity (PP_{eu}, in units of mg C m^{-2} d^{-1}) was estimated from the following equation:

$$PP_{eu} = 0.66125 \times P_{opt}^B \frac{E_o}{E_o + 4.1} C_{Sat} \times Z_{eu} \times D_{Irr}$$

where P_{opt}^B is the optimal rate of photosynthesis within the water column (mg C (mg chl)$^{-1}$ h^{-1}) and is a function of temperature, E_o is the surface daily photosynthetically active radiation (PAR, mol photons m^{-2} d^{-1}), C_{sat} is the surface chlorophyll concentration (mg chl m^{-3}) determined by satellite, Z_{eu} is the depth of the euphotic zone (m), and D_{Irr} is the photoperiod (h). P_{opt}^B was estimated from sea surface temperatures by the polynomial equation of Behrenfeld and Falkowski (1997b), and all P_{opt}^B values at temperatures less than $-1.0°C$ were set to 1.13.

Temperature, PAR, ice concentrations, and chlorophyll concentrations were derived from different satellite data sets. Different satellite data were mapped to the same grid as described below. We arbitrarily defined the Southern Ocean roughly as the region impacted by seasonal ice movements and hence set the northern boundary at 58°S. Ice concentrations and associated parameters (e.g., ice extent and area) were derived using data from the Special Sensor Microwave Imager (SSM/I) on the Defense Meteorological Satellite Program and mapped on a polar stereographic grid at a 25 × 25 km resolution. Ice concentrations were derived from satellite passive microwave data using the enhanced bootstrap algorithm used for Advanced Microwave Scanning Radiometer-EOS data and adapted for SSM/I data (e.g., Comiso et al., 2003; Comiso, 2004). Sea surface temperatures were derived from thermal infrared channels of the NOAA AVHRR as described in Comiso (2003). Pigment concentrations derived from SeaWiFS data were provided by the NASA Goddard Earth Sciences Distributed Active Archive Center. Surface temperature and pigment concentration data have been gridded in the same manner as the sea ice concentration data but on a 6.25 × 6.25 km resolution. Mean daily pigment concentrations were estimated using the standard SeaWiFS algorithm with OC4 (Version 4) calibration (Patt et al., 2003) and used to generate weekly (seven-day bins) and monthly data sets from 1997 to 2006. Photosynthetically active radiation data were extracted as part of the Sea-WiFS data but were not used in the estimates of productivity because a large fraction of the valuable polar data was inadvertently masked as ice covered by the SeaWiFS data processing group. We used a modeled PAR instead (which provided basically the same results) for much improved coverage. It is important to recognize that because of cloud and ice masking the weekly and monthly averages do not reflect true averages but are averages of daylight data (for each data element) available during clear-sky, ice-free conditions only.

Productivity was calculated on a daily basis and binned in a manner similar to that of chlorophyll. The gridding technique (Smith and Comiso, 2008) and the presence of clouds caused a large fraction of data elements (pixels) in the daily maps to have missing data. In the case where an empty pixel is surrounded by pixels with data, a simple interpolation technique is utilized to estimate the pigment level in the empty pixel. For larger data gaps, a combination of spatial and temporal interpolation was utilized. Such interpolation filled only a very small fraction of missing data in the daily maps, and for time series studies, weekly averages were produced as the basic product. In a similar manner, annual productivity was estimated by summing weekly averages over an entire year. Standard deviations were calculated for all pixels, but because of the variable number of data points within each pixel, we arbitrarily used only those locations where at least five means were available to calculate variations.

We recognize that regional algorithms have been developed for certain parts of the Southern Ocean (e.g., Ross Sea: Arrigo et al., 1998; Dierssen and Smith, 2000) and that these formulations provide a more accurate estimate of phytoplankton biomass in each area. We chose to use the output from the standard global algorithm to simplify the comparison of regions and of various years, to facilitate a comparison among all regions, and to avoid problems of defining boundaries of optically different regions. While this approach may introduce error into absolute estimates of productivity within a region, it provides a uniform basis to compute productivity throughout the Southern Ocean, as regional algorithms (some of which need more rigorous validation) are not available for all areas.

RESULTS

SPATIAL MEANS AND VARIABILITY

Annual productivity of the Southern Ocean is highly variable but also quite low relative to other oceans, as has been suggested based on discrete measurements (e.g., Smith and Nelson, 1986; Nelson et al., 1996; Tremblay and Smith, 2007). Much of the region off the continental shelf is oligotrophic and is characterized by primary production rates of less than 50 g C m^{-1} y^{-1} (Figure 1). Regions of

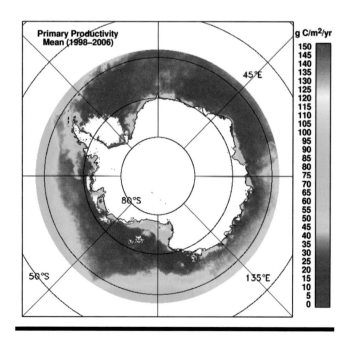

FIGURE 1. Mean (1998–2006) modeled productivity of the Southern Ocean as derived from a vertically integrated productivity model.

enhanced (threefold greater than the low-productivity off-shore areas) do occur on the continental shelf, with three areas being noteworthy: the Ross Sea, the Amundsen Sea, and Prydz Bay/East Antarctic shelf. Productivity in the Ross Sea is spatially extensive, but the greatest absolute productivity is in the Amundsen Sea region (150 g C m^{-1} y^{-1} at ~73°S, 110°W). It is interesting that this particular region has never been sampled because of the difficulty of gaining access by ships.

Productivity in the more northern regions (near the location of the Antarctic Circumpolar Current (ACC) and its associated fronts, e.g., Abbott et al., 2000) is elevated in the Pacific sector (between 45° and 135°W) and south of New Zealand (between 155°W and 165°E), averaging ~75 g C m^{-1} y^{-1}, and can be contrasted with the very low productivity waters of the South Atlantic and Indian Ocean sectors (Figure 1). Productivity of the South Atlantic is greater farther north than that in our selected study region (58°S; Moore and Abbott, 2000; Smith and Comiso, 2008), and the region we analyzed is also largely south of the ACC (Moore and Abbott, 2000) and largely free of frontal enhancements. The Indian Ocean sector is among the windiest areas on Earth, and hence deep mixing would be expected to occur. Regardless, the annual productivity in the southern Indian Ocean and South Atlantic areas is less than 20 g C m^{-1} y^{-1}, among the lowest anywhere in the world's oceans.

Computed standard deviations for the entire Southern Ocean suggest that while the absolute variations occur in the most productive continental shelf regions such as the Ross Sea, the relative spatial variations are actually greater elsewhere (Figure 2). For example, in the Ross Sea the standard deviation expressed as a percentage of the mean is only 2.8%, whereas in the southern Weddell Sea they range from 5.4% to 20%, suggesting the spatial variability in that location is much greater. This likely is due to the impact of ice, which varies greatly in this location interannually (Smith and Comiso, 2008). The highest productivity occurs in areas of polynyas; in the Ross Sea the standard deviation is not as large because the location of the polynya is basically the same from one year to another. Variations in the Amundsen Sea, the location of the productivity maximum, are also less than in other regions, being similar to those in the Ross Sea (~1.5%–3%). Variations in the South Atlantic can be substantial (~10% near the location of the Weddell Sea polynya and Maud Rise) as well. Conversely, the elevated productivity region in the Pacific sector north of 62°S exhibits quite low variability (generally less than 1%).

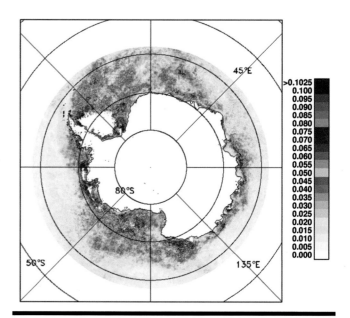

FIGURE 2. Standard deviation of the derived annual productivity values. Only those pixels where there were at least five years of data (from 1998 to 2006) were included. Black regions are those with fewer than five values; white areas have no data.

SEASONAL PRODUCTIVITY AND VARIABILITY ON MONTHLY SCALES

The broad seasonal progression of productivity in some regions of the Antarctic is relatively well known. For example, in the Ross Sea a rapid increase in phytoplankton biomass and productivity occurs in spring, and a decline begins in mid-December to early January. Much of the summer is characterized by relatively low biomass and productivity (Smith et al., 2000, 2003). Productivity in the West Antarctic Peninsula region also is characterized by a similar pattern (Ducklow et al., 2006), although the magnitude of the productivity is far less (Smith and Comiso, 2008). December productivity in the Southern Ocean parallels the annual pattern, with the maximum productivity occurring in the Amundsen and Ross seas and East Antarctic continental shelf (Figure 3). Clearly, the high-productivity areas are those of the continental shelf. Productivity north of 62°S is also higher in the Pacific sector. January productivity is characterized by increased rates and spatial extents in the Amundsen and Weddell seas, as well as at the tip of the Antarctic Peninsula, but by a decrease in the Ross Sea. February rates show a general decrease, with decreases being most noticeable in the East Antarctic region, the peninsula area, Amundsen Sea, and

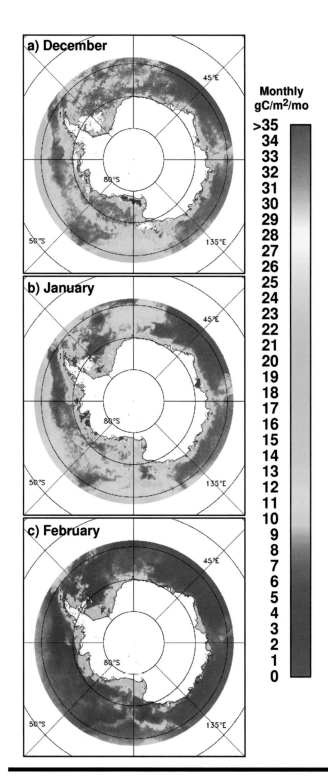

FIGURE 3. Mean monthly productivity of the Southern Ocean for the years 1998–2006 for (a) December, (b) January, and (c) February.

the Pacific sector north of 62°S. All sites show the generalized maximum in late spring or early summer, followed by a decrease, although the timing of various sites varies.

Variability on a monthly basis appears to be larger than on an annual basis (Figure 4). For example, relative variations in the Ross Sea are ~7% in all months, suggesting that the annual variations are somewhat dampened by the effects of long low-productivity periods. December variations are difficult to assess, as many locations have fewer than five years of data and hence no standard deviation was calculated. However, variability in general seems to increase slightly in February, which may reflect the relatively stochastic occurrence of storms (and hence deep mixing) during that period.

DISCUSSION

Primary productivity estimates in the Southern Ocean have been made for decades but have resulted in a biased picture of photosynthesis and growth. This is largely because historically, estimates have been made in ice-free waters (e.g., Holm-Hansen et al., 1977; El-Sayed et al., 1983), whereas polynyas, which are known to be sites of intensive productivity (Tremblay and Smith, 2007), have rarely been sampled. Additionally, open water regions of low production have largely been ignored, and sampling has concentrated on the high-productivity locations thought to support local food webs. The richness of upper trophic levels that has been observed for over 100 years (e.g., Knox, 1994) was so marked that it was assumed that primary production must occur to support this abundance. However, we now recognize that productivity in the Southern Ocean is not great (Smith and Nelson, 1986), particularly on an annual basis, and the abundant higher trophic level standing stocks and extensive biogenic sedimentary deposits are forced by food web efficiency, alternate food sources, and uncoupling of carbon with silica in biogeochemical cycles (Nelson et al., 1996).

With the advent of satellite oceanography, large, synoptic measurements of phytoplankton biomass became available. Such estimates in the Southern Ocean were far less common than in tropical and temperate waters, but they were very useful in showing the relationship of chlorophyll with ice distributions (Nelson et al., 1987; Sullivan et al., 1993), hydrographic features and fronts (Moore and Abbott, 2000), and depth (Comiso et al., 1993). In general, early satellite studies suggested that coastal zones and marginal ice zones were sites of large phytoplankton

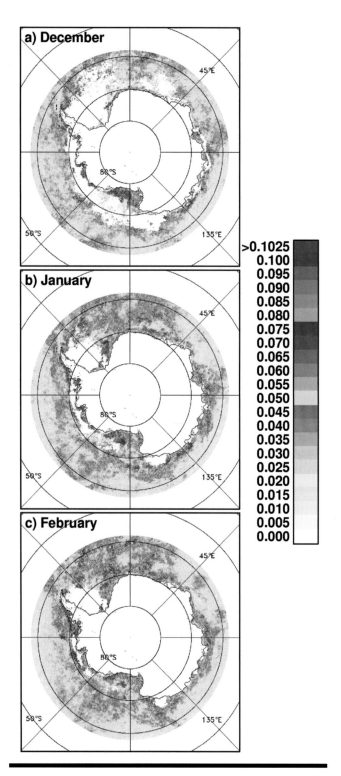

FIGURE 4. Standard deviations of the monthly productivity of the Southern Ocean for the years 1998–2006 for (a) December, (b) January, and (c) February. Black regions are those with fewer than five values; white areas have no data.

biomass accumulation (Sullivan et al., 1993; Arrigo and McLain, 1994). More refined treatments suggested that the Southern Ocean had a number of hot spots and short-lived increases in biomass (Moore et al., 1999) but, in large part, was extremely oligotrophic in nature.

For many years it was uncertain why the Antarctic was so oligotrophic. Many considered that vertical mixing created low-irradiance conditions, superimposed on the seasonal aspects of ice distributions and solar angle, both which restricted irradiance penetration into the surface (e.g., Smith and Nelson, 1985; Mitchell and Holm-Hansen, 1991). Macronutrients such as nitrate and phosphate were always in excess, and it was suggested that micronutrients such as iron or vitamin B-12 might limit production (e.g., Hart, 1934). However, reliable data on the concentrations of these micronutrients was lacking until the 1990s, when trace-metal clean measurements were made (e.g., Martin et al., 1990; Fitzwater et al., 2000). Iron concentrations were indeed found to be vanishingly small—in many cases less than 0.3 nM, even in coastal regions (Sedwick and DiTullio, 1997; Sedwick et al., 2000; Boyd and Abraham, 2001; Coale et al., 2003; de Baar et al., 2005). Furthermore, on the basis of laboratory studies and then field work, under low-irradiance conditions, iron demands increase; hence, the interactive effects between iron and light exacerbated the limitation, and this interaction was suggested to be of paramount importance in deeper, offshore regions (Boyd and Abraham, 2001; Smith and Comiso, 2008). Recently, it has been found that vitamin B-12 can limit or colimit phytoplankton growth in the Ross Sea (Bertrund et al., 2007), but the large-scale colimitation for the entire Southern Ocean remains to be demonstrated.

Other potential productivity-limiting factors have been addressed as well, such as grazing (Tagliabue and Arrigo, 2003) and temperature. However, herbivore biomass inventories are available only in selected regions and hence cannot be extrapolated over the entire Antarctic; furthermore, the effects of temperature have been considered to be of secondary importance in limiting growth and photosynthesis (Arrigo, 2007), although temperature may have a significant role in controlling assemblage composition.

It is useful to compare satellite means with other estimates that have been made, either via in situ measurements or numerical models. However, there are surprisingly few regions in the Southern Ocean that have adequate time series data to resolve the annual production signal; similarly, few regions have been the focus of intensive modeling. One region that has received assessments from both detailed measurements and numerical modeling is the

Ross Sea. Tremblay and Smith (2007, table 2) used the nutrient climatology compiled by Smith et al. (2003) and estimated the productivity by month and by year. The annual productivity based on nitrogen uptake was 155 g C m^{-1} y^{-1}, remarkably similar to the value estimated from our satellite model (Table 1). Smith and Gordon (1997) used measurements taken during November, along with other estimates, and calculated production to be 134 g C m^{-1} y^{-1}. Arrigo et al. (1998), using a numerical model, estimated productivity to be ~160 g C m^{-1} y^{-1}. The similarity between all of these estimates, either direct or indirect, and ours derived from satellite estimates and a vertically integrated production model is striking and gives us confidence that our procedure accurately assesses the production, despite the suggestion that chlorophyll retrievals from space in this area may contain significant errors (Arrigo et al., 1998). As the Ross Sea is the Antarctic's most spatial extensive phytoplankton bloom, the mean annual productivity is also near the maximum for the Antarctic. Our results suggest that the productivity of the Amundsen Sea may be slightly greater. The region is the site of a number of spring polynyas, and the optical properties of the water are likely similar to those in the Ross Sea. However, currently there are very limited in situ measurements available to confirm this substantial productivity.

It has been suggested that the high productivity of the Ross Sea is derived from substantial vertical stratification, early removal of ice, and adequate macro- and micronutrients for much of the growing season (Smith and Asper, 2001; Smith et al., 2003, 2006), coupled with limited grazing (Tagliabue and Arrigo, 2003). It has also been

shown that during some summers a large "secondary" bloom occurs (Peloquin and Smith, 2007) and that these blooms occur approximately every three years. Peloquin and Smith (2007) suggested that summer iron limitation is occasionally reduced or eliminated by the intrusion of Modified Circumpolar Deep Water onto the continental shelf by oceanographic processes. Such a process would contribute greatly to the increased February variability we observed at some locations. A similar pattern of oceanic circulation has been suggested for the Prydz Bay/East Antarctica region as well (Smith et al., 1984), and it would be interesting to know if a similar influence of currents is responsible for the high productivity we observed in the Amundsen Sea.

TEMPORAL PATTERNS OF PRODUCTIVITY IN THE SOUTHERN OCEAN

The data that are used to derive the mean productivity shown in Figure 1 have also been analyzed for temporal trends (Figure 5). Mean Antarctic productivity for the past decade has shown a significant increase; furthermore, this increase is driven by changes that are largely confined to January and February (Smith and Comiso, 2008). Models have suggested that the productivity of the Southern Ocean will increase under atmospheric temperature increases driven by CO_2 loading (Sarmiento and Le Quéré, 1996; Sarmiento et al., 1998; Behrenfeld et al., 2006). The change will result from increased ice melting, which, in turn, should increase stratification, rather than a direct temperature effect. An increase in stratification would increase

TABLE 1. Summary of annual productivity estimates and method of computation for various portions of the Southern Ocean. "Southern" means the assessment was confined to regions south of 75°S.

Region	Annual productivity (g C m^{-2} y^{-1})	Method of estimation	Reference
Ross Sea	112	biomass accumulation	Nelson et al. (1996)
Ross Sea (southern)	190	biomass accumulation	Smith and Gordon (1997)
Southern Ocean	95.4–208	bio-optical model	Behrenfeld and Falkowski (1997a)
Southern Ocean	105	bio-optical model	Arrigo et al. (1998)
Ross Sea	57.6 ± 22.8	nutrient deficits	Sweeney et al. (2000)
Southern Ocean	62.4	bio-optical model	Moore and Abbott (2000)
Ross Sea	151 ± 21	bio-optical model	Arrigo and van Dijken (2003)
Ross Sea (southern)	145	numerical model	Arrigo et al. (2003)
Ross Sea	84–218	nutrient deficits	Smith et al. (2006)
Ross Sea (southern)	153	nutrient deficits	Tremblay and Smith (2007)
Ross Sea (southern)	54–65	bio-optical model	Smith and Comiso (2008)
Southern Ocean	20–150	bio-optical model	this study

the net irradiance environment available to phytoplankton and also decrease the magnitude of the iron-irradiance interaction, resulting in a decreased iron demand. Should iron inputs and concentrations remain the same, then the increased productivity would result in large-scale increases in phytoplankton growth and productivity. The observed change in the productivity estimated from satellites are not necessarily indicative of the changes predicted by the models and may reflect shorter-term trends that have altered current patterns, atmospheric inputs of iron, or other factors. It should also be noted that models do not include any colimitation effects of vitamin B-12, and if this effect were significant throughout the Southern Ocean, then the increase in productivity would be smaller than predicted. Regardless, the observed increase in annual productivity was unexpected, and the data analysis should be continued (using the same methods) as far into the future as possible to confirm this pattern.

Smith and Comiso (2008) also attempted to ascertain if the satellite data could be used to detect changes in productivity on a regional scale. Given that certain regions are having significant alterations in ice concentrations (e.g., the West Antarctic Peninsula–Amundsen/Bellingshausen Sea sector has had a >7% decrease per decade in ice concentration, while the Ross Sea sector has had an increase of >5%; Kwok and Comiso, 2002), it might be expected that

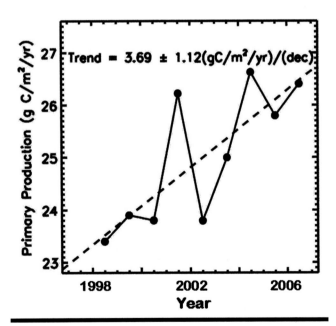

FIGURE 5. The temporal pattern of productivity for the entire Southern Ocean as derived from satellite data and a productivity model (from Smith and Comiso, 2008). The trend is derived from a linear regression of all points and is highly significant.

changes in productivity are accompanying these changes. However, the temporal variability in the estimates of productivity of these areas was too great to allow for any trends to be determined, so at this time, it is impossible to determine if changes in higher trophic levels are occurring because of food web effects (via energetics) or by habitat modification (e.g., loss of reproductive sites and decreases in reproductive success).

CONCLUSIONS

Tremendous advances have been made in our understanding of primary productivity in the Southern Ocean in the past 50 years. We have moved from an era of observational science into one that combines observations and experiments with large-scale assessments using data derived from multiple satellites and modeling using the same data. We recognize that the earlier assessments of productivity were biased by sampling and the nature of Antarctic productivity, and using unbiased techniques such as satellite data combined with robust models provides a means by which the temporal and spatial trends in phytoplankton production can be assessed. These methods have clearly demonstrated that the Southern Ocean as a whole is an oligotrophic area, with enhanced productivity on the continental shelves. Yet the shelf productivity is far from evenly distributed, and it is likely that oceanographic influences may play a large role in setting the maximum limits to production in the Southern Ocean.

It is suggested that the productivity of the entire Southern Ocean has increased significantly in the past decade, although the causes for such an increase remain obscure. Such changes have been predicted by numerical models, but it is far from certain that the observed changes are in fact related to climate change in the Antarctic. The short-term record also makes it difficult to interpret what the trend really means, especially in light of the possible effect of some climate modes like the Southern Hemisphere Annular Mode (Kwok and Comiso, 2002; Gordon et al., 2007). Only through extended analyses can such trends be confirmed and the causes for these changes ascertained. While increases in productivity of the magnitude shown may not induce major shifts in the ecology and biogeochemistry of the region, such changes, if they continue, may result in subtle and unpredicted impacts on the foods webs of the Antarctic ecosystem as well as changes in elemental dynamics. Knowledge of the environmental regulation of these changes in productivity is critical to the understanding of the ecology of the entire Southern Ocean and will provide insights into the potential changes that will undoubtedly occur in the coming years.

ACKNOWLEDGMENTS

The expert computer skills of Larry Stock of STX are gratefully acknowledged. This work was funded partially by National Sciences Foundation grants OPP-0087401 and OPP-0337247 (to WOS) and by the NASA Cryospheric Science Program (to JCC). This is VIMS contribution number 2955.

LITERATURE CITED

Abbott, M. R., J. G. Richman, R. M. Letelier, and J. S. Bartlett. 2000. The Spring Bloom in the Antarctic Polar Frontal Zone as Observed from a Mesoscale Array of Bio-optical Sensors. *Deep-Sea Research, Part II*, 47:3285–3314.

Arrigo, K. R. 2007. "Physical Control of Primary Productivity in Arctic and Antarctic Polynyas." In *Polynyas: Windows to the World's Oceans*, ed. W. O. Smith Jr. and D. G. Barber, pp. 239–270. Amsterdam: Elsevier.

Arrigo, K. R., and C. R. McClain. 1994. Spring Phytoplankton Production in the Western Ross Sea. *Science*, 266:261–263.

Arrigo, K. R., and G. L. van Dijken. 2003. Phytoplankton Dynamics within 37 Antarctic Coastal Polynya Systems. *Journal of Geophysical Research*, 108:3271, doi:10.1029/2002JC001739.

Arrigo, K. R., D. L. Worthen, A. Schnell, and M. P. Lizzote. 1998. Primary Production in Southern Ocean Waters. *Journal of Geophysical Research*, 103:15587–15600.

Arrigo, K. R., D. L. Worthen, and D. H. Robinson. 2003. A Coupled Ocean-Ecosystem Model of the Ross Sea: 2. Iron Regulation of Phytoplankton Taxonomic Variability and Primary Production. *Journal of Geophysical Research*, 108:3231, doi:10.1029/2001JC000856.

Behrenfeld, M. J., and P. Falkowski. 1997a. Photosynthetic Rates Derived from Satellite-Based Chlorophyll Concentration. *Limnology and Oceanography*, 42:1–20.

———. 1997b. A Consumer's Guide to Phytoplankton Primary Productivity Models. *Limnology and Oceanography*, 42:1479–1491.

Behrenfeld, M. J., R. T. O'Malley, D. A. Siegel, C. R. McClain, J. L. Sarmiento, G. C. Feldman, A. J. Milligan, P. G. Falkowski, R. M. Letelier, and E. S. Boss. 2006. Climate-Driven Trends in Contemporary Ocean Productivity. *Nature*, 444:752–755.

Bertrund, E. M., M. A. Saito, J. M. Rose, C. R. Riesselman, M. C. Lohan, A. E. Noble, P. A. Lee, and G. R. DiTullio. 2007. Vitamin B_{12} and Iron Colimitation of Phytoplankton Growth in the Ross Sea. *Limnology and Oceanography*, 52:1079–1093.

Boyd, P. W., and E. R. Abraham. 2001. Iron-Mediated Changes in Phytoplankton Photosynthetic Competence during SOIREE. *Deep-Sea Research, Part II*, 48:2529–2550.

Coale, K. H., X. Wang, S. J. Tanner, and K. S. Johnson. 2003. Phytoplankton Growth and Biological Response to Iron and Zinc Addition in the Ross Sea and Antarctic Circumpolar Current along 170°W. *Deep-Sea Research, Part II*, 50:635–653.

Comiso, J. C. 2000. Variability and Trends in Antarctic Surface Temperatures from in situ and Satellite Infrared Measurements. *Journal of Climate*, 13:1674–1696.

———. 2003. Warming Trends in the Arctic, *Journal of Climate*, 16:3498–3510.

———. 2004. Sea Ice Algorithm for AMSR-E. *Rivista Italiana di Telerilevamento*, 30/31:119–130.

———. 2009. *Polar Oceans from Space*. Berlin: Springer-Verlag.

Comiso, J. C., C. R. McClain, C. Sullivan, J. Ryan, and C. L. Leonard. 1993. CZCS Pigment Concentrations in the Southern Ocean and Their Relationships to Some Geophysical Parameters, *Journal of Geophysical Research*, 98:2419–2451.

Comiso, J. C., D. J. Cavalieri, and T. Markus. 2003. Sea Ice Concentration, Ice Temperature, and Snow Depth, Using AMSR-E Data. *IEEE Transactions on Geoscience and Remote Sensing*, 41:243–252.

de Baar, H. J. W., P. W. Boyd, K. H. Coale, M. R. Landry, A. Tsuda, P. Assmy, D. C. E. Bakker, Y. Bozec, R. T. Barber, M. A. Brzezinski, K. O. Buesseler, M. Boyé, P. L. Croot, F. Gervais, M. Y. Gorbunov, P. J. Harrison, W. T. Hiscock, P. Laan, C. Lancelot, C. S. Law, M. Levasseur, A. Marchetti, F. J. Millero, J. Nishioka, Y. Noriri, T. van Oiken, U. Riebesell, M. J. Rijkenberg, H. Saito, S. Takeda, K. R. Timmermans, M. J. W. Vedhuis, A. M. Waite, and C.-S. Wong. 2005. Synthesis of Iron Fertilization Experiments: From the Iron Age in the Age of Enlightenment. *Journal of Geophysical Research*, 110:C09S16, doi:10.1029/2004JC002601.

Dierssen, H. M., and R. C. Smith. 2000. Bio-optical Properties and Remote Sensing Ocean Color Algorithms for Antarctic Peninsula Waters. *Journal of Geophysical Research*, 105:26,301–26,312.

Dierssen, H. M., R. C. Smith, and M. Vernet. 2002. Glacial Meltwater Dynamics in Coastal Waters West of the Antarctic Peninsula. *Proceedings of the National Academy of Sciences*, 99(4):1790–1795.

Ducklow, H. W., W. Fraser, D. M. Karl, L. B. Quetin, R. M. Ross, R. C. Smith, S. E. Stammerjohn, M. Vernet, and R. M. Daniels. 2006. Water Column Processes in the West Antarctic Peninsula and the Ross Sea: Foodweb Structure and Interannual Variability. *Deep-Sea Research, Part II*, 53:834–852.

El-Sayed, S. Z., D. C. Biggs, and O. Holm-Hansen. 1983. Phytoplankton Standing Crop, Primary Productivity, and Near-Surface Nitrogenous Nutrient Fields in the Ross Sea, Antarctica. *Deep-Sea Research, Part A*, 30:871–886.

Fitzwater, S. E., K. S. Johnson, R. M. Gordon, K. H. Coale, and W. O. Smith Jr. 2000. Trace Metal Concentrations in the Ross Sea and Their Relationship with Nutrients and Phytoplankton Growth. *Deep-Sea Research, Part II*, 47:3159–3179.

Gordon, A. L., M. Visbeck, and J. C. Comiso. 2007. A Possible Link between the Great Weddell Polynya and the Southern Annular Mode. *Journal of Climate*, 20:2558–2571.

Hart, T. J. 1934. On the Phytoplankton of the Southwest Atlantic and Bellingshausen Sea. *Discovery Reports*, 8:1–268.

Holm-Hansen, O., S. Z. El-Sayed, G. A. Francescini, and R. L. Cuhel. 1977. "Primary Production and Factors Controlling Phytoplankton Growth in the Southern Ocean." In *Adaptations within Antarctic Ecosystems*, ed. G. A. Llano, pp. 11–50. Houston, Tex.: Gulf Publishing Company.

Knox, G. A. 1994. *The Biology of Southern Ocean*. London: Cambridge University Press.

Kwok, R., and J. C. Comiso. 2002. Spatial Patterns of Variability in Antarctic Surface Temperature: Connections to the Southern Hemisphere Annular Mode and the Southern Oscillation. *Geophysical Research Letters*, 29:1705, doi:10.1029/2002GL015415.

Martin, J. H., S. E. Fitzwater, and R. M. Gordon. 1990. Iron Deficiency Limits Phytoplankton Growth in Antarctic Waters. *Global Biogeochemical Cycles*, 4:5–12.

Mitchell, B. G., and O. Holm-Hansen. 1991. Observations and Modeling of the Antarctic Phytoplankton Crop in Relation to Mixing Depth. *Deep-Sea Research, Part A*, 38:981–1007.

Moore, J. K., and M. R. Abbott. 2000. Phytoplankton Chlorophyll Distributions and Primary Production in the Southern Ocean. *Journal of Geophysical Research*, 105:28,709–28,722.

Moore, J. K., M. R. Abbott, J. G. Richman, W. O. Smith Jr., T. J. Cowles, K. H. Coale, W. D. Gardner, and R. T. Barber. 1999. SeaWiFS Satellite Ocean Color Data at the U.S. Southern Ocean JGOFS Line Along 170°W. *Geophysical Research Letters,* 26:1465–1468.

Neale, P. J., R. F. Davis, and J. J. Cullen. 1998. Interactive Effects of Ozone Depletion and Vertical Mixing on Photosynthesis of Antarctic Phytoplankton. *Nature,* 392:585–589.

Neale, P. J., W. H. Jeffrey, C. Sobrino, J. D. Pakulski, J. Phillips-Kress, A. J. Baldwin, L. A. Franklin, and H.-C. Kim. 2009. "Inhibition of Phytoplankton and Bacterial Productivity by Solar Radiation in the Ross Sea Polynya." In *Smithsonian at the Poles: Contributions to International Polar Year Science,* ed. I. Krupnik, M. A. Lang, and S. E. Miller, pp. 299–308. Washington, D.C.: Smithsonian Institution Scholarly Press.

Nelson, D. M., W. O. Smith Jr., L. I. Gordon, and B. Huber. 1987. Early Spring Distributions of Nutrients and Phytoplankton Biomass in the Ice Edge Zone of the Weddell-Scotia Sea. *Journal of Geophysical Research,* 92:7181–7190.

Nelson, D. M., D. J. DeMaster, R. B. Dunbar, and W.O. Smith Jr. 1996. Cycling of Organic Carbon and Biogenic Silica in the Southern Ocean: Estimates of Large-Scale Water Column and Sedimentary Fluxes in the Ross Sea. *Journal of Geophysical Research,* 101: 18,519–18,531.

Patt, F. S., R. A. Barners, R. E. Eplee Jr., B. A. Franz, W. D. Robinson, G. C. Geldman, S. W. Bailey, J. Gales, P. J. Werdell, M. Wang, R. Frouin, R. P. Stumpf, R. A. Arnone, R. W. Gould Jr., P. M. Martinolich, V. Ramsibrahmanakul, J. E. O'Reilly, and J. A. Yoder. 2003. Algorithm Updates for the Fourth SeaWiFS Data Reprocessing. NASA Technical Memorandum NASA/TM-2003-206892. NASA Goddard Space Flight Center, Greenbelt, Md.

Peloquin, J. A., and W. O. Smith Jr. 2007. Phytoplankton blooms in the Ross Sea, Antarctica: Interannual Variability in Magnitude, Temporal Patterns, and Composition. *Journal of Geophysical Research,* 112:C08013, doi:10.1029/2006JC003816.

Sarmiento, J. L., T. M. C. Hughes, R. J. Stouffer, and S. Manabe.1998. Simulated Response of the Ocean Carbon Cycle to Anthropogenic Climate Warming. *Nature,* 393:245–249.

Sarmiento, J. L., and C. Le Quéré. 1996. Oceanic Carbon Dioxide Uptake in a Model of Century-Scale Global Warming. *Science,* 274: 1346–1350.

Sedwick, P. N., and G. R. DiTullio. 1997. Regulation of Algal Blooms in Antarctic Shelf Waters by the Release of Iron from Melting Sea Ice. *Geophysical Research Letters,* 24:2515–2518.

Sedwick, P. N., G. R. DiTullio, and D. J. Mackey. 2000. Iron and Manganese in the Ross Sea, Antarctica: Seasonal Iron Limitation in Antarctic Shelf Waters. *Journal of Geophysical Research,* 105: 11321–11336.

Smith, N. R., D. Zhaoqian, K. R. Kerry, and S. Wright. 1984. Water Masses and Circulation in the Region of Prydz Bay, Antarctica. *Deep-Sea Research, Part A,* 31:1121–1137.

Smith, W. O., Jr., and V. A. Asper. 2001. The Influence of Phytoplankton Assemblage Composition on Biogeochemical Characteristics and Cycles in the Southern Ross Sea, Antarctica. *Deep-Sea Research, Part I,* 48:137–161.

Smith, W. O., Jr., and J. C. Comiso. 2008. Influence of Sea Ice on Primary Production in the Southern Ocean: A Satellite Perspective. *Journal of Geophysical Research,* 113:C05S93, doi:10.1029/2007JC004251.

Smith, W. O., Jr., M. S. Dinniman, J. M. Klinck, and E. Hofmann. 2003. Biogeochemical Climatologies in the Ross Sea, Antarctica: Seasonal Patterns of Nutrients and Biomass. *Deep-Sea Research, Part II,* 47: 3083–3101.

Smith, W. O., Jr., and L. I. Gordon. 1997. Hyperproductivity of the Ross Sea (Antarctica) Polynya during Austral Spring, *Geophysical Research Letters,* 24:233–236.

Smith, W. O., Jr., J. Marra, M. R. Hiscock, and R. T. Barber. 2000. The Seasonal Cycle of Phytoplankton Biomass and Primary Productivity in the Ross Sea, Antarctica. *Deep-Sea Research. Part II,* 47: 3119–3140.

Smith, W. O., Jr., and D. M. Nelson. 1985. Phytoplankton Bloom Produced by a Receding Ice Edge in the Ross Sea: Spatial Coherence with the Density Field. *Science,* 227:163–166.

———. 1986. The Importance of Ice-Edge Blooms in the Southern Ocean. *BioScience,* 36:251–257.

Smith, W. O., Jr., A. R. Shields, J. A. Peloquin, G. Catalano, S. Tozzi, M. S. Dinniman, and V. A. Asper. 2006. Biogeochemical Budgets in the Ross Sea: Variations among Years. *Deep-Sea Research, Part II,* 53:815–833.

Sullivan, C. W., K. R. Arrigo, C. R. McClain, J. C. Comiso, and J. Firestone. 1993. Distributions of Phytoplankton Blooms in the Southern Ocean. *Science,* 262:1832–1837.

Sunda, W. G., and S. A. Huntsman. 1997. Interrelated Influence of Iron, Light and Cell Size on Marine Phytoplankton Growth. *Nature,* 390:389–392.

Sweeney, C., D. A. Hansell, C. A. Carlson, L. A. Codispoti, L. I. Gordon, J. Marra, F. J. Millero, W. O. Smith Jr., and T. Takahashi. 2000. Biogeochemical Regimes, Net Community Production and Carbon Export in the Ross Sea, Antarctica. *Deep-Sea Research, Part II,* 47: 3369–3394.

Tagliabue, A., and K. R. Arrigo. 2003. Anomalously Low Zooplankton Abundance in the Ross Sea: An Alternative Explanation. *Limnology and Oceanography,* 48:686–699.

Tremblay, J.-E., and W. O. Smith Jr. 2007. "Phytoplankton Processes in Polynyas." In *Polynyas: Windows to the World's Oceans,* ed. W. O. Smith Jr. and D. G. Barber, pp. 239–270. Amsterdam: Elsevier.

Vaughan, D. G., G. J. Marshall, W. M. Connolley, C. Parkinson, R. Mulvaney, D. A. Hodgson, J.C. King, C. J. Pudsey, and J. Turner. 2003. Recent Rapid Regional Climate Warming on the Antarctic Peninsula. *Climatic Change,* 60:243–274.

Chromophoric Dissolved Organic Matter Cycling during a Ross Sea *Phaeocystis antarctica* Bloom

David J. Kieber, Dierdre A. Toole, and Ronald P. Kiene

ABSTRACT. Chromophoric dissolved organic matter (CDOM) is ubiquitous in the oceans, where it is an important elemental reservoir, a key photoreactant, and a sunscreen for ultraviolet (UV) radiation. Chromophoric dissolved organic matter is generally the main attenuator of UV radiation in the water column, and it affects the remote sensing of chlorophyll *a* (chl *a*) such that corrections for CDOM need to be incorporated into remote sensing algorithms. Despite its significance, relatively few CDOM measurements have been made in the open ocean, especially in polar regions. In this paper, we show that CDOM spectral absorption coefficients (a_λ) are relatively low in highly productive Antarctic waters, ranging from approximately 0.18 to 0.30 m^{-1} at 300 nm and 0.014 to 0.054 m^{-1} at 443 nm. These values are low compared to coastal waters, but they are higher (by approximately a factor of two to three) than a_λ in oligotrophic waters at low latitudes, supporting the supposition of a poleward increase in a_{CDOM} in the open ocean. Chromophoric dissolved organic matter a_λ and spectral slopes did not increase during the early development of a bloom of the colonial haptophyte *Phaeocystis antarctica* in the Ross Sea, Antarctica, even though chl *a* concentrations increased more than one-hundred-fold. Our results suggest that Antarctic CDOM in the Ross Sea is not coupled directly to algal production of organic matter in the photic zone during the early bloom but is rather produced in the photic zone at a later time or elsewhere in the water column, possibly from organic-rich sea ice or the microbial degradation of algal-derived dissolved organic matter exported out of the photic zone. Spectral a_λ at 325 nm for surface waters in the Southern Ocean and Ross Sea were remarkably similar to values reported for deep water from the North Atlantic by Nelson et al. in 2007. This similarity may not be a coincidence and may indicate long-range transport to the North Atlantic of CDOM produced in the Antarctic via Antarctic Intermediate and Bottom Water.

David J. Kieber, Department of Chemistry, State University of New York College of Environmental Science and Forestry, Syracuse, NY 13210, USA. Dierdre A. Toole, Department of Marine Chemistry and Geochemistry, Woods Hole Oceanographic Institution, Woods Hole, MA 02543, USA. Ronald P. Kiene, Department of Marine Sciences, University of South Alabama, Mobile, AL 36688, USA. Corresponding author: D. Kieber (djkieber@esf.edu). Accepted 28 May 2008.

INTRODUCTION

Quantifying temporal and spatial variations in chromophoric dissolved organic matter (CDOM) absorption is important to understanding the biogeochemistry of natural waters because CDOM plays a significant role in determining the underwater light field. Chromophoric dissolved organic matter is the fraction of dissolved organic matter (DOM) that absorbs solar radiation in natural waters, including radiation in the UVB (280 to 320 nm), the UVA (320 to 400 nm), and the visible portion (400 to 700 nm) of the solar spectrum. For most natural waters, CDOM is the primary constituent that attenuates actinic

UVB and UVA radiation in the water column. Consequently, CDOM acts as a "sunscreen," providing protection from short wavelengths of solar radiation that can be damaging to aquatic organisms (Hebling and Zagarese, 2003). Chromophoric dissolved organic matter absorption is often also quite high in the blue spectral region, particularly in the subtropics and poles, accounting for a quantitatively significant percentage of total nonwater absorption (Siegel et al., 2002), complicating remote sensing of phytoplankton pigment concentrations and primary productivity (Carder et al., 1989; Nelson et al., 1998). In lakes and coastal areas with high riverine discharge, CDOM absorption in the blue region can be so large as to restrict phytoplankton absorption of light, thereby placing limits on primary productivity (e.g., Vodacek et al., 1997; Del Vecchio and Blough, 2004). Since CDOM absorption affects the satellite-retrieved phytoplankton absorption signal in most oceanic waters, especially coastal waters, CDOM absorption must be accounted for when using remotely sensed data (Blough and Del Vecchio, 2002). This necessitates a thorough understanding of the characteristics of CDOM and factors controlling its distribution in different areas of the ocean.

Sources of CDOM in the oceans are varied and, in many cases, poorly described. Potential sources include terrestrial input of decaying plant organic matter, autochthonous production by algae, photochemical or bacterial processing of DOM, and release from sediments (e.g., Blough et al., 1993; Opsahl and Benner, 1997; Nelson et al., 1998; Nelson and Siegel, 2002; Rochelle-Newall and Fisher, 2002a, 2002b; Chen et al., 2004; Nelson et al., 2004). The removal of CDOM in the oceans is dominated by its photochemical bleaching, but microbial processing is also important although poorly understood (Blough et al., 1993; Vodacek et al., 1997; Del Vecchio and Blough, 2002; Chen et al., 2004; Nelson et al., 2004; Vähätalo and Wetzel, 2004).

Absorption of sunlight by CDOM can affect an aquatic ecosystem both directly and indirectly (Schindler and Curtis, 1997). The bleaching of CDOM absorption and fluorescence properties as a result of sunlight absorption lessens the biological shielding effect of CDOM in surface waters. Chromophoric dissolved organic matter photobleaching may also produce a variety of reactive oxygen species (ROS), such as the hydroxyl radical, hydrogen peroxide, and superoxide (for review, see Kieber et al., 2003). Generation of these compounds provides a positive feedback to CDOM removal by causing further destruction of CDOM via reaction with these ROS.

Although CDOM has been intensively studied to understand its chemical and physical properties, previous research has primarily focused on CDOM cycling in temperate and subtropical waters. Very little is known regarding temporal and spatial distributions of CDOM in high-latitude marine waters. Studies in the Bering Strait–Chukchi Sea region and the Greenland Sea showed that absorption coefficients (a_λ) and spectral slopes (S) derived from CDOM absorption spectra at coastal stations were influenced by terrestrial inputs and comparable to a_λ and S values in temperate and tropical coastal sites (Stedmon and Markager, 2001; Ferenac, 2006). As the distance from the coastline in the Bering Strait and Chukchi Sea proper increased, there was a large decrease in a_λ from 1.5 to 0.2 m^{-1} at 350 nm. These a_λ were mostly higher than a_{350} observed in the open ocean at lower latitudes (Ferenac, 2006). However, corresponding spectral slopes were significantly lower (≤ 0.014 nm^{-1}) than open oceanic values in the Sargasso Sea and elsewhere (≥ 0.02 nm^{-1}; Blough and Del Vecchio, 2002), suggesting that the types of CDOM present in these contrasting environments were different, possibly owing to a residual terrestrial signal and lower degree of photobleaching in the Arctic samples.

As with Arctic waters, there is very little known regarding CDOM in Antarctic waters. To our knowledge, there are only three published reports investigating CDOM distributions in the Ross Sea and along the Antarctic Peninsula (Sarpal et al., 1995; Patterson, 2000; Kieber et al., 2007). A key finding of the Sarpal et al. study was that Antarctic waters were quite transparent in the UV ($a_\lambda < 0.4$ m^{-1} at $\lambda \geq$ 290 nm), even at coastal stations during a bloom of *Cryptomonas* sp. Patterson (2000) examined CDOM in several transects perpendicular to the Antarctic Peninsula coastline and found that CDOM absorption coefficients were low in the austral summer, with a_{305} ($\pm$SD) = 0.28 ($\pm$0.09) m^{-1} and a_{340} = 0.13 ($\pm$0.06) m^{-1}. Similarly low a_λ were observed by Kieber et al. (2007) in the upper water column of the Ross Sea ($a_{300} \sim 0.32$ m^{-1} and $a_{350} \sim 0.15$ m^{-1}) during the end of a *Phaeocystis antarctica* bloom when diatoms were also blooming (chl $a \sim 3.8$ μg L^{-1}).

Polar regions are unique in many ways that may influence CDOM optical properties. Sea ice may provide a rich source of ice-derived CDOM to melt water (Scully and Miller, 2000; Xie and Gosselin, 2005). Additionally, polar blooms can decay without significant losses to zooplankton, especially in the spring when zooplankton grazing can be minimal (Caron et al., 2000; Overland and Stabeno, 2004; Rose and Caron, 2007).

In the Ross Sea, soon after the opening of the Ross Sea polynya in the austral spring, a *Phaeocystis antarctica*–dominated bloom regularly occurs (Smith et al., 2000), especially in waters away from the ice edge where iron concentrations are lower and the water column is more deeply mixed. As is typical of polar regions, the massive phytoplankton production that is observed during the early stages of this bloom (in the early to mid austral spring) is not accompanied by significant micro- or macrozooplankton grazing (Caron et al., 2000). The spring bloom also appears to be a period of low bacterial abundance and activity (Ducklow et al., 2001), although bacteria do bloom during the later stages of the algal bloom, in early to mid summer, coinciding with an increase in dissolved and particulate organic carbon (Carlson et al., 2000).

Depending on physiological and hydrodynamic factors, this ecological decoupling between primary productivity and both microbial productivity and grazing may cause the phytoplankton to sink out of the photic zone (DiTullio et al., 2000; Becquevort and Smith, 2001; Overland and Stabeno, 2004). This may lead to a significant flux of organic matter to the ocean floor and to deepwater CDOM production. Export of the phytoplankton out of the photic zone may also lead to a decoupling of bloom dynamics and CDOM cycling.

Here we report on spatial and temporal patterns in CDOM spectra observed during the early stages of the 2005 austral spring *Phaeocystis antarctica* bloom in the seasonal Ross Sea polynya. Our results show that CDOM changed very little during a period when chl *a* concentrations increased more than one-hundred-fold. Implications of this finding for CDOM cycling in the Ross Sea are discussed.

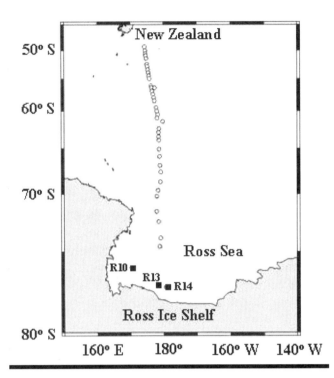

FIGURE 1. Locations of transect sampling stations south of New Zealand to the Ross Sea (open circles) and the main hydrographic stations that were occupied in the Ross Sea (solid black circles) during the NBP05-08 cruise. Latitude and longitude information for specific hydrographic stations (e.g., R10A and R10D) are given in figure captions 4, 5, 8 and 9.

METHODS

Ross Sea Site Description and Sampling

A field campaign was conducted aboard the R/V *Nathaniel B. Palmer* in the seasonal ice-free polynya in the Ross Sea, Antarctica, from 8 November to 30 November 2005 (Figure 1). During this time, the surface seawater temperature was approximately −1.8°C and the phytoplankton assemblage was dominated by colonial *Phaeocystis antarctica*. Three main hydrographic stations were occupied within the Ross Sea polynya for approximately seven days each (i.e., R10, R13, R14). Seawater samples were collected from early morning hydrocasts (0400-0700 local time) directly from Niskin bottles attached to a conductivity, temperature, and depth (CTD) rosette. Vertical profiles of a suite of routine measurements were obtained at each station including downwelling irradiance (and coupled incident surface irradiance), chl *a*, and CDOM absorption spectra. Additionally, a profile of dissolved organic carbon (DOC) was collected at one station (14F).

In addition to studying CDOM cycling in the Ross Sea, we also collected and analyzed surface water CDOM samples during our North-South transit from New Zealand through the Southern Ocean to the Ross Sea (28 October–7 November, 2005). Transect sampling for CDOM was conducted from ~49 to ~75°S. Details of the cruise track, sampling protocols, analyses conducted and meteorological and sea ice conditions for the southbound transect are presented in Kiene et al. (2007). The transect encompassed open waters of the Southern Ocean, the northern sea-ice melt zone, and ice-covered areas near the northern Ross Sea.

Chlorophyll *a* was determined fluorometrically by employing the acidification method described by Strickland and Parsons (1968). Briefly, 50–250 mL of seawater was filtered onto a 25-mm GF/C glass fiber filter (Whatman Inc., Floram Park, New Jersey) with low vacuum. Filters were placed in 5 mL of 90% HPLC-grade acetone and extracted for 24 h at −20°C. Chlorophyll fluorescence in the acetone extracts was quantified with a Turner Designs 10-AU fluorometer (Sunnyvale, Calafornia) before and after 80-μL addition of 10% HCl. Dissolved organic carbon samples were collected and concentrations were determined by employing the techniques outlined in Qian and Mopper (1996).

For nutrient and CDOM samples, seawater was collected directly from Niskin bottles by gravity filtration through a 20-μm Nitex mesh (held in a 47-mm-diameter polycarbonate (PC) filter holder) followed by a precleaned 0.2-μm AS 75 Polycap filter capsule (nylon membrane with a glass microfiber prefilter enclosed in a polypropylene housing). Silicone tubing was used to attach the PC filter to the Niskin bottle spigot and the Polycap to the PC filter outlet. Nutrient samples were collected into 50-mL polypropylene centrifuge tubes, while samples for CDOM were filtered into precleaned 80-mL Qorpak bottles sealed with Teflon-lined caps (see Toole et al., 2003, for details regarding sample filtration and glassware preparation). Nutrient samples were stored frozen at $-80°C$ until shipboard analysis by standard flow-injection techniques.

CDOM Absorption Spectra

Absorbance spectra were determined with 0.2-μm filtered seawater samples that were warmed to room temperature in the dark immediately after they were collected and then analyzed soon thereafter (generally within 24 h). Absorbance spectra were determined in a 100-cm path length, Type II liquid capillary waveguide (World Precision Instruments) attached to an Ocean Optics model SD2000 dual-channel fiber-optic spectrophotometer and a Micropack DH 2000 UV-visible light source. Prior to analysis, a sample or blank was first deaerated with ultrahigh purity He in an 80-mL Qorpak bottle and then pulled through the capillary cell slowly with a Rainin Rabbit peristaltic pump. Deaeration with He eliminated bubble formation in the sample cell, while increasing the pH slightly from 8.0 to 8.3. This pH change is not expected to affect absorption spectra, although this was not explicitly tested. The reference solution consisted of 0.2-μm-filtered 0.7-*M* NaCl prepared from precombusted (600°C, 24 h) high-purity sodium chloride (99.8%, Baker Analyzed) and dissolved in high-purity (18.2 MΩ cm) laboratory water obtained from a Millipore Milli-Q ultrapure water system (Millipore Corp., Billerica, Massachusetts). The sodium chloride solution was used to approximately match the ionic strength of the Ross Sea seawater samples and minimize spectral offsets due to refractive index effects. Even though a sodium chloride solution was used as a reference, sample absorbance spectra still exhibited small, variable baseline offsets (~0.005 AU). This was corrected for by adjusting the absorbance (A_λ) to zero between 650 and 675 nm where the sample absorbance was assumed to be

zero. The capillary cell was flushed after every fourth or fifth seawater sample with deaerated Milli-Q water and high-purity, distilled-in-glass-grade methanol (Burdick and Jackson, Muskegon, Michigan). Corrected absorbance values were used to calculate absorption coefficients:

$$a_\lambda = 2.303 A_\lambda / l, \tag{1}$$

where l is the path length of the capillary cell. Each sample was analyzed in triplicate, resulting in ≤2% relative standard deviation (RSD) in spectral absorbance values ≤400 nm. On the basis of three times the standard deviation of the sodium chloride reference, the limit of detection for measured absorption coefficients was approximately 0.002 m^{-1}. To characterize sample absorption, spectra were fit to the following exponential form (e.g., Twardowski et al., 2004):

$$a_\lambda = a_{\lambda_o} e^{-S(\lambda - \lambda_o)}, \tag{2}$$

where a_{λ_o} is the absorption coefficient at the reference wavelength, λ_o, and S is the spectral slope (nm^{-1}). Data were fit to a single exponential equation using SigmaPlot (SPSS Inc.). Slope coefficients were evaluated from 275 to 295 nm ($S_{275-295}$; $\lambda_o = 285$ nm) and from 350 to 400 nm ($S_{350-400}$; $\lambda_o = 375$ nm). These wavelength ranges were selected for study of spectral slopes instead of using broader wavelength ranges (e.g., 290–700 nm) because the former can be measured with high precision and better reflects biogeochemical changes in CDOM in the water column (Helms et al., 2008).

Optical Profiles

Vertical profiles of spectral downwelling irradiance ($E_d(z,\lambda)$) and upwelling radiance ($L_u(z,\lambda)$), as well as the time course of surface irradiance ($E_d(0^+,\lambda, t)$), were determined separately for ultraviolet and visible wavebands. Ultraviolet wavelengths were sampled using a Biospherical Instruments, Inc. (BSI, San Diego, California) PUV-2500 Profiling Ultraviolet Radiometer coupled with a continuously sampling, deck-mounted, cosine-corrected GUV-2511 Ground-based Ultraviolet Radiometer. Both sensors had a sampling rate of approximately 6 Hz and monitored seven channels centered at 305, 313, 320, 340, 380, and 395 nm, as well as integrated photosynthetically active radiation (PAR). Each channel had an approximate bandwidth of 10 nm, except for the 305-nm channel, whose bandwidth was determined by the atmospheric ozone cutoff and the PAR channel, which monitored the irradiance from 400 to 700 nm. The irradiance at several visible wavelength channels, centered at 412, 443, 490, 510, 555, and 665 nm, as well as PAR, were determined with a BSI PRR-600 Profiling Reflectance Radiometer coupled to a radiometrically matched surface reference sensor (PRR-610). Similarly, both PRR sensors had a sampling rate of approximately 6 Hz and an approximate bandwidth of 10 nm. The PUV-2500 was deployed multiple times a day (generally, three to five profiles per day) in free-fall mode, allowing it to sample at a distance of over 10 m from the ship, minimizing effects from ship shadow and instrument tilt (Waters et al., 1990). The PRR-600 was deployed several times per station in a metal lowering frame via the starboard side winch. Prior to each cast, the ship was oriented relative to the sun to minimize ship shadow. The GUV-2511 and PRR-610 were mounted to the deck, and care was taken to avoid shadows or reflected light associated with the ship's superstructure. To reduce instrument variability due to atmospheric temperature fluctuations, the GUV-2511 was equipped with active internal heating. All calibrations utilized coefficients provided by BSI, and the data were processed using standard procedures.

Spectral downwelling attenuation coefficients ($K_d(\lambda)$, m^{-1}) were derived from each PUV-2500 and PRR-600 profile as the slope of log-transformed $E_d(z, \lambda)$ versus depth. On the basis of water clarity, the depth interval for this calculation varied from < 10 m for shorter UV wavelengths up to 20-30 m for blue wavelengths of solar radiation. Daily mean $K_d(\lambda)$ were derived as the average of individual $K_d(\lambda)$ coefficients determined from each PUV and PRR profile, and station means were determined by averaging the daily $K_d(\lambda)$ coefficients.

RESULTS

SAMPLE STORAGE AND SPECTRAL COMPARISON

A storage test was conducted with seawater collected on 29 October 2005 (52°59.90′S, 175°7.76′E) during the transect from New Zealand to the Ross Sea. The sample was obtained from the ship's underway pump system that had an intake depth at approximately 4 m. Seawater was filtered directly from the pump line through a 0.2-μm AS 75 Polycap filter capsule into an 80-mL Qorpak bottle and stored in the dark at room temperature. When this sample was analyzed multiple times over a period of two weeks ($n = 8$), no change was observed in its absorption spectrum with respect to spectral absorption coefficients or spectral slopes. For example, a_{300} varied over a very narrow range from 0.196 to 0.202 m^{-1} with a mean

value of 0.197 m^{-1} and 3.1% RSD. This RSD is only slightly larger than the RSD for replicate analysis of the same sample when done sequentially (~2%). Likewise, the spectral slope from 275 to 295 nm ($S_{275-295}$) showed very little variation over time, ranging from 0.0337 to 0.0377 nm^{-1} (0.0358 nm^{-1} mean and 3.4% RSD). The $S_{350-400}$ varied somewhat more (11.8% RSD) due to the lower a_λ values, ranging from 0.0075 to 0.0111 nm^{-1}, with a mean value of 0.009 nm^{-1}. A storage study with two other samples that were collected along the transect showed similar results, with very little variability observed in either a_λ or S beyond the precision of sequential spectral measurements.

In addition to the storage study, absorption spectra obtained with the capillary waveguide system were compared to those obtained with the commonly used Perkin Elmer Lamda 18 dual-beam, grating monochromator spectrophotometer. There was no statistical difference in the spectral absorption coefficients obtained by these two spectrophotometers, except for considerably more noise in a_λ obtained with the Perkin Elmer spectrophotometer (Figure 2). The increased spectral noise seen with the Beckman spectrophotometer was expected due to the relatively short path length (0.10 m) and the extremely low absorbance values in the Ross Sea seawater samples (e.g., ~0.009 AU at 400 nm), which were close to the detection limit of this instrument. In contrast, a_λ spectra obtained

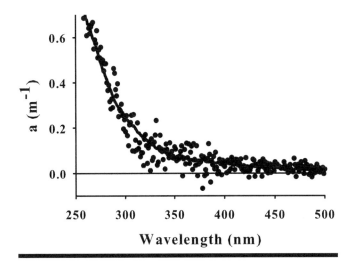

FIGURE 2. Comparison of spectral absorption coefficients determined with a Perkin-Elmer Lambda 18 dual-beam spectrophotometer (circles) and a capillary waveguide spectrophotometer (solid line). A 10-cm cylindrical quartz cell was used to obtain spectral absorption coefficients with the Perkin-Elmer spectrophotometer. Absorbance spectra were referenced against a 0.7 M NaCl solution.

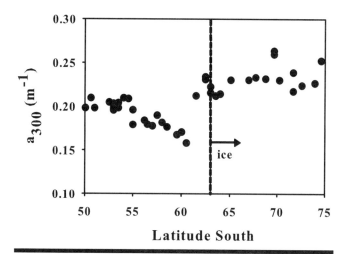

FIGURE 3. Sea surface a_{300} plotted as a function of degrees latitude south for the Oct–Nov 2005 transect from the Southern Ocean south of New Zealand to the Ross Sea. All data were obtained from water collected from the ship's underway seawater pump system (intake at approximately 4-m depth) that was filtered inline through a 0.2-μm AS 75 Polycap filter. The dashed line represents the approximate location of the northern extent of seasonal sea ice in our transect. For details regarding the transect, see Kiene et al. (2007).

with the capillary waveguide were much smoother owing to the much higher absorbance values due to the much longer path length (1 m) and the ability to spectrally average over several scans.

TRANSECT AND ROSS SEA CDOM ABSORPTION SPECTRA

Absorption coefficients obtained during our transect from New Zealand to the Ross Sea were generally low, as exemplified by a_{300} (Figure 3). Values for a_{300} ranged from 0.178 to 0.264 m^{-1}, with an average value of 0.209 m^{-1}. Interestingly, absorption coefficients at 300 nm were consistently higher in samples collected with significant ice cover (avg ± SD: 0.231 ± 0.014 m^{-1}) compared to a_{300} values collected in the Southern Ocean north of the sea ice (avg ± SD: 0.195 ± 0.017 m^{-1}) (Figure 3), possibly due to lower rates of photobleaching or release of CDOM from the sea ice into the underlying seawater (Scully and Miller, 2000; Xie and Gosselin, 2005). However, we cannot exclude the possibility that the ship caused some release of CDOM from the ice during our passage through it.

Absorption coefficients were also low within the Ross Sea during the development of the *Phaeocystis antarctica* bloom, even when surface waters were visibly green (chl

a = 4–8 μg L^{-1}). For example, the absorption coefficient spectrum at station R14F was remarkably similar to that obtained in the Sargasso Sea during July 2004 (Figure 4), even though the chl a content of these two water samples differed by two orders of magnitude (7.0 versus 0.08 μg L^{-1}, respectively). The main differences observed between the two spectra were seen at wavelengths less than approximately 350 nm, with the Sargasso Sea sample exhibiting a much higher spectral slope (e.g., $S_{275-295}$ of 0.0466 versus 0.0273 nm^{-1}) and the Ross Sea sample having a higher a_λ between ~300 and 350 nm. These differences are likely due to different autochthonous sources of CDOM as well as the presence of micromolar levels of nitrate in the Antarctic sample (and perhaps dissolved mycosporine amino acids (MAA) as well; see "Ross Sea Temporal Trends in CDOM" section) compared to the low nanomolar levels of nitrate in the surface Sargasso Sea sample.

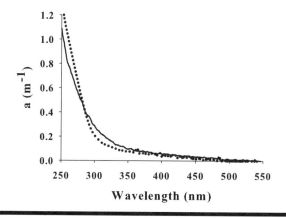

FIGURE 4. Comparison of spectral absorption coefficients determined with seawater collected from 50 m in the Sargasso Sea (30°55.5′N, 65°17.8′W) on 21 July 2004 (dotted line) and from 40 m in the Ross Sea (77°31.2′S, 179°79.8′W) on 26 November 2005 (station R14B, solid line). Both samples were 0.2-μm gravity filtered prior to analysis. The chl a concentration was 0.08 and 7.0 μg L^{-1} in the Sargasso Sea and Ross Sea, respectively. Absorption spectra in the Sargasso Sea were determined with a Hewlett Packard (HP) 8453 UV-Vis photodiode array spectrophotometer equipped with a 5-cm path length rectangular microliter quartz flow cell; the Sargasso spectrum was referenced against Milli-Q water (for details, see Helms et al., 2008). The small discontinuity at 365 nm is an artifact associated with the HP spectrophotometer (Blough et al., 1993).

DOWNWELLING ATTENUATION COEFFICIENTS

The optical clarity of the water column was reduced considerably from before the onset of the *Phaeocystis antarctica* bloom at station R10 to the end of the cruise at station R14. Before the onset of the *Phaeocystis antarctica* bloom (stations R10 and R13A–R13D), the photic zone exhibited a high degree of optical clarity, characteristic of type 1 open oceanic water (Mobley, 1994), with $K_d(\lambda)$ decreasing exponentially in the UV with increasing wavelength and dominated by absorption by CDOM (Figure 5). Prebloom $K_d(\lambda)$ shown in Figure 5 for station R10 were nearly the same as observed at stations R13A–R13D (data not shown). For station R10, $K_d(\lambda)$ ranged from 0.30 to 0.38 m^{-1} at 305 nm, 0.18–0.31 m^{-1} at 320 nm, and 0.05–0.15 m^{-1} at 395 nm. Because of low biomass (chl *a* $\leq$ 0.6 µg L^{-1}), the lowest values of $K_d(\lambda)$, and therefore highest degree of optical clarity, were observed in the visible between approximately 450 and 500 nm with $K_d(\lambda)$ ranging from 0.05 to 0.11 m^{-1}. When the bloom started to develop, the optical characteristics of the water, including the spectral structure of $K_d(\lambda)$, changed dramatically. Over an approximately three-week period, values of $K_d(\lambda)$ increased by a factor of six or more at some wavelengths, with peaks observed at two optical channels, 340 ± 10 and 443 ± 10 nm. At stations R13E and R14 (stations A through F) the bloom progressed to the point that the water column was more transparent to some wavelengths in the UV (e.g., 380 nm) relative to wavelengths in the blue portion of the solar spectrum (Figure 5).

ROSS SEA TEMPORAL TRENDS IN CDOM

Although UV and visible downwelling attenuation coefficients increased substantially when the *Phaeocystis antarctica* bloom was well developed in the Ross Sea (Figure 5), CDOM absorption coefficient spectra changed very little. To illustrate this point, an absorption coefficient spectrum of a 10-m sample taken before the onset of the bloom at station R10 was compared to a spectrum determined for a 10-m sample at station R14 when the water was visibly green (Figure 6). As can be seen from comparison of these two spectra, as well as from many other spectra not shown here, there was essentially no change in

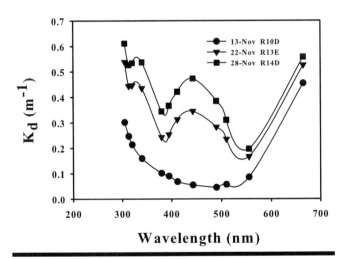

FIGURE 5. Spectral downwelling attenuation coefficients derived from PUV-2500 and PRR-600 profiles both before the *Phaeocystis antarctica* bloom (station R10D, circles) and during the development of the bloom (station R13E, triangles; station R14D, squares). Lines connecting the data do not represent a mathematical fit of the data. Water column profile cast locations are as follows: R10D, 13 November 2005 New Zealand (NZ) time at 76°5.74'S, 170°15.70'W; R13E, 22 November 2005 NZ time at 77°5.20'S, 177°24.49'W; and R14D, 28 November 2005 NZ time at 77°3.61'S, 178°49.06'E. All optical profiles were conducted at approximately 1200 local noon NZ time.

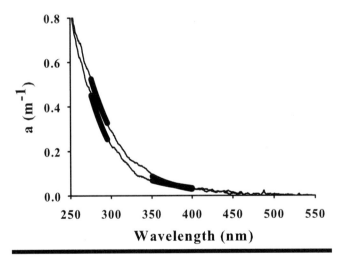

FIGURE 6. Spectral absorption coefficients plotted for 10-m samples from stations R10A (lower spectrum) and R14F (upper spectrum); latitude-longitude data for these stations are given in the Figure 8 caption. Thick lines represent the best fit of the data from 275 to 295 nm and 350 to 400 nm, employing nonlinear regression analysis (equation 2). For station R10A, $S_{275–295}$ = 0.0280 ± 0.0003 nm^{-1} (r^2 = 0.997) and $S_{350–400}$ = 0.0115 ± 0.0003 nm^{-1} (r^2 = 0.904). For station R14F, $S_{275–295}$ = 0.0237 ± 0.0004 nm^{-1} (r^2 = 0.986) and $S_{350–400}$ = 0.0117 ± 0.0005 nm^{-1} (r^2 = 0.916).

absorption coefficients or spectral slopes ($S_{350-400}$) at wavelengths greater than approximately 350 nm. At shorter wavelengths, absorption coefficients and spectral slopes ($S_{275-295}$) varied by 15%–30%, but with no consistent pattern among the many samples analyzed during a period when K_d(340 and 443) and chl a changed by more than a factor of 6 and 100, respectively.

Although there were generally only small changes in a_λ spectra and S, there was an indication of a discernable increase in absorption coefficients in the vicinity of 330–350 nm seen in a few sample spectra (station R14), with the presence of a small peak (or shoulder) noted in some cases. Previous results in the literature suggest that this peak may be due to the presence of MAA in the dissolved phase, possibly stemming from release by *Phaeocystis antarctica*, either through grazing, viral lysis, or direct release. The MAA are one of the primary UV-absorbing compounds detected in *Phaeocystis antarctica* (e.g., Riegger and Robinson, 1997; Moisan and Mitchell, 2001), and it would not be unreasonable for there to be some algal release of MAA into the dissolved phase. However, it is also possible that this UV absorption peak was an artifact of sample filtration (cf. Laurion et al., 2003). While artifacts associated with sample filtration were not rigorously tested in this study, they are probably minimal because we prescreened water by gravity through 20-μm Nitex mesh to remove large aggregates and *Phaeocystis* colonies and then used gravity (hydrostatic) pressure for filtration through a 0.2-μm AS 75 POLYCAP filter. When gentle vacuum filtration was tested on samples collected during the bloom, we often observed a 330- to 350-nm peak that was not seen in CDOM spectra of the same samples that were prescreened and gravity filtered. Vacuum filtration is not recommended and may explain the presence of a peak in spectra for some samples that were analyzed during a bloom in Marguerite Bay along the Antarctic Peninsula (Patterson, 2000).

The striking lack of change in CDOM spectra and spectral slopes during the development of the *Phaeocystis antarctica* bloom was also seen in temporal trends in surface a_λ. Using 340 nm as an example, surface values of a_{340} in the upper 10 m did not appreciably change from 8 November (0.0782 m^{-1}) to 29 November (0.0837 m^{-1}), while over the same time frame, chl a changed by more than a factor of 100 from 0.084 to 8.45 μg L^{-1} (Figure 7A). As with 340 nm, no significant changes in a_λ were observed at other wavelengths during the development of the bloom. Even though CDOM absorption coefficients did not change over time, downwelling attenuation coefficients increased dramatically (Figure 7B),

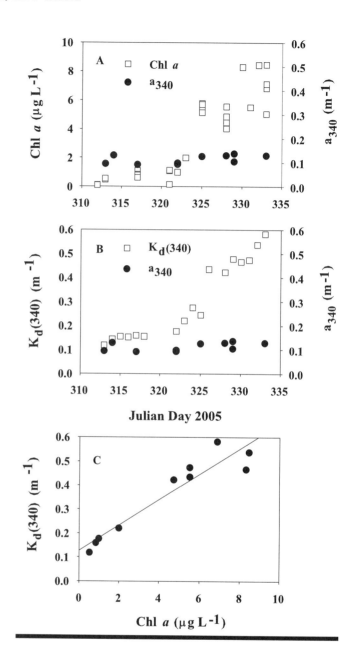

FIGURE 7. Temporal trends in (A) surface chl a and a_{340} and (B) K_d(340) and a_{340} from 8 November to 29 November 2005 (NZ time) in the Ross Sea, Antarctica. (C) Chlorophyll a plotted against K_d(340). In Figure 7C, the line denotes the best fit obtained from linear correlation analysis: $r^2 = 0.900$, K_d(340) = 0.053chl a + 0.128

paralleling increases in chl a (Figure 7C), especially in the vicinity of 340 and 443 nm (Figure 5), corresponding to particulate MAA and chl a absorption, respectively. The strong correlation between K_d(340) and chl a shown in Figure 7C was also seen when K_d(443) was plotted against chl a ($r^2 = 0.937$, data not shown). The nonzero

y-intercept in Figure 7C denotes the background $K_d(340)$ signal at very low chl a due to water, CDOM, and particles in the Ross Sea.

The lack of a clear temporal trend noted in a_λ surface values during the *Phaeocystis antarctica* bloom in November 2005 was also evident in a_λ and spectral slope depth profiles (Figures 8 and 9, respectively). Although we obtained multiple profiles at each station, results for only four CTD casts are shown in Figures 8 and 9 for clarity, with at least one CTD profile depicted for each main hydrostation (R10, R13, and R14). The absorption coefficient at 300 nm varied from approximately 0.18 to 0.30 m^{-1} in the upper 100 m, with no temporal trend observed; some of the lowest and highest values were observed early and late in the cruise (Figure 8A). In the upper 50 m, later in the cruise, a_{340} showed somewhat higher values at sta-

tions R13E and R14F compared to stations R10 and R13A (Figure 8B), as did chl a (Figure 8C). However, while a_{340} increased by 40%–60%, chl a increased by more than two orders of magnitude. It was therefore not surprising that variations in a_{340} did not correlate well with changes in chl a ($r^2 = 0.384$), as shown in Figure 8D.

Spectral slopes also did not vary with any consistent trend. $S_{275-295}$ showed less than 25% variation over depth and time, ranging from ~0.023 to 0.031 nm^{-1} (average 0.027 nm^{-1}, $n = 58$, 7% RSD) during the cruise. Trends in $S_{350-400}$ were more variable (range 0.009–0.017 nm^{-1}, average 0.012 nm^{-1}, $n = 58$, 15% RSD) but still showed no consistent trend with depth or time (Figure 9A and 9B). This variability was also seen in the ratio of the spectral slopes (Figure 9C), which showed no correlation to chl a ($r^2 = 0.143$; Figure 9D).

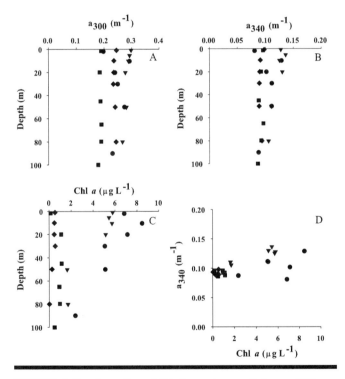

FIGURE 8. Depth profiles of (A) absorption coefficient at 300 nm, (B) absorption coefficient at 340 nm, and (C) chl a. (D) Plot of a_{340} versus chl a; linear correlation result is $a_{340} = 0.0046$chl a + 0.091 with $r^2 = 0.384$. Symbols are: diamonds, station R10A (CTD cast at 0754 local NZ time on 10 November 2005; 76°13.85′S, 170°18.12′W); squares, station R13A (CTD cast at 0817 local NZ time on 18 November 2005; 77°35.16′S, 178°34.57′W); triangles, station R13E (CTD cast at 0823 local NZ time on 22 November 2005; 77°12.61′S, 177°23.73′W); and circles, station R14F (CTD cast at 0734 local NZ time on 30 November 2005; 77°15.35′S, 179°15.35′E).

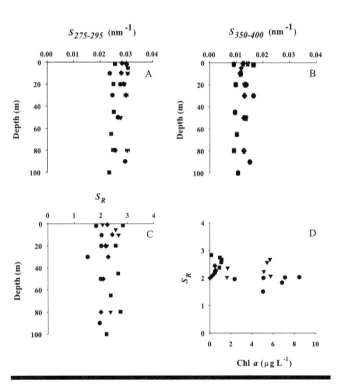

FIGURE 9. Depth profiles of (A) CDOM spectral slope from 275 to 295 nm, (B) CDOM spectral slope from 350 to 400 nm, and (C) the spectral slope ratio ($S_{275-295}$:$S_{350-400}$). Horizontal error bars denote the standard deviation. (D) Spectral slope ratio (S_R) plotted against chl a; linear correlation results were $S_R = -0.0447$chl a + 2.37, with $r^2 = 0.143$ (line not shown). For all four panels, symbols are: diamonds (station R10A), squares (station R13A), triangles (station R13E), and circles (station R14F). Cast times and station locations are given in Figure 8 caption.

DISCUSSION

CDOM absorption coefficients in the Southern Ocean and Ross Sea were consistently low throughout the cruise and along the transect south from New Zealand, with values significantly less than unity at wavelengths ≥ 300 nm (e.g., 0.15–0.32 m^{-1} at 300 nm). The a_λ values determined in this study are slightly lower than values reported in the Weddell–Scotia Sea confluence (Yocis et al., 2000) and along the Antarctic Peninsula (Sarpal et al., 1995; Yocis et al., 2000) (a_{300}, range 0.19–0.58 m^{-1}) and are similar to values obtained on a 2004–2005 Ross Sea cruise (a_{300}, range ~0.29–0.32 m^{-1}) during the latter stages of the *Phaeocystis antarctica* bloom and transition to a diatom-dominated bloom (Kieber et al., 2007). These published findings, along with results from our transect study and Ross Sea sampling, suggest that relatively low values of a_λ are a general feature of Antarctic waters. By comparison, a_{300} values in the Bering Strait–Chukchi Sea are higher, ranging from 0.3 to 2.1 m^{-1}, with an average of 1.1 m^{-1} ($n = 62$) (Ferenac, 2006). Similarly high a_{300} values in the Greenland Sea (Stedmon and Markager, 2001) suggest that a_λ values in the Antarctic are generally lower than those in Arctic waters, perhaps due to terrestrial inputs of DOM in the Arctic (Opsahl et al., 1999) that are lacking in the Antarctic.

Although Ross Sea absorption coefficients were similar to those in the Sargasso Sea at longer wavelengths >350 nm, absorption coefficient spectra were different in the Ross Sea at shorter wavelengths (Figure 4), with higher a_λ seen between approximately 290 and 350 nm. To illustrate this point further, we computed a_{325} on all casts and depths (in the upper 140 m) during our cruise ($n = 68$) in order to directly compare them to results obtained by Nelson et al. (2007) in the Sargasso Sea. The a_{325} values obtained during the *Phaeocystis antarctica* bloom were, on average ($\pm$ SD) 0.142 (± 0.017) and 0.153 (± 0.023) m^{-1} (with an RSD of 12% and 15%) before and during the bloom, respectively, with no temporal trends noted. If we consider a_{325} before the bloom (0.142 m^{-1}) and subtract the calculated contribution due to nitrate (present at 30 μM in the photic zone), then the average a_{325} value due to CDOM is 0.120 m^{-1}. This is approximately a factor of 2.5 higher than a_{325} values reported by Nelson et al. (2007) in the surface Sargasso Sea (~0.05 m^{-1} at 325 nm) and reported by Morel et al. (2007) in the South Pacific gyre.

While our a_{325} values are higher than those Nelson et al. (2007) found in the Sargasso Sea, they are comparable to those Nelson et al. (2007) reported in the Subpolar Gyre (~0.14–0.26 m^{-1}), consistent with a slight poleward trend of increasing a_{325} in open ocean waters due to a poleward decrease in CDOM photolysis rates and an increase in mixed layer depth (Nelson and Siegel, 2002). However, since not all wavelengths showed the same difference between samples (see Figure 4; e.g., a_λ <290 nm were smaller in the Ross Sea compared to the Sargasso Sea), care should be taken in extrapolating trends for all wavelengths given that there are likely regional differences in spectral shapes due to differences in CDOM source and removal pathways.

The supposition that CDOM photobleaching rates are slow in Antarctic waters is supported by field evidence. When 0.2-μm-filtered Ross Sea seawater samples in quartz tubes were exposed to sunlight for approximately eight hours, no measurable CDOM photobleaching was observed. This contrasts results from the Sargasso Sea or other tropical and temperate waters, where ~10% loss in CDOM absorption coefficients is observed after six to eight hours of exposure to sunlight (D. J. Kieber, unpublished results). This difference is likely driven by lower actinic fluxes at polar latitudes. However, differences in DOM reactivity cannot be ruled out. In addition to direct photobleaching experiments, no evidence for photobleaching was observed in a_{CDOM} depth profiles. At 300 nm, for example, absorption coefficients were uniform in the upper 100 m or showed a slight increase near the surface (Figure 8), a trend that is opposite of what would be expected if CDOM photolysis (bleaching) controlled near-surface a_λ. It is also possible that mixing masked photobleaching, but this was not evaluated.

ABSORPTION COEFFICIENT AT 443 nm

Understanding what controls spatial and temporal trends in near-surface light attenuation is critical to accurately interpret remotely sensed ocean color data from the Sea-viewing Wide Field-of-view Sensor (SeaWiFS) or future missions (see Smith and Comiso, 2009, this volume). One of the primary limitations in using satellite ocean color data to model CDOM distributions is the lack of directly measured CDOM spectra in the oceans for model calibration and validation, particularly in open oceanic environments and polar waters (Siegel et al., 2002). The 443 waveband corresponds to the chl *a* absorption peak and is often used in bio-optical algorithms for pigment concentrations, although model estimates suggest that CDOM and detrital absorption account globally for >50% of total nonwater absorption at this wavelength (Siegel et al., 2002). During our cruise, chl *a* concentrations varied one-hundred-fold, while a_{443} varied approximately 35% and showed no correlation to chl *a*. In the upper water column, a_{443} was, on average ($\pm$ SD) 0.032 ($\pm$0.011) m^{-1}, with no difference observed in prebloom values (0.031 $\pm$ 0.011 m^{-1}) compared to values obtained during the bloom (0.033 $\pm$ 0.012 m^{-1}). These observations fall within the range of wintertime zonally predicted values for southern latitudes between approximately 60° and 75°S (~0.009–0.05 m^{-1}) (Siegel et al., 2002) and suggest that the phytoplankton bloom is not directly responsible for the observed CDOM absorption.

While we do not have direct observations to calculate the contribution of CDOM absorption to total absorption, $K_d(\lambda)$ values allow us to assess the contribution of CDOM to total light attenuation. $K_d(\lambda)$ calculated from upper ocean optical profiles is the sum of component $K_d(\lambda)$ from pure water, CDOM, and particulate material (phytoplankton and detritus). The contribution from particulate material can be determined using $K_d(\lambda)$ from pure water (Morel and Maritorena, 2001) in conjunction with measured CDOM absorption coefficients. To a first approximation the majority of the particulate matter is expected to be living phytoplankton, as the Ross Sea is spatially removed from sources of terrigenous material. At the prebloom station R10A, the chl *a* concentration in the upper 30 m was, on average ($\pm$SD), 0.51 ($\pm$0.04) μg L^{-1} and K_d(443) was relatively low (0.0684 m^{-1}). Pure water contributed 14.5% of the total attenuation at 443 nm while CDOM accounted for 42.8% ($\pm$4.7%) (avg $\pm$ RSD) of the nonwater absorption, with 57.2% ($\pm$4.7%) accounted for by particles. At the bloom station R14D, the average chl *a* concentration was an order of magnitude greater (6.87 $\pm$ 1.4 μg L^{-1}), and pure water contributed 2.1% of the total attenuation at 443 nm. Chromophoric dissolved organic matter accounted for only 3.5% ($\pm$0.9%) of the total nonwater attenuation, with particles contributing the remaining 96.5% ($\pm$0.9%). Not surprisingly, this confirms that the attenuation of blue and green wavelengths was dominated by particles and not by dissolved constituents during the bloom.

Many of the current suite of satellite algorithms (e.g., OC4v4, O'Reilly et al., 2000) have been shown to poorly predict chl *a* in the Southern Ocean, potentially because of the unique optical properties of large *Phaeocystis antarctica* colonies or the assumption that water column optical properties covary with chl *a* (e.g., Siegel et al., 2005). Our results confirm that semianalytical approaches, which individually solve for optical components, are necessary to describe the decoupling of CDOM and particulate mate-

rial during *Phaeocystis antarctica* blooms in the Ross Sea and ultimately allow accurate chl *a* retrievals.

Spectral Slope

The spectral slope (*S*) varies substantially in natural waters, and it has been used to provide information about the source, structure, and history of CDOM (Blough and Del Vecchio, 2002). However, while spectral slopes have been reported in the literature for a range of natural waters, they are nearly impossible to compare because of differences in how *S* values have been determined and because different wavelength ranges have been considered (Twardowski et al., 2004). Indeed, when we employed a nonlinear fitting routine to determine the spectral slope over several broad wavelength ranges, a range of *S* values was obtained for the same water sample [e.g., 0.0159 nm^{-1} (290–500 nm), 0.0124 nm^{-1} (320–500 nm), 0.0118 nm^{-1} (340–500 nm), 0.0133 nm^{-1} (360–500 nm), 0.0159 nm^{-1} (380–500 nm), 0.0164 nm^{-1} (400–500 nm)]. These variations in the slope indicate that Antarctic a_λ spectra do not fit a simple exponential function, as also observed by Sarpal et al. (1995) for samples along the Antarctic Peninsula. Therefore, instead of computing *S* over relatively broad wavelength ranges, we chose instead to compute *S* over two relatively narrow wavelength ranges proposed by Helms et al. (2008), 275–295 nm and 350–400 nm. These wavelength ranges were chosen because they can be determined with high precision and they are less prone to errors in how the data are mathematically fit relative to broad wavelength ranges (e.g., 290–700 nm; Helms et al., 2008). Additionally, the ratio, S_R, for these two wavelength ranges should facilitate comparison of different natural waters. In our study, the spectral slope between 275 and 295 nm was in all cases significantly higher than at 350–400 nm (~0.028 nm^{-1} versus ~0.013 nm^{-1}, respectively), and S_R was low, ranging between 1 and 3, with an average value of 2.32 (e.g., Figure 9C).

Our S_R are similar to coastal values observed in the Georgia Bight (avg $\pm$ SD: 1.75 $\pm$ 0.15) and elsewhere even though a_λ in coastal areas are much higher than we observed in the Ross Sea (e.g., >1 m^{-1} versus <0.3 m^{-1} at 300 nm, respectively). Likewise, the S_R values we found in the Ross Sea are much lower than those observed in open oceanic sites, where values as high as 9 or more have been observed (Helms et al., 2008). Helms et al. (2008) found a strong positive correlation between S_R and the relative proportion of low molecular weight DOM versus high molecular weight (HMW) DOM in the sample. If the results of Helms et al. can be extrapolated to Antarctic waters, then our low S_R results would suggest that the Ross Sea samples contained a relatively high proportion of HMW DOM compared to what is observed in oligotrophic waters. The relatively higher molecular weight DOM and low S_R in the Ross Sea may be related to the lower photobleaching rates that are observed in the Antarctic, since photobleaching is the main mechanism to increase S_R and remove HMW DOM (Helms et al., 2008).

CDOM SOURCE

The CDOM present in coastal areas near rivers and in estuaries in subtropical-temperate and northern boreal latitudes is predominantly of terrestrial origin (e.g., Blough et al., 1993; Blough and Del Vecchio, 2002; Rochelle-Newall and Fisher, 2002a), but in the open ocean, as in the Antarctic, terrigenous CDOM is only a minor component of the total DOM pool (Opsahl and Benner, 1997; Nelson and Siegel, 2002).

Phytoplankton are expected to be the main source of CDOM in the open ocean, although they are not thought to be directly responsible for CDOM production (Bricaud et al., 1981; Carder et al., 1989; Del Castillo et al., 2000; Nelson et al., 1998, 2004; Rochelle-Newall and Fisher 2002b; Ferenac, 2006). Our results are consistent with this finding (Figure 7). With no substantial grazing pressure (Rose and Caron, 2007, and as noted by our colleagues D. Caron and R. Gast during our cruise to the Ross Sea in early November 2005) and very low bacterial activity (Ducklow et al., 2001; Del Valle et al., in press), it is not surprising that CDOM a_{300} and a_{340} changed very little during the bloom. In fact, a_{300} did not apparently increase even during the latter stages of the Ross Sea *Phaeocystis antarctica* bloom when the microbial activity was higher (Kieber et al., 2007: fig. 5). This finding is rather remarkable since DOC is known to increase by ~50% during the *Phaeocystis antarctica* bloom from ~42 to >60 μM in the Ross Sea (Carlson et al., 1998). We also observed a DOC increase during our cruise from background levels (~43 μM at 130 m) to 53-μM DOC near the surface (based on one DOC profile obtained at our last station, R14F, on 30 November 2005). This difference suggests that the DOC increase was due to the release of nonchromophoric material by *Phaeocystis antarctica*. Field results support this supposition, showing that the main DOC produced by *Phaeocystis antarctica* is carbohydrates (Mathot et al., 2000).

The temporal and spatial decoupling between DOC and CDOM cycles in the Ross Sea photic zone indicate that CDOM was produced later in the season or elsewhere in the water column. Since evidence from Kieber et al. (2007) suggests that additional CDOM did not accumulate later in the season, it was likely produced elsewhere. Previous studies have shown that sea ice is a rich source of CDOM (Scully and Miller, 2000; Xie and Gosselin, 2005). It is therefore possible that the pack ice along the edges of the Polynya was an important source of CDOM in the photic zone, especially the bottom of the ice, which was visibly light brown with ice algae. It is also possible that CDOM was produced below the photic zone and reached the photic layer via vertical mixing. Several lines of evidence indicate that Ross Sea *Phaeocystis antarctica* may be exported out of the photic zone (DiTullio et al., 2000; Rellinger et al., in press) and perhaps reach the ocean floor (~900 m) (DiTullio et al., 2000), as seen in the Arctic. Arctic algal blooms often occur in the early spring when the water is still too cold for significant zooplankton grazing and bacterial growth (Overland and Stabeno, 2004). As a consequence, the algae sink out of the photic zone and settle to the ocean floor rather than being consumed, thereby providing a DOM source for long-term CDOM production in dark bottom waters. A similar phenomenon may occur in the Ross Sea. The possibility that CDOM may be generated in deep waters, with no photobleaching, might explain the high photosensitizing capacity of this CDOM for important reactions like DMS photolysis (Toole et al., 2004).

Deepwater production of CDOM in the Ross Sea would explain why our a_{325} values are comparable to those observed by Nelson et al. (2007: figs. 8–9) in deep water (~0.1–0.2 m^{-1}) and nearly the same as would be predicted on the basis of values in Antarctic Bottom Water and Antarctic Intermediate Water (average of ~0.13–0.14 m^{-1}). Although speculative, it is possible that CDOM is exported from the Southern Ocean to deep waters at temperate-subtropical latitudes, which would be consistent with CDOM as a tracer of oceanic circulation (Nelson et al., 2007).

CONCLUSIONS

Despite the necessity of understanding the spatial and temporal distributions of CDOM for remote sensing, photochemical, and biogeochemical applications, few measurements have been made in the Southern Ocean. Our results indicate that Antarctic CDOM shows spectral properties that are intermediate between what is observed in coastal environments and properties observed in the main oceanic gyres. We suggest this trend is largely due to slow photobleaching rates and shading from *Phaeocystis antarctica* and other bloom-forming species that contain substantial MAA.

While CDOM spectral absorption coefficients are low in Antarctic waters, they are generally higher than surface water a_λ in low-latitude, open-ocean waters, such as the Sargasso Sea, supporting the supposition of a poleward increase in a_{CDOM} in the open ocean. Our results suggest that CDOM in the Ross Sea is not coupled directly to algal production of organic matter in the photic zone. This indicates that case I bio-optical algorithms, in which all in-water constituents and the underwater light field are modeled to covary with chl *a* (e.g., Morel and Maritorena, 2001), are inappropriate. The decoupling of the phytoplankton bloom and CDOM dynamics indicates that CDOM is produced from sea ice or the microbial degradation of algal-derived dissolved organic matter that was exported out of the photic zone. Ross Sea CDOM absorption coefficients are similar in magnitude to values in Antarctic-influenced deep waters of the North Atlantic (Nelson et al., 2007), suggesting long-range transport of CDOM produced in the Ross Sea via Antarctic Intermediate and Bottom Water.

ACKNOWLEDGMENTS

This work was supported by the NSF (grant OPP-0230499, DJK; grant OPP-0230497, RPK). Any opinions, findings, and conclusions or recommendations expressed in this paper are those of the authors and do not necessarily reflect the views of the NSF. The authors gratefully acknowledge the chief scientists for the October–December 2005 Ross Sea cruise, Wade Jeffery (University of West Florida) and Patrick Neale (Smithsonian Environmental Research Center). Thanks are also extended to Patrick Neale, Wade Jeffery, and their research groups for collection of the optics profiles, and the captain and crew of the *Nathanial B. Palmer* for technical assistance. We also thank Joaquim Goes (Bigelow Laboratory for Ocean Sciences), Helga do S. Gomes (Bigelow Laboratory for Ocean Sciences), Cristina Sobrino (Smithsonian Environmental Research Center), George Westby (State University of New York, College of Environmental Science and Forestry: SUNY-ESF), John Bisgrove (SUNY-ESF), Hyakubun Harada (Dauphin Island Sea Lab, University of South Alabama), Jennifer Meeks (Dauphin Island Sea Lab, University of South Alabama), Jordan Brinkley (SUNY-ESF), and Daniela del Valle (Dauphin Island Sea Lab, University of South Alabama) for their technical help with sampling during this study.

LITERATURE CITED

Becquevort, S., and W. O. Smith Jr. 2001. Aggregation, Sedimentation and Biodegradability of Phytoplankton-Derived Material During Spring in the Ross Sea, Antarctica. *Deep-Sea Research, Part II*, 48: 4155–4178.

Blough, N. V., and R. Del Vecchio. 2002. "Chromophoric DOM in the Coastal Environment." In *Biogeochemistry of Marine Dissolved Organic Matter*, ed. D. A. Hansell and C. A. Carlson, pp. 509–546. San Diego: Academic Press.

Blough, N. V., O. C. Zafiriou, and J. Bonilla. 1993. Optical Absorption Spectra of Waters from the Orinoco River Outflow: Terrestrial Input of Colored Organic Matter to the Caribbean. *Journal of Geophysical Research*, 98:2271–2278.

Bricaud, A., A. Morel, and L. Prieur. 1981. Absorption by Dissolved Organic Matter of the Sea (Yellow Substance) in the UV and Visible Domains. *Limnology and Oceanography*, 26:43–53.

Carder, K. L., R. G. Steward, G. R. Harvey, and P. B. Ortner. 1989. Marine Humic and Fulvic Acids: Their Effects on Remote Sensing of Ocean Chlorophyll. *Limnology and Oceanography*, 34:68–81.

Carlson, C. A., H. W. Ducklow, D. A. Hansell, and W. O. Smith Jr. 1998. Organic Carbon Partitioning during Spring Phytoplankton Blooms in the Ross Sea Polynya and the Sargasso Sea. *Limnology and Oceanography*, 43:375–386.

Carlson, C. A., D. A. Hansell, E. T. Peltzer, and W. O. Smith Jr. 2000. Stocks and Dynamics of Dissolved and Particulate Organic Matter in the Southern Ross Sea, Antarctica. *Deep-Sea Research, Part II* 47:3201–3225.

Caron, D. A., M. R. Dennett, D. J. Lonsdale, D. M. Moran, and L. Shalapyonok. 2000. Microzooplankton Herbivory in the Ross Sea, Antarctica. *Deep-Sea Research, Part II*, 47:3249–3272.

Chen, R. F., P. Bissett, P. Coble, R. Conmy, G. B. Gardner, M. A. Moran, X. Wang, M. W. Wells, P. Whelan, and R. G. Zepp. 2004. Chromophoric Dissolved Organic Matter (CDOM) Source Characterization in the Louisiana Bight. *Marine Chemistry*, 89:257–272.

Del Castillo, C. E., F. Gilbes, P. G. Coble, and F. E. Muller-Karger. 2000. On the Dispersal of Riverine Colored Dissolved Organic Matter over the West Florida Shelf. *Limnology and Oceanography*, 45:1425–1432.

del Valle, D. A., D. J. Kieber, D. A. Toole, J. C. Brinkley, and R. P. Kiene. In press. Biological Consumption of Dimethylsulfide (DMS) and Its Importance in DMS Dynamics in the Ross Sea, Antarctica. *Limnology and Oceanography*.

Del Vecchio, R., and N. V. Blough. 2002. Photobleaching of Chromophoric Dissolved Organic Matter in Natural Waters: Kinetics and Modeling. *Marine Chemistry*, 78:231–253.

———. 2004. Spatial and Seasonal Distribution of Chromophoric Dissolved Organic Matter and Dissolved Organic Carbon in the Middle Atlantic Bight. *Marine Chemistry*, 89:169–187.

DiTullio, G. R., J. M. Grebmeier, K. R. Arrigo, M. P. Lizotte, D. H. Robinson, A. Leventer, J. P. Barry, M. L. VanWoert, and R. B. Dunbar. 2000. Rapid and Early Export of *Phaeocystis antarctica* Blooms in the Ross Sea, Antarctica. *Nature*, 404:595–598.

Ducklow, H., C. Carlson, M. Church, D. Kirchman, D. Smith, and G. Steward. 2001. The Seasonal Development of the Bacterioplankton Bloom in the Ross Sea, Antarctica, 1994–1997. *Deep-Sea Research, Part II*, 48:4199–4221.

Ferenac, M. A. 2006. Optical Properties of Chromophoric Dissolved Organic Matter (CDOM) in the Bering Strait and Chukchi Sea. Master's thesis, College of Environmental Science and Forestry, State University of New York, Syracuse.

Hebling, E. W., and H. Zagarese, eds. 2003. *UV Effects in Aquatic Organisms and Ecosystems*. Comprehensive Series in Photochemical and Photobiological Sciences, Vol. 1. Cambridge, U.K.: Royal Society of Chemistry.

Helms, J. R., A. Stubbins, J. D. Ritchie, E. C. Minor, D. J. Kieber, and K. Mopper. 2008. Absorption Spectral Slopes and Slope Ratios as Indicators of Molecular Weight, Source and Photobleaching of Chromophoric Dissolved Organic Matter. *Limnology and Oceanography*, 53:955–969.

Kieber, D. J., B. M. Peake, and N. M. Scully. 2003. "Reactive Oxygen Species in Aquatic Ecosystems." In *UV Effects in Aquatic Organisms and Ecosystems*, ed. E.W. Hebling and H. Zagarese, pp. 251–288. Comprehensive Series in Photochemical and Photobiological Sciences, Vol. 1. Cambridge, U.K.: Royal Society of Chemistry.

Kieber, D. J., D. A. Toole, J. J. Jankowski, R. P. Kiene, G. R. Westby, D. A. del Valle, and D. Slezak. 2007. Chemical "Light Meters" for Photochemical and Photobiological Studies. *Aquatic Sciences*, 69: 360–376.

Kiene, R. P., D. J. Kieber, D. Slezak, D. A. Toole, D. A. Del Valle, J. Bisgrove, J. Brinkley, and A. Rellinger. 2007. Distribution and Cycling of Dimethylsulfide, Dimethylsulfoniopropionate, and Dimethylsulfoxide During Spring and Early Summer in the Southern Ocean South of New Zealand. *Aquatic Sciences,* 69:305–319.

Laurion, I., F. Blouin and S. Roy. 2003. The Quantitative Filter Technique for Measuring Phytoplankton Absorption: Interference by MAAs in the UV Waveband. *Limnology and Oceanography: Methods*, 1:1–9.

Mathot, S., W. O. Smith Jr., C. A. Carlson, D. L. Garrison, M. M. Gowing, and C. L. Vickers. 2000. Carbon Partitioning Within *Phaeocystis antarctica* (Prymnesiophyceae) Colonies in the Ross Sea, Antarctica. *Journal of Phycology*, 36:1049–1056.

Mobley, C. D. 1994. *Light and Water: Radiative Transfer in Natural Waters*. San Diego: Academic Press.

Moisan, T. A., and B. G. Mitchell. 2001. UV Absorption by Mycosporine-Like Amino Acids in *Phaeocystis antarctica* Karsten Induced by Photosynthetically Available Radiation. *Marine Biology*, 138: 217–227.

Morel, A., and S. Maritorena. 2001. Bio-optical Properties of Oceanic Waters: A Reappraisal. *Journal of Geophysical Research*, 106: 7163–7180.

Morel, A., B. Gentili, H. Claustre, M. Babin, A. Bricaud, J. Ras, and F. Tieche. 2007. Optical Properties of the "Clearest" Natural Waters. *Limnology and Oceanography*, 52:217–229.

Nelson, N. B., and D. A. Siegel. 2002. "Chromophoric DOM in the open ocean." In *Biogeochemistry of Marine Dissolved Organic Matter*, ed. D. A. Hansell and C. A. Carlson, pp. 547–578. San Diego: Academic Press.

Nelson, N. B., D. A. Siegel, and A. F. Michaels. 1998. Seasonal Dynamics of Colored Dissolved Material in the Sargasso Sea. *Deep-Sea Research, Part I* 45:931–957.

Nelson, N. B., C. A. Carlson, and D. K. Steinberg. 2004. Production of Chromophoric Dissolved Organic Matter by Sargasso Sea Microbes. *Marine Chemistry*, 89:273–287.

Nelson, N. B., D. A. Siegel, C. A. Carlson, C. Swan, W. M. Smethie Jr., and S. Khatiwala. 2007. Hydrography of Chromophoric Dissolved Organic Matter in the North Atlantic. *Deep-Sea Research, Part I* 54:710–731.

Opsahl, S., and R. Benner. 1997. Distribution and Cycling of Terrigenous Dissolved Organic Matter in the Ocean. *Nature*, 386:480–482.

Opsahl, S., R. Benner, and R. M. W. Amon. 1999. Major Flux of Terrigenous Dissolved Organic Matter through the Arctic Ocean. *Limnology and Oceanography*, 44:2017–2023.

O'Reilly, J. E., S. Maritorena, D. A. Siegel, M. C. O'Brien, D. A. Toole, F. P. Chavez, P. Strutton, G. F. Cota, S. B. Hooker, C. R. McClain, K. L. Carder, F. Muller-Karger, L. Harding, A. Magnuson, D. Phinney, G. F. Moore, J. Aiken, K. R. Arrigo, R. Letelier, and M. Culver. 2000. Ocean Color Chlorophyll-*a* Algorithms for SeaWiFS, OC2 and OC4: Version 4. In *SeaWiFS Postlaunch Calibration and Validation Analyses: Part 3*, ed. S. B. Hooker and E. R. Firestone, pp. 9–23. NASA Technical Memorandum, No. 2000-206892, Volume 11. NASA Goddard Space Flight Center, Greenbelt, Md.

Overland, J. E., and P. J. Stabeno. 2004. Is the Climate of the Bering Sea Warming and Affecting the Ecosystem? *Eos, Transactions, American Geophysical Union*, 85:309–310, 312.

Patterson, K. W. 2000. Contribution of Chromophoric Dissolved Organic Matter to Attenuation of Ultraviolet Radiation in Three Contrasting Coastal Areas. Ph.D. diss., University of California, Santa Barbara.

Qian, J., and K. Mopper. 1996. Automated High-Performance, High-Temperature Combustion Total Organic Carbon Analyzer. *Analytical Chemistry*, 68:3090–3097.

Rellinger, A. N., R. P. Kiene, D. Slezak, D. A. del Valle, H. Harada, J. Bisgrove, D. J. Kieber, and J. Brinkley. In press. Occurrence and Turnover of DMSP and DMS in the Deep Waters of the Ross Sea, Antarctica. *Deep Sea Research, Part I*.

Riegger, L., and D. Robinson. 1997. Photoinduction of UV-Absorbing Compounds in Antarctic Diatoms and *Phaeocystis antarctica*. *Marine Ecology Progress Series*, 160:13–25.

Rochelle-Newall, E. J., and T. R. Fisher. 2002a. Chromophoric Dissolved Organic Matter and Dissolved Carbon in Chesapeake Bay. *Marine Chemistry*, 77:23–41.

———. 2002b. Production of Chromophoric Dissolved Organic Matter Fluorescence in Marine and Estuarine Environments: An Investigation into the Role of Phytoplankton. *Marine Chemistry*, 77: 7–21.

Rose, J. M., and D. A. Caron. 2007. Does Low Temperature Constrain the Growth Rates of Heterotrophic Protists? Evidence and Implications for Algal Blooms in Cold Waters. *Limnology and Oceanography*, 52:886–895.

Sarpal, R. S., K. Mopper, and D. J. Kieber. 1995. Absorbance Properties of Dissolved Organic Matter in Antarctic Waters. *Antarctic Journal of the United States*, 30:139–140.

Schindler, D. W., and P. J. Curtis. 1997. The Role of DOC in Protecting Freshwaters Subjected to Climatic Warming and Acidification from UV Exposure. *Biogeochemistry*, 36:1–8.

Scully, N. M., and W. L. Miller. 2000. Spatial and Temporal Dynamics of Colored Dissolved Organic Matter in the North Water Polynya. *Geophysical Research Letters*, 27:1009–1011.

Siegel, D. A., S. Maritorena, N. B. Nelson, D. A. Hansell, and M. Lorenzi-Kayser. 2002. Global Distribution and Dynamics of Colored Dissolved and Detrital Organic Materials. *Journal of Geophysical Research*, 107:3228, doi:10.1029/2001JC000965.

Siegel, D. A., S. Maritorena, N. B. Nelson, and M. J. Behrenfeld. 2005. Independence and Interdependencies of Global Ocean Color Properties: Reassessing the Bio-optical Assumption, *Journal of Geophysical Research*, 110:C07011, doi:10.1029/2004JC002527.

Smith, W. O., Jr., and J. C. Comiso. 2009. "Southern Ocean Primary Productivity: Variability and a View to the Future." In *Smithsonian at the Poles: Contributions to International Polar Year Science*, ed. I. Krupnik, M. A. Lang, and S. E. Miller, pp. 309–318. Washington, D.C.: Smithsonian Institution Scholarly Press.

Smith, W. O., Jr., J. Marra, M. R. Hiscock, and R. T. Barber. 2000. The Seasonal Cycle of Phytoplankton Biomass and Primary Productivity in the Ross Sea, Antarctica. *Deep-Sea Research, Part II*, 47:3119–3140.

Stedmon, C. A., and S. Markager. 2001. The Optics of Chromophoric Dissolved Organic Matter (CDOM) in the Greenland Sea: An Algorithm for Differentiation between Marine and Terrestrially

Derived Organic Matter. *Limnology and Oceanography*, 46: 2087–2093.

Strickland, J. D. H., and T. R. Parsons. 1968. A Practical Handbook of Seawater Analysis. *Bulletin of the Fisheries Research Board of Canada*, 167:1–311.

Toole, D. A., D. J. Kieber, R. P. Kiene, D. A. Siegel, and N. B. Nelson. 2003. Photolysis and the Dimethyl Sulfide (DMS) Summer Paradox in the Sargasso Sea. *Limnology and Oceanography*, 48:1088–1100.

Toole, D. A., D. J. Kieber, R. P. Kiene, E. M. White, J. Bisgrove, D. A. del Valle, and D. Slezak. 2004. High Dimethylsulfide Photolysis Rates in Nitrate-Rich Antarctic Waters. *Geophysical Research Letters*, 31:L11307, doi:10.1029/2004GL019863.

Twardowski, M. S., E. Boss, J. M. Sullivan, and P. L. Donaghay. 2004. Modeling the Spectral Shape of Absorption by Chromophoric Dissolved Organic Matter. *Marine Chemistry*, 89:69–88.

Vähätalo, A. V., and R. G. Wetzel. 2004. Photochemical and Microbial Decomposition of Chromophoric Dissolved Organic Matter during Long (Months-Years) Exposures. *Marine Chemistry*, 89:313–326.

Vodacek, A., N. V. Blough, M. D. DeGrandpre, E. T. Peltzer, and R. K. Nelson. 1997. Seasonal Variation of CDOM and DOC in the Middle Atlantic Bight: Terrestrial Inputs and Photooxidation. *Limnology and Oceanography*, 42:674–686.

Waters, K. J., R. C. Smith, and M. R. Lewis. 1990. Avoiding Ship-Induced Light-Field Perturbation in the Determination of Oceanic Optical Properties. *Oceanography,* 3:18–21.

Xie, H., and M. Gosselin. 2005. Photoproduction of Carbon Monoxide in First-Year Sea Ice in Franklin Bay, Southeastern Beaufort Sea. *Geophysical Research Letters,* 32:L12606. doi:10.1029/2005GL022803.

Yocis, B. H., D. J. Kieber, and K. Mopper. 2000. Photochemical Production of Hydrogen Peroxide in Antarctic Waters. *Deep-Sea Research, Part I* 47:1077–1099.

Capital Expenditure and Income (Foraging) during Pinniped Lactation: The Example of the Weddell Seal (*Leptonychotes weddellii*)

Regina Eisert and Olav T. Oftedal

ABSTRACT. Weddell seals, like many true seals (Phocidae), store nutrients in body tissues prior to lactation and then expend these "capital reserves" in pup rearing. During lactation, 40% or more of the initial mass of a lactating Weddell seal may be expended to cover the combined costs of maternal metabolism and milk production. However, most lactating Weddell seals also begin active diving to depths of 300 m or more by three to four weeks postpartum, and dietary biomarker data indicate that at least 70% of Weddell seals forage in late lactation. Thus, Weddell seals may employ a combined capital and income (foraging) strategy. Determining the relative importance of capital expenditures and food consumption to maternal reproduction will require accurate measurement of maternal energy expenditure, the magnitude of milk production, changes of maternal nutrient stores over lactation and the success of foraging efforts. Alternative scenarios include the following: (1) prey consumption is opportunistic rather than essential because body reserves of Weddell seals are sufficient for reproduction, (2) foraging is necessary only in those females (such as small or young seals) that have limited body stores relative to lactation costs, and (3) successful foraging is critical to the lactation strategy of this species. If alternative 2 or 3 is correct, the drops in pup production observed in Erebus Bay (McMurdo Sound, Ross Sea) during years of unusually heavy ice accumulation may reflect changes in foraging opportunities due to adverse impacts of heavy ice on primary production and on prey populations. Further study is needed on the effects of annual, cyclic, or long-term changes in prey abundance on Weddell seal reproduction.

INTRODUCTION

Mammalian reproduction is characterized by a period of lactation in which large quantities of nutrients are transferred from mother to young (Oftedal, 1984b). This process puts a great physiologic demand on the mother, who must either acquire the additional nutrients needed for milk secretion by increased food consumption, mobilize nutrients from stored reserves in the body, or employ some combination of both (Oftedal, 2000). Along the continuum from intensive foraging to sole dependence on stored reserves, mammals that rely mostly on feeding can be characterized as "income breeders," whereas those that rely on stored reserves are "capital breeders" (Jönsson, 1997). Income breeders are highly influenced by local climatic conditions that impact immediate food supply, whereas capital breeders should be relatively independent of food resources

Regina Eisert Conservation Ecology Center, National Zoological Park, Smithsonian Institution, P.O. Box 37012, MRC 5507, Washington, DC 20013-7012, USA. Olav T. Oftedal, Smithsonian Environmental Research Center, 647 Contees Wharf Road, Edgewater, MD 21037, USA. Corresponding author: R. Eisert (eisertr@si.edu). Accepted 28 May 2008.

during lactation by virtue of their previously stored body reserves.

Among Antarctic mammals, two groups rely heavily on stored reserves during lactation: baleen whales (suborder Mysticeti) and true seals (family Phocidae). Baleen whales, such as the blue whale (*Balaenoptera musculus*), fin whale (*Balaenoptera physalus*), humpback whale (*Megaptera novaeangliae*), and minke whale (*Balaenoptera acutorostrata*), migrate to Antarctic waters to forage on seasonal abundances of prey, such as krill, squid, and fish, and deposit large amounts of fat and other body constituents at this time (Lockyer, 1981, 1984; Oftedal, 1997). However, these baleen whales migrate back to subtropical or temperate regions to give birth and lactate. Stored energy and nutrients fuel most or all of lactation as these species feed little if at all at the calving grounds (Oftedal, 1997). Thus, baleen whales export substantial quantities of nutrients from the Southern Ocean to more temperate regions. By contrast, phocid seals, such as southern elephant seal (*Mirounga leonina*), crabeater seal (*Lobodon carcinophagus*), Ross seal (*Ommatophoca rossii*), leopard seal (*Hydrurga leptonyx*), and Weddell seal (*Leptonychotes weddellii*), both feed and lactate in Antarctic areas. Elephant seals typically remain on land and fast throughout a three to four week lactation (Arnbom et al., 1997) and are thus true capital breeders. On the basis of data from satellite-linked dive recorders, Ross seals are also capital breeders, as they haul out on pack ice for only about 13 days in mid-November to give birth and lactate (Blix and Nordøy, 2007). Unfortunately, little is known about reproduction in crabeater or leopard seals, but Weddell seals appear to employ a hybrid breeding approach: partly capital use and partly food consumption.

The ability to rely solely on stored reserves to support the energy and substrate demands of lactation is limited by body size (Oftedal, 2000). Nutrient reserves increase in direct proportion to body mass ($BM^{1.0}$), but rates of energy expenditure (including lactation) increase in proportion to body mass raised to the power of 3/4 ($BM^{0.75}$). Thus, the capacity to support metabolism and lactation from body stores alone increases with body size, and larger species can support metabolism and lactation from stored reserves for longer periods of time. The benefit of being able to store large quantities of nutrients for subsequent use was likely an important factor in the evolution of large body size in both seals and whales.

At 400–500 kg, the female Weddell seal is one of the largest of the phocid seals and has long been assumed to rely on stored reserves for lactation (Tedman and Green, 1987). If so, lactating Weddell seals should be relatively immune to environmental variables that affect local food supply in the areas where they give birth and lactate. However, population censuses have indicated tremendous variation (>50%) in annual pup production associated with changes in ice conditions in Erebus Bay in the Ross Sea (R. Garrott, Montana State University, personal communication, 2007). It is not known whether this variation is related to ice-related changes in prey abundance and diversity or to some other consequence of sea ice accumulation, such as navigational difficulties for seals traveling under the ice. A step in addressing this issue is to evaluate the importance of stored reserves versus acquisition of food to lactation performance of the Weddell seal.

In this paper we briefly discuss breeding strategy, mass change, lactation performance, and foraging by Weddell seals, with comparisons to other phocid species. This paper is a preliminary contribution based on a project in 2006–2007 examining energy expenditure, milk production, and changes in body reserves in lactating Weddell seals in McMurdo Sound, Antarctica.

EVOLUTION OF CAPITAL BREEDING AMONG PHOCID SEALS

Animals that employ capital breeding incur energetic costs associated with the deposition, transport, and mobilization of stores (Jönsson, 1997). The resulting energetic inefficiency is thought to favor "income breeding" except in specific circumstances such as uncertainty or inadequacy of food at the time of reproduction (Jönsson, 1997). However, among some capital breeders, such as phocid seals that fast during lactation, a major benefit appears to be abbreviation of lactation, with consequent reduction of maternal metabolic overhead and the time devoted to pup rearing. Milk production from stored reserves is also much more efficient than production based on food consumption (Agricultural Research Council, 1980), especially if foraging requires significant effort. This permits an increase in the proportion of energy available for transfer to the offspring (Fedak and Anderson, 1982; Costa et al., 1986). At the extreme, lactation is reduced to as little as four days in the hooded seal, with up to 88% of the energy transferred to pups incorporated into tissue growth (Bowen et al., 1985; Oftedal et al., 1993). Thus, it is not clear that capital breeding is always more energetically costly than income breeding. A variety of other parameters, including animal size, food availability, transport costs, neonatal developmental state, and type of maternal care, are thought to be important to the evolution of capital breeding systems (Boyd, 1998; Trillmich and Weissing, 2006; Houston et al., 2006).

There is also uncertainty whether maternal capital expenditure is limited primarily by energy or by nutrient stores, such as protein. In the fasting state, catabolized protein is lost continually from the body (Nordøy et al., 1990; Owen et al., 1998), and lactating mammals must export milk protein to support offspring growth. Yet excessive loss of body protein leads to progressive and eventually lethal loss of function (Oftedal, 1993; Liu and Barrett, 2002). Animals that fast during lactation typically produce milks that are low in both protein and carbohydrate (Oftedal, 1993). As both protein and carbohydrate in milk potentially derive from amino acids (either directly or via gluconeogenesis), this suggests that high protein demands may be selected against during the evolution of capital breeding (Oftedal, 1993). In the grey seal (*Halichoerus grypus*), daily milk production and final offspring mass were significantly correlated with initial maternal protein but not initial fat stores (Mellish et al., 1999a), despite the fact that most of maternal body energy reserves are stored as fat. Although phocid seals are often thought to be unusually efficient at conserving protein during fasting, this assumption may have to be reconsidered (Eisert, 2003). Thus, capital breeding may be limited by the size of protein stores as well as by the magnitude of energy stores.

Seals are the best-studied group of mammalian capital breeders (Oftedal et al., 1987a; Costa, 1991; Boness and Bowen, 1996; Boyd, 1998; Mellish et al., 2000; Oftedal, 2000; Schulz and Bowen, 2004). Otariid seals remain ashore for approximately one week after giving birth and transfer approximately 4% of body protein and 12% of body energy to their pups, after which they undertake regular foraging trips to sea (Oftedal et al., 1987a; Costa, 1991; Oftedal, 2000). This strategy of an initial fasting period followed by foraging cycles occurs in at least one phocid, the harbor seal *Phoca vitulina* (Boness et al., 1994), and perhaps in other species that feed during lactation [e.g., bearded seal *Erignathus barbatus*, harp seal *P. groenlandica*, and ringed seal *P. hispida* (Lydersen and Kovacs, 1996, 1999)]. However, many large phocids fast throughout the lactation period [e.g., land-breeding grey seal *H. grypus*, hooded seal *Cystophora cristata* and elephant seals *Mirounga angustirostris* and *M. leonina* (Fedak and Anderson, 1982; Costa et al., 1986; Oftedal et al., 1993; Arnbom et al., 1997)]. As the true seals (family Phocidae) encompass a wide spectrum from mixed capital-income to extreme capital breeding, this family is an excellent model system for testing hypotheses about the evolution of capital breeding strategies. Factors thought to have favored the evolution of

extreme capital breeding in phocids include large body size (Boness and Bowen, 1996; Oftedal, 2000), limited availability of food (Boyd, 1998), the impact of unstable nursing substrates (Oftedal et al., 1987a; Lydersen and Kovacs, 1999), and reduction of maternal metabolic overhead costs (Fedak and Anderson, 1982; Costa, 1991).

WEDDELL SEAL: EXAMPLE OF AN INTERMEDIATE STRATEGY?

The Weddell seal represents an interesting, if not fully understood, example of a species where a continuum of capital to mixed capital-income breeding strategies may occur within the same population. Lactating Weddell females fast and remain with their offspring for at least the first week postpartum, but on the basis of a new biomarker method of detecting feeding (Eisert et al., 2005), at least 70% of females feed to some extent during the latter half of a lactation period that lasts six to eight weeks (Bertram, 1940; Kaufmann et al., 1975; Thomas and DeMaster, 1983). During late lactation, an increase in diving activity (Hindell et al., 1999; Sato et al., 2002) and a decrease in rates of maternal mass loss relative to pup mass gain have also been observed (Hill, 1987; Testa et al., 1989). However, the importance of food intake to the energy and nutrient budgets or to reproductive success of lactating Weddell seals is not known, nor has the magnitude of capital expenditure (depletion of maternal body stores) been studied. Three scenarios appear possible: (1) Females are able to complete lactation without food intake but take prey opportunistically (until recently, the prevailing belief). (2) Because of individual differences in nutrient stores and reproductive demand, some females (such as small or young females) have an obligatory need for food intake, while others do not. (3) Food intake is an essential part of the lactation strategy of this species because maternal body stores are inadequate in the face of such an extended lactation period (the longest of any phocid).

Uncertainty regarding the dependency of lactating Weddell seals on local food resources complicates efforts to interpret the influence of environmental factors on maternal condition (Hill, 1987; Hastings and Testa, 1998), pup growth and survival (Bryden et al., 1984; Tedman, 1985; Tedman and Green, 1987; Testa et al., 1989; Burns and Testa, 1997), and population dynamics (Stirling, 1967; Siniff et al., 1977; Testa, 1987; Hastings and Testa, 1998). A strong dependency, in some or all females, on local food resources for successful lactation might limit breeding colonies to areas of local prey abundance or result in the vulnerability of populations to annual or long-term changes in prey availability, as might occur due to changes in sea ice or shifts in water currents.

MASS CHANGES DURING WEDDELL SEAL LACTATION

Prior work on Weddell seals has focused primarily on mass changes of mothers and their pups, under the assumption that if mothers are fasting, there should be correspondence between maternal mass loss, maternal milk output, and pup mass gain, as is the case in other true seals that fast throughout lactation. In these species, maternal body mass and age are strong determinants of total milk energy output and, consequently, of pup growth and weaning mass (Iverson et al., 1993; Fedak et al., 1996; Arnbom et al., 1997; Mellish et al., 1999b). By contrast, females feed during a variable proportion of lactation in almost half of extant phocid species (Bonner, 1984; Oftedal et al., 1987a; Boness et al., 1994; Boness and Bowen, 1996; Lydersen and Kovacs, 1999; Eisert, 2003). Bowen et al. (2001a) found that the positive correlation of maternal body mass with pup weaning mass was much weaker in harbor seals than in species that fast during lactation, presumably because supplementary feeding results in a partial decoupling of maternal mass loss and milk transfer to the pup. Similar patterns have been found in ice-breeding

grey seals *H. grypus* and harp seals *P. groenlandica* (Baker et al., 1995; Lydersen and Kovacs, 1996, 1999).

Extant data for Weddell seals are more complex. Weddell seal females certainly lose a large amount of body mass: for example, females that we studied in 2006 and 2007 lost 40% of their two-day postpartum mass during about 40 days lactation (Figure 1). The daily mass loss of 1.0% of initial mass is lower than values of 1.5%–3.4% for fasting and lactating females of the northern elephant seal, southern elephant seal, land-breeding gray seal, and hooded seal (Costa et al., 1986; Carlini et al., 1997; Mellish et al., 1999a, 1999b), but Weddell seal lactation is so prolonged that overall mass loss (42%) is equal to or greater than that in the other species (14%–39%). If mass loss is standardized to a lactation length of 42 days, initial mass predicts 66% of the variation in mass loss, indicating that large females lose more mass than small females (Figure 2). Is this because large females expend more energy (on metabolism and milk production) or because they feed less? Females that lose more mass also support more mass gain by their pups: pup mass gain was positively correlated to maternal mass loss (Figure 3). Tedman and Green (1987) found a similar strong positive correlation ($r = 0.85$, $P < 0.001$) between maternal mass loss and pup mass gain, whereas data from studies by Hill (1987) and Testa et al. (1989) indicate a much weaker correlation between maternal mass loss and pup mass gain ($r = 0.16$, $P = 0.005$, $n = 35$).

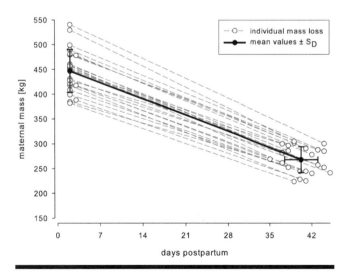

FIGURE 1. Change in body mass of lactating Weddell seals from early (2–3 days postpartum) to late (35–45 days postpartum) lactation at Hutton Cliffs, Erebus Bay, McMurdo Sound. Data were obtained from 24 females in 2006 and 2007. Average rate of mass loss was 1.0% of initial mass per day.

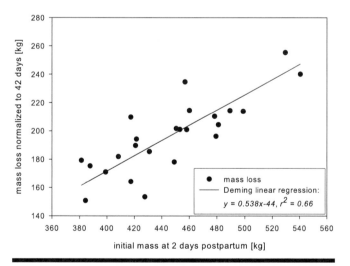

FIGURE 2. Relationship of maternal mass loss to initial maternal mass of lactating Weddell seals. Initial mass was measured at two to three days postpartum. Mass loss was normalized to 42 days and compared to initial mass by Deming linear regression. Data are from the same 24 females at Hutton Cliffs, Erebus Bay, McMurdo Sound, as in Figure 1.

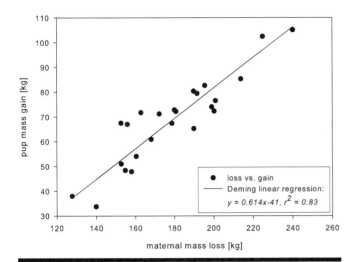

FIGURE 3. Pup mass gain in relation to maternal mass loss of lactating Weddell seals. Mother and pup data are paired (*n* = 24) and reflect the same time periods (from 2–3 days to 35–45 days postpartum) for both. Pup gain and maternal loss were compared by Deming linear regression.

This difference could stem from differences in the masses of animals studied: in our study and in that of Tedman and Green (1987) mean female mass was about 450 kg at the beginning of lactation, whereas the average in Hill's study was 406 kg. This suggests that the strength of the correlation of maternal mass loss and pup mass gain may increase with maternal size. Assuming that decoupling of maternal mass loss and pup growth in the Weddell seal can be attributed to foraging, feeding may be obligatory for small females but optional or opportunistic for large females (Testa et al., 1989).

ISOTOPIC MEASUREMENTS OF EXPENDITURES

Change in body mass alone is, at best, an imprecise measure of energy expenditure (Blaxter, 1989) and is invalid if animals are obtaining significant energy from food. The very high costs of lactation entail both metabolic costs (such as the energy expenditure associated with maternal attendance of pups and the energetic cost of milk synthesis) and substrate costs (the energy transferred into milk as fat, protein, carbohydrate, and minor constituents). Currently, the only method of accurately assessing metabolic energy expenditure in wild animals is the doubly labeled water (DLW) technique in which differences in the kinetics of hydrogen and oxygen isotopes provide an estimate of carbon dioxide production (see reviews by Nagy, 1980, and Speakman, 1997). Because of the high economic cost of ^{18}O-labeled water, this procedure has usually been applied to mammals of small body size (Speakman, 1997); among phocids it has been applied to pups (e.g., Kretzmann et al., 1993; Lydersen and Kovacs, 1996). However, the DLW method may provide valuable insight into maternal metabolic expenditures during lactation, as reported for sea lions and fur seals (e.g., Arnould et al., 1996; Costa and Gales, 2000, 2003). In Weddell seals it would be particularly interesting to know if metabolic energy expenditures vary in accord with diving activity, stage of lactation, and food consumption. In animals that fast, one would expect metabolic rates to decline over the course of the fast, whereas energy expenditures should increase with increases in activity and in association with digestion and metabolism of food constituents (e.g., Blaxter, 1989; Speakman, 1997). However, there remain a number of technical issues to overcome, including selection of an appropriate model of isotope behavior and estimation of average respiratory quotient (RQ, ratio of carbon dioxide production to oxygen consumption), which differs between fasting and feeding animals. Model and RQ errors can directly impact energetic estimates and thus need to be assessed (Speakman, 1997). There are also logistic problems in accurately administering water isotopes to large, unsedated animals living in very cold and windy environments, but these are not prohibitive: in 2006 and 2007, we successfully dosed about 20 lactating Weddell seals in Erebus Bay, McMurdo Sound, with doubly labeled water; sample analyses are still in progress.

The DLW method does not, however, measure export of substrates via milk. It is therefore also necessary to measure milk yield and milk composition to estimate reproductive costs associated with the output of milk constituents (Oftedal, 1984b). The most widely used method for estimating milk production in seals relies on the dilution of hydrogen isotope–labeled water in nursing young (e.g., Costa et al., 1986; Oftedal and Iverson, 1987; Oftedal et al., 1987b; Tedman and Green, 1987; Lydersen et al., 1992; Iverson et al., 1993; Lydersen and Hammill, 1993; Oftedal et al., 1993; Lydersen and Kovacs, 1996; Oftedal et al., 1996; Lydersen et al., 1997; Mellish et al., 1999a; Arnould and Hindell, 2002). If milk is the exclusive source of water (both free and metabolic) for the offspring, then milk consumption can be estimated from water turnover and milk composition (Oftedal and Iverson, 1987). The accuracy of this method depends on the ability to correct estimates of milk intake for isotope recycling (Baverstock and Green, 1975; Oftedal, 1984a), for changes in pool size (Dove and Freer, 1979; Oftedal,

1984a), and for any water obtained by offspring from sources other than milk (Holleman et al., 1975; Dove, 1988), such as consumption of prey, snow, or seawater and metabolic water production. Isotope studies have demonstrated that milk energy output in seals is inversely proportional to lactation length: seals with very short lactations, such as species that breed on unstable pack ice, have much higher daily energy outputs than species that breed on stable substrates, such as land and fast ice (Oftedal et al., 1987a).

The sole published attempt at measuring milk production in Weddell seals employed two isotopes (^2H and ^{22}Na) to determine if pups were ingesting water from sources other than milk (Tedman and Green, 1987). Tedman and Green argued that if pups were obtaining all or most of their water from milk, the sodium intake predicted from milk consumption (calculated milk intake from ^2H turnover multiplied by milk sodium content) would be similar to that estimated from turnover of ^{22}Na. As the observed discrepancy was not large, they concluded that intake of seawater or sodium-containing prey must have been minor (Tedman and Green, 1987). However, large (20%) underestimation of sodium intake occurs in ^{22}Na turnover measurements on suckling young (Green and Newgrain, 1979), and Tedman and Green (1987) do not state whether this error was corrected for in their study. The potential importance of nonmilk water as a confounding effect in isotope studies warrants further study, especially as Weddell pups have been observed to grab snow in their mouths and may consume it. At present, the Tedman and Green (1987) data are the only published data on Weddell seal lactation, and the estimated milk yield of about 3.5 kg/d or 160 kg milk over the lactation period has been cited repeatedly in comparative studies (e.g., Oftedal et al., 1987a, 1996; Costa, 1991; Boness and Bowen, 1996; Oftedal, 2000) but is in need of reevaluation.

In order to avoid possible errors caused by consumption of food or water by nursing Weddell seal pups, we recommend use of a two-hydrogen isotope method originally developed for terrestrial herbivores in which the suckling young begin to feed on solid foods during lactation (e.g., Holleman et al., 1975, 1988; Wright and Wolff, 1976; Oftedal, 1981; Dove, 1988; Carl and Robbins, 1988; Reese and Robbins, 1994). Water containing tritium (^3HHO) is given to the mother and water containing deuterium (^2H_2O) is given to offspring so that their body water pools are separately labeled. Thus, water turnover in mother and offspring can be measured independently.

In the pup, tritium concentrations rise so long as tritium intake (via milk water) exceeds tritium loss (via excretion), reaching a plateau when intake and loss are equal. In a Weddell seal pup this occurs after about two weeks (Figure 4). As tritium loss can be estimated from the rate of water turnover of the pup (measured from deuterium kinetics) and tritium intake equals milk tritium concentration multiplied by milk water intake, modeling of isotope fluxes allows calculation of mean water intake from milk. Unlike single isotope methods, this procedure allows milk water intake by the pup to be distinguished from influx of water from all other sources, such as drinking, feeding, and metabolic water production. Once milk water intake is known, milk production can be calculated from milk composition. We applied this dual-isotope method on about 20 Weddell pups in Erebus Bay, McMurdo Sound, in 2006 and 2007.

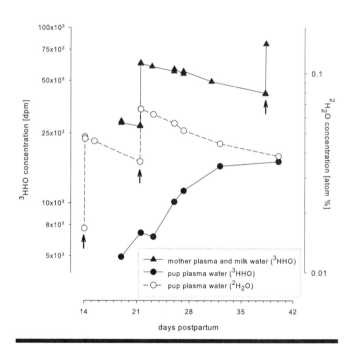

FIGURE 4. Illustration of the dual-isotope procedure for a Weddell seal mother and her pup. The mother was administered tritium-labeled (^3HHO) water and the pup was given deuterium-labeled water (^2H_2O) by intravenous infusion at the times indicated by vertical arrows. While deuterium levels (^2H_2O) declined following administration, tritium levels (^3HHO) in the pup rose towards a plateau level, indicating that tritium intake via milk water exceeded tritium losses of the pup over this time period. Deuterium was measured by isotope ratio mass spectrometry, and tritium was measured by scintillation counting. Mathematical modeling of isotope behavior indicated that milk intake was about 2.5 kg over this period.

MONITORING FOOD CONSUMPTION DURING THE LACTATION PERIOD

If Weddell seals did not enter the water during lactation, it would be obvious that they must be fasting, but this is not the case. Weddell seal mothers usually remain on the ice with their pups for the first one to two weeks of lactation, but then most mothers begin diving bouts that typically increase in frequency and length as lactation proceeds. The diving behavior of Weddell seals, including lactating females as well as nursing, weaned, and yearling animals, has been extensively investigated with time-depth recorders, or TDRs, including satellite-uplinked instruments (e.g., Kooyman, 1967; Testa et al., 1989; Burns et al., 1997, 1999; Castellini et al., 1992; Sato et al., 2002, 2003; Williams et al., 2004; Fuiman et al., 2007). The recent development of instrumentation that records directional information (Harcourt et al., 2000; Davis et al., 2001; Hindell et al., 2002; Mitani et al., 2003) allows examination of dive behavior in three-dimensional space. Although food intake requires diving, even deep diving need not entail food consumption. In other words, one cannot equate dive records to actual food intake unless food intake can be independently confirmed (Testa et al., 1989).

This has led to development of a number of different methods to monitor food intake. Classically, the diet of the Weddell seal has been examined by stomach content analysis (Bertram, 1940; Dearborn, 1965; Plötz, 1986; Plötz et al., 1991), but lethal methods are no longer employed, and gastric lavage of adults requires extensive restraint or chemical immobilization. Scat analysis can provide information on those prey that have identifiable indigestible parts (Burns et al., 1998; Lake et al., 2003) or even residual prey DNA (Casper et al., 2007) in the scats. However, the relative proportions of prey are difficult to quantify without extensive feeding trials to develop correction factors for the differential rates of digestion of prey. This is not feasible in free-ranging Weddell seals. In addition, the identity of the animal producing the scat and the time it was produced are often unknown. Occasionally, Weddell seals are observed to bring large prey, such as Antarctic toothfish (*Dissostichus mawsoni*) to holes in the ice (e.g., Caelhaem and Christoffel, 1969). Such observations can be extended by deploying animal-borne underwater cameras (Marshall, 1998; Davis et al., 1999; Bowen et al., 2002; Fuiman et al., 2002; Sato et al., 2002, 2003; Fuiman et al., 2007). Although dives in which potential prey are visible have been termed "foraging dives" (Fuiman et al. 2007), it is difficult to determine the success

of prey capture attempts from the images obtained. Of course, the images provide valuable information on hunting methods of seals at depth.

Another approach is to attach instruments in the mouth or digestive tract of seals to record feeding events. Sensors have been glued to the jaw of the seal that detect opening of the mouth (Bornemann et al., 1992; Plötz et al., 2001), but prey capture may be difficult to distinguish from other jaw movements during social behavior (e.g., threats and bites). Temperature-transmitting thermistors have been introduced into the stomach to monitor changes in the temperature of stomach contents associated with ingestion of cold items, such as ectothermic fish (Bornemann, 1994; Hedd et al., 1996; Austin et al., 2006a, 2006b; Kuhn and Costa, 2006). However, stomach temperature is also affected by other factors such as water ingestion, gastric blood flow, thermal mass of gastric contents and thermistor location, so that validation studies are essential to interpretation (Ponganis, 2007). Instruments may also require considerable intervention to attach (e.g., prolonged anesthesia), may alter animal behavior, or may require recaptures for data acquisition. Thus, there is still a need for a simple method of determining when food is actually consumed by free-living seals.

As an alternative approach, food energy intake of seals has been estimated from changes in whole-body water flux using isotope-labeled water (Costa, 1987; Bowen et al., 2001b). This method relies on the assumption that uptake of water from sources other than food (e.g., drinking) is minimal (Costa, 1987; Bowen et al., 2001b), yet seals are known to voluntarily consume both freshwater and seawater (Skalstad and Nordøy, 2000; Lea et al., 2002). Lactating Weddell seals have been observed to eat snow (Eisert and Oftedal, unpublished observations). This may lead to errors of unknown magnitude in both the detection and quantitation of food intake.

As a result of the difficulties in detecting and quantifying food intake, the energetics of lactation in the Weddell seal and in other species that feed during lactation are not well described (Schulz and Bowen, 2004). However, this may be improved by combining isotope methodology with new techniques for detecting feeding using biomarkers (Eisert et al., 2005). This approach allows food intake to be confirmed at a specific point in time from the presence in body fluids of dietary *biomarkers*, i.e., specific compounds that are absorbed intact from prey but are not generated by normal metabolic processes in the predator. On the basis of studies in Weddell seals, we have identified two suitable compounds, arsenobetaine (AsB) and trimethylamine

N-oxide (TMAO) (Eisert, 2003; Eisert et al., 2005). Both are specific to, and apparently ubiquitous in, marine prey yet are neither stored nor synthesized by higher vertebrates and in mammals are eliminated rapidly from the circulation following ingestion (Edmonds and Francesconi, 1977, 1987, 1988; Yancey et al., 1982; Vahter et al., 1983; Al-Waiz et al., 1987, 1992; Van Waarde, 1988; Cullen and Reimer, 1989; Brown et al., 1990; Shibata et al., 1992; Smith et al., 1994; Svensson et al., 1994; Zhang et al., 1999; Lehmann et al., 2001). The biomarker method provides information on recent food intake within a timescale of hours to days, in contrast to fatty acid signatures or stable isotopes in fluids or tissue samples, which integrate food intake over a period of months (Iverson et al., 1997a, 1997b; Brown et al., 1999).

Investigations of the incidence of foraging in lactating Weddell seals using the biomarker method (Eisert et al., 2005) revealed that (1) ~70% of females studied in late lactation (>27 days postpartum) had concentrations of AsB and TMAO indicative of recent food intake, (2) most females appear to fast for the first three to four weeks of lactation, in agreement with observed dive activity (Hindell et al., 2002), and (3) feeding may commence as early as eight to nine days postpartum in some females. These results suggest that the onset of feeding may vary substantially among lactating seals, and the possibility remains that some females fast throughout lactation. To clarify the dose-response and kinetic characteristics of AsB and TMAO in seals, we conducted validation trials in which varying doses of biomarkers were fed to juvenile hooded seals (*Cystophora cristata*) in captivity at the University of Tromsø in collaboration with E. S. Nordøy and A. S. Blix. Plasma TMAO peaked in about six to eight hours after intake and returned to low levels within 30 hours. Thus, biomarker methods may clarify whether a dive bout within a 24-hour period is associated with food capture, a considerable improvement over arbitrary assignment of dive shapes to foraging or nonforaging categories based on untested assumptions about prey hunting behavior.

ONTOGENY OF FORAGING IN WEDDELL SEAL PUPS

A disconnect between maternal mass loss and pup mass gain could also arise because (1) pups begin to forage independently during the lactation period, leading to mass gain without corresponding maternal loss, or (2) variation in the pattern of energy deposition (e.g., fat versus protein) alters the pattern of pup mass gain independent of maternal expenditures.

A prolonged period of dependence is characteristic of mammals in which development of social relationships appears to be important, such as in elephants, many primates, and some odontocete whales (West et al., 2007). However, phocid seals typically wean their pups abruptly, with departure of the mother from the breeding colony. Foraging by suckling pups has so far been described for only two phocid species, the ringed seal *Phoca hispida* and the bearded seal *Erignathus barbatus* (Lydersen and Kovacs, 1999). Nursing Weddell seal pups commence diving at about two weeks of age and, on average, perform in excess of 20 dives per day (Burns and Testa, 1997). Although mothers and pups may at times dive together (Sato et al., 2002, 2003), it is unclear whether this entails any "teaching" of the pup with regards to location, type, or capture of prey. There is a single published observation of the presence of milk and crustacean prey in the stomach of a Weddell seal pup (Lindsey, 1937), and pups have occasionally been observed bringing captured fish to the surface (K. Wheatley, University of Tasmania, personal communication, May 2004). It is possible that feeding by nursing pups could reflect an inadequate rate of maternal energy transfer during lactation (e.g., Hayssen, 1993), but it is not known if feeding by pups is common or exceptional in this species.

UNCERTAINTIES ABOUT THE WEDDELL SEAL STRATEGY

Much remains to be learned about the relative importance of foraging (income) versus stored reserves (capital) in the lactation strategies of Weddell seals at both individual and population levels. Weddell seals clearly rely extensively on stored reserves, but whether these are sufficient to support the demands of lactation in some or all females is uncertain. Foraging is much more prevalent during the lactation period than previously thought, but the magnitudes of energy and nutrient intakes are not known.

It seems likely that access to food resources is important to reproductive success at least during the second half of lactation, when most females forage. In years when heavy multiyear ice has failed to break out of McMurdo Sound due to giant icebergs that have blocked egress to the north, the numbers of Weddell pups born has been reduced by up to 50%–65% (R. Garrott, personal communication, 2007). By blocking light penetration the ice undoubtedly reduced primary productivity in McMurdo Sound, and this could result in a reduction in prey resources for Weddell seals. This may have led mothers to seek out alternative breeding sites in closer proximity to food resources, although the mechanism by which such choice is made is not known.

It would be especially valuable to examine the variation in foraging success and reproductive performance in different areas in the Antarctic where availability of food resources varies in time and space. How flexible are the reproductive strategies of Weddell seals? Does the relative importance of income versus capital breeding vary among populations or among years? How could the reproductive success of the Weddell seal be impacted by changes in ice or currents associated with global warming? In a world of change, we need sufficient background information on the resource needs of species to be able to predict future population trends.

ACKNOWLEDGMENTS

Weddell seal research at Hutton Cliffs, Erebus Bay, McMurdo Sound, Antarctica, in 1999 was supported by the Lottery Science Board New Zealand and the New Zealand Antarctic Program. Research at this site in 2006 and 2007 was supported by the National Science Foundation Office of Polar Programs (NSF-OPP award ANT-0538592) and authorized by permits issued by the National Marine Fisheries Service Office of Protected Resources (permit 763-1485-00) and NSF-OPP (Antarctic Conservation Act permit 2007-001). We thank our field teams for their hard work and dedication.

LITERATURE CITED

Agricultural Research Council. 1980. *The Nutrient Requirements of Ruminant Livestock*. Slough, U.K.: Commonwealth Agricultural Bureaux.

Al-Waiz, M., S. C. Mitchell, J. R. Idle, and R. L. Smith. 1987. The Metabolism of ^{14}C-Labelled Trimethylamine and Its N-Oxide in Man. *Xenobiotica*, 17(5):551–558.

Al-Waiz, M., M. Mikov, S. C. Mitchell, and R. L. Smith. 1992. The Exogenous Origin of Trimethylamine in the Mouse. *Metabolism—Clinical and Experimental*, 41:135–136.

Arnbom, T., M. A. Fedak, and I. L. Boyd. 1997. Factors Affecting Maternal Expenditure in Southern Elephant Seals during Lactation. *Ecology*, 78(2):471–483.

Arnould, J. P. Y., and M.A. Hindell. 2002. Milk Consumption, Body Composition and Pre-weaning Growth Rates of Australian Fur Seal (*Arctocephalus pusillus doriferus*) Pups. *Journal of Zoology*, 256: 351–359.

Arnould, J. P. Y., I. L. Boyd, and J. R. Speakman. 1996. The Relationship between Foraging Behaviour and Energy Expenditure in Antarctic Fur Seals. *Journal of Zoology*, 239:769–782.

Austin, D., W. D. Bowen, J. I. McMillan, and D. J. Boness. 2006a. Stomach Temperature Telemetry Reveals Temporal Patterns of Foraging Success in a Free-Ranging Marine Mammal. *Journal of Animal Ecology*, 75:408–420.

Austin, D., W. D. Bowen, J. I. McMillan, and S. J. Iverson. 2006b. Linking Movement, Diving, and Habitat to Foraging Success in a Large Marine Predator. *Ecology*, 87:3095–3108.

Baker, S. R., C. Barrette, and M. O. Hammill. 1995. Mass Transfer during Lactation of an Ice-Breeding Pinniped, the Grey Seal (*Halichoerus grypus*), in Nova Scotia, Canada. *Journal of Zoology*, 236: 531–542

Baverstock, P., and B. Green. 1975. Water Recycling in Lactation. *Science*, 187:657–658.

Bertram, G. C. L. 1940. The Biology of the Weddell and the Crabeater Seals. *British Graham Land Expedition Scientific Report*, 1:1–139.

Blaxter, K. L. 1989. *Energy Metabolism in Animals and Man*. Cambridge: Cambridge University Press.

Blix, A. S., and E. S. Nordøy. 2007. Ross Seal (*Ommatophoca rossii*) Annual Distribution, Diving Behaviour, Breeding and Moulting, off Queen Maud Land, Antarctica. *Polar Biology*, 30:1449–1458.

Boness, D. J., and W. D. Bowen. 1996. The Evolution of Maternal Care in Pinnipeds. *Bioscience*, 46(9):645–654.

Boness, D. J., W. D. Bowen, and O. T. Oftedal. 1994. Evidence of a Maternal Foraging Cycle Resembling That of Otariid Seals in a Small Phocid, the Harbor Seal. *Behavioural Ecology and Sociobiology*, 34(2):95–104.

Bonner, N.W. 1984. Lactation Strategies in Pinnipeds: Problems for a Marine Mammalian Group. *Symposia of the Zoological Society of London*, 51:253–272.

Bornemann, H. 1994. Untersuchungen zum Fressverhalten der Weddellrobbe (*Leptonychotes weddellii*) in der Antarktis. Ph.D. diss., Freie Universität Berlin, Berlin.

Bornemann, H., E. Mohr, and J. Plötz. 1992. Recording the Feeding Behavior of Freely Moving Animals Using the Example of Freely Diving Weddell Seals (*Leptonychotes weddellii*). *Zentralblatt für Veterinärmedizin, Reihe A*, 39(3):228–235.

Bowen, W. D., O. T. Oftedal, and D. J. Boness. 1985. Birth to Weaning in Four Days: Remarkable Growth in the Hooded Seal, *Cystophora cristata*. *Canadian Journal of Zoology*, 63:2841–2846.

Bowen, W. D., S. L. Ellis, S. J. Iverson, and D. J. Boness. 2001a. Maternal Effects on Offspring Growth Rate and Weaning Mass in Harbour Seals. *Canadian Journal of Zoology*, 79(6):1088–1101.

Bowen, W.D., S. J. Iverson, D. J. Boness, and O. T. Oftedal. 2001b. Foraging Effort, Food Intake and Lactation Performance Depend on Maternal Mass in a Small Phocid Seal. *Functional Ecology*, 15(3): 325–334

Bowen, W.D., D. Tully, D. J. Boness, B. M. Bulheier, and G. J. Marshall. 2002. Prey-Dependent Foraging Tactics and Prey Profitability in a Marine Mammal. *Marine Ecology Progress Series*, 244:235–245.

Boyd, I. L. 1998. Time and Energy Constraints in Pinniped Lactation. *American Naturalist*, 152(5):717–728.

Brown, D.J., I. L. Boyd, G. C. Cripps, and P. J. Butler. 1999. Fatty Acid Signature Analysis from the Milk of Antarctic Fur Seals and Southern Elephant Seals from South Georgia: Implications for Diet Determination. *Marine Ecology Progress Series*, 187:251–263.

Brown, R. M., D. Newton, C. J. Pickford, and J. C. Sherlock. 1990. Human Metabolism of Arsenobetaine Ingested with Fish. *Human and Experimental Toxicology*, 9(1):41–46.

Bryden, M., M. Smith, R. Tedman, and D. Featherston. 1984. Growth of the Weddell Seal, *Leptonychotes weddelli* (Pinnipedia). *Australian Journal of Zoology*, 32:33–41.

Burns, J. M., and J. W. Testa. 1997. "Developmental Changes and Diurnal and Seasonal Influences on the Diving Behaviour of Weddell Seal (*Leptonychotes weddellii*) Pups." In *Antarctic Communities:*

Species, Structure and Survival, ed. B. Battaglia, J. Valencia, and D. H. Walton, pp. 328–334. Cambridge: Cambridge University Press.

Burns, J. M., J. F. Schreer, and M. A. Castellini. 1997. Physiological Effects on Dive Patterns and Foraging Strategies in Yearling Weddell Seals (*Leptonychotes weddellii*). *Canadian Journal of Zoology*, 75: 1796–1810.

Burns, J. M., S. J. Trumble, M. A. Castellini, and J. W. Testa. 1998. The Diet of Weddell Seals in McMurdo Sound, Antarctica as Determined from Scat Collections and Stable Isotope Analysis. *Polar Biology*, 19(4):272–282.

Burns, J. M., M. A. Castellini, and J. W. Testa. 1999. Movements and Diving Behavior of Weaned Weddell Seal (*Leptonychotes weddellii*) Pups. *Polar Biology*, 21(1):23–36.

Caelhaem, I., and D. A. Christoffel. 1969. Some Observations of the Feeding Habits of a Weddell Seal, and Measurements of Its Prey *Dissostichus mawsoni* at McMurdo Sound, Antarctica. *New Zealand Journal of Marine and Freshwater Research*, 3(2):181–190.

Carl, G. R., and C. T. Robbins. 1988. The Energetic Cost of Predator Avoidance in Neonatal Ungulates: Hiding versus Following. *Canadian Journal of Zoology*, 66:239–246.

Carlini, J. I., G. A. Daneri, M. E. I. Marquez, G. E. Soave and S. Poljak. 1997. Mass Transfer from Mothers to Pups and Mass Recovery by Mothers during the Post-breeding Foraging Period in Southern Elephant Seals (*Mirounga leonina*) at King George Island. *Polar Biology*, 18:305–310.

Casper, R. M., S. N. Jarman, F. E. Deagle, N. J. Gales, and M. A. Hindell. 2007. Detecting Prey from DNA in Predator Scats: A Comparison with Morphological Analysis, Using Arctocephalus Seals Fed a Known Diet. *Journal of Experimental Marine Biology and Ecology*, 347:144–154.

Castellini, M. A., G. L. Kooyman, and P. J. Ponganis. 1992. Metabolic Rates of Freely Diving Weddell Seals—Correlations with Oxygen Stores, Swim Velocity and Diving Duration. *Journal of Experimental Biology*, 165:181–194.

Costa, D. P. 1987. "Isotopic Methods for Quantifying Material and Energy Intake of Free-Ranging Marine Mammals." In *Approaches to Marine Mammal Energetics*. Volume 1, ed. A.C. Huntley, D. P. Costa, G. A. J. Worthy, and M. A. Castellini, pp. 43–66. Lawrence, Kans.: Allen Press.

Costa, D. P. 1991. "Reproductive and Foraging Energetics of Pinnipeds: Implications for Life History Patterns." In *Behaviour of Pinnipeds*, ed. D. Renouf, pp. 300–344. London: Chapman and Hall.

Costa, D. P., and N. J. Gales. 2000. Foraging Energetics and Diving Behavior of Lactating New Zealand Sea Lions, *Phocarctos hookeri*. *Journal of Experimental Biology*, 203:3655–3665.

———. 2003. Energetics of a Benthic Diver: Seasonal Foraging Ecology of the Australian Sea Lion, *Neophoca cinerea*. *Ecological Monographs*, 73:27–43.

Costa, D. P., B. J. Le Boeuf, A. C. Huntley, and C. L. Ortiz. 1986. The Energetics of Lactation in the Northern Elephant Seal, *Mirounga angustirostris*. *Journal of Zoology*, 209:21–33.

Cullen, W. R., and K. J. Reimer. 1989. Arsenic Speciation in the Environment. *Chemical Reviews*, 89(4):713–764.

Davis, R. W., L. A. Fuiman, T. M. Williams, S. O. Collier, W. P. Hagey, S. B. Kanatous, S. Kohin, and M. Horning. 1999. Hunting Behaviour of a Marine Mammal beneath the Antarctic Fast Ice. *Science*, 283(5404):993–996.

Davis, R. W., L. A. Fuiman, T. M. Williams, and B. J. I. S. Le Boeuf. 2001. Three-Dimensional Movements and Swimming Activity of a Northern Elephant Seal. *Comparative Biochemistry and Physiology, Part A*, 129(4):759–770.

Dearborn, J. H. 1965. Food of Weddell Seals at McMurdo Sound, Antarctica. *Journal of Mammalogy*, 46(1):37–43.

Dove, H. 1988. Estimation of the Intake of Milk by Lambs, from the Turnover of Deuterium- or Tritium-Labelled Water. *British Journal of Nutrition*, 60:375–387.

Dove, H., and M. Freer. 1979. The Accuracy of Tritiated Water Turnover Rate as an Estimate of Milk Intake in Lambs. *Australian Journal of Agricultural Research*, 30:725–739.

Edmonds, J. S., and K. A. Francesconi. 1977. Isolation, Crystal Structure and Synthesis of Arsenobetaine, the Arsenical Constituent of the Western Rock Lobster *Panulirus longipes cygnus* George. *Tetrahedron Letters*, 18:1543–1546.

———. 1987. Transformations of Arsenic in the Marine Environment. *Experientia*, 43(5):553–557.

———. 1988. The Origin of Arsenobetaine in Marine Animals. *Applied Organometallic Chemistry*, 2:297–302.

Eisert, R. 2003. Energy Metabolism of Weddell Seals (*Leptonychotes weddellii*) during the Lactation Period. Ph.D. diss., Lincoln University, Canterbury, New Zealand.

Eisert, R., O. T. Oftedal, M. Lever, S. Ramdohr, B. H. Breier, and G. K. Barrell. 2005. Detection of Food Intake in a Marine Mammal Using Marine Osmolytes and Their Analogues as Dietary Biomarkers. *Marine Ecology Progress Series*, 300:213–228.

Fedak, M. A., and S. S. Anderson. 1982. The Energetics of Lactation: Accurate Measurements from a Large Wild Mammal, the Grey Seal (*Halichoerus grypus*). *Journal of Zoology*, 198:473–479.

Fedak, M. A., T. Arnbom, and I. L. Boyd. 1996. The Relation Between the Size of Southern Elephant Seal Mothers, the Growth of Their Pups, and the Use of Maternal Energy, Fat and Protein During Lactation. *Physiological Zoology*, 69(4):887–911.

Fuiman, L. A., R. W. Davis, and T. M. Williams. 2002. Behavior of Midwater Fishes under the Antarctic Ice: Observations by a Predator. *Marine Biology*, 140(4):815–822.

Fuiman, L. A., K. M. Madden, T. M. Williams, and R. W. Davis. 2007. Structure of Foraging Dives by Weddell Seals at an Offshore Isolated Hole in the Antarctic Fast-Ice Environment. *Deep-Sea Research, Part II*, 54:270–289.

Green, B., and K. Newgrain. 1979. Estimation of Milk Intake of Sucklings by Means of ²²Na. *Journal of Mammalogy*, 60:556–559.

Harcourt, R. G., M. A. Hindell, D. G. Bell, and J. R. Waas. 2000. Three-Dimensional Dive Profiles of Free-Ranging Weddell Seals. *Polar Biology*, 23(7):479–487.

Hastings, K. K., and J. W. Testa. 1998. Maternal and Birth Colony Effects on Survival of Weddell Seal Offspring from McMurdo Sound, Antarctica. *Journal of Animal Ecology*, 67(5):722–740.

Hayssen, V. 1993. Empirical and Theoretical Constraints on the Evolution of Lactation. *Journal of Dairy Science*, 76(10):3213–3233.

Hedd, A., R. Gales, and D. Renouf. 1996. Can Stomach Temperature Telemetry Be Used to Quantify Prey Consumption by Seals? A Reexamination. *Polar Biology*, 16(4):261–270.

Hill, S. E. B. 1987. Reproductive Ecology of Weddell Seals (*Leptonychotes weddelli*) in McMurdo Sound, Antarctica. Ph.D. diss., University of Minnesota, Minneapolis.

Hindell, M. A., R. G. Harcourt, D. Thompson, and J. R. Waas. 1999. Evidence for Foraging during Lactation in the Weddell Seal. Paper presented at the 13th Biennial Conference on the Biology of Marine Mammals. Society for Marine Mammalogy, Wailea, Maui, Hawaii.

Hindell, M. A., R. Harcourt, J. R. Waas, and D. Thompson, 2002. Fine-Scale Three-Dimensional Spatial Use by Diving, Lactating Female Weddell Seals *Leptonychotes weddellii*. *Marine Ecology Progress Series*, 242:275–284

Holleman, D. F., R. G. White, and J. R. Luick. 1975. New Isotope Methods for Estimating Milk Intake and Milk Yield. *Journal of Dairy Science*, 58:1814–1821.

Holleman, D. F., R. G. White, and P. G. Lambert. 1988. Analytical Procedures for Estimating Milk Intake and Yield in Steady-State and

Non-steady-State Systems. *Journal of Dairy Science*, 71(5):1189–1197.

Houston, A. I., P. A. Stephens, I. L. Boyd, K. C. Harding, and J. M. McNamara. 2006. Capital or Income Breeding? A Theoretical Model of Female Reproductive Strategies. *Behavioral Ecology*, 18: 241–250.

Iverson, S. J., W. D. Bowen, D. J. Boness, and O. T. Oftedal. 1993. The Effect of Maternal Size and Milk Energy Output on Pup Growth in Gray Seals (*Halichoerus grypus*). *Physiological Zoology*, 66(1): 61–88.

Iverson, S. J., J. P. Y. Arnould, and I. L. Boyd. 1997a. Milk Fatty Acid Signatures Indicate Both Major and Minor Shifts in the Diet of Lactating Antarctic Fur Seals. *Canadian Journal of Zoology*, 75(2): 188–197.

Iverson, S. J., K. J. Frost, and L. F. Lowry. 1997b. Fatty Acid Signatures Reveal Fine Scale Structure of Foraging Distribution of Harbor Seals and Their Prey in Prince William Sound, Alaska. *Marine Ecology Progress Series*, 151(1–3):255–271.

Jönsson, K. I. 1997. Capital and Income Breeding as Alternative Tactics of Resource Use in Reproduction. *Oikos*, 78(1):57–66.

Kaufmann, G. W., D. B. Siniff, and R. Reichle. 1975. "Colony Behavior of Weddell Seals, *Leptonychotes weddellii*, at Hutton Cliffs, Antarctica." In *Biology of the Seal: Proceedings of a Symposium Held in Guelph, Canada, 14–17 August 1972*, ed. K. Ronald and A. W. Mansfield, pp. 228–246. Rapports et Procès-Verbaux des Réunions, No. 169. Charlottenlund Slot, Denmark: Conseil International pour l'Exploration de la Mer.

Kooyman, G. L. 1967. "An Analysis of Some Behavioral and Physiological Characteristics Related to Diving in the Weddell Seal." In *Biology of the Antarctic Seas III*, ed. G. A. Llano and W. L. Schmitt, pp. 227–261. Antarctic Research Series, No. 11. Washington, D.C.: American Geophysical Union.

Kretzmann, M. B., D. P. Costa, and B. J. Leboeuf. 1993. Maternal Energy Investment in Elephant Seal Pups: Evidence for Sexual Equality? *American Naturalist*, 141(3):466–480.

Kuhn, C. E., and D. P. Costa. 2006. Identifying and Quantifying Prey Consumption Using Stomach Temperature Change in Pinnipeds. *Journal of Experimental Biology*, 209:4524–4532.

Lake, S., H. R. Burton, and J. van den Hoff. 2003. Regional, Temporal and Fine-Scale Spatial Variation in Weddell Seal Diet at Four Coastal Locations in East Antarctica. *Marine Ecology Progress Series*, 254:293–305.

Lea, M.A., F. Bonadonna, M. A. Hindell, C. Guinet, and S. D. Goldsworthy. 2002. Drinking Behaviour and Water Turnover Rates of Antarctic Fur Seal Pups: Implications for the Estimation of Milk Intake by Isotopic Dilution. *Comparative Biochemistry and Physiology, Part A*, 132(2):321–331.

Lehmann, B., E. Ebeling, and C. Alsen-Hinrichs. 2001. Kinetik von Arsen im Blut des Menschen nach einer Fischmahlzeit. [Kinetics of Arsenic in Human Blood after a Fish Meal.] *Gesundheitswesen*, 63(1):42–48

Lindsey, A. A. 1937. The Weddell Seal in the Bay of Whales, Antarctica. *Journal of Mammalogy*, 18(2):127–144.

Liu, Z. Q., and E. J. Barrett. 2002. Human Protein Metabolism: Its Measurement and Regulation. *American Journal of Physiology*, 283(6): E1105–E1112.

Lockyer, C. 1981. "Growth and Energy Budgets of Large Baleen Whales from the Southern Hemisphere." In *Mammals in the Seas*. Volume 3, pp. 379–487, FAO Fisheries Series, No. 5. Rome: Food and Agriculture Organization of the United Nations.

Lockyer, C. 1984. "Review of Baleen Whale (Mysticeti) Reproduction and Implications for Management." In *Reproduction in Whales, Dolphins, and Porpoises: Proceedings of the Conference, Cetacean Reproduction, Estimating Parameters for Stock Assessment and Management*, ed. William F. Perrin, Robert L. Brownell, and Douglas P. DeMaster, pp. 27–50. Reports of the International Whaling Commission, Special Issue, No. 6. Cambridge: International Whaling Commission.

Lydersen, C., and M. O. Hammill. 1993. Activity, Milk Intake and Energy Consumption in Free-Living Ringed Seal (*Phoca hispida*) Pups. *Journal of Comparative Physiology B*, 163:433–438.

Lydersen, C., M. O. Hammill, and M. S. Ryg. 1992. Water Flux and Mass Gain During Lactation in Free-Living Ringed Seal (*Phoca hispida*) Pups. *Journal of Zoology*, 228:361–369.

Lydersen, C., and K. M. Kovacs. 1996. Energetics of Lactation in Harp Seals (*Phoca groenlandica*) from the Gulf of St Lawrence, Canada. *Journal of Comparative Physiology*, 166(5):295–304.

———. 1999. Behaviour and Energetics of Ice-Breeding, North Atlantic Phocid Seals during the Lactation Period. *Marine Ecology Progress Series*, 187:265–281.

Lydersen, C., K. M. Kovacs, and M. O. Hammill. 1997. Energetics during Nursing and Early Postweaning Fasting in Hooded Seal (*Cystophora cristata*) Pups from the Gulf of St Lawrence, Canada. *Journal of Comparative Physiology B*, 167(2):81–88.

Marshall, G. J. 1998. CRITTERCAM: An Animal-Borne Imaging and Data Logging System. *Marine Technology Society Journal*, 32(1): 11–17.

Mellish, J. E., S. J. Iverson, and W. D. Bowen. 1999a. Variation in Milk Production and Lactation Performance in Grey Seals and Consequences for Pup Growth and Weaning Characteristics. *Physiological and Biochemical Zoology*, 72(6):677–690.

Mellish, J. E., S. J. Iverson, W. D. Bowen, and M. O. Hammill. 1999b. Fat Transfer and Energetics during Lactation in the Hooded Seal: The Roles of Tissue Lipoprotein Lipase in Milk Fat Secretion and Pup Blubber Deposition. *Journal of Comparative Physiology B*, 169(6):377–390.

Mellish, J. E., S. J. Iverson, and W. D. Bowen. 2000. Metabolic Compensation during High Energy Output in Fasting, Lactating Grey Seals (*Halichoerus grypus*): Metabolic Ceilings Revisited. *Proceedings of the Royal Society of London, Series B*, 267(1449):1245–1251.

Mitani, Y., K. Sato, S. Ito, M. F. Cameron, D. B. Siniff, and Y. Naito. 2003. A Method for Reconstructing Three-Dimensional Dive Profiles of Marine Mammals Using Geomagnetic Intensity Data: Results from Two Lactating Weddell Seals. *Polar Biology*, 26(5):311–317.

Nagy, K. A. 1980. CO_2 Production in Animals: Analysis of Potential Errors in the Doubly Labeled Water Method. *American Journal of Physiology*, 238:R466–R473.

Nordøy, E. S., O. C. Ingebretsen, and A. S. Blix. 1990. Depressed Metabolism and Low Protein Catabolism in Fasting Grey Seal Pups. *Acta Physiologica Scandinavica*, 139(2):361–369.

Oftedal, O. T. 1981. Milk, Protein and Energy Intakes of Suckling Mammalian Young: A Comparative Study. Ph.D. diss., Cornell University, Ithaca, N.Y.

———. 1984a. Lactation in the Dog: Milk Composition and Intake by Puppies. *Journal of Nutrition*, 114:803–812.

———. 1984b. Milk Composition, Milk Yield and Energy Output at Peak Lactation: A Comparative Review. *Symposia of the Zoological Society of London*, 51:33–85.

———. 1993. The Adaptation of Milk Secretion to the Constraints of Fasting in Bears, Seals and Baleen Whales. *Journal of Dairy Science*, 76(10):3234–3246.

———. 1997. Lactation in Whales and Dolphins: Evidence of Divergence Between Baleen and Toothed Species. *Journal of Mammary Gland Biology and Neoplasia*, 2:205–230.

———. 2000. Use of Maternal Reserves as a Lactation Strategy in Large Mammals. *Proceedings of the Nutrition Society*, 59(1):99–106.

Oftedal, O. T., and S. J. Iverson. 1987. "Hydrogen Isotope Methodology for the Measurement of Milk Intake and Energetics of Growth in

Suckling Young." In *Approaches to Marine Mammal Energetics,* ed. A. D. Huntley, D. P. Costa, G. A. J. Worthy, and M. A. Castellini, pp. 67–96. Lawrence, Kans.: Allen Press.

Oftedal, O .T., D. J. Boness, and R. A. Tedman. 1987a. "The Behavior, Physiology, and Anatomy of Lactation in the Pinnipedia." In *Current Mammalogy,* Volume 1, ed. H. Genoways, pp. 175–245. New York: Plenum Press.

Oftedal, O.T., S. J. Iverson, and D. J. Boness. 1987b. Milk and Energy Intakes of Suckling California Sea Lion *Zalophus californianus* Pups in Relation to Sex, Growth, and Predicted Maintenance Requirements. *Physiological Zoology,* 60(5):560–575.

Oftedal, O. T., W. D. Bowen, and D. J. Boness. 1993. Energy Transfer by Lactating Hooded Seals and Nutrient Deposition in Their Pups during the 4 Days from Birth to Weaning. *Physiological Zoology,* 66(3):412–436.

———. 1996. Lactation Performance and Nutrient Deposition in Pups of the Harp Seal, *Phoca groenlandica,* on Ice Floes off Southeast Labrador. *Physiological Zoology,* 69(3):635–657.

Owen, O. E., K. J. Smalley, D. A. D'alessio, M. A. Mozzoli, and E. K. Dawson. 1998. Protein, Fat, and Carbohydrate Requirements during Starvation: Anaplerosis and cataplerosis. *American Journal of Clinical Nutrition,* 68(1):12–34.

Plötz, J. 1986. Summer Diet of Weddell Seals (*Leptonychotes weddellii*) in the Eastern and Southern Weddell Sea, Antarctica. *Polar Biology,* 6(2):97–102.

Plötz, J., W. Ekau, and P. J. H. Reijnders. 1991. Diet of Weddell Seals *Leptonychotes weddellii* at Vestkapp, Eastern Weddell Sea (Antarctica), in Relation to Local Food Supply. *Marine Mammal Science,* 7(2):136–144.

Plötz, J., H. Bornemann, R. Knust, A. Schröder, and M. Bester. 2001. Foraging Behaviour of Weddell Seals, and Its Ecological Implications. *Polar Biology,* 24(12):901–909.

Ponganis, P. J. 2007. Bio-logging of Physiological Parameters in Higher Marine Vertebrates. *Deep-Sea Research, Part II,* 54:183–192.

Reese, E. O., and C. T. Robbins. 1994. Characteristics of Moose Lactation and Growth. *Canadian Journal of Zoology,* 72:953–957.

Sato, K., Y. Mitani, M. F. Cameron, D. B. Siniff, Y. Watanabe, and Y. Naito. 2002. Deep Foraging Dives in Relation to the Energy Depletion of Weddell Seal (*Leptonychotes weddelli*) Mothers during Lactation. *Polar Biology,* 25(9):696–702.

Sato, K., Y. Mitani, H. Kusagaya, and Y. Naito. 2003. Synchronous Shallow Dives by Weddell Seal Mother-Pup Pairs during Lactation. *Marine Mammal Science,* 19(2):384–395.

Schulz, T. M., and W. D. Bowen. 2004. Pinniped Lactation Strategies: Evaluation of Data on Maternal and Offspring Life History Traits. *Marine Mammal Science,* 20(1):86–114.

Shibata, Y., M. Morita, and K. Fuwa. 1992. Selenium and Arsenic in Biology: Their Chemical Forms and Biological Functions. *Advances in Biophysics,* 28:31–80.

Siniff, D. B., D. P. DeMaster, R. J. Hofman, and L. L. Eberhardt. 1977. An Analysis of the Dynamics of a Weddell Seal Population. *Ecological Monographs,* 47(3):319–335.

Skalstad, I., and E. S. Nordøy. 2000. Experimental Evidence of Seawater Drinking in Juvenile Hooded (*Cystophora cristata*) and Harp Seals (*Phoca groenlandica*). *Journal of Comparative Physiology B,* 170(5–6):395– 401.

Smith, J. L., J. S. Wishnock, and W. M. Deen. 1994. Metabolism and Excretion of Methylamines in Rats. *Toxicology and Applied Pharmacology,* 125(2):296–308.

Speakman, J. R. 1997. *Doubly Labelled Water: Theory and Practice.* London: Chapman and Hall.

Stirling, I. 1967. Population Studies on the Weddell Seal. *Tuatara,* 15(3): 133–141.

Svensson, B.-G., B. Åkesson, A. Nilsson, and K. Paulsson. 1994. Urinary Excretion of Methylamines in Men with Varying Intake of Fish from the Baltic Sea. *Journal of Toxicology and Environmental Health,* 41(4):411–420.

Tedman, R. 1985. "The Weddell Seal, *Leptonychotes weddelli,* at McMurdo Sound, Antarctica: Milk Production in Relation to Pup Growth." In *Studies of Sea Mammals in Southern Latitudes,* ed. J. K. Ling and M. M. Bryden, pp. 41–52. Sydney: South Australia Museum.

Tedman, R., and B. Green. 1987. Water and Sodium Fluxes and Lactational Energetics in Suckling Pups of Weddell Seals (*Leptonychotes weddellii*). *Journal of Zoology,* 212:29–42.

Testa, J. W. 1987. Long-Term Reproductive Patterns and Sighting Bias in Weddell Seals (*Leptonychotes weddellii*). *Canadian Journal of Zoology,* 65(5):1091–1099.

Testa, J. W., S. E. B. Hill, and D. B. Siniff. 1989. Diving Behavior and Maternal Investment in Weddell Seals (*Leptonychotes weddellii*). *Marine Mammal Science,* 5(4):399–405.

Thomas, J. A., and D. P. DeMaster. 1983. Diel Haul-out Patterns of Weddell Seal (*Leptonychotes weddellii*) Females and Their Pups. *Canadian Journal of Zoology,* 61(9):2084–2086.

Trillmich, F., and F. J. Weissing. 2006. Lactation Patterns of Pinnipeds Are Not Explained by Optimization of Maternal Energy Delivery Rates. *Behavioral Ecology and Sociobiology,* 60:137–149.

Vahter, M., E. Marafante, and L. Dencker. 1983. Metabolism of Arsenobetaine in Mice, Rats and Rabbits. *Science of the Total Environment,* 30:197–211.

Van Waarde, A. 1988. Biochemistry of Non-protein Nitrogenous Compounds in Fish Including the Use of Amino Acids for Anaerobic Energy Production. *Comparative Biochemistry and Physiology, Part B,* 91(2):207–228

West, K. L., O. T. Oftedal, C. Carpenter, B. J. Krames, M. Campbell, and J. C. Sweeney. 2007. Effect of Lactation Stage and Concurrent Pregnancy on Milk Composition in the Bottlenose Dolphin (*Tursiops truncatus*). *Journal of Zoology,* 273(2):148–160.

Williams, T. M., L. A. Fuiman, M. Horning, and R.W. Davis. 2004. The Cost of Foraging by a Marine Predator, the Weddell Seal *Leptonychotes weddellii:* Pricing by the Stroke. *Journal of Experimental Biology,* 207:973–982.

Wright, D. E., and J. E. Wolff. 1976. Measuring Milk Intake of Lambs Suckling Grazing Ewes by a Double Isotope Method. *Proceedings of the New Zealand Society of Animal Production,* 36:99–102.

Yancey, P. H., M. E. Clark, S. C. Hand, R. D. Bowlus, and G. N. Somero. 1982. Living with Water Stress: Evolution of Osmolyte Systems. *Science,* 217:1214–1222.

Zhang, A. Q., S. C. Mitchell, and R. L. Smith. 1999. Dietary Precursors of Trimethylamine in Man: A Pilot Study. *Food and Chemical Toxicology,* 37(5):515–520.

Latitudinal Patterns of Biological Invasions in Marine Ecosystems: A Polar Perspective

Gregory M. Ruiz and Chad L. Hewitt

ABSTRACT. Biological invasions in coastal ecosystems have occurred throughout Earth's history, but the scale and tempo have increased greatly in recent time due to human-mediated dispersal. Available data suggest that a strong latitudinal pattern exists for such human introductions in coastal systems. The documented number of introduced species (with established, self-sustaining populations) is greatest in temperate regions and declines sharply at higher latitudes. This observed invasion pattern across latitudes may result from differences in (1) historical baseline knowledge, (2) propagule supply, (3) resistance to invasion, and (4) disturbance regime. To date, the relative importance of these mechanisms across geographic regions has not been evaluated, and each may be expected to change over time. Of particular interest and concern are the interactive effects of climate change and human activities on marine invasions at high latitudes. Shifts in invasion dynamics may be especially pronounced in the Northern Hemisphere, where current models predict not only an increase in sea surface temperatures but also a rapid reduction in sea ice in the Arctic. These environmental changes may greatly increase invasion opportunity at high northern latitudes due to shipping, mineral exploration, shoreline development, and other human responses.

INTRODUCTION

The extent and significance of biological invasions in coastal marine ecosystems has become increasingly evident in recent years. On multiple continents, studies have described invasions by nonnative marine species, occurring primarily in shallow waters of bays and estuaries (e.g., Cohen and Carlton, 1995; Cranfield et al., 1998; Orensanz et al., 2002; Hewitt et al., 2004; Kerckhof et al., 2007; Fofonoff et al., in press). Although the ecological effects of most invasions have not been explored, it is evident that some nonnative species exert strong effects on the structure and function of invaded coastal ecosystems (Ruiz et al., 1999; Carlton, 2001; Grosholz, 2002).

Marine invasions have occurred throughout Earth's history, occurring sometimes as punctuated events in geologic time that correspond to changes in climate and dispersal barriers (e.g., Vermeij, 1991a, 1991b). However, invasions in modern time differ from those of the past, especially with respect to spatial and temporal scale. Most invasions are now driven primarily by the human-mediated transfer of organisms, instead of natural dispersal processes. As one consequence,

Gregory M. Ruiz, Smithsonian Environmental Research Center, 647 Contees Wharf Road, Edgewater, MD 21037, USA. Chad L. Hewitt, Australian Maritime College, University of Tasmania, Bag 1370, Launceston, Tasmania 7250, Australia. Corresponding author: G. Ruiz (ruizg@si.edu). Accepted 28 May 2008.

the potential range of dispersal is arguably less constrained than in the past, without the need for geographic adjacency. Marine organisms are now often moved quickly by humans across great distances and dispersal barriers (e.g., ocean basins, hemispheres, and continents), which were previously insurmountable in ecological timescales for most coastal species.

Human transport of organisms also has increased the rate of invasions in recent time. It is clear that the documented rate of marine invasions from human causes has increased dramatically, especially in the past 100–200 years, in many global regions (e.g., Cohen and Carlton, 1998; Hewitt et al., 1999, 2004; Wonham and Carlton, 2005). The current tempo of invasions may, in fact, be unprecedented, resulting from the massive and growing scope of global trade, but it remains challenging to estimate actual rates of invasion that adequately control for potential biases (Ruiz et al., 2000). Nonetheless, a broad consensus exists that the pace of invasions has increased sharply in many well-studied regions.

Despite considerable literature on patterns and processes of marine invasion, there is surprisingly little analysis of latitudinal patterns of invasion. In this paper, we review the current state of knowledge about human-mediated invasions (hereafter invasions or introductions) along a gradient from temperate to polar marine ecosystems, and we consider possible effects of climate change on invasions at high-latitudes. An extension of this comparison to tropical latitudes is the focus of future analyses.

TEMPERATE-POLAR PATTERN OF INVASIONS

For marine systems, most introductions (established, self-sustaining populations of nonnative species) are documented from temperate latitudes, including North America, Australia, Europe, New Zealand, and South America (see Cranfield et al., 1998; Hewitt et al., 1999, 2004; Reise et al., 1999; Ruiz et al., 2000; Hewitt, 2002; Orensanz et al., 2002; Castilla et al., 2005; Kerckhof et al., 2007; CIESM, 2007). While scores to hundreds of nonnative species are known from single bays and estuaries in temperate regions, few invasions are known from similar high-latitude sites, especially in polar regions.

This pattern is illustrated by the sharp decline in documented introductions with increasing latitude along western North America (Figure 1). In an analysis of available literature and collection records, Ruiz et al. (2006a) examined the number of nonnative marine invertebrate species reported from 12 large bays and estuaries (each including

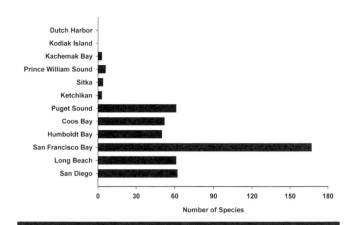

FIGURE 1. Total number of nonnative marine invertebrate species with established populations in bays along western North America. Data are summarized from species reported in the literature and collections in each of 12 sites from California to Alaska (from Ruiz et al., 2006a).

commercial ports) between 32° and 61°N latitude. For the six southernmost sites, from California to Washington, the number of documented introductions ranged from 50 to 170 species, with the largest number reported for San Francisco Bay (often the initial site for reported introductions that spread to other bays; see Cohen and Carlton, 1995, for further discussion). In contrast, the six northern sites in Alaska were at least one order of magnitude lower in the number of known introductions, ranging from 0 to 5 species.

For the entire Arctic (≥66°N), we are aware of only one nonnative marine species that is known to have an established population. The Alaskan king crab, *Paralithodes camtschaticus*, was intentionally introduced to the White Sea in the 1960s to establish a fishery and now occurs abundantly from Russia to Norway (Jorgensen, 2005). While other nonnative species have been reported for Arctic bioregions (e.g., Streftaris et al., 2005), it appears that such occurrences either have not been documented above 66°N or are not known to exist as established populations.

For the Antarctic (>60°S), two nonnative species have been reported recently, both on the Antarctic Peninsula, but neither are known to have established populations. Two specimens of the North Atlantic spider crab *Hyas araneus* were found in collections from 1986, including one male and one female (Tavares and De Melo, 2004). In addition, the European green alga *Ulva intestinalis* was also reported (Clayton, 1997); however, the morphological identification may be suspect. While these two species, and perhaps others, may have invaded the Antarctic, this has not been confirmed to date (Lewis et al., 2003, 2004; Clarke et al., 2005).

To some extent, the observed differences in nonnative species richness across latitudes may reflect bias in search effort and taxonomic knowledge, which undoubtedly declines from temperate regions to the poles. It is virtually certain that other nonnative species are present at high latitudes and have not been recognized because of either lack of sampling or insufficient taxonomic and biogeographic resolution. However, such differences in historical baseline are unlikely to account for the overall latitudinal pattern, especially when considering the larger, conspicuous organisms (e.g., decapods, shelled molluscs, and ascidians). This is further supported by recent surveys in Alaskan waters that found a paucity of nonnative sessile invertebrates relative to other sites in the continental United States (Ruiz et al., 2006a, unpublished data).

The poleward decline in invasions apparently results from latitudinal differences in propagule supply of nonnative species, resistance (or susceptibility) to invasion, or disturbance regimes. These may operate alone or in combination to produce the observed pattern of nonnative species richness. There exists theoretical and empirical support for the role of each factor in invasion dynamics (see Ruiz et al., 2000, and references therein), although these have not been evaluated for latitudinal patterns of marine invasions. Below, we consider each of these potential mechanisms and how they may contribute to observed patterns in further detail, focusing particular attention on western North America.

DIFFERENCES IN INVASION MECHANISMS ACROSS LATITUDES

PROPAGULE SUPPLY

The delivery pattern of organisms (propagules) greatly affects the likelihood of established populations. Propagule supply can be further divided into multiple components, including total number of propagules and the frequency (rate) and magnitude of inocula. Assuming suitable environmental conditions exist for a species to persist (including survival, growth, and successful reproduction), the likelihood of establishment is generally expected to increase with an increase in each component (Ruiz and Carlton, 2003; Lockwood et al., 2005; Johnston et al., in press).

Most marine introductions are thought to result from species transfers by vessels and live trade. For North America, at least 50% of introduced marine species have been attributed to commercial ships, which move species associated with their underwater surfaces and also in ballasted materials (Ruiz et al., 2000; Fofonoff et al., 2003; see Carlton, 1985, for description of the history and use of solid ballast and ballast water). After shipping, live trade is the second largest mechanism (vector) of marine introductions to North America, resulting from species transfers for aquaculture, fisheries, bait, and aquaria (e.g., Cohen and Carlton, 1995; Carlton, 2001; Fofonoff et al., in press); invasions from live trade include both the target species of interest as well as many associated species, such as epibiota, parasites, and pathogens. These two vectors are active and often dominant throughout the world, although their relative importance certainly varies in space and time (e.g., Cranfield et al., 1998; Hewitt et al., 1999; 2004; Orensanz et al., 2002; Wasson et al., 2001; Castilla et al., 2005; see also Ribera and Boudouresque, 1995; Ribera Siguan, 2003; Hewitt et al., 2007).

Once established, nonnative species often spread along the coast from the initial site of introduction. Some introduced marine species can expand their range in a new territory to encompass hundreds of kilometers (e.g., Grosholz, 1996; Thresher et al., 2005). This spread may occur by a combination of natural dispersal and anthropogenic means, depending upon the circumstances. Thus, invasion to a particular location can result by an initial introduction from distant sources or spread from an adjacent population. In general, proximity to potential source populations may often increase the chances of colonization, especially for the latter.

The current level of human activity, and especially shipping and live trade, is relatively low in polar regions, limiting opportunity for human-mediated transfers (e.g., Lewis et al., 2003, 2004). Moreover, the arrival of nonnative organisms from adjacent regions by natural dispersal is also likely to be low, resulting from a combination of low prevalence of nonnative species in adjacent regions and also the considerable distances or barriers that exist between potential sources for invasion of polar habitats.

It is informative to compare the magnitude of commercial shipping to various regions of the United States (Figure 2). For 2004–2005, far fewer ship arrivals occurred in Alaska compared to other regions at lower latitudes. Unlike the latter regions, most ship arrivals to Alaska were from domestic sources, originating from other U.S. ports (particularly those on the west coast) instead of foreign ports.

Importantly, even the current level of shipping to Alaska is only a very recent development, increasing substantially over just the past few decades. Although these temporal changes in shipping have not been fully quantified, an

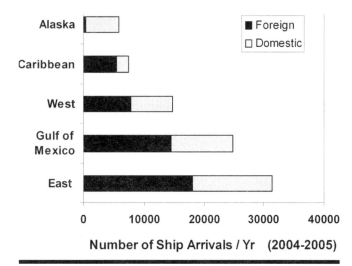

FIGURE 2. Estimated number of commercial ship arrivals per year (2004–2005) to regions of the United States. (Data are from Miller et al., 2007.)

obvious increase has occurred. This is best exemplified for oil tankers. Recent studies show a large number of marine organisms are delivered to Alaska in the ballast water of oil tankers. In 1998, it was estimated that oil tankers discharged a mean volume of 32,715 m³ of ballast water per arrival to Port Valdez (61°N), containing an average density of 12,637 plankton per m³ (as sampled by 80-μm mesh net, $n = 169$ vessels, chain-forming diatoms excluded; Hines and Ruiz, 2000). Most of these ships came from ports in California and Washington that are a potential source for many nonnative species (Figure 1). Over 17,000 oil tankers have arrived to Port Valdez since 1977, when the Alyeska pipeline was completed (Alyeska Pipeline Service Company, 2008). Prior to this date, tanker trade to Port Valdez simply did not exist.

While we can consider the number of arrivals to be a coarse proxy for ship-mediated propagule supply to a region, especially for a specific trade route and ship type (as above), this approach has clear limitations. Considerable variation exists among ships, voyage routes, and seasons in both the density and diversity of associated organisms (Smith et al., 1999; Coutts, 1999; Verling et al., 2005). In addition, the changing patterns of ship movements and trade present radically different invasion opportunities that are not captured in assessing the number of arrivals at one point in time (Hewitt et al., 1999, 2004; Minchin, 2006). As a result, the extent of species transfers by ships to locations is poorly resolved for any time period. Similar limitations exist for most other transfer mechanisms in coastal ecosystems, making it challenging to estimate the

actual propagule supply of nonnative species and provide direct comparisons across latitudes.

Despite existing information gaps, the magnitude of nonnative propagule supply (both historically and presently) has undoubtedly been low in polar regions. Historically, whaling and sealing activities, particularly in the Southern Ocean (Murphy, 1995), provided some opportunity for ship-mediated species transfer. Today, modern shipping continues to provide a transfer mechanism to high latitudes in both hemispheres (Hines and Ruiz, 2000; Lewis, 2003, 2004). However, compared to temperate latitudes, the number of ship arrivals and the diversity of routes (source ports) for the Arctic Ocean and Southern Ocean have been extremely limited. Rafting of marine species to the poles also appears to be low relative to lower latitudes (Barnes, 2002). Finally, natural dispersal of nonnative species is likely to be uncommon to both poles, perhaps especially in the Southern Hemisphere where distance and the Antarctic Circumpolar Circulation appear to create a significant dispersal barrier (see reviews by Clarke et al., 2005, and Barnes et al., 2006).

RESISTANCE TO INVASIONS

Independent of propagule supply, high latitudes may be more resistant (less susceptible) to invasions. This can result from environmental resistance, whereby physical or chemical conditions in the recipient environment are not conducive to survivorship, reproduction, and population growth. Alternatively, biotic resistance can result from predators, competitors, food resources or other biological interactions that limit colonization success.

There is support for environmental resistance to polar invasions due to the current temperature regime. In the Antarctic, low temperature is considered to be responsible through geologic time for the low diversity of decapod crustaceans, sharks, and other taxonomic groups and is also thought to operate today as a potential barrier to colonization (Thatje et al., 2005a, 2005b; Barnes et al., 2006; but see Lewis et al., 2003). This is, perhaps, best illustrated by research on lithodid crabs, which are physiologically unable to perform at the current polar temperatures (Aronson et al., 2007).

In the Northern Hemisphere, using environmental niche models, deRivera et al. (2007) found that the northern ranges of some introduced species (the crab *Carcinus maenas*, the periwinkle *Littorina saxatilis*, the ascidian *Styela clava*, and the barnacle *Amphibalanus improvisus*) along western North America are not limited by temperature. While none of these species appeared capable of colonizing the Arctic Ocean under current climatic conditions, their estimated ranges all included Alaskan waters (where they do not presently occur). Thus, available analyses indicate both Antarctic and Arctic waters are currently beyond the thermal tolerance for some species, but the extent to which invasions can occur in these polar regions is not known.

Temperature may often serve as a barrier to polar invasions by directly limiting larval development rate, which is highly temperature dependent (Thatje et al., 2003, 2005a, 2005b; deRivera et al., 2007). Many species are able to persist and grow at cold temperatures as juveniles or adults, compared to larvae that require warmer water for successful development to metamorphosis. High latitudes can also have short seasons when sufficient food exists to sustain larval development. These direct and indirect effects of temperature are thought to have greatly favored nonplanktotrophic larvae at high latitudes (see Thatje et al., 2005a, and references therein).

Aside from food limitation, the potential importance of biotic resistance for high-latitude marine invasions is largely unexplored. Specifically, it is not clear whether competition or predation would greatly affect invasion establishment at high latitudes, especially in comparison to more temperate regions. As discussed by deRivera et al. (2007), it is conceivable that biotic interactions operate to reduce the likelihood of invasions to Alaska, despite suitable environmental conditions, but this hypothesis has not been tested empirically. More broadly, understanding biotic resistance to invasion is a critical gap in marine systems.

DISTURBANCE REGIME

Disturbance can play an important role in invasion dynamics through a variety of mechanisms. In general, the role of disturbance in invasion ecology has focused on changes in biotic interactions, thereby reducing biotic resistance to invasion. This can result from changes in competition that affect availability of resources, such as open space for colonization, food, or nutrients. Alternatively, changes in predation pressure can increase invasion opportunities. While disturbance agents may operate directly to affect competition or predation, they can also have an indirect effect of these interactions. For example, changes in sediment or nutrient loading may cause a change in resident community structure (including species composition or abundance) that affects the strength of biotic interactions for newly arriving species.

In marine systems, literature on the role of disturbance in invasions has focused primarily on anthropogenic sources of disturbance (e.g., Ruiz et al., 1999; Piola and Johnston, 2006). Past studies have especially considered effects of fisheries exploitation, changes to habitat structure (whether physical or biological in nature), and chemical pollution. Invasions themselves have also been considered an important source of disturbance in cases where invasions either have (1) negative effects on resident biota by reducing biotic resistance (Grosholz, 2005) or (2) positive effects on newly arriving species by providing habitat, hosts, or food resources that were previously limiting (Simberloff and Von Holle, 1999).

Anthropogenic disturbance can clearly play an important role in invasion dynamics, in terms of both establishment and abundance of nonnative species, for which there is strong theoretical and empirical underpinning. While considered likely to be a key factor in the high diversity of nonnative species in some estuaries, such as San Francisco Bay (Cohen and Carlton, 1998), the relative contribution of disturbance to observed invasion histories is not well understood, as there are many confounding variables that vary among sites (Ruiz et al., 1999).

The magnitude of local and regional sources of anthropogenic disturbance has been low in high-latitude and polar marine systems to date, compared to lower latitudes, reflecting the low level of human activities. In contrast, climate change represents a global-scale and human-mediated disturbance, with pronounced effects expected for high latitudes (Arctic Climate Impact Assessment, 2005; Intergovernmental Panel on Climate Change (IPCC), 2007). While several researchers have begun to explore the potential effects of climate change to marine invasions (Stachowicz et al., 2002; Occhipinti-Ambrogi, 2007), they have focused primarily on effects of temperature at mid-latitudes. Below, we expand this scope to examine potential direct and indirect effects of projected temperature changes at high latitudes, considering especially the response of human activities and implications for changes in propagule supply, invasion resistance, and local/regional disturbance.

EFFECTS OF CLIMATE CHANGE ON INVASIONS

Climate change is expected to affect many dimensions of coastal ecosystems, including temperature regimes, sea level, upwelling, ocean currents, storm frequency and magnitude, and precipitation patterns, which will influence land-sourced runoff, leading to changes in nutrients and turbidity (IPCC, 2007). Shifts in these key physical processes are expected to cause myriad and complex changes to the structure, dynamics, and function of biological communities. The magnitude and rate of climate change are the focus of ongoing research, as are the expected changes to coastal ecosystems.

One of the clear effects of climate change is elevated sea surface temperature, which is expected to be greatest at high latitudes and includes the complete loss of Arctic sea ice in the summer (IPCC, 2007). While models estimate the seasonal disappearance of Arctic sea ice in the next 50–100 years, empirical measures suggest ice loss is occurring at a more rapid rate (Serreze et al., 2007; Stroeve et al., 2007, 2008). In contrast, no trend in sea ice change has been detected in the Antarctic (Cavalieri et al., 2003; but see Levebvre and Goosse, 2008). In Table 1, we consider some consequences of climate change in polar ecosystems for invasions, comparing potential responses in the Arctic and Antarctic. Our goal is to explore how the direct effects of climate and indirect effects on human activities (in response to climatic shifts and associated opportunities) may affect invasion dynamics at high latitudes.

Temperature is expected to have a direct effect on environmental resistance to invasion. It is clear that thermal regime sets range limits of many species, and these species are expected to shift in response to changing temperatures (Stachowicz et al., 2002; Occhipinti-Ambrogi, 2007). The projected changes for the Arctic and Antarctic waters should allow species invasions (both natural and human-mediated) to occur that are not possible now due to constraints in thermal tolerance and possibly food availability (e.g., Thatje et al., 2005a; deRivera et al., 2007; Aronson et al., 2007). Thus, we hypothesize increased invasions at both poles (Table 1), caused by natural dispersal and human-aided transport. However, the rate of new invasions may differ greatly between Arctic and Antarctic ecosystems, depending upon the interaction of temperature, propagule supply, and invasion resistance.

Currents are expected to shift as a component of climate change and will no doubt affect propagule supply. While considerable uncertainty exists about changes in ocean currents, we hypothesize (Table 1) that especially strong effects of currents on propagule supply may occur across the Arctic Ocean due to (1) loss of sea ice, potentially allowing greater water movement, and (2) the continuous nature of the shoreline, providing adjacent source communities for transport. It appears likely that these adjacent communities will increase in species richness with rising temperature as many native and nonnative species expand their northern range limits in response. We posit that currents would therefore operate with temperature to facilitate species transport and coastwise spread across the Arctic. While currents can also supply larvae to the Antarctic (Barnes et al., 2006), we do not expect an analogous and increasing role with temperature rise there (Table 1),

TABLE 1. Hypothesized effects of climate change on invasion dynamics in Arctic and Antarctic ecosystems. A plus (+) indicates projected increase in invasion resulting from specified independent variables and response variables (mechanisms that affect invasion dynamics); a dash (—) indicates no expected effect or ambiguous outcome.

Agent	Independent variable(s)	Response variable(s)	Projected changes for invasions	
			Arctic	Antarctic
Climate	Temperature	Environmental resistance	+	+
	Currents	Dispersal	+	—
Commercial shipping	Number of ship transits	Dispersal, disturbance	+	—
	Shift in trade routes	Dispersal	+	—
Shoreline development	Port development	Dispersal, disturbance, new habitat	+	—
	Shoreline development	Disturbance, new habitat	+	—
	Mineral extraction	Dispersal, disturbance, new habitat	+	—
Fisheries	Natural stocks	Dispersal, disturbance	+	—
	Aquaculture	Dispersal, disturbance, new habitat	+	—
Tourism	Number of visits	Dispersal, disturbance	+	+
Debris	Quantity of debris	Dispersal, disturbance	+	—

due in part to the great distances from other coastal habitats and adjacent populations as well as the nature of the continuous Antarctic Circumpolar Circulation that creates a significant dispersal barrier.

There is considerable historical precedent for trans-Arctic exchange of biota between the Pacific and the Atlantic. Vermeij (1991a) documented 295 species of molluscs that crossed the Arctic Ocean from the Pacific to the Atlantic (261 species) or in the reverse direction (34 species) after the opening of the Bering Strait in the early Pliocene. This analysis included both species that took part in the interchange and species that were descended from those that did. While the faunal exchange occurred in geologic time, it may have been punctuated and also underscores the potential for such current-mediated transport in the future. We are now exploring further the environmental conditions under which this interchange occurred to better understand its implication for expected climate change in the Arctic. It is also noteworthy that a diatom species of Pacific origin, *Neodenticula seminae*, was recently discovered in the North Atlantic, where it now appears to be well established (Reid et al., 2007). The species, detected from collections in 1998, is thought to be a recent trans-Arctic exchange, although the possibility of ship-mediated introduction via ballast water cannot be excluded.

In response to projected temperature changes in polar regions, we expect major shifts in the level of many human activities that will affect marine invasion dynamics at high latitudes and elsewhere. Moreover, we hypothesize that the human responses and effects on invasions will be asymmetrical, with the greatest changes in the Northern Hemisphere (Table 1). The greatest effects (and greatest asymmetries) are likely to result from increases in commercial shipping and shoreline development, followed by fisheries and tourism.

As sea ice disappears in the Arctic, the opportunities for shipping and mineral (especially oil) exploitation increase dramatically. If the Arctic becomes safe for navigation, its use for commercial shipping would have strong economic incentive, reducing transit times and fuel costs. For example, the Northwest Passage between Europe and Asia is estimated to be approximately 9,000 km shorter than transiting the Panama Canal (Wilson et al., 2004). In addition, there is added expense (use fees) and often delays associated with the Panama Canal. Currently, 13,000–14,000 vessels transit the Panama Canal per year (Ruiz et al., 2006b), and approximately 75% of these vessels are on routes in the Northern Hemisphere. Thus, a large number of vessels could benefit from using an Arctic trade route, especially when considering additional ships

now transiting the Suez Canal that may also save time and expense on this new route.

A deflection of shipping routes into the Arctic has several likely consequences from an invasion perspective. First, this would greatly increase the number of ships transiting the polar waters and thereby increase the delivery of nonnative propagules associated with hulls and ballast tanks to high latitudes. The per-ship magnitude of this supply is not immediately clear as it depends upon source. Second, the source ports for transiting vessels would increase the diversity of organisms being delivered. Because few ships now visit Arctic water, they certainly do not include the full selection of geographic source ports (and associated biotic assemblages) of ships now transiting the Panama and Suez canals. Third, ships also have chemical discharges, whether intended or accidental (such as oil spills and leaching of active antifouling compounds), which represent a form of disturbance that may affect invasion resistance.

On a broader geographic scale, we expect the decrease in transit time may greatly improve survivorship of organisms associated with ballast water because survivorship in transit is time-dependent (Verling et al., 2005). The same is likely to be true for organisms on ships' hulls. Improved survivorship for either or both would result in increased propagule supply to subsequent ports of call, including major ports in Asia, Europe, and North America. While survivorship of shipborne organisms is time-dependent, the relative effects of transiting warm (Panama Canal) versus cold (Arctic) water will also affect the magnitude of change in mass flux of organisms among existing temperate ports. A cold temperature may serve to lower metabolic requirements, extending competency and survivorship of associated organisms. However, the overall effects of ambient temperature are likely to be complex, varying with species and source regions, and remain to be explored.

With warming temperatures and retreating sea ice, we expect a potentially large increase in shore-based activities in the Arctic, especially due to increase in mineral extraction and export. We consider three different but related activities that can result in increased invasion opportunity.

1. Commercial port development will occur on some scale to support oil extraction offshore, where large reserves exist. This will result in some increase in (1) propagule supply by ships, (2) local disturbance from chemical discharges from ship and port operations, and (3) local disturbance in the creation of novel habitat (rip rap, piers, etc.) associated with shoreline modifications. The latter is especially relevant given that many nonnative species are

found on such artificial substrates (Cohen and Carlton, 1995; Hewitt et al., 2004; Glasby et al., 2007), which may be especially important focal areas for colonization. If local export of oil occurs by shipping, this could greatly increase the scale of port development as well as propagule supply, as exemplified by oil export from Port Valdez (see above).

2. The scope of shoreline development, and especially associated habitat alteration and disturbance (as outlined above), is likely to exceed that for commercial shipping alone. Specifically, we expect some level of development to support oversight of territorial jurisdiction among Arctic countries, shore-based mineral extraction, tourism, and fisheries. It is difficult to gauge the potential scale of such development, although it is noteworthy that several countries have recently increased their presence in the Arctic (including military and surveying activities) in support of claims to Arctic territory and underlying mineral resources.

3. Offshore mineral extraction itself will also create opportunities for increased dispersal of propagules as well as some disturbance. It is not uncommon to use mobile drilling platforms for oil exploration, where the platforms are towed among sites at slow speeds. Although little studied, this movement can occur over great distances (i.e., across ocean basins) and may result in the transport organisms at much greater densities than found on operating ships because (1) the platforms sometimes reside at previous sites for long periods, accumulating dense assemblages of organisms, and (2) the speed of transport is relatively slow, increasing the chance that organisms will remain associated. To our knowledge, strategies to assess or to reduce the associated risk of species transfers have not been explored for mobile drilling platforms. As with port development, offshore oil platforms, when fixed, create artificial (novel) habitats and have some risk of chemical discharge, and both types of disturbance may affect susceptibility to invasion.

For the Antarctic, we do not expect commercial shipping or shoreline development to occur to any great extent, simply because the same economic drivers do not exist there at this point in time. There are not major shipping routes that would benefit from transiting near Antarctica, and access to mineral and other resources is restricted under the Antarctic Treaty System.

The potential exists for fisheries to expand much more rapidly in the Arctic than in the Antarctic. This difference results in large part from access. The Arctic is in relatively close proximity to current centers of population and human activity, and a considerable history of fisheries at northern

high latitudes already exists in the Arctic. In contrast, access to fisheries resources in Southern Ocean waters >60°S is managed under the Antarctic Treaty System, specifically the Convention on the Conservation of Antarctic Marine Living Resources. It is difficult to say whether aquaculture would occur to any extent in high-latitude systems; however, current aquaculture trends indicate that it is highly likely. As discussed for commercial shipping, fisheries activities can increase the levels of propagule supply and disturbance, with the latter resulting from operation of ships (and discharges), removing predators and competitors, and creating physical disturbance with fishing gear (especially bottom trawls; Thrush et al., 1995).

Tourism is already a growing industry to both the Arctic and Antarctic, and we expect this trend to continue. As with fishing, the scope for growth appears greater in the Arctic, simply because of distance and access (including cost). As most tourism occurs by ships, the potential consequences for invasions are as outlined previously.

Finally, we predict an increase in the quantity of human-derived floating debris to occur in the Arctic and surrounding high latitudes in the Northern Hemisphere, coincident with increased levels of shipping, shoreline development, fisheries, and tourism, as these are all potential sources for floating debris. While Barnes (2002) reported relatively few organisms colonizing floating debris at high latitudes, the number may also increase under warmer temperatures. Further, in the absence of sea ice in the summer, the potential for longer-distance transport of floating material across the Arctic exists. Thus, we surmise that floating debris may play an important future role in the inoculation and, especially, regional spread of species in the Arctic, in contrast to much smaller changes expected in the Antarctic.

CONCLUSIONS

At the present time, very few introduced species are known from marine ecosystems at high latitudes in either hemisphere, especially for polar regions. This low number most likely results from a combination of low propagule supply of nonnative species and environmental resistance to invasion due to cold water temperatures and seasonal fluctuations in resources. The relative lack of anthropogenic disturbance may also serve to limit invasion opportunity.

With projected increases in temperature and the disappearance of Arctic sea ice in summer, we should expect invasions to increase as (1) temperatures fall within the thermal tolerance limits of organisms that are arriving and (2) human-mediated responses to climate change increase the propagule supply and decrease the resistance to invasion (to the extent it exists) through disturbance. The change in invasion risk at high latitudes is expected to increase most in the Northern Hemisphere, driven by potentially large scale increases in the level of commercial shipping and shoreline development (especially associated with extraction of mineral resources). Fisheries, tourism, and floating debris also are likely to increase the opportunity for invasions, but to a much smaller degree.

The consequences of climate change for invasions at high latitudes deserve serious attention from a conservation and management perspective. While global shifts in climate (especially temperature) are underway and serve to increase chances of polar invasions, it appears that human responses to climate change will largely determine the number of invasions that occur. Although nonnative species can arrive to polar ecosystems by natural dispersal (Barnes et al., 2006), these regions are relatively isolated geographically, and the scope for human transport is far greater. Significant efforts should now focus on understanding and reducing the transfer of nonnative species to the poles, aiming to avoid the high number and significant impacts of introductions experienced in temperate waters.

Efforts to minimize invasion risk at lower latitudes have employed several approaches that are applicable and should be adopted in polar regions. These are conceptually simple, focusing especially on (1) prevention or reduction of species transport by human activities and (2) detection of invasions by nonnative species. In many nations, regulations exist to greatly reduce the delivery of organisms that pose some risk of invasions (Ruiz and Carlton, 2003). While these sometimes focus on specific species that are known to survive or cause significant impacts in a region, many strategies are now aimed at reducing transfers of all organisms associated with a known vector, especially because the number of potential species is vast and the risks of colonization and impacts are simply not known (i.e., have not been examined) for most species. As an example, this approach of vector management is now being applied to commercial ships in many countries, where ships are required to treat their ballast water before discharging in coastal areas, reducing the concentrations of all coastal organisms (e.g., Minton et al., 2005).

A comprehensive effort to reduce species transfers should include an assessment of potential human-mediated vectors as the basis for developing and implementing vector management (Ruiz and Carlton, 2003). For polar systems, policies could be adopted immediately to reduce

transfers by commercial ships, extending efforts developed in temperate latitudes, since ships' ballast water and hulls are known to carry a risk of invasions (Ruiz et al., 2000; Fofonoff et al., 2003; Hewitt et al., 2004). Analyses of additional present and future vectors, such as oil drilling platforms and fisheries activities, would be obvious next steps to estimate the potential magnitude of species transfers and to consider options for vector management.

In addition to vector management, efforts to detect invasions and to measure temporal changes in invasions should be established in polar regions. Ideally, this would include an initial baseline survey and repeated surveys through time designed explicitly to test hypotheses about invasions (e.g., Ruiz and Hewitt, 2002) and address several management needs. First, these data would provide a measure of whether invasions are occurring and help identify specific vector(s) for management, providing feedback on how well management strategies are working to limit invasions (Ruiz and Carlton, 2003). Second, resulting detections of new invasions would also enable efforts to eradicate or control invasions, as deemed desirable.

These strategies for prevention and detection are easily understood, but implementation is not so easy to achieve. Often, there are issues related to resources (time and funding), limiting the desired scope of effort. In addition, there can be issues related to jurisdiction that further complicate implementation, resulting from political (geographic) boundaries and institutional (legal) authorities. Unfortunately, in temperate marine systems, these impediments to effective management strategies are often not overcome until a threshold of significant ecological or economic impacts is reached.

Since few invasions are known for polar systems to date, the opportunity now exists to implement management and policy that would greatly limit invasions and their unwanted impacts in these unique communities. Given the transboundary aspects of polar systems, there is a clear need for international cooperation and agreements in this area. We hope this article stimulates actions to evaluate and reduce invasion risks at high latitudes, applying the principals, methods, and experiences from temperate marine systems around the globe.

ACKNOWLEDGMENTS

We wish to thank Michael Lang at the Smithsonian Institution Office of the Under Secretary for Science for the opportunity to participate in the IPY Symposium. The content of this manuscript benefited from discussions with Gail Ashton, Paul Fofonoff, Amy Freestone, Tuck Hines, Mark

Minton, Whitman Miller, and Brian Steves, all of Smithsonian Environmental Research Center; Catherine deRivera, University of Portland; and Gretchen Lambert. Research in Alaska was supported by National Sea Grant Program, Prince William Sound Citizens' Advisory Council, Smithsonian Institution, and U.S. Fish and Wildlife Service.

LITERATURE CITED

Aleyeska Pipeline Service Company. About Us. *http://www.alyeska-pipe .com/about.html* (accessed 2 May 2008).

Arctic Climate Impact Assessment. 2005. *Arctic Climate Impact Assessment.* New York: Cambridge University Press.

Aronson, R., S. Thatje, A. Clarke, L. Peck, D. Blake, C. Silga, and B. Seibel. 2007. Climate Change and Invasibility of the Antarctic Benthos. *Annual Review of Ecology and Systematics,* 38:129–154.

Barnes, D .K. A. 2002. Invasions by Marine Life on Plastic Debris. *Nature,* 416:808–809.

Barnes, D. K. A., D. A. Hodgson, P. Convey, C. S. Allen, and A. Clarke. 2006. Incursion and Excursion of Antarctic Biota: Past, Present, and Future. *Global Ecology and Biogeography,* 15:121–142.

Carlton, J. T. 1985. Transoceanic and Interoceanic Dispersal of Coastal Marine Organisms: The Biology of Ballast Water. *Oceanography and Marine Biology: An Annual Review,* 23:313–371.

———. 2001. Introduced Species in US Coastal Waters: Environmental Impacts and Management Priorities. Pew Ocean Commissions, Arlington, Virginia.

Castilla, J. C., M. Uribe, N. Bahamonde, M. Clarke, R. Desqueyroux-Faúndez, I. Kong, H. Moyano, N. Rozbaczylo, B. Santilices, C. Valdovinos, and P. Zavala. 2005. Down under the Southeastern Pacific: Marine Non-indigenous Species in Chile. *Biological Invasions,* 7:213–232.

Cavalieri, D., C. Parkinson, and K. Vinnikov. 2003. 30-Year Satellite Record Reveals Contrasting Arctic and Antarctic Decadal Sea-Ice Variability. *Geophysical Research Letters,* 30(18):1970, doi:10.1029/2003GL018031.

CIESM. CIESM Atlas of Exotic Species in the Mediterranean. http://www.ciesm.org/online/atlas/intro.htm (accessed 1 June 2007).

Clarke, A., D. K. A. Barnes, and D. A. Hodgson. 2005. How Isolated is Antarctica? *Trends in Ecology and Evolution,* 20:1–3.

Clayton, M. N., C. Weincke, and H. Kloser. 1997. New Records of Temperate and Sub-Antarctic Marine Benthic Macroalgae from Antarctica. *Polar Biology,* 17:141–149.

Cohen, A. N., and J. T. Carlton. 1995. Biological Study: Non-indigenous Aquatic Species in a United States Estuary: A Case Study of the Biological Invasions of the San Francisco Bay and Delta. NTIS Report PB96-166525. U.S. Fisheries and Wildlife and National Sea Grant College Program, Springfield, Va.

———. 1998. Accelerating Invasion Rate in a Highly Invaded Estuary. *Science,* 279:555–558.

Coutts, A. D. M. 1999. Hull Fouling as a Modern Vector for Marine Biological Invasions: Investigation of Merchant Vessels Visiting Northern Tasmania. Master's thesis, Australian Maritime College, Launceston, Tasmania.

Cranfield, H. J., D. P. Gordon, R. C. Willan, B. A. Marshall, C. N. Battershill, M. P. Francis, W. A. Nelson, C. J. Glasby, and G. B. Read. 1998. Adventive Marine Species in New Zealand. NIWA Technical Report 34. National Institute of Water and Atmospheric Research, Wellington, New Zealand.

deRivera, C. E., B. P. Steves, G. M. Ruiz, P. Fofonoff and A. H. Hines. 2007. Northward Spread of Marine Nonindigenous Species along Western North America: Forecasting Risk of Colonization in Alaskan Waters Using Environmental Niche Modeling. Final Report. Regional Citizens' Advisory Council of Prince William Sound and the U.S. Fish and Wildlife Service, Anchorage, Alaska.

Fofonoff, P. W., G. M. Ruiz, B. Steves, and J. T. Carlton. 2003. "In Ships or on Ships? Mechanisms of Transfer and Invasion for Non-native Species to the Coasts of North America." In *Invasive Species: Vectors and Management Strategies,* ed. G. M. Ruiz and J. T. Carlton, pp. 152–182. Washington, D.C.: Island Press.

Fofonoff, P. W., G. M. Ruiz, A. H. Hines, B. D. Steves, and J. T. Carlton. In press. "Four Centuries of Estuarine Biological Invasions in the Chesapeake Bay Region." In *Marine Bioinvasions: Ecology, Conservation, and Management Perspectives,* ed. G. Rilov and J. Crooks. New York: Springer-Verlag.

Glasby, T. M., S. D. Connell, M. G. Holloway, and C. L. Hewitt. 2007. Facilitation of Marine Biological Invasions—The Role of Habitat Creation. *Marine Biology,* 151:887–895.

Grosholz, E. D. 1996. Contrasting Rates of Spread for Introduced Species in Terrestrial and Marine Systems. *Ecology,* 77:1680–1686.

———. 2002. Ecological and Evolutionary Consequences of Coastal Invasions. *Trends in Ecology and Evolution,* 17:22–27.

———. 2005. Recent Biological Invasion May Hasten Invasional Meltdown by Accelerating Historical Introductions. *Proceedings of the National Academy of Sciences,* 102:1088–1091.

Hewitt, C. L. 2002. The Distribution and Diversity of Tropical Australian Marine Bio-Invasions. *Pacific Science,* 56(2):213–222.

Hewitt, C. L., M. L. Campbell, R. E. Thresher, and R. B. Martin, eds. 1999. *Marine Biological Invasions of Port Phillip Bay, Victoria.* CRIMP Technical Report, No. 20. Hobart, Australia: CSIRO Division of Marine Research.

Hewitt, C. L., M. L. Campbell, R. E. Thresher, R. B. Martin, S. Boyd, B. F. Cohen, D. R. Currie, M. F. Gomon, M. J. Keogh, J. A. Lewis, M. M. Lockett, N. Mays, M. A. McArthur, T. D. O'Hara, G. C. B. Poore, D. J. Ross, M. J. Storey, J. E. Watson, and R. S. Wilson. 2004. Introduced and Cryptogenic Species in Port Phillip Bay, Victoria, Australia. *Marine Biology,* 144:183–202.

Hewitt, C. L., M. L. Campbell, and B. Schaffelke. 2007. Introductions of Marine Macroalgae—Accidental Transfer Pathways and Mechanisms. *Botanica Marina,* 50:326–337.

Hines, A. H., and G. M. Ruiz. 2000. Biological Invasions of Cold-Water Coastal Ecosystems: Ballast-Mediated Introductions in Port Valdez/ Prince William Sound, Alaska. Final Report. Regional Citizens' Advisory Council of Prince William Sound, Anchorage, Alaska.

Intergovernmental Panel on Climate Change. 2007. *Climate Change 2007: Synthesis Report. Contribution of Working Groups I, II, and III to the Fourth Assessment Report of the Intergovernmental Panel on Climate Change.* Geneva: Intergovernmental Panel on Climate Change.

International Maritime Organization. GloBallast Programme. http://globallast.imo.org (accessed 2 May 2008).

Johnston, E. L., R. Piola, and G. Clark. In press. "The Role of Propagule Pressure in Marine Invasions." In *Marine Bioinvasions: Ecology, Conservation, and Management Perspectives,* ed. G. Rilov and J. Crooks. New York: Springer-Verlag.

Jorgensen, L. L. 2005. Impact Scenario for an Introduced Decapod on Arctic Epibenthic Communities. *Biological Invasions,* 7:949–957.

Kerckhof, F., J. Haelters, and S. Gollasch. 2007. Alien Species in the Marine and Brackish Ecosystem: The Situation in Belgian Waters. *Aquatic Invasions,* 2:243–257.

Levebvre, W., and H. Goosse. 2008. Analysis of the Projected Regional Sea-Ice Changes in the Southern Ocean During the Twenty-First Century. *Climate Dynamics,* 30:59–76.

Lewis, P. N., C. L. Hewitt, M. Riddle, and A. McMinn. 2003. Marine Introductions in the Southern Ocean: An Unrecognised Hazard to Biodiversity. *Marine Pollution Bulletin,* 46:213–223.

Lewis, P. N., M. Riddle, and C. L. Hewitt. 2004. Management of Exogenous Threats to Antarctica and the Sub-Antarctic Islands: Balancing Risks from TBT and Non-indigenous Marine Organisms. *Marine Pollution Bulletin,* 49:999–1005.

Lockwood, J. L., P. Cassey, and T. Blackburn. 2005. The Role of Propagule Pressure in Explaining Species Invasions. *Trends in Ecology and Evolution,* 20:223–228.

Miller, A. W., K. Lion, M. S. Minton, and G. M. Ruiz. 2007. Status and Trends of Ballast Water Management in the United States. Third Biennial Report of the National Ballast Information Clearinghouse. U.S. Coast Guard, Washington, D.C.

Minchin, D. 2006. "The Transport and the Spread of Living Aquatic Species." In *The Ecology of Transportation, Managing Mobility for the Environment,* ed. J. Davenport and J. L. Davenport, pp. 77–97. Dordrecht, Germany: Springer.

Minton, M. S., E. Verling, A. W. Miller, and G. M. Ruiz. 2005. Reducing Propagule Supply by Ships to Limit Coastal Invasions: Effects of Emerging Strategies. *Frontiers in Ecology and the Environment,* 6: 304–308.

Murphy, E. J. 1995. Spatial Structure of the Southern-Ocean Ecosystem—Predator-Prey Linkages in Southern-Ocean Food Webs. *Journal of Animal Ecology,* 64:333–347.

Occhipinti-Ambrogi, A. 2007. Global Change and Marine Communities: Alien Species and Climate Change. *Marine Pollution Bulletin,* 55: 342–352.

Orensanz, J. M., E. Schwindt, G. Pastorino, A. Bortolus, G. Casas, G. Darrigran, R. Elías, J. J. López Gappa, S. Obenat, M. Pascual, P. Penchaszadeh, M. L. Piriz, F. Scarabino, E. D. Spivak, and E. A. Vallarino. 2002. No Longer the Pristine Confines of the World Ocean: A Survey of Exotic Marine Species in the Southwestern Atlantic. *Biological Invasions,* 4:115–143.

Piola, R. F., and E. L. Johnston. 2006. Differential Resistance to Extended Copper Exposure in Four Introduced Bryozoans. *Marine Ecology Progress Series,* 311:103–114

———. 2008. Pollution Reduces Endemic Diversity and Increases Invader Dominance in Hard-Substrate Communities. *Diversity and Distributions,* 14(2):329–342.

Reid, P. C., D. G. Johns, E. Edwards, M. Starr, M. Poulin, and P. Snoeijs. 2007. A Biological Consequence of Reducing Arctic Ice Cover: Arrival of the Pacific Diatom *Neodenticula seminae* in the North Atlantic for the First Time in 800 000 Years. *Global Change Biology* (2007) 13:1910–1921, doi:10.1111/j.1365-2486 .2007.01413.

Reise, K., S. Gollasch, and W. J. Wolff. 1999. Introduced Marine Species of the North Sea Coasts. *Helgoländer Meeresuntersuchungen,* 52: 219–234.

Ribera, M. A., and C. F. Boudouresque. 1995. Introduced Marine Plants with Special Reference to Macroalgae: Mechanisms and Impact. *Progress in Phycological Research,* 11:187–268.

Ribera Siguan, M. A. 2003. "Pathways of Biological Invasions of Marine Plants." In *Invasive Species: Vectors and Management Strategies,* ed. G. M. Ruiz and J. T. Carlton, pp. 183–226. Washington, D.C.: Island Press.

Ruiz, G. M., and J. T. Carlton. 2003. "Invasion Vectors: A Conceptual Framework for Management." In *Invasive Species: Vectors and Management Strategies,* ed. G. M. Ruiz and J. T. Carlton, pp. 459–504. Washington, D.C.: Island Press.

Ruiz, G. M., and C. L. Hewitt. 2002. "Toward Understanding Patterns of Coastal Marine Invasions: A Prospectus." In *Invasive Aquatic Species of Europe,* ed. E. Leppakoski, S. Olenin, and S. Gollasch, pp. 529–547. Dordrecht: Kluwer Academic Publishers.

Ruiz, G. M, P. W. Fofonoff, A. H. Hines, and E. D. Grosholz. 1999. Nonindigenous Species as Stressors in Estuarine and Marine Communities: Assessing Invasion Impacts and Interactions. *Limnology and Oceanography,* 44:950–972.

Ruiz, G. M., P. W. Fofonoff, J. T. Carlton, M. J. Wonham, and A. H. Hines. 2000. Invasion of Coastal Marine Communities in North America: Apparent Patterns, Processes, and Biases. *Annual Review of Ecology and Systematics,* 31:481–531.

Ruiz, G. M., T. Huber, K. Larson, L. McCann, B. Steves, P. W. Fofonoff, and A. H. Hines. 2006a. Biological Invasions in Alaska's Coastal Marine Ecosystems: Establishing a Baseline. Final Report. Prince William Sound Regional Citizens' Advisory Council and U.S. Fish and Wildlife Service, Anchorage, Alaska.

Ruiz, G. M., J. Lorda, A. Arnwine, and K. Lion. 2006b. "Shipping Patterns Associated with the Panama Canal: Effects on Biotic Exchange?" In *Bridging Divides: Maritime Canals as Invasion Corridors,* ed. S. Gollasch, B. S. Galil, and A. N. Cohen, pp. 113–126. Dordrecht, Germany: Springer.

Schaffelke, B., and C. L. Hewitt. 2007. Impacts of Introduced Macroalgae. *Botanica Marina,* 50:397–417.

Serreze, M. C., M. M. Holland, and J. Stroeve. 2007. Perspectives on the Arctic's Shrinking Sea-Ice Cover. *Science,* 315(5818):1533–1536, doi:10.1126/science.1139426.

Simberloff, D., and B. Von Holle. 1999. Positive Interactions of Nonindigenous Species: Invasional Meltdown? *Biological Invasions,* 1:21–32.

Smith, L. D., M. J. Wonham, L. D. McCann, G. M. Ruiz, A. H. Hines, and J. T. Carlton. 1999. Invasion Pressure to a Ballast-Flooded Estuary and an Assessment of Inoculant Survival. *Biological Invasions,* 1:67–87.

Stachowicz, J. J., J. R. Terwin, R. B. Whitlatch, and R. W. Osman. 2002. Linking Climate Change and Biological Invasions: Ocean Warming Facilitates Nonindigenous Species Invasions. *Proceedings of the National Academy of Sciences,* 99:15,497–15,500.

Streftaris, N., A. Zenetos, and E. Papathanassiou. 2005. Globalization in Marine Ecosystems: The Story of Non-indigenous Marine Species across European Seas. *Oceanography and Marine Biology: An Annual Review,* 43:419–453.

Stroeve, J., M. M. Holland, W. Meier, T. Scambos, and M. Serreze. 2007. Arctic Sea Ice Decline: Faster Than Forecast. *Geophys. Res. Lett.,* 34:L09501, doi:10.1029/2007GL029703.

Stroeve, J., M. Serreze, S. Drobot, G. Shari, M. Holland, J. Maslanik, W. Meier, and T. Scambos. 2008. Arctic Sea Ice Plummets in 2007. *Eos, Transactions of the American Geophysical Union,* 89:13–14

Tavares, M., and G. A. S. De Melo. 2004. Discovery of the First Known Benthic Invasive Species in the Southern Ocean: The North Atlantic Spider Crab *Hyas araneus* Found in the Antarctic Peninsula. *Antarctic Science,* 16:129–131.

Thatje, S., S. Schnack-Schiel, and W. E. Arntz. 2003. Developmental Trade-offs in Subantarctic Meroplankton Communities and the Enigma of Low Decapod Diversity in High Southern Latitudes. *Marine Ecology Progress Series,* 260:195–207.

Thatje, S, C. D. Hillenbrand, and R. Larter. 2005a. On the Origin of Antarctic Marine Benthic Community Structure. *Trends in Ecology and Evolution,* 20:534–540.

Thatje, S., K. Anger, J. A. Calcagno, G. A. Lovrich, H.O. Portner, and W. E. Arntz. 2005b. Challenging the Cold: Crabs Reconquer the Antarctic. *Ecology,* 86:619–625.

Thresher, R. E., C. Proctor, G. M. Ruiz, R. Gurney, C. MacKinnon, W. Walton, L Rodriguez, and N. Bax. 2003. Invasion Dynamics of the European Green Crab, *Carcinus maenas,* in Australia. *Marine Ecology Progress Series,* 142:867–876.

Thrush, S. F., J. E. Hewitt, V. J. Cummings, and P. K. Dayton. 1995. The Impact of Habitat Disturbance by Scallop Dredging on Marine Benthic Communities: What Can Be Predicted from the Results of Experiments? *Marine Ecology Progress Series,* 129:141–150.

Verling, E., G. M. Ruiz, L. D. Smith, B. Galil, A. W. Miller, and K. Murphy. 2005. Supply-Side Invasion Ecology: Characterizing Propagule Pressure in Coastal Ecosystems. *Proceedings of the Royal Society of London, Series B,* 272:1249–1256.

Vermeij, G. J. 1991a. When Biotas Meet: Understanding Biotic Interchange. *Science,* 253:1099–1104.

———. 1991b. Anatomy of an Invasion: The Trans-Arctic Interchange. *Paleobiology,* 17:281–307.

Wasson, K., C. J. Zabin, L. Bedinger, M. C. Diaz, and J. S. Pearse. 2001. Biological Invasions of Estuaries without International Shipping: The Importance of Intraregional Transport. *Biological Invasions,* 102:143–153.

Wilson, K. J., J. Falkingham, H. Melling, and R. De Abreu. 2004. "Shipping in the Canadian Arctic." In *Proceedings of the IEEE International Geoscience and Remote Sensing Symposium, 2004, IGARSS '04.* Volume 3, pp. 1853–1856. Piscataway, N.J.: IEEE Press.

Wonham, M., and J. T. Carlton. 2005. Cool-Temperate Marine Invasions at Local and Regional Scales: The Northeast Pacific Ocean as a Model System. *Biological Invasions,* 7(3):369–392.

Cosmology from Antarctica

Robert W. Wilson
and Antony A. Stark

ABSTRACT. Four hundred thousand years after the Big Bang, electrons and nuclei combined to form atoms for the first time, allowing a sea of photons to stream freely through a newly transparent universe. After billions of years, those photons, highly redshifted by the universal cosmic expansion, have become the cosmic microwave background (CMB) radiation we see coming from all directions today. Observation of the CMB is central to observational cosmology, and the Antarctic plateau is an exceptionally good site for this work. The first attempt at CMB observations from the plateau was an expedition to the South Pole in December 1986 by the Radio Physics Research group at Bell Laboratories. No CMB anisotropies were observed, but sky noise and opacity were measured. The results were sufficiently encouraging that in the austral summer of 1988–1989, three CMB groups participated in the "Cucumber" campaign, where a temporary site dedicated to CMB anisotropy measurements was set up 2 km from South Pole Station. These were summer-only campaigns. Wintertime observations became possible in 1990 with the establishment of the Center for Astrophysical Research in Antarctica (CARA), a National Science Foundation Science and Technology Center. The CARA developed year-round observing facilities in the "Dark Sector," a section of Amundsen–Scott South Pole Station dedicated to astronomical observations. The CARA scientists fielded several astronomical instruments: Antarctic Submillimeter Telescope and Remote Observatory (AST/RO), South Pole Infrared Explorer (SPIREX), White Dish, Python, Viper, Arcminute Cosmology Bolometer Array Receiver (ACBAR), and Degree-Angular Scale Interferometer (DASI). By 2001, data from CARA, together with that from Balloon Observations of Millimetric Extragalactic Radiation and Geophysics (BOOMERANG—a CMB experiment on a long-duration balloon launched from McMurdo Station on the coast of Antarctica) showed clear evidence that the overall geometry of the universe is flat, as opposed to being positively or negatively curved. In 2002, the DASI group reported the detection of polarization in the CMB. These observations strongly support a "concordance model" of cosmology, where the dynamics of a flat universe are dominated by forces exerted by the mysterious dark energy and dark matter. The CMB observations continue on the Antarctic plateau. The South Pole Telescope (SPT) is a newly operational 10-m-diameter offset telescope designed to rapidly measure anisotropies on scales much smaller than 1°.

Robert W. Wilson and Antony A. Stark, Smithsonian Astrophysical Observatory, 60 Garden Street, Cambridge, MA 02138, USA. Corresponding author: R. W. Wilson (rwilson@cfa.harvard.edu).
Accepted 25 June 2008.

INTRODUCTION

Cosmology has made tremendous strides in the past decade; this is generally understood within the scientific community, but it is not generally appreciated that some of the most important results have come from Antarctica. Observational cosmology has become a quantitative science. Cosmologists describe the universe by a model with roughly a dozen parameters, for example, the Hubble constant, H_0, and the density parameter, Ω. A decade ago, typical errors on these parameters were 30% or greater; now, most are known within 10%. We can honestly discriminate for and against cosmological hypotheses on the basis of quantitative data. The current concordance model, Lambda–Cold Dark Matter (Ostriker and Steinhardt, 1995), is both highly detailed and consistent with observations. This paper will review the contribution of Antarctic observations to this great work.

From the first detection of the cosmic microwave background (CMB) radiation (Penzias and Wilson, 1965), it was understood that deviations from perfect anisotropy would advance our understanding of cosmology (Peebles and Yu, 1970; Harrison, 1970): the small deviations from smoothness in the early universe are the seeds from which subsequent structure grows, and these small irregularities appear as differences in the brightness of the CMB in various directions on the sky. When the universe was only 350,000 years old, the CMB radiation was released by electrons as they combined with nuclei into atoms for the first time. Anisotropies in the CMB radiation indicate slight differences in density and temperature that eventually evolve into stars, galaxies, and clusters of galaxies. Observations at progressively higher sensitivity by many groups of scientists from the 1970s through the 1990s failed to detect the anisotropy (cf. the review by Lasenby et al., 1998). In the course of these experiments, observing techniques were developed, detector sensitivities were improved by orders of magnitude, and the effects of atmospheric noise became better understood. The techniques and detectors were so improved that the sensitivity of experiments came to be dominated by atmospheric noise at most observatory sites. Researchers moved their instruments to orbit, to balloons, and to high, dry observatory sites in the Andes and in Antarctica. Eventually, CMB anisotropies were detected by the Cosmic Background Explorer satellite (COBE; Fixsen et al., 1996). The ground-based experiments at remote sites also met with success. The spectrum of brightness in CMB variations as a function of spatial frequency was measured by a series of ground-based and balloon-borne experiments, many of them located in the Antarctic. The data were then vastly improved upon by the Wilkinson Microwave Anisotropy Probe (WMAP; Spergel et al., 2003). The future Planck satellite mission (Tauber, 2005), expected to launch in 2008, will provide high signal-to-noise data on CMB anisotropy and polarization that will reduce the error on some cosmological parameters to the level of 1%.

Even in the era of CMB satellites, ground-based CMB observations are still essential for reasons of fundamental physics. Cosmic microwave background radiation occurs only at wavelengths longer than 1 mm. The resolution of a telescope (in radians) is equal to the observed wavelength divided by the telescope diameter. To work properly, the overall accuracy of the telescope optics must be a small fraction of a wavelength. Observing the CMB at resolutions of a minute of arc or smaller therefore requires a telescope that is 10 m in diameter or larger, with an overall accuracy of 0.1 mm or better. There are no prospects for an orbital or airborne telescope of this size and accuracy in the foreseeable future. There is, however, important science to be done at high resolution, work that can only be done with a large ground-based telescope at the best possible ground-based site—the Antarctic plateau.

DEVELOPMENT OF ASTRONOMY IN THE ANTARCTIC

Water vapor is the principal source of atmospheric noise in radio observations. Because it is exceptionally cold, the climate at the South Pole implies exceptionally dry observing conditions. As air becomes colder, the amount of water vapor it can hold is dramatically reduced. At 0°C, the freezing point of water, air can hold 83 times more water vapor than saturated air at the South Pole's average annual temperature of −49°C (Goff and Gratch, 1946). Together with the relatively high altitude of the South Pole (2850 m), this means the water vapor content of the atmosphere above the South Pole is two or three orders of magnitude smaller than it is at most places on the Earth's surface. This has long been known (Smythe and Jackson, 1977), but many years of hard work were needed to realize the potential in the form of new astronomical knowledge (cf. the recent review by Indermuehle et al., 2006).

A French experiment, Emission Millimetrique (EMILIE) (Pajot et al., 1989), made the first astronomical observations of submillimeter waves from the South Pole during the austral summer of 1984–1985. Emission Millimetrique was a ground-based, single-pixel bolometer dewar operating at $\lambda 900\mu m$ and fed by a 45-cm off-axis mirror. It had successfully measured the diffuse galactic emission while operating on Mauna Kea in Hawaii in 1982, but the accuracy of the result had been limited by sky noise (Pajot et al., 1986). Martin A. Pomerantz, a cosmic ray researcher at Bartol Research Institute, encouraged the EMILIE group to relocate their experiment to the South Pole (Lynch, 1998).

There they found better observing conditions and were able to make improved measurements of galactic emission.

Pomerantz also enabled Mark Dragovan, then a researcher at Bell Laboratories, to attempt CMB anisotropy measurements from the pole. Dragovan et al. (1990) built a lightweight 1.2-m-offset telescope and were able to get it working at the pole with a single-pixel helium-4 bolometer during several weeks in January 1987 (see Figure 1). The results were sufficiently encouraging that several CMB groups (Dragovan et al., 1989; Gaier et al., 1989; Meinhold et al., 1989; Peterson et al., 1989) participated in the "Cucumber" campaign in the austral summer of 1988–1989, where three Jamesway tents and a generator were set up at a temporary site dedicated to CMB anisotropy 2 km from South Pole Station in the direction of the international date line. These were summer-only campaigns, where instruments were shipped in, assembled, tested, used, disassembled, and shipped out in a single three-month-long summer season. Considerable time and effort were expended in establishing and then demolishing observatory facilities, with little return in observing time. What little observing time was available occurred during the warmest and wettest days of midsummer.

Permanent, year-round facilities were needed. The Antarctic Submillimeter Telescope and Remote Observatory (AST/RO; Stark et al., 1997, 2001) was a 1.7-m-diameter offset Gregorian telescope mounted on a dedicated permanent observatory building. It was the first radio telescope to operate year-round at the South Pole. The AST/RO was started in 1989 as an independent project, but in 1991 it be-

FIGURE 1. Mark Dragovan, Robert Pernic, Martin Pomerantz, Robert Pfeiffer, and Tony Stark with the AT&T Bell Laboratories 1.2-m horn antenna at the South Pole in January 1987. This was the first attempt at a CMB measurement from the South Pole.

came part of a newly founded National Science Foundation Science and Technology Center, the Center for Astrophysical Research in Antarctica (CARA, http://astro.uchicago.edu/cara; cf. Landsberg, 1998). The CARA fielded several telescopes: White Dish (Tucker et al., 1993), Python (Dragovan et al., 1994; Alvarez, 1995; Ruhl et al., 1995; Platt et al., 1997; Coble et al., 1999), Viper (Peterson et al., 2000), the Degree-Angular Scale Interferometer (DASI; Leitch et al., 2002a), and the South Pole Infrared Explorer (SPIREX; Nguyen et al., 1996), a 60-cm telescope operating primarily in the near-infrared K band. These facilities were housed in the "Dark Sector," a grouping of buildings that includes the AST/RO building, the Martin A. Pomerantz Observatory building (MAPO), and a new "Dark Sector Laboratory" (DSL), all located 1 km away from the main base across the aircraft runway in a radio quiet zone.

The combination of White Dish, Python, and University of California at Santa Barbara 1994 (Ganga et al., 1997) data gave the first indication, by 1997, that the spectrum of spatial anisotropy in the CMB was consistent with a flat cosmology. Figure 2 shows the state of CMB anisotropy measurements as of May 1999. The early South Pole experiments, shown in green, clearly delineate a peak in CMB anisotropy at a scale $\ell = 200$, or 1°, consistent with a flat $\Omega_0 = 1$ universe. Shortly thereafter, the Balloon Observations of Millimetric Extragalactic Radiation and Geophysics (BOOMERANG)-98 long-duration balloon experiment (de Bernardis et al., 2000; Masi et al., 2006, 2007; Piacentini et al., 2007) and the first year of DASI (Leitch et al., 2002b) provided significantly higher signal-to-noise data, yielding $\Omega_0 = 1$ with errors less than 5%. This was a stunning achievement, definitive observations of a flat universe balanced between open and closed Friedmann solutions. In its second year, a modified DASI made the first measurement of polarization in the CMB (Kovac et al., 2002; Leitch et al., 2002c). The observed relationship between polarization and anisotropy amplitude provided a detailed confirmation of the acoustic oscillation model of CMB anisotropy (Hu and White, 1997) and strong support for the standard model. The demonstration that the geometry of the universe is flat is an Antarctic result.

SITE TESTING

One of the primary tasks for the CARA collaboration was the characterization of the South Pole as an observatory site (Lane, 1998). It proved unique among observatory sites for unusually low wind speeds, the complete absence of rain, and the consistent clarity of the submillimeter sky.

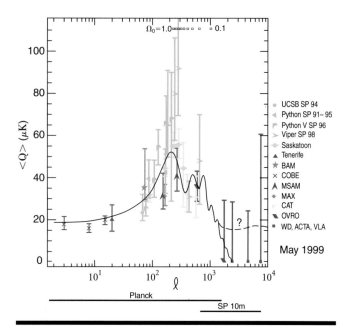

FIGURE 2. Microwave background anisotropy measurements as of May 1999, prior to the launch of BOOMERANG, the deployment of DASI, and the launch of WMAP. South Pole experimental results are shown in green. Note that the peak at $\ell = 200$ is clearly defined, indicating a flat universe ($\Omega_0 = 1$). Abbreviations are as follows: UCSB SP 94 = a campaign at the South Pole in 1994 by the University of California at Santa Barbara sponsored by NSF; BAM = Balloon-borne Anisotropy Measurement; COBE = Cosmic Background Explorer; MSAM = Medium Scale Anisotropy Measurement experiment; MAX = Millimeter Anisotropy eXperiment; CAT = Cosmic Anisotropy Telescope; OVRO = Owens Valley Radio Observatory; WD = White Dish; ACTA = Australia Telescope Compact Array; VLA = Very Large Array.

Schwerdtfeger (1984) and Warren (1996) have comprehensively reviewed the climate of the Antarctic plateau and the records of the South Pole meteorology office. Chamberlin (2002) analyzed weather data to determine the precipitable water vapor (PWV), a measure of total water vapor content in a vertical column through the atmosphere. He found median wintertime PWV values of 0.3 mm over a 37-year period, with little annual variation. The PWV values at South Pole are small, stable, and well-understood.

Submillimeter-wave atmospheric opacity at South Pole has been measured using sky dip techniques. Chamberlin et al. (1997) made over 1,100 sky dip observations at 492 GHz ($\lambda 609\mu m$) with AST/RO during the 1995 observing season. Even though this frequency is near a strong oxy-

gen line, the opacity was below 0.70 half of the time during the austral winter and reached values as low as 0.34, better than ever measured at any other ground-based site. From early 1998, the $\lambda 350\mu m$ band has been continuously monitored at Mauna Kea, Chajnantor, and the South Pole by identical tipper instruments developed by S. Radford of the National Radio Astronomy Observatory and J. Peterson of Carnegie Mellon University and CARA. The 350-μm opacity at the South Pole is consistently better than at Mauna Kea or Chajnantor.

Sky noise is caused by fluctuations in total power or phase of a detector caused by variations in atmospheric emissivity and path length on timescales of order one second. Sky noise causes systematic errors in the measurement of astronomical sources. This is especially important at the millimeter wavelengths for observations of the CMB: at millimeter wavelengths, the opacity of the atmosphere is at most a few percent, and the contribution to the receiver noise is at most a few tens of degrees, but sky noise may still set limits on observational sensitivity. Lay and Halverson (2000) show analytically how sky noise causes observational techniques to fail: fluctuations in a component of the data due to sky noise integrate down more slowly than $t^{-1/2}$ and will come to dominate the error during long observations. Sky noise at South Pole is considerably smaller than at other sites, even comparing conditions of the same opacity. The PWV at the South Pole is often so low that the opacity is dominated by the dry-air component (Chamberlin and Bally, 1995; Chamberlin, 2002); the dry-air emissivity and phase error do not vary as strongly or rapidly as the emissivity and phase error due to water vapor. Lay and Halverson (2000) compared the Python experiment at the South Pole (Dragovan et al., 1994; Alvarez, 1995; Ruhl et al., 1995; Platt et al., 1997; Coble et al., 1999) with the Site Test Interferometer at Chajnantor (Holdaway et al., 1995; Radford et al., 1996) and found that the amplitude of the sky noise at the South Pole is 10 to 50 times less than that at Chajnantor (Bussmann et al., 2004).

The best observing conditions occur only at high elevation angles, and at the South Pole this means that only the southernmost 3 steradians of the celestial sphere are accessible with the South Pole's uniquely low sky noise, but this portion of sky includes millions of galaxies and cosmological sources, the Magellanic clouds, and most of the fourth quadrant of the galaxy. The strength of the South Pole as a millimeter and submillimeter site lies in the low sky noise levels routinely obtainable for sources around the south celestial pole.

TELESCOPES AND INSTRUMENTS AT THE SOUTH POLE

Viper was a 2.1-m off-axis telescope designed to allow measurements of low-contrast millimeter-wave sources. It was mounted on a tower at the opposite end of MAPO from DASI. Viper was used with a variety of instruments: Dos Equis, a CMB polarization receiver operating at 7 mm; the Submillimeter Polarimeter for Antarctic Remote Observing (SPARO), a bolometric array polarimeter operating at $\lambda 450\mu m$; and the Arcminute Cosmology Bolometer Array Receiver (ACBAR), a multiwavelength bolometer array used to map the CMB. The ACBAR is a 16-element bolometer array operating at 300 mK. It was specifically designed for observations of CMB anisotropy and the Sunyaev–Zel'dovich effect (SZE). It was installed on the Viper telescope early in 2001 and was successfully operated until 2005. The ACBAR has made high-quality maps of SZE in several nearby clusters of galaxies and has made significant measurements of anisotropy on the scale of degrees to arcminutes (Runyan et al., 2003; Reichardt et al., 2008).

The Submillimeter Polarimeter for Antarctic Remote Observing (SPARO) was a nine-pixel polarimetric imager operating at $\lambda 450\mu m$. It was operational on the Viper telescope during the early austral winter of 2000. Novak et al. (2000) mapped the polarization of a region of the sky (~0.25 square degrees) centered approximately on the Galactic Center. Their results imply that within the Galactic Center molecular gas complex, the toroidal component of the magnetic field is dominant. The data show that all of the existing observations of large-scale magnetic fields in the Galactic Center are basically consistent with the "magnetic outflow" model of Uchida et al. (1985). This magnetodynamic model was developed in order to explain the Galactic Center radio lobe, a limb-brightened radio structure that extends up to one degree above the plane and may represent a gas outflow from the Galactic Center.

The Degree Angular Scale Interferometer (DASI; Leitch et al., 2002a) was a compact centimeter-wave interferometer designed to image the CMB primary anisotropy and measure its angular power spectrum and polarization at angular scales ranging from two degrees to several arcminutes. As an interferometer, DASI measured CMB power by simultaneously differencing on several scales, measuring the CMB power spectrum directly. The DASI was installed on a tower adjacent to MAPO during the 1999–2000 austral summer and had four successful winter seasons. In its first season, DASI made measurements of CMB anisotropy that confirmed with high accuracy the "concordance" cosmological model, which has a flat geometry, and made significant contributions to the total stress energy from dark matter and dark energy (Halverson et al., 2002; Pryke et al., 2002). In its second year, DASI made the first measurements of "E-mode" polarization of the CMB (Leitch et al., 2002c; Kovac et al., 2002).

The Antarctic Submillimeter Telescope and Remote Observatory (AST/RO) was a general-purpose 1.7-m-diameter telescope (Stark et al., 1997, 2001) for astronomy and aeronomy studies at wavelengths between 200 and 2,000 μm. It was operational from 1995 through 2005 and was located in the Dark Sector on its own building. It was used primarily for spectroscopic studies of neutral atomic carbon and carbon monoxide in the interstellar medium of the Milky Way and the Magellanic Clouds. Six heterodyne receivers and a bolometer array were used on AST/RO: (1) a 230-GHz superconductor-insulator-superconductor (SIS) receiver (Kooi et al., 1992), (2) a 450- to 495-GHz SIS quasi-optical receiver (Zmuidzinas and LeDuc, 1992; Engargiola et al., 1994), (3) a 450- to 495-GHz SIS waveguide receiver (Walker et al., 1992; Kooi et al., 1995), which could be used simultaneously with (4) a 800- to 820-GHz fixed-tuned SIS waveguide mixer receiver (Honingh et al., 1997), (5) the Pole Star array, which deployed four 800- to 820-GHz fixed-tuned SIS waveguide mixer receivers (see http://soral.as.arizona.edu/pole-star; Groppi et al., 2000; Walker et al., 2001), (6) the Terahertz Receiver with NbN HEB Device (TREND), a 1.5-THz heterodyne receiver (Gerecht et al., 1999; Yngvesson et al., 2001), and (7) the South Pole Imaging Fabry-Perot Interferometer (SPIFI; Swain et al., 1998). Spectral lines observed with AST/RO included CO $J = 7 \rightarrow 6$, CO $J = 4 \rightarrow 3$, CO $J = 2 \rightarrow 1$, HDO $J = 1_{0,1} \rightarrow 0_{0,0}$, [C I] $^3P_1 \rightarrow {}^3P_0$, [C I] $^3P_2 \rightarrow {}^3P_1$, and [^{13}C I] $^3P_2 \rightarrow {}^3P_1$. There were four acousto-optical spectrometers (AOS; Schieder et al., 1989): two low-resolution spectrometers with a bandwidth of 1 GHz, an array AOS with four low-resolution spectrometer channels with a bandwidth of 1 GHz for the PoleSTAR array, and one high-resolution AOS with 60-MHz bandwidth. The Antarctic Submillimeter Telescope and Remote Observatory produced data for over a hundred scientific papers relating to star formation in the Milky Way and the Magellanic Clouds. Among the more significant contributions is a submillimeter-wave spectral line survey of the Galactic Center region (Martin et al., 2004) that showed the episodic nature of starburst and black hole activity in the center of our galaxy (Stark et al., 2004).

The Q and U Extra-Galactic Sub-mm Telescope (QUEST) at DASI (QUaD; Church et al., 2003) is a CMB polarization experiment that placed a highly symmetric antenna feeding a bolometer array on the former DASI mount at MAPO, becoming operational in 2005. It is capable of measuring amplitude and polarization of the CMB on angular scales as small as 0.07°. The QUaD has sufficient sensitivity to detect the conversion of E-mode CMB polarization to B-mode polarization caused by gravitational lensing in concentrations of dark matter.

Background Imaging of Cosmic Extragalactic Polarization (BICEP) (Keating et al., 2003; Yoon et al., 2006) is a millimeter-wave receiver designed to measure polarization and amplitude of the CMB over a 20° field of view with 1° resolution. It is mounted on the roof of the Dark Sector Laboratory and has been operational since early 2006. The design of BICEP is optimized to eliminate systematic background effects and thereby achieve sufficient polarization sensitivity to detect the component of CMB polarization caused by primordial gravitational waves. These measurements test the hypothesis of inflation during the first fraction of a second after the Big Bang.

The South Pole Telescope is a 10-m-diameter off-axis telescope that was installed during the 2006–2007 season (Ruhl et al., 2004). It is equipped with a large field of view (Stark, 2000) that feeds a state-of-the-art 936-element bolometer array receiver. The initial science goal is a large SZE survey covering 4,000 square degrees at 1.3′ resolution with 10 μK sensitivity at a wavelength of 2 mm. This survey will find all galaxy clusters above a mass limit of $3.5 \times 10^{14} \, M_\odot$, regardless of redshift. It is expected that an unbiased sample of approximately 8,000 clusters will be found, with over 300 at redshifts greater than one. The sample will provide sufficient statistics to use the density of clusters to determine the equation of state of the dark energy component of the universe as a function of time.

CONCLUSIONS

Observations from the Antarctic have brought remarkable advances in cosmology. Antarctic observations have definitively demonstrated that the geometry of the universe is flat. These observations were made possible by excellent logistical support offered for the pursuit of science at the Antarctic bases. The cold climate and lack of water vapor provide atmospheric conditions that, for some purposes, are nearly as good as space but at greatly reduced cost. Antarctica provides a platform for innovative, small instruments operated by small groups of sci-

entists as well as telescopes that are too large to be lifted into orbit. In the future, Antarctica will continue to be an important site for observational cosmology.

LITERATURE CITED

Alvarez, D. L. 1995. Measurements of the Anisotropy in the Microwave Background on Multiple Angular Scales with the Python Telescope. Ph.D. diss., Princeton University, Princeton, N.J.

Bussmann, R. S., W. L. Holzapfel, and C. L. Kuo. 2004. Millimeter Wavelength Brightness Fluctuations of the Atmosphere above the South Pole. *Astrophysical Journal*, 622:1343–1355.

Chamberlin, R. A. 2002. "Comparisons of Saturated Water Vapor Column from Radiosonde, and mm and submm Radiometric Opacities at the South Pole." In *Astronomical Site Evaluation in the Visible and Radio Range*, ed. J. Vernin, Z. Benkhaldoun, and C. Muñoz-Tuñón, p. 172–178. ASP Conference Proceedings, Vol. 266. San Francisco: Astronomical Society of the Pacific.

Chamberlin, R. A., and J. Bally. 1995. The Observed Relationship Between the South Pole 225 GHz Atmospheric Opacity and the Water Vapor Column Density. *International Journal of Infrared and Millimeter Waves*, 16:907.

Chamberlin, R. A., A. P. Lane, and A. A. Stark. 1997. The 492 GHz Atmospheric Opacity at the Geographic South Pole. *Astrophysical Journal*, 476:428.

Church, S., P. Ade, J. Bock, M. Bowden, J. Carlstrom, K. Ganga, W. Gear, J. Hinderks, W. Hu, B. Keating, J. Kovac, A. Lange, E. Leitch, O. Mallie, S. Melhuish, A. Murphy, B. Rusholme, C. O'Sullivan, L. Piccirillo, C. Pryke, A. Taylor, and K. Thompson. 2003. QUEST on DASI: A South Pole CMB Polarization Experiment, *New Astronomy Review*, 47:1083–1089.

Coble, K., M. Dragovan, J. Kovac, N. W. Halverson, W. L. Holzapfel, L. Knox, S. Dodelson, K. Ganga, D. Alvarez, J. B. Peterson, G. Griffin, M. Newcomb, K. Miller, S. R. Platt, and G. Novak. 1999. Anisotropy in the Cosmic Microwave Background at Degree Angular Scales: Python V Results. *Astrophysical Journal Letters*, 519:L5.

de Bernardis, P., P. A. R. Ade, J. J. Bock, J. R. Bond, J. Borrill, A. Boscaleri, K. Coble, B. P. Crill, G. De Gasperis, P. C. Farese, P. G. Ferreira, K. Ganga, M. Giacometti, E. Hivon, V. V. Hristov, A. Iacoangeli, A. H. Jaffe, A. E. Lange, L. Martinis, S. Masi, P. V. Mason, P. D. Mauskopf, A. Melchiorri, L. Miglio, T. Montroy, C. B. Netterfield, E. Pascale, F. Piacentini, D. Pogosyan, S. Prunet, S. Rao, G. Romeo, J. E. Ruhl, F. Scaramuzzi, D. Sforna, and N. Vittorio. 2000. A Flat Universe from High-Resolution Maps of the Cosmic Microwave Background Radiation. *Nature*, 404:955.

Dragovan, M., S. R. Platt, R. J. Pernic, and A. A. Stark. 1989. "South Pole Submillimeter Isotropy Measurements of the Cosmic Microwave Background." In *Astrophysics in Antarctica*, ed. D. J. Mullan, M. A. Pomerantz, and T. Stanev, p. 97, New York: AIP Press.

Dragovan, M., A. A. Stark, R. Pernic, and M. A. Pomerantz. 1990. Millimetric Sky Opacity Measurements from the South Pole. *Applied Optics*, 29:463.

Dragovan, M., J. Ruhl, G. Novak, S. R. Platt, B. Crone, R. Pernic, and J. Peterson. 1994. Anisotropy in the Microwave Sky at Intermediate Angular Scales. *Astrophysical Journal Letters*, 427:L67.

Engargiola, G., J. Zmuidzinas, and K.-Y. Lo. 1994. 492 GHz Quasioptical SIS Receiver for Submillimeter Astronomy. *Review of Scientific Instruments*, 65:1833.

Fixsen, D. J., E. S. Chang, J. M. Gales, J. C. Mather, R. A. Shafer, and E. L. Wright. 1996. The Cosmic Microwave Background Spectrum from the Full COBE FIRAS Data Set. *Astrophysical Journal*, 473: 576–587.

Gaier, T., J. Schuster, and P. Lubin. 1989. "Cosmic Background Aniso-tropy Studies at 10° Angular Scales with a HEMT Radiometer." In *Astrophysics in Antarctica*, ed. D. J. Mullan, M. A. Pomerantz, and T. Stanev, p. 84. New York: AIP Press.

Ganga, K., B. Ratra, J. O. Gundersen, and N. Sugiyama. 1997. UCSB South Pole 1994 Cosmic Microwave Background Anisotropy Measurement Constraints on Open and Flat- Lambda Cold Dark Matter Cosmogonies. *Astrophysical Journal*, 484:7.

Gerecht, E., C. F. Musante, Y. Zhuang, K. S. Yngvesson, T. Goyette, J. Dickinson, J. Waldman, P. A. Yagoubov, G. N. Goltsman, B. M. Voronov, and E. M. Gershenzon. 1999. NbN Hot Electron Bolomet-ric Mixers_A New Technology for Low Noise THz Receivers. *IEEE Transactions on Microwave Theory and Techniques*, 47:2519.

Goff, J. A., and S. Gratch. 1946. Low-Pressure Properties of Water from -160 to 212 F. *Transactions of the American Society of Heating and Ventilating Engineers*, 52:95.

Groppi, C., C. Walker, A. Hungerford, C. Kulesa, K. Jacobs, and J. Kooi. 2000. "PoleSTAR: An 810 GHz Array Receiver for AST/RO." In *Imaging Radio Through Submillimeter Wavelengths*, ed. J. G. Man-gum and S. J. E. Radford, p. 48. ASP Conference Series, No. 217. San Francisco: Astronomical Society of the Pacific.

Halverson, N. W., E. M. Leitch, C. Pryke, J. Kovac, J. E. Carlstrom, W. L. Holzapfel, M. Dragovan, J. K. Cartwright, B. S. Mason, S. Padin, T. J. Pearson, A. C. S. Readhead, and M. C. Shepherd. 2002. Degree Angular Scale Interferometer First Results: A Measurement of the Cosmic Microwave Background Angular Power Spectrum. *Astrophysical Journal*, 568:38.

Harrison, E. R. 1970. Fluctuations at the Threshold of Classical Cosmol-ogy. *Physical Review D*, 1:2726.

Holdaway, M. A., S. J. E. Radford, F. N. Owen, and S. M. Foster. 1995. Fast Switching Phase Calibration: Effectiveness at Mauna Kea and Chajnantor. Millimeter Array Technical Memorandum 139. Na-tional Radio Astronomy Observatory, Charlottesville, Va.

Honingh, C. E., S. Hass, K. Hottgenroth, J. Jacobs, and J. Stutzki. 1997. Low-Noise Broadband Fixed-Tuned SIS Waveguide Mixers at 660 and 800 GHz. *IEEE Transactions on Applied Superconductivity*, 7:2582.

Hu, W., and M. White. 1997. A CMB Polarization Primer. *New Astron-omy*, 2:323.

Indermuehle, B. T., M. G. Burton, and S. T. Maddison. 2006. A History of Astronomy in Antarctica. *Publications of the Astronomical Soci-ety of Australia*, 22:73.

Keating, B. G., P. A. R. Ade, J. J. Bock, E. Hivon, W. L. Holzapfel, and A. E. Lange, H. Nguyen, and K. W. Yoon. 2003. "BICEP: A Large Angular Scale CMB Polarimeter." In *Polarimetry in Astronomy*, ed. S. Fineschi. *Proceedings of SPIE*, 4843:284–295.

Kooi, J. W., C. Man, T. G. Phillips, B. Bumble, and H. G. LeDuc. 1992. A Low-Noise 230 GHz Heterodyne Receiver Employing a 0.25μm² Area Nb/AlOₓ/Nb Tunnel Junction. *IEEE Transactions on Micro-waves Theory and Techniques*, 40:812.

Kooi, J. W., M. S. Chan, B. Bumble, H. G. LeDuc, P. L. Schaffer, and T. G. Phillips. 1995. 230 and 492 GHz Low-Noise SIS Waveguide Receivers Employing Tuned Nb/ALOₓ/Nb Tunnel Junctions. *Inter-national Journal of Infrared and Millimeter Waves*, 16:2049.

Kovac, J. M., E. M. Leitch, C. Pryke, J. E. Carlstrom, N. W. Halverson, and W. L. Holzapfel. 2002. Detection of Polarization in the Cosmic Microwave Background Using DASI. *Nature*. 420:772.

Landsberg, R. H. 1998. Education and Outreach from the End of the Earth. *Bulletin of the American Astronomical Society*, 30:903.

Lane, A. P. 1998. "Submillimeter Transmission at South Pole." In *Astrophysics from Antarctica*, ed. G. Novak and R. H. Landsberg, p. 289. ASP Conference Series, No. 141. San Francisco: Astronom-ical Society of the Pacific.

Lasenby, A. N., A. W. Jones, and Y. Dabrowski. 1998. "Review of Ground-Based CMB Experiments." Proceedings of the Moriond

Workshop, Fundamental Parameters in Cosmology, Les Arcs, France.

Lay, O. P., and N. W. Halverson. 2000. The Impact of Atmospheric Fluc-tuations on Degree-Scale Imaging of the Cosmic Microwave Back-ground. *Astrophysical Journal*, 543:787.

Leitch, E. M., C. Pryke, N. W. Halverson, J. Kovac, G. Davidson, S. LaRoque, E. Schartman, J. Yamasaki, J. E. Carlstrom, W. L. Hol-zapfel, M. Dragovan, J. K. Cartwright, B. S. Mason, S. Padin, T. J. Pearson, A. C. S. Readhead, and M. C. Shepherd. 2002a. Experi-ment Design and First Season Observations with the Degree Angu-lar Scale Interferometer. *Astrophysical Journal*, 568:28.

Leitch, E. M., J. E. Carlstrom, N. W. Halverson, J. Kovac, C. Pryke, W. L. Holzapfel, and M. Dragovan. 2002b. "First Season Observa-tions with the Degree Angular Scale Interferometer (DASI)." In *Ex-perimental Cosmology at Millimetre Wavelengths*, ed. M. de Petris and M. Gervasi, p. 65–71. AIP Conference Proceedings, No. 616. Melville, N.Y.: American Institute of Physics.

Leitch, E. M., J. M. Kovac, C. Pryke, J. E. Carlstrom, N. W. Halverson, W. L. Holzapfel, M. Dragovan, B. Reddall, and E. S. Sandberg. 2002c. Measurement of Polarization with the Degree Angular Scale Interferometer. *Nature*, 420:763.

Lynch, J. T. 1998. "Astronomy & Astrophysics in the U. S. Antarctic Program." In *Astrophysics from Antarctica*, edited by G. Novak and R. H. Landsberg, p. 54. ASP Conference Series, No. 141. San Francisco: Astronomical Society of the Pacific.

Martin, C. L., W. M. Walsh, K. Xiao, A. P. Lane, C. K. Walker, and A. A. Stark. 2004. The AST/RO Survey of the Galactic Center Region. I. The Inner 3 Degrees. *Astrophysical Journal, Supplement Series*, 150:239.

Masi, S., P. A. R. Ade, J. J. Bock, J. R. Bond, J. Borrill, A. Boscaleri, P. Cabella, C. R. Contaldi, B. P. Crill, P. de Bernardis, G. de Gasperis, A. de Oliveira-Costa, G. de Troia, G. di Stefano, P. Ehlers, E. Hivon, V. Hristov, A. Iacoangeli, A. H. Jaffe, W. C. Jones, T. S. Kisner, A. E. Lange, C. J. MacTavish, C. Marini Bettolo, P. D. Mason, P. Maus-kopf, T. E. Montroy, F. Nati, L. Nati, P. Natoli, C. B. Netterfield, E. Pascale, F. Piacentini, D. Pogosyan, G. Polenta, S. Prunet, S. Ric-ciardi, G. Romeo, J. E. Ruhl, P. Santini, M. Tegmark, E. Torbet, M. Veneziani, and N. Vittorio. 2006. Instrument, Method, Brightness, and Polarization Maps from the 2003 Flight of BOOMERanG, *Astronomy and Astrophysics*, 458:687.

Masi, S., P. A. R. Ade, J. J. Bock, J. R. Bond, J. Borrill, A. Boscaleri, P. Cabella, C. R. Contaldi, B. P. Crill, P. de Bernardis, G. de Gasperis, A. de Oliveira-Costa, G. de Troia, G. di Stefano, P. Ehlers, E. Hivon, V. Hristov, A. Iacoangeli, A. H. Jaffe, W. C. Jones, T. S. Kisner, A. E. Lange, C. J. MacTavish, C. Marini Bettolo, P. Mason, P. D. Mauskopf, T. E. Montroy, F. Nati, L. Nati, P. Natoli, C. B. Netter-field, E. Pascale, F. Piacentini, D. Pogosyan, G. Polenta, S. Prunet, S. Ricciardi, G. Romeo, J. E. Ruhl, P. Santini, M. Tegmark, E. Torbet, M. Veneziani, and N. Vittorio. 2007. The Millimeter Sky as Seen with BOOMERanG. *New Astronomy Review*, 51:236.

Meinhold, P. R., P. M. Lubin, A. O. Chingcuanco, J. A. Schuster, and M. Seiffert. 1989. "South Pole Studies of the Anisotropy of the Cosmic Microwave Background at One Degree." In *Astrophysics in Ant-arctica*, ed. D. J. Mullan, M. A. Pomerantz, and T. Stanev, p. 88. New York: AIP Press.

Nguyen, H. T., B. J. Rauscher, S. A. Severson, M. Hereld, D. A. Harper, R. F. Lowenstein, F. Morozek, and R. J. Pernic. 1996. The South Pole Near Infrared Sky Brightness. *Publications of the Astronomi-cal Society of the Pacific*, 108:718.

Novak, G., J. L. Dotson, C. D. Dowell, R. H. Hildebrand, T. Renbarger, and D. A. Schleuning. 2000. Submillimeter Polarimetric Observa-tions of the Galactic Center, *Astrophysical Journal*, 529:241.

Ostriker, J. P., and P. J. Steinhardt. 1995. The Observational Case for a Low Density Universe with a Non-Zero Cosmological Constant. *Nature*, 377:600–602.

Pajot, F., R. Gispert, J. M. Lamarre, R. Peyturaux, J.-L. Puget, G. Serra, N. Coron, G. Dambier, J. Leblanc, J. P. Moalic, J. C. Renault, and R. Vitry. 1986. Submillimetric Photometry of the Integrated Galactic Emission. *Astronomy and Astrophysics,* 154:55.

Pajot, F., R. Gispert, J. M. Lamarre, R. Peyturaux, M. A. Pomerantz, J. L. Puget, G. Serra, C. Maurel, R. Pfeiffer, and J. C Renault. 1989. Observations of the Submillimetre Integrated Galactic Emission from the South Pole. *Astronomy and Astrophysics,* 223:107.

Peebles, P. J. E., and J. T. Yu. 1970. Primeval Adiabatic Perturbation in an Expanding Universe. *Astrophysical Journal,* 162:815.

Penzias, A. A., and R. W. Wilson. 1965. A Measurement of Excess Antenna Temperature at 4080 Mc/s. *Astrophysical Journal,* 142: 419–421.

Peterson, J. 1989. "Millimeter and Sub-millimeter Photometry from Antarctica." In *Astrophysics in Antarctica,* ed. D. J. Mullan, M. A. Pomerantz, and T. Stanev, p. 116. New York: AIP Press.

Peterson, J. B., G. S. Griffin, M. G. Newcomb, D. L. Alvarez, C. M. Cantalupo, D. Morgan, K. W. Miller, K. Ganga, D. Pernic, and M. Thoma. 2000. First Results from Viper: Detection of Small-Scale Anisotropy at 40 GHz, *Astrophysical Journal Letters,* 532:83.

Piacentini, F., P. A. R. Ade, J. J. Bock, J. R. Bond, J. Borrill, A. Boscaleri, P. Cabella, C. R. Contaldi, B. P. Crill, P. de Bernardis, G. de Gasperis, A. de Oliveira-Costa, G. de Troia, G. di Stefano, E. Hivon, A. H. Jaffe, T. S. Kisner, W. C. Jones, A. E. Lange, C. Marini-Bettolo, S. Masi, P. D. Mauskopf, C. J. MacTavish, A. Melchiorri, T. E. Montroy, F. Nati, L. Nati, P. Natoli, C. B. Netterfield, E. Pascale, D. Pogosyan, G. Polenta, S. Prunet, S. Ricciardi, G. Romeo, J. E. Ruhl, P. Santini, M. Tegmark, M. Veneziani, and N. Vittorio. 2007. CMB Polarization with BOOMERanG 2003. *New Astronomy Review,* 51:244.

Platt, S. R., J. Kovac, M. Dragovan, J. B. Peterson, and J. E. Ruhl. 1997. Anisotropy in the Microwave Sky at 90 GHz: Results from Python III. *Astrophysical Journal Letters,* 475:L1.

Pryke, C., N. W. Halverson, E. M. Leitch, J. Kovac, J. E. Carlstrom, W. L. Holzapfel, and M. Dragovan. 2002. Degree Angular Scale Interferometer First Results: A Measurement of the Cosmic Microwave Background Angular Power Spectrum. *Astrophysical Journal,* 568:38.

Radford, S. J. E., G. Reiland, and B. Shillue. 1996. Site Test Interferometer. *Publications of the Astronomical Society of the Pacific,* 108: 441.

Reichardt, C. L., P. A. R. Ade, J. J. Bock, J. R. Bond, J. A. Brevik, C. R. Contaldi, M. D. Daub, J. T. Dempsey, J. H. Goldstein, W. L. Holzapfel, C. L. Kuo, A. E. Lange, M. Lueker, M. Newcomb, J. B. Peterson, J. Ruhl, M. C. Runyan, and Z. Staniszewski. 2008. High Resolution CMB Power Spectrum from the Complete ACBAR Data Set. ArXiv e-prints 0801.1491. http://adsabs.harvard.edu.ezp-prod1.hul .harvard.edu/abs/2008arXiv0801.1491R.

Ruhl, J. E., M. Dragovan, S. R. Platt, J. Kovac, and G. Novak. 1995. Anisotropy in the Microwave Sky at 90 GHz: Results from Python II. *Astrophysical Journal Letters,* 453:L1–L4.

Ruhl, J. E., P. A. R. Ade, J. E. Carlstrom, H. M. Cho, T. Crawford, T. M. Dobbs, C. H. Greer, N. W. Halverson, W. L. Holzapfel, T. M. Lantin, A. T. Lee, J. Leong, E. M. Leitch, W. Lu, M. Lueker, J. Mehl, S. S. Meyer, J. J. Mohr, S. Padin, T. Plagge, C. Pryke, D. Schwan, M. K. Sharp, M. C. Runyan, H. Spieler, Z. Staniszewski, and A. A. Stark. 2004. The South Pole Telescope. *Proceeding of SPIE,* 5498:11–29.

Runyan, M. C., P. A. R. Ade, J. J. Bock, J. R. Bond, C. Cantalupo, C. R. Contaldi, M. D. Daub, J. H. Goldstein, P. L. Gomez, W. L. Holzapfel, C. L. Kuo, A. E. Lange, M. Lueker, M. Newcomb, J. B. Peterson, D. Pogosyan, A. K. Romer, J. Ruhl, E. Torbet, and D. Woolsey. 2003. First Results from the Arcminute cosmology Bolometer Array Receiver. *New Astronomy Reviews,* 47:915.

Schieder, R., V. Tolls, and G. Winnewisser. 1989. The Cologne Acousto Optical Spectrometers. *Experimental Astronomy,* 1:101.

Schwerdtfeger, W. 1984. *Weather and Climate of the Antarctic.* Amsterdam: Elsevier.

Smythe, W. D., and B. V. Jackson. 1977 Atmospheric Water Vapor at South Pole. *Applied Optics,* 16:2041.

Spergel, D. N., L. Verde, V. Hiranya, E. Peiris, M. R. Komatsu, C. L. Nolta, M. Bennett, G. Halpern, N. Hinshaw, A. Jarosik, M. Kogut, S. S. Limon, L. Meyer, G. S. Page, J. L. Tucker, E. Weiland, E. Wollack, and E. L. Wright. 2003. First-Year Wilkinson Microwave Anisotropy Probe (WMAP) Observations: Determination of Cosmological Parameters. *Astrophysical Journal, Supplement Series,* 148:175.

Stark, A. A. 2000. "Design Considerations for Large Detector Arrays on Submillimeter-Wave Telescopes." In *Radio Telescopes,* ed. H. R. Butcher. *Proceedings of SPIE,* 4015:434.

Stark, A. A., R. A. Chamberlin, J. Cheng, J. Ingalls, and G. Wright. 1997. Optical and Mechanical Design of the Antarctic Submillimeter Telescope and Remote Observatory (AST/RO). *Review of Scientific Instruments,* 68:2200.

Stark, A. A., J. Bally, S. P. Balm, T. M. Bania, A. D. Bolatto, R. A. Chamberlin, G. Engargiola, M. Huang, J. G. Ingalls, K. Jacobs, J. M. Jackson, J. W. Kooi, A. P. Lane, K.-Y. Lo, R. D. Marks, C. L. Martin, D. Mumma, R. Ojha, R. Schieder, J. Staguhn, J. Stutzki, C. K. Walker, R. W. Wilson, G. A. Wright, X. Zhang, P. Zimmermann, and R. Zimmermann. 2001. The Antarctic Submillimeter Telescope and Remote Observatory (AST/RO). *Publications of the Astronomical Society of the Pacific,* 113:567.

Stark, A. A., C. L. Martin, W. M. Walsh, K. Xiao, A. P. Lane, and C. K. Walker. 2004. Gas Density, Stability, and Starbursts near the Inner Lindblad Resonance of the Milky Way. *Astrophysical Journal Letters,* 614:L41.

Swain, M. R., C. M. Bradford, G. J. Stacey, A. D. Bolatto, J. M. Jackson, M. Savage, and J. A. Davidson. 1998. Design of the South Pole Imaging Fabry-Perot Interferometer (SPIFI). *Proceedings of SPIE,* 3354:480.

Tauber, J. A. 2005. "The Planck Mission." In *New Cosmological Data and the Values of the Fundamental Parameters,* ed. A. Lasenby and D. A. Wilkinson, p. 86. IAU Symposium and Colloquium Proceedings Series, No. 201. San Francisco: Astronomical Society of the Pacific.

Tucker, G. S., G. S. Griffin, H. T. Nguyen, and J. S. Peterson. 1993. A Search for Small-Scale Anisotropy in the Cosmic Microwave Background. *Astrophysical Journal Letters,* 419:L45.

Uchida, Y., K. Shibata, and Y. Sofue. 1985. Origin of the Galactic Center Lobes. *Nature,* 317:699.

Walker, C. K., J. W. Kooi, W. Chan, H. G. LeDuc, P. L. Schaffer, J. E. Carlstrom, and T. G. Phillips. 1992. A Low-Noise 492 GHz SIS Waveguide Receiver. *International Journal of Infrared and Millimeter Waves,* 13:785.

Walker, C., C. Groppi, A. Hungerford, K. Kulesa, C. Jacobs, U. Graf, R. Schieder, C. Martin, and J. Kooi. 2001. PoleSTAR: A 4-Channel 810 GHz Array Receiver for AST/RO. Twelfth International Symposium on Space Terahertz Technology, 14–16 February 2001, NASA Jet Propulsion Laboratory, Pasadena, Calif.

Warren, S. G. 1996. "Antarctica." In *Encyclopedia of Weather and Climate,* edited by S. H. Schneider, p. 32. New York: Oxford University Press.

Yngvesson, K. S., C. F. Musante, M. Ji, F. Rodriguez, Y. Zhuang, E. Gerecht, M. Coulombe, J. Dickinson, T. Goyette, J. Waldman, C. K. Walker, A. A. Stark, and A. P. Lane. 2001. Terahertz Receiver with NbN HEB Device (TREND)—A Low-Noise Receiver User Instrument for AST/RO at the South Pole. Twelfth International Symposium on Space Terahertz Technology, 14–16 February 2001, NASA Jet Propulsion Laboratory, Pasadena, Calif.

Yoon, K. W., P. A. R. Ade, D. Barkats, J. O. Battle, E. M. Bierman, J. J. Bock, J. A. Brevik, H. C. Chiang, A. Crites, C. D. Dowell, L. Duband, G. S. Griffin, E. F. Hivon, W. L. Holzapfel, V. V. Hristov, B. G. Keating,

J. M. Kovac, C. L. Kuo, A. E. Lange, E. M. Leitch, P. V. Mason, H. T. Nguyen, N. Ponthieu, Y. D. Takahashi, T. Renbarger, L. C. Weintraub, and D. Woolsey. 2006. "The Robinson Gravitational Wave Background Telescope (BICEP): A Bolometric Large Angular Scale CMB Polarimeter." In *Millimeter and Submillimeter Detectors and Instrumentation for Astronomy III,* ed., J. Zmuidzinas, W. S. Holland, S. Withington, and W. D. Duncan. *Proceedings of SPIE,* 6275, 62751K(2006), doi:10.1117/12.672652.

Zmuidzinas, J., and H. G. LeDuc. 1992. Quasi-Optical Slot Antenna SIS Mixers. *IEEE Transactions on Microwave Theory and Techniques,* 40:1797.

Feeding the Black Hole at the Center of the Milky Way: AST/RO Observations

Christopher L. Martin

ABSTRACT. Feeling a bit hungry? Imagine that you only received one meal every few million years and that when you ate it, it was a gigantic Thanksgiving feast. That sort of gorging might give you quite a stomach ache! The black hole at the center of our galaxy seems to go through just this cycle of feast and famine, but as the turkey dinner arrives, it bursts into a tremendous display of fireworks. Instead of turkey, a black hole eats a vast platter of dust and gas that is compressed and stressed as it reaches the inner part of the galaxy. This compression causes the formation of a plethora of large short-lived stars that go supernova shortly after their birth. These supernova fireworks would then be sufficiently intense to make the center of the galaxy one of the brightest objects in our night sky while at the same time sterilizing any life that might be nearby. How does this matter get to the center of the galaxy and when can we expect the next burst of fireworks? At this very moment the dinner plate for the black hole at the center of the Milky Way is being assembled, and a group of astronomers from the South Pole is looking at the menu. Dinner will be served in about 10 million years.

ANTARCTIC SUBMILLIMETER TELESCOPE AND REMOTE OBSERVATORY

Observing the gas in the center of our galaxy requires an instrument that is sensitive to its emissions. While the bulk of the baryonic matter in our universe is simply hydrogen, it is surprisingly difficult to observe. Rather than detecting the hydrogen directly, tracers such as carbon monoxide (CO) are used instead to determine the density, temperature, and dynamics of the hydrogen with which it is well mixed. The Antarctic Submillimeter Telescope and Remote Observatory (AST/RO, Figure 1), located at 2847 m altitude at the Amundsen-Scott South Pole Station, was built in 1995 to study the emissions of these tracers. One might reasonably ask, why would one put a telescope like this at the bottom of the Earth? The South Pole has very low water vapor, high atmospheric stability, and a thin troposphere, making it exceptionally good for submillimeter observations (Chamberlin et al., 1997; Lane, 1998). Technically, AST/RO is a 1.7-m-diameter, offset Gregorian telescope capable of observing at wavelengths between 200 μm and 1.3 mm (Stark et al., 2001). The observations of the center of the Milky Way described here were taken during the austral winter seasons of 2001–2004 by the telescope's dedicated winter-over staff.

Christopher L. Martin, Oberlin College, Department of Physics and Astronomy, 110 North Professor Street, Oberlin, OH 44074, USA (chris.martin@oberlin.edu). Accepted 25 June 2008.

FIGURE 1. The Antarctic Submillimeter Telescope and Remote Observatory (AST/RO) as it appeared shortly after its construction in 1995 with the main Amundsen-Scott South Pole Station in the background.

WHAT DOES THE GALACTIC CENTER LOOK LIKE WHEN SEEN BY AST/RO?

Figure 2 presents spatial–spatial (l, b) maps integrated over velocity for the three transitions AST/RO has observed in the Galactic Center. The first thing you might notice when looking at the maps is that the Galactic Center appears to be made up of clouds rather than stars. This is because the frequencies of light observed by AST/RO are sensitive to the dust and gas between the stars rather than the stars themselves. Looking beyond this, the next most striking result is that CO $J = 4 \rightarrow 3$ emission in the Galactic Center region is essentially coextensive with the emission from the lower J transitions of CO. This contrasts sharply with the outer galaxy where CO $J = 4 \rightarrow 3$ emission is rather less extensive than CO $J = 1 \rightarrow 0$. On the other hand, CO $J = 7 \rightarrow 6$ emission is very compact and constrained to just a few key regions, indicating high densities and temperatures in those regions. Four major cloud complexes are seen in the maps, from left to right: the complex at $l \approx 1.3°$, the Sgr B complex near $l \approx 0.7°$, the Sgr A cloud near $l \approx 0.0°$, and the Sgr C cloud near $(l \approx -0.45°, b \approx -0.2°)$. As noted by Kim et al. (2002), the CO $J = 7 \rightarrow 6$ emission is much more spatially confined than the lower-J CO transitions. In contrast, the [CI] (atomic carbon) emission is comparable in spatial extent to the low-J CO emission, but its distribution appears somewhat more diffuse (less peaked). The Sgr C cloud is much less prominent in the [CI] map than in the other five transitions (Ojha et al., 2001). In order to understand what this gas is doing, we need to combine the data taken with AST/RO with data from other sources, and we need a broader understanding of the dynamics of the Galactic Center.

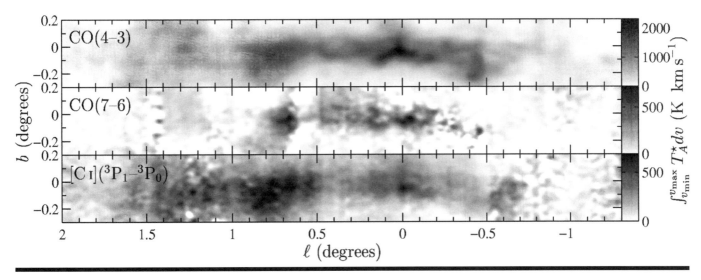

FIGURE 2. Spatial–spatial (l, b) integrated intensity maps for the three transitions observed with AST/RO. Transitions are identified at the left on each panel. The emission is integrated over all velocities where data are available. All three maps have been smoothed to the same 2′ resolution. Electronic versions of results from this region as published in Martin et al. (2004) may be requested from the author via e-mail.

WHAT IS THIS GAS DOING?

Much has been learned about dense gas in the Galactic Center region through radio spectroscopy. Early observations of $F(2 \rightarrow 2)$ OH absorption (Robinson et al., 1964; Goldstein et al., 1964) suggested the existence of copious molecular material within 500 pc of the Galactic Center. This was confirmed by detection of extensive $J = 1 \rightarrow 0$ ^{12}CO emission (Bania, 1977; Liszt and Burton, 1978). Subsequent CO surveys (Bitran, 1987; Stark et al., 1988; Bitran et al., 1997; Oka et al., 1998) have measured this emission with improving coverage and resolution. These surveys show a complex distribution of emission, which is chaotic, asymmetric, and nonplanar; there are hundreds of clouds, shells, arcs, rings, and filaments. On scales of 100 pc to 4 kpc, however, the gas is loosely organized around closed orbits in the rotating potential of the underlying stellar bar (Binney et al., 1991). Some CO-emitting gas is bound into clouds and cloud complexes, and some is sheared by tidal forces into a molecular intercloud medium of a kind not seen elsewhere in the galaxy (Stark et al., 1989). The large cloud complexes, Sgr A, Sgr B, and Sgr C, are the among the largest molecular cloud complexes in the galaxy ($M > 10^{6.5}$ M_{sun}). Such massive clouds must be sinking toward the center of the galactic gravitational well as a result of dynamical friction and hydrodynamic effects (Stark et al., 1991). The deposition of these massive lumps of gas upon the center could fuel a starburst or an eruption of the central black hole (Genzel and Townes, 1987; Stark et al., 2004).

To better understand the molecular gas of the Galactic Center, we need to determine its physical state—its temperature and density. This involves understanding radiative transfer in CO, the primary tracer of molecular gas. Also useful would be an understanding of the atomic carbon lines, [CI], since those lines trace the more diffuse molecular regions, where CO is destroyed by UV radiation but H_2 is still present.

Hence, a key project of the Antarctic Submillimeter Telescope and Remote Observatory reported by Martin et al. (2004) has been the mapping of CO 4–3 and CO 7–6 emission from the inner Milky Way, allowing determination of gas density and temperature. Galactic Center gas that Binney et al. (1991) identify as being on x_2 orbits has a density near $10^{3.5}$ cm^3, which renders it only marginally stable against gravitational coagulation into a few giant molecular clouds. This suggests a relaxation oscillator mechanism for starbursts in the Milky Way, whereby inflowing gas accumulates in a ring at 150-pc radius until the critical density is reached and the resulting instability leads to the sudden formation of giant clouds and the deposition of 4×10^7 M_{sun}, of gas onto the Galactic Center. Depending on the accretion rate near the inner Lindblad resonance, this cycle will repeat with a timescale on the order of 20 Myr, leading to starbursts on the same timescale. When we analyze our data (Stark et al., 2004), we observe gas approaching this density and thus beginning the next stage of its long descent in the black hole at the heart of our galaxy. In the Thanksgiving feast analogy, the gas that we can see coagulating on these outer orbits and beginning its slow trip inward is the future dinner for the black hole at the center of our galaxy. When it arrives at the center of the galaxy, it will provide the fuel for a burst of star formation activity (a starburst) at the very heart of the Milky Way and, hence, for the fireworks that will light up our night skies in the millennia to come.

ACKNOWLEDGMENTS

This research was supported in part by the National Science Foundation under NSF grant number ANT-0126090 and was conducted with the assistance of the many collaborators of the Antarctic Submillimeter Telescope Remote Observatory (AST/RO).

LITERATURE CITED

Bania, T. M. 1977. Carbon Monoxide in the Inner Galaxy. *Astrophysical Journal,* 216:381–403.

Binney, J., O. E. Gerhard, A. A. Stark, J. Bally, and K. I. Uchida. 1991. Understanding the Kinematics of Galactic Centre Gas. *Monthly Notices of the Royal Astronomical Society,* 252:210–218.

Bitran, M., H. Alvarez, L. Bronfman, J. May, and P. Thaddeus. 1997. A Large Scale CO Survey of the Galactic Center Region. *Astronomy and Astrophysics, Supplement Series,* 125:99–138.

Bitran, M. E. 1987. CO in the Galactic Center: A Complete Survey of CO Emission in the Inner 4 kpc of the Galaxy. Ph.D. diss., University of Florida, Gainesville.

Chamberlin, R. A., A. P. Lane, and A. A. Stark. 1997. The 492 GHz Atmospheric Opacity at the Geographic South Pole. *Astrophysical Journal,* 476:428–433.

Genzel, R., and C. H. Townes. 1987. Physical Conditions, Dynamics, and Mass Distribution in the Center of the Galaxy. *Annual Review of Astronomy and Astrophysics,* 25:377–423.

Goldstein, S. J., E. J. Gundermann, A. A. Penzias, and A. E. Lilley. 1964. OH Absorption Spectra in Sagittarius. *Nature,* 203:65–66.

Kim, S., C. L. Martin, A. A. Stark, and A. P. Lane. 2002. AST/RO Observations of CO $J = 7 \rightarrow 6$ and $J = 4 \rightarrow 3$ Emission toward the Galactic Center Region. *Astrophysical Journal,* 580:896–903.

Lane, A. P. 1998. "Submillimeter Transmission at South Pole." In *Astrophysics From Antarctica,* ed. G. Novack and R. H. Landsberg, p. 289. Astronomical Society of the Pacific Conference Series, No. 141. San Francisco: Astronomical Society of the Pacific.

Liszt, H. S., and W. B. Burton. 1978. The Gas Distribution in the Central Region of the Galaxy. II—Carbon Monoxide. *Astrophysical Journal,* 226:790–816.

Martin, C. L., W. M. Walsh, K. Xiao, A. P. Lane, C. K. Walker, and A. A. Stark. 2004. The AST/RO Survey of the Galactic Center Region I. The Inner 3 Degrees. *Astrophysical Journal, Supplement Series,* 150:239–262.

Ojha, R., A. A. Stark, H. H. Hsieh, A. P. Lane, R. A. Chamberlin, T. M. Bania, A. D. Bolatto, J. M. Jackson, and G. A. Wright. 2001. AST/RO Observations of Atomic Carbon near the Galactic Center. *Astrophysical Journal,* 548:253–257.

Oka, T., T. Hasegawa, F. Sato, M. Tsuboi, and A. Miyazaki. 1998. A Large-Scale CO Survey of the Galactic Center. *Astrophysical Journal, Supplement Series,* 118:455–515.

Robinson, B. J., F. F. Gardner, K. J. van Damme, and J. G. Bolton. 1964. An Intense Concentration of OH Near the Galactic Centre. *Nature,* 202:989–991.

Stark, A. A., J. Bally, G. R. Knapp, and R. W. Wilson. 1988. "The Bell Laboratories CO Survey." In *Molecular Clouds in the Milky Way and External Galaxies,* ed. R. L. Dickman, R. L. Snell, and J. S. Young, p. 303. New York: Springer-Verlag.

Stark, A. A., J. Bally, R. W. Wilson, and M. W. Pound. 1989. "Molecular Line Observations of the Galactic Center Region." In *The Center of the Galaxy: Proceedings of the 136th Symposium of the International Astronomical Union,* ed. M. Morris, p. 129. Dordrecht: Kluwer Academic Publishers.

Stark, A. A., J. Bally, O. E. Gerhard, and J. Binney. 1991. On the Fate of Galactic Centre Molecular Clouds. *Monthly Notices of the Royal Astronomical Society,* 248:14P–17PP.

Stark, A. A., J. Bally, S. P. Balm, T. M. Bania, A. D. Bolatto, R. A. Chamberlin, G. Engargiola, M. Huang, J. G. Ingalls, K. Jacobs, J. M. Jackson, J. W. Kooi, A. P. Lane, K.-Y. Lo, R. D. Marks, C. L. Martin, D. Mumma, R. Ojha, R. Schieder, J. Staguhn, J. Stutzki, C. K. Walker, R. W. Wilson, G. A. Wright, X. Zhang, P. Zimmermann, and R. Zimmermann. 2001. The Antarctic Submillimeter Telescope and Remote Observatory (AST/RO). *Publications of the Astronomical Society of the Pacific,* 113:567–585.

Stark, A. A., C. L. Martin, W. M. Walsh, K. Xiao, A. P. Lane, and C. K. Walker. 2004. Gas Density, Stability, and Starbursts near the Inner Lindblad Resonance of the Milky Way. *Astrophysical Journal Letters,* 614:L41–L44.

HEAT: The High Elevation Antarctic Terahertz Telescope

Christopher K. Walker and Craig A. Kulesa

ABSTRACT. The High Elevation Antarctic Terahertz Telescope (HEAT) is a proposed 0.5-m THz observatory for automated, remote operation at the summit of Dome A, the highest point on the Antarctic plateau. The altitude of Dome A combined with the extreme cold and dry conditions prevalent there make it the best location on Earth for conducting many types of astronomical observations. The HEAT will operate at wavelengths from 150 to 400 micrometers and will observe the brightest and most diagnostic spectral lines from the galaxy. It will follow PreHEAT, an NSF-funded 450-micrometer tipper and spectrometer that was deployed to Dome A in January 2008 by the Polar Research Institute of China. PreHEAT is one of several instruments designed to operate with the University of New South Wales' Plateau Observatory (PLATO). A 1.5-THz (200-micrometer) receiver channel will be installed onto PreHEAT in Austral summer 2008–2009. PreHEAT/HEAT and PLATO operate autonomously from Dome A for up to a year at a time, with commands and data being transferred to and from the experiment via satellite daily. The Plateau Observatory is the Dome A component of the multinational Astronomy at the Poles (AstroPoles) program, which has been endorsed by the Joint Committee for the International Polar Year (IPY).

INTRODUCTION

From the Milky Way to high-redshift protogalaxies, the internal evolution of galaxies is determined to a large extent by the life cycles of interstellar clouds, as shown in Figure 1. These clouds are largely comprised of atomic and molecular hydrogen and atomic helium, which are notoriously difficult to detect under normal interstellar conditions. Atomic hydrogen is detectable via the 21-cm spin-flip transition and provides the observational basis for current models of a multiphase galactic interstellar medium (ISM). Its emission is insensitive to gas density and does not always discriminate between cold ($T \sim 70$ K) atomic clouds and the warm ($T \sim 8000$ K), neutral medium that is thought to pervade the galaxy. Furthermore, neither atomic helium nor molecular hydrogen (H_2) have accessible emission line spectra in the prevailing physical conditions in cold interstellar clouds. Thus, it is important to probe the nature of the ISM via rarer trace elements. Carbon, for example, is found in ionized form (C^+) in neutral clouds, eventually becoming atomic (C), then molecular as carbon monoxide (CO) in dark molecular clouds.

Christopher Walker and Craig Kulesa, University of Arizona, 933 North Cherry Avenue, Tucson, AZ 85721, USA. Corresponding author: C. Walker (cwalker@as.arizona.edu). Accepted 25 June 2008.

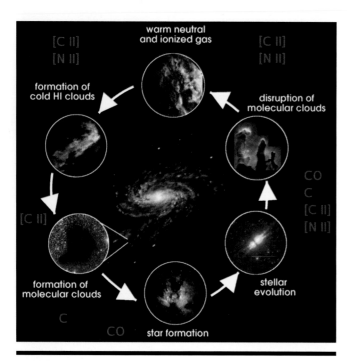

FIGURE 1. The High Elevation Antarctic Terahertz Telescope (HEAT) will observe the fine-structure lines of N^+, C^+, C, and CO that probe the entire life cycle of interstellar clouds. In particular, HEAT will witness the transformation of neutral atomic clouds into star-forming clouds, the interaction of the interstellar medium (ISM) with the young stars that are born from it, and the return of enriched stellar material to the ISM by stellar death.

Although we are now beginning to understand star formation, the formation, evolution, and destruction of molecular clouds remains shrouded in uncertainty. The need to understand the evolution of interstellar clouds in the context of star formation has become a central theme of contemporary astrophysics. Indeed, the National Research Council's most recent decadal survey has identified the study of star formation as one of the key recommendations for new initiatives in this decade.

HEAT SCIENCE GOALS

Via resolved C^+, C, CO, and N^+ THz line emission, the High Elevation Antarctic Terahertz Telescope (HEAT) uniquely probes the pivotal formative and disruptive stages in the life cycles of interstellar clouds and sheds crucial light on the formation of stars by providing new insight into the relationship between interstellar clouds and the stars that form in them, a central component of galactic

evolution. A detailed study of the ISM of the Milky Way is used to construct a template to interpret global star formation in other spiral galaxies.

The minimum science mission of HEAT is to make significant contributions to achieving the three major science goals described below. Using the proposed instrument and observing methodology, the minimum mission is expected to be achievable in a single season of survey operation from Dome A.

GOAL 1: OBSERVING THE LIFE CYCLE OF INTERSTELLAR CLOUDS

The formation of interstellar clouds is a prerequisite for star formation, yet the process has not yet been observed! The HEAT is designed with the unique combination of sensitivity and resolution needed to observe atomic clouds in the process of becoming giant molecular clouds (GMCs) and their subsequent dissolution into diffuse gas via stellar feedback.

GOAL 2: MEASURING THE GALACTIC STAR FORMATION RATE

The HEAT will probe the relation between the gas surface density on kiloparsec scales and the N^+−derived

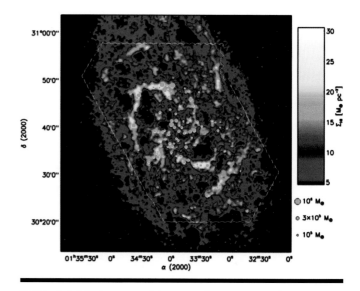

FIGURE 2. The location of GMCs in the nearby spiral galaxy M33 are overlaid upon an integrated intensity map of the HI 21-cm line (Engargiola et al., 2003). These observations show that GMCs are formed from large structure of atomic gas, foreshadowing the detailed study of GMC formation that HEAT will provide in the Milky Way.

star formation rate, so that we might be able to better understand the empirical Schmidt law used to estimate the star-forming properties of external galaxies (Schmidt, 1959; Kennicutt et al., 1998).

GOAL 3: CONSTRUCTING A MILKY WAY TEMPLATE

C^+ and N^+ will be the premier diagnostic tools for terahertz studies of external galaxies with large redshifts (e.g., with Atacama Large Millimeter Array, or ALMA). In such spatially unresolved galaxies, however, only global properties can be measured. The HEAT observations will yield detailed interstellar studies of the widely varying conditions in our own Milky Way galaxy and serve as a crucial diagnostic template or "Rosetta Stone" that can be used to translate the global properties of more distant galaxies.

PROPERTIES OF THE PROPOSED SURVEY

The HEAT's science drivers represent a definitive survey that would not only provide the clearest view of interstellar clouds and their evolution in the galaxy but would also serve as the reference map for contemporary focused studies with space, suborbital, and ground observatories. The following properties define the science requirements for the HEAT survey.

HIGH-RESOLUTION SPECTROSCOPIC IMAGING

Techniques commonly used to diagnose the molecular ISM include submillimeter continuum mapping of dust emission (Hildebrand et al., 1983) and dust extinction mapping at optical and near-infrared wavelengths (Lada et al., 1994). Large-format detector arrays in the infrared are now commonplace, and with the advent of bolometer arrays, both techniques have performed degree-scale maps of molecular material. However, these techniques have limited applicability to the study of the structure of the galactic ISM due to the complete lack of kinematic information.

The confluence of many clouds along most galactic lines of sight can only be disentangled with spectral line techniques. Fitting to a model of galactic rotation is often the only way to determine each cloud's distance and location within the galaxy. With resolution finer than 1 km/s, a cloud's kinematic location can even be distinguished from other phenomena that alter the line shape, such as tur-

bulence, rotation, and local effects, such as protostellar outflows. These kinematic components play a vital role in the sculpting of interstellar clouds, and a survey that has the goal of understanding their evolution *must* be able to measure them. The HEAT will easily resolve the intrinsic profiles of galactic interstellar lines, with a resolution of <0.4 km/s up to 370 km/s of spectrometer bandwidth, comparable to the galactic rotational velocity.

A TERAHERTZ GALACTIC PLANE SURVEY

Molecular line surveys have been performed over the entire sky in the light of the 2.6 mm $J = 1–0$ line of ^{12}CO, and they have been used to synthesize our best understanding of the molecular content of the galaxy. Still, our understanding of the evolution of galactic molecular clouds is woefully incomplete. As already described in the HEAT Science Goals section, the dominant spectral lines of the galaxy are the fine-structure far-infrared and submillimeter lines of C, CO, C^+, and N^+. They probe and regulate all aspects of the formation and destruction of star-forming clouds. They will provide the first barometric maps of the galaxy and illuminate the properties of clouds and their life cycles in relation to their location in the galaxy. They will highlight the delicate interplay between (massive) stars and the clouds which form them, a critical component of galactic evolution. A terahertz survey will dramatically enhance the value of existing millimeter-wave CO observations by providing critical excitation constraints.

ARCMINUTE ANGULAR RESOLUTION AND FULLY SAMPLED MAPS

Good angular resolution is a critical aspect of improvement for a new galactic survey. Previous surveys of [N II] and [C II] were limited to very small regions (KAO and ISO) or had low angular resolution (COBE and BICE) (Bennett et al., 1994; Nakagawa et al., 1998). The HEAT will fully sample both species over large regions of sky to their diffraction-limited resolution of 1.7' and 1.3', respectively. Arcminute resolution with proper sampling is crucial to disentangling different clouds and cloud components over large distances in the galaxy. For example, the Jeans length for star formation in a GMC is approximately 0.5 pc. This length scale is resolved by HEAT to a distance of 500 pc at CO $J = 7–6$ and [C I] and 1200 pc at [C II]. Warm and cold HI clouds and GMCs can be resolved well past 10 kpc.

HIGH SENSITIVITY

The HEAT's high sensitivity is due mostly to the superlative atmospheric conditions expected above Dome A, Antarctica. The extreme cold and exceptional dryness allow ground-based observations into the otherwise forbidden terahertz windows. A plot of the expected atmospheric transmission for excellent winter observing conditions at Dome A versus the comparable opacity at the South Pole is plotted in Figure 3. The high elevation, cold atmosphere, and benign wind conditions at Dome A definitively open the terahertz windows to ground-based observatories and cannot be matched anywhere else on Earth. The implications for the sensitivity to each spectral line is discussed below.

CO J = 7–6 and [C I] J = 2–1

We aim to detect all CO and C^0 to $A_V = 1$–2, where most hydrogen has formed H_2 and CO is just forming. This extinction limit corresponds to $N(CO) \sim 5 \times 10^{15}$ cm^{-2} and $N(C) = 1.6 \times 10^{16}$ cm^{-2} for integrated intensities of 3 K k/ms in CO $J = 7$–6 and 1.8 K km/s in [C I]. These sensitivity limits are achievable (three sigma) within 1.6 and 5 minutes, respectively, of integration time at 810 GHz in median winter atmospheric conditions on Dome

A with an uncooled Schottky receiver. Limits on line emission in that time would constrain the gas density, based upon the line brightness of millimeter wave transitions.

N^+ and C^+

The fine-structure lines of ionized carbon and nitrogen represent the dominant coolants of the interstellar medium of the galaxy and star-forming galaxies. Indeed, the integrated intensity of the 158-micrometer C^+ line alone represents ~1% of the bolometric luminosity of the galaxy! As such, these lines are relatively easy to detect in the ISM. Our most demanding requirements for detection of C^+ and N^+ lie in the search for the formation of giant molecular clouds (via C^+) and the measurement of the diffuse warm ionized medium in the galaxy (via N^+). A flux limit of 2 K km/s will detect N^+ in warm HI as far away as the molecular ring, achievable in good winter weather in three minutes with velocity smoothing to 3 km/s, appropriate for hot ionized gas. Similarly, the accumulation of GMCs from many cold neutral clouds of atomic hydrogen occurs at low relative column densities of ~5×10^{20} cm^{-2}. Since essentially all carbon in such clouds is ionized, $N(C^+) \sim 10^{17}$ cm^{-2}. At the $T = 70$ K common in cold atomic clouds and $n_H = 10^3$ cm^{-3}, the expected C^+ line emission would be 2.5 K km/s, detectable with a Schottky receiver in 10 minutes in excellent winter weather on Dome A. The three sigma limit achievable with deep integrations (two hours) with HEAT would reach $n_H = 10^2$ cm^{-3}. This pressure limit would readily determine whether interstellar material causing significant infrared extinction but without CO is gravitationally bound and likely to be a forming molecular cloud or is simply a line of sight with numerous overlapping diffuse HI clouds.

LARGE-AREA MAPPING COVERAGE OF THE GALACTIC PLANE

From previous CO surveys it is known that the scale height of CO emission toward the inner galaxy is less than one degree (Dame et al., 1987, 2001). The BICE balloon experiment demonstrated that the C^+ distribution is more extended but is still confined to $|b| < 1$. Interstellar pressure, abundances, and physical conditions vary strongly as a function of galactocentric radius, so it is necessary to probe the inner galaxy, the outer galaxy and both spiral arms and interarm regions to obtain a statistically meaningful survey that encompasses the broad dynamic range of physical conditions in the galaxy. We propose therefore to probe the entire galactic plane as seen from Dome A ($0°$ $> l > -120°$). An unbiased survey will be undertaken, ul-

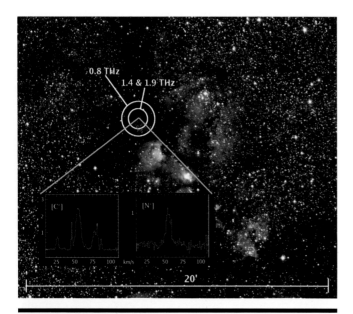

FIGURE 3. Each of HEAT's heterodyne beams is overlaid upon a 2MASS infrared image of NGC 6334. The beams will measure high-resolution spectra in the 0.81-, 1.46-, and 1.90-THz bands, respectively; a small portion (25%) of each is shown as synthetic spectra of NGC 6334.

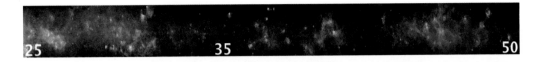

FIGURE 4. An 8.3-micrometer map of the galactic plane from the molecular ring through the Scutum-Crux spiral arm (-20° > *l* > -55°). The yellow rectangle highlights the region to be explored by HEAT in its first season at Dome A. A definitive chemical and kinematic survey of star-forming clouds in [C I] *J* = 2–1 and ^{12}CO *J* = 7–6 of 40 square degrees (~10 square degrees in [C II] and [N II] emission) can be performed in a single season using Schottky receivers. No other site on Earth allows routine access to both far-infrared lines.

timately covering up to 240 square degrees ($-1° < b < 1°$); however, 80 square degrees in two years will be targeted by the Schottky receiver system described here. Figure 4 demonstrates the sky coverage of HEAT's survey of the inner galaxy, with the first season coverage highlighted in yellow. It will probe three crucial components of the galaxy: the molecular ring, the Crux spiral arm, and the interarm region. The remaining sky coverage will be provided by a future upgraded instrument package from the Netherlands Institute for Space Research (SRON), featuring a cryocooled 4 K superconductor insulator superconductor and hot-electron bolometer system. The "inner" galaxy survey will coincide with Galactic Legacy Infrared Mid-Plane Survey Extraordinaire (GLIMPSE), a Spitzer Space Telescope (SST) Legacy Program (Benjamin et al., 2003). Above *l* = 90°, most of the CO emission is located at higher galactic latitude, so *l* and *b* "strip mapping" will locate the target regions, generally following the outskirts of CO *J* = 1–0 distribution (Dame et al., 1987, 2001), and the best-characterized star-forming regions in the galaxy. The observing program will be designed to maximize synergies with the "Cores to Disks" SST Legacy program (Evans et al., 2003) and other SST GTO programs.

HEAT INSTRUMENTATION OVERVIEW

The HEAT will be a fully automated, state-of-the-art terahertz observatory designed to operate autonomously from Dome A in Antarctica. The combination of high altitude (4,100 m), low precipitation, and extreme cold make the far-infrared atmospheric transmission exceptionally good from this site. In Figure 5 we present a plot of the expected atmospheric transmission above Dome A as a function of wavelength (Lawrence, 2004), indicating that winter weather at Dome A approaches (to order of magnitude) the quality of that achieved by the Stratospheric Observatory for Infrared Astronomy (SOFIA). The wavelengths of several important astrophysical lines are indicated with

arrows. The HEAT is designed to take advantage of these unique atmospheric conditions and observe simultaneously in [C II] (158 micrometer), [N II] (205 micrometer), and CO *J* = 7–6 and [C I] (370 micrometer).

A conceptual drawing of HEAT is shown in Figure 6. For robustness and efficiency, the telescope and instrument are integrated into a common optical support structure. The HEAT will be mounted on top of the University of New South Wales' Plateau Observatory (PLATO), which was deployed to Dome A in January 2008. The Plateau Observatory is the successor to the Automated Astrophysical Site-Testing International Observatory (AASTINO) deployed to Dome C in 2003, and it provides power and

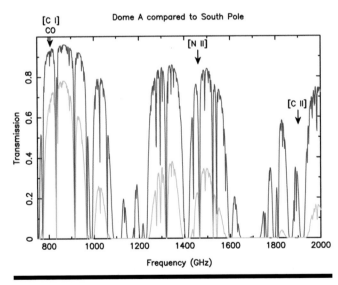

FIGURE 5. Terahertz atmospheric transmission for good (twenty-fifth percentile) winter conditions for the South Pole (bottom line) and Dome A (top line), derived from PWV measurements at the South Pole, atmospheric models from Lawrence (2004), and actual automatic weather station data collected during 2005 from Dome A. The PWV content for each model atmosphere is 210 and 50 micrometers, respectively. Arrows indicate the wavelengths of the [N II], [C II], and CO/[C I] lines.

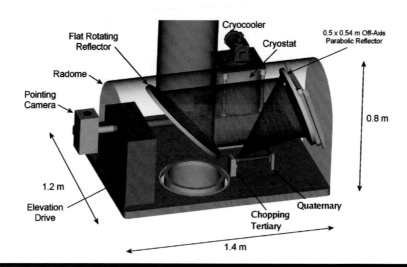

FIGURE 6. The HEAT telescope has an effective collecting area of 0.5 m. Elevation tracking is accomplished by rotating the 45° flat reflector. The entire telescope structure is warmed by waste heat from the PLATO instrument module below. The Schottky mixers used in the instrument package are efficiently cooled to 70 K using a reliable off-the-shelf closed-cycle cryocooler.

communications for the HEAT telescope and instrument. The total power budget for HEAT, including cryogenics, telescope drive system, and instrument control system, is maximally 600 W, which is readily provided by efficient, high-reliability generators within PLATO. Data transfer and control of HEAT will be done via Iridium satellite through the PLATO facilities. The combined HEAT and PLATO facility is functionally equivalent to a space-based observatory.

The HEAT will be able to calibrate observations through several means. (1) A vane with an ambient temperature absorbing load will be located at the cryostat entrance window, allowing standard chopper wheel calibration to be performed. (2) HEAT will routinely perform sky dips to compute the atmospheric optical depth in each of its three wavelength bands. (3) HEAT will regularly observe a standard list of calibration sources. (4) The PLATO currently hosts PreHEAT, a 450-micrometer tipper and spectrometer that measures atmospheric transmission. Its measurements will be coordinated with HEAT spectral line observations to provide cross calibration.

LOGISTICS: DEPLOYMENT TO DOME A

Antarctic science has reached a level of maturity where several options exist for fielding instruments on remote sites. For Dome A, these options include the following:

1. (Chinese) Traverse from Zhongshan Station to Dome A: PLATO and its complement of instruments (includ-

ing PreHEAT) were deployed to Dome A by a 1300-km Chinese traverse from the coastal Zhongshan station in January 2008. The expedition was a collaborative effort with the Polar Research Institute of China, the National Astronomical Observatory of China, and the Nanjing Institute of Astronomical Optics Technology. Upgrades to PreHEAT and the installation of the full HEAT experiment could potentially be deployed in a similar manner.

2. (American) Twin Otter air support: If a Chinese traverse brings PLATO (in 2007–2008) and HEAT to Dome A (in 2009–2010), U.S. Antarctic Program Twin Otter air support would allow personnel to be flown in from the South Pole or the forthcoming AGAP field camps (such as AGO3) to facilitate the HEAT installation. Furthermore, the HEAT experiment is small enough to be deployed by Twin Otter.

3. (Australian) An Australian Antarctic Division CASA 212 cargo flight directly from Mawson/Davis to Dome A may be possible for transport of the HEAT experiment, with subsequent flights to support fuel and/or personnel for the HEAT installation.

SUMMARY

At this writing, the pathfinder for HEAT, PreHEAT, is operating autonomously from a PLATO module recently deployed to the summit of Dome A by the Polar Research Institute of China. Because of the altitude and extreme cold/dry conditions known to exist at Dome A, the atmospheric opacity above the site is expected to be the lowest on Earth, making it ideal for far-infrared/terahertz observatories. Our hope is that HEAT will follow quickly on the heels of PreHEAT and provide a powerful new window to the universe.

LITERATURE CITED

Bennett, C. L., D. J. Fixsen, G. Hinshaw, J. C. Mather, S. H. Moseley, E. L. Wright, R. E. Eplee Jr., J. Gales, T. Hewagama, R. B. Isaacman, R. A. Shafer, and K. Turpie. 1994. Morphology of the Interstellar Cooling Lines Detected by COBE. *Astrophysical Journal,* 434:587–598.

Benjamin, R. A., E. Churchwell, B. L. Babler, T. M. Bania, D. P. Clemens, M. Cohen, J. M. Dickey, R. Indebetouw, J. M. Jackson, H. A. Kobulnicky, A. Lazarian, A. P. Marsten, J. S. Mathis, M. R. Meade, S. Seager, S. R. Stolovy, C. Watson, B. A. Whitney, M. J. Wolff, and M. G. Wolfire. 2003. GLIMPSE: I. An SIRTF Legacy Project to Map the Inner Galaxy. *Publications of the Astronomical Society of the Pacific,* 115:953–964.

Dame, T. M., H. Ungerechts, R. S. Cohen, E. J. Geus, de, I. A. Grenier, J. May, D. C. Murphy, L.-Å Nyman, and P. Thaddeus. 1987. A Composite CO Survey of the Entire Milky Way. *Astrophysical Journal,* 322:706.

Dame, T. M., D. Hartmann, and P. Thaddeus. 2001. The Milky Way in Molecular Clouds: A New Complete CO Survey. *Astrophysical Journal,* 547:792.

Engargiola, G., R. L. Plambeck, E. Rosolowsky, and L. Blitz. 2003. Giant Molecular Clouds in M33. I. BIMA All-Disk Survey. *Astrophysical Journal, Supplement Series,* 149:343–363.

Evans, N. J., II, and the Cores to Disks (c2d) Team. 2003. From Molecular Cores to Planet-forming Disks: A SIRTF Legacy Program. *Publications of the Astronomical Society of the Pacific,* 115:965–980.

Hildebrand, R. H. 1983. The Determination of Cloud Masses and Dust Characteristics from Submillimetre Thermal Emission. *Quarterly Journal of the Royal Astronomical Society,* 24:267.

Kennicutt, R. C. 1998. The Global Schmidt Law in Star-Forming Galaxies. *Astrophysical Journal,* 498:541.

Lada, C. J., E. A. Lada, D. P. Clemens, and J. Bally. 1994. Dust Extinction and Molecular Gas in the Dark Cloud IC 5146. *Astrophysical Journal,* 429:694.

Lawrence, J. S. 2004. Infrared and Submillimetre Atmospheric Characteristics of High Antarctic Plateau Sites. *Publications of the Astronomical Society of the Pacific,* 116:482.

Nakagawa, T., Y. Y. Yui, Y. Doi, H. Okuda, H. Shibai, K. Mochizuki, T. Nishimura, and F. J. Low. 1998. Far-Infrared [CII] Line Survey Observations of the Galactic Plane. *Astrophysical Journal, Supplement Series,* 115:259–269.

Schmidt, M. 1959. The Rate of Star Formation. *Astrophysical Journal,* 129:243.

Watching Star Birth from the Antarctic Plateau

N. F. H. Tothill, M. J. McCaughrean, C. K. Walker, C. Kulesa, A. Loehr, and S. Parshley

ABSTRACT. Astronomical instruments on the Antarctic plateau are very well suited to observing the formation of stars and their associated planetary systems since young stars emit their light at the wavelengths at which Antarctica offers the most striking advantages. Antarctic telescopes have already brought new insights into the physics of star formation and the molecular clouds where it occurs. During the International Polar Year (IPY), new sites will be opened up to astronomical exploitation, with the prospect of new capabilities in the drive to understand how stars and planets form.

INTRODUCTION

Stars are one of the main engines of evolution in the universe. They convert mass to light and hydrogen and helium into heavier elements; massive stars compress and disrupt nearby gas clouds by the action of their ionizing radiation and their stellar winds. However, the formation and early evolution of stars are not well understood: they form inside clouds of molecular gas and dust, which are opaque to visible light but transparent to infrared light and submillimeter-wave radiation. These wavebands are thus crucial to our understanding of the formation of stars: the young stars themselves radiate infrared light, which can penetrate the dark clouds, while submillimeter-wave observations can trace the gas and dust that make up the clouds.

N. F. H. Tothill, School of Physics, University of Exeter, Stocker Road, Exeter EX4 4QL, UK; also Smithsonian Astrophysical Observatory, 60 Garden Street, Cambridge, MA 02138, USA. M. J. McCaughrean, School of Physics, University of Exeter, Stocker Road, Exeter EX4 4QL, UK. C. K. Walker and C. Kulesa, Steward Observatory, University of Arizona, Tucson, AZ 85721, USA. A. Loehr, Smithsonian Astrophysical Observatory, 60 Garden Street, Cambridge, MA 02138, USA. S. Parshley, Department of Astronomy, Cornell University, Ithaca, NY 14853, USA. Corresponding author: N. F. H. Tothill (nfht@astro.ex.ac.uk). Accepted 25 June 2008.

ANTARCTIC SUBMILLIMETER TELESCOPE AND REMOTE OBSERVATORY OBSERVATIONS OF MOLECULAR CLOUDS

The main constituents of molecular clouds, hydrogen and helium gases, are effectively invisible to us: both molecular hydrogen and atomic helium have very few low-energy transitions that could be excited at the low temperatures prevailing in interstellar space. We therefore rely on tracers—gas and dust that are readily excited at low temperatures and readily emit at long wavelengths. The most basic of these tracers is carbon monoxide (CO), which is the most abundant molecule in these gas clouds after hydrogen (H_2) and helium (He).

The lower-energy (low-*J*) transitions of CO emit radiation at wavelengths of 0.8–3mm, and are easily detected from high, dry, mountaintop sites in the temperate zones. At shorter wavelengths, the higher energy mid-*J* transitions can be detected only through a very dry atmosphere. The Antarctic plateau provides the largest fraction of such dry weather of any observing site in the world, and, sited at Amundsen-Scott South Pole Station, the Antarctic Submillimeter Telescope and Remote Observatory (AST/RO; Stark et al., 2001) is designed to take full advantage of these conditions.

The mid-*J* transitions (from CO 4–3 up to CO 7–6) are particularly interesting for their ability to probe the physical conditions of the molecular gas from which they arise: in particular, they can only be excited in gas with density comparable to a critical density (about 10^4 molecules cm^{-3} for CO 4–3); emission in these transitions implies the presence of dense gas. By also observing the molecular clouds in lower-*J* transitions, AST/RO is able to trace the velocity structure of the gas clouds and to estimate the gas temperature, thus providing a suite of measurements of the physical conditions of the gas clouds where stars form.

Nearby Low-Mass Star-Forming Regions

All the nearest star-forming molecular clouds (within a few hundred parsecs; a parsec (pc) is a standard astronomical distance unit: 1 pc = 3.09×10^{16} m = 3.26 light-years) form low-mass stars. Because of their proximity, they subtend large areas on the sky (of the order of square degrees), requiring large amounts of time to map them properly. The Antarctic Submillimeter Telescope and Remote Observatory is very well suited to this task: its small mirror gives it a comparatively large beam, which, in turn, allows large areas to be mapped quickly. The highly transparent Antarctic atmosphere provides long stretches of very clear air in winter, which allows large blocks of time to be allocated to mapping these clouds at comparatively high frequencies. The clouds themselves are less dense and cooler than the giant molecular clouds that form the majority of stars, and many of the stars form in isolation, rather than in clusters. It is therefore often assumed that mid-*J* transitions of CO are not excited in these regions and are so difficult to detect that they no longer make good tracers. The AST/RO mapped large areas of two nearby cloud complexes, Lupus and Chamaeleon (named after the constellations in which they are found), in the CO 4–3 transition, finding significant emission. With a brightness temperature of the order of 1K, this CO 4–3 emission must come from molecular gas that is dense

enough to thermalize the transition and warm enough to have a Rayleigh-Jeans temperature of a few Kelvin.

The Lupus star-forming region consists of a complex of molecular clouds lying about 150 pc from Earth, associated with a large number of young stars. The clouds are readily visible in optical photographs of the sky as clumpy, filamentary dark patches (Figure 1)—indeed, this is how these clouds were first discovered (Barnard, 1927). The Lupus complex lies to one side of the Scorpius–Centaurus OB Association (Sco-Cen), a huge collection of very massive young stars lying in the southern sky. On the other side of Sco-Cen, the rho Ophiuchi star-forming region displays clusters of massive young stars whose interaction with their natal molecular gas produces highly visible nebulae. By comparison to rho Ophiuchi, Lupus is quiescent—it is rather lacking in massive stars and has no large cluster, the young stars being much more spread out. One might therefore assume that Lupus would also lack the dense, warm molecular gas found in abundance in rho Ophiuchi.

However, the AST/RO data show detectable CO 4–3 emission throughout the Lupus clouds, with very strong emission in a few hot spots. By comparing this emission to the more easily excited ^{13}CO 2–1 (Figure 2), it is possible to estimate the physical conditions of the gas (Figure 3). The gas making up the bulk of the clouds is quite warm (probably >10K) and close to the critical density. The clumps within the cloud seem to be denser but not much cooler, and some are warm (around 20K). The data suggest that one of the hot spots in Lupus III is very warm (perhaps as much as 50K) but not dense enough to fully excite the 4–3 transition. The hot spot at the northwestern end of the Lupus I filament also appears to be warm and not very dense but has broader lines, implying more turbulent motion in the gas. While the elevated temperature in Lupus III can be explained by the proximity of the fairly massive young stars HR 5999 and 6000 (visible in Figure 1, lying in the dark cloud), there are no comparable stars near the end of the Lupus I filament. Clearly, the Lupus clouds show significant diversity in their physical conditions and, hence, in the environments in which stars are formed.

Being more easily excited, emission in the isotopically substituted ^{13}CO 2–1 line is distributed throughout the molecular gas and is less discriminating as a probe of the physical conditions of the gas. But because it is so widely distributed, it is an excellent tracer of the velocity field of the gas. The ability of AST/RO to map large areas allows us to fully sample the gas velocity field over degree-scale fields. Maps of the centroid velocity of the ^{13}CO 2–1 line show strong velocity gradients in several locations in the complex, usually

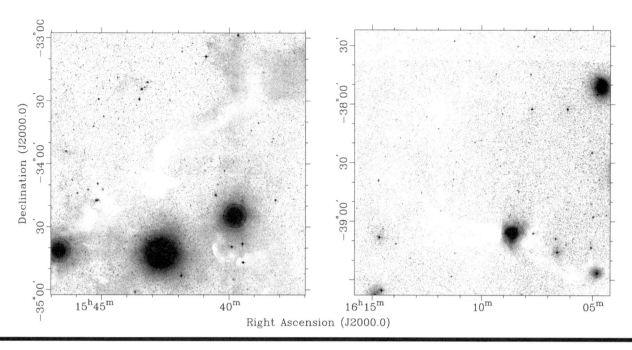

FIGURE 1. Two of the molecular clouds that make up the Lupus complex, visible as dark patches against the stars: (left) Lupus I and (right) Lupus III. The ridge in Lupus I is about 5 pc long. Images taken from the Digital Sky Survey (Lasker et al., 1990).

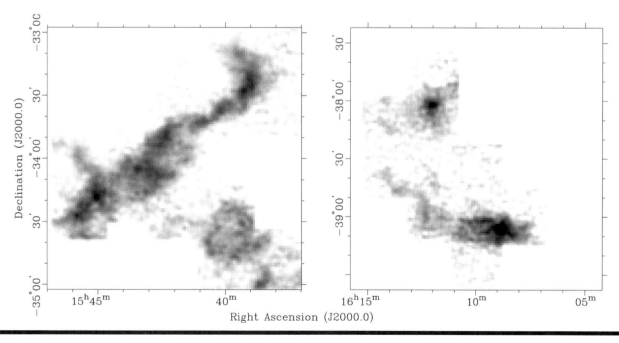

FIGURE 2. The same clouds as in Figure 1, mapped in the millimeter-wave emission of ^{13}CO 2–1. The isotopically substituted CO traces the dark cloud structure very well (N. F. H. Tothill, A. Loehr, S. C. Parshley, A. A. Stark, A. P. Lane, J. I. Harnett, G. Wright, C. K. Walker, T. L. Bourke, and P. C. Myers, unpublished manuscript).

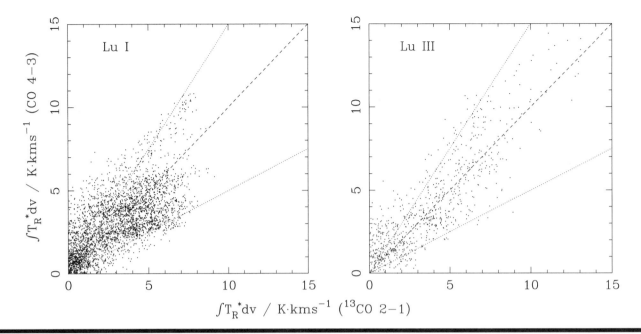

FIGURE 3. Comparison of CO 4–3 and ^{13}CO 2–1 emission from Lupus I and III clouds. The different physical conditions of the hot spots in the two clouds show up in the different distributions, but the bulk of each cloud is quite similar to that of the other (N. F. H. Tothill, A. Loehr, S. C. Parshley, A. A. Stark, A. P. Lane, J. I. Harnett, G. Wright, C. K. Walker, T. L. Bourke, and P. C. Myers, unpublished manuscript).

over quite small distances (about 0.5 pc), but in Lupus I, a different pattern emerges, of a shallow and rather uneven velocity gradient along the filament, coupled with a strong gradient across the filament. This gradient across the filament is coherent over at least 2 pc of the filament's length. The presence of such a large coherent structure in a region whose activity appears quite stochastic is remarkable; it may have arisen from external influences, presumably from Sco-Cen. The massive stars in Sco-Cen are quite capable of affecting nearby clouds; the rho Ophiuchi region on the other side of Sco-Cen is clearly influenced by the nearby OB association. There are some signs of a supernova remnant to the northwest of the Lupus I filament, which could have a strong dynamical effect on the gas.

NEW OBSERVING SITES IN THE ANTARCTIC AND ARCTIC

The factors that make the South Pole such a good site to detect the submillimeter-wave radiation from the clouds around young stars are likely to be found in many other locations on the Antarctic plateau and even at some sites in the Arctic. With the astronomical potential of the Antarctic plateau established, it is possible to evaluate other sites in the polar regions as potential observatories.

Projects to evaluate the potential of several polar sites are taking place during the International Polar Year: Astronomy from the Poles (AstroPoles) is a general program to study all the sites listed below, while STELLA ANTARCTICA concentrates on a more detailed study of the characteristics of the Franco-Italian Concordia station on Dome C.

The meteorology of Antarctica is dominated by the katabatic flow, as the air loses heat by contact with the radiatively cooled snow surface, loses buoyancy, and sinks down the slope of the ice sheet, leading to a downward-flowing wind. Most of the atmospheric turbulence is concentrated in a boundary layer between this flow and the ice, a layer which gets deeper farther downslope.

ANTARCTICA: DOME A

Dome A is the highest point on the plateau and has less atmosphere to get in the way than any other site. However, it also lacks infrastructure: in the absence of a year-round station, all instruments must be fully autonomous. Traverses to Dome A and astronomical site testing are being undertaken by the Polar Research Institute of China, in collaboration with an international consortium. This consortium, including Chinese institutions, the Universities of New South Wales, Arizona, and Exeter, and Caltech, is constructing and deploying the Plateau Observatory (PLATO), an automated unmanned site-testing observatory (Lawrence et al., 2006). One of the instruments on PLATO, PreHEAT, is designed to characterize the site quality at submillimeter wavelengths and to map the $J = 6-5$ emission of isotopically substituted ^{13}CO from massive star-forming regions and giant molecular clouds. It will be succeeded by the High Elevation Antarctic Terahertz Telescope (HEAT), a 0.5-m-aperture telescope designed to function around 0.2 mm wavelength. The HEAT will map the fine-structure emission from atomic and ionized carbon and nitrogen, together with CO 7–6, to trace the evolution and recycling of the interstellar medium in our galaxy. The prospects for PreHEAT and HEAT at Dome A are discussed in more detail in Walker and Kulesa (2009, this volume).

At the top of the continent, the boundary layer at Dome A may be only 3 to 4 m thick, which would make it much easier to place a telescope above the boundary layer, into what is likely to be very stable air with very good seeing. Other experiments on PLATO will test these predictions about the boundary layer at Dome A and sketch out its potential as a future observatory site.

ANTARCTICA: DOME C

Dome C is significantly higher than the South Pole (around 3200 m elevation) and lies on a local maximum of the ice sheet along the ridge running through East Antarctica. It is likely to enjoy better conditions than the South Pole but not such good conditions as Dome A. Recent measurements (Lawrence et al., 2004) show the boundary layer to be about 30 m deep, with clear-air seeing above the layer estimated to be better than 0.3 arcseconds. Although Dome C probably enjoys better submillimeter atmospheric transparency than the South Pole, infrared astronomy seems more likely to be its greatest strength: the combination of excellent seeing, very little cloud cover, low thermal background (due to the cold air), and the presence of a year-round crewed station with strong logistical support makes it possible to build an infrared facility telescope with a primary mirror diameter of 2 m or more, which would be competitive with the largest telescopes elsewhere in the world (Burton et al., 2005). Detailed site testing at Concordia is being carried out by the IPY program STELLA ANTARCTICA and by members of the European Commission–funded network "Antarctic Research—A European Network for Astronomy" (ARENA). In the near future, this should lead to the construction and validation of a model of the boundary layer that allows telescopes to be designed to take advantage of the unusual conditions at this site. Two

small telescopes are in the process of being designed and deployed to Concordia: Antarctica Search for Transiting Extrasolar Planets (ASTEP) is an optical time series experiment, designed to monitor the brightness of nearby stars and watch for the fluctuations as their planets transit. The International Robotic Antarctic Infrared Telescope (IRAIT) is a 0.8-m-aperture infrared telescope to carry out wide-field infrared surveys and to test the site characteristics for a larger infrared telescope.

GREENLAND: SUMMIT

The atmosphere above the Greenland ice cap in winter is also dominated by katabatic flow. The peak of the ice cap (Summit station, at latitude 72°N) is therefore analogous to Dome A in Antarctica, albeit less extreme: lower (3200 m), warmer (about −42°C in good observing conditions), etc. Nonetheless, it should share many characteristics of Antarctic plateau sites, such as cold, dry, stable air. It has its own advantages: it is crewed year-round and access is easy in summer, possible in winter; it also has access to the northern sky, which is invisible from Antarctica. All these factors combine to give Summit excellent potential as an observatory site. There is also room for synergy with Antarctic observatories in order to cover more of the sky and to prototype and test equipment at a more easily accessible location.

ELLESMERE ISLAND

The northern tip of Ellesmere Island in Canada lies very close to the North Pole and thus offers at least one of the advantages of very high latitude sites, namely, the ready availability of 24-hour darkness with small changes in source elevation. Since this part of Ellesmere Island is rocky, with mountain peaks rising above the permanent sea ice, it is likely to have rather different meteorology to the smooth ice caps in Greenland and Antarctica. Automated weather stations have been placed on several candidate rocky peaks on the northern coast, and the first results of this basic site testing are expected shortly.

CONCLUSIONS

Understanding the process of star formation requires the observation of infrared light (to see the young star through the gas and dust around it) and submillimeter waves (to estimate the physical conditions of the molecular gas itself). Observations from the Antarctic plateau offer large advantages in both of these regimes, demonstrated by the AST/RO observations of nearby molecular clouds, which yield a picture of quite different molecular clouds: Lupus I has strong coherent velocity gradients and may have been externally influenced, while Lupus III has been heated by associated young stars.

During the International Polar Year, efforts to test the suitability of other sites for astronomy are under way: Concordia Station on Dome C is likely to be an excellent infrared site and is the best known. Other sites (Dome A, Summit, and Ellesmere Island) are at much earlier stages of characterization.

ACKNOWLEDGMENTS

Arctic astronomical projects are being coordinated, for Ellesmere Island by Ray Carlberg (University of Toronto) and Eric Steinbring (Herzberg Institute of Astrophysics), and for Greenland by Michael Andersen (Niels Bohr Institute). The AstroPoles and STELLA ANTARCTICA programs are led by Michael Burton (University of New South Wales) and Eric Fossat (University of Nice), respectively.

The ARENA network is coordinated by Nicolas Epchtein (University of Nice) and funded by the European Commission under the 6th Framework Programme. Operations at Dome A are carried out by the Polar Research Institute of China. The AST/RO was supported by the National Science Foundation's Office of Polar Programs under ANT-0441756. We also acknowledge financial support from the University of Exeter.

LITERATURE CITED

Barnard, E. E. 1927. Catalog of 327 Dark Objects in the Sky. Chicago: University of Chicago Press.

Burton, M. G., J. S. Lawrence, M. C. B. Ashley, J. A. Bailey, C. Blake, T. R. Bedding, J. Bland-Hawthorn, I. A. Bond, K. Glazebrook, M. G. Hidas, G. Lewis, S. N. Longmore, S. T. Maddison, S. Mattila, V. Minier, S. D. Ryder, R. Sharp, C. H. Smith, J. W. V. Storey, C. G. Tinney, P. Tuthill, A. J. Walsh, W. Walsh, M. Whiting, T. Wong, D. Woods, and P. C. M. Yock. 2005. Science Programs for a 2-m Class Telescope at Dome C, Antarctica: PILOT, the Pathfinder for an International Large Optical Telescope. *Publications of the Astronomical Society of Australia*, 22:199–235.

Lasker, B. M., C. R. Sturch, B. J. McLean, J. L. Russell, H. Jenker, and M. M. Shara. 1990. The Guide Star Catalog. I—Astronomical Foundations and Image Processing. *Astronomical Journal*, 99: 2019–2058, 2173–2178.

Lawrence, J. S., M. C. B. Ashley, A. Tokovinin, and T. Travouillon. 2004. Exceptional Astronomical Seeing Conditions above Dome C in Antarctica. *Nature*, 431:278–281.

Lawrence, J. S., M. C. B. Ashley, M. G. Burton, X. Cui, J. R. Everett, B. T. Indermuehle, S. L. Kenyon, D. Luong-Van, A. M. Moore, J. W. V. Storey, A. Tokovinin, T. Travouillon, C. Pennypacker, L. Wang, and D. York. 2006. Site Testing Dome A, Antarctica. *Proceedings of SPIE*, 6267:51–59.

Stark, A. A., J. Bally, S. P. Balm, T. M. Bania, A. D. Bolatto, R. A. Chamberlin, G. Engargiola, M. Huang, J. G. Ingalls, K. Jacobs, J. M. Jackson, J. W. Kooi, A. P. Lane, K.-Y. Lo, R. D. Marks, C. L. Martin, D. Mumma, R. Ojha, R. Schieder, J. Staguhn, J. Stutzki, C. K. Walker, R. W. Wilson, G. A. Wright, X. Zhang, P. Zimmermann, and R. Zimmermann. 2001. The Antarctic Submillimeter Telescope and Remote Observatory (AST/RO). *Publications of the Astronomical Society of the Pacific*, 113:567–585.

Walker, C. K., and C. A. Kulesa. 2009. "HEAT: The High Elevation Antarctic Terahertz Telescope." In *Smithsonian at the Poles: Contributions to International Polar Year Science*, ed. I. Krupnik, M. A. Lang, and S. E. Miller, pp. 373–380. Washington, D.C.: Smithsonian Institution Scholarly Press.

Antarctic Meteorites: Exploring the Solar System from the Ice

Timothy J. McCoy, Linda C. Welzenbach, and Catherine M. Corrigan

ABSTRACT. The collection of meteorites from the Antarctic plateau has changed from a scientific curiosity to a major source of extraterrestrial material. Following initial meteorite recoveries in 1976, the U.S. National Science Foundation, the National Aeronautics and Space Administration (NASA), and the Smithsonian Institution formed the U.S. Antarctic Meteorite program for the collection, curation, classification, and distribution of Antarctic meteorites, which was formalized in 1981. The Smithsonian provides classification and serves as the long-term curatorial repository, resulting in explosive growth of the Smithsonian meteorite collection. After 30 field seasons, more than 80% of the Smithsonian collection now originates from Antarctica. In addition to curation and classification, Smithsonian staff provide administrative leadership to the program, serve on field expeditions, and provide specimens for outreach and display. Given the relatively pristine state and ancient terrestrial ages of these meteorites, they provide perhaps our best sampling of the material in our solar system. Meteorites from the Moon were first recognized among the Antarctic meteorites in 1981, as was the first martian meteorite the next year. In 1996, debate erupted about evidence for past microbial life in an Antarctic martian meteorite, and that debate spurred the launch of two rovers to explore Mars. Among meteorites thought to have originated on asteroids, ingredients for ancient life may have survived much higher temperatures than previously envisioned during early planetary melting and differentiation. The ongoing collection of Antarctic meteorites will enrich the scientific community and Smithsonian Institution in specimens and knowledge about our solar system.

METEORITES FROM ANTARCTICA

Serendipitous finds of meteorites from Antarctica were documented as early as 1912 (Adelie Land), and several such finds occurred in the early 1960s as scientific investigations in Antarctica increased (Lazarev, 1961; Thiel Mountains, 1962; Neptune Mountains, 1964). In 1969, with the recovery of nine meteorites in the Yamato Mountains by Japanese glaciologists, meteorites went from being mere curiosities to becoming a focus of exploration. While most accumulations of multiple meteorites represent a single fall that broke up in the atmosphere and showered an area with stones, this discovery suggested a unique concentration mechanism. These nine meteorites represented six different types, including two rare chondrites (primitive meteorites formed in the solar nebula) and a diogenite

Timothy J. McCoy, Linda C. Welzenbach, and Catherine M. Corrigan, Department of Mineral Sciences, National Museum of Natural History, Smithsonian Institution, Washington, DC 20560-0119, USA. Corresponding author: T. J. McCoy (mccoyt@si.edu). Accepted 25 June 2008.

(a rock formed by melting on the surface of an asteroid) (Shima and Shima, 1973).

The concentration mechanism (Figure 1) is tied to the 12 million km² of Antarctic ice sheet, which acts as an ideal catchment area for fallen meteorites (Harvey, 2003). As the East Antarctic ice sheet flows toward the margins of the continent, its progress is occasionally blocked by mountains or obstructions below the ice. In these areas, old, deep, blue ice is pushed to the surface, carrying the meteorites along with it. Strong katabatic winds cause massive deflation, removing large volumes of ice and preventing the accumulation of snow on the stranded deposits of meteorites. The end result is a representative sampling of meteorite falls.

Of additional significance is the terrestrial residence time of these rocks. Antarctic meteorites record terrestrial ages ranging from tens of thousands to two million years (Welten et al., 1997) and yet are less weathered than meteorites found in temperate climates. The newly fallen meteorites are quickly frozen and preserved into the thickening ice sheet, reducing the amount of weathering and contamination. The relatively pristine state of the samples allows studies that were previously difficult or impossible. The lack of weathering also means that much smaller me-

teorites survive and thus provide a broader sample of the material in our solar system.

ANTARCTIC METEORITE PROGRAM

The Japanese began regular collecting expeditions to the Antarctic in 1973, collecting a modest 12 meteorites. In 1974, they returned hundreds of meteorites. During this same period, University of Pittsburgh meteorite scientist Bill Cassidy submitted three proposals to the National Science Foundation (NSF) to fund a U.S. expedition to find other suitable areas of meteorite accumulation. When word of the Japanese success finally reached the NSF, after it had rejected the three previously submitted proposals, support was granted for a 1976–1977 expedition. Cassidy was joined by Ed Olsen (Field Museum, Chicago) and Keizo Yanai (National Institute for Polar Research, Tokyo) to search in areas accessible by helicopter from McMurdo Station to Allan Hills. Nine specimens were found that season. These early days of Antarctic meteorite collection are wonderfully recounted in Cassidy (2003). The meteorites were curated by Olsen

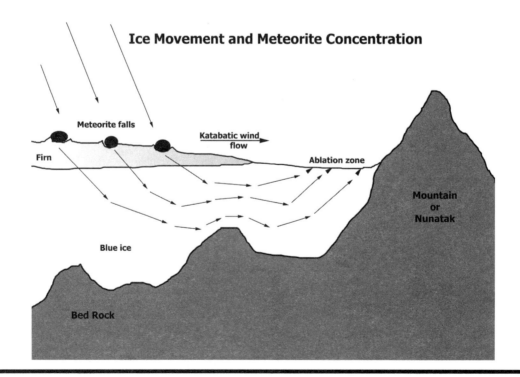

FIGURE 1. Diagram illustrating the mechanism by which Antarctic meteorites are concentrated in specific locations . See text for description of this process.

at the Field Museum, and pieces were distributed in an ad hoc fashion to the research community.

Despite the modest numbers for this joint U.S.–Japanese team, it was clear that this was merely the tip of the iceberg and that large numbers of meteorites from the cleanest environment on Earth were soon to be recovered in Antarctica. An ad hoc committee was convened on 11 November 1977 in Washington, D.C. The meeting included representatives of NSF (Mort Turner), the field party (William Cassidy), the Smithsonian Institution (SI, Brian Mason of the Natural History Museum and Ursula Marvin of the Astrophysical Observatory), National Aeronautics and Space Administration (NASA, Don Bogard of Johnson Space Center and Bevan French of NASA headquarters), and the scientific community (including Jim Papike) (Antarctic Meteorite Working Group, 1978). This meeting produced "a plan for the collection, processing, and distribution of the U.S. portion of the Antarctic meteorites collected during 1977-78" (Antarctic Meteorite Working Group, 1978:13). However, much of the groundwork for this system of interagency cooperation (which ultimately was formalized as the three-agency agreement between NASA, NSF, and SI) and distribution of samples was laid before the meeting. Brian Mason (Smithsonian Institution, personal communication, 2004) recounted a conversation with Mort Turner where the opinion expressed was that meteorites collected by U.S. field expeditions should properly become U.S. government property. It was agreed that NASA would provide short-term curation modeled on, but less rigorous than, standards for lunar rock curation, while the Smithsonian would assume responsibility for classification and long-term curation and storage.

The collection effort evolved into what is now known as the Antarctic Search for Meteorites (ANSMET). Thirty full seasons have now been completed with the recovery of more than 16,000 meteorites—more than were collected over the entire Earth in the previous 500 years. The field party grew from three members initially, with six to eight members during much of its history, and peaked at 12 members split between two field parties, with one supported by NASA with the specific objective of increasing the collection of martian meteorites. The NSF Division of Polar Programs, with decades of experience in exploring the harsh Antarctic environment, provides support for the ANSMET. Currently, the ANSMET program is run by Ralph Harvey, an associate professor at Case Western Reserve University. Each year, teams of four to eight scientists work together collecting meteorites in remote field locations for about six weeks during the austral summer (November–January). Their primary goal is

to recover a complete and uncontaminated sampling of meteorites. Systematic searches are conducted as a series of 30-m-wide parallel transects by snowmobile on areas of snow-free blue ice. If the concentration is high, transects by snowmobile are replaced by searching on foot, ensuring the recovery of meteorites as small as 1 cm in diameter. Many stranding surfaces are large enough to require several seasons in the same area.

It is interesting to note that as the program evolved, the number of meteorites recovered changed dramatically. Starting with 11 meteorites in 1976, ANSMET averaged ~200 meteorites per year from 1976 to 1984, before ramping up to an average of nearly 600 meteorites from 1985 to 2001. This average is remarkable given the cancellation of the 1989 field season due to logistical problems and the intentional exploration of areas with greater and lesser numbers of meteorites to average out the curatorial workload from year to year. During 2002–2006, an average of more than 900 meteorites was recovered each year, including two seasons of 1200+ meteorites.

The astounding success of the Antarctic meteorite programs of the United States and Japan have spurred a number of other efforts, including those from Europe (EUROMET) (Folco et al., 2002) and China (Lin et al., 2002). Indeed, a few privately funded expeditions have actually recovered meteorites in Antarctica. These events caused the Antarctic Treaty Organization to encourage member countries to take measures to protect this valuable scientific resource. The U.S. government, through the NSF, responded by implementing a federal regulation (45 CFR 674; National Science Foundation, 2003) that codified, for the first time, collection and curatorial standards used by the U.S. Antarctic Meteorite Program. It is important to note that other national governments and government consortia (e.g., EUROMET) adhere to similar standards, although each has standards adapted to their unique situation.

SMITHSONIAN'S ROLE IN THE U.S. ANTARCTIC METEORITE PROGRAM

While the Smithsonian's role has primarily been in classification and curation, it has been greatly strengthened by the participation of several SI staff in the field efforts over the years (Figure 2). Ursula Marvin of the Smithsonian Astrophysical Observatory, who played a pivotal role in both the initial formation and long-term management of the program over the next three decades, was the first Smithsonian participant in 1978–1979 and returned in 1981–1982, joined by Bob Fudali of the Division of

FIGURE 2. Linda Welzenbach collects an achondrite meteorite at Larkman Nunatak during the 2006–2007 ANSMET field season.

Meteorites, a long-time associate of Cassidy. Subsequently, Fudali (1983–1984, 1987–1988), meteorite collection managers Twyla Thomas (1985–1986) and Linda Welzenbach (2002–2003, 2006–2007), and postdoctoral fellows Sara Russell (1996–1997) and Cari Corrigan (2004–2005) served on the ANSMET field parties.

While the collection effort was shared by many, the classification of Antarctic meteorites has been largely the responsibility of two individuals, Brian Mason and Tim McCoy. Mason volunteered his services during the formative stages of the program, and it would be hard to have found a more perfect individual to undertake the challenge of classifying thousands of individual meteorites. During his tenure at the American Museum of Natural History in New York and subsequently at the Smithsonian Institution, Mason had examined virtually every type of mete-

orite known, pioneered the use of mineralogical data in the classification of meteorites in his seminal 1963 paper (Mason, 1963), and, when faced with an unusual Antarctic meteorite, could quickly recall other similar meteorites he had examined during his long career. During his long tenure with the ANSMET program, Mason would go on to classify more than 10,000 individual meteorites, including a considerable number of Japanese meteorites during a visit to the National Institute of Polar Research in 1982. McCoy was hired in large part because of his experience and interest in classification of and research on Antarctic meteorites and has overseen classification, with the help of Welzenbach and a cadre of students and postdoctoral fellows, of more than 5,000 meteorites.

After macroscopic descriptions are completed at NASA's Johnson Space Center, a small chip is sent to the Smithsonian for classification. In the earliest days of the program, a thin section was prepared for every meteorite, and mineral compositions were measured using the electron microprobe. As the numbers of meteorites ramped up between 1984 and 1988, it became clear that this laborious, time-consuming technique was producing an unacceptably large backlog of meteorites awaiting classification. Mason saw a need for a quicker technique to separate and classify the myriad of equilibrated ordinary chondrites. In 1987, he returned to a technique he had successfully applied in the 1950s and early 1960s—oil immersion. The rapid determination of the composition of a few olivine grains from each meteorite then became and remains the method by which 80%–90% of all U.S. Antarctic meteorites are classified.

Unequilibrated ordinary, carbonaceous, and enstatite chondrites and achondrites are sent for thin section preparation, along with some meteorites that cannot be confidently classified due to brecciation, shock, or severe weathering. The Smithsonian's Antarctic thin-section library now contains over 5,000 thin sections, and ~200 new sections are prepared each year. Mineral compositions (olivine and orthopyroxene for most chondrites; olivine, pyroxene, and plagioclase for achondrites) are determined using the JEOL JXA-8900R electron microprobe. The Smithsonian prepares brief descriptions, tables of data, and digital petrographic images that are published in the *Antarctic Meteorite Newsletter* (Satterwhite and Righter, 2006), which is also posted on the Web. Antarctic iron meteorites, which are found at very modest rates, are permanently transferred. The Smithsonian has unique capabilities for processing iron meteorites and handles all processing, curatorial, and classification of irons. For more than 30 years, the responsibility for the description and curation of Antarctic meteorites fell to Roy S. Clarke Jr., whose specialty in the metallography of iron meteorites and oversight of the non-Antarctic collection made him an ideal choice. While all meteorites are classified, the Smithsonian's major task is identifying those specimens that are of particular interest to scientists and that would be worthy of further study. Figure 3 illustrates the results of these efforts, indicating the number of samples recovered, the total number of meteorites, and the subset of meteorites that are not equilibrated ordinary chondrites. The number of meteorites recovered increased steadily from an average of ~300 (1977–1984) to greater than 1,000 per year (2002–2006) as collecting techniques improved and field parties grew in size and number. The number of samples was sometimes greater than the number of meteorites due to the collection of a small number of terrestrial rocks mistaken for meteorites. The number of the most scientifically interesting specimens, those other than equilibrated ordinary chondrites (e.g., unequilibrated ordinary chondrites, carbonaceous and enstatite chondrites, achondrites, and irons), remained constant at ~50/year. (The sharp dip in 1989 was due to a cancelled field season.) The apparent disconnect between the number collected and those of greatest scientific interest is due to the occurrence of meteorites that break up in the atmosphere and possibly shower local areas with thousands of individual fragments. While most scientific studies focus on the small subset of the most interesting specimens, the collection as a whole still offers clues to ice movements related to concentration mechanism and the influx of meteoritic material to Earth over time (Harvey, 2003). Only through systematic collection and classification of all the meteorites can these latter studies be undertaken.

The other major obligation of the SI in the U.S. Antarctic Meteorite Program was serving as the long-term curatorial facility for specimens (Figure 4). In 1983, the SI opened its Museum Support Center in Suitland, Maryland. This state-of-the-art collections facility is centered on four pods (football-field-sized buildings ~50 feet (~15 m) high)

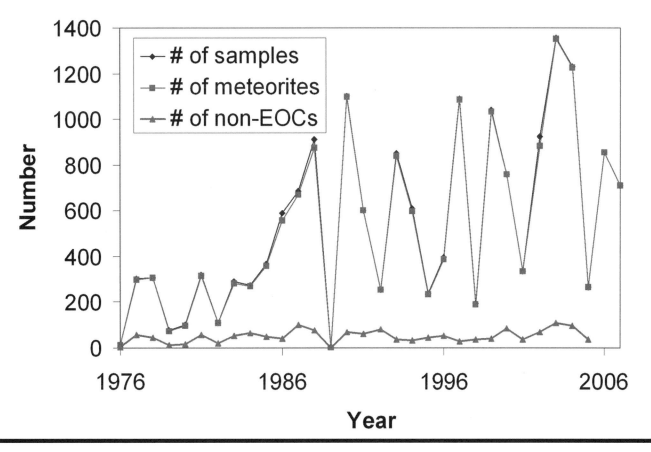

FIGURE 3. The number of samples and recovered meteorites and those meteorites that are not equilibrated ordinary chondrites (EOCs) from 1977 to 2007.

FIGURE 4. Meteorite storage laboratories at the Smithsonian Museum Support Center in Suitland, Maryland, modeled on the facility used for lunar rocks at NASA's Johnson Space Center. The water- and oxygen-free nitrogen gas in the cabinets keeps meteorites from oxidizing and free from contamination by environmental pollutants such as organic compounds, heavy metals, and salts, which could reduce the scientific value of the specimens. Photo by Chip Clarke, SI.

connected by a corridor of offices and laboratories. Shortly after this facility opened, planning began for building what became essentially a duplicate of the dry nitrogen storage facility for Antarctic meteorites at Johnson Space Center in Houston, and the new museum storage facility opened in the fall of 1986. The first significant transfer (126 specimens) of Antarctic meteorites to the Smithsonian occurred in 1987. Regular annual transfers from Johnson Space Center to the museum began in 1992, and the flow of meteorites increased tremendously in 1998. At that point, the Meteorite Processing Laboratory at Johnson Space Center was essentially full, and the subsequent influx of newly recovered meteorites necessitated the transfer of large numbers of specimens to the SI. By the end of 2004, more than 11,300 individual specimens had been transferred to the museum. When coupled with the chips and thin sections used for the initial classification, Antarctic meteorites now represent more than 80% of named meteorites in the Smithsonian collection and more than 70% of all specimens. These percentages alone demonstrate the spectacular impact of the Antarctic Meteorite Program on the Smithsonian's meteorite collection.

During the 30 years of the U.S. Antarctic Meteorite Program, Smithsonian personnel have fulfilled a number of other roles. The program is managed by a three-member Meteorite Steering Group with representatives from NASA, NSF, and the Smithsonian. Recommendations on sample allocations are made by the Meteorite Working Group, a 10-member panel that also includes members of the academic and research communities. Smithsonian personnel from both the Natural History Museum and the Astrophysical Observatory have actively participated or led these committees throughout the history of the program. Additionally, the Smithsonian provides selected samples of Antarctic meteorites for exhibits throughout the world, including meteorites on display at the Crary Science and Engineering Center in McMurdo Station, perhaps the southernmost display of Smithsonian objects.

SCIENTIFIC VALUE OF ANTARCTIC METEORITES

While the U.S. Antarctic Meteorite Program has had a dramatic influence on the size of the Smithsonian meteorite collection, it is the information that these priceless samples hold that is of greatest benefit. While listing the full range of scientific discoveries is beyond the scope of this paper, we list a few examples.

Brian Mason and Smithsonian volcanologist Bill Melson published the first book-length treatise on Apollo 11 samples in 1970 (Mason and Melson, 1970), and Mason remained involved in the study of lunar samples through the end of the Apollo Program. In 1982, Mason described the Antarctic meteorite ALH A81005 as containing clasts that "resemble the anorthositic clasts described from lunar rocks" (Mason, 1983). From his earlier work, Mason knew this was the first lunar meteorite but presented his findings in a typically understated manner so as not to undercut the considerable research that would be forthcoming. Today, we recognize more than three dozen distinct lunar meteorites. A remarkable feature of these meteorites is that they commonly exhibit very low abundances of the radioactive element thorium. In contrast, the area sampled by the Apollo missions on the equatorial near side of the Moon typically has elevated thorium concentrations indicative of the thin crust and extensive volcanism that occurred in that region. For this reason, lunar meteorites are thought to represent a much broader representative sampling of the lunar surface and are the subject of intense scrutiny as the U.S. plans for a return to the Moon (Korotev et al., 2003).

The realization that lunar meteorites had been launched by impacts from the surface of the Moon and escaped the heating that many predicted would melt them completely reinvigorated debate about whether certain meteorites actually originated on Mars. This debate was largely settled in 1981, when Don Bogard and colleagues at Johnson Space Center showed that gases trapped inside impact melt pockets in the Antarctic meteorite EET A79001 matched those measured in the martian atmosphere by the Viking lander. These samples, now numbering several dozen, provide the only materials from Mars that we have in our laboratories. Although they lack geologic context, study of these rocks has posed many of the questions driving Mars exploration. This was never more true than when McKay et al. (1996) argued that ALH 84001 contained evidence of past microbial life in the form of distinctive chemical, mineralogical, and morphological features. Although the result has been vigorously debated for over a decade, it is clear that this single paper reinvigorated NASA's Mars Exploration Program. The founding of the NASA Astrobiology Institute and the launch of the Mars Exploration Rovers Spirit and Opportunity, which continue to operate after three years on the surface of Mars and on which the senior author is a team member, were spurred in part by the idea that ancient life may have existed on Mars. It is truly remarkable that a modest program of collecting meteorites—the poor man's space probe—prompted the initiation of major research and spacecraft efforts!

Among the significant advances in meteoritics within the last decade, one of the most noteworthy is the recognition of meteorites that are intermediate between the primitive chondrites formed as sediments from the solar nebula and achondrites that sample differentiated bodies with cores, mantles, and crusts, like Earth. These meteorites, termed primitive achondrites, experienced only partial melting and differentiation, after which the process was halted. These meteorites may offer our best clues to how our own planet differentiated. While such meteorites have been known for more than a century, they were few in number and largely viewed as curiosities. The vast numbers of meteorites recovered from Antarctica have pushed these meteorites into prominence, as major groupings have emerged. Among these meteorites, one is truly remarkable. Graves Nunatak (GRA) 95209 contains metal veins that sample the earliest melting of an asteroid as it began to heat up more than 4.5 billion years ago (McCoy et al., 2006). These veins record a complex history of melting, melt migration, oxidation-reduction reactions, intrusion into cooler regions, cooling, and crystallization. The single most remarkable feature of this meteorite is the presence of millimeter-size metal grains that contain up to a dozen graphite rosettes tens of micrometers in diameter. Within a single metal vein, carbon isotopic compositions ($\delta^{13}C$) can range from -50 to $+80‰$. These graphite grains formed not in the parent asteroid during melting but during nebular reactions. This isotopic heterogeneity is even more remarkable when we consider that a single millimeter-sized metal grain within this meteorite has a greater carbon isotopic heterogeneity than all the natural materials on Earth. Despite extensive heating, this asteroid did not achieve a homogeneous carbon isotopic composition. In a very real way, this sample gives us a glimpse into the processes that occurred in the solar nebula during the birth of our solar system as well during the heating, melting, and differentiation of our Earth.

CONCLUSIONS

The meteorite collection and the insights provided by the influx of a tremendous number of Antarctic meteorites continue to enrich the Smithsonian collections and offer opportunities for research among its staff. Much of the current emphasis is in the burgeoning field of astrobiology. Understanding the fate of carbon during the differentiation of planets forms another link in understanding this fundamental element from its birth in other stars to the role it plays today in biologic evolution. Scientists at the Smithsonian use these meteorites to ask fundamental questions that they then set about answering through participation in spacecraft missions to the Moon, Mars, asteroids, and comets. Rather than supplanting meteorites as a major source of information, samples returned from these bodies will make Antarctic meteorites more scientifically valuable as they continue to provide the framework as we continue to ask and answer the questions of our solar system's birth, evolution, and destiny.

ACKNOWLEDGMENTS

This paper reports the results of an effort shared by hundreds of individuals over three decades. These include the members of the meteorite search teams, the curatorial teams at Johnson Space Center and the Smithsonian Institution, the administrative support at NASA, the National Science Foundation, and the Smithsonian, and the efforts of thousands of scientists who have studied Antarctic meteorites. Among these, Don Bogard (NASA Johnson Space Center), Ursula Marvin (Smithsonian Astrophysical Observatory), and Bill Cassidy (University of Pittsburgh) have given us insights over the years into the formative stages of the U.S. Antarctic Meteorite Program. Our current partners in the curatorial and collection efforts Ralph Harvey (Case Western Reserve University), John Schutt (ANSMET), Kevin Righter (NASA Johnson Space Center), and Cecilia Satterwhite (Jacobs) have been particularly helpful, as have our colleagues at the Smithsonian, Brian Mason, Roy S. Clarke Jr., and the late Gene Jarosewich, who preceded us in these efforts and have been unfailingly supportive. We dedicate this paper to our colleague Gene Jarosewich, who never wavered in his enthusiasm for meteorites.

LITERATURE CITED

Antarctic Meteorite Working Group. 1978. Antarctic Meteorite Newsletter, No. 1(1). http://www-curator.jsc.nasa.gov/antmet/amn/previous_newsletters/ANTARTIC_METERORITE_NEWSLETTER_VOL_1_NUMBER_1.pdf (accessed 15 August 2008).

Cassidy, W. A. 2003. *Meteorites, Ice, and Antarctica: A Personal Account*. Cambridge: Cambridge University Press.

Folco, L., A. Capra, M. Chiappini, M. Frezzotti, M. Mellini, and I. E. Tabacco. 2002. The Frontier Mountain Meteorite Trap. *Meteoritics and Planetary Science*, 37:209–228.

Harvey, R. 2003. The Origin and Significance of Antarctic Meteorites. *Chemie der Erde*, 63:93–147.

Korotev, R. L., B. L. Jolliff, R. A. Zeigler, J. J. Gillis, and L. A. Haskin. 2003. Feldspathic Lunar Meteorites and Their Implications for Compositional Remote Sensing of the Lunar Surface and the Composition of the Lunar Crust. *Geochimica et Cosmochimica Acta*, 67:4895–4923.

Lin, C.-Y., F. S. Zhang, H.-N. Wang, R.-C. Wang, and W.-L. Zhang. 2002. "Antarctic GRV9927: A New Member of SNC Meteorites." Thirty-third Annual Lunar and Planetary Science Conference, March 11–15, Lunar and Planetary Institute, Houston, Tex.

Mason, B. H. 1963. Olivine Composition in Chondrites. *Geochimica et Cosmochimica Acta*, 27:1011–1023

———. 1983. Antarctic Meteorite Newsletter, No. 6 (1). http://curator.jsc.nasa.gov/antmet/amn/previous_newsletters/ANTARTIC_METERORITE_NEWSLETTER_VOL_6_NUMBER_1.pdf (accessed 15 August 2008).

Mason, B. H., and W. G. Melson. 1970. *The Lunar Rocks*. New York: Wiley-Interscience.

McCoy, T. J., W. D. Carlson, L. R. Nittler, R. M. Stroud, D. D. Bogard, and D. H. Garrison. 2006. Graves Nunataks 95209: A Snapshot of Metal Segregation and Core Formation. *Geochimica et Cosmochimica Acta*, 70:516–531.

McKay, D. S., E. K. Gibson, K. L. Thomas-Keprta, H. Vali, C. S. Romanek, S. J. Clemett, X. D. F. Chiller, C. R. Maechling, and R. N. Zare. 1996. Search for Past Life on Mars: Possible Relic Biogenic Activity in Martian Meteorite ALH84001. *Science*, 273:924–930.

National Science Foundation. 2003. U.S. Regulations Governing Antarctic Meteorites. 45 CFR Part 674. http://www.nsf.gov/od/opp/antarct/meteorite_regs.jsp (accessed 15 August 2008).

Satterwhite, C., and K. Righter, eds. 2006. Antarctic Meteorite Newsletter. http://curator.jsc.nasa.gov/antmet/amn/amn.cfm (accessed 15 August 2008).

Shima, M., and M. Shima. 1973. Mineralogical and Chemical Composition of New Antarctica Meteorites. *Meteoritics*, 8:439–440.

Welten, K. C., C. Alderliesten, K. Van der Borg, L. Lindner, T. Loeken, and L. Schultz. 1997. Lewis Cliff 86360: An Antarctic L-chondrite with a terrestrial age of 2.35 million years. *Meteoritics and Planetary Science*, 32:775–780.

Index